"*The Long Journey Home* is an ambitious attempt to address the multifaceted problem of sexual abuse, an issue that is often overlooked in our churches. The book is comprehensive in scope, covering the prevalence and types of sexual abuse, its immediate and long-term consequences upon victims, survivors, and abusers, the theological and spiritual dimensions and implications, reviews of current research, and practical guidelines for ministry and healing. Over two-dozen contributors provide multiple levels of insight into sexual abuse, from scholarly investigation to the personal and practical. Most noteworthy is the emphasis on the use of Scripture in understanding the fundamental spiritual issues of sexual abuse and in directing survivors, perpetrators, ministers, counselors, and the community of faith toward ultimate healing found in God. I recommend this book for anyone dealing with sexual abuse, and, in particular, students, pastors, and care givers who seek a better understanding of the problem and desire to be more effective ministers of the Gospel."

—IAN F. JONES
PROFESSOR OF PSYCHOLOGY AND COUNSELING
BAPTIST COMMUNITY MINISTRIES' CHAIR OF PASTORAL COUNSELING
NEW ORLEANS BAPTIST THEOLOGICAL SEMINARY

"*The Long Journey Home* offers a unique contribution to the subject of undeserved, horrifyingly hurtful suffering associated with sexual abuse. As editor and contributor, Dr. Schmutzer has gathered a collection of specialists to address the problem from three different perspectives: social sciences, theological disciplines, and pastoral care. However, sexual abuse isn't merely theoretical, philosophical, or theological. It is deeply personal. Therefore, of significant importance is this book's value to pastors, counselors, and churches who are dealing with (or will deal with) the complex causes and consequences connected with sexual abuse."

—LARRY J. WATERS
ASSOCIATE PROFESSOR OF BIBLE EXPOSITION
DALLAS THEOLOGICAL SEMINARY

"*The Long Journey Home* is the fruit of excellent work blending theology, ministry, and psychology concerning sexual abuse and healing into a magnificent resource. The church has struggled for centuries to walk with abuse survivors and become an advocate in their healing. This book equips us to face their journey with hope and justice. I feel it is about time Christian practitioners have been able to publish something of this caliber to address such a painful issue."

—RON CLARK
GEORGE FOX EVANGELICAL SEMINARY

"It is no secret that the darkness and horrors of sexual abuse are all too prevalent within the Christian community. Tragically, for too many years the Church has responded to such darkness with silence. As a result, this darkness has spread and left a broad trail of destruction along its way . . . the destruction of individual lives, families, church communities, and the glorious witness of Christ. Through this great tragedy, we must be reminded that all is not hopeless and lost. There is hope, much hope, because we worship the God of truth and light who is moving in mighty ways by demonstrating love to those who knew no love, hope to those who had no hope, and the power of His Gospel to those who had only associated the Gospel with abuse and pain. Dr. Schmutzer's new collaborative book, *The Long Journey Home*, will undoubtedly be one way

God uses to demonstrate such Gospel-centered hope to so many inside and outside of His Church who have been effected by abuse. Written by a collection of experts who have spent entire careers addressing and confronting the various facets of this sin, *The Long Journey Home* is the most comprehensive and well informed book on this subject from a Gospel-centered perspective. As one who spends his days laboring alongside the Christian community in addressing the issue of abuse, I am greatly encouraged by the depth and spirit that fill the pages of *The Long Journey Home*. This book should be required reading for all Christian leaders and anyone else whose life has been impacted by the horrors of abuse."

—BASYLE TCHIVIDJIAN
PROFESSOR OF LAW
LIBERTY UNIVERSITY SCHOOL OF LAW

"The trauma and heinousness of sexual abuse leaves me speechless. Unfortunately, many of us pastors and ministry professionals are clueless. Andrew J. Schmutzer's excellent work helps change that and more; it gives us tested insights and strategies to unpack abuse and facilitate healing in Christ. I have seen this first hand. Andrew's teaching and counseling ministry in our church—his church—has been a beacon of light for so many stuck in the shadows of shame."

—ROB BUGH
SENIOR PASTOR
WHEATON BIBLE CHURCH

"This collection of vital information holistically addresses issues of abuse that are deeply complex and tender. Hope is offered from many voices that is personal, biblical, and insightful. Many survivors, counselors, pastors, and family members are sure to find the understanding they have longed for and help for which they have prayed. This book has a very important message."

—PAMELA MACRAE
ASSISTANT PROFESSOR OF PASTORAL STUDIES
MOODY BIBLE INSTITUTE

"Andrew J. Schmutzer's *The Long Journey Home* is an outstanding compendium of resources from the social sciences, the helping professions, theology, and pastoral care focused on understanding and caring for those who have been sexually abused. Schmutzer has accomplished the monumental task of weaving together the writings of over twenty-six social scientists, clinicians, church leaders, and survivors telling their personal stories into one coherent volume. It is an amazing accomplishment. Every church leader has in their congregation survivors of sexual abuse and has opportunity like no one else to speak healing words into their lives. *The Long Journey Home* will enable seminarians, church leaders, and helping professionals to become instruments of hope and healing."

—DIANA R. GARLAND
DEAN
BAYLOR SCHOOL OF SOCIAL WORK

The Long Journey Home

The Long Journey Home

Understanding and Ministering to the Sexually Abused

A collaborative address from psychology,
theology, and pastoral care

EDITED BY
ANDREW J. SCHMUTZER

WIPF & STOCK · Eugene, Oregon

THE LONG JOURNEY HOME
Understanding and Ministering to the Sexually Abused

Resource Publications
An Imprint of Wipf and Stock Publishers
199 W. 8th Ave., Suite 3
Eugene, OR 97401
www.wipfandstock.com

ISBN 13: 978-1-60899-395-6

Manufactured in the U.S.A.

This book is dedicated to:

—*Those who have yet to face their journey*

—*Those who have just begun their journey*

—*Those who need guidance in their journey*

—*Those who have made peace with their journey*

—*Those who were overcome by their journey*

"Not all who wander are lost."

—J. R. R. Tolkien

"What is forgotten is unavailable,
and what is unavailable cannot be healed."

—Henri J. M. Nouwen

"If no one remembers a misdeed or names it publically, it remains invisible.
To the observer, its victim is not a victim and its perpetrator is not a
perpetrator; both are misperceived because the suffering of the one
and the violence of the other go unseen. A double injustice occurs—the first when the
original deed is done and the second when it disappears."

—Miroslav Volf

Contents

Contents

Preface

THE VISION FOR THIS book began with my own experience as a survivor. As I began studying the issue of sexual abuse (SA), I quickly realized that the subject was not only complex but, unfortunately, the various professions with a stake in the issue were often talking past each other or just ignoring discussions they were not adequately trained to follow. From scientific studies on post-traumatic stress disorder (PTSD) to analysis of Old Testament rape laws, embodiment theology to family systems theory, liturgy for corporate healing to new research on how forgiveness lowers blood pressure—this all deserves to be heard. But I felt that such innumerable talks needed to be drawn into a more *cohesive dialogue*, like key pieces forming a grand puzzle. There was obviously a flood of literature out there, from popular memoirs to academic articles and idiosyncratic stuff in between. There are social surveys, gender studies, and books by "group-x" for "group-x" regarding "group-x," but very little discussion on SA that intentionally valued other professions and showed it in generous dialogue. Unfortunately, some of the best research on SA never filters down to the abused. So I found some other professionals who understood this need and were eager to lend their skills.

The Long Journey Home has both in-depth analysis and sweeping vision to address abuse. What emerged includes description and prescription, personal reflection and some tough questions, all geared toward helping Christian leaders understand and minister to the sexually abused. From the outset, I saw the book functioning as a much-needed *bridge* between the disciplines of psychology, theology, and pastoral care (see Contents). While each profession has developed its own set of technical terms surrounding SA (needed in the respective trades, see Glossary), the effect has also tended to shut out other conversation partners. So here is a collaboration of disciplines, working together from a broad faith-perspective within the Christian tradition. Contrary to some opinions, combining theology and the social sciences for SA has not been tried and found wanting; it has been found difficult and largely left untried.

As I am writing this, a Salt Lake City Jury has found fifty-nine-year-old Brian David Mitchell guilty of kidnapping Elizabeth Smart (then fourteen, in 2002) for the purpose of having sex. I took some notes. I mention this case because it illustrates the complexity that often surrounds SA and the necessity of *coordinative modalities* of learning for a fuller understanding and advocacy.

Mitchell, accompanied by his wife, Wanda Eileen Barzee (age sixty-six) is a self-proclaimed prophet who goes by the name "Immanuel." Mitchell is an excommunicated Mormon who has written a manifesto embracing polygamy. He considers Elizabeth his wife, attempting to rename her "Remnant-Who-Will-Return," a likely reference to

Shear-yashub in Isaiah 7:3. Mitchell knew Elizabeth because her mother had hired him to work on the family's house. For Mitchell, Elizabeth's nine-month disappearance was not a kidnapping, but a "call from God." Each day during his trial, Mitchell would enter the courtroom singing hymns from an LDS hymnal.

To symbolically sever her ties to family, Mitchell forced her to burn her pajamas worn on the night she was abducted. She later found a safety pin from her pajamas in the ashes and secretly kept it. Elizabeth was raped almost daily, forced to drink alcohol, use drugs, and view pornography. Once when she did try to escape, Mitchell and Barzee told her that the next time she would be killed by a sword-wielding angel. Elizabeth was so terrified that on the day police located her, she said she was someone else, Augustine Marshall. She later stated, "I felt terrible that the detective hadn't pushed harder and had just walked away." Is this kind of thinking adequately understood?

Reflecting on her story, several points should be noted. Mitchell had threatened to kill her family if Elizabeth spoke out, brainwashing was involved—but the safety pin was a kind of transitional object for Elizabeth to her prior life. Do we simply call Mitchell mentally ill and decry "patriarchal religion?" Mitchell's profile was clearly delusional, anti-social, and also narcissistic. His world view was shaped by facets of Mormon culture and doctrine (polygamy is no longer held). The context of socialization and tradition does play a role. Does the faith community adequately value victim impact statements that might critique these religious traditions? The fact that so many people of faith have been abused, and then "abandon" their faith should be enough to bring the psychologist and pastor into sober dialogue.

Recall that Mitchell was known to the Smart family. Most victims know their abusers, which compounds issues of anger, betrayal, and shame. For her part, Elizabeth returned from Paris, France, nine years later for the trial—she was completing her LDS missionary service. She is Mormon herself. How are therapists trained to work with religion? Just what parts of a victim's life should therapy focus on? Elizabeth's own family was strongly opposed to Mitchell even being charged with any sexual abuse crimes, fearing the detail that she would have to give in the trial. Was her parents' fear entirely for her sake? Who suffers more from silence: the abuser, the family, or the abused? Who sets the agenda?

Do police and social workers adequately understand shame-based social systems and the tenacity of religious convictions? Is culture and faith to be dismissed as outdated or a nuisance? Well, consider that Elizabeth was handcuffed and placed in the back of a squad car. What does that communicate! Sadly, cases large enough to compete with the Olympics are probably going to be known by the name of the perpetrator, not the victim—Elizabeth. Nor is every abuse survivor, even those molested once, able to show the resilience of Elizabeth Smart. Are church leaders adequately trained for this kind of complexity? Not every survivor gets a "guilty" verdict to help with closure. She wants to be a lawyer. I wonder why? My point is that addressing SA is bigger than all of us. Every professional discipline is needed. It is time to work together!

What Makes this Book Unique

The Long Journey Home is a collection of specialists meeting to discuss and speak into the complexities SA. Much like doctors in consultation for a person with cancer, *The Long Journey Home* is, as Nancy Nason–Clark and Steve McMullin describe it, "trans-disciplinary triage." Twenty-six contributors—thirteen women and thirteen men—used their academic training and professional and ministerial experience. The result is twenty-three chapters collected under three headings: (1) Understanding Sexual Abuse through the Social Sciences, (2) Engaging Sexual Abuse through the Theological Disciplines, and (3) Addressing Sexual Abuse through Pastoral Care.

The chapters are written at a semi-technical level. The tone of the book is instructional, pastoral, and at times almost investigative. Readers may feel like they are seated at a table, surrounded by a team of concerned professionals discussing their own situations and offering strategies to help the abused, instruct leaders, and guide the church. The universal problem of SA requires a more universal approach, so the language is overall, intentionally inclusive. Gender specific treatments are already out there. Contributors worked from their own training, insight, and passion. Beyond a broad Christian commitment, there was no intention to use one method, one school of thought, or to arrive at any set of conclusions—*The Long Journey Home* uses multivalent methods in a multidimensional dialogue. The result is a rich ferment of discussion and maybe a few differing opinions. But enough lines have already been drawn in the sand. In the address of SA, it is time for disagreement at a higher level.

Also included are five Stories of Survivors who boldly share from their own lives. For various reasons, readers may need to hear or reference a personal story, a survivor's account in their own words; these are important as well. Each chapter closes with Questions for Discussion and additional resources For Further Reading. The questions highlight vital points in the chapter, press the reader to contemplate certain scenarios and contemporary social views, and offer suggestions to engage various aspects of SA in the classroom of academy as well as ministries of the community and local church. So the questions are written with various professions in view. Whether the reader wants an introductory treatment of a given issue or a more advanced discussion in a professional journal, the reading list is always offered to help guide the user—college professor or pastor, group leader or counselor. Regardless, the desire of all the contributors is to partner with Christian leaders who want to address SA in a more focused, proactive, and redemptive manner.

Finally a glossary, some written prayers for survivors, and a bibliography close out the volume. Prompted by the asterisk (*) in the text of the book (including the footnotes), the glossary alphabetically defines around five hundred terms used by therapists, theologians, and pastors. Following a interdisciplinary dialogue requires such tools. For many glossary terms, cross-references are offered for a more in-depth understanding for the reader (e.g., *Family Dysfunction* also refers the reader to *Boundary Confusion* and *Enmeshed Relationship*). The written prayers are addressed below. While For Further Reading has a broader appeal, the extensive bibliography may be valued more by the student, counselor, or specialist. It not only contains the sources used in the chapters, but also many other scholarly resources on aspects of SA. A list of helpful web resources has also been provided for survivors and caretakers, alike.

How to Use This Book

Within psychology, theology, and pastoral care, the interests and needs of many professions and ministries are represented and also overlap. *The Long Journey Home* offers an *arc of understanding*. So I thought I would offer a few suggestions to help maximize use of this book.

- Begin in one of the above three fields with which you are most familiar, but don't stop there! Work toward the most unfamiliar discipline; don't neglect it (e.g., theology). Sexual abuse is not mono- but multi-factorial, so listen to the insights and concerns of other professional voices at the table.

- If you are a teacher, encourage the students to thoroughly engage the Questions for Discussion. By design, these questions will pull from many opinions, perspectives, and backgrounds.

- If you are a survivor, try to find a counselor, pastor, or trusted friend to read this material with you. Or, join a support group where you can reflect, process, and grieve as you need to. Your own journey of healing can be a slow "spiral upwards." Give yourself some time, but quality information is vital.

- Pastors and Christian leaders, you will find much in these chapters to bolster your current policies, develop your sermons and seminars, and assist in your search for professional counselors that can help. These chapters recommend many creative ideas to inform the abused in your congregation that you care and are willing to walk with them. Many ideas are offered here to develop healing services for the abused. There are many biblical texts from the Old and New Testament that need to be preached, taught, and employed in articulate and sensitive ways for the sexually wounded.

- The Written Prayers for Survivors are offered primarily to *give survivors needed words*. Help survivors write their own. Therapists can use these prayers in support groups. Counselors can use them as diagnostic tools to see what emotions a survivor identifies with. In these prayers, survivors have a mode of expression that does not hide their anger, sense of betrayal, or fear that God himself may have abandoned them. In them, survivors always find that Jesus suffered in ways amazingly similar to their experiences. Pastors can use some of these prayers for healing services designed for the abused. Such prayers can be an aid when teaching or helping others lament and redeem their pain.

- For therapists and Christians leading support groups, the discussion questions can be very helpful to raise issues, prompt differing perspectives, process experiences, and represent viewpoints that might not have been considered. This is important in shaping a generous dialogue and teaching others the skills of advocacy.

- For instructors leading classes on sexuality, trauma, counseling the abused, or pastoral ethics, and so on, I encourage you to dig deep in all areas. The entire book can be used in the class. Especially important for counseling and therapy is becoming familiar with the glossary of terms surrounding SA. The Stories of Survivors are excellent case studies. Educators and therapists can use these to illustrate the different issues and complexities commonly faced by survivors, their social contexts, and communities of faith.

- If you are a grieving parent, friend, sibling, or spouse, find a counselor or church leader to work with you through particular chapters of this book. Try to understand how you can help support your child, friend, or family member or spouse. A counselor or pastor can also help you find some literature listed in For Further Reading.

In short, here is a mine of ideas to help understand and minister to the sexually abused. There is room at the table, come join the dialogue!

> We are not alone in our sadness, loneliness, longing, frustration, disorientation and confusion, anger, guilt, anxiety, fear, and helplessness. Others, too, are daunted by challenges to reshape their daily lives and recast the next chapters of their life stories. In this shared plight, others know us as fellow travelers who struggle to find our way again in worlds transformed by loss.

—Thomas Attig
Andrew J. Schmutzer
Easter, 2011

Acknowledgments

IN A RESOURCE LIKE this, many people need to be acknowledged. I must thank every contributor who stepped in to add their voice, expertise, and empathy to the dialogue. I learned so much from you all. I also want to thank Drs. Terri S. Watson and Richard E. Butman (Wheaton College) for their encouragement to take on this project. Dr. James Wood, Assistant Professor of Counseling Psychology (Moody Theological Seminary–Michigan) had a significant hand in compiling the glossary. Dr. Watson also helped review it. For the three women and two men who agreed to share their stories, thanks for your courage and grace. I must also thank my student, David Ulrich, for his help compiling the bibliography and his critique of the written prayers and portions of my chapter. I also want to thank my wife, Ashley, whose empathy was a torch of healing light. She believed in this project from the beginning, and gave me the time, profound feedback, and encouragement to complete it.

Introduction

Facing the Many Challenges of Healing and Helping

RICHARD E. BUTMAN, PhD

IT SHOULD BE PAINFULLY obvious to women and men of faith that we are living "after Eden"—and south of "Jerusalem." For those of us who aspire to be *world citizens* and *global Christians*, we don't have to look very far to see horrific examples of deception, evil, injustice, and sin in our own country and abroad. Abject poverty, widespread coercion and exploitation of women and children, wars and rumors of war, and the depletion of the earth's limited resources bombard our consciousness on a regular basis. We were called to responsible dominion and healthy relatedness in the Creation Mandate in Genesis. Yet, we can all cite examples of this dominion having gone awry—and the relatedness being powerfully distorted. *Apart from the ravages of war, this is perhaps no more painfully evident than in the reality of verbal, emotional, physical, and sexual abuse.*

How are we to understand such widespread exploitation and injustice? Initially, we need to consider what it means to be created in the image and likeness of God. Every human being should be considered of infinite worth, if only because they reflect something of God's character. Yet, the reality of the fall has somewhat marred that image (i.e., we are all broken, finite, and sinful creatures). Yet, the hope of the resurrection and the reality of the incarnation remind us that there is still hope—and a reason for faithfulness. If how we care for widows and orphans are one of the marks of true Christian character, convictions, and compassion, then there are many ways we ought to become more cognizant of the awful, far-reaching, and painful realities of verbal, emotional, physical, and sexual abuse if we mean to become imitators of Christ in word and deed. Such awareness demands both an individual and collective response at many levels (e.g., in our families, in our communities, and in our churches).

The Long Journey Home is a book about what it means to love boldly, courageously, and even fearlessly in a world in which caring can be so obviously distorted. The sheer statistical reality of abuse and violence should alert us to the fact that truth can be twisted and distorted—and authority can be misinterpreted and appropriated in ways that leave victims feeling hopeless, helpless, and powerless. Anyone who has carefully read the research on the reality of abuse and violence in our culture—including our Christian churches and ministries—quickly discovers that *these are complex issues that reflect multi-dimensional causal factors* that can be biological, psychosocial, sociocultural, and spiritual. People become perpetuators of abuse and violence for a host of factors that reflect sins of omission and commission, both personal and collective. For those of us prone to reductionism in our thinking about complex social issues, engaging in the sin of "nothing-but-ism" is especially tempting. Simply put, we are not entirely clear about the complex and diverse factors that prompt abuse and violence. Sadly, we often know even less about the short-term and long-term impact on victims. What is clear, however, is that the denial and distortion of abuse and violence—be it from the perspective of the victim or perpetuator of aggression—is tempting. Indeed, life would be infinitely easier if we could deny the existence of the distasteful—and the awful reality of the intergenerational effects of coercion and exploitation.

We do know something of the importance of our creational heritage—and the power of the healing community. Awareness and understanding of the issues are prerequisite for healing and change. We do know that hope can be restored in even some of the most difficult and challenging situations. Perhaps it is best "caught" rather than "taught" when trust and respect have been destroyed. We also know that there is no set of techniques that can fix it—but that it does need to be worked through in the context of safe and supportive relationships—ideally, in the context of faith-based communities that have an almost exquisite sense of timing, tact, and sensitivity. *We do know that although it takes relationships to "break" people—it also takes people to help people heal.* And those people need to be attentive, respectful, and active listeners—perhaps more willing to be a fan, friend, and facilitator than an "expert." But perhaps most important is the ability to understand more of the experience of those who have had their trust and faith so significantly shattered. This indeed is challenging and difficult work, since it requires a kind of involvement and investment that few of us are really willing to undertake. Perhaps it is our own willingness to hear the experiences of those who have been exploited—and our desire to face these tragedies together—that really are at the core of the corrective emotional experience. Learning to be both affiliative and assertive (again)—and finding others who can help us become healthy and whole (again)—appears to be the heart of the matter. Those of us who want to help must be willing to enter into their world and learn from them what it means to have courage, to believe and trust (again), and to stay faithful to our values, vision, and mission when it seems like everything has gone wrong. In short, it requires biblical, realistic hope—not arrogant optimism or pseudo-solutions to complex and difficult problems.

This is a much-needed book for women and men of faith who want to understand more of what it means to stand together with people who so often feel confused, demoralized, and isolated. Our caring response begins with understanding abuse from the perspectives of both general (Part I) and special revelation (Part II). The importance of good thinking on these matters cannot be overstated. Finally, the themes will be addressed through the perspectives of pastoral care and professional intervention (Part III). I'd encourage you to do the hard work of exploring the issues through the foundational sections before considering some of the fine insights offered in the chapters on what it means to care deeply about restoring these individuals to greater measures of health, holiness, and happiness. Abuse and violence are by definition incredibly difficult constructs to really grasp. Well-intentioned efforts to "be helpful" may be misguided—even toxic—if we don't fully grasp the nature of that responsible dominion having gone awry and that healthy relatedness being distorted. I commend to you the whole of this well-edited volume. The message for hope and healing that it offers our culture, our churches, and our ministries is desperately needed in the early part of the beginning of the twenty-first century.

RICHARD E. BUTMAN, PHD
PROFESSOR OF PSYCHOLOGY (WHEATON COLLEGE)
LICENSED CLINICAL PSYCHOLOGIST

PART ONE

Understanding Sexual Abuse through the Social Sciences

1

Definitions and Prevalence Rates
of Sexual Abuse

Quantifying, Explaining, and Facing a Dark Reality

Steven R. Tracy, PhD

> I have written about *rape many times during the last fourteen years . . . It is difficult for many to imagine how one's life changes after living through an experience of terror. I cannot imagine how my life might have been had I not been raped. I have little connection to my life prior to the rape. Rape forced me to start over. In a very disturbing way I experienced the *trauma of being torn from the womb and immediately recognizing that even while clothed, I am naked; even in a family, I am alone; even speaking, I am silenced; and even living, I am dying.[1]

*S*EXUAL ABUSE (SA) IS an incredibly complex and ugly subject. It is difficult and confusing to contemplate the possibility of vast numbers of fellow human beings all around us who stand naked while clothed, silenced while speaking, alone in a family, and dying while living. What should we make of this testimony? Is Ruth's life-altering rape experience the rare exception, or is sexual abuse really as prevalent as many secular experts would have us believe? What exactly constitutes sexual abuse? Is it increasing or decreasing in frequency? What light does Scripture shed on the reality of sexual abuse? These are the critical questions we will seek to answer in this chapter.

GOSPEL MOTIVATION FOR A CLOSE LOOK
AT SEXUAL ABUSE

Until quite recently, physical and sexual abuse were not well understood, analyzed, or addressed. This changed dramatically in the 1970s when various professionals began writing detailed treatments on abuse. Many of these authors were secular or religiously liberal feminists who analyzed and addressed abuse by attacking *patriarchy, men, and even

---

1. Schmidt, "After the Fact," 14.

religion.[2] This is particularly evident in two of the earliest treatments of sexual abuse. In her classic work on childhood sexual abuse, *The Best Kept Secret*, Florence Rush argued that *child sexual abuse (CSA) has been widespread historically and presently due to patriarchy fueled by religion, particularly Christianity.[3] Similarly, in *Against Our Will*, one of the first modern detailed treatments of rape, Susan Brownmiller argued that from prehistoric times to the present, rape has been widespread and "is nothing more or less than a conscious process by which *all men* keep *all women* in a state of fear."[4] Thankfully, since the 1970s the sexual abuse literature has become more nuanced and balanced. Yet the fact remains that a high percentage of sexual abuse research and outreach is done by secular professionals and organizations.

Thus, it is important to note that Christians have the greatest motivations imaginable for grappling with and responding to the ugly reality of sexual abuse. *Christian motivation for sexual abuse ministry can be summed up with a single, pregnant phrase: "the gospel."* The message of Christianity, the "good news" of the gospel, is that the innocent world God created has been corrupted and ravaged by sin. Sin infects and harms every person who walks the earth, resulting in a world of pain and evil, including sexual abuse. Incredibly, Jesus—the holy, divine Creator—voluntarily entered human history and took on human flesh for one primary purpose—to be fatally abused so that he could break the power of sin, death, and Satan.[5] Jesus experienced physical and verbal abuse as well as sexual humiliation from being publicly crucified naked. Jesus summarized his ministry as a divine anointing to set captives free and release the oppressed (Luke 4:18–19). He showed particular love and care for the sexually broken.[6] *His earthly ministry was characterized by focused outreach to the marginalized, oppressed, and abused.*[7] It was also characterized by unflinching public warnings against abuse and clashes with spiritual and physical abusers.[8] In summary, the gospel impels Christians to face the reality of widespread human sin, including abuse. It also impels us to confront abusers and minister to their victims.

SEXUAL ABUSE DEFINITIONS AND PREVALENCE

The Challenge

It should be noted at the outset of this discussion that accurate understandings of the *prevalence of sexual abuse are exceedingly difficult for several reasons: (1) Diverse definitions of sexual abuse lead to diverse and at times conflicting data. (2) Sexual abuse is

2. See for instance, Dobash and Dobash, *Violence against Wives*. Two later classic works written from the same militant conceptual framework are Warshaw, *I Never Called It Rape* and Dworkin, *Letters from a War Zone*.

3. Rush, *The Best Kept Secret*. Rush first presented her child sexual abuse hypothesis in a seminal speech at a New York Radical Feminist Conference in April 1971.

4. Brownmiller, *Against Our Will*, 5.

5. Cf. Isah 53:3–6; Col 2:13–15; Heb 2:14–15.

6. Cf. Matt 21:31–32; Luke 7:36–50; John 4:4–26; 8:3–11.

7. Cf. Matt 9:9–13; 18:1–14; 19:13–15; 21:12–16, 28–46; 13:10–17; 14:21–24; 15:1–32; 18:9–14; 21:1–3.

8. Cf. Matt 15:1–9; 23:11–36; Mark 3:1–6; Luke 13:31–35; 20:45–47.

humiliating and traumatizing for victims, making self-reports of sexual abuse notoriously unreliable, which can also lead to conflicting data. There is a strong consensus among experts that sexual abuse is seriously underreported and minimized by victims, and that it is one of the most underreported crimes in America. For instance, the National Violence Against Women Survey found that only one in five adult women reported their rapes to police.[9] (3) Sexual abuse is painful and ugly for non-victims, creating a powerful innate *denial mechanism that often overrides clear evidence of abuse. This helps explain the extremely low rates of disclosure and prosecution of sexual abuse, particularly when perpetrated by family members.[10] Denial of abuse is a widespread problem in the church and virtually every other social institution.

Definitions

It is essential that we construct precise definitions of "sexual abuse." To do so, we will break this down into two subsets: (1) child sexual abuse and (2) adult sexual abuse. *Child sexual abuse is the exploitation of a minor for the sexual gratification of another person through sexual contact or sexual interaction.*[11] This definition encompasses a much broader range of behaviors than many people realize, including contact and non-contact abuse.

Abusive sexual contact encompasses a wide spectrum of increasingly intrusive types of contact: sexual kissing, touching clothed breasts, touching clothed pubic areas, touching/fondling breasts, touching/fondling genitals, oral sex, and intercourse. Abusive sexual interaction involves such acts as deliberate exposure of a minor to pornography, sexual acts, or one's own sexual organs (i.e., *exhibitionism). While some of these types of sexual abuse are clearly much less severe than others, all are illegal in the United States, all are morally wrong, and all have the potential to create great damage.[12]

Adult sexual abuse is "any sexual act in which the woman or man does not consent."[13] In defining CSA the initiation, objections, and/or responses of the child to sexual activity are irrelevant since there is an intrinsic power and developmental disparity between adults and children (or children and adolescents). In defining adult sexual abuse, however, the critical factor is *consent*. Often misunderstandings of sexual abuse result from a wrong focus on the relationship between the individuals—e.g., it is rape if a stranger forces sex, may not be rape if it is a cohabiting partner, and is certainly not rape if it is a husband. But relationship is not the issue. Sexual intercourse is a most intimate and powerful human act, and regardless of the nature of the relationship or previous sexual activity, *no one has*

---

9. Tjaden and Thoennes, *Extent, Nature, and Consequences of Rape Victimization.*

10. Judith Lewis Herman argues that reported cases of incest represent less than 10 percent of the actual instances, *Father-Daughter Incest*, 223–24. Catherine Cameron found that of the seventy-two women in her study who had experienced childhood sexual abuse, they had been assaulted by over two hundred different people, predominantly family members, and yet not a single individual had been charged with a crime, *Resolving Childhood Trauma*, 268.

11. Tracy, *Mending the Soul*, 27. See also, Allender, *The Wounded Heart*, 48.

12. For the specific legal definitions of child abuse based on federal and state legislation, go to "definitions" on the Child Information Gateway website: http://www.childwelfare.gov/systemwide/laws_policies/statutes/define.cfm.

13. Toronto Crisis Center, "Rape," 62.

a right to force sex acts on someone else. Force can include direct physical aggression and/or assault as well as threats or other forms of *coercive control.

Sexual Abuse Prevalence

There is overwhelming data from numerous research studies indicating that in the United States and around the world, sexual abuse is tragically widespread and prevalent.

Child Sexual Abuse

One of the most respected and thorough studies of child abuse is the National Incidence Study of Child Abuse and Neglect. The Fourth, and most recent National Incidence Study was released early in 2010. It revealed the following about CSA:

- An estimated 135,000 children were sexually abused in 2005/2006, a 36 percent decrease from the previous National Incidence Study of 1993.

- Girls were sexually abused at a rate over five times that of boys.

- Black children were sexually abused at a rate almost twice that of white children.

- Children in low socioeconomic families were three-and-a-half times more likely to be sexually abused.

- 37 percent of sexually abused children were abused by a biological parent, and another 23 percent were abused by a step-parent.

- 87 percent of sexually abused children were abused by a male.[14]

There has been much discussion of the fact that government statistical rates for CSA declined markedly between the Third and Fourth Incidence Studies. This may, in part, reflect the positive impact of abuse prevention and response strategies, though it may also be explained by other factors such as changes in *Child Protective Agencies data collection and increased conservativism within Child Protective Services (CPS).[15]

Even if this statistical decline represents a real decrease in abuse, our children are still experiencing dramatic rates of abuse. For instance, a recent large national survey of youth victimization (ages two to seventeen years old) found that, in the study year, over half of the youth had experienced a physical assault, more than one in eight had experienced some form of child maltreatment, one in twelve had experienced a sexual victimization; only 29 percent had no direct or indirect violent victimization.[16] Numerous studies conducted in the past decade reveal high rates of child sexual abuse in America. More specifically, a meta-analysis of twenty-two American studies, using both national and regional sampling data, indicates that 30 to 40 percent of girls and 13 percent of

---

14. Sedlak et al., *Fourth National Incidence Study of Child Abuse and Neglect.*

15. For an analysis of this decline, see Jones et al., "Why is Child Sexual Abuse Declining?" 1139–58.

16. Finkelhor et al., "The Victimization of Children and Youth," 5–25.

boys experience childhood sexual abuse.[17] Other more recent studies of childhood sexual abuse rates for women have revealed prevalence rates from 24 to 32 percent.[18]

Finally, we should note that sexual exploitation of children and youth via the Internet is a huge and apparently growing problem. A recent Justice Department report estimates that there are more than 1 million pornographic images of children on the Internet, and one single child pornography site reportedly received 1 million hits in one month.[19] A recent analysis of peer-to-peer network content on the Internet found that the most prevalent searches and the top two most prevalent filenames returned as query hits were child-pornography related. The median age searched for was thirteen years old.[20]

Adolescent and Young Adult Sexual Abuse

There is evidence that rates of sexual abuse among adolescent and young adult women has risen rather dramatically.[21] One recent general population study of women found that 38 percent of all respondents reported at least one experience of sexual abuse in their lifetime, but for the women thirty-one years old and younger, almost 42 percent reported sexual abuse.[22] According to a US Department of Justice report, the researchers discovered "by the end of four years of college, 79 percent of women had experienced at least one incident of sexual victimization in their lifetimes."[23] The data also shows that for college students, over 70 percent of completed, attempted, or threatened rapes took place on a date, and the majority (60 percent) of the rapes occurred in the victim's home.[24] Another Department of Justice source on dating violence asserts that 5 percent of college women experience a completed or attempted rape each year and 51 percent of college males admit perpetrating one or more sexual assault incidents during college.[25] Alarmingly high sexual assault rates are also being seen among high school age adolescents. In one major study of dating violence, 20 percent of American high school girls report being physically or sexually assaulted by a male partner.[26]

Another closely related issue is sexual harassment among college students. In a recent study which defined sexual harassment in a strict and narrow manner as "*unwanted* and *unwelcome* sexual behavior which interferes with your life," almost two-thirds of col-

17. Bolen and Scannapieco, "Prevalence of Child Sexual Abuse," 281–313.

18. Briere and Elliott, "Prevalence and Psychological Sequelae of Self-Reported Childhood Physical and Sexual Abuse in a General Population Sample of Men and Women," 1205–22.

19. Wortley and Smallbone, *Child Pornography on the Internet*, 12.

20. Steel, "Child Pornography in Peer-to-Peer Networks," 560–68.

21. Casey and Nurius, "Trends in the Prevalence and Characteristics of Sexual Violence," 629–44.

22. Ibid., 635–37.

23. *Violence against Women*, 1. For an excellent discussion of the research on date rape, see Cook and Koss, "More Data Have Accumulated Supporting Date and Acquaintance Rape as Significant Problems for Women," 97–116.

24. Fisher et al., *The Sexual Victimization of College Women*.

25. "Campus Dating Violence Fact Sheet." See also, Adams-Curtis and Forbes, "College Women's Experiences of Sexual Coercion," 91–122.

26. Silverman et al., "Dating Violence against Adolescent Girls and Associated Substance Abuse, Unhealthy Weight Control, Sexual Risk Behavior, Pregnancy, and Suicidality," 572–79.

lege students had experienced sexual harassment, less than 10 percent reported it, males and females were equally likely to be harassed, but females were significantly more likely to be upset by it.[27]

Adult Rape

The threat of sexual abuse does not end when one reaches adulthood, though adulthood is strongly impacted by experiences of prior sexual abuse. Sexual abuse *survivors are much more likely to be *re-victimized than are the non-abused.[28] More specifically, two out of every three people who are sexually victimized will be re-victimized.[29] This is part of the "cascading effect" of unhealed sexual abuse. In terms of general prevalence of rape among American adults, we can note the following. One out of six women is a victim of rape. *Specifically, an estimated 18 million women and almost 3 million men in the United States have been raped.*[30] *Intimate partner sexual assault is the most common sexual assault, with 14 to 25 percent of women reporting sexual assault by their intimate partners at some time during the relationship.[31] The National Violence Against Women Survey reported that almost 25 percent of women and 7.6 percent of men were raped and/or physically assaulted by a current or former spouse, cohabitating partner, or date at some time in their lifetime.[32] Prevalence of rape differs by age group, with the highest being one in five women ages eighteen to forty-nine, one in six women ages fifty to fifty-nine, and one in fifteen women age sixty and older.[33] *Finally, we should note that while most of the literature on rape deals with female victims, sexual assault is also a serious problem for males.* It is estimated that one in every ten rape victims is male in the United States, and about 2.78 million men have experienced an attempted or completed rape in their lifetime.[34]

Global Sexual Abuse Prevalence

South Africa has the highest documented sexual assault rates in the world. A recent survey by the country's Medical Research Council found that 27 percent of the men interviewed had raped someone, 46 percent of the self-confessed rapists had raped two or more women or girls, and one in five of the rapists were HIV+.[35] *These rates mean that currently a woman born in South Africa has a greater chance of being raped than she has of learning to read.*

27. Hill and Silva, *Drawing the Line*, 2–16; emphasis original.

28. Arata, "Child Sexual Abuse and Sexual Revictimization," 135–64. Also, Roodman and Clum, "Victimization Rates and Method Variance," 183–204.

29. Classen et al., "Sexual Revictimization," 103–29.

30. Tjaden and Thoennes, *Extent, Nature, and Consequences of Rape Victimization*.

31. McFarlane and Malecha, *Sexual Assault among Intimates*. Experts estimate that 10 to 14 percent of married women experience marital rape, Bennice and Resick, "Marital Rape," 228–46.

32. Tjaden and Thoennes, *Extent, Nature, and Consequences of Intimate Partner Violence*.

33. Ibid.

34. Rape, Abuse, and Incest National Network at: http://www.rainn.org; accessed May 21, 2009.

35. Jewkes et al., *Understanding Men's Health and Use of Violence*. See also, Kapp, "Rape on Trial in South Africa," 718–19.

The most comprehensive recent study of global sexual abuse was published by the World Health Organization in 2005.[36] This study was composed by teams that collected information from more than 24,000 women from fifteen sites in ten countries. This study corroborated previous findings about the staggering global prevalence of sexual abuse.[37] This study specifically found that the proportion of partnered women who had ever experienced physical or sexual violence, or both, by an intimate partner in their lifetime, ranged from 15 to 71 percent, with most sites falling between 29 and 62 percent. Overall, the percentage of women who reported sexual abuse by a partner ranged from 6 percent in Japan, Serbia, and Montenegro to 59 percent in Ethiopia, with the majority of settings falling between 10 and 50 percent. The proportion of women physically forced into intercourse ranged from 4 percent in Serbia and Montenegro to 46 percent in provincial Bangladesh and Ethiopia. *Nearly one third of Ethiopian women reported being physically forced by a partner to have sex against their wills within the previous twelve months.* Younger women, especially those ages fifteen to nineteen years old, were at higher risk of "current" (within the previous twelve months) physical or sexual violence, or both, by a partner in all settings except Japan and Ethiopia. The combined prevalence of physical and sexual violence by a non-partner after the age of fifteen years old ranged from 5 percent in Ethiopia to 65 percent in Samoa.

Historically, sexual abuse has often increased during times of war. Recent global conflicts have dramatically repeated this pattern. For instance, during the Bosnian conflict in the 1990s, tens of thousands of women were systematically raped, particularly by Serbians.[38] Similarly, one major survey found that in Liberia's recent civil war, 75 percent of the women had been raped, most having been *gang raped.[39] Unfortunately, sexual violence does not necessarily end when large-scale fighting ends. It has the potential to impact an entire generation and can result in a long-term elevation of sexual assault rates. Perhaps the most salient example of this is found in the Democratic Republic of the Congo. Even though a series of wars with invading foreign armies and widespread civil war has ended, its sexual violence has not abated and is the worst in the world in terms of sheer numbers as well as level of brutality.[40] Tens of thousands of women and children, and numbers of men, are estimated to be raped in just one single eastern province.[41] Similarly, a 2007 survey in post-war Liberia found that 12 percent of girls ages seventeen and under acknowledged having been sexually abused in some way in the previous eighteen months.[42]

---

36. *WHO Multi-country Study on Women's Health and Domestic Violence against Women.*

37. For instance, a meta-analysis of 169 international studies found that the global lifetime sexual abuse prevalence rate for females is 25 percent and 8 percent for males, World Health Organization, "Comparative Risk Assessment."

38. Allen, *Rape Warfare.*

39. Kristof, "After Wars, Mass Rapes Persist."

40. Wakabi, "Sexual Violence Increasing in Democratic Republic of Congo," 15–16.

41. Gettleman, "Rape Epidemic Raises Trauma of Congo War."

42. Kristof, "After Wars, Mass Rapes Persist."

Surprisingly little detailed research has been conducted to determine sexual abuse prevalence rates among *evangelicals. The data we do have suggests that sexual abuse rates among evangelicals are at parity with the general population. For instance, in 1989 the Christian Reformed Church commissioned a research study to determine prevalence of abuse in their denomination. The findings were based on adults' self-reports. Given what we know about abuse victims' tendency to deny and minimize abuse, these prevalence findings are undoubtedly lower than actual abuse rates experienced. Twelve percent of the respondents reported having been sexually abused.[43] A frequently cited sexuality survey of two thousand Christian women conducted by three well-respected evangelical social scientists revealed that 50 percent of the women surveyed reported they had experienced unwanted sexual touch.[44]

The Current "Trajectory" of Sexual Abuse Rates

While there is considerable debate regarding the current trajectory of sexual abuse, most experts agree that CSA has declined in recent years, though there is no consensus regarding the near future. It also seems apparent that sexual abuse rates among adolescent and young adults have risen markedly in recent years. Unfortunately, there are solid reasons to believe abuse rates among young adults will remain precipitously high and may rise even more in the future. In particular, I believe the increasing *sexualization of young girls,[45] the widespread usage and influence of pornography,[46] and the recent *"hook up" trend threaten to further elevate sexual abuse rates among female adolescents and young adults.[47] Globally, there is evidence that physical and sexual violence against women is increasing.[48] War, increased *sex trafficking, disintegration of the family, and the proliferation of Internet pornography are all likely factors in this increase, which does not appear likely to abate soon.

BIBLICAL/THEOLOGICAL EXPLANATION
OF SEXUAL ABUSE PREVALENCE

Scripture does not sanitize human nature or the accounts of Jewish and Christian leaders. Rather, Scripture teaches that Adam and Eve's disobedience plunged the human race into universal sin and *depravity and this resulted in large-scale abuse. The first account of physical abuse in Scripture (Gen 4:2–16) is found in the very next chapter after the account of the first human sin. Only two chapters later we find that moral corruption, particularly abuse, was so pervasive that God decided to destroy the human race (Gen

---

43. Annis and Rice, "A Survey of Abuse Prevalence in the Christian Reformed Church," 7–40.

44. Hart et al., *Secrets of Eve*, 181.

45. See Durham, *The Lolita Effect*, and also, Levin and Kilbourne, *So Sexy So Soon*.

46. Jensen, "Cruel to Be Hard," 33–34, 45–48. See also: Paul, *Pornified*; and Russell, *Dangerous Relationships*.

47. Anonymous M.D., *Unprotected*. See also, Stepp, *How Young Women Pursue Sex, Delay Love, and Lose at Both*.

48. Watts and Zimmerman, "Violence against Women," 1232–37.

6:11–13). Throughout the rest of Genesis we find accounts of *incest (19:30–38), kidnapping and forced slavery (14:1–12), attempted *homosexual gang rape (19:4–5), and heterosexual rape (34:1–4). These incidents include abuse between family members, abuse committed or potentially allowed by spiritual leaders, as well as abuse committed by pagans. Scripture reveals that abuse is not the exception to human relations; it is all too common even among believers.

For instance, "Righteous Lot offered his own daughter to be raped by wicked men."[49] Abraham, the father of the Jewish nation and exemplar of faith, twice protected himself by exposing his wife to sexual abuse by a pagan monarch. His son, Isaac, also one of the patriarchs of Israel, did exactly the same thing.[50] David, the greatest human monarch in Jewish history, was guilty of murder and either adultery or rape. He also failed to protect his own daughter from being raped by a family member, and he engaged in a *conspiracy of silence with her rapist.[51] Christians in the Corinthian church engaged in a form of incest that was more perverted than that practiced by their pagan neighbors (1 Cor 5:1). The Apostle Paul, affirming that abuse is a wide-spread human behavior, cites physical and verbal abuse as concrete evidence of the universal depravity of the human race (Rom 3:13–16). He also states that abuse will become even more prevalent in the last days (2 Tim 3:1–4). In short, due to innate human sinfulness, those with more power, regardless of their religious identity or family ties, often take advantage of those with less power through physical and sexual abuse.

CONCLUSION

Sexual abuse across the age span is tragically prevalent in the United States and around the world. Biblical teaching on universal human depravity and abuse sheds much light on the dynamics of contemporary sexual abuse. It also explains its prevalence. As painful as it is to accept this ugly reality, we must, for abuse is a gospel issue.

QUESTIONS FOR DISCUSSION

1. Explain how sexual abuse is a gospel issue? Coming from your own faith tradition, what elements of the gospel do you see that need greater depth, clarity, or definition in order to adequately address the reality of sexual abuse and violence? List the ways and policies in which your church fleshes out the "ethics" of the gospel. What key areas need further thought and development?

2. Why do Christians have such an effective platform to both "call out" the abusers and bring healing to the abused? List some biblical texts you could use to explain this. Historically, how do most Christians respond to sexual abuse? Why? Compare this to other "healing ministries" local churches have. What makes it uniquely difficult to respond to sexual abuse?

49. Cf. Gen 19:7–8; 2 Pet 2:7.

50. Cf. Gen 12:10–20; 20:1–18; 26:1–11.

51. Cf. 2 Samuel 11; 13:7, 20–39.

3. What biblical passages or theological principles are most helpful in explaining the prevalence of sexual abuse? List some biblical examples in which Jesus ministers to various forms of sexual exploitation. What commonalities emerge from these passages? Brainstorm various ways these passages could be discussed, preached, and used to craft or improve a church policy that addresses sexual abuse.

4. What is the best way to define sexual abuse? What is the distinction between contact and non-contact sexual abuse? List some precise examples. Interview a mature survivor willing to give his or her insight, especially if you are crafting literature or a church policy to address sexual abuse. Are you presently aware of any cases of *wife/marital rape among your acquaintances? Discuss *mandated reporting with a counselor or social worker to get a better understanding of the responsibilities various professional community leaders have (e.g., counselors, nurses, pastors, and educators).

5. Whether in a home, church, or on a college campus, where has sexual abuse most recently been reported in your area? If there was a conspiracy of silence, how did it manifest itself? If you have any friends or family members who are missionaries, ask them to explain how the combination of sexual abuse, war, and political corruption has played out in sexual abuse. How would a sexual abuse survivor feel in your church? Are victims' stories ever mentioned?

FOR FURTHER STUDY

Allender, Dan B. *The Wounded Heart: Hope for Adult Victims of Childhood Sexual Abuse.* Rev. ed. Colorado Springs: NavPress, 1995.

Buchwald, Emilie, Pamela R. Fletcher, and Martha Roth, *Transforming a Rape Culture.* Rev. ed. Minneapolis: Milkweed Editions, 2005.

Clark Kroeger, Catherine and James R. Beck, eds. *Women, Abuse, and the Bible: How Scripture Can Be Used to Hurt or Heal.* Grand Rapids: Baker, 1996.

Loseke, Donileen, Richard Gelles, and Mary Cavanaugh, eds. *Current Controversies on Family Violence.* 2nd. ed. Thousand Oaks, CA: Sage, 2005.

National Clearinghouse on Child Abuse and Neglect Information. http://nccanch.acf .hhs.gov.

National Sexual Violence Resource Center. www.nsvrc.org.

Tracy, Steven. *Mending the Soul: Understanding and Healing Abuse.* Grand Rapids: Zondervan, 2005.

United States Department of Justice, Office on Violence against Women. http://www .usdoj.gov/ovw.

World Health Organization, Department of Gender, Women, and Health. http://www .who.int/gender/en.

2

The Dynamics of the Sexually Abusing Family

A Family Systems Perspective

CHERYL CLAYWORTH BELCH, MA, MTS, DMIN, CFLE

IN RECENT YEARS, PUBLIC attention has been drawn to the prevalence of *depression, behavioral problems, abusive relationships, broken marriages, violence, and *suicidal ideation within our communities. Many speculate as to the reasons behind such chaos, especially with this season of war, terrorism, and economic recession placing additional stress on the family. Perhaps the most startling factor is the emerging recognition of the problem of *intrafamilial sexual abuse and the devastation it leaves behind. *Once considered to be a rarity, it is now reported to range from 5 percent to 15 percent in the general population and possibly even greater among high-risk groups such as families dealing with serious chemical dependencies.*[1]

In this chapter, I will examine the dynamics of the sexually abusing family and support the claim that *family dysfunction, as considered from a *systems perspective, contributes to the abuse of children and adolescents by parenting figures and by older siblings. To accomplish this, I will briefly mention some of the past and present theories that regulate society's feelings toward *incest, as well as present a general overview of *systems theory, focusing on the family structure, which regulates the family's capacity to function and maintain the *status quo. These principles of *family system theory will be used to give understanding to the family dynamics during occurrences of incest by a parental figure and/or a sibling.

DEFINITION OF INCEST

Although there are variations in the legal definitions of incest, most researchers state that when it comes to the victimization of a *minor,[2] incest includes "all forms of erotic sexual

---

1. Madock, "Healthy Family Sexuality," 134.

2. The age of a minor, for the purposes of this discussion, is referring to the age of protection from sexual exploitation, which for many countries is under the age of eighteen. However, the age of sexual consent varies between countries, states, and provinces depending on the activity: US—sixteen (federal level), Canada—fourteen, United Kingdom—sixteen, New Zealand—sixteen, Pakistan—eighteen for men and sixteen for women, and so on. Look up the legal ages in your area by examining your local government regulations and policies regarding sexual abuse.

contacts, sexual demands or threats initiated by any adult who is related to the child by family ties or surrogate family ties."[3] Sue Blume further explains:

> [I]ncest, as both *sexual abuse and abuse of power, is violence that does not require force . . . *it is abuse because it doesn't take into consideration the needs or the wishes of the child*, rather meeting the needs of the 'caretaker' at the child's expense . . . incest can be seen as the imposition of sexually inappropriate acts, or acts with sexual overtones, or any use of a minor child to meet the sexual or emotional needs of one or more persons who derive authority through ongoing emotional bonding with that child.[4]

This extended explanation would include sexual abuse (SA) between siblings, which will be discussed later in the chapter.

CONVENTIONAL UNDERSTANDING: "THE INCEST TABOO"

There have been occurrences of incest recorded since ancient times, and for the most part, it has been considered to be a violation of social or *cultural norms. In Scripture, we find the example of David's son, Amnon, premeditating and committing incest with his half-sister, Tamar (2 Samuel 13). Even in that *patriarchal society and culture, this treachery was considered to be so destructive that it ruins the life of a young virgin. While her father, David, was angry, it was her brother Absalom who took revenge into his own hands and later killed his half-brother, Amnon.

In the past, it seems that cultural limitations regarding sexual relationships followed a similar line to what was considered to be socially acceptable in the rules of marriage and to guard against inbreeding. Several theories have emerged from this discussion as having some impact on the occurrence of incest: the Westermarck theory, Freud's *psychoanalysis, and Bowlby's *attachment theory.

In the early 1900s, Edward Westermarck made the observation that:

> [T]here was the remarkable absence of erotic feeling between persons living very closely together from childhood . . . sexual indifference is combined with the positive feeling of aversion when the act is thought of . . . People who have been living closely together from childhood are as a rule near relatives. Hence, their aversion to sexual relations with one another displays itself in custom and in law as a prohibition of intercourse between near kin.[5]

Thus, one may have some concerns if preschool siblings are separated due to custody issues or foster care, and brought together again as adolescents.

In Freud's perspective, "an incestuous love-choice was the first one and that it was only later . . . that the intense bonds between primary kin are *repressed."[6] In this theory, the parent of the opposite sex is considered to be the first love-object of the child, but these feelings are eventually repressed and interest changes to extrafamilial members of

3. Vander Mey and Neff, "Adult-Child Incest," 550.
4. Blume, *Secret Survivors*, 4; emphasis added.
5. Westermarck, *The History of Human Marriage*, 80.
6. Patterson, "Coming too Close, Going too Far," 97.

the opposite sex, as the child enters later stages of psychosexual development. This process is known as "the *Oedipal/Electra complex."[7]

Bowlby's attachment theory is a biologically-based system of behavior between an attachment figure (usually the parent) and the child. When attachment figures are available and responsive, the child develops a strong sense of security that becomes internalized. This enables the child to separate from the attachment figure, believing that upon his or her return, the child will be welcomed and nurtured. An insecurely attached child, in their internalized perception of themselves in relation to their attachment figure, has an unconscious expectation that the other is not available to them, often due to past experiences of abandonment (e.g., parental divorce), separation (e.g., a lengthy hospitalization), death of a parental figure, or inconsistent care. Thus, the child tends to cling to caregivers and be dependent in relationships.[8] Therefore, this could create more of a risk of sexual abuse by a trusted authority figure.

Much discussion has ensued as a result of these theories as well as other paradigms, which consider economic, "evolutionary,"[9] and cultural perspectives. The bottom line indicates that in most cultures incest is considered to be crossing the boundaries of acceptable familial relationship.

PRESENT PERSPECTIVES ON INCEST

*Shockingly, it is estimated that more than 90 percent of all *childhood sexual abuse (CSA) is perpetrated by family members, friends of family members, or other individuals that children know.*[10] Christine Courtois states that "incest between an adult and related child or adolescent is now recognized as the most prevalent form of child sexual abuse and as one with great potential for damage to the child."[11] Incest and child abuse laws *mandate responsible individuals to report their knowledge of any such incidences. However, secrecy, shame, threats, religious beliefs, and loyalty to family members often block disclosure by young victims. Despite the availability of supportive treatment and rehabilitation centers, women's and family shelters, and *support groups, many families remain locked in the continuing cycle of abuse and hopelessness.

Efforts to understand the causes of sexual abuse and its resolution have typically centered around two perspectives: the offender's and the family's. The former focuses on the physiology and psychological functioning of offenders. Often, society views sexual abuse as poor *impulse control or as a transient problem.[12] Since most of the research material is collected from *perpetrators serving time in prison, the worker doesn't have the benefit

7. Corey, *Theory and Practice of Counseling and Psychotherapy*, 67.

8. Bowlby, *Separation*, 213–16.

9. Some current perspectives consider the evolutionary aspect of "survival of the fittest" as reason against incest by protecting the gene pool from potential mutations caused by inbreeding.

10. Ferrara, *Child Sexual Abuse*, 43.

11. Courtois, *Healing the Incest Wound*, 12.

12. Smith, *Sexual Offending Against Children*, 188.

of understanding the family history or dynamics that may have contributed to the abuse.[13] In the author's opinion, these areas are vital in understanding the relationships between family members that create the potential for incest and the feelings of entrapment that keep the cycle operating. Thus, I will focus on the family dynamics through the perspective of family systems.

Overview of Family Systems Theory

Proponents of this theory describe the family as a system, consisting of unique components (i.e., family members) *in which they belong, relate, and impact one another through a series of consistent interacting patterns.* Since the behavior of members arises within this social system, individuals can only be understood within the context of the whole family system. As well, the family is simultaneously a whole system and a part of larger systems (e.g., culture, environment, religious heritage) that bring about external pressures and mutual influences on the individual members and the family as a whole, creating change and development. *Thus, change and conflict are a constant as individuals both influence and are influenced by their environment.*

Change is also a normal requirement as a family matures and advances through the various developmental stages of life—from its inception as a couple to its expansion into future generations. However, systems tend to be *self-regulating, that is, various roles and manners of relating between family members become *normalized and tend to operate in specific ways for substantial periods of time. *Feedback mechanisms become threatened with the stress of possible change, and the family system attempts to maintain the stability of operating in familiar patterns, known as *homeostasis. Thus, feedback serves as a regulatory function to maintain the status quo, but it can also provide the motive for change within the system.[14] The function of the family system, as well as the potential for incest, can be determined by the *manner* of operation of three main features: family structure, subsystems, and boundaries.

FAMILY STRUCTURE

Family Norms

Each family system is organized by an invisible web of consistent, functional demands and expectations that make up the *family structure and determine how, when, and to whom family members relate. Each family has its own unique set of explicit and implicit rules, roles, and transactions that are considered to be the norm of family functioning. Many of these norms have been *internalized by the parents from their own family of origin, their negotiations with each other, their religious belief system,[15] and interactions

---

13. Child Welfare Information Gateway, *Casual Models of Sexual Abuse*, 3.

14. Walsh and McGraw, *Essentials of Family Therapy*, 5–8.

15. In many families, religious beliefs shape such elements as authority, expectations, roles, loyalties, family secrets, openness of communication (or lack thereof), boundaries, and the level of shame and betrayal, especially if help is sought *outside* the family (or religious) system, even to the extent of shunning or shaming. Given these variables, one can imagine the rampant nature of sexual abuse in fundamental reli-

with their environment. Children accept and obey these norms as part of their sense of belonging to the family unit.

Hierarchical Power Systems

The structure of the family is also governed by the fact that each family unit has a *hierarchical power structure or status which dictates the authority and decision-making process within the family. Ideally, the parents have a greater level of authority than children since parents have the responsibility of socializing the children to conform to acceptable family, social, religious, and cultural norms. Over time a democratic exchange is encouraged as children mature, *differentiate, and become more autonomous within the family.

Thus, the system regulates itself by maintaining the accustomed patterns of transaction as much as possible and resisting any change that goes beyond its level of tolerance. Yet, the family structure must be able to adapt when circumstances change. The existence of the system depends on the range of patterns and the flexibility to mobilize alternative transaction patterns in order to meet the needs of a new situation without losing the continuity that serves as a frame of reference to the family members.[16]

Subsystems

Each family system consists of *subsystems, which "can be formed by generation, by sex, by interest, or by function . . . Each individual belongs to different subsystems, in which he has power and where he learns differentiated skills."[17] For example, a woman can be a wife, mother, sister, daughter, and granddaughter, each of which requires different complementary relationships and various subsystems. Subsystems are alliances that can be activated to serve certain family goals. The three main subsystems within the family system consist of: spousal, parental, and sibling subsystems.

Spousal Subsystem

The spousal subsystem consists of the adult or marital dyad, which ideally negotiates its roles and operates as a united and complementary team. This subsystem teaches children about intimacy and commitment in relationships.

Parental Subsystem

The parental subsystem is usually composed of parents but may include other persons in a caregiving role. This subsystem has the major responsibility for child guidance, limit setting, nurturance, protection, and discipline. The ideal result of these processes is a child, adequately *socialized to become an independent and fully functioning member of society, who has the capacity for intimate relationships and the ability to live a meaningful

---

gious sects who isolate themselves from the world beyond their faith community. In such social constructs, the church community is not a sanctuary of safety and healing for the victim of incest or *spousal rape, but instead places fault on the victim and fosters *spiritual incest that further isolates and adds to their powerlessness. For an excellent resource on how religious beliefs impact the family system, see Burton's "Religion and Family" in For Further Reading.

16. Minuchin, *Families and Family Therapy*, 51–53.

17. Ibid., 52.

and purposeful life. Appropriate "boundaries surrounding this subsystem would allow a child to have access to both parents, yet exclude the child from spousal functions."[18]

Sibling Subsystem

The sibling subsystem serves as the child's first peer group in which the child learns skills of negotiation, cooperation, competition, mutual support, and conflict resolution to be used both within their intrafamilial and extrafamilial worlds.

BOUNDARIES

"Boundaries are determined by a set of rules that define who participates in the subsystem and how the individuals participate. The nature of the boundaries has an impact on the functioning of the subsystem as well as the entire family unit."[19] The degree of permeability determines the quality of the boundary, with semi-permeable[20] being the optimal amount. This allows for transactions that are positive and growth producing to enter the family system, while blocking those that cause *dysfunction. The theory describes three types of boundaries between subsystems as being on a continuum: rigid, clear, and diffuse.

Rigid Boundaries

Rigid boundaries permit minimal interaction or communication within and between other subsystems. Otherwise known as disengaged, these families and individuals are autonomous to the extreme of being isolated from the rest of the family and/or community. *Maximum privacy is exchanged for minimum support and protection.*

Clear Boundaries

Clear boundaries are firm yet flexible, and are a necessity for healthy family functioning. They provide "an ideal balance between support, nurture, and inclusion on the one hand, and freedom to experiment, *individuate, and be one's own person on the other hand."[21]

Diffuse Boundaries

"Diffuse boundaries provide minimal privacy and maximum interaction."[22] Family members have a heightened sense of belonging and become overly dependent on each other, requiring them to sacrifice their autonomy. Often it's difficult to determine who is responsible for what, since lines of authority are blurred so that the stress of one individual or subsystem is owned by all.

So what does a family system need in order to adapt to changes required in maintaining function during family development and through crises produced by interaction with external systems? *The healthy family system incorporates good communication, clear*

---

18. Ibid., 57.

19. Walsh and McGraw, *Essentials of Family Therapy*, 50.

20. A semi-permeable boundary has the capacity to adapt by making appropriate structural changes during situational stress or developmental growth, while maintaining proper restrictions and *self-regulation.

21. Becvar and Becvar, *Family Therapy*, 178.

22. Walsh and McGraw, *Essentials of Family Therapy*, 51.

boundaries, flexible roles, a sense of self, and relationships with family members that are supportive, nurturing, and respectful. When observing the family dynamics surrounding incest, it is significant to note areas of family system dysfunction in order to give hope for resolution and rehabilitation so that families become the places of safety, nurture, and growth, as God intended them to be. The incestuous family has distinguishing characteristics that we will now consider.

GENERAL CHARACTERISTICS OF AN INCESTUOUS FAMILY

Wodarski and Johnson describe the common characteristics of an incestuous family; Gil notes *many similarities to a physically abusive family: low self-esteem, low frustration tolerance, impulsivity, feelings of helplessness, lack of problem-solving skills, isolation, despair, exaggeration of patriarchal norms, emotional and sexual estrangement between spouses, *parentification of a child, poor sexual and physical boundaries, abuse of power, fear of authority, *denial, emotional deprivation, lack of *empathy, poor parenting skills, personal stress, social stress, economic stress, substance abuse, and either a *sexualized or *repressive atmosphere.*[23] Within this list, we can note family dysfunction according to family systems theory: abuse of power within the subsystems; diffuse boundaries around the parental subsystem resulting in a *"parentified child"[24]; rigid boundaries surrounding the family system, causing isolation from external resources; diffuse boundaries between and within the parental-child subsystems and the sibling subsystem, abolishing personal privacy; inability for the family system to adapt to external and internal stressors; closed communication; diffuse boundaries within the subsystems, causing family members to take on inappropriate responsibilities—to name a few. By examining the dynamics of families in which incest by parental figures is occurring and those that involve sibling incest, we will notice an overlap of *dysfunctional patterns and some that are unique to each.

Parental-figure Incest

Both male and female parental figures sexually abuse children. However, Tracy Peter notes that statistics in Canada and the United States identify that only 2 to 3 percent of convicted child *molesters are females. That said, *sexual assault by female family members is underreported* due to the fact that inappropriate, lingering touch or the rubbing of the child's genitals (for the purpose of adult sexual arousal), can be disguised within regular family duties, such as bathing children.[25] Since further research is needed in the area of female perpetrators, this section of the chapter will focus on paternal incest by the biological father or step-father and the common opinions regarding the role of the mother figure.

---

23. Wodarski and Johnson, "Child Sexual Abuse," 159–161. See also, Gil, *Sexualized Children*, 102–117.

24. Boszormenyi-Nagy and Spark, *Invisible Loyalties*, 158, suggest that a parentified child is very loyal and will take on the role of physical and psychological guardian for a parent if he or she senses an unmet need for comfort.

25. Peter, "Exploring Taboos," 1112.

PROFILE FACTORS

God created children to be dependent on parents for their *socialization, safety, provision for physical and emotional needs, and spiritual direction. As a result, each child naturally seeks answers to the questions—"Am I loved? Do I belong?" Since we were created in God's *image as "persons-in-relationship" (Gen 1:27; 2:18), these needs for love and belonging are part of who we are as human beings. *An adult who has not had these questions answered adequately within his or her own childhood experience brings this emotional deprivation into the family unit in which they are now parenting.* American clinical studies discovered that men who had sexual contact with their daughters had commonly experienced the desertion of a father figure at a young age or were emotionally deprived in their family of origin and, thus, had minimal opportunities to learn and internalize social constraints within the parent-child relationship. If the perpetrator's father was present, he tended to be harsh and authoritarian. Hence, the abuser had this strong ambivalence of hating and fearing his own father, as well as admiring and respecting him to the point of being left with an ungratified longing for an affectionate relationship with him.[26] There is also a good chance that he was abused in some manner as a child, resulting in low self-esteem, loss of personal power, and feelings of helplessness. *In order to gain some control, he may seek comfort in pornography and other secretive sexual pastimes rather than developing intimacy and open communication within the spousal subsystem.* His sense of self is, not as an autonomous person, but one of need and dependency. Meiselman states findings that "economic deprivation is a special characteristic of the incest group,"[27] although incest also occurs in other economic classes.

If his female partner was a victim of childhood abuse, there may be issues of trust and intimacy within the spousal subsystem, especially in the area of sexual intimacy. She may be promiscuous in other relationships and/or *frigid within the spousal partnership—either way, she expresses her fear of intimacy. This creates poor communication and disengagement within the spousal subsystem.

ABUSE OF POWER: A CORE CHARACTERISTIC OF REPRESSED FAMILIES

Usually, there is an abuse of power—often provoking a rigid patriarchal pattern of relating within the spousal subsystem—creating a repressive atmosphere; the wife is subordinated in power and status to the level of the sibling subsystem. In such cases, wives and children are considered to be "possessions" of the father figure and, therefore, must obey. Overt conflict and confrontation are discouraged; communication about sexual matters is considered to be *taboo. Threats, intimidation, and various *shaming mechanisms control the family members and maintain family secrets, a *conspiracy of silence. *Personal privacy among individuals is nonexistent, and boundaries surrounding the family system are rigid so that family members are isolated from external support.*

*The *authoritarian father lacks a secure sense of his masculine identity but attempts to compensate for his feelings of inadequacy by projecting an image of *role competence. He is*

26. Meiselman, *Incest*, 85–86.

27. Ibid., 85.

usually perceived by those outside the family system as a respectable, hard-working family man, *often with strict religious and moral standards.* Outwardly, he is often intolerant of deviant sexual practices, teaching his children that all sexual thoughts, feelings, and bodily sensations are shameful and sinful, thereby creating within the child an *overbearing conscience* manifested through feelings of guilt and shame. Yet, inwardly he may lead a disorganized personal life, resulting in a cyclical pattern of drunkenness (i.e., anesthetizing his personal pain), violence, remorse, and repentance.[28] This domineering figure uses rationalization for his participation in incest, explaining that he was just "teaching a point," confirming some "spiritual reality," or somehow "showing interest" in what he never had—a caring father. After all, doesn't God command him to take charge of his family? Are not wives commanded to "submit" to their husbands (Eph 5:22–24; Col 3:18), and children to "obey" their parents (Eph 6:1–3; Col 3:20)? Sometimes the Church's teaching on family relationships doesn't include the whole message of God, which also commands *mutual respect* (Eph 5:21), and responsibility for all family members, as well as emphasizing God's loving concern for children, his most vulnerable creation (Matt 18:1–10). Such scenarios also reveal spiritual incest. However, Scripture cannot be used to defend or hide an abusive leader or family situation.

ENABLER ROLES

If the mother figure is emotionally distanced from the family, dealing with her own pain and low self-esteem, she *abdicates her responsibility (i.e., under-functioning) in her roles as "mother," "nurturer," and "protector." Often, a "special relationship" takes place between the father and the oldest daughter as she steps in—as a parentified child—to fill the vacated maternal role, assume excessive caretaking responsibilities (i.e., over-functioning), and attempt to meet the emotional needs of the father. Bradshaw claims that this *enmeshment of boundaries is "a way that children take on the covert needs of a family system"[29] in order to maintain system function. This *role-reversal between mother and daughter contributes to estrangement and jealousy between them, while the alliance between the father and daughter creates a new subsystem to the detriment of the spousal subsystem. This emotional relationship easily becomes *sexualized, particularly if the father is abusing alcohol, which tends to remove inhibitions to socially unacceptable urges lying below the surface. Gil explains the dynamics: "the parent-child relationship provides the inequality in status and the necessary dependency the individual craves, and it is in this relationship that self-esteem momentarily returns, feelings of dominance prevail, some sexual gratification occurs, and pain finds a respite."[30] Much of this description applies specifically to the *"repressed family."

THE SEXUALIZED FAMILY

Gil also refers to the *"sexualized family," a family system that has "an inordinate preoccupation with sex. They use "sexual language, make sexual innuendos . . . sexualize their

---

28. Ibid., 91–111.

29. Bradshaw, *Healing the Shame that Binds You*, 49.

30. Gil, *Sexualized Children*, 105.

intimate contact, respect few if any boundaries, stimulate each other with sexual informa-tion . . . nudity takes on dimensions of *exhibitionism and *voyeurism."[31] Children are exposed prematurely to adult patterns of behavior, including incestuous contact. *Power and control may be distributed along gender lines in that males are taught a lack of respect for females*; pornography, which is openly available for children to view, teaches sons that men invariably force themselves on women in a sexual manner. This psychological form of sexual abuse often causes children to use inappropriate *sexualized behavior.[32] *Daughters learn to equate acceptance, intimacy, and love as inseparable from sexual behavior, and thus, often behave seductively toward others as an attempt to make up for their unmet emotional needs.* As children enter into the adolescent stage of dating, family control over their af-fectionate and sexual expression is threatened, creating *intergenerational conflict even to the extent of the premature departure of the adolescent from the family home.

The type of sexualized behavior that is practiced may not only be impacted by gender but also culturally and economically. There is the double standard of the Latino family, for example, in which one aspect of the male *"machismo" suggests that *his virility is asserted through sexual conquests.* Although the "Latina" may be flirtatious, *she is held responsible to protect her virginity* in all circumstances (even from father-daughter incest) since her marital value depends on it, *as well as her family's dignity.*[33] In addition, in some poverty-stricken Asian cultures, mothers leave their daughters unprotected from father-daughter incest due to their need to become migrant laborers in another country. Yet, even in religious cultures that normalize the practice of *child-brides, the victims experience a feeling of deep shame and oppression.

THE COLLUSIVE PARTNER

So what is the role of the "other parent" in all of this? Is the non-abusing parent, usually the mother, fully aware of the incestuous crime against her child, and if so, is she equally responsible for the victimization? In many cases, the mother figure is immersed in her own emotional pain and "toxic shame . . . which gives a sense of worthlessness, a sense of failing and falling short as a human being."[34] In order to counter these feelings and to minimize *cognitive dissonance, family members rely on *defense mechanisms—the most powerful being *"denial,"[35] especially if the mother has also been a victim of child-hood abuse.

Twisted religious views of relationships can also create ethical passivity—God's sov-ereignty can functionally "trump" the need for relational accountability between family members. Such perspectives enable the mother to engage in distorted thought patterns, which can lead to rationalizations of *symptomatic behaviors.[36] At times, the mother

31. Ibid., 110–11.

32. Ibid., 112.

33. Fontes, "Sin Verguenza," 61–81.

34. Bradshaw, *Healing the Shame that Binds You,* 10.

35. Key to this chapter, denial is an inability to recognize certain feelings and experiences that may threaten aspects of reality.

36. Maddock, "Healthy Family Sexuality," 134.

ignores the ongoing abuse, hides behind rigid domestic roles, emotionally disconnects from the family, and may refuse to engage sexually with her partner, leaving her daughter to fulfill his needs. This situation identifies the mother as a *collusive partner in the crime. This ultimate abandonment by both parents leaves the child without a safe refuge and to experience the world as a dangerous place.

Usually, the mother is shocked at the discovery of incest within her home, *but in hindsight, she may recognize some clues about its presence.* Yet, whether or not the mother is fully aware of the abuse, she is still left in a *dilemma of loyalty.* She is forced to choose between two family members and the two most vital roles on which she may base her identity—her role of spouse/partner and that of mother. Entering into this decision is the duty she may feel toward her marriage. *After all, within her marriage vows she covenanted before God to be loyal to her spouse for a lifetime, which is why rationalized and rigid roles can enable avoidance and "false closure."* How can she charge him with a criminal offence? As well, "to choose 'for the child' means women are likely to exchange economic dependence on men for dependence on state benefits and low-paid work or alternatively to replace dependence on one man with dependence on another,"[37] since the option of single parenting or being without a relationship is beyond her comprehension, religiously and socially. In some cultures, the removal of the patriarch from the home is considered to cause more family disruption than the abuse itself. *Thus, many women tend to base their decision on their own survival and that of the family system, rather than on the protection of their child. As a result, incest may continue for years at the child's expense, maintained by the need of homeostasis within the family system.*

Sibling Incest

There is much debate among researchers as to the extent of damage caused by sibling sexual contact and of the criteria that qualifies it as abuse. "Sibling incest is often viewed as less traumatic to the victim than incest which involves an adult and a child because no generational boundary is violated."[38] This makes the incident easier to hide but more difficult to determine if the act was consensual or *coercive. Hardy suggests that:

> [S]ome sexual behavior between siblings may not be abusive, provided there is less than a four- to five-year age difference, the children are young [i.e., before puberty], there is no betrayal of trust, the behavior is the result of natural curiosity and experimentation, and the children are not traumatized by the behavior or by disapproving adults.[39]

However, Brennan's definition accounts for occasions in which *trauma can result—"sibling incest is sexual interaction beyond age-appropriate exploration such that *older siblings, possessing significant age, power, or resource differences, may be considered abusive.*"[40] Such activity is deemed to consist of everything from unwanted sexual advances, sexual

37. Hooper, *Mothers Surviving Child Sexual Abuse*, 81.
38. Canavan et al., "The Female Experience of Sibling Incest," 130.
39. Hardy, "Physical Aggression and Sexual Behavior among Siblings," 256.
40. Brennan, "Sibling Incest Within Violent Families," 287; emphasis added.

leers, forcing a sibling to view pornographic material, touching or fondling, up to and including intercourse.[41]

Although sibling sexual abuse may be the most common form of incest,[42] it is greatly underestimated by society and under-reported, due to parental opinions that it is merely harmless, developmental curiosity of children. *Part of this attitude can be attributed to parental denial, due to the fact that it may bring attention to relational deficits within the family, and/or incur memories of the parents' own childhood victimization.* Parents also may assume guilt for neglecting to monitor the responsibility, trust, and power that they have attributed to one of their older children. This is particularly the case in single-parent families in which the mother is often emotionally and/or physically absent, leaving an older child in charge of his or her siblings. Parenting skills may also be deficient when it comes to making, and consistently enforcing, family regulations and boundaries. Divided family loyalties—especially when abuse occurs between stepsiblings—make it very difficult for parents to report to *Child Protective Agencies that one child is an offender with the possible consequences that he or she will be removed from the home. As well, a daughter within a patriarchic family system, buried in shame, feels that her disclosure will be ignored, or that she will be blamed for possible dissolution of the family and harshly punished. As a result, she sacrifices her autonomy for the sake of homeostasis of the family system, feeling helpless, powerless, and invariably experiencing depression.

TYPES OF SIBLING INCEST

Sibling incest tends to fall under two subtypes: power-oriented incest and nurturance-oriented incest.[43]

Power-oriented Incest

Power-oriented incest involves a more powerful perpetrator coercing an unwilling victim. The offender violates the trust of the younger victim by using force, threats, bribes, or the offer of special attention in order to continue the abuse. Since the perpetrator has easy access to the victim(s), the abuse is protected by family secrecy and may continue well into adolescence. *The family is often isolated, with severe sanctions about discussing family life outside the home, but with blurred boundaries among family members such that other forms of abuse may already be occurring.* It is common for older siblings to help in caretaking duties of younger siblings, especially when parents are overstressed and overburdened with responsibility, but misuse of power and authority can lead to abuse in various forms. If the more powerful sibling has experienced sexual abuse himself, he or she may force sexual activity on a much younger sibling through violence or coercion.[44] Kiselica and Morrill-Richards claim that "when the family structure supports power imbalances, rigid

---

41. Kiselica and Morrill-Richards, "Sibling Maltreatment," 150.

42. Carlson et al., "Sibling Incest," 20.

43. Canavan et al., "The Female Experience of Sibling Incest," 130. These categories are also noted by Carlson, et al, "Sibling Incest," 22.

44. Canavan et al., "The Female Experience of Sibling Incest," 131.

gender roles, differential treatment of siblings, and lack of parental supervision, there is an increased risk of sibling abuse."[45]

Nurturance-oriented Incest

Nurturance-oriented incest denotes two siblings who begin engaging in sexual behaviors on a consensual basis, whereupon one sibling no longer wishes to participate but is pressured to do so.[46] In these instances, boundaries blur within the sibling subsystem and the resulting sexual behavior is a misguided attempt to show affection, empathy, and comfort in families experiencing parental abuse and neglect. In both "sexualized families" that normalize seductive behavior and enforce secrecy surrounding extramarital affairs and "sexually repressed families," who paradoxically increase children's curiosity in the forbidden, there are contributing factors that bind the participants to silence. A systems perspective of the family maintains that *many factors contribute to sibling incest and that all family members are victims due to the complication of the family dynamics.*[47]

SOME FUTURE DIRECTIONS

This chapter has discussed the dynamics within a sexually abusing family and pointed to dysfunctional organizational and *power structures within the family system as major contributing factors in the occurrence of parental-figure incest and sibling sexual abuse. In realizing the powerful hold that feedback mechanisms have in sustaining the status quo of family function, and the place of *cyclical transactional patterns within family history, *we realize that stopping the abuse is not enough—the underlying family dynamics themselves need to be addressed.* So how does one accomplish this feat? In my opinion, education is prevention.

Thus, we must approach the enormous task of teaching families healthy ways of relating, both through family therapy and the preventive means of family life education. General education, in an age-appropriate manner, is essential in schools, community centers, and churches on such topics as conflict and stress management, communication skills, self-esteem, assertiveness, family roles, healthy sexuality, intimacy, abuse prevention, and parenting skills. Facilitators, knowledgeable in family of origin issues, offer significant input in identifying strengths and potential problem areas during premarital counseling and marriage enrichment programs. And, since single parent families are especially vulnerable to incest when a parent enters another relationship, support groups would be informative about the realities and stresses of blending families in parenting, family loyalties, and increased opportunities for conflicting values.

As well, there are areas requiring further study. Family connectedness and the *hierarchy of power are necessary components to be examined in our multi-cultural society, in which one's identity is *enmeshed in extended family relations and where multiple generations live under one roof. In addition, further research is necessary in areas that are

---

45. Kiselica and Morrill-Richards, "Sibling Maltreatment," 148.

46. Carlson et al., "Sibling Incest," 22.

47. Canavan et al., "The Female Experience," 139.

underreported, as in male victimization and the dynamics surrounding female perpetrators. As we move forward in our learning and, in turn, intervene in the lives of others, may God use us as instruments of healing and protection for vulnerable families within our communities.

QUESTIONS FOR DISCUSSION

1. How would you advise the non-offending spouse within a Christian marriage in which parental incest has been disclosed? Consider the following scenarios in your answer. If she calls the child protective agency, her husband will likely be charged, removed from the family, and sent to jail (or the child may be removed from the family, creating further trauma). If she doesn't carry through with the laws of the country, what message does she send her victimized child? How does accusing her husband impact the loyalty that she covenanted to him in her marriage vows: "for better or for worse . . . until death do us part?" Discuss the ramifications if she does report her spouse and the subsequent impact on the rest of the family. Can and should the marriage be restored?

2. What is the role of the faith community in preventing and supporting families who are dealing with the impact of incest? What role should *survivors play in the church, family ministries, and support groups? What areas in your church have you seen survivors utilized or placed in areas of care and leadership? List several contributions that a family systems approach makes to "family pastors" and their concerns in local church ministries.

3. In what areas of family life education could the church or community develop programs to encourage healthy family relationships and healthy sexuality? What age groups would you target? How do cultural views of sexuality and the family shape policies—at the state and church levels? Based on this chapter, what specific areas of "family ministry" need more careful explanation, definition, or intervention-like address?

4. Explain how the "sexualized family" operates. Make a list of social ideologies and influences in society today that contribute to the sexualized family. How do various members of a sexualized family contribute to this collective problem? Compare and contrast the *repressed family* and the *sexualized family*. If a church leadership insists that the abuser repent and join a support group and the abused child resume life within the family—what might a family systems perspective help these leaders understand about this family and the child's needs? How does the cultural context shape the "permeability" of family boundaries? What other factors need to be considered when addressing sexuality (e.g., the "purity talk") to teens?

5. Explain how an abusing family's role-reversals and rationalizations (e.g., parentification, *collusion, etc.) foster "family secrets," keep members from finding outside help, and prevent the family from healing. Considering Westermarck's theory, would removing children from the home and separating them from each other during the

first three to six years of life due to parental abuse, set up the children for potential sibling incest when they are older? How might this impact the policies of child protective agencies?

FOR FURTHER READING

Balswick, Jack O. and Judith K. Balswick. *The Family: A Christian Perspective on the Contemporary Home*. 3rd Edition. Grand Rapids: Baker Academic, 2007.

Burton, Laurel A. ed. *Religion and the Family: When God Helps*. Binghamton, NY: The Hayworth Press, 1992.

Canavan, Margaret M. et al. "The Female Experience of Sibling Incest." *Journal of Marital and Family Therapy* 18 (1992): 129–142.

Hooper, Carol-Ann. "Working it Out." In *Mothers Surviving Child Sexual Abuse*. Abingdon, Oxfordshire: Taylor & Francis Ltd., 1992, 80–110.

Maddock, James W. "Healthy Family Sexuality: Positive Principles for Educators and Clinicians." *Family Relations* 38 (1989): 130–136.

Nasjleti, Maria. "Suffering in Silence: The Male Incest Victim." *Child Welfare* 59 (1980): 269–275.

Scott, Marshall S. "Honor thy Father and Mother: Scriptural Resources for Victims of Incest and Parental Abuse." *Journal of Pastoral Care* 42 (1988): 139–148.

Thornton, Jennifer A. et al. "Intrafamilial Adolescent Sex Offenders: Family Functioning and Treatment." *Journal of Family Studies* 14 (2008): 362–375.

Ramsey-Klawsnik, Holly. "Elder Sexual Abuse within the Family." *Journal of Elder Abuse & Neglect* 15 (2003): 43–58.

3

Sexually Abusive Relationships

Their Kinds and Dynamics

Joyce Wagner, PhD

THERE ARE SEVERAL TYPES of sexually abusive relationships. With each type of relationship comes a unique set of dynamics for both victims and their offenders.[1] For the purposes of this chapter, sexually abusive relationships will be grouped into three sections:

- *Sexual abuse (SA) involving children and adolescents (i.e., *child sexual abuse [CSA], *incest, *molestation),

- Sexual assault (i.e., *stranger rape, *date/acquaintance rape, *spousal/intimate partner rape),

- *Paraphilias (i.e., *exhibitionism, *voyeurism).[2]

Each section will be broken down into a historical understanding of the issue followed by a present understanding of victims and offenders. The chapter will conclude with a discussion of the future direction and some unresolved needs regarding these issues.

CHILD SEXUAL ABUSE, INCEST, AND MOLESTATION

The typical depiction of CSA may be a father molesting his daughter, however, the picture is actually much broader and includes prostitution, *ritualistic abuse, and even *female circumcision. The common characteristics of CSA include non-consensual sexual contact, violence, non-physical force (e.g., control and manipulation), secrecy, and entrapment. *While feelings of helplessness and hopelessness are common among victims, feelings of ambivalence and retraction are common among offenders.*[3]

---

1. Gilmartin, *Rape, Incest, and Child Sexual Abuse*, 138–158. See also, Maltz, *The Sexual Healing Journey*, 15–28.

2. Other less common but equally disturbing types of sexual abuse include: *sadistic sexual abuse, sexual violence,*sexual harassment, gender attacks, and *gay bashing.

3. Dienemann et al., *Issues in Mental Health Nursing*, 499–513; Ferguson and Mullen, *Childhood Sexual Abuse*, 35–52; Green, "Children Traumatized by Physical Abuse," 134–54; Leserman, "Sexual Abuse History," 906–15.

Historical Understanding

Ancient societies' histories abound with examples of CSA, including *infanticide, child slavery, and the use of children for adult sexual gratification. In Greece, *pederasty was even lauded among top citizens, including Aristotle.[4] Incest also held a prominent place in Greek mythology in which incest among the gods was frequent. Incest was also prevalent in Roman (e.g., Claudius, Agrippa, Nero) and Egyptian cultures; in Persia incestuous marriage was directly recommended (e.g., Cleopatra).[5]

During the Middle Ages children were viewed as miniature adults and sexual abuse was rampant. Until approximately the sixteenth century, children were viewed as insignificant property—essentially *chattel—with parents having nearly unlimited power over them.[6] The turnaround of societal views on CSA is credited largely to the *Jesuits, who stressed childhood innocence, expressed *empathy for children, and attempted to end the practice of children and adults sleeping together.[7] Despite these changes, in colonial America children were commonly viewed in *economic* terms and thus were easy marks for violence. Standard Puritan child-rearing practices would now be considered abusive, and sadly, the Bible was often misused to sanction harsh treatment.[8]

In the late 1800s the legal struggle for children's rights began informally in America with the case of Mary Ellen. Given up to New York City's Department of Charities at the age of three, Mary Ellen was handed over to a family who both neglected (i.e., did not allow her to go outside, did not provide adequate clothing, food, or shelter) and abused her (i.e., burned, hit, cut, whipped). Concerns from several neighbors were filed and the case was given to a Methodist caseworker. *After being turned away by police, the caseworker sought help from the Society for the Protection and Care of Animals (SPCA) because there were no laws governing the protection of children.* Eventually the case was won, resulting in the foundation of the first Society for the Prevention of Cruelty to Children (SPCC) in 1874.[9] Gilmartin summarizes this insidious pattern of societal tolerance of CSA, stating:

> [W]e have a lengthy history of ignoring the fact that incest and child sexual abuse exist, minimizing the serious impact and the traumatizing nature of these experiences, buying into the mythology which surrounds this subject, victimization, and acknowledging the "less serious" forms of child sexual victimization which deny that organized or cultic forms could be real.[10]

Present Understanding

Presently, what is known about children and adolescents who are at greatest risk for CSA include those who are unplanned, unwanted, of minority status, or premature. Also at risk

---

4. DeMause, *The History of Childhood*, 46.

5. Serrano and Gunsburger, "An Historical Perspective of Incest," 70–80.

6. Schetky and Green, *Child Sexual Abuse*, 25.

7. Ibid., 25.

8. Schroeder, *Dinah's Lament*, 4–10.

9. By 1967 all US states finally had statutes on child abuse.

10. Gilmartin, *Rape, Incest, and Child Sexual Abuse*, 78.

are those with difficult temperaments, those with behavioral problems, and those who fail to bond with the mother.[11] Those abused as infants or toddlers typically come from low-income, minority households run by a single parent, typically a mother.[12] In contrast, those abused as adolescents typically come from two-parent, Caucasian, middle-income families where the abuse occurs by fathers.[13]

A great deal of research has been conducted regarding those who abuse children and adolescents. In general, offenders who abuse children are known collectively as *pedophiles. Not all pedophiles offend children; however, what is known clinically is typically from those who do and get caught. Research suggests the rate of pedophilia is rare[14] although there are differing results with regard to education, socio-economic status, and ethnicity.[15] Those at greatest risk for offending, according to the US Department of Health and Human Services (DHHS), includes young parents, those with several young children, substance abusers, those with a history of poor *impulse control or violence, and those who suffered physical abuse as children.[16]

The marital relationship also plays a role in pedophilia, with couples who exhibit poor communication and conflict resolution skills being at higher risk, in part because *their children often become cast in parental roles as a result of the discord.*[17] Serious consideration of environmental factors, including poverty, lack of a social support network, unemployment, homelessness/inadequate housing, frequent moving, *acculturative stress, and the experience of discrimination based on minority group status, must all be considered.[18]

Child molesters are older and more passive than other sexual offenders. *In many cases child molesters also know their victims on a relational basis,* versus many sexual offenders who choose strangers to victimize.[19] Child molesters often have a history of adverse family relations, along with poor *attachment patterns. Relationally they are considered incompetent in regard to interactions with the opposite sex. In general these individuals are preoccupied or fearful of adult romantic relationships; such fears of rejection and evaluation make it easier to interact with children. Child molesters have also experienced

11. Rodrigues-Srednicki and Twaite, *Understanding, Assessing, and Treating Adult Victims of Childhood Abuse*, 1–28.

12. Straus et al., *Behind Closed Doors*, 123–153.

13. Kelly, *Surviving Sexual Violence*, 138–158.

14. Approximately > 3 percent of males. Seto, "Pedophilia: Psychopathology and Theory," 164–82.

15. Camilleri and Quinsey, "Pedophilia: Assessment and Treatment," 183–212.

16. Other factors playing a part in the making of a pedophile include: inadequate *coping skills, poor social skills, isolation, the modeling of violence within their family of origin, CSA, parents with a history of mental illness such as *anti-social behavior, *depression or *somatic complaints, and low self-esteem. Clinically, pedophiles also struggle with anxiety, depression, personality problems, and other paraphilias such as exhibitionism, voyeurism, public masturbation, and *sadism (Kelly, *Surviving Sexual Violence*, 138–158).

17. Seto, "Pedophilia," in *Sexual Deviance*, 164–182; emphasis added.

18. Kelly, *Surviving Sexual Violence*, 138–158.

19. Camilleri and Quinsey, "Pedophilia: Assessment and Treatment," 183–212.

more consenting and non-consenting sexual activity with children.[20] *Professionally, they are more likely to have held a professional position, although they demonstrate highly emotional and *intrusive behaviors.* These patterns, along with low self-worth, a high level of general empathy but low victim empathy, and *cognitive distortions create a profile of a likely abuser.[21]

*Role confusion and a blurring of physical and psychological boundaries characterize incestuous families.[22] These families typically fall into one of the following three categories.

Types of Incestuous Families

1. *Father-dominant:* families where the father is *authoritarian while the mother is devalued, silent, fearful, and emotionally distant.[23]

2. *Mother-dominant:* families where the mother is self-absorbed while the husband struggles with inadequacy.[24]

3. *Chaotic/disorganized families:* families that are characterized by neglect, abandonment, and substance abuse. In these households the parents *abdicate responsibility to children. As the children become *parentified, the door is opened further for the father to become their nurturer.[25]

Several theories try to explain the behavior of pedophiles. One rationale offered by Seto asserts that "it is possible that pedophiles and non-pedophiles share the same curiosity about seeing other children nude when they were children themselves, but pedophiles remain fixed at this stage and do not develop a sexual attraction to postpubertal individuals as they reach puberty."[26] *Neurological abnormalities have also been reported along with lower scores on intelligence tests among offenders. Others purport the behavior to be the cycle of CSA, which often perpetuates itself (see discussion below).

Cycles and Patterns in the Incestuous Family

Much work has been done in recent years to understand this cycle of CSA. Allender's now classic work outlines how the stage is set for abuse, as the child is singled out as the "little adult," leading to *role distortion and role confusion. Next, there is some violation of boundaries, such as giving little or no privacy to the child. This type of home-life pro-

20. Clinically these individuals have experienced higher levels of CSA and sexual confusion along with a highly *sexualized childhood (Connolly and Woollons, "Childhood Sexual Experience and Adult Offending," 119–32).

21. Wood and Riggs, "Predictors of Child Molestation," 259–275.

22. Green, "Children Traumatized by Physical Abuse," 134–54.

23. The father in this type of household views his offensive behaviors as "sex education" (Langberg, *Counseling Survivors of Sexual Abuse*, 64); see "*collusive partner" in Glossary.

24. The father in this type of household prefers pornography, *compulsive masturbation, and/or pederasty to normal marital relations (Langberg, *Counseling Survivors*, 64).

25. Ibid.

26. Seto, "Pedophilia," in *Sexual Deviance*, 166.

duces a *relational* hunger—"a sense of being needed but nevertheless demeaned, making it difficult for the child to trust her perceptions and feelings."[27] The result is a child who is "left *empty*, committed to pleasing, boundary-less, burdened, and bound to a family or a parent whose desire becomes the bread of hope for the hungry child."[28]

THE "SEQUENCE" OF ABUSE

Allender discusses the typical sequence of abuse throughout his work. Below is a summary, illustrated in a diagram.

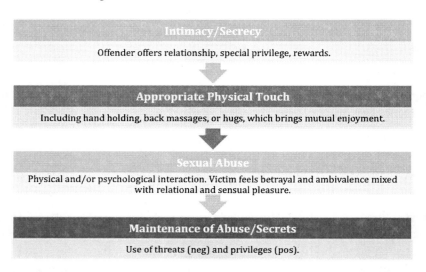

As detailed in the diagram, the offender sets up a slippery slope of desensitization where the child is *groomed—slowly prepared to accept sexual abuse. *By gradually gaining the child's trust and confidence through the use of the ordinary behaviors, the offender systematically tests the child's boundaries to determine whether he or she is likely to report a violation* (e.g., inappropriate touch, talk, humor, etc.). Once the child has been lured into the offender's subtle web and the sexual abuse has begun, the offender can often easily perpetuate the cycle by keeping the child *emotionally confused* regarding the nature of the relationship by shifting roles and preying on the child's own sense of shame, loyalty, and a desire to please.

SEXUAL ASSAULT/RAPE, DATE/ACQUAINTANCE RAPE, MARITAL PARTNER RAPE

Legally, *rape can be defined as: "penetration of the vagina or anus without legitimate consent."[29] In the United States, 62 percent of victims of sex crimes are under age sixteen, and 29 percent are under the age of eleven.[30] Worldwide, overall sexual assault figures

27. Allender, *Wounded Heart*, 91–110.

28. Ibid., 95; emphasis added.

29. Bachar and Koss, "From Prevalence to Prevention," 117–42.

30. It is estimated that 84 percent of victims know their attacker (Kroeger and Nason-Clark, *No Place*

range from 2 to 56 percent.[31] Researchers have also studied the various motivations behind rape, *determining sex, aggression, impulsivity, *sexual diffusion, and power to be the primary determinants.*[32] Marital or intimate partner rape is defined as sexual abuse perpetrated by one spouse on the other, or a sexual partner in any long-term committed relationship.[33]

Historical Understanding

Historical accounts of sexual assault are few, largely because women have been considered property of men under English law until recently. *It was not until the 1970s that sexual assault became a legal issue*; at that time the crime needed to meet the following three criteria: (1) carnal knowledge, (2) force or the threat of force, (3) and lack of consent.[34] Even with these criteria however, attacks were often interpreted narrowly. An *adversarial legal system essentially put the victim "on trial," implicitly blaming that victim. The 1970s also brought about reform in rape laws, which insisted on increasing the overall concern for the rape *survivor.[35] In contrast to earlier cases, victims were not required to corroborate their story and less examinations of victim's sexual history surfaced in court.[36]

Present Understanding

Presently, what is known about the factors that put individuals at a higher risk for a sexual assault include a past sexual victimization, a history of multiple sexual partners, and alcohol use. Nontraditional sex roles and the acceptance of interpersonal violence also play a role.[37] Demographically speaking, victims of *intimate partner sexual assault grew up in a home that contained violence; they may have also endured CSA. As an adult they are often African American, young, unemployed, divorced, and often have been raped outside of the marriage.[38] Those who are separated or divorced are at much greater risk to be assaulted by a previous partner. Those in a *lesbian relationship also report up to 50

---

for Abuse, 9–13).

31. Bachar and Koss, "From Prevalence to Prevention," 117–42.

32. For further research regarding the four types of offense behaviors found in sexual assaults, see Hazlewood and Wolbert Burgess, *Practical Aspects of Rape*; Lauer, *The Truth About Rape*, 159.

33. Worldwide, 7.7 million women are affected by marital/intimate partner rape; these numbers jump to 40 to 50 percent among battered women (Martin et al., "A Review of Marital Rape," 329–47); see "*wife rape" in Glossary.

It is estimated that an intimate partner has committed 33 percent of all female murders (Mahoney et al., "Violence against Women by Intimate Relationship Partners," 143–78; Wendy Maltz, *The Sexual Healing Journey*, 15–28).

34. Bennice and Resick, "Marital Rape," 228–46.

35. In 1978 John Rideout became the first husband prosecuted for marital rape, though he was eventually acquitted. However, his case did succeed in raising overall awareness of marital rape (Bennice and Ressick, "Marital Rape," 228–46).

36. Ibid.

37. Ibid.

38. Ibid.

percent more sexual battering within their current relationships;[39] such reports indicate that abuse is more chronic.[40] As would be assumed, *victims more often than not stay in these relationships due to fear, finances, and the fantasy that things will change.*[41] However, this wishful thinking rarely materializes, leaving these individuals with many of the consequences listed above. In addition, however, victims who have endured intimate-partner abuse also incur additional *judicial and medical bills, and have a higher incidence of job loss as a result of their chronic abuse.[42]

As with those who offend children and adolescents, much research has been done regarding rapists. The demographic profile of a sexual assailant includes individuals who, as children, experienced neglect, CSA, traumatic brain injuries, adverse family relations, and poor *attachment patterns, especially with their fathers. As adults, offenders are often high school dropouts, substance abusers, or blue-collar workers with a low socioeconomic status.[43]

The offender's cognitions also play a crucial role in their desire to rape. These include sexual preoccupation, deviant arousal, hypersexuality, and skewed beliefs about appropriate masculinity.[44] Along with these thoughts are rape-supportive beliefs, or offense-supportive *schemas, used by the offender to draw inferences about their victim's beliefs, desires, and future intentions.[45] A sense of *entitlement, *machismo mentality, and control are also present. Ironically, these offenders view the world as a dangerous place where actions cannot be controlled, particularly in the face of strong urges and impulses. These *cognitive distortions, which are entrenched in the individual and therefore difficult to change, cause the person to misinterpret their world and therefore provide a strong "justification" for rape.[46]

Clearly, there are many puzzle pieces that must come together to form a rapist. Marshall and Barbaree's Integrated Theory of Sexual Offenders[47] (see diagram below) outlines the various factors that often work together to *trigger a sexual assault.[48] When considering the *etiology of this type of *psychopathology, as Yarhouse et al., points out,

---

39. Ibid.

40. Martin, Taft, and Resick. "A Review of Marital Rape," 329–47.

41. Kroeger and Nason-Clark, *No Place for Abuse*, 9–13.

42. Mahoney, Williams, and West, "Violence Against Women," 143–78.

43. Clinically these individuals are hypersensitive, insecure, distrustful, and hostile toward women. They are emotionally lonely; some have engaged in CSA, exhibitionism, and burglary (Bard et al., "A Descriptive Study of Rapists and Child Molesters," 203–20; Connolly and Woollons, "Childhood Sexual Experience and Adult Offending: An Exploratory Comparison of Three Groups," 119–32).

44. Ryan, "Further Evidence for a Cognitive Component of Rape," 579–604.

45. These include viewing women as dangerous, unknowable, and deceptive sexual objects who are sexually preoccupied and therefore highly receptive to sexual advances (Ward, "Sexual Offenders' Cognitive Distortions as Implicit Theories," 491–507).

46. Criassati, "Sexual Violence Against Women," 401–22.

47. Marshall and Barbaree, "An Integrated Theory of Sexual Offending," 363–85.

48. Ward and Beech's Integrated Theory of Sexual Offending (ITSO) is another comprehensive framework designed to outline various factors that contribute to make a sexual offender. For more information, see Ward and Beech, "An Integrated Theory of Sexual Offending," 21–38.

it is extremely important to employ this type of *comprehensive framework* in order to best understand these individuals.[49]

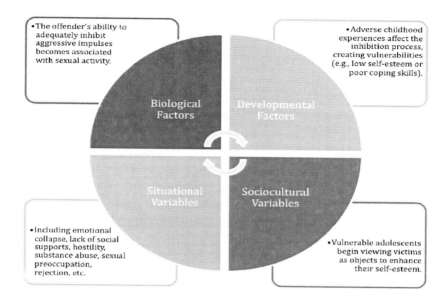

PARAPHILIAS: EXHIBITIONISM AND VOYEURISM

The term paraphilia comes from the Greek words *para* ("beyond," "amiss," "altered") and *philia* ("love"). Paraphilias first appears in American psychiatry in 1934 to specify a subclass of *psychosexual disorders and to replace the word *perversion*.[50] Currently, the *Diagnostic and Statistical Manual of Mental Disorders (DSM-IV-TR)* defines the broad class of paraphilias as "recurrent, intense, sexually arousing fantasies, sexual urges, or behaviors generally involving nonhuman objects, the suffering or humiliation of oneself or one's partner, or children or other non-consenting persons that occur over a period of at least six months."[51] Common paraphilias include exhibitionism or deliberate exposure[52] and voyeurism, including sexually suggestive e-mail messages and *telephone scatalogia.[53] The profile of an offender is someone who has had contact with the criminal justice system in their midtwenties. Offenders are primarily male; their victims, typically young women and children.[54] On a related note, a growing phenomenon in our technological age is also the creation of *"sexting"—where people use cell phones or computers to share sexually explicit photos and/or videos of themselves. At present our judicial system is wrestling with how to handle sexting cases, wrestling with whether the material transmitted should

49. Yarhouse et al., *Modern Psychopathologies*, 310–340.

50. Money and Lamacz, "Paraphilia not Otherwise Specified: Psychopathology and Theory," 384.

51. American Psychiatric Association, *Diagnostic and Statistical Manual of Mental Disorders*, 566.

52. Law enforcement estimates that 4.3 percent of males and 2.1 percent of females engage in exhibitionist/exposure behaviors (Milner, Dopke, and Crouch, "Paraphilia not Otherwise Specified," 384–418).

53. Lavin, "Voyeurism: Psychopathology and Theory," 305–19.

54. Milner, Dopke, and Crouch, "Paraphilia not Otherwise Specified," 384–418.

be considered pornographic, the rights of the individuals in the pictures/videos, the rights of those transmitting such data, and whether such cases are best handled legally or left in the hands of parents.[55]

There are no known *prevalence rates for voyeurism, although Mann and her colleagues assert "it is generally assumed that the majority of men and women who chanced upon an opportunity to observe a woman or man undressing would stop and take a look."[56] Part of the nonchalance that seems to surround voyeuristic behavior seems to have come from the belief "there's no harm in looking."[57] This behavior has become *normalized through peep shows and pornography to the point where, while perhaps not healthy or desirable, it is hardly considered deviant. While accurate statistics are very difficult to obtain, recent estimates compiled by respected news and research organizations claim that every second $3,075.64 is being spent on pornography. Every second 28,258 Internet users are viewing pornography. In that same second 372 Internet users are typing adult search terms into search engines. Every 39 minutes a new pornographic video is being created in the United States.[58] As Mann et al., also points out, this type of tolerance may be dangerous, in part because "what little information there is about voyeurs suggests *voyeurism is rarely found as a pure condition*, and in cases where aggressive fantasy is involved, it may signal risk of more serious sexual offending."[59]

Historical Understanding

Voyeurism is also not a new subject. The term "Peeping Tom" originated from the tale of Lady Godiva, a noblewoman who rode naked through the streets of Coventry, England.[60] French psychiatrist Ernest-Charles Lasègue first used the word exhibitionism in 1877 to describe the powerful urges some individuals have to display their genitals without any attempt to form a relationship.[61] During the mid-1900s, East and Hubert determined "true exhibitionists" to be those who used the practice either as a means of sexual relief or as a prelude to intercourse. For those unable to have intercourse, either because they were abnormal or incapable of the normal approach to courtship, the behavior was viewed as a substitute.[62]

---

55. Duffy, *3rd Circuit Bars Prosecution Threat for Teen 'Sexting.'*

56. Mann and her colleagues further assert that voyeuristic behaviors are potentially equal among women and men (Mann et al., "Voyeurism," 320–55).

57. Such thinking reflects John Stuart Mill's utilitarian concept known as "The Harm Principle," which holds an action can only be banned if it causes harm to someone, not if it is harmful in itself.

58. Jerry Ropelato, "Pornography Statistics."

59. Mann et al., "Voyeurism," 326; emphasis added.

60. The infamous ride occurred with the understanding that the townspeople would keep their doors and windows shut in return for a decrease in oppressive taxation. All obeyed the rules but a tailor named Tom who watched and was struck either blind or dead as a consequence.

61. Lavin, "Voyeurism," 305–319.

62. Ibid.

Current Understanding

While estimates of victims are difficult to determine, it is estimated that 1.6 million youth between the ages of two and seventeen years old are victims of exhibitionism yearly.[63] The impact to these victims seems to be minimal, with some describing the incident as slightly affecting their marital or sexual adjustment. In contrast, the impact to the offender and their family is significant, as the behaviors tend to occur frequently and in public making the likelihood of arrest, stigma, and stress high.[64]

Again, while information regarding victims is somewhat scarce, much research has been conducted regarding various paraphilia offenders. The *DSM-IV-TR*, for example, outlines sixteen types of paraphilias. It is safe to say the various groups who make up the different types of offenders are *heterogeneous, but in general they are individuals whose sexual motivation is impaired by brain-based disorders or disinhibitions.[65] In 1975, Mead outlined three types of telephone scatophilia. With the first, the caller immediately uses profanity and/or makes obscene propositions, typically to adolescents. In the second type, or the "ingratiating seducer," the ploy is subtler with the caller often providing a plausible story about prior introductions, admiration from afar, or mutual friends; this talk, how-ever, soon leads to offensive suggestions. With the third type, "the trickster" uses some type of ruse, such as a survey or impersonation of a female, in order to discuss personal matters; this talk soon leads to offensive suggestions.[66]

In 1982 Masters and his colleagues also outlined three types of general voyeurs. The first boasts about himself and his sexual organs, and he describes his masturbation. The second makes sexual and other threats toward the listener. The third attempts to manipu-late the respondent into revealing intimate sexual or otherwise private information about herself.[67]

Kurt Freund developed the *Courtship Disorder Theory* as one means to explain vari-ous paraphilias. According to this model, some people are unable to move through the normal steps of courting/mating rituals and therefore develop one of the paraphilias as a compensation mechanism.[68] The normal steps of courting or mating consist of look-ing for and appraising potential sexual partners, having pretactile interactions with these potential partners, engaging in tactile interaction, and finally participating in sexual intercourse.[69] Correspondingly, a disturbance of the first stage manifests as voyeurism, a disturbance of the second manifests as exhibitionism or telephone scatologia, a distur-bance of the third manifests as *frotteurism, and absence of any courtship behavior phases

63. Murphy and Page, "Exhibitionism," 61–75.

64. Ibid.

65. General paraphiliac behaviors include excessive sexual appetite, sexual preoccupation, repetitive and impulsive enactment of sexual behavior, compulsive masturbation, protracted promiscuity, pornography dependence, cybersex, and telephone sex dependence (American Psychiatric Association, *Diagnostic and Statistical Manual of Mental Disorders*, 569).

66. Mead, "Coping with Obscene Phone Calls," 127–28.

67. Masters et al., *Human Sexuality*, 342–343.

68. Freund, et al., *Archives of Sexual Behavior*, 369–379.

69. Ibid., 369–379.

manifests as *biastophilia.[70] Freund's model is well known and has been empirically tested to some degree, but with mixed results.[71] Fruend's theory is also the only one to address issues specifically related to exhibitionism and, if correct, proves that various paraphilias *are not stand-alone disorders but rather individual symptoms of a single disorder.*

Overall, those at greatest risk for developing exhibitionism appear to be those coming from *dysfunctional family systems—although not from families with CSA or physical abuse—with poor child-parent bonding. These individuals also have difficulties with relationships, general *emotional regulation, and *antisocial cognitions. Their personalities tend to be shy, inhibited and nonassertive.[72]

As with the other paraphilias, the age of onset for voyeurs is believed to be young, in this case prior to the age of fifteen. The individual is typically heterosexual, possesses an average or elevated sex drive, a history of minor thefts and limited social interactions. Cognitively, there may be issues with mental retardation, although the individual likely completed high school and some college and now holds a menial job.[73]

SOME FUTURE DIRECTIONS

The consequences of sexually violent behavior among victims are far-reaching.[74] Among the multitude of troubling affects is the knowledge that many victims of sexual violence become victims again. This *re-victimization may be due to chronic feelings of low worth or helplessness, the need to gain a sense of control, or the belief that they simply deserve to be treated poorly—continuing the vicious cycle of abuse.[75] During the last two decades, much has been written regarding *best practice treatment strategies for many who have been victims of sexual abuse. Holistic treatment centers also exist to help many survivors dealing with the aftermath of sexual abuse. For Christians, it may be particularly gratifying to see the excellent writings and techniques now available for this specific segment of society. What remains to be seen however, even as observed throughout this chapter, *are continued efforts to help determine ways to identify high-risk targets and then to educate our broader society regarding prevention strategies to employ.* Along with this type

---

70. Murphy and Paige, "Exhibitionism," 61–75.

71. Results of these studies generally reveal that exhibitionism is typically found in conjunction with other disorders (Ibid.).

72. Clinically, exhibitionistic behaviors are found in conjunction with: mood disorders, substance abuse, ADHD, child molestation, and several other paraphilias including *frottage, voyeurism, and rape (Morin and Levenson, "Exhibitionism," 76–101).

73. Clinically, voyeuristic behaviors are found in conjunction with low-self esteem, anger, *psychosis, alcohol abuse, and several other paraphilias including exhibitionism, frotteurism, pedophilia, rape, and sadism (Matek, "Obscene Phone Callers," 113–30; Pakhomou, "Methodological Aspects of Telephone Scatalogia," 178–85).

74. The effects of sexual abuse are covered elsewhere in this volume. Suffice it to say that abuse affects the person at every level (i.e., physically, emotionally, cognitively, psychologically, relationally, and spiritually).

75. Allender, *The Wounded Heart*, 113–188; Gilmartin, *Rape, Incest, and Child Sexual Abuse*, 15–28; Green, "Children Traumatized," 134–54; Jackson and March, "Post-traumatic Stress Disorder," 276–300; Langberg, *Counseling Survivors*, 69–74; idem, *On the Threshold of Hope*, 85–135; Lauer, *The Truth about Rape*, 119–262.

of psychoeducation would be continued research into minority groups (e.g., the elderly, chronic mentally ill men, lesbians, developmentally disabled individuals, etc.), who are particularly at high risk for this type of victimization.[76]

Unresolved needs also exist regarding sexual offenders. Overall, it is difficult to conduct research on this group, in large part because it is hard to get good sample sizes and funding; moreover, the subject material is delicate in nature. Existing research also suggests *sexually violent offenders are particularly difficult to treat and resistant to change. While not the definitive statement, one well known—the Sex Offender Treatment and Evaluation Project (SOTEP)—was a valid, funded program that followed treatment completers, dropouts, and nonparticipants for close to twenty years. *The bottom line showed no significant differences between the three groups with regard to *recidivism* in terms of sexual or violent offenses committed.[77] There are also difficulties with measurements for several of the sexually violent categories. Moreover, many of the terms and definitions used in the *DSM-IV-TR* are vague, arbitrary, and difficult to quantify or lack adequate operational definitions.[78]

Researchers agree that developmentally sensitive assessment methods are needed to study the course of pedophilia over the lifespan, especially to test the hypothesis that this sexual preference emerges around puberty and is stable over time.[79] Technology to guide the process for this does not currently exist and some believe it would be unethical and/or undesirable. In order for treatment to work, neurohormonal or psychological mechanisms controlling sexual preferences must also be addressed.[80] Most believe that research into neurological difficulties is warranted.

Richard Laws suggests a preventative public health approach to address many of the issues of sexual violence.[81] With this approach there would be emphasis on the primary causes of sexual violence in order to prevent the deviant behavior from starting. There would also be an investment of time and money, exploring secondary level causes where adolescents exhibiting deviant behavior would be identified and appropriate *interventions performed. At the tertiary level, individuals have already entered into the criminal justice system, typically with entrenched patterns of *deviant sexual behavior.

If such a comprehensive approach were to exist, Laws contends there would need to be an "ongoing, systematic collection, analysis, and interpretation of health data," versus the scattered systems in place right now.[82] There would also be research into the factors

76. Cermak and Molidor, "Male Victims of Child Sexual Abuse," 385–401; Roberto et al., "Sexual Abuse of Vulnerable Young and Old Men," 1009–1023; Stoddard et al., "Sexual and Physical Abuse," 407–20.

77. Marques et al., "Effects of a Relapse Prevention Program on Sexual Recidivism," 79–107.

78. For instance, there is no distinction between pedophiles and child molesters. The terminology for sexual assault is also missing. Under the paraphilia section there is the mention of biastophilia and *erotophonophilia. However, most rapists would not fit the criteria of someone with a paraphilia and therefore these distinctions are not helpful (Gannon and Ward, "Rape: Psychopathology and Theory," 336–55).

79. The selection of sexual preference is believed to happen partly during early brain development (Camilleri and Quinsey, "Pedophilia: Assessment and Treatment," 183–212).

80. Ibid.

81. Laws, "The Public Health Approach," 611–28.

82. This particular research is gaining momentum but needs to be more specific, matching the offender

placing an individual at higher risk for an unhealthy consequence. Additionally, there also needs to be the development and evaluation of programs "based on knowledge about modifiable risk factors identified in step two."[83] Finally, there would also need to be a dissemination of information on what works with offenders in order to help make their lives healthier and more fulfilling, while not removing the focus on risk factors associated with interpersonal violence, abuse, and recidivism. Such a system sounds promising, yet *at present there is no coordinated national or international effort to fund this type of research*.[84]

QUESTIONS FOR DISCUSSION

1. How do various *systems* (e.g., families, the church, the workplace, etc.) keep sexual abuse, sexual assault, and other types of sexual victimization in a *conspiracy of silence? What are the implications for the various parties involved (e.g., victimizer, victim, family, church leadership, tax-payer, etc.) when such abuse is hidden? What are the implications of bringing sexual abuse to light? How can you help to raise awareness within your personal or professional realm?

2. What types of prevention and/or *advocacy efforts are you aware of that exist to help those who have been or are currently being sexually abused, assaulted, or otherwise sexually violated? Are these efforts sufficient to reach the population you are concerned about? If not, what type of prevention/advocacy efforts should exist? How can various systems better collaborate (e.g., family, community organizations, counseling programs, mental health education, churches, etc.) to promote prevention/advocacy efforts? What is the cost (i.e., time, money, etc.) of such efforts?

3. Knowing what you do, how would you specifically advise one of your colleagues who happened to be sitting next to a Christian who had been sexually violated?

   a. What would you say? What things would you avoid saying? What part would God and Christian faith play in your conversation?

   b. How would your conversation change if the person had been sexually abused, sexually assaulted, or otherwise victimized?

   c. How would your conversation change depending on your role (e.g., friend, pastor, health provider, family member, counselor, etc.)?

   d. How could you best prepare yourself (or a colleague) for one of these conversations?

4. What part do you think the Internet and technology plays with each of the areas mentioned (e.g., child sexual abuse [CSA], sexual assault, and paraphilias)? Are you aware of how the Internet and technology affects those you serve? What are the larg-

---

with the intervention (Laws, "The Public Health Approach," 611–628).

83. Ibid.

84. Some speculate that this is because the US appears more focused on other problem areas, such as terrorism, rather than stopping sexual abuse (Laws, "The Public Health Approach," 611–628).

est and most troubling aspects of this technology (e.g., Internet addiction, *cybersex, pornography, social media, sexting, virtual addiction, etc.)? Do you have any formal policies in place at work or place of worship to address the issues surrounding the Internet and/or technology? What about personally? What kind of accountability measures do you have in place?

5. What were your personal reactions to this chapter? Which type of individual do you think it would be "easiest" to help (e.g., victim of sexual abuse, sexual assault, other type of sexual victimization)? Why? Which type of individual would be hardest" to help? Why? What if you were called upon to help an offender—what would your reaction be? Would you be able to help that person? Why or why not?

FOR FURTHER READING

Allender, Dan. *The Wounded Heart: Hope for Adult Victims of Childhood Sexual Abuse.* Colorado Springs, CO: Navpress, 2005.

Gilmartin, Pat. *Rape, Incest, and Child Sexual Abuse.* New York, NY: Garland Publishing, Inc., 1994.

Laws, D. Richard, and William T. O'Donohue. *Sexual Deviance: Theory, Assessment, and Treatment.* 2nd ed. New York, NY: The Guilford Press, 2008.

Langberg, Diane M. *Counseling Survivors of Sexual Abuse.* Carol Stream, IL: Tyndale House Publishers, 1997.

———. *On the Threshold of Hope: Opening the Door to Healing for Survivors of Sexual Abuse.* Wheaton, IL: Tyndale House Publishers, 1999.

Lauer, Teresa M. *The Truth About Rape: Emotional, Spiritual, Physical, and Sexual Recovery from Rape.* Gold River, CA: Raperecovery.com, 2002.

Maltz, Wendy. *The Sexual Healing Journey: A Guide for Survivors of Sexual Abuse.* New York, NY: Harper Collins, 2001.

Rodrigues-Srednicki, Ofelia, and James A. Twaite. *Understanding, Assessing, and Treating Adult Victims of Childhood Abuse.* Lanham, MD: The Rowman and Littlefield Publishing Group, 2006.

Schetky, Diane H., and Arthur H. Green. *Child Sexual Abuse: A Handbook for Health Care and Legal Professions.* Florence KY: Routledge Publishers, 1988.

Schroeder, Joy A. *Dinah's Lament: The Biblical Legacy of Sexual Violence in Christian Interpretation.* Minneapolis, MN: Augsburg Fortress Press, 2007.

4

Characteristics and Typologies of Sex Offenders

Understanding Abusers and the Risks They Pose

Justin Smith, PsyD

EXAMINING SEX OFFENDERS IS a taxing endeavor because sex crimes represent the worst of fallen humanity. While Christianity commonly embraces the notion of human *depravity, sex offenses put a horrifying face on the capacity of one human to torture[1] and debase another.[2] And while many crimes contain victims, sex crimes are particularly notable because they necessitate both a victim and *physical* contact with the offender.[3]

Sex crimes are more than the seizure of one person's property by another. Sex offenses involve one person suffering while another derives pleasure, sometimes because of the other's suffering.[4] Given the proximity of the offender to the victim during a sex crime, even when the *perpetrator does not receive direct gratification from the victim's suffering he or she persists in the crime and the pleasure derived from it while in the presence of the victim and the victim's pain and objections. The perpetrator of *sexual abuse (SA) must be constitutionally capable of taking from another person, causing another

---

1. Given God's intent in creating sex to be pleasurable and emotionally bonding, torture is an appropriate term: "anguish of body or mind; something that causes agony or pain; the infliction of intense pain to punish, coerce, or afford *sadistic pleasure; distortion of a meaning" (*Merriam-Webster Online Dictionary*, s.v. "Torture," http://www.merriam-webster.com/dictionary/torture [accessed November 25, 2009]). For an introduction to God's intent for sex see Gen 2:18–25; Song 1:2; 2:3–7; Matt 19:4–9; 1 Cor 6:13–20; and 1 Cor 7:1–5.

2. Consider the effects of sexual abuse in the biblical account of Tamar in 2 Sam 13:12–20. Note the similarity of Tamar's language, and her subsequent condition with the definition of debase: "to lower in status, esteem, quality, or character; to reduce the intrinsic value of" (*Merriam-Webster Online*, s.v. "Debase," http://www.merriam-webster.com/dictionary/torture [accessed November 25, 2009]). For a summary of the current psychological literature on the impact of rape, see Logan et al., "Victimization Manifestations and Vulnerability Factors," 17–49.

3. Physical interaction may be visual as in the case of *exhibitionism, which although classified as a sex offence, is not considered "hands on" or violent. Exhibitionism is not a painless crime, however, as the intent is often to produce shock in the victim, with the offender deriving pleasure from his or her seeing the reaction of the victim.

4. While Jam 4:1–4 seems to explain the general concept of sin as *covetousness*, how does one explain the "desires" of Jam 1:14 involving taking pleasure from the suffering of another person? This cruelty seems more in keeping with the unnatural depravity described in Rom 1:28–32.

person pain, and experiencing pleasure in the presence of that person's pain and suffering. The capacity to perpetrate such evil seems beyond the realm of normal human behavior, beyond normal "total depravity."

SPECIAL PROBLEM, COMMON EXPLANATION

The immediate reaction of many people, including graduate students, seminarians, and survivors of abuse, is that *sex offenders are uniquely different from the rest of the population. *They* are different from *us*. While sex crimes are morally disturbing, the tendency to differentiate people who do certain bad things from other people is a common social phenomenon of creating "in groups" (i.e., *us*) and "out groups" (i.e., *not us*). This dynamic allows for a certain psychological distance between our self-identification as reasonably good and law-abiding citizens and the categorization of "others," in this case the sex offender, as horribly corrupt and evil. It also allows for a distancing between socially acceptable behavior and the damnable behavior of the sex offender.

Sex offenders are often *stereotyped as mentally ill drifters like Brian David Mitchell, a self-proclaimed preacher who pled insanity to charges of kidnapping and assaulting fourteen-year-old Elizabeth Smart. His long matted hair, disheveled beard, and dead stare featured prominently in the news. However, women who commit sex offenses are often viewed as confused or as victims themselves of some larger dynamic.[5] Unfortunately the distinction between sexual abuser and non-abuser is not nearly as dramatic as the stereotypes portray.

Tracking the Rates

At the current rate of conviction for sex offenses, 1 to 2 percent of the male population will be convicted of a sex offense.[6] In the first fifteen years since Congress passed the Wetterling Act in 1994, there have been 686,515 individuals who have been registered as

---

5. Consider the cases of Mary Kay Letourneau or Amanda Knox, who have been depicted as troubled, confused, or scared but rarely as manipulative, cruel, or as sex offenders, despite crimes that would quickly draw condemnation had the offender been male. American college student Knox was convicted of holding down her roommate while Knox and two boyfriends taunted, assaulted, tortured, and then stabbed the roommate to death during a drug-sex binge in Italy. *Good Morning America* describes Knox as a young, timid, and scared woman needing to be comforted by prison guards when hearing the verdict (Mooney, "Amanda Knox's Prison Cell," http://www.abcnews.go.com/GMA/AmandaKnox/amanda-knoxs-prison-cell/story?id=9329773 [accessed December 19, 2009]). CNN's description of the crime, however, has a vengeful Knox taunting her male companions into assaulting the victim, torturing and taunting the victim, and then stabbing the victim in the neck (Messia, "Amanda Knox tortured, killed roommate, prosecutor says in closing," http://www.cnn.com/2009/CRIME/11/20/amanda.knox.trial.arguments/index.html [accessed December 19, 2009]). An African male barely in puberty accused of a crime with some similarities although no attempt to kill the victim receives little such sympathy. Fourteen-year-old Liberian refugee Steven Tuopeh held down a girl for approximately ten minutes while several boys assaulted her. He was charged in adult court with seven charges with little commentary on his developmental maturity despite having an interpreter in court and being evaluated for competence to stand trial (Kiefer and Ferraresi, "Not guilty plea entered in alleged rape of Phoenix girl, 8," http://www.azcentral.com/news/articles/2009/08/10/2 0090810liberia0810-onl.html [accessed December 19, 2009]).

6. Marshall, *The prevalence of convictions for sexual offending*, http://www.homeoffice.gov.uk/rds/pdfs/r55.pdf [accessed November 28, 2009].

sex offenders in America.[7] Despite how disturbing these figures are, they do not unmask the true extent of sexual abuse or dispel the notion of sex offender as categorically different from the rest of the population.

To understand the extent of human sexual depravity, one needs to examine not the growing number of registered offenders but the number of victims of sexual abuse. For the past twenty years the *prevalence of sexual abuse among American women has remained in the 20 to 25 percent range, with rates for men between 10 to 20 percent.[8] Given the low rates of reporting sexual assaults and the prevalence of assaults against children who have a diminished capacity to report, rates of reported sex crimes are dwarfed by estimated rates. Data within the sex offender treatment community suggests that an American woman has a 50 percent chance of being sexually assaulted at least once in her lifetime.[9] The contrast between statistics of sex offenders and sexual abuse victims should not be surprising as only a fraction of rapes actually result in a conviction.[10] Consequently, sex offenders represent only a small minority of individuals who commit sexual abuse. The high rates of sexual abuse cannot be attributed to a few *serial offenders either. While some offenders are clearly serial offenders, the majority of convicted sex offenders are never convicted of a new offense, even when tracked for up to twenty years.[11]

If the number of perpetrators of sexual abuse is between 20 to 50 percent of the male population, as opposed to 1 to 2 percent, then sexually abusive behavior is not that unusual and neither is the sexual abuser. Theologically the harsh division between offender and non-offender does not stand up either. Human depravity is pervasive both across society and within the individual.[12] Each person is a sexual being with urges that seek to be expressed but which need to be controlled and contained within socially (and biblically) acceptable parameters. Likewise, each person is prone to manipulate others for his or her own ends.[13] Lastly, while religious and humanistic groups like to proclaim advancement of civilization or obtainable "illumination" that allows for the elimination of interpersonal violence, the capacity for human violence remains universal.[14]

7. Officially the Jacob Wetterling Crimes Against Children and Sexually Violent Offender Act, which mandated every state centralize the registration of sex offenders. *Megan's Law* was an amendment added two years later, requiring community notification (National Center for Missing & Exploited Children [2009]. http://www.missingkids.com/en_US/documents/sex-offender-map.pdf [accessed November 28, 2009]).

8. There has been disagreement on exact rates of abuse since Charcot and Freud studied female *hysteria in the 1880s. For a current review see Steve Tracy's chapter on the prevalence of sexual abuse. Judith Herman presents a concise and readable history of the struggle to accept sexual abuse as anything more than a rare occurrence in her 1992 seminal work, *Trauma and Recovery*.

9. Marshal, "Diagnosing and Treating Sexual Offenders."

10. Only 7.5 percent of reported rapes result in prosecution, and most assaults are not reported. Logan et al., *Women and Victimization*, 183.

11. Hanson, "Stability and Change," 17.

12. For a good discussion of biblical anthropology, see Hoekema, *Created in God's Image*.

13. For an interesting discussion of communication as manipulation, see Dorothy Stroh Becvar and Raphael J. Becvar, *Family Therapy: A Systemic Integration*, 202.

14. The belief in ever-increasing good resulting in the ushering in of the *millennium was widespread within Protestant Christianity at the turn of the twentieth century. The Great War of 1914 dispelled this notion and most *Evangelical Christians have held to a pre-millennial or amillennial view of *eschatology since.

Not only is violence universal, but it often occurs between those who love each other. Noted *forensic psychologist and author of *The Mark of Cain*, Reid Meloy, has noted that, "One of the great paradoxes of human existence is that most interpersonal violence occurs between people who are attached or bonded to each other."[15] This finding is consistent with research that shows that *most sexual assaults are not by strangers but by individuals who know each other and are often related*.[16] The sex offender "monster" is often our brother, uncle, grandfather, or family friend. Scripture records the first act of violence as being by a family member (Gen 4:8). Sexual perversion is listed as accompanying the spread of wickedness on the earth before the flood, and the threat of sexual violence is involved in the destruction of Sodom (Gen 6:1–6; 19:4–11).[17] There are also numerous biblical examples of sexual offenses involving family members.[18]

WHAT DISTINGUISHES THE SEXUAL ABUSER

Disregarding Boundaries

What seems to characterize the person who commits a sexual offense from the person who does not is the individual's *behavior*, not their mental health or constitution. If all persons have sexual impulses and the capacity to be manipulative and potentially violent, perhaps the questions should be: "Why don't people offend?" instead of, "Why do people offend?" "What constrains some people and fails to constrain others?"

To cross the line, so to speak, the offender must violate several *internal* and *external* barriers. First, the offender must move from a passive desire or impulse to acting on an urge. This requires breaking societal norms and laws. Some sexual offenses involve extensive preplanning and preparation.[19] Secondly, the offender must violate moral or religious prohibitions in the form of personal conscience. Thirdly, the offender must override sympathy and compassion for the victim. Some sex offenders actually justify their behavior as being desired or pleasing to the victim. Many *pedophiles, for example, *groom their victims through the development of trust and a special status. They may coerce a trusting victim rather than threaten and force a resisting victim. While this does not diminish the *trauma for the victim, it allows the offender the mental protection of not seeing the victim appear to suffer at the time of the *molestation. The ability of these offenders to arouse their victims can be a source of great pride, while the memory of being aroused during a sexual offense can be extremely shaming and psychologically traumatic for victims.

15. Melroy, "Pathologies of Attachment, Violence, and Criminality," 509.

16. N. Gibbs, "Can These Parents Be Saved?" 54–57.

17. The first rape detailed is the defiling of Dinah by her neighbor in Genesis 34. A particularly graphic portrayal of the rape of the Levite's concubine is detailed in Judges 19.

18. Lot's daughters commit incest with their father (Gen 19:30–38), Judah commits incest with Tamar (Genesis 38), Amnon rapes his sister Tamar (2 Samuel 13), Absalom rapes his father's concubines (2 Sam 16:20–23).

19. While some sexual crimes are acts of opportunity, others involve extensive grooming of the victim, particularly children; preparations to create opportunity as in some abductions or gaining access to particular victims; or elaborate mental rehearsal before executing an offense.

Disregarding Distress

The ability of most sexual offenders to continue in a sex act, while observing obvious distress in the victim, is a particularly troubling aspect of working with sex offenders. How can one human derive sexual pleasure from an experience that is causing pain and alarm to another human? While there are sexual *sadists, the answer often is that sexual crimes are not about sexual pleasure. *Sex crimes can be about the feeling the offender gets from exercising power over another or even causing humiliation to the victim.* In the biblical case of Absalom's rebellion against David, he is advised to rape his father's concubines publically so that "all Israel will hear that you have made yourself a stench to your father, and the hands of all who are with you will be strengthened" (2 Sam 16:21–22). *Rape has historically proliferated during warfare both as the result of the loss of social control and as a means of punishing the vanquished.[20] Counter-intuitively, many sexually violent offenders are unable to perform sexually during their crime. Sadly, this reality leads to increased violence and repeated sexual acts as the offender seeks the gratification he fantasized about *before* the crime but was unable to achieve *during* the offense.[21]

For the non-offender, the distinguishing characteristics of not offending are the ability to contain or appropriately channel sexual urges, keeping manipulative behavior within socially acceptable parameters, adhering to legal standards of behavior, following a moral code of conduct, and allowing compassion for others to curtail interpersonal harm. With this type of distinction it is clear that many non-offenders toy at the edges of pro-offender thinking and behavior. Indeed, many individuals dwell on pro-offender thoughts and harbor pro-offender attitudes. Violent thoughts are correlated with subsequent violent acts just as negative attitudes toward women and the acceptance of violence as a problem-solving strategy accompany *domestic violence.[22]

Poor Self-Regulation and Outrageous Behavior

There is a relationship between viewing violent and *coercive pornography and sexual aggression. The view that pornography was linked to sexual violence was dismissed for many years, but meta-analysis over the past ten years has demonstrated that the relationship between pornography and sexual activity is grounded in solid research and not just religious rhetoric. In particular, violent pornography and attitudes supporting sexual aggression are correlated with sexual aggression toward women.[23]

Generally poor *self-regulation, including poor *impulse control, is one of the strongest predictors of sexual offending.[24] This speaks for the need of the non-offender to adhere to both internal and external standards and expectations. This advice is consistent

20. Lalumiere et al., *The Causes of Rape*, 9–30.

21. This was the experience of a number of civilly committed sex offenders this author worked with. Similar findings are common in the sex offender treatment community and literature (David Thornton, personal communication with author, November 29, 2009).

22. See the discussion of the MacArthur Violence Risk Assessment Study in Monahan, "Violence Risk Assessment," 527–540.

23. Lalumiere et al., *The Causes of Rape*, 148.

24. Conroy, "Evaluation of Sexual Predators," 463–484.

with biblical teaching to exercise self-control of one's thought life, attitudes, and words as a precursor to one's behavior.[25]

While society is inclined to seek horrendous events that cause people to become sex offenders, the truth may be far more horrific. Sex offenders are like other people. The dividing line may be narrow and may be unglamorous, as sex offenders give ground in little ways over time until they commit acts that may have at one time seemed outrageous but have become justifiable for some reason(s). This notion of a progression of *sexualized thoughts and behavior is foundational to the concept of *sexual addiction.[26]

SEX OFFENDER OR SEXUAL ABUSER?

Having established that sexual abuse covers a wide range of behaviors and undoubtedly involves a significant portion of the population, what can be said about sex offenders? Offenders are a subset of sexual abusers. They have not only committed sexual abuse but they have committed a specific sexual crime as defined by society. This means that they were charged with a sexual crime, apprehended, tried, and found guilty by a court of law. Estimates are that only one in fifty rapes result in a conviction.[27] While it would be helpful to study and understand all perpetrators of sexual abuse, much of our knowledge is limited to those who have been apprehended. The sex offender population will be discussed because they are the abusers who are available for examination. The distinction between these three population groups—(1) people who have not sexually abused others, (2) people who have sexually abused others but are not sex offenders for various reasons, (3) and those who are convicted sex offenders—is important because we can examine differences between the sex offender population and the population of non-sex offenders.

Without belaboring the point, the term sex offender is a legal and *forensic one. A person may have committed sexual abuse, but if that person is not apprehended, not convicted, or released for technical reasons then the person is not a sex offender. And a person is a sex offender if the legal system determines he or she is. Many lay persons, for example, might not consider either public urination or two sexually active teenagers, for example, a sex offense, but in many states, those who take such actions are.

A significant distinction is made between sex offenders and *sexually violent offenders or *predators (SVP). Most states have enacted laws allowing for the *civil commitment of individuals who are deemed at high risk of reoffending in a violent manner. The usefulness of a civil commitment is that individuals who are not eligible for incarceration can still be detained. Many civilly committed SVPs have completed their prison sentences,

---

25. Cf. Rom 12:1–3; 1 Cor 9:24–27; 2 Cor 10:5–6; Phil 4:8–9; Titus 1:7–8; James 3.

26. There is disagreement within mental health disciplines over the use of *addiction* as applied to sexual behavior. People who work with offenders often do not use the term *addiction* since it suggests to some diminished culpability. The head of the US Marshals Service makes this point in Bourke, "Response from the Researcher," 8, 65. Counselors who work with individuals who are not charged with a crime may use the term *addiction* as a useful conceptualization for treatment. If you are new to the concept of sex as an addiction, two classic works include: Carnes, *Out of the Shadows*, and Sexaholics Anonymous, *Sexaholics Anonymous*.

27. Even in cases where the victim is able to identify the assailant, only about 25 percent of assault cases result in an arrest and about 7.5 percent of women who reported partner sexual assault to the police reported the offender was prosecuted (Logan et al., "Justice System Options and Responses," 174–186).

were found not guilty of sex crimes because of a mental illness, or were not competent to be tried for sex offenses due to mental illness. Civil commitment is based upon the same legal reasoning (and typically through the same government agency) that allows for the hospitalization of someone threatening suicide or homicide.[28]

IDENTIFYING AND TREATING SEX OFFENDERS: UNDERSTANDING ASSESSMENT AND RISK

There is a growing body of research on sex offenders, including identifying variables associated with heightened risk of reoffending (i.e., *recidivism), positive treatment outcomes and effects, and understanding the role of the brain in *deviant sexual behavior.[29] While there has been a general move toward treatment outcome research over the past twenty years,[30] this has been a particularly acute issue for clinicians working with sex offenders. *Counseling a sex offender has consequences for both the future quality of life of the offender and those individuals who come into contact with the offender in the future.* Decisions about what type of treatment to provide, how long to continue treatment, and how much involuntary oversight should be provided by corrections, probation, parole, or civil commitment authorities needs to be based on information and decision making that is as reliable as possible. Given a counselor's duty to protect the public, *all sex offender treatment is, to some extent, an assessment of the risk the offender poses to others.*[31] As Dennis M. Doren states:

> A *risk assessment involving a sexual offender usually means there is a potential real-life high cost to be paid by someone. Depending on the evaluation's recommendation, an offender's freedom to be in the community may be at stake . . . [and if] the offender gains freedom as a result of the evaluation, the placement of the offender in the community increases the risk for new victimization of law-abiding members of society.[32]

Given the consequences involved in assessing sex offenders, assessment of risk needs careful scrutiny. Predictions of future dangerousness based upon clinical judgment alone have been found to be wrong more than 50 percent of the time.[33] In other words, decisions would be more accurate if made by flipping a coin than based solely upon the clinical judgment of a mental health practitioner. Factors historically held to be predictive of risk, such as race, education, history of depression, history of having been sexually abused, and *denial are not correlated with recidivism.[34] Clinicians without specific training in the

---

28. For a good summary of the history of civil commitment of sexual predators, see Conroy, "Evaluation of sexual predators," 463–484.

29. Wilson, "Editor's Note," http://www.newsmanager.commpartners.com/atsa.textonly/2009-12-16/index.html (accessed December 18, 2009).

30. Lambert and Ogles, "The Efficacy and Effectiveness of Psychotherapy," 139–193.

31. Duty to protect is a legal responsibility of mental health providers based on the case of Tarasoff v. Regents of the University of California, 17 Cal. 3d 425, 551 P.2d 334, 131 Cal. Rptr. 14 (Cal. 1976).

32. Doren, "Recidivism Risk Assessments," 3.

33. Conroy, "Evaluation of Sexual Predators," 468–469.

34. Hanson and Monique T. Bussiere, "Predicting Relapse," 348–362.

assessment and treatment of sex offenders should refrain from making recommendations to courts or employers about sex offenders. Even clinicians with specialized training in sex offender treatment are susceptible to biases that put the population at risk. A survey of sex offender treatment specialists found that two-thirds doubted rehabilitation for violent sex offenders was possible while at the same time 63 percent believed that the sex offenders they treated would not reoffend![35]

An alternative to clinical judgment alone is to use *actuarial assessments. Like most psychological assessments, knowing the limitations and strengths of the tool is crucial in receiving an accurate or meaningful answer. Actuarial risk assessments focus on the probability of a specific outcome. Even the best instrument will not tell a counselor or court that a specific person will offend at a certain time, at a certain place, or in a certain manner. *Actuarial instruments establish a degree of possibility in the present*—a probability which remains accurate regardless of future behavior.[36] When establishing insurance rates, actuaries find that an eighteen-year old male is at higher risk for an accident claim whether or not he has an accident in the next year. Likewise, an individual who legitimately falls within a low-risk population may offend in the future, just as an individual who possesses sufficient criteria to be deemed at high-risk for offending may not offend within the next five years and so on.

Many *referring agencies dislike actuarial results because they want to know if a specific person will or will not commit a crime in the future. However, the best a clinician can do is to provide an assessment of *probability* and then let the referring agency decide how much risk they are willing to accept. The wise clinician will refrain from guaranteeing anyone will *never* commit a crime. The future is known only to God. Scriptures attest that godly people do fail and sinners can repent and change their ways.[37]

GENERAL CHARACTERISTICS OF SEX OFFENDERS: STATIC FACTORS

The best predictor of future behavior is past behavior. This is true for the sex offender as with most all other human behavior. While it might be tempting to write off the sex offender as incorrigible, research shows that "once detected, most sexual offenders are never reconvicted for a new sexual offence."[38] Unfortunately, the cost to new victims for those who do reoffend necessitates careful scrutiny of all offenders. Looking at those factors most highly correlated with reoffending and those theories of treating offenders that have shown the most empirical support is probably the best method of understanding the general characteristics and typologies of sex offenders.

---

35. Engle et al., "The Attitudes of Members of the Association for the Treatment of Sexual Abusers toward Treatment, Release, and Recidivism of Violent Sex Offenders," 17–24.

36. Doren, "Recidivism Risk Assessments," 11.

37. See 2 Samuel 11 for the fall of David and 1 Cor 6:9–11 and 2 Cor 5:17 for the transformation in character after coming to faith in Christ.

38. Hanson, "Stability and Change," 17.

Some Characteristics and Illustrations

The first characteristic of a sex offender is a person who has demonstrated the capacity and willingness to overcome personal, religious, and societal prohibitions against sexual offending and to risk legal consequences for such behavior by engaging in a sexual crime. Through offending behavior they become a part of a population that is at a greater risk of future offending than the non-offending population. Research shows that *the highest correlations to repeat offending are sexual interest in children, any deviant sexual interests, and prior sexual offenses.*[39] Characteristics of offenders then include deviant sexual interests and a history of having acted on deviant sexual impulses.[40]

Secondary factors appear to be clustered around general character issues more related to criminality in general than *sexual deviance per se. They include having any victims who were strangers, having started but then failed to complete sex offender treatment, any prior criminal behavior, early age of onset of sexual offending, and an *antisocial personality disorder. This second set of factors is related to a more general defiant disposition. The *Diagnostic and Statistical Manual of Psychiatric Disorders (DSM-IV-TR) defines Antisocial Personality Disorder as "a pervasive pattern of disregard for, and violation of, the rights of others that begins in childhood or early adolescence and continues into adulthood."[41] Hanson and Bussiere also found that sex offenders were as likely to reoffend with non-sexual offenses as they were with sexual ones.[42] It appears sex offenders can be sub-grouped into those who are driven primarily by their sexual deviance and those whose sex offenses are a part of a larger drive for thrill seeking and *entitlement combined with a reckless violation of the rights of others, aggression, a lack of remorse, and poor behavior control.

A third group of characteristics highlight specific demographics that bridge the first two groups. These features are not as highly correlated as the first two groups but bear some examination. The age of the offender is a risk factor. As age increases there is a general decline in aggression and criminality,[43] although some older individuals certainly continue to commit crimes and pose a risk to the public.[44] Other characteristics that fall into this third category include never having been married, having any male victims, the

39. Hanson and Bussiere, "Predicting Relapse," 348–362.

40. In this capacity, deviant also refers to any sexual conduct considered illegal, included forced sex and sex with minors.

41. American Psychiatric Association, *Diagnostic and Statistical Manual of Mental Disorders*, 645–650.

42. Hanson and Bussiere, "Predicting Relapse," 348–362. The rate of recidivism for new sexual offenses was 13.4 percent after five years while the recidivism rate for non-sexual offenses by sex offenders was 12.2 percent after five years.

43. Hanson and Morton-Bourgon, "The Accuracy of Recidivism Risk Assessments for Sexual Offenders," 1–21.

44. Ellef Ellefson was civilly committed as a sexually violent predator at the age of ninety-five, over sixty years after his first sexual offence. He was 103 when he passed away in a secure treatment facility in Wisconsin, having convictions for assaulting minors dating from 1937 to 1990 (Tribune Staff, "State's Oldest Inmate, Former La Crosse Resident, Dies.")

presence of unrelated victims, and diverse sex crimes.[45] *Among child molesters, research has shown that same-sex offenders have the highest recidivism rates.*[46]

An example of how these factors might be examined together to determine a level of risk is the Static-99.[47] This instrument weighs factors to give a four-category risk level, from low to high. The factors examined include: (1) the age of the offender, (2) whether the offender has ever lived with a significant other for more than two years, (3) any prior convictions for non-sexual violent offenses, (3) prior sex offenses, (4) any unrelated victims, (5) any victims who were strangers, (6) and any male victims.

Understanding static risk factors requires careful thought. One could conclude that a young, unattached individual with a criminal history, a prior sexual offense against a stranger, and an interest in young boys is at high risk for committing a future sex crime. While this profile would fit serial killers such as Jeffrey Dahmer or John Wayne Gacy,[48] it would not be indicative of the person the average American is most at risk from. *Most sex offenses are committed by family members and acquaintances, not by strangers.*

DYNAMIC CHARACTERISTICS OF SEX OFFENDERS

While many clinical or *dynamic factors historically thought to be predictive of sexual offending have not been empirically shown to be associated with future risk of offending, interest in dynamic factors has returned because while actuarial or static factors can be helpful in understanding offenders, static factors are not amenable to treatment and "the relationships between any single risk factor and recidivism are small."[49] While dynamic factors were initially theory driven, the growing body of research on offender recidivism has shown "strong evidence in support of dynamic risk factors for general offenders."[50] As risk assessment has grown more sophisticated, more individuals have been committed for treatment. The growing body of offenders in treatment has contributed to the need to find empirically supported treatments—a complicated quest at best given that risk is measured by static factors while treatment outcome must be based upon dynamic factors.[51]

Criminogenic Factors

Dynamic factors which bear consideration include those associated with general *criminogenic factors and those associated more specifically with *partner violence and sexual offending. Criminogenic or antisocial factors include hostility, irresponsibility, impulsivity,

---

45. Hanson and Bussiere, "Predicting Relapse," 348–362.

46. Quinsey et al., *Violent Offenders*, 132.

47. Harris et al., *Static-99 Coding Rules Revised 2003*, 1–84.

48. Chua-Eoan, "The Top 25 Crimes of the Century," http://www.Time.com/time/2007/crimes/16.html; accessed January 18, 2010.

49. Hanson and Morton-Bourgon, "The Accuracy of Recidivism Risk Assessments for Sexual Offenders," 1.

50. Ibid., 2.

51. Obviously an individual's offense and victim history cannot be changed by treatment. Since treatment cannot lower risk by changing static factors, treatment must target dynamic factors and changes in these factors must be shown to reduce risk if offender treatment is to continue as a viable endeavor.

low self-control, *pro-offending attitudes and beliefs, and substance abuse.[52] Hanson has identified the most acute dynamic factor appearing in research as negative moods such as anger or loneliness.[53] Self-regulation and poor self-control appear highly correlated with criminal behavior. "Individuals who commit crimes tend to change jobs and residences, have unrealistic plans for the future, and engage in a variety of high risk behaviors (e.g., drinking, driving fast, or maintaining unsafe work practices)."[54] While Hanson and Bussiere's 1998 meta-analysis of risk factors did not find alcohol abuse a statistically significant factor, a consistent relationship has since been found between alcohol and drug abuse and crime, in general, and rape, in particular.[55] *Triggering events that provide acute risk factors would be short-term states such as subjective distress and intoxication.

Cognition Factors

Cognition appears to play a strong role in sex offending as with most behavior. Various theories and approaches nuance the role cognition plays in the *etiology and treatment of offending. Childhood exposure to sexual stimuli and experiences may result in subsequent mental fantasies reinforced by masturbation. Sexual deviance may be the result of reinforced deviant arousal patterns and concurrent *cognitive distortions.[56] Cognitions can also form into more elaborate beliefs about the world and the roles one plays in the world. These *schemas form "filters" through which the world is experienced and understood. Environmental cues may be misread, creating self-reinforcing behavior and beliefs. A man who believes women will reject him, for example, is likely to act dismissively toward women, increasing the likelihood of their rejecting him. *Examples of pro-offending schemas include beliefs that the male sex drive is uncontrollable, that women enjoy being forced upon, that children enjoy sex and are not harmed unless physically injured, and so forth.*[57]

Cognition can also play a role in strengthening the positive traits of a certain course of behavior, increasing the behavior's desirability, justifying the behavior, and weakening one's resolve to abstain from the behavior. Cognition is understood to play a significant role in addictive behavior and abstinence or sobriety. Relapse prevention models seek to identify triggers or environmental situations that activate thoughts, memories, and the desire to engage in certain addictive behavior.[58] Cognitive rehearsal of deviant sexual fantasies and viewing of violent pornography increases the desirability of this behavior

52. Hanson and Morton-Bourgon, "The Accuracy of Recidivism Risk Assessments for Sexual Offenders," 1–21.

53. Hanson, "Stability and Change," 25.

54. Ibid., 24.

55. Lalumiere et al., *The Causes of Rape*, 146.

56. For a summary of *Abel's Cognitive Distortion Theory*, see Ward et al., *Theories of Sexual Offending*, 117–122.

57. For a summary of *Schema Theories*, see Ward et al., *Theories of Sexual Offending*, 123–133. For a primer on targeting schemas in sex offender treatment, see Mann and Shingler, "Schema-driven Cognition in Sexual Offenders," 173–185.

58. For a summary of *Relapse Prevention and Self-Regulation Models*, see Ward et al., *Theories of Sexual Offending*, 213–235.

while weakening the resolve to refrain from engaging in criminal behavior. Treatment for sex offenders often targets an "*offense cycle," seeking to identify and avoid triggers while channeling fantasies toward socially acceptable sexual expression.[59] Gerry Blasingame has developed a "relapse prevention ladder" model, which would apply to most addictive behavior as well as sex offending.[60] Individuals are susceptible to poor choices when hungry, angry, lonely, or tired. They then progress up through a series of poor choices, including isolating behavior, employing cognitive distortions, dwelling on fantasies of acting out, and eventually seeking or creating opportunities to offend.

Cognition represents a dynamic risk factor and window into the characteristics of the sex offender when deviant sexual behavior is fantasized or dwelt upon, sexual offenses are planned and rehearsed, deviant sexual fantasies are reinforced, and pro-offending schemas are maintained. In this light, viewing violent pornography, telling jokes that objectify women, or using language that demeans women are not "harmless." Prominent pastors and politicians who engage in sexual indiscretions at the expense of their marriages and careers have probably allowed enactment fantasies and cognitive distortions of need and entitlement to overwhelm more logical reasoning. Current theorists hold that avoiding risk and consequences is probably insufficient to prevent relapse. A "good lives" model has been proposed that combines relapse prevention with a focus on living a better kind of life. While a secular theory, the Good Lives Model advocates a "redemptive identity script," a self-identity focused on success and not failure.[61]

Interpersonal Violence

Interpersonal violence, including sexual crimes, appears to be driven largely by dynamic factors associated with *attachment deficits or threats. While danger is often associated with strangers, it is significant that "most interpersonal violence occurs between people who are attached or bonded to each other."[62] *Typically the most intense human emotions are generated by the formation, maintenance, or loss of close attachment relationships.*[63] Attachment problems are evident in various mental disorders such as Antisocial Personality Disorder (BPD) and *Borderline Personality Disorder. Healthy attachment is absent in *psychopathy. This kind of person is more likely to use violence in a predatory or instrumental fashion.

Individuals who are incapable of forming healthy attachments are most vulnerable to perpetrating intimate partner violence.[64] Having an insecure or anxious attachment, being shamed by a caregiver as a child, and witnessing violence directed toward one's self or mother is a triad predictive of domestic battery as an adult. Batterers can be grouped much like sex offenders: (1) those who are aggressive and antisocial in general, (2) those

---

59. For a summary of *Offence Cycles*, see Ward et al., *Theories of Sexual Offending*, 237–260.
60. Blasingame, *Developmentally Disabled Persons with Sexual Problems.*
61. Ward and Stewart, "The Treatment of Sex Offenders," 645–673.
62. Melroy, "Pathologies of Attachment, Violence, and Criminality," 509.
63. Bowlby, *The Making and Breaking of Affectional Bonds*, 130.
64. Melroy, "Pathologies of Attachment, Violence, and Criminality," 514.

who are *dysphoric—angry, moody, hypersensitive to slights, (3) and those who exhibit violent and controlling behavior exclusively within the home.[65]

Attachment Disturbance

Attachment issues have been postulated to be dynamic factors particular to sex offenders.[66] Child molesters are thought to have social and attachment deficits, which make children of particular interest. Adults who groom children may feel overwhelmed or inadequate with adult partners who are chronological peers but socially more mature and savvy. Children and cognitively or developmentally disabled victims may be targeted because their innocent, trusting nature demands less and gives more within a less sophisticated emotional relationship. Particularly for the non-caregiver, adult perpetrators can come and go in the life of the young victim and engage in a relatively controlled emotional relationship. Intimacy deficits, including conflicts within intimate relationships and emotional identification with children, were shown to have some of the largest effect sizes of all dynamic factors in a meta-analysis of recidivism follow-up studies.[67]

Melroy has presented both theoretical and empirical support for attachment disturbances as a dynamic factor in *stalking.[68] The stalker obsesses about the victim and the relationship between the offender and the victim. A healthy, secure attachment is absent; replaced by obsessive fantasies typically including *rumination and the elaborate planning and rehearsal of behavior designed to bring the offender into close proximity with the victim. Melroy has shown rates of violence in stalking to be very high, ranging from 25 percent to over 50 percent among previous sexual partners. Those with fearful or preoccupied attachment disturbances are most likely to engage in stalking behavior. Those who are under-aroused, with avoidant attachments are least likely to stalk but most likely to be severely violent, sadistic, and to target strangers.

SEX OFFENDERS: SEXUALLY ACTIVE MINORS
AND CHILDREN WHO RAPE

In the heightened public attention on sex crimes, laws governing sex offenders have been extended to include *minors. Underage offenders typically fall into two categories: (1) sexually active minors who cannot legally consent to sex, (2) and minors who engage in behaviors that would be considered criminal even if age were not a factor.

All states have established laws that govern when individuals are old enough to consent to sexual activity. *Society believes that individuals need a certain maturity to be able to make the decision to engage in sexual behavior, particularly intercourse.* The consequences

---

65. For a good summary of the role of attachment in violence and pathology, see Melroy, "Pathologies of Attachment, Violence, and Criminality," 509–526.

66. For a summary of *Theories of Intimacy Deficits* in sex offenders, see Ward et al., *Theories of Sexual Offending*, 181–196.

67. The study was conducted by Hanson and Morton-Bourgon in 2004, as reported in Hanson, "Stability and Change," 23–24.

68. Melroy, "Pathologies of Attachment, Violence, and Criminality," 519–521.

can be life-long. When an adult engages in intercourse with a minor this is often called
*statutory rape. Concerns of older men exploiting younger girls are the basis for statu-
tory rape laws—consequently the young victim does not have to prove the adult used or
threatened force. Age alone does not constitute maturity. Certain levels of disability are
also given differential legal protection, the intent being to protect individuals with cognitive disabilities from exploitation by more sophisticated adults. In reality, attempting to
nuance maturity would be nearly impossible. Consequently, laws governing maturity are
based on chronological age and legal classification of disability, sometimes based on the
notion of mental age.

So-called *Romeo and Juliet laws* have been passed in most states to address situations
where adolescents are close in age and in a dating relationship. Minors who are near the age
of majority and within a year or two of their partner are deemed guilty of a minor offense
and are often not included in sex offender laws that require life-long registration as a sex
offender. Even so, many states retain laws on the books allowing sexually active teenagers to be charged with serious crimes. Minors who are younger, typically under sixteen or
fourteen, or when there is a larger age difference, often three to five years or more, are more
likely to be considered victims of sexual crimes. The partner is often considered guilty of a
sex crime without consideration of whether the minor "agreed" to the sexual behavior. The
seventeen-year-old who has sex with a thirteen-year-old boyfriend or girlfriend is likely to
be prosecuted regardless of whether the thirteen-year-old was "willing."[69]

Moral and ethical issues surrounding consent have drawn less attention than other
aspects of family law and sex offending law. Some states, for example, have set the age of
consent to marry below what other states have for consent to engage in sex, resulting in
two legally married teenagers finding themselves sex offenders in another state.[70] Similar
statutes regulating the ability to give consent were used to keep the mentally ill and disabled from procreating during the 1920s and 1930s.[71] While laws governing the sex lives
of adults are now largely considered inappropriate, complexities remain over how to govern healthy sexuality in institutions and other settings with disabled adults.

SEX OFFENDERS: INCEST

*Incest is a troubling offense; a crime and moral affront that bears many common traits
with other sex crimes and yet is unique given the relationship between the offender and
victim. Incest can be a focused crime or it may share many factors with pedophilia and
the molestation of children by extended- or non-family members.

---

69. Each state has its own statutes governing sexual crimes. Most are now able to be accessed online.
For example, the State of Arizona has harsher penalties for sexual crimes committed against a victim under
the age of fifteen, or if the offender is a parent, teacher, licensed counselor, and so forth (Arizona State
Legislature, *A.R.S. section 13-1405*, 49th Legislature, 1st Regular Session). http://www.azleg.state.az.us/
ArizonaRevisedStatutes.asp.

70. This was the case when the author worked as a Social Work Supervisor with child protective services
and a young couple moved into Wisconsin from another state. The District Attorney's office mandated the
couple live apart until the younger of the two was of age in Wisconsin.

71. See Grobb, *The Mad Among Us*, 141–162.

Rape and molestation within families is morally prohibited (Leviticus 18). When perpetrated against an adult, the incest offender bears the most similarities with rapists. In the biblical example of Amnon and Tamar, both appear to be adults, and although they were half-siblings they did not live in the same house (2 Sam 13:7, 13). However Amnon uses his family position to gain access to Tamar, and the family first silences the victim and then does not punish the offender, leading to further violence (2 Sam 13:6, 20–22, 32).

Society has been slow to provide legal protection to victims of *domestic abuse, including rape and sexual abuse. Laws governing conduct within families are spread across family, criminal, and juvenile courts. Many early rape laws were designed to protect the property of the father/husband and not the rights of the daughter/wife. In the United States, *advocacy for the rights of women and children were initially based on laws passed to protect against animal cruelty. While one might imagine courts in the 1820s ruling that men had the legal right to use physical discipline on their wives, as recently as 1989 the Supreme Court ruled that the government does not have a responsibility to rescue a child from maltreatment but instead has a responsibility to "protect the people from the State, not to insure that the State protected them from each other."[72]

Historically, the mental health community has also been slow to come to the assistance of incest survivors. Neither Jean-Martin Charcot nor Sigmund Freud, both early clinicians who worked with traumatized women, were sympathetic to either the role of women or reports of sexual abuse. Freud turned his patient's reports of sexual molestation *against them*, determining that their accounts were either fantasies or the fulfillment of the victim's own desires.[73] The notion of women "wanting" rape and sexual exploitation persists in society in the form of both the "rape myth" and the indifferent reactions to reports of child sexual abuse.

Incest, while morally repugnant, still flourishes because society tends to give adults, and men in particular (husbands and fathers), leeway in what happens within the confines of the home. The incestuous offender typically has: (1) greater access to the victim, (2) time and opportunity to groom the victim, (3) a persistent presence with which to coerce or enforce silence and compliance from the victim, (4) emotional and economic leverage over the family, should legal action be pursued, (5) and a social or religious structure that is reluctant to intervene. Unlike other crimes, child abuse and incest are usually addressed by child welfare and not law enforcement. Family preservation may have *statutory weight, and government agencies are discouraged from entering children into formal proceedings. After an abused child is removed from the home, reunification may be a primary objective.[74] Too often, punishment for the offender, whether in society or church, is seen to be at odds with the best interests of the child and the family.

---

72. Bradley v. State, 1 Miss. 156, 157 (1824). DeShaney v. Winnebago County, 109 S. Ct. 998 (1989). For a brief history of domestic laws in the United States, see Hess and Brinson, "Mediating Domestic Law Issues," 63–103. Another good source is Logan et al., "Justice System Options and Responses," 161–194.

73. Herman, *Trauma and Recovery*, 7–32.

74. Wisconsin Statute 48.01 Title and Legislative Purpose.

Incest and Re-victimization

If a child is found to have been abused, it is the victim who is typically removed from the home, often in the back of a police car. The *symbolic* message is clear—the child is at fault. This "blame-the-victim" mentality is *re-victimizing and not unique to incest, but *in incest the victim is placed in the position of having to seek safety and justice at the expense of family unity and sustenance.*[75] Removing the offending figure (usually the father) may cost the family its income and social status, threatening both family cohesion and the mother's primary emotional support. Unfortunately, the incestuous offender and family at large may threaten the victim directly or may threaten others the child cares about. Too often, the non-offending parent may dismiss indications of incest and even direct reports of incest because of feared consequences for the family.

Tragically, victims of sexual abuse sometimes disclose crimes only to find the perpetrator is allowed to remain in the home while the family gets treatment rather than the offender receiving punishment. *Victims who disclose once but are not adequately believed or protected are less inclined to report subsequent abuse.* In effect the perpetrator's hand is strengthened as is the family's *conspiracy of silence. Child and adolescent victims may also endure abuse in the belief that they are protecting younger siblings or even the non-offending parent.

Incest Offenders: Risk and Characterization

Risk factors for incest are similar to those of other types of child abuse. Sexual abuse is more likely in homes with domestic violence, substance abuse, poverty, and single-parent status.[76] In general, risks of offending are higher when the potential victim is more vulnerable and the potential offender has more stressors, including intimacy deficits and fewer supports.

If incest offenders could be characterized, there would probably be two primary categories. The first group of incest offenders is that group of individuals for whom incest is just one of many forms of child abuse, *spousal rape, or other criminal behavior. These offenders are either generally anti-social and commit many offenses repeatedly over time or they display a pattern of domestic violence. The second group is not generally anti-social but conforms to social expectations in other settings. Research on sex offenders has found that "among child molesters, heterosexual father-daughter incest offenders (who have no other victims) exhibit the lowest recidivism rates."[77] For these offenders, the defining characteristic appears to be the *cognitive distortions* surrounding power, intimacy, and access within the family structure.

---

75. This author worked as a child protective service supervisor with a neighboring judge who acquitted a man of rape, ruling that the five-year old victim's provocative and flirtatious behavior was responsible for her own incestuous molestation (Ward et al., *Theories of Sexual Offending*, 170).

76. Kathryn Kuehnle, "Child Sexual Abuse Evaluations," 437–439.

77. Quinsey et al., *Violent Offenders*, 132.

CONCLUSION

Sex crimes represent some of the darkest aspects of humanity. While all humanity has the ability for evil, those who commit sexual offenses have demonstrated the presence of sexual deviance and a willingness to override personal as well as societal constraints on behavior. While not all offenders repeat their offenses, many do. The destructiveness of sexual crimes and the propensity of offenders to traumatize new victims necessitates that the church and the broader treatment community understand the characteristics of sex offenders and find ways to reduce both the number of offenders and the number of offenses they commit.

QUESTIONS FOR DISCUSSION

1. In what ways do we all have the potential to sexually abuse another person? List several factors that distinguish the disturbed person with a history of sexual abuse. Think of a recent sexual abuse case in your area: in what ways are male and female predators treated differently by the press, clinicians, and society at large? For all these questions above, is there a difference between what you think the answers are and how you feel about the answers?

2. Why do you think 20 to 25 percent of women will experience sexual abuse, but only 1 to 2 percent of men will be convicted of a sexual crime? List some factors that contribute to this disparity. List several things the church can do to address the ignorance and misconceptions from a biblical perspective. What are some concrete things that can be done in your community to address this disparity and better inform people? For men and women headed into ministry, how can seminaries help train people to address sexual crimes?

3. What should the church be doing to address the number of female victims of sexual abuse? How can the worship and liturgy better acknowledge the reality of sexually wounded and broken people? What obligation does the church have to address the offenders? What can the church uniquely offer to offenders? Do some research in your area: what complex concerns are churches struggling with when it comes to relating to offenders? What are the latest policies and practices that you know churches are implementing to address offenders wanting to worship? What should a quality church policy look like to appropriately address offenders? Have you adequately talked with victims and parents about their concerns with offenders in the church?

4. Why do you think most sexual violence occurs between people who know each other and ostensibly love each other? Make a list of biblical passages that can be sensitively used to preach, teach, and better educate people? What are some characteristics of incestuous families and their "family systems" that help explain this family violence (consider other chapters in this volume on this subject)?

5. Has sexual offending become the unpardonable sin? What stereotypes (existing in various professions) are prohibiting effective help being given to offenders? To what extent should the church welcome the offender back into their fellowship? To what

extent should the offender be kept "outside the camp"? Think of a recent scenario of an offender in your church or faith community—how was it handled? What needs to be done differently?

6. Do *mandatory reporting laws ostracize family members of the offender? How should the church minister to the family of the offender? List some ways the church can come alongside public laws and assist in care, accountability, and protection. Does your church or faith community have a proactive ministry for the needs of offenders? Explain. Are churches and mental health services working together in your area? Explain.

FOR FURTHER READING

Baumeister, Roy F. *Evil: Inside Human Violence and Cruelty*. New York, NY: Henry Holt, 1999.

Beech, Anthony R., Leam A. Craig, and Kevin D. Browne, eds. *Assessment and Treatment of Sex Offenders: A Handbook*. New York, NY: Wiley, 2009.

Carnes, Patrick. *Out of the Shadows: Understanding Sexual Addiction*. Minneapolis: CompCare. 1983.

Doren, Dennis M. *Evaluating Sex Offenders*. Thousand Oaks, CA: Sage, 2002.

Hare, Robert D. *Without Conscience: The Disturbing World of the Psychopaths Among Us*. New York, NY: Guilford, 1993.

Laws, D. Richard and William T. O'Donohue, eds. *Sexual Deviance, Second Edition: Theory, Assessment, and Treatment*. New York, NY: Guilford, 2008.

Salter, Anna. *Predators: Pedophiles, Rapists, and Other Sex Offenders*. New York, NY: Basic, 2004.

Sexaholics Anonymous. *Sexaholics Anonymous*. Simi Valley, CA: SA Literature. 1989.

Seto, Michael C. *Pedophilia and Sex Offending Against Children: Theory, Assessment, and Intervention*. Washington, DC: American Psychological Association, 2007.

Struthers, William M. *Wired for Intimacy: How Pornography Hijacks the Male Brain*. Downers Grove, IL: IVP, 2009.

5

The Role of Dissociation in Sexual Abuse

Current Research and Approaches in Healing

Heather Davediuk Gingrich, PhD

SINCE THE MID 1980s I have been working with adult survivors of *sexual abuse (SA), some of whom fit diagnostic criteria for *dissociative identity disorder (DID).[1] Observing that the *dissociative symptoms that were so obviously manifested in those with DID were also present, albeit more subtly, in survivors of *childhood sexual abuse (CSA) who did not have a *dissociative disorder, I began to experiment with techniques I had been trained to use with DID clients, finding them beneficial in work with my other SA survivors.

In this chapter I will briefly describe how *dissociation has been conceptualized in the past and I will examine some current models. I will then discuss assessment of dissociative symptoms and the treatment techniques that make use of an SA client's dissociative abilities.

CONCEPTUALIZING DISSOCIATION: BRIEF HISTORICAL OVERVIEW

Both late eighteenth and early nineteenth century proponents of *animal magnetism and *hypnosis, as well as clinicians working with *hysteria in the mid- and late nineteenth century, conceptualized dissociation as divisions in consciousness.[2] Janet's development of a dissociation theory to explain hysteria and hypnosis, in addition to Prince's well-known multiple personality case of Miss Beauchamp, were instrumental in making the study of dissociation popular in the early twentieth century.[3]

Although Freud included dissociation in his list of *defense mechanisms, interest in dissociation waned in the 1930s as the psychoanalytic concept of *repression was em-

---

1. Formerly called *Multiple Personality Disorder. There has been skepticism in the popular media as well as the mental health field about whether DID even exists. I believe that this is the result of misconceptions and misinformation with regard to how DID develops and how the symptoms commonly manifest.

2. Van der Hart and Dorahy, "History of the Concept of Dissociation," 3–11.

3. Ibid., 11–12.

braced, supplanting dissociative explanations.[4] A resurgence of interest in dissociation since the 1980s can be attributed to: (1) increased diagnosis of and physiological research into multiple personality disorder, (2) interest in *post-traumatic stress syndromes (e.g., PTSD) where dissociative symptoms are exhibited, (3) greater public awareness of child abuse, (4) and renewed interest in hypnosis.[5] This has led to the current proliferation of ways of conceptualizing dissociation.[6]

Current Definition

Dissociation can be defined as a disruption in the usually integrated functions of consciousness, memory, identity, perception of the environment, sensation, and motor function. The first part of this definition is the one used in the *Diagnostic and Statistical Manual of Mental Disorders (DSM-IV-TR)*.[7] It is focused almost exclusively on the compartmentalization of mental events such as thoughts, feelings, memories, and attitudes. The expanded definition includes *somataform Dissociation, which involves not only psychological but *somatic symptoms.[8] This definition is consistent with early conceptualizations of dissociation, dissociation across cultures, and recent critics who have decried the narrowness of the *DSM-IV* definition.[9]

Normal vs. Pathological Dissociation

Dissociative experiences are not necessarily *pathological. For example, it is not uncommon for individuals to become so absorbed in a task that they lose track of how much time has passed by. Similarly, identification with characters in a novel or movie can be so intense that it is possible to temporarily forget one's own reality. Such experiences of absorption and imaginative involvement are dissociative in nature, but can be viewed as normal.[10]

Repetitive tasks that may not require a conscious decision to perform (i.e., *automatisms) can also be viewed as normal dissociative experiences. People who work on factory assembly lines, for example, can become so accustomed to doing the same thing over and

---

4. Chu and Bowman, "Trauma and Dissociation," 5–20.

5. Putnam, *Diagnosis and Treatment of Multiple Personality Disorder*, 4–6.

6. Van der Hart and Dorahy, "History of the Concept of Dissociation," 18–19.

7. American Psychiatric Association, *Diagnostic and Statistical Manual of Mental Disorders* (Text revision. Washington, DC: Author, 2000).

8. Nijenhuis, "Somatoform dissociation," 7–32.

9. Nemiah, "Dissociation, Conversion, and Somatization," 248–260; Saxe et al., "Somatization in Patients with Dissociative Disorders," 1329–34. Saxe et al. pointed out, for example, that hysteria, although defined in different ways over the past 150 years, has always involved dissociation *and* somatization as prominent features. Nemiah wrote that it was only in 1980, with the advent of the DSM-III, that a separate category was created for dissociative disorders, with conversion disorders (i.e., physical symptoms with a psychological cause) subsumed under *somatoform disorders. In my own clinical experience with counselees who dissociate, somatoform components have been prominent (see later discussion of the BASK model and body memories).

10. Carlson, "Studying the Interaction between Physical and Psychological States with the Dissociative Experiences Scale," 41–58.

over that their minds may not be on their work at all. I sometimes ask my students who, at some point in time, have stepped out of the shower and not been able to remember whether or not they have washed their hair, and a majority will raise their hands. It is as though the body seemingly performs such tasks on its own. Unless work performance or personal hygiene suffers, these types of experiences would not be considered abnormal.

Mystical spirituality also has its dissociative components. A deep sense of God's presence through mediation and prayer, or charismatic experiences of *glossolalia are altered states of consciousness that are dissociative but can be deeply meaningful.

There has been some debate in the literature as to whether dissociative experiences are best understood on a *continuum* or as discrete categories (i.e., *typology model*). Proponents of a continuum model view dissociation as a range of experiences with normal dissociation at one end to more severe, pathological dissociation (e.g., DID/dissociative disorders) at the other.[11] Those who advocate a typology model categorize individuals as either *low*, *medium*, or *high* dissociators.[12] While adherents to both models imply that the higher the degree of dissociation, the greater the level of pathology, the cross-cultural literature suggests that significant impairment must be present and the symptoms considered evidence of illness in the indigenous culture in order to be considered pathological.[13] *Therefore, it is important to distinguish between normal dissociative experiences and problematic dissociative symptoms in any given individual.*

Dissociation and Early Childhood Trauma

A strong association between early childhood *trauma, particularly SA, and dissociation has been reported worldwide.[14] *Neurological and cognitive functions are rapidly formed early in a child's development, laying the necessary foundations crucial for subsequent healthy development.[15] Discrete, fragmented behavioral states are normative in early infancy.[16] Newborns, for example, have no ability to regulate their emotions. When they are hungry they may scream at the top of their lungs, their whole bodies getting into the act as they flail arms and legs with scrunched up, red faces. But when given the breast or bottle they immediately switch states. Their bodies instantly relax; they stop crying and may even make contented gurgling noises.

As children get older they are expected to exhibit more integration between states. If, for example, a hungry five-year-old has a temper tantrum when food is not immediately

11. Watson, "Investigating the Construct Validity of the Dissociative Taxon," 298–305.

12. Putnam et al., "Patterns of Dissociation in Clinical and Nonclinical Samples," 673–679.

13. Castillo, "Dissociation," 101–123. In other words, it is possible for individuals to show evidence of a high degree of dissociation without necessarily having a mental health issue.

14. Gingrich, "Trauma and Dissociation in the Philippines," 245–269. Published simultaneously in *Trauma and Dissociation in a Cross-Cultural Perspective*, 245–269; idem, "Assessing Dissociative Symptoms and Dissociative Disorders in College Students in the Philippines," 403–418.

15. Ford, "Neurobiological and Developmental Research," 31–58; Elizabeth Carlson et al., "Dissociation and the Development of the Self," 39–52.

16. Putnam, *Dissociation in Children and Adolescents*, 151–179.

available, it is likely grounds for disciplinary action. If an adult shows such behavior it would be viewed as totally inappropriate.

With sensitive and nurturing parenting, secure *attachments form which aid in the development of a more continuous, integrated sense of self and experience. For instance, if a caregiver responds to the cries of the infant, determines the reason for the crying, and takes action to alleviate the problem,[17] the infant learns that the parent can be counted on, providing a sense of safety and security.[18] Although the infant's *affect is initially regulated externally, that is, through the caregiver's responsiveness to her needs,[19] as the child develops she develops the capacity to begin to regulate her own emotions as she learns to *self-soothe.[20] Good parenting therefore, not only impacts attachment, and thereby the ability of individuals to function well in relationships throughout their lives, but also has a positive effect on their ability to integrate their experiences and develop a healthy sense of self.

Traumatic experiences interfere with this process of integration.[21] *Abuse at the hands of parents is particularly destructive due to the increased element of betrayal.*[22] Attachment is greatly impacted when the very people who are supposed to be providing a safe haven for the child are the ones hurting him or her.[23] Yet young children are totally dependent on their caregivers for survival. Even if the SA was not due to *incest, attachment with parents can be adversely affected as children may not understand why their parents are not protecting them.

Dissociation can become an adaptive way for abused children to somehow cope with their reality, both with respect to the trauma itself[24] as well the challenges these children face with respect to attachment.[25] For example, an incest victim who is *raped in the early morning hours by her father is in the horrendous position of having to sit down at the breakfast table with her *perpetrator and act as though nothing has happened. Using dissociation, the child can *compartmentalize* the memory of being raped, effectively shutting it away, so that when she eats with her father at the breakfast table, then goes to school, she has no conscious awareness of what happened to her even minutes before. Since children dissociate easily, this process can become effortless.[26] *While non-traumatized children tend*

17. E.g., If the infant is hungry he is fed, if his diaper is dirty it is changed, and if a noise has startled him he is picked up and soothed.

18. Bowlby, *A Secure Base.*

19. The process works in the same way for males and females, as both can be SA survivors.

20. Thumb-sucking or a pacifier may be initial ways that a baby learns to self-soothe. A little later a favorite blanket or stuffed animal can serve to comfort the child when caregivers are not available. Once a child develops language they can use self-talk to calm themselves down. For example, she can say to her doll, "Mommy says we can have a cookie if we let her finish her phone call without bugging her."

21. Liotte, "Attachment and Dissociation," 53–65.

22. Freyd et al., "The State of Betrayal Trauma Theory," 295–311.

23. Bowlby, "A Secure Base."

24. DePrince and Freyd, "Trauma-induced Dissociation," 135–150.

25. Lyons-Ruth et al., "From Infant Attachment Disorganization to Adult Dissociation," 63–86.

26. See the preceding discussion on discrete behavioral states and the development of increased integration through the process of socialization.

to lose their ability to dissociate as they get older, abused children may retain that capacity out of necessity. SA survivors are, therefore, more prone to dissociation in adulthood due to the detrimental impact of the abuse on their development, including impeding the formation of secure attachment figures and/or their need for dissociation as a psychological *defense against the trauma.

THE BASK MODEL

The *BASK model of dissociation[27] can be especially helpful when working with SA. BASK is an acronym that describes various components of experience or memory: *Behavior, Affect, Sensation,* and *Knowledge.* Any aspect of a particular experience can be dissociated from the rest. For example, an SA *survivor may have no memory of an entire abuse incident or some aspect of it, but still experience the affect (**A**) attached to the event. One SA client woke up regularly at 3:48 a.m. terrified, but having no idea why. Eventually she recalled that her father regularly raped her at about that time most nights of her childhood. Initially she had no *conscious* knowledge (**K**) of this series of events because the cognitive aspects were dissociated even though she was fully aware of the emotion (**A**) that corresponded to it. *Conversely, SA survivors could have full cognitive memory of an abuse incident yet display no emotion as they describe the horrendous details to you.* In this case, the affect is the BASK component that is dissociated.

Sensation (**S**) refers to physical aspects of the experience, whether pain, pleasure, or some other aspect of *somatoform dissociation. For example, SA survivors may experience physical pain (e.g., in the pelvic or genital area) and not know why until they make the connection to a specific abuse incident that resulted in just such pain.[28] Behavior (**B**) may also be dissociated from the other BASK components. SA (female) survivors who continually run from committed, intimate relationships with men but are totally unaware of the connection of this to their fears of *re-victimization are a good example. Another illustration is a woman who vomited every time she and her husband had intercourse, but made no conscious link between that behavior and the SA she had cognitive memory (**K**) of as a child.

Any one of these BASK components, or various combinations, can be dissociated from each other at various times for any SA survivor. The same principles, however, are in operation for SA survivors who have dissociative disorders. For those with DID, for instance, dissociated parts of self may be built around clusters of events, or smaller fragments of self may compartmentalize a particular emotion or aspect of an event. *In all cases of SA, a major part of the healing process involves *reintegration of these BASK components.*

---

27. Braun, "The BASK Model of Dissociation," 16–23.

28. Dissociated sensation is sometimes referred to as *body memories* in the SA literature.

IDENTIFYING DISSOCIATIVE SYMPTOMS

Clinical Observation

While formal assessment instruments can be important in determining the degree to which an SA client dissociates, even the decision to administer such tests are based on initial clinical observations of symptoms. Therefore it is important for anyone involved in helping those with SA to recognize the signs. The BASK model has been discussed in the previous section as a way of conceptualizing dissociation. However diagnostic criteria for *DSM-IV-TR* dissociative disorders and post-traumatic stress disorder (PTSD) also include symptoms that are relevant to recognizing dissociation in SA survivors.

BASK and DSM-IV-TR Dissociative Symptom Areas

Learning to recognize when BASK components are not integrated is one way to determine that an SA client is dissociating. These components may *present as: behavior that seems to make no sense (**B**); emotions that appear random, are exaggerated, or are absent (**A**); unexplained pain or physical complaints (**S**); or small or large memory gaps (**K**).

There are five dissociative symptom areas that are associated with the *DSM-IV-TR* dissociative disorders that can also be an aid to recognizing dissociation: (1) amnesia, (2) depersonalization, (3) derealization, (4) identity confusion, and (5) identity alteration.[29]

Amnesia refers to the memory gaps discussed earlier; the K component of the BASK model. While amnesia may be present for past abuse memories, the clinician should also check for current memory problems. "Missing" hours or days of time, not recognizing people who call them by name, not remembering buying certain items, being told they did something they do not remember doing, forgetting daily routines, and frequently being called a liar are all examples of the dissociative symptom of amnesia. In counseling, there can be *intrainterview amnesia.[30]

Depersonalization, a sense of disconnection from self and body, is commonly experienced by SA survivors. Depersonalization may take the form of watching themselves do something from a distance rather than being an active participant in an event. For instance, during an abuse incident a child may have the sense of "watching from the ceiling" or from "a spot on the wall" while someone is "hurting the little boy on the bed." Depersonalization may also take the form of not recognizing themselves in the mirror or distortion of body parts.[31] It may also take the form of "I know I'm the one holding the pen and writing in the journal, but it doesn't feel like it's me!"

Derealization has to do with distorted perceptions of surroundings or other people. This can take the form of seeing the world as though through a fog or a tunnel, or things just seeming strange. Full post-traumatic *flashback experiences are ultimately derealization experiences; the SA survivor is seeing and experiencing things and people that are

---

29. Steinberg, "Advances in the Clinical Assessment of Dissociation," 146–163.

30. I.e., The client not remembering what was said earlier in the session.

31. E.g., Seeing their hands the size of a young child's hands or their leg at an unrealistic angle from their body.

not actually there. Sometimes individuals will confuse daydreams with reality. In therapy, derealization can take the form of the SA client confusing the therapist with the abuser.

Identity Confusion is particularly problematic for SA survivors with *dissociative disorder not otherwise specified (DDNOS)[32] or DID. However, other SA survivors can also experience more than usual angst about who they are.

Identity Alteration, that is, feeling and/or acting as though they are different people, is severe in DID and in some types of DDNOS. However SA survivors who do not meet *diagnostic criteria for the above disorders may still exhibit mild to moderate identity alteration. Therefore, most SA survivors I know resonate with the concept: "parts of self." *When a deeply wounded, terrified, or rebellious child or teenaged part of self appears, it can look like immaturity to an outsider.* Mood changes may accompany identity alteration, which can result in misdiagnoses of mood disorders (particularly *bipolar disorder) or anxiety disorders.

Relationship of Dissociation to Post-traumatic Stress Disorder

Two of the key diagnostic criteria for post-traumatic stress disorder involve *reexperiencing* of the traumatic event and *avoidance* of it.[33] *Post-traumatic reexperiencing symptoms such as flashbacks, *nightmares, and overwhelming affect are common in SA survivors as are *numbing of affect and avoidance of potentially *triggering situations.

FLASHBACKS AND NIGHTMARES

If viewed through the lenses of the BASK model, flashbacks can be seen as the result of dissociated aspects of experience being triggered into awareness. A full flashback[34] could be explained as all four BASK components being triggered at once.[35] Alternately, a full flashback could be described as all five dissociative symptom areas being triggered.

A partial flashback could potentially take the form of a frightening visual image without the client reexperiencing any physical symptoms and without impacting their immediate behavior. In this case the SA survivor would be fully aware that what they are seeing, terrifying as it seems, is not actually happening now. In terms of BASK, the S and B components remain dissociated in this example while the A and K components are reexperienced. With regard to the five dissociative symptom areas, note the following scenarios: the client's amnesia is being challenged (e.g., "This couldn't have really happened!"), they are experiencing mild to moderate derealization (e.g., "I know I'm here at work, but my childhood bedroom is superimposed on my office environment"), mild to moderate depersonalization (e.g., "That little kid looks like me as a child, but surely isn't really me"), potentially some identity confusion (e.g., "What kind of person am I that I'm

---

32. DDNOS can be similar to DID except that fragmented parts of self do not actually take over *executive functioning* of the body.

33. American Psychiatric Association, *Diagnostic.*

34. I.e., A flashback so intense that the abuse is fully relived to the extent that it feels as though it is actually happening "here-and-now."

35. E.g., The cognitive memory bursting into awareness (K), experience of overwhelming terror (A), physical sensations of heart racing, choking and pain (S), and sense of fending off the perpetrator (B).

imagining such disgusting things?"), and mild identity alteration (e.g., "That little kid has no business messing up my work day").

Reexperiencing of SA in the form of nightmares can be similar to flashbacks. For example, some flashbacks can involve a full reenactment of the SA involving all BASK components. Others may differ in content from the actual SA incident, but still bring to awareness affect that has been dissociated. For instance, the terror may feel real, but in the dream it is associated with being chased by a monster rather than by being abused by a perpetrator. In this way cognitive knowledge is still dissociated; the individual remains amnestic to the actual abuse incident.

DIFFICULTIES WITH *AFFECT REGULATION

As mentioned earlier, SA survivors tend either to be flooded with emotions or have *blunted affect, sometimes swinging back and forth between the two extremes. This kind of intense affect can be viewed as part of post-traumatic reexperiencing. Restricted affect, on the other hand, can be seen as part of post-traumatic *avoidance.

BODY MEMORIES

Body memories are related to the Sensation component of the BASK model. Physical pain, pleasure, marks on the skin, and unexplained bruising and bleeding can all be potential reexperiencing symptoms of past SA.

ASSESSMENT INSTRUMENTS

Numbers of good assessment instruments for measuring dissociative experiences, dissociative symptoms, and dissociative disorders exist. Based on my work I would like to recommend two.

The *Dissociative Experiences Scale—II (DES)[36] is an excellent, brief, screening tool for assessing how much an individual dissociates. It has been translated into dozens of languages and used extensively in research both in North America and internationally. With only twenty-eight items, it takes less than thirty minutes to complete and only a few minutes to score. The DES looks at both normal and pathological dissociation, so it is not considered a diagnostic instrument. While the over-all score is indicative of the degree of dissociation, examining responses to individual test items also can be immensely helpful in counseling. Best of all, it can be found online and downloaded free of charge.[37] There is also a similar scale for adolescents[38] as well as a checklist that adults can complete as they observe potentially dissociative children.[39]

The *Structured Clinical Interview for DSM-IV-TR Dissociative Disorders (SCID-D)[40] is a semi-structured diagnostic interview developed to systematically assess the presence,

---

36. Carlson and Putnam, "An Update on the Dissociative Experiences Scale," 16–27.
37. The DES can be obtained at http://www.traumaawareness.org/id15.html as well as other sites.
38. Armstrong et al., "Development and Validation of a Measure of Adolescent Dissociation," 491–497.
39. Putman et al., "Development, Reliability, and Validity of a Child Dissociation Scale," 731–741.
40. Steinberg, "Advances," 146–163.

severity, and *phenomenology of the five *DSM-IV-TR* dissociative symptom areas. It can be used to assess the use of dissociative symptoms in individuals without psychiatric illness and those with psychiatric disorders, as well as make *DSM-IV-TR* diagnoses in the five dissociative disorders. The SCID-D is considered the "gold standard" for assessing dissociative disorders.[41] For a counselor with an extensive SA practice, buying the manual, score sheets, and questionnaires could be a worthwhile investment. No formal training on using the SCID-D is required as the manual provides the necessary instructions for administration, scoring, and interpretation.

USE OF AN ADULT CLIENT'S DISSOCIATIVE CAPACITIES AS AN AID TO TREATMENT

One of the key benefits of recognizing dissociative symptoms in SA clients is *the potential to harness their ability to dissociate for constructive use in the healing process.*

Symptom Stabilization

Perhaps the most exciting therapeutic discovery I have made in my almost thirty years in the counseling field has been learning how to use dissociation to help stabilize symptoms. Anyone who has done much work with SA can likely identify with the overwhelming feelings of helplessness experienced by the therapist when confronted with their SA clients' continual crisis situations. The post-traumatic reexperiencing symptoms of flashbacks, nightmares, and overwhelming affect can be particularly difficult to cope with for both SA clients and their counselors.

INTRODUCTION OF CONCEPT "PARTS OF SELF"

Identifying the dissociative symptom of identity alteration can be very useful to the counselor. The SA survivor's sense of not always feeling like the same person is what enables them to so easily identify with the concept of "different parts of self." *Some SA clients already express themselves in this manner, while others are relieved at being offered a way of talking that so closely fits their experience.*

As this language may seem strange to the average person, I tend to attempt to *normalize the concept as I introduce it by telling SA clients that we all have parts of us that we know and others of which we are not aware.[42] However, my concerns about a potential negative reaction from my SA clients have almost always been unfounded because they tend to so easily "get it."

The Negotiation Process

Once an SA survivor acknowledges that they are not aware of all parts of self, this concept can be used to manage symptoms. *My underlying assumption is that although symptoms*

---

41. Welburn et al., "Discriminating Dissociative Identity Disorder from Schizophrenia and Feigned Dissociation on Psychological Tests and Structured Interview," 109–130.

42. At a very basic level I believe this to be true as even individuals who are not highly dissociative are not fully aware of all aspects of themselves. After all, "The heart is deceitful above all things and desperately wicked: who can know it?" (Jer 17:9 KJV).

may feel totally out of control, they are actually under the control of SA clients; that at some level they are allowing the symptom to manifest. For example, if a client is having post-traumatic nightmares every night, some part of them is allowing the nightmares to come. The same is true of flashbacks, body memories, and other reexperiencing symptoms.

I have come to see such symptoms as *cries for help*, red flags that some part of the SA survivor is waving as an indication that something needs attention. The problem is that not everything can be resolved at once, as healing from SA is often a long, grueling process. Managing a particular symptom involves acknowledging the cry for help, then negotiating with that part of the SA survivor that has been allowing the symptom to surface.

Ideomotor Signaling

I have found the use of *ideomotor signaling to be the easiest way to facilitate the negotiation process. This is a technique that involves the use of finger signals to communicate with a dissociated aspect of self. For example, Jane is struggling with nightly, terrifying dreams that are greatly impacting her ability to sleep and as a result, her ability to cope well during the day. I would first introduce Jane to the "parts of self" idea, after which I would see if it makes sense to her that "some part" of her is allowing the nightmares to surface. I would then say something like the following: "Jane, I wonder if you'd be willing to let me talk to this part of you by using 'yes' and 'no' finger signals? There is nothing mystical about this; it is merely a short-cut, a way to bypass what you are consciously aware of so that the part of you that is allowing the nightmares to come has a chance to communicate."

My graduate counseling students have a hard time believing that this does not freak clients out! However, as *SA survivors already naturally use dissociation, I think the process is more intuitive for them than it is for non-dissociative individuals*. Of course, I would make sure I have developed good rapport with an SA client before introducing such a technique.

Next, I explain to Jane what she can expect if she consents, and go over the finger signals. I use the baby finger as a "yes" signal and the index finger as a "no" signal, but this can be modified. I also reassure her that she can stop the process at any point in time, incorporating a slightly raised hand as a "stop" signal in case she has trouble verbalizing her desire to interrupt the process. I tell Jane to merely allow her fingers to respond without thinking consciously about what the answers are.

I then suggest that Jane close her eyes to cut down on distraction, after which I invite "all parts of Jane" to listen in. I briefly introduce myself because not all parts of Jane necessarily know who I am, saying something like "My name's Heather. I'm a counselor who Jane came to see about some issues in her life." I then go over the finger signals once more, as not all parts of Jane were necessarily listening in on my earlier conversations with Jane. Then I initiate discussion of the problem symptom area in the following fashion: "Jane has been telling me about nightmares that are very disturbing to her. Is the part of Jane that has control of the nightmares listening in?" If the "yes" finger twitches, I will go on, saying, "Jane and I realize that the nightmares are an indication that she needs to work on something. The problem is that rather than helping right now, the nightmares are making it even harder for Jane to heal because she isn't getting enough sleep. If Jane agrees to eventually deal with the issue that the nightmare represents, would you agree to stop the nightmares for at least a number of months?" There is a very good chance that given this information, the part of Jane that controls the nightmares will respond "yes" through the finger signals, and the nightmares will disappear!

Of course, it doesn't always go this smoothly. If there is no indication that the targeted part of Jane is listening, I'll say, "Could some other parts of Jane let the part of her that controls the nightmares know that I have some questions to ask her?" If there is still resistance I'll say, "Could some other part of Jane either speak to me directly, or let Jane know through her thoughts what the hesitation is?" In this way the counselor is serving the function of a *mediator* and will need to adapt as the situation requires.

Flashbacks can be controlled through a similar negotiation process, as can *suicidal ideation, somatic symptoms, and affect. I once had a client come to her session after having gone to the ER because of vaginal hemorrhaging. The doctors had been unable to find any reason for the bleeding; they had merely attempted to staunch the flow. Suspecting a possible body memory connected to the client's SA, I asked if any part of her knew why she was bleeding, getting a positive response. While it did not instantly stop after the negotiation process, the flow was significantly reduced and was gone within a few days. This bought time until the client was at a point, months later, where she could work through the associated abuse memory.

Alternative Negotiating Techniques

If either the counselor or the client is uncomfortable with the use of ideomotor signaling, similar principles can be applied without use of the finger signals. The disadvantage is that the counselor then has to rely on a *verbal* response, either directly from the dissociated part of the client, or by the dissociated part somehow getting the message through to the client. I generally find it easier to initially get a definitive response through ideomotor signaling until the client has better access and can give voice to the dissociated aspects of self. However, the key to successful symptom management is in understanding both the meaning of the symptom as well as the importance of the negotiation process. Counselors working with SA can then find their own means of negotiation.

PROCESSING TRAUMA: WORKING
THROUGH THE TRAUMATIC MEMORIES

The ability of SA survivors to dissociate can also be used during the memory-work phase of therapy. The methods discussed above for managing symptoms can also be used to help pace memory work and order priorities. For example, if a number of issues seemed pressing, I would ask "all parts of Jane" to determine where to start. If we were doing particularly difficult memory work, I would invite "all parts of Jane" to give input as to whether the timing was right to deal with this particular memory, determine when she had processed enough for one session, and to help keep her safe between sessions. As safety and symptom stabilization are considered prerequisites to doing the actual trauma processing work, I previously would have worked enough with dissociated aspects of the client that I would not necessarily be limited to "yes/no" questions, but could rely on the client to have developed better skills at internal communication between parts of self. In the case of severely dissociated SA clients, dialogue could potentially be directly between the counselor and other parts of self.

A BRIEF NOTE ON WORKING WITH DISSOCIATION IN CHILDREN AND ADOLESCENTS[43]

*Longitudinal studies of the general population have shown that individuals dissociate to the greatest extent in early childhood and that dissociative experiences gradually decrease throughout adolescence and early adulthood, after which levels tend to stabilize.[44] *As long as the focus in the treatment of dissociative adults remains reintegration of the whole person and/or their experiences*, I believe that there is little danger that the techniques discussed in the previous section will increase dissociation. However, as even healthy children and adolescents have not fully integrated their experiences and/or sense of self, there is the potential danger that a helper could inadvertently reinforce dissociative behavior through initiating contact with parts of self which may not have yet concretized because of their developmental stage. Instead, interacting with whatever dissociative part of the child spontaneously presents itself can be helpful. In *play therapy, dissociated aspects of self may be projected onto puppets or stuffed animals, in which case the toy can be addressed. Treatment of dissociative children, if currently in a non-abusive, safe environment can be relatively short-term compared to treatment of dissociative adults. Therefore, I would encourage those who work with children to become skilled at recognizing childhood dissociative symptoms so that long years of treatment in adulthood can potentially be avoided.

CONCLUSION

While there is a separate literature for treating those with dissociative disorders, many facets of treatment are similar. If an SA client is showing even mild to moderate dissociative symptoms, the techniques discussed in this chapter will be helpful. If an SA client is diagnosable with DID or another dissociative disorder, the same principles apply. In fact, unless forced to give a diagnosis for insurance purposes, I simply talk with all of my SA clients about the process of dissociation, letting them determine over time where they fall on the dissociative continuum.

For readers wanting more information about working with dissociation I highly recommend the *International Society for the Study of Trauma and Dissociation* (ISSTD). Their

---

43. See the bibliography on children and dissociation posted on www.isst-d.org for further information about the treatment of dissociative children.

44. Ogawa et al., "Development and the Fragmented Self," 855–879. Welburn et al., "Discriminating Dissociative Identity Disorder from Schizopherenia and Feigned Dissociation on Psychological Tests and Structured Interview," 109–130.

website[45] contains an extensive bibliography of helpful resources, provides guidelines for treatment, offers email discussion groups, and lists component groups in geographical locations worldwide. It also gives information about conferences, training opportunities, and client referral sources. While it is a secular organization, it includes many Christians among its members.

QUESTIONS FOR DISCUSSION

1. You are encouraging Sandy, a SA survivor, to get some counseling. She tells you that she does not feel upset about what happened to her, has *forgiven her perpetrator, and has already put the abuse behind her. How would you determine whether she has indeed been healed or whether she is merely dissociating her affect?

2. When you look into the mirror one day, a terrified young child stares back at you. Shocked, you turn away and are disturbed to notice that your hand has shrunk to one-quarter the size it should be for an adult. Which two dissociative symptoms can be used to explain these experiences?

3. While you are introducing "parts of self" language to an SA survivor, he interrupts you, saying, "Does this mean you think I have multiple personalities?" How would you use the dissociative continuum model to address his concern (whether or not you suspect DID)?

4. Upon hearing that you are using ideomotor signaling with an SA survivor, your pastor accuses you of using New Age techniques that are demonically influenced. How would you counteract this accusation, knowing what you do about dissociation? This chapter mentioned symptoms and *indigenous cultures*. Discuss the implications of this for diagnosis and treatment. Interview a missionary or crisis counselor who has worked with sexual trauma in two-thirds world countries. How does culture shape dissociative symptoms and the perceptions of them? How can *spiritual formation programs incorporate people with dissociative issues into healing *rituals and practices?

5. In the midst of processing an abuse memory, your counselee looks at you and begins screaming, "Get away from me! Stop hurting me!" How can you use the concept of dissociation to explain what is happening? Discuss particular movies or TV series you have seen that illustrate these types of dissociation? Why do you believe these particular dissociative symptoms were highlighted in the movie or TV program?

FOR FURTHER READING

Courtois, Christine A. and Judy D. Ford. *Treating Complex Traumatic Stress Disorders: An Evidence-Based Guide.* New York, NY: Guilford Press, 2009.

Dell, Paul F. and John A. O'Neil. *Dissociation and the Dissociative Disorders: DSM-V and Beyond.* New York, NY: Taylor & Francis, 2009.

45. See www.isst-d.org.

Gingrich, Heather D. "Stalked by Death: Cross-Cultural Trauma Work with a Tribal Missionary." *Journal of Psychology and Christianity* 21 (2002): 262–265.

———. "Dissociative Symptoms in Filipino College Students." *Philippine Journal of Psychology* 37 (2004): 50–78.

———. "Complex Traumatic Stress Disorders in Adults." *Journal of Psychology and Christianity* 28 (2009): 269–274.

Putman, Frank W. *Dissociation in Children and Adolescents: A Developmental Perspective.* New York, NY: Guilford, 1997.

Rhoades, George Jr. and Vedat Sar. *Trauma and Dissociation in a Cross-Cultural Perspective: Not Just a North American Phenomenon.* New York, NY: Haworth Press, 2005.

Steinberg, Marlene. *Interviewer's Guide to the Structured Clinical Interview for DSM-IV Dissociative Disorders (SCID-D) Revised.* Washington, DC: American Psychiatric Press, 1994.

———, and Maxine Schnall. *The Stranger in the Mirror: Dissociation, the Hidden Epidemic.* New York, NY: Cliff Street Books, 2001.

6

Wife Rape: Personal Realities and Hope for the Future

Gary H. Strauss, EdD

CONSIDER THE FOLLOWING THREE scenarios:

For six years she had been beaten and raped repeatedly by her own husband. He was a "smooth talker" who always said it would never happen again—but it always did. Victoria tried to leave him many times but couldn't support three young children as a fast-food worker.[1]

In June of 1994, Karen's husband of four years threatened her with a knife. She acted immediately to get an *order of protection. He stayed away for three weeks, but one Saturday morning she awoke to find him at the bedroom door with the same knife. He punched her, tied and gagged her, and raped her. "He was trying to punish me for having gone to court to protect myself," Karen says. "This was definitely about power and control, not sex or lust."[2]

He attacked around midnight, choking her, dragging her by her hair, brutally raping her over and over again. But as the husband of his victim, this violent rapist may receive only 1.5 years imprisonment and, perhaps, none at all. A stranger committing the same crime could receive 14 years.[3]

A CRIME IGNORED NO LONGER

These three stories are horrendous, both in tone and focus. The terror each of these women experienced is graphically portrayed. What is experienced every day by so many women in a large country like the USA, and countless more throughout the world, is almost impossible to grasp. National and international data is increasingly available that makes it clear that *sexual abuse (SA) is a severe and universal problem. This broad category of

---

1. The Voices and Faces Project: Survivor Stories, http://www.voicesandfaces.org/survivor_victoria.asp; accessed August10, 2009.

2. Ibid.

3. McElroy, "Spousal Rape Case Sparks Old Debate," http://www.foxnews.com/story.0,2933,147725,00.html; accessed August 8, 2009.

abuse includes the domestic component which itself contains the narrower category of *spousal sexual abuse.

This chapter specifically addresses the sexual abuse of a wife or girlfriend by her husband or boyfriend by means of *rape. It is vital to begin by defining this vicious act in order to provide an adequate understanding of and response to this harsh reality of *wife rape. This phenomenon must be recognized as something that occurs on a continuum ranging from the unquestionably criminal acts described above to those experiences that many, if not the majority, would even today reject as examples of wife rape.

It is also my intention to provide an adequate consideration of wife rape within the context of the personal experience of the victims themselves. So in this chapter, I want to encourage the reader to give careful thought to the violence against women, and particularly wives and girlfriends, if this violence is to be reduced. This reduction is vital to increase the percentage of women who can live with a greater sense of safety, hope, and delight in their relationships; rather than enduring in those relationships as they live in fear or an experience of sexual assault. Against this backdrop it is also important to consider the biblical perspective of marriage to understand God's intended context for marital sexual intimacy. My hope is that the following discussion will help us all, from layperson to credentialed professional, to respond in a manner that celebrates the biblical mandate to care for one another and for all those who we may encounter who have been hurt.

THE AUTHOR'S PERSONAL EXPERIENCE AND PERSPECTIVE

The phenomenon of *spousal rape, wife rape, *marital rape, or rape in marriage, whatever label might be used, is known to be a universal problem, no doubt dating back to early human history.[4] Possible biblical examples include the level of evil that caused such regret to the heart of God that he brought a worldwide flood upon all humanity. This biblical account likely included marital sexual abuse, including wife rape (cf. Gen 6:1–8). David, the beloved king of Israel, may have physically forced himself upon Bathsheba. I find this difficult, since he later respected her time of grieving following the death of her husband, a death arranged by David himself. Regardless, *David seriously violated her, having essentially forced her into an adulterous relationship and then taking her as his wife following Uriah's death* (cf. 2 Sam 11:27; 12:9).

*While men and women both engage in *domestic violence against their spouses or partners, spousal rape within heterosexual, intimate relationships must be identified as exclusively a male act.*[5] Over the thirty-five-plus years of my professional practice as a teaching psychologist and a *psychotherapist, I have never encountered any literature, news report, or personal account of a man being raped by his wife. My research has also not come across a single reference to such behavior on the part of wives. It is commonly known that husbands are killed with poison, guns, and knives; others have experienced the mutilation or even severing of genital organs, and still many others (undoubtedly the

4. For an examination of rape in antiquity, see Deacy and Pierce, *Rape in Antiquity.*

5. Pagelow, "Marital Rape," chap 9.

majority of those men who have been assaulted by their wives) have been brutalized by beatings with fists or other instruments of bodily harm.[6] But women, obviously, cannot forcibly penetrate their husband's body with their sexual organ as men can do to their wives or girlfriends, thereby making it impossible for wives to inflict upon their husbands what men have been inflicting upon their wives for millennia.[7]

In light of this fact, as a husband for over fifty years and as a father and grandfather to women, and because I deeply love and treasure these three women in my immediate family, I experience a filial and paternal part of me that is deeply grieved and angered by those of my gender who have engaged in wife rape. I personally consider this act to be heinous, overwhelmingly humiliating, exceedingly disrespectful, and physically and emotionally traumatic for the victims. I also consider it a cowardly act of manipulating or physically overpowering their less physically strong wives. And here I must separate this personal and emotional reaction from my professional perspective.

Many years of practice as a psychotherapist has helped me come to at least partially understand and accept the reality of the various "demons" with which many men struggle, often rooted in the deep pain and subsequent anger that has been experienced in their developmental histories that violent men recount. Don't misunderstand: these histories are an explanation, not a justification. I am thankful that I have been able to be caring and *empathic with such men and hopefully helpful to those with whom I have worked. Nevertheless, my focus in this chapter is primarily on the suffering of the wives and girlfriends—their incidences, their vulnerability, and some of the factors that have been identified that correlate with intimate sexual violence on the part of both the wives and their husbands.

TERMS AND DEFINITIONS

Examination of the current literature reveals that there are several terms and definitions that are important to this discussion. I will continue to refer to this as "wife rape," in keeping with my observation that the wife is the only spouse that can be truly raped. There are legal as well as socio-cultural definitions, each contributing to our overall understanding of both the essential nature and the range of behavior surrounding wife rape.

Raquel Bergen, in her study dealing with what she terms *marital rape*, defines the act as follows: "While the legal definition varies within the United States, marital rape can be defined as any unwanted intercourse or penetration (vaginal, anal, or oral) obtained by force, threat of force, or when the wife is unable to consent."[8]

---

6. For a recent critique of an article addressing the higher level of domestic violence committed by women than by men returning from involvement in the Middle East wars, see http://pajamasmedia.com/blog/stacy-bannerman's-domestic-violence-hoax/?singlepage=true; accessed October 7, 2010.

7. Voices and Faces, an organization seeking to address the issue of sexual assault, lists on its website a number of myths about rape, http://www.voicesandfaces.org/rape.asp; accessed August 10, 2009. The one pertinent to this point is the following: "*Myth*: It is impossible for a husband to sexually assault his wife. *Fact*: Regardless of marital or social relationship, if a woman does not consent to sexual activity, she is being sexually assaulted. In fact, 14 percent of women are victims of rape committed by their husband."

8. Bergen, "Marital Rape," http://new.vawnet.org/category/Main_Doc.php?docid=248; accessed September 28, 2010. See Bergen, *Wife Rape*; Pagelow, "Adult Victims of Domestic Violence," 87–120; Russell,

Diana Russell, in the publication of her landmark study begun in 1977, reports that at that time in California and most other states:

> [F]orcible rape included: (1) forced intercourse (vaginal-penile penetration), or (2) intercourse obtained by threat of force, in which a husband threatens to force his wife to yield to his unwanted behavior, or (3) intercourse when consent is impossible because the victim is unconscious, severely drugged, asleep, or in some other way totally helpless.[9]

Several observations emerge from this. First, *rape is not essentially about sex but rather about issues of *entitlement, power, uncontrolled anger, and in many cases, punishment.* The second scenario at the beginning of the chapter illustrates this. A second observation is that *intimate partner sexual assault involves imposing "any *unwanted* intercourse or penetration" upon the wife by her husband.[10] So it is important to recognize that *husbands never have the right to impose unwanted sexual activity*. Until quite recently, his right to impose himself was legally assumed to be legitimate because of the marital contract.[11]

In Russell's identification of the forms of "forcible rape," we can observe three possible levels of force being used by the husband. Wives who have experienced the highest level, what might be called *brute force*, have known the reality of powerlessness as they've experienced their own limits of strength in resisting the rape. Those who have experienced the *threat of force* have also known the harsh reality of manipulation, having their fears played upon. They know the emotional pain of experiencing their husband's exploitation. They know feelings of weakness and their fear of being physically forced. The women understand that if they resist their husband's threats, they may receive even more bodily harm than if they comply immediately. And those wives who have been raped in a totally helpless state know the reality of being treated as an object. It seems likely that these women feel very little, if any, sense of personhood in their marriages; all the more when these experiences occur numerous times.

Russell also cites a *feminist-preferred definition, which includes "any sexual intimacy forced on one person by another."[12] She states that her preferred definition is a "compromise between the traditional legal definition and the more modern, feminist-influenced definition, to include forced oral and anal sex as well as forced digital penetration."[13] She makes it clear that she is not including a broad range of other forced acts of intimacy, though she acknowledges that some sociologists would include these acts under the definition of *wife rape*.

I personally agree with such sociologists: any act of sexual intimacy that is forced upon a wife, either directly or by threat—including acts imposed upon a wife in a helpless state—is by its very nature a serious violation of the wife. Such an experience can be as

---

Rape in Marriage.

9. Russell, *Rape in Marriage*, 42–43.

10. Bergen, "Marital Rape"; Pagelow, "Adult Victims."

11. See the helpful analysis of Schroeder, *Dinah's Lament*.

12. Katz and Mazur, *Understanding the Rape Victim*, 11.

13. Russell, *Rape in Marriage*, 43.

violating as forced penetration. This reflection on the definition of wife rape acknowledges the sense of violation a wife experiences in response to *any* act of sexual intimacy forced or imposed upon her by her husband. This definition also helps sensitize both present and future husbands to the seriousness of the sexually intimate behaviors they would choose to engage in with their wives. Obviously counselors, pastors, and spiritual mentors also need to manifest sensitivity in their work with these wives and their husbands.

It is also necessary to sensitize wives to the meaning of the behaviors they may experience in their marriages. Some may not identify this behavior as personally violating as a rape or a rape-type experience. Russell notes this same lack of behavior identification: "Only six of the eighty-seven victims of wife rape (7 percent) mentioned their experience with their husbands in answer to the one direct question on rape (*At any time in your life, have you ever been the victim of rape, or attempted rape?*)"[14] She further notes that there may have been understandable reasons for them not to respond affirmatively, though it would have been a most logical point in the interview for those questioned to acknowledge such an experience.

Citing prevalence data, Bergen observes that when the research includes "women who felt emotionally coerced to have 'unwanted sex' with their intimate partner, the prevalence is much higher."[15] Further, she notes that a national study conducted by Basile found that 34 percent of the women surveyed reported that they had experienced "unwanted sex with their partner—most frequently as a result of marital obligation."[16] This observation adds another issue of concern for wives, namely, the need to seriously consider what is legitimately to be included within the range of "marital obligations."

THE PREVALENCE OF WIFE RAPE

Russell's conclusions from her work in San Francisco provide a baseline regarding prevalence of wife rape. She stated that "approximately one in every seven women who has ever been married in our San Francisco sample was willing to disclose an experience of sexual assault by their husbands that met our quite conservative definition of rape."[17] Since women also appear vulnerable to not identifying forced experiences with their husbands as a rape or other forms of sexual assault for various reasons, the likely prevalence of wife rape, even more broadly defined, was 14.28 percent of all married woman in Russell's study.

Russell reported that of the various relationships between victim and assailant at the time of the first rape, the marriage relationship accounted for the highest number of women (seventy-one women), with "acquaintance" (forty-seven) and "lover or ex-lover" (forty-three) accounting for the next highest numbers.[18] Two additional perpetrator-victim relationships that were also significant in terms of numbers were "date" (twenty-six)

14. Ibid., 52–53.

15. Bergen, "Marital Rape," 2.

16. Basile, "Prevalence of Wife Rape and Other Intimate Partner Sexual Coercion in a Nationally Representative Sample of Women," 511–524.

17. Russell, *Rape in Marriage*, 57.

18. These relational levels moved from stranger through a total of ten different levels, concluding with husband or ex-husband and other relative.

and "boyfriend" (fifteen). The fourth largest category was that of "stranger" (thirty-one) with the sixth largest category being that of "authority figure" (twenty).[19]

Bergen estimates "that over 7 million women have been raped by their intimate partners in the United States," which was based on the findings of a study published in 1998 that she identified as "the largest US study of violence to date," a report published online after 2005.[20] This estimate indicates that intimate partner rape occurs in pandemic proportions.

A comprehensive review of wife rape or marital rape was published in 2007, thirty years following the groundbreaking work of Russell and her assistants.[21] Three decades following Russell's figure of more than 14 percent, this recent review reports rates of wife rape ranging from 10 percent to 14 percent of all married women. This data offers broad support for the rate Russell first observed and indicates that the incidence of wife rape has remained relatively consistent. The review also reveals that comparative studies show that *"marital rape is the most common form of rape."*[22]

What I believe is most significant about these statistics is that they indicate that *women have more to fear from the men they do know*, particularly the men with whom they have been or are sexually intimate, especially husbands. The category of authority figure (noted above) is also significant in that the examples identified—including doctors, teachers, employers, ministers, therapists, and policemen—are all individuals a woman would naturally tend to trust and with whom she might allow herself to be more emotionally vulnerable. These observations speak quite clearly about the poor job our society does in raising and socializing its men to be valuing, protecting, and sensitive to the best interests of the women with whom they have relationships.

It may be that determining the best possible estimate of wife rape is not essential or even that important, other than to state unequivocally that the incidence, whatever that estimate might be, is totally unacceptable, particularly in Western cultures that pride themselves on support of human rights. Doing everything to reduce the current prevalence rate is vital. My hope is that spousal rape legislation will help reduce these rates and raise new levels of awareness in society.

SPOUSAL RAPE LEGISLATION

Legislation limiting a husband's right to treat his wife as he pleases has been very slow in coming. In her chapter entitled "Marital Rape," Pagelow states, "Blackstone, the renowned English legal scholar, described marriage under the common law of England as the merger of husband and wife into a single identity."[23] She notes that the precedent for this common law position finds it roots in the view of Sir Matthew Hale, a seventeenth

19. Russell, *Rape in Marriage*, 65.

20. Bergen, "Marital Rape."

21. Martin et al., "A Review of Marital Rape," 329–347; Sachs and Gomberg, "Intimate Partner Sexual Abuse," 265–274.

22. Ibid., Section 4.4; emphasis added. Included is a 1990 update by Russell.

23. Pagelow, "Marital Rape," 214–15; citing Lauren M. Weitzman.

century Chief Justice, which was published in 1736 after his death. Sir Hale believed that because a wife has entered into a binding contract with her husband by common consent, she has given herself to her husband, a position she cannot retract. As of July 1980, only three states, New Jersey, Oregon, and Nebraska, had completely eliminated the marital rape exemption from their laws. It has been partially eliminated in four additional states: California, Hawaii, Minnesota, and Iowa. Though limited progress is being made in the United States, lawmakers in thirteen states had extended the freedom of husbands to rape their wives to include men who were living with women to whom they were not married.[24]

As of 2007, Martin, Taft, and Resick report that the federal government and all fifty states had outlawed marital rape though there were yet thirty-two states which allowed a partial exemption, in which the allowances could involve the amount of force used and the inability of the wife to consent to sexual intercourse.[25] At present, there remain exemptions in some states.[26]

International Law

While some progress has been made internationally, more and stronger laws are needed. According to a document published in 2003 by the United Nations Development Fund for Women (UNIFEM),[27] six nations in Africa, six nations in Asia and the Pacific (with legislation pending in Thailand), eleven nations in Eastern Europe and the Commonwealth of Independent States, primarily former Soviet Block nations,[28] six nations in Latin America and the Caribbean, and seventeen nations in Western Europe have laws sanctioning wife rape. Most of these laws are identified as non-specific legislation, in which certain exemptions may exist. Among these nations, only five have crafted specific legislation stipulating the exact conditions in which sexual assault by husbands can be prosecuted. These are South Africa, Zimbabwe, the Philippines, Cypress, and Sweden. As of the publication date for the UNIFEM document, *there were no Arab states that had any spousal rape legislation.*

Quite recently, laws that had been passed in Afghanistan following the overthrow of the Taliban were revised to legalize marital rape. These applied only to the Shiite minority. However, international condemnation of these legal conditions resulted in a suspended

24. Russell, *Rape in Marriage*, 21.

25. Martin et al., "A Review of Marital Rape," Section 1, Legal History.

26. Washington Coalition of Sexual Assault Programs, Summary of Spousal Rape Laws, (2009). http://www.wcsap.org/pdf/Spousal%20Rape%20Statutes%202009.pdf; accessed October 29, 2009. A number of organizations exist that are actively pursuing efforts to address the continuing problem of wife rape, including further refinement of marital rape laws. These include such organizations as the National Center for the Victims of Crime (http://www.ncvc.org/ncvc/main.aspx?dbID=dash_Home), the Washington Coalition of Sexual Assault Programs (http://www.wcsap.org), and the American Bar Association Commission on Domestic Violence (http://www.abanet.org/domviol/).

27. United Nations Development Fund for Women, *Not a Minute More: Ending Violence Against Women.* 2003. Data gathered from a variety of documents dated 1997–2003.

28. Several nations of which are predominantly Muslim and did not have spousal rape legislation as of 2003.

enforcement with modifications being made to some of these laws.[29] Obviously, there is more work to be done in the United States and the rest of the world that focuses on attitudes, practices, and legal sanctions involving the rape of women by their husbands.

CHARACTERISTICS OF RAPED WIVES AND HUSBANDS WHO RAPE

In their review of wife rape related studies, Martin, Taft, and Resick concluded that few studies have found a significant association of demographic variables with wife rape.[30] However, the associations that they did find with increased vulnerability for wife rape includes younger age, racial/cultural minorities, both lower and higher levels of education (conflicting results from different studies), unemployment of the wife, divorce and separation (even when restraining orders are in place), violence in the victim's family of origin, and having previously experienced non-marital rape.[31]

Moving Toward Prevention and Intervention

Each of these related factors raises important implications for prevention and *intervention. Among them are:

- the need for wives to carefully evaluate what type of protection they require and to find sources of protection from husbands who have shown physical and/or sexual violence prior to divorce or separation,

- the need to work proactively with men and boys regarding their attitudes, *socialization, and behavior toward women (particularly wives, girlfriends, and mothers),

- the need to work with wives who have a history of childhood abuse,

- the need to organize a *support group in your community or church that includes recovering wives who can help support recent victims,

- the need to provide funds and support for young wives as well as couples who are not in a position to contribute meaningfully to the financial well-being of the family.

Much more could be said regarding how best to pursue prevention and intervention, for which there is not space in this chapter—but these suggestions can help cast a vision.[32]

---

29. Faiez, "Are Afghans Revising Laws That Will Legalize Marital Rape?" http://blog.taragana.com/n /afghan-govt-drafts-revision-of-marriage-law-criticized-as-legalizing-marital-rape-104326/; accessed October 29, 2009.

30. Martin et al., "A Review of Marital Rape," Section 5.4, Victim Factors.

31. This is hypothesized to be a function of the husband's anger, jealousy, and a lack of power and control in the relationship.

32. The costs of counseling and other professional care can be one more obstacle that wives (and children) do not need added to their already difficult situation. Strategic intervention, therapy, and pastoral care for such women may require church funds to help offset rising costs.

ADDRESSING HUSBANDS WHO RAPE

Where husbands who rape are concerned, there are key similarities and differences to note between them and their wives. The two most similar characteristics are: (1) *perpetrator unemployment and (2) the existence of violence in the husband's family of origin. Prior socialization in violence serves as a *modeling experience. Such a history indicates that men may be more vulnerable than women to the impact of general violence, including the witnessing or domestic sanctioning of violence. When men have grown up around domestic violence, they can *present serious dysfunction. This dysfunction can also stem from exposure to childhood violence perpetrated by various individuals, not just parents, but also witnessing assaults by the child's parents on one another.

The factors observed that were distinctly different between (raping) husbands and (victimized) wives include:

- marital conflicts over the frequency of sex and the type of sex acts to be pursued,
- the desire for sex after violent activity in the relationship (i.e., men relating sex to force),
- the impersonal nature of the sexual experience,
- a greater degree of fantasy involving sexual *coercion,
- sexual aggression in the marriage,
- alcohol and drug use,
- *hypermasculine men rationalizing wife rape,
- an enjoyment of the "rape narrative,"
- a tendency to believe in "wifely duty" that justifies a man in using force,
- and being domineering and hostile toward women.

Again, it seems obvious that the difference between the associated factors relating to men who violate their wives and those factors relating to women who are violated speak deeply to the issue of male socialization in our society. This issue is not limited to ours only, with South Africa possibly being the most alarming regarding *corrective rape and rape in general.[33] In a description of a resource for those responding to violence against women from diverse cultures, it is reported that, "Each year, millions of women immigrate to the United States and Canada who are victims of domestic violence in their former countries of residence, as well as their new homes in North America."[34] It can be assumed that at least some of this violence is wife rape. Additionally, pornography has been observed to play a contributing role in violence committed against women by many husbands.[35] This only adds to the imperative that our society must work to combat

33. South Africa's Rape Epidemic; from www.salon.com/mwt/broadsheet/2009/06/18/southafricarape/; accessed September 24, 2009.

34. Intermedia, *Facing Diversity: Responding to Violence against Women from Diverse Cultures*; from www.intermedia-inc.com/title.asp?sku+FA02&subcatID=29; accessed August 17, 2009.

35. The viewing of pornography by so many husbands is an issue with which I have had considerable experience in my clinical work, but this is beyond the scope of this chapter. I recommend that the reader

violent attitudes and behavior toward women in general and, specifically, toward wives, girlfriends, and mothers on the part of husbands, boyfriends, and sons.

BIBLICAL PERSPECTIVES REGARDING MARITAL SEX

Going back to "the beginning," it is hard for me to conclude that Adam and Eve did not experience at least some degree of sexual intimacy prior to the *Fall. God instructed them to "be fruitful and multiply" (Gen 1:28) and intended for a man to "hold fast to his wife, and they [were to] become one flesh" (2:24). These texts are more thoroughly addressed in other chapters. From my years of teaching Human Sexuality, I should note that attraction and sexual desire are universal and natural to humanity, a capacity that is biologically and psychologically innate. Since God observed that all he had made was "very good" (1:31), which had to include these natural elements of sexuality, I do not believe we can limit sexual intimacy to a fallen experience, a view that gave rise to the concept of sexual intercourse being viewed as carnal knowledge. Since the Bible does not clearly state that sexual intimacy was experienced before the Fall, however, we can only speculate about the occurrence.

The writer of the book of Hebrews provides a clear perspective regarding how marriage and intercourse are to be viewed. We read, "Let marriage be held in honor among all, and let the marriage bed be undefiled, for God will judge the sexually immoral and adulterous" (13:4). *This respectful attitude and a commitment to "undefiled" behavior is exactly what we all, particularly we men, need to internalize and manifest, seeking to increasingly impact and promote transformation of our culture in every possible way.*

In Eph 5:25–28, the Apostle Paul takes the matter to a higher level when he instructs husbands:

> "[L]ove your wives, as Christ loved the church and gave himself up for her, that he might sanctify her, having cleansed her by the washing of water with the word, so that he might present the church to himself in splendor, without spot or wrinkle or any such thing, that she might be holy and without blemish. In the same way husbands should love their wives as their own bodies. He who loves his wife loves himself."

It is clear that Jesus and his self-sacrificial love is the model for all men in their attitudes toward and treatment of their wives. With this model, there is obviously no basis to impose or force one's wife in an unwanted sexual experience. Furthermore, Paul notes that such unilateral and sacrificial love (Greek, *agapeo*) and respectful care for one's wife is a manifestation of a love that is *characterized as nourishing* and cherishing one's own body. Observe then, how Paul repeats the design of creation (Gen 2:24) regarding "leaving, cleaving, and becoming one flesh." Not only should the couple's unity motivate the husband to care for his wife, but this unity is also an *illustration*—the unity of husband and wife and the unity of Christ and the church are a profound mystery (Eph 5:32).

What strikes me about this linking of marital intimacy and the relationship of Christ with his church is that human marital intercourse is hereby elevated to a living symbol of the divine groom and bride. Just as the Tabernacle and sacrificial system of the Old

consider the pornography related resources in For Further Reading at the close of this chapter.

Testament were tangible symbols of God's yet-to-be-completed plan of redemption, so is marriage in the New Testament, of which the church is the culmination. *This pairing raises marital sexuality to a "high and holy level," which Christians, above all others, must revere and protect.*

The Song of Songs presents yet another picture of the quality of marital intimacy that God intends for humanity. There is no question that the King and the Shulamite woman experienced the absolute ecstasy of love described by Sternberg as including the three dimensions of *passion*, *intimacy*, and *commitment*.[36] The words of the Shulamite capture the quality of love that is vividly described throughout the book: "He brought me to the banqueting house, and his banner over me was love" (2:4).

Several passages in the New Testament deserve careful consideration, since a husband (or wife) could incorrectly interpret them to support his abusive behavior. The body for Christians is not only a sacred sanctuary but houses the divine presence—*sexual violation harms both sanctuary and divine presence* (1 Cor 3:16–17; 6:18–20). In 1 Cor 7:1–2, Paul states that though he prefers celibacy, the reality of sexual temptation and society's immorality means, "each man should have his own wife and each woman her own husband" (7:2b; cf. Matt 19:10–12). If Paul is addressing men here, then the husband who may be looking for biblical support for demanding sex from his wife could misapply this kind of text for his own purposes.

There is no biblical warrant here for sexual abuse of any kind. Observe that Paul goes on to state that *the authority over the bodies of both husband and wife belong not to the self but to the other spouse* (7:4). Both husband and wife should be committed to providing sexual intimacy to one another as an act of love and *mutual* submission. This is the issue we briefly consider next.

In Eph 5:22–25, Paul reminds wives "to submit to your own husbands, as to the Lord" (v. 22). The rationale he provides is that the husband is "the head of the wife even as Christ is the head of the church" (v. 23) and that "as the church submits to Christ, so also wives should submit in everything to their husbands" (v. 24). Since most English translations use the word *submit* in verse 22,[37] it can easily be argued that submission is the primary duty of the wife, from which the husband may be somewhat "exempt." This not only a misreading the passage, but sadly, one I have heard over the years in my experience with Christian men.

In particular, Paul admonishes husbands to "love [their] wives, as Christ loved the church and gave himself up for her" (v. 25), which raises the bar to an unachievable level in terms of perfection. Thank God, increasing Christlikeness, to which the Father commits himself in Rom 8:29, makes it possible to love and give of ourselves for the sake of our wives more and more over time.

---

36. Sternberg, "Triangular Theory of Love"; retrieved from http://academics.tjhsst.edu/psych/oldPsych/Sternberg/; accessed October 2, 2010. See Sternberg and Sternberg Weis, *The New Psychology of Love*.

37. Some translations put the word "submit/be subject" in italics in v. 22 (NASB), indicating that it is not present in the Greek text, but is implied from v. 21 (cf. Col 3:18–19 for a similar listing of the *household code). It is not insignificant that the early *lectionaries* (i.e., readings used for private and public worship) of the church began a new day's reading with v. 22, a fact that likely caused the verb to be added to v. 22.

As often noted, a key to the submission issue is found in verse 21, in which the word *submit* occurs in the Greek text. *Mutual submission is the overarching principle in verse 21, teaching that all believers live under the lordship of Christ, "submitting" to each other.* Paul makes it clear that one of the evidences of being filled with the Spirit is submitting to one another. We are all, men and women, husbands and wives alike, to submit to each other. This is the foundation for the more specific expressions we need to pursue in our relationships with various parties. I view these as respectfully cooperating with one's husband on the part of the wife and self-sacrificial love being showered on the wife by the husband (cf. 1 Pet 2:13–14; 3:1–2, 7). Karen H. Jobes summarizes this New Testament principle of *reciprocity*, "The wife and the husband are to serve each other, perhaps in gender-differentiated ways, but with both emulating the self-denying servanthood of their Lord Jesus Christ."[38] Significantly, husbands receive the longest instruction in the household code (vv. 25-33) and in it, Paul never instructs husbands to be dominant over their wives. In fact, only children are to "obey" (6:1), implying a qualitative difference between submission and obedience. Against the backdrop of domestic violence in general, and our discussion of wife rape in particular, Scot McKnight offers a helpful insight:

> I believe in a wife submitting to her husband, *but I don't believe the husband ever has the right to demand it.* In fact, I know that when I am worthy of submission, my wife submits; and when I am unworthy of it, she does not. *My responsibility as a husband is to be worthy.*[39]

CONCLUSION

It is commonly recognized in the fields of psychology and law enforcement that it is the capacity for *empathy that enables us to feel sorrow for and anger on behalf of those who are victimized. *These emotions can be a source of energy to help us engage in efforts to help others and to bring change to our culture.*

Much of what I have written is informational. I have made brief observations about specific issues that still need to be addressed through efforts to prevent abuse and intervene on behalf of both victims and abusers. I propose two basic courses of action that need to be pursued by Christians and non-Christians alike. The first is to *seriously consider becoming involved in social and political action* designed to encourage greater compliance with the unanimous resolution signed by every nation that is a member of the UN at the conference held in Beijing in September of 1995.[40] This resolution guarantees that every woman has the right to respond as she wishes to sexual approaches, saying either yes or no, specifically including wives.[41]

---

38. Jobes, *Esther*, 90.

39. Ibid., citing McKnight, *1 Peter*, 191–192; emphasis added.

40. As reported in the *NY Times*. National Clearinghouse on Marital and Date Rape, "Mexican Supreme Court's Women's Human Rights Violation Overridden!" Retrieved from http://ncmdr.org/sumary.html; accessed August 17, 2009.

41. I recognize that increased reliance on international law and treaties by the United States is a complex and controversial issue. The major fear, as I recently heard the matter discussed (October 8, 2010 by Dr.

The article cited here describes the impact of women's rights groups in achieving the overturn of the Mexican Supreme Court's ruling that "forcing a spouse to have sex is not rape but a mere 'undue exercise of a right.'"[42] Considering that two of the three justices who authored the decision were women, one of whom was a Mexican delegate to the UN Conference on Women held in Nairobi, such efforts must not be limited to attempting to influence male legislators and judges, but women as well who likely have been *acculturated to unwittingly *collude with the men in their society. Such collusion can be observed in the enforcement of *infiblulation or other forms of *female circumcision by the women themselves, of a particular family or village.[43]

The second course of action is to capitalize on every opportunity one has to influence both men and women to rethink their view of marital sexuality. To that end, I offer the following comparison of what I observe to be the two primary approaches to sexual intimacy. The first is the pursuit of *personal gratification* as the primary motive. This motive is pervasive and can be readily seen in our society's promotion of the adage popularized by Woodstock, "If it feels good, do it!"[44]

David Shaw, the author of *The Pleasure Police*, decried the influence of President Carter when he raised concern about pleasure as the primary motive in relationships. Yet, my observation as a therapist is that the unbridled pursuit of personal pleasure, particularly if manifested by a husband at the expense of his wife, largely results in a breakdown of mutual fulfillment, trust, and commitment in a sexual relationship, accompanied by symptoms of severe *depression in the wife. It must also be recognized that what motivates a man to rape his wife goes beyond the pursuit of mere self gratification and is most often attributed to issues of power and control.[45]

Instead, when sexual intimacy is mutually pursued as a celebration of the love relationship in a marriage, *with the pleasuring of one's partner rather than oneself being the primary motive*, the inevitable result is a strengthening of the love and respect each partner has for the other and an increased level of fulfillment, physically and emotionally. The results of this approach over the many years of my therapeutic practice and in the relationships of couples I have known as friends and colleagues, it occurs to me that this approach to marriage and sexual intimacy is a significant application of the "The Golden Rule," expressed approximately two thousand years ago by Jesus when he stated quite simply, "Treat others exactly as you would have them treat you" (Luke 7:31 MLB).

James Dobson and his guest, Michael Farris, JD), is that such reliance will inevitably result in the increasing loss of national freedom and rights, such as parental rights (see www.parentalrights.com). Yet, there may be legitimacy in some international cooperation regarding the issue of women's rights.

42. National Clearinghouse on marital and Date Rape, "Mexican Supreme Court's Women's Human Rights Violation Overridden!"; http://ncmdr.org/sumary.html.

43. World Health Organization, "FGM [female genital mutilation] defined"; retrieved from www.circumstitions.com/FGM-defined.html; accessed October 31, 2009.

44. Klein, "'If It Feels Good, Don't Do It,' A Review of David Shaw's *The Pleasure Police*," 25.

45. Doak, *Violent Relationships*, chap 3.

QUESTIONS FOR DISCUSSION

1. What thoughts and feelings do you have after reading the introductory scenarios describing three experiences of wife rape? On the other hand, what if you were one of the participants in each of those situations—as the wife or as the husband? Now describe your feelings. Have you known of wife rape among your acquaintances? What was the outcome of that situation? How do you view such examples of sexual violence now, after reading this chapter?

2. How would you like others to respond to you if you had experienced this kind of sexual violence, either as the wife or the husband? If you heard of this kind of abuse happening with a couple you knew, what would your response be? As a pastor or Christian leader, what have you done when such situations came to light?

3. How do you anticipate responding to such a situation if the wife or the husband was a sibling of yours? A missionary friend? A co-worker? Take some time to draw up a plan of action for your response. As a counselor, what steps do you pursue unique to these cases?

4. How might you as a community or church leader attempt to engage your community or church members to become more sensitized and informed about the issue of wife rape? As a pastor or teacher, can you think of any biblical texts you could preach or teach differently? As a leader in your church, do you address wife rape in your "family ministries" program? If not, why not?

5. Based on your practice as a therapist, what are the short- and long-term effects of wife rape? What kind of support group is needed? At the level of *post-traumatic stress syndrome (PTSD), how does wife rape compare with *stranger rape? *Date Rape? What are the professional resources that you would want to have available, depending on the specific role you might have—a family therapist, a wife, a husband, a family member or close friend, a community or church leader?

6. If you are a medical or a mental health professional but have had little occasion to work with a rape situation, what types of training and experience would you wish to have to best prepare you? Where can such training and experience be found? How does *spiritual formation speak into domestic violence and cases of wife rape? What can seminaries do to better train men and women to address this kind of sexual violence?

7. As a helping agent (pastor, therapist, social worker, medical specialist), how do you anticipate responding to a woman who has been raped by her husband for the first time? To a woman who has experienced repeated rape events? How might your approach differ or be the same in these scenarios?

FOR FURTHER READING

Pornography

Cramer, Elizabeth, Judith McFarlane, Barbara Parker, Karen Soeken, Concepcion Silva, and Sally Reel. "Violent Pornography and Abuse of Women: Theory to Practice." *Violence and Victims* 13 (1990): 319–332.

Donnerstein, Edward and Leonard Berkowitz. "Victim Reactions in Erotic Films as a Factor in Violence Against Women." *Journal of Personality and Social Psychology* 41 (1981): 710–724.

Haid, Gert Martin, Neil M. Malamuth, and CarlinYuen. "Pornography and Attitudes Supporting Violence against Women: Revisiting the Relationship in Non-experimental Studies. *Aggressive Behavior* 36 (2010): 14–20.

Linz, Daniel G., Edward Donnerstein, and Steven Penrod. "Effects of Long-term Exposure to Violent and Sexually Degrading Depictions of Women." *Journal of Personality and Social Psychology* 55 (1988): 758–768.

Page, Stewart. "The Turnaround on Pornography Research: Some Implications for Psychology and Women." *Canadian Psychology/Psychologie Canadienne* 31 (1990): 359–367.

Russell, Diana E. H. and Nadine Strossen. "Pornography: Is it Harmful to Women?" In *Women, Men, & Gender: Ongoing Debates*, edited by Mary Roth Walsh, 155–179. New Haven, CT: Yale University Press, 1997.

Struthers, M. William. *Wired for Intimacy: How Pornography Hijacks the Male Brain*. Downers Grove, IL: IVP, 2009.

Wife Rape, Intimate Partner Violence

Bergen, Raquel Kennedy. "Studying Wife Rape." *Violence Against Women* 10 (2004): 1407–1416.

———. *Wife Rape: Understanding the Response of Survivors and Service Providers*. Newbury Park, CA: Sage Publications, 1996.

Campbell, Rebecca, Megan R. Greeson, and Deborah Bybee. "The Co-Occurrence of Childhood Sexual Abuse, Adult Sexual Assault, Intimate Partner Violence, and Sexual Harassment: A Mediational Model of Posttraumatic Stress Disorder and Physical Health Outcomes." *Journal of Consulting and Clinical Psychology* 76 (2008): 194–207.

Ferro, Christine, et al. "Current Perceptions of Marital Rape: Some Good and Not-So-Good News." *Journal of Interpersonal Violence* 23 (2008): 764–779.

Mahoney, Patricia, et al. "Violence Against Women by Intimate Relationship Partners." In *Sourcebook on Violence Against Women*, edited by Claire M. Renzetti, et al, 143–178. Thousand Oaks, CA: Sage Publishers, 2001.

Munge, Bethany A., et al. "The Influence of Length of Marriage and Fidelity Status on Perception of Marital Rape." *Journal of Interpersonal Violence* 22 (2007): 1332–1339.

Panuzio, Jillian and David DiLillo. "Physical, Psychological, and Sexual Intimate Partner Aggression Among Newlywed Couples: Longitudinal Prediction of Marital Satisfaction." *Journal of Family Violence* 25 (2010): 689–699.

Resick, Patricia A. and Monica Schnicke. *Cognitive Processing Therapy for Rape Victims: A Treatment* Manual. Interpersonal *Violence: The Practice Series.* Newbury Park, CA: Sage Publications, 1993.

Web Sites

Spousal Rape: A Woman's Secret Shame, www.buzzle.com/editorials/12-21-2005-84604 .asp.

Spousal Rape Laws Continue to Evolve, www.womensenews.org/story/rape/090701 /spousal-rape-laws-continue-evolve.

Hidden Hurt: Domestic Violence Information: Marital Rape, www.hiddenhurt.co.uk /Articles/maritalrape.htm.

7

The Impact of Sexual Abuse on Sexual Identity

*Exploring the Relationship between Childhood Sexual Abuse
and Adult Sexual Identity*

ELISABETH C. SUAREZ, PHD,
AND MARK A. YARHOUSE, PSYD

JORGE SAT DOWN ACROSS *from his pastor. He had difficulty keeping eye contact. The pastor, too, struggled getting the conversation going, but he knew that Jorge had called the meeting with him, and he sensed it was something difficult to talk about. Hesitantly and filled with emotion, Jorge shared that he had been sexually abused as a child by a male neighbor and a good friend of the family. Jorge was struggling today with thoughts about what that abuse meant about him as a man. He has not dated much due to his shame. Was there something about him or something he did that drew the family friend to him? Does this experience mean that he's *gay? Where does he fit in at the church? Does the pastor know of a counselor who could help him change his *sexual orientation?*

*Hui-Shiang approached the Director of Women's Programs at her church. She has been struggling with *depression, and friends had told her to speak to a church leader. She has had difficulty concentrating lately and her boyfriend is concerned about her erratic behavior and mood swings. Hui-Shiang shared that her boyfriend of six months is really interested in her, and that he initiates physical contact, such as hugs or kisses, but that her body does not seem to respond. She likes him but she doesn't want to be close to him in a romantic way. She is wondering if there is something wrong with her. As the Director probes further, she finds that Hui-Shiang was sexually abused in her teen years by her father. She had made a silent promise at that time not to stir up sexual feelings until she was married. However, she finds it much easier to be close to women, and she is not sure what this means about her sexuality.*

Jorge and Hui-Shiang represent two people whose sexual confusion needs to be more fully understood in the context of their theological views. They face unique challenges that others will not face, and they are looking for accurate information about the relationship between their experiences of *sexual abuse (SA) and their current sense of their *sexual identity. The messages from the media seem to promote *homosexuality as a *genetic* predisposition and viable alternative lifestyle, but their understanding of Scripture clearly shows homosexuality to be a sin.

90

DEFINITIONS AND CLARIFICATIONS

Sexual abuse occurs when sexuality is used in a way that is not invited, an unwelcomed sexual advance usually (but not always) from a person of power or authority. *The psychological ramifications of sexual abuse include loss of trust, fear, anxiety, uncontrollable crying, *numbness, *dissociation, and other negative *emotional sequelae.* The relational problems that can later result include difficulty maintaining proper emotional and physical boundaries with others and fear of relational vulnerability. In dating relationships, sexual abuse *survivors may be controlling and rigid in their physical affection. *Relationally, they can either share indiscriminately or shut down emotionally or do both in different situations.*

Sexual identity refers to the act of labeling oneself based upon one's sexual preferences. Common sexual identity labels include gay, straight, *lesbian, and *bisexual. Other common labels include questioning, curious, and *queer. Labeling often corresponds with the perceived amount of *same-sex attraction (SSA) a person feels, but this is not always the case. Sometimes it is associated with "acting out" behavior, how much a person follows up their feelings with same-sex physical interactions.

Those who struggle with sexual identity questions or concerns tend to report a higher risk of depression, anxiety, substance use, sexually transmitted disease, and other emotional and physical health concerns. In mainstream psychology circles, these elevations are often thought of as a result of being a *sexual minority in a heterosexual culture. However, these elevations also exist in the most gay-affirming cultures, which have raised the question for some: is it only the marginalization that leads to such elevations or is there is something inherently unstable in the experience itself? In societies where homosexuality is not celebrated, gay individuals are marginalized, which can result in feelings of isolation, loneliness, anxiety, and depression. But since the homosexual-identified individual can also have higher than normal feelings of *detachment, sadness, and depression in gay-affirming cultures, questions remain as to why that occurs. This chapter addresses the relationship between sexual abuse and sexual identity questions and labeling.

PAST UNDERSTANDING OF HOMOSEXUALITY: THEORIES ON "CAUSES"

One belief that seems to circulate among conservative Christian circles asserts that sexual abuse is the *cause* of homosexuality, particularly for women. A young girl, abused by a male relative or trusted family friend, rejects all males as unsafe, turning to women to meet their emotional and physical needs. An extreme and violent response that may be tied to a similar linear and overly simplistic understanding of homosexuality can be seen in attempts to "cure" lesbian women through forced sex acts.[1]

Another perspective on the causes of homosexuality is based somewhat on *psychoanalytic theory in which early parent-child relationships are implicated in the cause of

---

1. In an effort to "cure" lesbians, some men engage in what is being called *corrective rape* in order to "change" the woman's sexual orientation. This form of sexual violence has been reported particularly in war-torn countries like South Africa; see Kelly, "Raped and Killed for Being a Lesbian."

homosexuality.[2] The theory is perhaps more developed in its account of male homosexuality than female homosexuality, but it would suggest that, for males, there is a damaging experience growing up with an *absent, distant, or critical father and an over-involved or *close-binding mother. Essentially, the male does not feel secure in himself as a male.[3]

What is said to happen is that, consciously and unconsciously, a young male grows in his personality and sense of himself as a male after the model he has in his father.[4] This will include attractions to the opposite sex. According to this theory, the normal outcome is identification with a father who loves him and a mother who supports that identification. In situations where there is no available father or father-figure—or where the father is rejecting and/or critical—that male identification is threatened. The mother is important, too, insofar as she could undermine the identification by being critical of the father or men in general. She could also bond so much with the boy that emotional separation is impossible. The theory posits that the result of such a compromised sense of male identity is *homoerotic attraction.[5]

This theory is tied to one specific model of treatment for homosexuality referred to as *"reparative therapy," which is a secular theory but one that is popular in some conservative Christian circles.[6] It is reparative in that it asserts that homosexuality represents a healthy and appropriate drive that is, in some significant ways, derailed in childhood and that is expressed as sexual attraction to the same sex in adolescence or adulthood. The derailing that occurs is believed to be a *trauma experienced in childhood, hence the connection to *childhood sexual abuse (CSA) as one such traumatic experience that might set the stage for later development of homosexuality.

Few reparative therapists publish studies to support this theory today. Most practitioners rely on their own clinical experiences and look for support from older studies conducted in the 1960s. For example, the Bieber study is probably one of the most influential studies in this regard.[7] It was a study of over one hundred male homosexuals and one hundred male heterosexuals in which the family dynamics described above were present, at least in part. Fathers of male homosexuals were reported to be more distant, detached, or rejecting in relation to their sons. Also consistent with psychoanalytic theory, the mothers of the male homosexuals were reported to have *enmeshed relationships with their sons. Although these parent-child connections may be present (suggesting a correlation or relationship), there has not been a well-designed study to support claims of a direct cause and effect (suggesting causation). Today these family dynamics are viewed by proponents as compelling, but they are really based on older studies that would need to be updated and improved to meet contemporary, rigorous standards of social science research.

2. Moberly, *Homosexuality*, 2–16.

3. Yarhouse, *Homosexuality and the Christian*, 70–73.

4. Jones and Yarhouse, *Homosexuality*, 54.

5. Ibid.

6. It was probably most popular in the mid- to late-1990s, following the publication of *Reparative Therapy for the Homosexual Male* by Joseph Nicolosi.

7. Bieber et al., *Homosexuality*, 85–115.

The Bieber et al. findings were based on the recollections of psychoanalysts who worked with the patients. Critics have pointed out that there is no way to confirm these family dynamics; that it is possible that the analysts were noting dynamics they would expect to find given their training; or that these dynamics reflect those male homosexuals who are seeking help; or that *biological antecedents could have contributed to the homosexual orientation that was then the impetus for the fathers' rejection (rather than the parent-child relationship being causal).

Ray Evans published a smaller study intended to address some of these concerns.[8] The data was from the *self-report (rather than the report by analysts) of male homosexuals who had not been in analysis or *psychotherapy. Fewer than one-third of the male homosexuals reported the parent-child dynamics expressed in the earlier study. On the other hand, over 10 percent of the male heterosexuals reported the dynamics that were noted to cause homosexuality. This data seemed to contradict Beiber's claims; the larger percentage of the study did not contain the family dynamics claimed to lead to homosexuality.

Although most researchers today are not looking at parent-child dynamics to explain the cause of homosexuality, more recent studies[9] have looked at family patterns or possible childhood traumas that some might view as predicting homosexuality given the psychoanalytic and reparative model of understanding homosexuality. For example, a recent study[10] reported no significant differences between homosexuals and heterosexuals in their recall of their relationship with their fathers. Indeed, the homosexual men in the study reported "warmer" (rather than "colder" or "distant") relationships with their fathers (and mothers) than did their heterosexual counterparts. Thus, the psychoanalytic perception of a difficult or distant paternal relationship being a condition for homosexuality was not supported. *The prevailing understanding is that while environment may play a role in homosexuality to some extent, the parent-child relationship as posited in classic psychoanalytic theory does not have the kind of empirical support from research.* This does not, however, mean that clinicians do not still rely upon such theories in their practice.

We mentioned above that few analytic clinicians or reparative therapists publish studies today on the *etiology of homosexuality. Of course, it is more common in the analytic tradition to publish *case analyses of persons who have been seen in psychoanalysis, rather than conduct a large-scale study. We do not see many large-scale studies directly addressing this topic from this perspective, and it is unlikely that we will. Psychoanalysts tend to emphasize case studies of therapy and their implications rather than large, quantitative research experiments. This makes it much more difficult to either confirm or disconfirm the psychoanalytic theory of homosexuality.

8. Evans, "Childhood Parental Relationships of Homosexual Men," 129–135.

9. See, for example, Wilson and Spatz Widom, "Does Physical Abuse, Sexual Abuse, or Neglect in Childhood Increase the Likelihood of Same-Sex Sexual Relationships and Cohabitation? A Prospective 30-Year Follow-Up," 63–74; Alanko et al., "Psychiatric Symptoms and Same-Sex Sexual Attraction and Behavior in Light of Childhood Gender Atypical Behavior and Parental Relationships," 1–11.

10. Alanko et al., "Psychiatric Symptoms and Same-Sex Sexual Attraction and Behavior in Light of Childhood Gender Atypical Behavior and Parental Relationships," 1–11.

Although the theory may be popular among some who provide services to change sexual orientation, and while it has also been a popular theory in some Christian ministry circles, we are beginning to see a more critical consumption of psychoanalytic theory in some Christian ministry circles. For example, in the book *The Complete Christian Guide to Understanding Homosexuality* edited by Joe Dallas and Nancy Heche, we not only find coverage of psychoanalytic theory as a *developmental theory, but we also see a greater awareness of the difficulty in finding evidence to support the theory, regardless of how popular it may be. Dallas and Heche also caution the reader not to assume that such parent-child relationships explain all experiences of homosexuality:

> We don't, after all, know all homosexual people, much less their family histories. And to presume that because X number of homosexuals we've seen in treatment had a certain family experience then therefore all homosexuals share that experience is presumptuous and smacks of arrogance.[11]

The authors also recognize the importance of such histories in the lives of individual people seeking help in ministry, which they then see as valuable to minister to; rather than a template that is held onto by a ministry and placed over the experiences of those seeking help.

CONTEMPORARY UNDERSTANDING OF THE ISSUE: DISTINGUISHING SSA AND ORIENTATION

As we turn to a contemporary understanding of the issue, we want to help the reader make several important distinctions between key terms. We can begin by distinguishing between same-sex attraction (SSA), a homosexual orientation, and a *gay identity. Same-sex attraction refers to one's sexual and/or emotional attraction or connection with a person of the same gender. Sexual orientation, however, is a more stable and enduring experience of sexual and/or emotional attraction or connection with a person or persons of the same gender. *The difference between attraction and orientation is a difference in degree and also how persistent, enduring, or sustained the attraction is over time.* Orientation is typically reported by people as more stable over time, although this too can vary and seems to be more fluid among females than males.[12] Gay identity refers to a more contemporary understanding of who a person is. It is a *self-defining* attribution (i.e., "I am gay") that takes attraction to the same sex or orientation toward the same sex and integrates that attraction or orientation into an identity.

Same-Sex Behavior: Causes and Contributing Factors

In addition to this distinction between attraction, orientation, and identity, it is also important to recognize same-gender sexual behavior. Same-gender sexual behavior can be an expression of attraction, orientation, or identity. It can also exist on its own independently of attraction, orientation, or identity.

11. Dallas and Heche, *The Complete Christian Guide to Understanding Homosexuality*, 206.

12. Dimond, *Sexual Fluidity*, 61–70.

What causes attraction, orientation, identity, and behavior? Most of the scientific research on this question has been dedicated to finding a *cause* of homosexual orientation. *When we look at that research, most experts today recognize that both *nature and nurture contribute to a person having a homosexual orientation.* As already noted, in the past the broader mental health profession, and conservative Christians, focused on nurture as the key contributing factor in the development of a homosexual orientation. More recently, this area of research has been largely neglected in favor of the *biological hypothesis*, namely, that nature trumps nurture in determining sexual orientation. *The neglect of this research appears to be due to the appeal in contemporary society of what appears to be a more scientific approach steeped in experimental design and biological *reductionism*—the idea that human experience can be reduced to biological explanations. Also, in terms of research design, many challenges exist for how to even conduct a rigorous study where multiple potential contributing factors can make the results harder to understand. The state of this research today is that both nature and nurture contribute to sexual orientation and that the contributing factors are probably weighted differently for different people. The research suggests some "push" in the direction of homosexuality from nature, *but that push is not determinative—that is, the possible predisposition does not make someone homosexual as such.* It is not like eye color or hair color in terms of the relationship between *genotype and *phenotype. Environmental factors, or nurture, may also contribute, and it is difficult to say what those contributing factors are and how much weight they have in influencing sexual orientation.

Sexual Abuse and Sexual Identity

As we mentioned, less research has been conducted on attraction, identity, or behavior. Much more attention has been paid to orientation, in large part because it has been both vilified in the past by some in the church and society and also heralded by some in the gay community as an immutable characteristic of a class of persons. This brings us to our present understanding of the research in the area of sexual abuse and its impact on sexual identity. *The research does suggest that people who say they have a history of CSA are more likely to say they have a homosexual orientation than those who do not report CSA.*[13] We want to acknowledge that fact while also asking about how best to understand these findings. This is not a comprehensive review of all possible studies, but a review of some of the more well-known studies of the relationship between CSA and sexual identity or orientation.

There is a connection between a history of sexual abuse and being a sexual minority. In an extensive review of the literature on sexual abuse of boys, William Holmes and Gail Slap reported that "Abused adolescents, particularly those victimized by males, were

---

13. In one large, national study of sexual experiences in the US by Laumann and his colleagues, adults who said they had a history of CSA were three times more likely to report a homosexual orientation than those who did not report childhood sexual abuse. See Laumann et al., *The Social Organization of Sexuality*.

Balsam et al., ("Victimization Over the Lifespan," 477–487) compared lesbian, gay, bisexual (LGB) and heterosexual siblings and reported higher rates of childhood emotional abuse, physical abuse, and sexual abuse among LGB siblings as compared to heterosexual siblings.

up to seven times more likely to self-identify as gay or bisexual than peers who had not been abused."[14] Studies have also shown that people with a history of sexual abuse have a higher likelihood of reporting a homosexual orientation, having gender identity questions, experiencing same-sex attraction, and engaging in same-sex behavior regardless of self-identification as a sexual minority, that is, encompassing a gay identity. This connection appears to be true whether the *perpetrator of the abuse is of the same sex or the opposite sex.[15] These studies are typically descriptive of a relationship between reported sexual abuse and reported sexual identity. However, this connection between sexual abuse and sexual identity labeling should not be understood as a directly causal connection. *Due to the complex nature of the ramifications of sexual abuse, it would be reductionistic to say that only one reason is what causes sexual identity labeling* or the questions or confusion that may be reflected in labeling.[16] Many conditions and factors appear to play a role in understanding and determining sexual identity and sexual orientation. The mistake that is often made by individuals in society is to assume that the reason people have a non-heterosexual orientation is because of past sexual abuse. However, the causes of homosexuality are likely much more complex than that.

We need to be careful not to draw conclusions from descriptive studies that one is causing the other. There could be a number of reasons for sexual identity questions to arise and sexual abuse may or may not be one of those considerations. Part of what is challenging here is that *sexual abuse may itself be related to sexual identity questions or even behavior*, but it may not lead to a fundamental difference in sexual orientation.

A thirty-year *longitudinal study by Wilson and Widom, who followed sexually abused (and physically abused and neglected) children,[17] also compared findings with

14. Holmes and Slap, "Sexual Abuse of Boys," 1859; see also Shrier and Johnson, "Sexual Victimization of Boys," 1189–1193.

In a more recent study (Austin et al., "Sexual Violence Victimization History and Sexual Risk Indicators in a Community-Based Urban Cohort of 'Mostly Heterosexual' and Heterosexual Young Women," 1015–1020) based on the Nurses' Health study of about sixty-three thousand women, lesbian and bisexual women reported higher rates of CSA (19 percent and 20 percent respectively) than did heterosexual women (9 percent).

15. In one of the few studies that looked specifically at whether sexual abuse was done by someone of the same sex, Tomeo et al., ("Comparative Data of Childhood and Adolescence Molestation in Heterosexual and Homosexual Persons," 535–541) collected data from 943 college-age students. They reported higher rates of childhood molestation by persons of the same sex among GLB men and women than among their heterosexual peers. Twenty-two percent of lesbian and bisexual women and only 1 percent of heterosexual women reported molestation by another woman. Forty-six percent of gay and bisexual men and 7 percent of heterosexual men reported molestation by another man.

16. The word "labeling" in this context refers to the act of categorizing oneself (or being categorized by others) based upon one's same-sex sexuality, mannerisms and voice inflection, or other factors, such as one's beliefs and values, gender identity, and so on. It is not used here in a pejorative manner but merely as an act of recognition of how one sees oneself or is seen by others.

17. See, for example, the study by Corliss et al., ("Reports of Parental Maltreatment During Childhood in a United States Population-Based Survey of Homosexual, Bisexual, and Heterosexual Adults," 1165–1178), in which they reported on data from the National Survey of Midlife Depression in the United States. They reported that homosexual and bisexual men were more likely than heterosexual men to report emotional and physical maltreatment in childhood by their mother or guardian and more likely to report physical maltreatment by their father or guardian. When they looked at the experiences of females, Corliss et al. reported

children who were not abused nor neglected.[18] While childhood physical abuse and ne-glect was not associated with homosexual behavior or same-sex relationships as adults, there was a relationship between CSA and later homosexual partners in adulthood. The men who had been victims of CSA were more likely to report homosexual experiences in adulthood, although they did not tend to report *cohabitation with the same sex or ongoing relationships that might be more characteristic of a homosexual orientation or gay identity. It is possible that CSA *complicated* their sexual identity and led to some experimentation but not a fundamental sense of orientation or identity. Interestingly, in this study the relationship between CSA and adult homosexual experiences was present for men but not for women.

Jones and Yarhouse reported on ninety-eight homosexuals seeking to change their sexual orientation through involvement in a religious ministry.[19] This was a study of people who were seeking change of sexual orientation from homosexual to heterosexual through involvement in a Christian ministry. The researchers reported higher than expected rates of CSA in their sample.

What Can We Conclude from this Review?

Most victims of CSA do not identify themselves as having a homosexual orientation. Further, most people who report a homosexual orientation or a gay identity do not also report a history of CSA. So while sexual abuse could certainly complicate a person's un-derstanding of their sexual identity ("Does the fact that I, being a male, was abused by another male mean that I am gay?"), we should not fall into the trap of treating it as though it were the specific causal mechanism that directly results in homosexuality. There are a multitude of factors that can influence a person's sexual orientation. *Pinpointing CSA as a sole contributor is short-sighted at best.* But the questions that are raised are important for us to reflect upon further.

Recall that in the thirty-year longitudinal study mentioned above by Wilson and Widom, the men who had been victims of CSA were more likely to report homosexual experiences in adulthood but apparently not a gay identity—at least not in ongoing same-sex relationships. A likely outcome of CSA may be a tendency to explore one's sexuality through engagement in same-sex relationships. *The person may express interest and/or engage in relationships with same-gendered individuals as they process the impact of the sexual abuse on their identity.* But such experiences may also lead a person to seek help from a trusted adult or trained professional.

It should also be noted, for instance, that some people may be distressed by their abuse as much as they are distressed by their attractions or orientation. For example, in the Jones and Yarhouse study, all ninety-eight persons seeking change of sexual orienta-tion were *help-seeking* persons; they had sought out professionals to help navigate their

---

that homosexual and bisexual women were more likely to report higher rates of physical maltreatment by their mother or father or guardian.

18. Wilson and Widom, "Does Physical Abuse, Sexual Abuse, or Neglect in Childhood Increase the Likelihood of Same-sex Sexual Relationships and Cohabitation? A Prospective 20-year Follow-up," 63–74.

19. Jones and Yarhouse, *Ex-Gays?*

understanding of their sexual orientation.[20] They were, on average, more distressed than the average person in the general population, but they were also less distressed than the average person who is in professional counseling. *It is possible that part of that help-seeking is due to their history of sexual abuse.* The emotional and relational effects of CSA can be devastating and can directly interfere with the formation of healthy relationships, leading the individual to seek help. We want to at least be cautious not to think that all gay or homosexual persons would have CSA as part of their history.

The relationship between CSA and future *sexual risk-taking behavior is rather strong. In several studies, past sexual abuse was a predictor of sexual risk-taking behavior in adulthood.[21]

In summary, sexual abuse can complicate sexual identity and its formation. It can lead a person to question their sexual identity. It can contribute to risk-taking behavior and a tendency to seek help for related concerns. In terms of providing care to these individuals, *we recommend that a person first receive help addressing the aftereffects of sexual abuse before addressing sexual identity issues and concerns.* Individuals need to resolve the effects of sexual abuse and its aftermath as a first step toward resolving any sexual identity confusion.

SOME FUTURE DIRECTIONS AND UNRESOLVED ISSUES

Due to the fluidity of sexual identity, and because it is not fully developed until late teens or early twenties, it is hard to know the effect of sexual abuse on sexual identity when the abuse occurs in children and teens. One can look retrospectively to see where their sexual identity is and ask if sexual abuse affected it, but we need to do further research to determine whether sexual identity changes when faced with sexual trauma and how we as counselors and church leaders should best deal with the aftermath. Although homosexuality is over-represented in sexually abused people, the causes of homosexuality are not adequately known. There are many contributors to sexual identity, and sexual abuse may or may not be one of them. We need to be able to sift out the ramifications of sexual abuse and determine whether those are contributors to sexual identity.

The Need for Empathy and a Safe Environment

Sometimes the response by well-meaning people to the abuse can be just as potentially damaging to a young person as the abuse itself, depending upon the nature of what has happened. *People with sincere hearts and relatively pure motivations can react in ways that alienate or ostracize the survivor.* For example, asking a survivor why they did not tell someone sooner about their sexual abuse can easily be interpreted as though one wanted the abuse and got what they deserved. Limiting the individual's ministry opportunities due to previous abuse can stigmatize the victim and perpetuate the feeling that they are being punished for someone's sin against them. *It is important for people in the church*

---

20. Jones and Yarhouse, *Ex-Gays?*

21. Kalichman et al., "Trauma Symptoms, Sexual Behaviors, and Substance Abuse," 1–15. See also Lenderking et al., "Childhood Sexual Abuse Among Homosexual Men," 205–253.

and in *pastoral care to create an environment in which revelations of abuse can be heard in a non-judgmental, loving way.* A caregiver who is aware of sexual identity issues can create an environment in which the person can experience acceptance so that they can, in time, begin to explore the event and their own sense of identity in a way that is not tied prematurely to identity labels. We need to raise more awareness to help people respond appropriately to revelations of sexual abuse, so that they do not label that person prematurely or overreact to the abuse itself.

Clergy Training in Sexual Identity Concerns: Some Recommendations

When we reflect on unresolved issues, the first and foremost concern is the need for adequate training of pastoral care providers in the area of sexual abuse and sexual identity issues. Many people will seek the help of a spiritual leader or mentor when dealing with the aftereffects of abuse and determining whether or how these factors might contribute to sexual identity concerns. *We recommend Christian leaders get some training in the pastoral care of victims of sexual abuse.* Increased knowledge and *empathy skills are necessary to create an environment where a survivor of sexual abuse can be both vulnerable and safe. Attending trainings and workshops that define and model caring responses to admissions of sexual identity confusion are vital to having a sensitive reaction to a person's confession of such confusion.

Another suggestion for pastors and pastoral care providers is to be intentionally available to these needs in your local church. Let the congregation know that you care about victims of sexual violence and are willing to talk about it in an open, caring, and judgment-free manner. You are, in essence, giving permission for people to come and talk to you and receive help. This can be done through sermons, Sunday school classes, announcements for *support groups, quality literature, and so on.

Having a list of *community referrals gives quick and easy access to trained professionals. *Clergy need to acquaint themselves with agencies that specialize in sexual trauma, and specifically with a therapist who can comfortably explore sexual identity.* Having a list of competent male and female counselors whom you have met and highly recommend is foundational to knowing that the victim is in "good hands."

From a pastor's perspective, you have the unique ability to address theological issues and questions that arise. Doubts about God's love and presence can be addressed with a sound *hermeneutic of the Scriptures. Victims need to be reassured that they are loved and accepted, and that they won't be abandoned during this difficult journey. Even after referral to a qualified professional, it is vital to remain available to the victim and ready to give spiritual direction and prayer. It is crucial to be a sustained presence in his or her life, a person available for spiritual counsel and support.

It is also important that pastors and pastoral care workers be able to assess a situation and know the limits of their ability to help. For example, when a person in the church reveals that they are questioning their sexuality due to a sexual abuse situation, prayerfully listen and evaluate the severity of the crisis. If the sexual abuse is a recent occurrence, make sure that appropriate agencies have been notified. If it was in the past, evaluate the current needs of the victim and the impact of the sexual abuse on their life.

In pastoral care itself, be mindful of the impact of labels on people. It can be helpful to make a three-tier distinction between: (1) same-sex attractions, (2) homosexual orientation, (3) and gay identity.[22] Ask the person to describe their experience and their emotions surrounding the incident rather than prematurely forming an identity based upon those experiences.

Additionally, it is also important to know the *limits of confidentiality for clergy in your county, state, province, or country. *Mandated reporting may be required for any knowledge of CSA, especially if the offender is still in proximity to *minors and has access to them. In cases in which there are no legal obligations, a pastor or Christian leader may still feel an obligation to work with the person on reasonable steps to safeguard potential victims with whom the offender is in contact.

Christian workers need to acquaint themselves with the stages that people go through during a crisis.[23] With sexual trauma, men and women are shocked and can't believe that it has happened to them. Once they come to terms with the situation really happening, their awareness can lead to emotional upheaval (e.g., intense fear, bitter anger or rage, uncontrollable crying, etc.). Eventually, they come to accept that God will use this situation for his glory. Being able to *forgive their abuser and possibly find resolution are crucial but difficult steps in their healing process. Other chapters in this book address issues of healing and forgiveness, and what they are *not*.

This chapter has broadly reviewed the impact of sexual abuse on the sexual identity of men and women survivors. Looking at the past and present understandings in the psychological and counseling literature shows a complicated and intricate relationship between sexual abuse and sexual identity. The church has a unique position in helping victims of sexual abuse to understand their sexual identity along with their identity in Christ. Trained counselors can help survivors of sexual abuse explore the ramifications of CSA and establish their sexual identity. Pastoral care workers can be better trained to understand the issues related to sexual abuse and create a welcoming environment in the church for victims to heal.

---

22. Yarhouse, "Same-Sex Attraction, Homosexual Orientation, and Gay Identity," 201–212.
23. Kubler-Ross, *On Death and Dying*.

QUESTIONS FOR DISCUSSION

1. How have current understandings of the relationship between sexual abuse and sexual identity challenged conventional views of a causal link between the two? What are some examples of "labels" you hear in your community? Do these labels serve the speaker or person(s) in question? Compare scenarios where such labels have damaged relationships; what insights and alternative actions could be taken in the future?

2. If you are a counselor, how has your understanding of sexual abuse and sexual identity changed? What are the struggles you face in your practice regarding clients and sexual identity? What is a pastoral care-giving response to a person who is questioning his or her sexual identity in light of past sexual abuse? Regardless of your profession, what areas of training do you need in order to better address issues of sexual abuse (SA) and same-sex attraction (SSA)?

3. Why is it important to address sexual abuse first rather than sexual identity? As discussed in this chapter, what are some elements that can make sexual identity so complex? What can pastors (and seminaries) do better to teach people and educate the next generation on these issues? In what ways to you feel *spiritual formation programs can speak into the lives of men and women struggling with SSA? How has this chapter helped define the issues surrounding sexual identity for your faith community?

4. As you understand the issues of sexual abuse, what should be the church's response? How was the last "revelation" of sexual abuse and/or sexual orientation addressed in your church? How could both leadership and laity have responded even better? What do you think spiritual maturity should look like for a believer struggling with their sexual identity? Describe a scenario where a survivor was seeking help and the family or church reacted, leaving the person *revictimized. List some lessons to be learned from this.

5. As you understand the issues of sexual identity, what should be the church's response? List three challenges your church is facing regarding sexual identity issues and how they are addressing them. What are some specific ways that pastors and counselors can work together more intentionally to address sexual identity issues? Does your denomination or local church have written policies on issues of sexual abuse and sexual identity? Are they adequate? Why or why not? What is the policy of your church regarding abuse survivors or people struggling with SSA who also wish to serve in church ministries? How could those policies be strengthened in light of this chapter?

FOR FURTHER READING

Allender, Dan B. *The Wounded Heart: Hope for Adult Victims of Childhood Sexual Abuse.* Colorado Springs, CO: NavPress, 2008.

Balswick, Judith K., and Jack O. Balswick. "Chapter 11: Sexual Abuse: A Violation Deep Within the Soul." In *Authentic Human Sexuality: An Integrated Christian Approach*, 204–220. Downers Grove, IL: InterVarsity Press, 1999.

Hallman, Janelle. *The Heart of Female Same-Sex Attraction: A Comprehensive Counseling Resource.* Downers Grove, IL: InterVarsity Press, 2008.

Kroeger, Catherine C., and James R. Beck. "Chapter 9: Sexual Abuse Survivors in the Church; Chapter 11: From Victim to Survivor and Beyond." In *Healing the Hurting: Giving Hope & Help to Abused Women*, 163–179. Grand Rapids, MI: Baker Books, 1998.

Lew, Mike. "Chapter 4: Sexuality, Homophobia, and Shame." In *Victims No Longer: Men Recovering from Incest and Other Sexual Child Abuse*, 54–64. New York, NY: HarperCollins, 1990.

Rosenau, Douglas E. "Chapter 24: Survivors of Sexual Abuse." In *A Celebration of Sex: A Guide To Enjoying God's Gift of Sexual Intimacy*, 2nd ed., 309–320. Nashville, TN: Thomas Nelson, 2002.

Yarhouse, Mark A. *Homosexuality and the Christian: A Guide for Pastors, Parents, and Friends.* Minneapolis, MN: Bethany House, 2010.

———. "Same-Sex Attraction, Homosexual Orientation, and Gay Identity: A Three-Tier Distinction for Counseling and Pastoral Care." *Journal of Pastoral Care & Counseling* 59 (2005): 201–212.

PART TWO

Engaging Sexual Abuse
through the Theological Disciplines

8

A Theology of Sexuality and its Abuse

Creation, Evil, and the Relational Ecosystem

ANDREW J. SCHMUTZER, PHD

THERE IS A MYSTERY to sexuality that demands respect. The most treasured relation-ships in Scripture—personal, national, and divine—draw deeply on sexual imagery: "as a bridegroom rejoices over his bride, so will your God rejoice over you" (Isah 62:5b, cf. Rev 21:2, 9).[1] Paul's language to the Corinthians also employs sacred motifs of sexuality: "I promised you to one husband, to Christ, so that I might present you as a pure virgin to him" (2 Cor 11:2b). Appropriately, Brueggemann states:

> [F]aith that must resort to the most erotic imagery to speak about a covenantal relation-ship that operates at the deepest levels of trust and intimacy is useful indeed . . . the outcome of such usage is a relationship *glorious in its intimacy* and *costly in its brokenness.* The Bible understands that sexuality is the ultimate arena of *cost and joy.*[2]

So how does a sexually abused child carry *both* cost and joy into their adult life? How does a young woman anticipate her marriage—"glorious in its intimacy"—when her own father has sexually betrayed her during her years of nurture, leaving his child with a defining experience "costly in its brokenness?" Sexuality may be "personal," but it is never private.[3] *Whether in brokenness or gloriousness, sexuality functions within a grand web of embodied relationships that are fragile, connected, and enduring.*

---

1. Translations reflect the TNIV, unless otherwise noted or author's translation (AT). The language in this context refers to the "Bride [be'ulah] of God" in marriage (v. 4, cf. Isah 54:5). In Hosea 2:19 God declares of Israel, "I will betroth you to me forever; I will betroth you with [ב] righteousness and justice, with [ב] love and compassion" (AT). The Hebrew preposition in 2:19–20[21–22] is a *bêt* of *price*, here alluding to the cost of bridal gifts (cf. Gen 29:18). This construction can also connote "risk" (Arnold and Choi, *A Guide to Biblical Hebrew Syntax*, 106). John the Baptist speaks of Jesus as the "Bridegroom" (John 3:25–30), as Jesus also calls himself (Matt 9:14–15). In Revelation, John hears the thunderous announcement: "the wedding of the Lamb has come and his bride has made herself ready" (Rev 19:7b). For an illuminating discussion of early ascetic interpretation, see Clark, "The Celibate Bridegroom and His Virginal Brides," 1–25.

2. Brueggemann, "Sexuality," 195; emphasis added.

3. By "sexuality," I mean the *embodied physical behavior of people and the various sexual parts of their bodies involved in expression that is sexual—and therefore *intra-relational* and so beyond mere "acts." This embodied behavior necessarily includes interactive emotions, sensation, and memory (see Gravett, "Sex, Sexuality," 5:199; also the stimulating theological discussion on redemptive memory by Volf, *The End of Memory*).

SEXUAL ABUSE, SCRIPTURE AND THEOLOGY:
A MESSY OBLIGATION

In this chapter we focus on a *biblical theology of sexuality primarily through the texts of creation (Genesis 1–3). Secondarily, we will observe how sexuality and its desecration reverberates through Scripture: in narratives of sexual violation (e.g., 2 Samuel 13), in Jesus' prescriptive model for human sexual behavior (Mark 10:6–9), and in Paul's letter of moral exhortation (1 Thess 4:1–8). Throughout, however, our chief interest is in the significance of the *relational dynamics* that surround sexuality and its violation, including agency, consequences, *intergenerational transmission, and the way sin, evil, and community are portrayed in violence that is sexual in nature.

Using a biblical theological approach enables us to highlight literary, historical, and thematic trajectories in these texts. Further, a combination of these elements, within the context of Christian faith, forms a "plausibility structure"[4] of Scriptural reading that is sensitive to the on-going truths of these biblical stories—both the *horizontal* and *vertical* realities of human sexuality.[5] After all, the "horizontal dimensions of biblical theology cannot be separated from the vertical ones: love of neighbor is practiced within the claim divine love makes upon humankind."[6] Note this relational dynamic that James K. Mead highlights in his useful definition:

> Biblical theology seeks to identify and understand the Bible's theological message and themes, as well as how the Bible witnesses to those themes and *to whom* and *by whom* it declares that message. The outcome of such investigation will lead us to hear what the Bible says about God's being, words, and actions; *about God's relationship to all creation, especially humankind; and about the implications this divine-human encounter has for relationships between human beings.*[7]

The literature on gender, sexuality, and *sexual ethics is a veritable explosion[8] as there are diverse groups, approaches, and issues at stake.[9] Adequately addressing people

4. Moberly, *The Theology of the Book of Genesis*, 7.

5. For a helpful application of biblical theology to ministry, see House, "Biblical Theology and the Wholeness of Scripture," 267–79.

6. Mead, *Biblical Theology*, 242. Note how Jesus' explanation of bi-directional love in Matt 22:35–40 draws both from the "Shema" (Deut 6:5) and Lev 19:18 (cf. Mark 12:30).

7. Ibid; emphasis added. Focusing on history, literature, and anthropology, we will not be investigating the philosophical implications better addressed in other disciplines.

8. For a helpful survey of contemporary Catholic moralists, see Keenan, "Contemporary Contributions to Sexual Ethics," 148–167; a centrist treatment is Hollinger, *The Meaning of Sex*; a liberationist and activist treatment is Ipsen, *Sex Working and the Bible*; a stimulating discussion, especially for its analysis of *wife/ marital rape and the rape of men, is feminist scholar Scholz, *Sacred Witness*; a provocative anthology of essays largely from a theologically liberal perspective is Kamitsuka, *The Embrace of Eros, Bodies, Desires, and Sexuality in Christianity*; a conservative *evangelical treatment is Heimbach, *True Sexual Morality*; a innovative and historical-critical discussion is Carr, *The Erotic Word*; a progressive and pluralistic collection of diverse methodologies (e.g., history, psychology, literature, gender, ritual, cognitive science, etc.) exploring the relationship between humans and the divine as gendered and sexual is Nissinen and Uro, *Sacred Marriages*; an *exegetical and magisterial discussion of Old Testament texts is Davidson, *Flame of Yahweh*, esp. his bibliography (659–801).

9. In same-sex discussions in Catholic circles, for example, *classicists* use "a fixed anthropology that does not yield to experience or contemporary social-scientific claims," while "*revisionists* employ a personalist

who have a history of *sexual abuse (SA) is a complex undertaking. It requires a *multiplex* approach: an interplay of social-sciences, pastoral *empathy, and relational categories capable of addressing the "attack-factor" of physical violation, *intrafamilial betrayal, biblical *anthropology, and the *disorganized relational associations that can be both cause and effect. Along with the victim's psychological damage are also composite issues of *spiritual incest and *theological* trauma—healing for victims often requires "chasing down" the God who never showed up or worse, sat passively by![10] In fact, the complexity of issues surrounding SA—chaos at numerous levels—is part of the reason our understanding of SA needs a more holistic articulation and implementation, making trans-disciplinary studies like this necessary.

For many reasons, studying the brokenness of SA alongside Scripture—of an already mysterious sexuality—creates a "messy obligation." Understanding and responding to the sexually abused means we are committed to the *revealed truth* of Scripture as well as the *observed truth* of empirical studies,[11] which help illuminate the victim's lived-experience.[12] *When revealed truth and observed truth merge, then the complexity of the human condition is in fullest view—the "treasure in jars of clay" (2 Cor 4:7).*

CREATION THEOLOGY: THE BACKDROP OF SEXUALITY

In Genesis we find "a theological understanding of the Old Testament *on its own ground.*"[13] Here is the canonical "downbeat" of sexuality, a sexuality rooted in *creation theology. Paradoxically, the Creator's intention for human sexuality can appear all the more vibrant when we consider the demise of Eden. While it may seem counter-intuitive, *we are aided in a theology of sexuality by acknowledging the state of the broken world as we know it—the world that victims of abuse know in uniquely painful ways.*

Eden Is Long Gone: Facing a Collective Reality

Creation's portrait of human sexuality is deeply fractured. This rupture of biblical sexuality exists in every class, country, culture, and religious expression. When, for example: por-

---

and relational anthropology" (Keenan, "Contemporary Contributions," 149; emphasis added); so Keenan, who notes the critique of current Catholic moralists against each other's views. The issue of *same-sex attraction (SSA) is driving much of this discussion in Catholic circles. Similar Protestant discussions include Seitz, "Sexuality and Scripture's Plain Sense," 319–339; and Miller, "What the Scriptures Principally Teach," 286–296.

10. See Habakkuk's sharp protest (of lament) to a God slow to respond to the problems of his own people, neither hearing nor intervening in the face of serious injustices (1:1–4). For some helpful theological address of divine relationality and absence, see Burnett, *Where is God?*, Brueggemann, *An Unsettling God*, and Garrett, "Why, God, Why?" 1–33.

11. In key places Scripture exhorts people to scrutinize or investigate something: "go to the ant; *study* its ways and *learn*" (Prov 6:6 JPS); "*Consider* the lilies of the field, how they grow; they neither toil nor spin" (Matt 6:28b NRSV, cf. Prov 30:25–28; Job 12:7; 14:2). Accurately experiencing this life is more important than securing it (Williams, *Those Who Ponder Proverbs*, 50).

12. The helpful terms and discussion of Biddle, *Missing the Mark*, xi–xii; see also Green, *Body, Soul, and Human Life*, 1–34.

13. Rendtorff, *Canon and Theology*, 88; emphasis original.

nography remains so well funded, affecting children, women, and men; when women are victimized through *corrective rape in war-torn countries like Africa; when a 170-page manual on child *molestation circulates that details step-by-step, how to find, *groom, and molest children;[14] when human *sex trafficking exploits children and young women like *"chattel" on a global market; when young girls must endure *female circumcision; when boys are sexually abused throughout the world but shame, *cultural mores,[15] and male *stereotypes keep them quiet; when women are maimed or burned in *"honor killing" for breaking sectarian relational *taboos; when protestant churches sensitively pray about infertility on Mother's Day but won't acknowledge the sexually abused sitting in the same room;[16] when the Catholic Church remains so dogmatic about adult contraception but criminally silent about child sexual abuse of epidemic proportion—*the portrait of biblical sexuality is indeed fractured!*

In his book *Sex in the Bible*, J. Harold Ellens captures the moral gravity of our time when he laments that, "we increasingly witness the progressive unfolding of the horror of sexual abuse and other forms of sexual aberration in all societies on this planet, particularly in religious communities."[17] Singling out the religious communities and the leaders of our faith traditions is a haunting but necessary remark. *Any shepherd who preys on their sheep by sexually abusing them is a profound illustration of corrosive hypocrisy—to faith, body, and community* (Ezekiel 34).

It has been estimated that in a fifty-two-year period (1950–2002), at least fifty thousand young people were abused by priests.[18] What major Western country has not had the sexual abuse crisis hit their community of faith? Through symbolism or other means, *there is now a need for collective *restitution and healing on an international and inter-faith scale* (Psalm 32). On the model of South Africa's *Truth and Reconciliation Commission*,[19] the international faith community needs to demonstrate a renewed welcome to their sexually violated, standing in solidarity with the betrayed in the name of our Wounded Lamb who

---

14. A report that emerged from Central Florida concerning Phillip R. Greaves II and his "How-To-*Pedophilia" book; see: http://www.wftv.com/news/24862761/detail.html; accessed October 13, 2010.

15. A personal friend of mine is a missionary working primarily with Arab women in the Middle East. She tells of two young women in a *support-type group who were engaged to be married but, as she found out, they were understandably petrified to tell their male fiancées that they were not virgins (a horrific dishonor in that culture), having been sexually abused as children. After some time, both women agreed to disclose their "soiled pasts" to their fiancées. They reported back, the men had *not* rejected them—both men revealed that they too had been sexually abused!

16. To acknowledge the sexually abused (young and old) in their congregations, churches could consider placing a single white rose (for purity) at the front of the sanctuary and dedicating the entire service to all forms of violence in their congregation, *including sexual abuse*. Leaders should remind victims that virginity is given, not stolen. Using *Holy Innocents' Day* (Dec 28; cf. Matt 2:16) is appropriate, when Herod ordered the killing of children. Who is being hurt more by the "sacred silence" of churches?

17. Ellens, *Sex in the Bible*, x.

18. Beste, "Mediating God's Grace Within the Context of Trauma," 245–246; idem, *God and the Victim*, esp. 1–16 and 37–57. Some organizations estimate that there are 39 million survivors of childhood sexual abuse (CSA) in the USA alone (see darkness2light.org).

19. Tutu, *No Future without Forgiveness*; Barnes Lampman, *God and the Victim*, and more recently, de Gruchy, *Reconciliation*, esp. 147–180; Browning and Reed, *Forgiveness, Reconciliation, and Moral Courage*.

stands "as slain" (Rev 5:6a).[20] The eternal scarring of the Savior is extremely meaningful to the sexually violated. This biblical text holds out a precious truth and a healing paradox for abused people still struggling with the effects of their *trauma: at the center of the throne John no longer sees the Lion (5:5), but now a Lamb (5:6). John's theology of Christ's *victory through sacrifice* "emphasizes the lasting benefits of his sacrificial death and resurrection."[21] *Christ did not die to save humans from their humanity, but to authenticate and redeem it.*[22] Through the scarred Christ, a holistic redemption is provided.

Various cultural forces have exacerbated this fracturing of sexuality, including: "The modern 'turn to the subject,' the inordinate preoccupation with 'I,'"[23] the ever-destructive religious hypocrisies, and various social movements defined by *power structures have, for example, called into question the foundational claims of biblical sexuality.[24] In many ways, the church has blunted its own authority on sexual ethics. Too much preaching on "little sins" has shrunk our hearts. What imagination do people have left for *epic* waves of human violation sweeping our globe?[25] Abuse victims are further diminished when fellow humans repackage others' pain, rather than sitting with the broken. Unfortunately, as Walter Brueggemann has observed:

> The practical outcome of this compartmentalization in the contemporary church is that so-called conservatives tend to take careful account of the most rigorous claims of the Bible concerning sexuality, and are indifferent to what the Bible says about economics. Mutatis mutandis, so-called liberals relish what the Bible says in de-

20. Revelation uses "lamb" (contra "lion," v. 5) twenty-eight times exclusively to designate the resurrected, victorious Christ (5:9; 7:14; 12:11; 13:8; 17:14, cf. John 1:29, 36). As a perfect past participle, *esphagmenon* ("having been slain"; including the perfect "having taken his stand," cf. 13:3) expresses an on-going condition as a result of the past act of being slain (cf. Rev 13:8). Greg Beale states, "The translation 'as *though* slain' is unnecessary and misleading, as if the Lamb only looked slain but was not; 'as slain' is best" (*The Book of Revelation*, 352). Peter Hicks captures the weight of a scarred God in Rev 5:6 with the following theological points: (1) What was being done on the cross was huge, (2) What was being done on the cross was being done by the triune God, (3) What was being borne on the cross was being borne by the triune God, (4) What was done on the cross is forever in the triune God (Hicks, *The Message of Evil and Suffering*, 78–82); see also Moltmann, *The Crucified God*.

21. Mounce, *The Book of Revelation*, 144, 146. I am speaking here of the sacrifice of Christ in his death and resurrection. The resurrection of Christ should not be used to dismiss or ignore the real suffering of abuse victims, nor should survivors view their victimization as any sort of "sacrifice." Christ's sacrifice was costly, but it was also *voluntary* suffering (John 10:18; Phil 2:7–8; cf. John 17:5; 2 Cor 8:9). For a discussion of how key biblical texts (e.g., "living sacrifice," Rom 12:1) can sound terrorizing to abuse victims who may read with a hermeneutic of self-involvement, see my "Spiritual Formation and Sexual Abuse: Embodiment, Community, and Healing," 81–82 (see For Further Reading).

22. Biddle, *Missing the Mark*, 73.

23. Brueggemann, "Listening," 125; also Twenge and Campbell, *The Narcissism Epidemic*. When human trauma must be legitimized through power differentials, "tribal affiliations," and aggressive gender ideologies, the *postmodern *hermeneutic of "suspicion" proves ill suited to adequately empathize with the *totalizing* condition of a broken *humanity*.

24. See the introductory discussion of Gagnon, "Sexuality," and Yao-Hwa Sung, "Culture and Hermeneutics," 739; 150–55, respectively.

25. Miller, "Sermons That are Now? What a Novel Idea!" 11.

manding ways about economics, but tread lightly around what the Bible says about sexuality.[26]

Clearly, a representative policy on sexual abuse is desperately needed, one that can transcend our differences, and I believe a collective voice may yet be found to address this issue.

Serious fracture is also evident when entire populations use stock phrases like: "my sex life"—an ethical *oxymoron—they betray a lack of interpersonal understanding, steeped instead in ideologies of autonomy and hyperindividualism. Rather, as Christian Gostecnik reminds us, "[S]exuality is and remains the arena where the most important relational configurations play out, and with all their power point to a *transcendence and sacredness of interpersonal and *family system relationships.*"[27] Yet without an adequate perspective of the relational web comes a tragic minimizing of a deeply relational form of trauma. What has withered outside Eden is the very foundation for an interconnectedness that is also accountable.

Learning from Eden's Loss: Reclaiming a Collective Conscience

Persons are parts of relationships. Addressing SA requires a more theologically integrative anthropology—*including the contextualizing nature of lived-experience.* Also needed is a more respectful appraisal of cultural assumptions that define personhood, assumptions operating in and outside the church.[28] Historically, theology has assumed a rather Western and "fixed" anthropology: essentially *dualistic, excessively individualized, culturally "flat," and an experientially minimalist view of personhood.[29] *However, through creation, Scripture offers a vision of moral community that also defines personal morality.*[30] Creation theology mediates the two extremes of collective *fatalism and hyperindividualism.[31] In creation theology, *both* individual and collective realities are anchored and affirmed.

Understandably, personal violence and relational loss can foster a sharp distaste for the finitude and contingency of creation as part of its goodness.[32] "In creation is a recognition of *the worth of limitation* . . . that which is limited and finite constitutes the very place in which God's being is exhibited."[33] But such creaturely (inter-)dependence can appear like reckless vulnerability. Sexually violated people naturally tend to "wall-up" and "close in"; post-violation, relational vulnerability can simply seem too costly. Yet there is hope. Creation teaches

26. Brueggemann, *An Unsettling God*, 188 n.23.

27. Gostecnik, "Sexuality and the Longing for Salvation," 589; emphasis added.

28. Yao-Hwa Sung, "Culture and Hermeneutics," 150–55.

29. Research in altered neurobiology, neurodevelopmental factors, and the *dissociative continuum surrounding trauma are raising the profile of the environment's role in "brain molding" and what shapes the person at the deepest levels (see www.ChildTrauma.org; also Murphy, *Bodies and Souls, or Spirited Bodies?*). On a more general level, see the stimulating discussions of Green, *Body, Soul, and Human Life*; Corcoran, *Rethinking Human Nature*.

30. Divito, "Anthropology, OT Theological," 1:173; emphasis added.

31. Klingbeil, "Between 'I' and 'We,'" 335.

32. Rego, *Suffering and Salvation*, 216.

33. Ibid., quoting Kennedy, *Deus Humanissimus*, 86; emphasis original.

an exalted anthropology; humankind is dignified through the *image of God (discussed below). Outside Eden, people still retain their ability to choose and the dignity of agency, enabling a journey of healing *within* community. Collective conscience—whether celebrating or restoring it—means that personal morality is operating within moral community.

Buried in the profound damage of sexual abuse lay the vestiges of a Creator's intended design for sexual personhood. John MacMurray rightly claims that "personal existence is *constituted* by the relation of persons"—the personal self has "its being in relationships."[34] This reality of "situatedness" in biblical anthropology highlights ethical elements functioning within the "*I–Thou*" and "*We*" of personhood. It is this relational dynamic that highlights the devastation factor of *human-induced* trauma and the enduring consequences of sexual violation.[35] Neither sexuality nor its abuse can be adequately grasped outside of Creation's view of *being-in-relation*. These implications run deep, both for violation and healing. For example, "All memories are communal," argues theologian Miroslav Volf. "Individuals do not remember alone but as members of a group."[36] Acknowledging these realities of personhood, we turn to Genesis 1.

Sexuality Rooted in Doxology

Genesis 1:1–2:3 functions as the first exposition.[37] The poetic cadence of this initial unit is *theo-centric* *doxology, "a world-making *liturgy that invites the congregation to respond in regular *litany, 'it is good ... very good.'"[38] As theologized history,[39] creation theology has also spawned numerous creation-psalms. In fact, so central was creation to Israel's faith and hope that "Israel spoke about Yahweh's creation activity above all in hymnic praise" (e.g., Psalms 8, 18, 65, 104, 148).[40] Creation is *worded-forth*, according to the "moral imagination"[41] of the Creator. Divine speech is effective, for the Creator to speak is to manifest (Gen 1:3, 6, 9, 11, etc.).[42] What God makes is more than "good" (vv. 10, 12, 18, 25); the concluding evaluation is "very good" (1:31)—*only after the creation of humankind. Elohim* is the transcendent, wholly-other, universal King (cf. 1 Sam 12:12; Ps 95:3–7).[43] But God is not sexed, he is *supra-sexual*. The God of biblical creation is unique. "Outside Israel all gods or goddesses are sexed

34. MacMurray, *Self as Agent*, 17; emphasis original.

35. According to Beste, *human-induced* trauma carries a greater impact (*God and the Victim*, 38). While cancer and car wrecks may also produce forms of PTSD, one still passively "*contracts* a disease" or is "*involved* in a collision"—but the active violation from another human being makes the trauma of SA, the contravening of one's will, uniquely devastating.

36. Volf, *The End of Memory*, 99; also citing Halbwachs, "The Social Frameworks of Memory," 38.

37. The language of Wenham, *Story as Torah*, 24, 27.

38. Brueggemann, "Creation," 40. Similarly, Gordon J. Wenham speaks of Gen 1:1–2:3 as "a hymnic overture to the book" (*Story as Torah*, 24).

39. Wenham, *Exploring The Old Testament*, 15, 16; similarly, Waltke, *Old Testament Theology*, 39–40.

40. Hermisson, "Observations on the Creation Theology in Wisdom," 123.

41. For discussion of "moral imagination," see Brown, *The Ethos of the Cosmos*, esp. 46–52.

42. God's "act of speech" is his work. This is why in judgment, God falls silent (Genesis 7–8)—chaos reasserts itself in the *un-creation* of the flood (cf. Amos 8:11).

43. J. Gordon McConville calls Kingship "the root metaphor" ("The Judgment of God in the Old Testament," 25).

. . . goddesses all over the world are directly and inescapably linked to sexuality."[44] In contrast to the ancient Near Eastern cultures,[45] as John N. Oswalt explains:

> [H]uman sexual behavior is specifically desacralized. Nothing happens to God or to nature when a man and a woman have sex together . . . Sex is a divinely willed characteristic of creation, but it is not a characteristic of ultimate reality. *As a result, the Bible builds specific boundaries around the practice of sex . . . God is beyond the limits of our sexuality.* So, these prohibitions on sex outside of heterosexual marriage are not the work of prudes. They are a revelation of the boundaries inside of which the Creator intended us to find blessing and not curse.[46]

Nevertheless, as John Goldingay explains: "God can be bodily enough to be seen (e.g., Exod 24:9–11) and specifically has, for example, eyes, a nose, a face, arms, hands and a womb—everything but genitals."[47] Since God is neither male nor female, *human sexuality is a result of creation, not a quality of a sexual Creator.*[48]

---

44. Oswolt, *The Bible Among the Myths*, 72, 73; see esp. 63–84. *Enuma Elish*, the early second millennium B.C.E. Babylonian account of creation contains a recital of the generation of the gods (theogony) that leads to the creation of humans and the world:

> When on high the heaven had not been named,
> Firm ground below had not been called by name,
> There was nothing but primordial Apsu, their begetter,
> *And* Mummu-Tiamat, she who bore them all,
> Their waters commingling as a single body;
> No reed hut had been matted, nor marsh land had appeared,
> When no gods whatever had been brought into being,
> Uncalled by name, their destinies undetermined—
> Then it was that the gods were formed within them.
> Lahmu and Lahamu were brought forth, by name they were called.

(Arnold and Beyer, "Enuma Elish," 32).

45. Evidence of the human sexual and divine combined in ritual has been found in Middle Assyrian lead figurines. This ritual intercourse, with *amuletic* property, depicts a man standing and the woman resting on an altar. Similar models of male and female sexual organs were found in the temple of Ishtar at Ashur and are connected with her cult as the goddess of physical love and prostitution (Green and Baird, "Prostitution and Ritual Sex," 236).

46. Oswolt, *The Bible Among the Myths*, 74, 75; emphasis added.

47. Goldingay, *Old Testament Theology*, 1:102–103. Female imagery for God employs metaphors of rich relational involvement, e.g., a woman in childbirth (Isah 42:14; cf. Deut 32:18) and a comforting mother (Isah 66:13).

In stark contrast to the non-sexual portrait of God, pagan religion and magic also saw demons as either male or female, not sexually neutral. The sex and sexuality of demons is particularly evident in magical documents from Mesopotamia. Female "Lilith" demons who murdered infants were especially evil. Female Liliths were also sexually seductive spirits that would attack men at night, stealing their semen. Male Lilith demons were thought to seduce women through their dreams. Thus, sexually producing demons after their own kind was a common belief. Human sexual dreams were viewed as evidence of demonic seduction, and many ancient Jews held that such dreams constituted a sort of marriage, one only dissolved by a formal divorce or "*gēt*" (Billington, "Ancient Exorcists, Demons, and the Name of Jesus: Part One," 18, 20).

48. "Sex," in *Dictionary of Biblical Imagery*, 776; emphasis added.

SEXUALITY DELIBERATELY CONNECTING GENESIS 1 AND 2

The doxology of creation moves from earth (1:2) to "earthling" (1:26), inanimate to the animate, chaos to rest. "All of creation—the natural world and humans together—stands in relationship to God and is a suitable vehicle of God's presence."[49] Yet, rising in complexity and agency, the creation of humankind on *Day 6* is twice the length (149 words [vv. 26–31]) of its corresponding *Day 3* (69 words [vv. 9–13]). The doxology culminates with humankind (1:26–28), the pinnacle of God's eight creative acts.[50]

The 2nd exposition (2:4–4:26) amplifies the origin (2:7, 21–22) and sexuality of humankind (2:18, 23–25). The viewpoint shifts from a cosmic panorama (Genesis 1) to the "ground-level" particulars of the human pair (Genesis 2). Tying these two expositions together are foundational theological themes with sexuality framing them all. Observe the following diagram.

SEXUALITY AMONG THE THEMES OF GENESIS 1 & 2

	Theme		Domain	Related Significance
Gen 1	*Sexuality*	(1:26–27)	humankind	[+ Divine Speech, v. 26]
	Dominion	(1:28)	animals	[Pos. Law/Command, v. 28]
	Food	(1:29–30)	land	
Gen 2	Food	(2:8–17)	land	[Neg. Law/Prohib., vv. 16–17]
	Dominion	(2:18–20)	animals	
	Sexuality	(2:21–25)	humankind	[+ Human Speech, v. 23]

Using *chiastic structure, sexuality is the framing theme, highlighting theological focus. Law not only establishes *boundaries* in the best interests of human life, but law is also God's gracious gift and pre-dates rebellion.[51] "The law is given because God is concerned about *the best possible life* for *all* of God's creatures."[52] *Whether as boundary or blessing, God's directives foster life: for procreation (1:28) and relational protection (2:16–17).* God's provision of food moves from the introduction of image bearers—sexuality in the *Creation Mandate (1:26–27, discussed below)—to sexuality in vulnerability (2:21–25). The two sexes who have "dominion" over the animals (1:28; cf. Ps 8:6–8[7–9]) in turn define their sexual uniqueness in contrast to the animals (2:20, 24). "Procreation is shared

49. Simkins, *Creator and Creation*, 131.

50. Not surprisingly, this elevation of the human order finds echoes elsewhere in Scripture: "kings . . . rulers . . . young men and women, old men and children. Let them praise the name of the LORD"; "praise him in his mighty heavens. Praise him for his acts of power," cf. Pss 148:11–13a; 150:1b–2a; cf. 8:4–6[5–7]; Phil 2:7–10.

51. Birch et al., *A Theological Introduction to the Old Testament*, 51, 52. While the word for "sin, guilt" (ʿāôn) is not used until Cain's punishment (Gen 4:13)—after Adam and Eve's expulsion—the couple are similarly judged for *rebellion*, breaking the LORD's command (2:16–17), which God mentions *twice* (cf. 3:11b; 17a).

52. Fretheim, "Law in the Service of Life," 186; emphasis original.

by humankind with the animal world (Gen 1:22, 28); sexuality is not."[53] Animals multiply "according to their kinds" (1:25), but humans, "according to our likeness" (1:26; 5:3).[54] The gravity of sexual abuse is better understood next to a deeper understanding of the grandeur of humankind made in God's image.

The Image of God: Under-kings in Stewardship

The study of the image of God is essentially the study of Western understanding of humanity.[55] In Gen 1:26–28 we find core theological values. Here, sexuality participates in a holistic anthropology. Unfortunately, texts like Gen 1:26 and 27 are typically read in isolation from their larger context, and even God's dignifying speech. A *close reading reveals the literary contour of 1:26–28. God's speech—both creative and appointing—actually encircles v. 27; the Creator's "Let us" (v. 26, 1st person address) culminates with his priest-like blessing: "Be fruitful" (v. 28, 2nd person blessing). My following translation and semantic layout contextualizes the vital subjects of "humankind," "image of God," "rule," and "male and female" in an interplay of divine speech (vv. 26, 28) and a narrator's report (v. 27). *Significantly, human sexuality is defined within community, granted a royal context, and tasked with an ethical mission.*

IMAGE OF GOD (GEN 1:26–28):
RESEMBLANCE AND RELATIONSHIP IN LITERARY STRUCTURE

Announcement:		"Let us make humankind (*ādām*) in our <u>image</u> . . . our likeness" (26a)
Purpose:		"so that THEY may <u>rule over</u> (*rādâ*): fish, birds, creepers" (26b)
	A	So created (*wybārā'*) God the human being (*hāādām*) in *his* <u>image</u> (27a)
Report:	B	in *the* image of God he created him (27b)
	B'	male (*zākār*) and female (*něqēbâ*) he created THEM (27c)
	A'	Then blessed (*wybārek*) God THEM and God said to THEM (28aα)
Blessing[1]	(= *endowment*):	"Be fruitful. . . multiply . . . fill. . . subdue it" (28aβ)
Blessing[2]	(= *commission*):	"<u>rule over</u> (*rādâ*): fish, birds, creepers" (28b)

From the outset, the syntax underscores *relationships in purpose*. In *performative utterance, the more intimate "Let us make" now replaces the impersonal "Let there be" (cf. v. 14). The ruling community is specifically tasked—"*so that* they may rule over . . . fish, birds, creepers" (vv. 26b, 28b).[56] "They" who are anticipated to "rule" (v. 26b, *rādâ*)

53. Trible, *God and the Rhetoric of Sexuality*, 15.

54. Mentioned four times in Scripture, bestiality refers to sexual acts performed with animals (Exod 22:19[18]; Lev 18:23; 20:15–16; Deut 27:21; cf. "perversion," Tanak). Bestiality inverts the created order by mixing image bearers with animals (Gen 1:27–28), and is condemned as "confusion" (Heb. *tebel*). The nations purged from Canaan were guilty of these abominations (Lev 20:23).

55. Goldingay, *Old Testament Theology*, 1:102, quoting Emil Brunner and Gunnlauger A. Jónsson.

56. In Hebrew, the prefixed verbal form with *wāw* conjunctive ("so that they may rule over," v. 26b) following the cohortative ("let us make," v. 26a) expresses *purpose* (GKC §109f; Van Leeuwen, "Form, Image," *NIDOTTE*, 4:645; F. J. Stendebach, "*tselem*" *TDOT*, 12:394; A. J. Schmutzer, *Be Fruitful and Multiply*, 166–

are the same community (v. 28a, "them") blessed with "rule" in the Creation Mandate (v. 28b, *rādâ*).[57] The Mandate blessing ignites life, giving it direction, purpose, and ethical mission (Gen 2:15; Psalm 8).[58] *Human sexuality is presupposed within the relational and ethical dynamic of the Mandate.*[59]

Notice that humankind was made in "dialogue" for dialogue—the man will only be heard when there is woman, a corresponding being to speak to (2:23).[60] *Rhetorically, the "divine plural" (= "us") from the heavenly stage *initiates* a mission that the "human plural" (= "them") *enacts* on the earthly stage. Bracketing the entire unit, God's speech is both informative (1:26) and empowering (1:28).

Highlighting the historical and cultural context, biblical theology sees God's angelic court in the plural "us" (cf. 1 Kgs 22:19–22; Isah 6:8).[61] Humankind is cast as the terrestrial counterpart to God's heavenly entourage.[62] God's experience of community now spills over into a new arena, "deepening and broadening the community of relationships that already exists in the divine realm."[63]

As the image of God, humankind both *represents* and *resembles* God.[64] Rooted in the "stuff of earth" (2:7), humankind as the "image of God" has "a physical nature shared

186). More recent translations are starting to reflect this purpose (so TNIV, NET, cf. NEB).

57. Reading Gen 1:28a ("Be fruitful, increase in number, fill the earth") as a command to bear children is a worn out misreading, confusing the *form* of the text (grammatical imperative) with its *function* (genre of blessing). Genesis 1:28 is God's *blessing* to accomplish, not humankind's *command* to breed (cf. 24:60; 49:22–26). A further problem is that this misreading also isolates *reproduction* (v. 28a) from *governance* (v. 28b).

58. My emphasis here is of humankind in a power-sharing relationship with their Creator, operating within a redemptive trajectory. By contrast, the *Cultural Mandate* is the classic expression of civilizing-dominion in (Dutch) Reformed Covenant Theology and has overplayed the Covenant of Works (Gen 2:15–17), thereby flattening and distorting the significance of 1:26–28. See the critique of Wook Chung, "Toward the Reformed and Covenantal Theology of Premillennialism," 133–46, esp. 134–35.

59. Mathews, *Genesis 1–11:26*, 1:158.

60. B. C. Birch et al., *Theological Introduction*, 49.

61. The "angelic court" view allows for the ontological *Trinity in Christian theology, but does not require its expression at this juncture in revelatory history. In addition to ignoring the ancient Near Eastern historical context, a key problem with the Trinitarian reading in Gen 1:26 is that the other four uses of the plural pronoun with reference "God" (3:22; 11:7; Isah 6:8) do not seem to have the Trinity in view (Waltke, *Genesis*, 64). Goldingay speaks for the vast majority of Old Testament scholarship when he notes: ". . . this [the Trinity] would be lost on Genesis's audience" (*Old Testament Theology*, 1:98, n.90). For other key biblical references to the "angelic court," see Job 1:6; 2:1; 38:7; Pss 29:1–3; 89:6–8[5–7]; 40:1–6; Dan 10:12–13; Luke 2:8–14; see also Joüon, *A Grammar*, §§113e, 136d; Stendebach, "*tselem*," *TDOT*, 12:394; Newsom, "Angels," *ABD*, 1:248–253, esp. "The Divine Council," 249; Mullen, Jr., "Divine Assembly," *ABD*, 2:214–217; Heiser, "Divine Council," 112–116; Walton, *Ancient Near Eastern Thought and the Old Testament*, 93–97.

62. McBride, Jr., "Divine Protocol," 16. Compare with Psalm 148, which uses the same *bi-partite* structure to portray the angels in praise (vv. 1–7), followed by the agents of the earthly realm (vv. 8–14)—the cosmos in antiphonal chorus.

63. Olson, "Genesis," 4.

64. Some of the more recent literature to cogently address the complex issue of the "image of God" include: Niskanen, "The Poetics of Adam," 417–36; Schmutzer, *Be Fruitful and Multiply*, 89–204; Herring, "A 'Transubstantiated' Humanity," 480–94; Middleton, *The Liberating Image*; Waltke, *An Old Testament Theology*, 211–30.

with the rest of the world and a unique form of liveliness that came from God."[65] In the theology of creation, the stone statues used by ancient Near Eastern kings are replaced by God's living emblems. So Goldingay perceptively notes, if the "we" includes God's heavenly entourage, it "would fit with the fact that God and God's aids all have human form when they appear on earth" (e.g., Genesis 18–19).[66] Further, the fact that: "You have crowned him with glory and honor" (Ps 8:5[6]) coronates human under-kings (Pss 21:5[6]; 45:3–4[4–5]) with the dignity of their Cosmic King (Pss 29:1–4; 96:6–7; 145:5). "Glory and honor" are distinguishing characteristics shared by God and his vice-regents,[67] but a royalty that is now *democratized* to all of humankind, not one gender, one class of people, or ancient kings who thought they were demigods. "*The first human beings are themselves royal figures, living in a royal garden and exercising royal authority there.*"[68]

Following the above diagram, Gen 1:26–28 shows that *ādām* refers to the category of "human being" to which the individual belongs; that is, collective humankind as "male" and "female" (v. 27c). The Old Testament does not use *ādām* to distinguish one individual from another.[69] The terms and literary structure of this passage shows that neither gender nor *hierarchy is at issue here; at focus is the image-bearer as God's *agent* in earthly stewardship.[70]

As image-bearers, their difference lies in sexual structure. Significantly, *the terms "male" (zākār) and "female" (nĕqēbâ, v. 27c) refer to their capacity as sexual beings, thus making sexual potency—alongside the royal status of image-bearing—the gravitational center of this passage.* As the above diagram shows, sexuality is an assumption celebrated in the blessing that immediately follows (v. 28). Not until we come to Gen 2:23 do we find the terms "man" ('îš) and "woman" ('iššâ) used by God's agents. Only in Gen 2:23 are social relationships evident—gender, as we tend to think of it.[71] But our diagram illustrates more.

The *chiasm in the center *report* communicates some unique emphases.[72] Together, (A, A') "so created" and "then blessed"[73] underscores the fact that human creation is be-

65. Goldingay, *Old Testament Theology*, 1:99.

66. Ibid., 1:98, n.90.

67. A powerful illustration is found when God "calls out" Job; he states: "Do you have an arm like God's? . . . Adorn yourself with *majesty and splendor*, and clothe yourself with *honor and glory* . . . Then I will confess to you that your own right hand can deliver you" (40:9a, 10, 14 HCSB).

68. Goldingay, *Old Testament Theology*, 1:100; emphasis added.

69. Hess, "Adam," *Dictionary of the Old Testament*, 19.

70. That some would argue for man and woman being created from an original bisexual, androgynous "golem" or asexual being (i.e., 2:23) is exegetically unfounded and historically naïve (so Bal, *Lethal Love*, 113–116). Unfortunately, such *deconstructive arguments continue, disparaging male and female by idealizing androgyny as the sexual unity of one body, even as the intent of Paul's writings. This only adds to the confusion (see Wright Knust, *Unprotected Texts*). For a critique of such interpretation, see Noort, "The Creation of Man and Woman in Biblical and ancient Near Eastern Traditions," 6–10.

71. Waltke, *Old Testament Theology*, 221. This is confirmed elsewhere by the same use of "male" and "female" when reproduction is the issue (cf. Gen 6:9; 7:9). "Woman" ('iššâ) is used by the narrator in v. 22, but my focus is on the interpersonal understanding of the man reflected in his speech.

72. Adapted from Walsh, *Style and Structure in Biblical Hebrew Narrative*, 106.

73. The sound play (i.e., paronomasia, *wybārā', wybārk;*) underscores the uniqueness of human creation

yond a neutral event—"Let us" was salvific and doxological.[74] Used three times in v. 27, "create" (*bārā'*) communicates *product* rather than process (cf. "make," v. 26), further highlighting the special nature of "the human being" (*hāādām*, v. 27a). Further, the core subunits (B, B'): "in the image of God" and "male and female" are *topically* stressed. The structure of subunits "B" are *explicative* verbless phrases, not the "normal" Hebrew word order. In other words, moving from the articular form ("*the* human being," v. 27a) to the collective singular (B: "him/it," v. 27b)[75] presents "male" (*zākār*) and "female" (B': *nĕqēbâ*, v. 27c) as *two types of the same generic human being*, agents of the same mission. We now consider how sexuality and mission merge.

Royal Custodians in Ethical Mission

Sexuality operates in the context of a divinely delegated and other-oriented mission. God's vice-regents are custodians in an ethical trust. The mission in Gen 1:28 is a theological *hendiadys, or pairing of two interrelated parts: (1) *endowment* for reproduction, (2) and *commission* for governance (see above diagram). Aberrant notions of sexuality tend to divide: a severance of reproduction from governance, a dismissal of society from self, or an elevation of personal choice over social obligation. But moored to the image of God, the context of human sexuality is ethical mission—*from* God and *for* others. Sexuality has a "nested existence"[76] in a web of relationships that originates with the Creator who considerately observed, "It is not good for the man to be alone" (Gen 2:18). God "allows himself to be affected, to be touched by each of his creatures. He adopts the community of creation as his own milieu."[77]

While endowment addresses sexual reproduction, it is never separated from the commission of ruling (cf. 1:26, 28)—the stewardship of governance. Sexuality has an orienting vision in which God has interjected moral order and ethical coherence.[78] To produce and care is to mimic the Creator (cf. 2:5, 15). Humankind is intended to co-create with God (Gen 4:1; 5:3). The same ethical mission means that "subduing" (v. 28a) in creation theology is the task of earthly *development*, whereas "ruling" (v. 28b) grants humankind the necessary position to achieve this harnessing of earthly life.[79] But abuse defies both dignity and vision. *Theologically, sexual abuse is: ethical mission in reverse, custodians in sabotage of their royal family, a distortion of delegated authority, a plundering of fellow-image bearers, a degrading of the redemptive horizon, and a marring of connecting metaphors for God.* The grand web of relationships is broken.[80]

---

within artistic literary writing.

74. Loader, *The Septuagint, Sexuality, and the New Testament*, 28–29.

75. The Hebrew 3ms suffix ("him/it," v. 27b; cf. 5:1) functions as a *collective* singular and recent translations now focus on this collectivity, simply translating "them" (TNIV, NLT, NET, NRSV).

76. Murphy, "The Resurrection Body and Personal Identity," 202–218.

77. Moltmann, *God in Creation*, 279.

78. Fretheim, *God and World in the Old Testament*, 282.

79. Fretheim, "The Book of Genesis," 1:346.

80. On the comprehensive damage to the realms of personhood, see Schmutzer, "Spiritual Formation and Sexual Abuse," 67–86.

Doxology gives dominion legitimacy.[81] *Theirs is not a dominion of power, but power for dominion.* Thus, both doxology and dominion must be held together, for worship without human authority is *abdication and human power without the context of praise becomes self-serving human regency.[82] God blessed the sexual human being for ethical mission. Sexual intimacy is unique, a *merging* of blessed man and woman (1:28), of a "male" and "female" who are structurally compatible with each other, possessing "the right degree of likeness and unlikeness to make the merger truly complimentary" (2:23–24).[83]

The theological force of God's blessing reissued to Noah portrays the Creator in some degree of accommodation to sustain his redemptive program, *recalibrating* the original Mandate for a new era—involved, but never calling it "good" again (Gen 9:1–7). Significant to the renewal of the Mandate mission with Noah is the reality that the image of God remains *intact* (Gen 9:1, 6, 7; Jam 3:9).[84] Renewed law assures that moral order reflects the created order, thereby sustaining and extending God's creative work. Several implications for ministering to the sexually abused can be noted from our discussion.

IMAGE OF GOD: IMPLICATIONS FOR PERSONHOOD AND ABUSE

First, regarding gender. Notice that the two pronouns ("our" [2x], v. 26a) underscore a *theomorphic* perspective (i.e., having the form of God), as "our image" and "our likeness" fix their point of reference in God, not in "him" or "herself."[85] God models a common humanity, not our gender specificity.[86] Moreover, the structure of the passage shows that the narrator's report culminates with a depiction of genders in unity ("them," v. 27c). *Throughout Genesis 1–2, God addresses them as persons, not genders—persons in a "community of need."*[87] Theologically, healing a victim implies restoring a community. While the Mandate is given to rule the earth, there is no Mandate for humans to rule each other.[88] As Patrick D. Miller notes, "Once the declaration is made that it is as man and as woman that God has created human beings, *then the story speaks of them only in the plural.*"[89]

Sexual abuse only compounds the survivor's struggle to define their gendered identity, a point addressed in other chapters. Our analysis shows that the difference in sexed bodies of men and women actually grounds their intricate *interdependence.*[90] What has

---

81. Brueggemann, *The Message of the Psalms*, 37–38.

82. Ibid., 38.

83. Gagnon, "Sexuality," 747.

84. Cf. 1 Cor 11:7; Col 1:15. The intact image is increasingly noted by scholars from various disciplines; see bio-ethicist, Kilner, "Humanity in God's Image," 601–17. "By the grace of the Creator the new humanity is created in the 'image of Christ' (cp. 1 Cor 15:49) and through his perfect obedience achieves life and glory for believers as his adopted children (e.g., Rom 8:17, 30; 9:23; 2 Cor 4:4, 6; Col 3:9–10)"; (Mathews, *Genesis 1–11:26*, 164).

85. van Wolde, "Rhetorical, Linguistic and Literary Features in Genesis 1," 149.

86. Volf, *Exclusion and Embrace*, 172.

87. Miller, "Man and Woman," 311–312; emphasis added.

88. Middleton, *The Liberating Image*, 204–205.

89. Miller, "Man and Woman," 311; emphasis added. Marking God's dialogue with *them*, plural forms occur fifteen times in four verses (vv. 26–29), a muted reality in English translations.

90. Volf, *Exclusion and Embrace*, 186.

exhausted itself is the contemporary insistence, notes Allison Weir, especially among some *feminists, that identity is necessarily based on subject-object opposition, requiring the *exclusion* of the other.[91] In other words, a theology of sexuality is not found in *neutralizing* gender differences (i.e., "neither-one-nor-the-other"), nor *synthesizing* gender (i.e., "not-the-one-and-the-other"), but as Miroslav Volf explains, "affirming gender differences while at the same time positing one gender identity as always internal to the other" (i.e., "not-without-the-other"; cf. Gen 2:18, 23–24).[92] *What will help victims of abuse are models of identity that consciously include difference and identity*—rather than excluding difference and identity through theories of opposition, class, or sanctioned stereotypes.[93]

Second, regarding embodied personhood. As a survivor myself, I understand how "oppositional logic" has rightly attempted to empower the oppressed voice by securing dignity and personal autonomy, but secondary problems have also resulted. Politics no longer recognizes any roots or accountability to theology; rather, it is quite the opposite. And this has raised another problem—the *disembodied* victim. Here's the issue: if image is cognitive capacity, the *imago Dei is *reason*; if worship is central, the image is *spiritual*; if the aesthetic is primary, then image is *creativity*; if image is Trinitarian, emotion-filled relationship, then image is *relational*.[94] Notice that the net result of all these emphases is locating God's image in the *interior* of the person.[95] This, however, is a serious misstep for a theology of sexuality, much less addressing physical violence that is sexual in nature. A holistic biblical anthropology, what Patrick Miller calls a "Christian anthropology" of differentiation and interdependencies,[96] requires a greater balance of internal and external realities of personhood. Living and wounding is spatio-temporal; so is healing.

The push to define "image-through-equality" (true as that may be), especially in recent Trinitarian theologies has, unfortunately and unnecessarily, resulted in minimizing *corporality or ignoring the *embodied realities* of personhood altogether.[97] While gender

91. Ibid., quoting Weir, *Sacrificial Logistics*, 3.

92. Volf (*Exclusion and Embrace*, 187), summarizing the views of Daniel Boyarin and Rosemary Radford Ruether (Boyarin, *A Radical Jew*, 195; Radford Ruether, "Christian Anthropology and Gender," 251), respectively.

93. Volf (*Exclusion and Embrace*, 186–187), quoting Weir, *Sacrificial Logistics*, 3, 7. Both sexuality and gender find foundational address in the Creation Mandate of Gen 1:26–28 and 2:18–24. Men and women cannot be defined simply by what women and men are *not* (Ibid., 187), definition *via negativa*, the way of negation. Inclusion is sustained through difference. More biblical-theological work is needed here. John Giles' story illustrates how sanctioned stereotypes can operate. When he tried to speak of his sexual abuse perpetrated by his own mother, he was called a liar and told this was his "patriarchal fantasy" (Giles, "Forgiving the Unforgivable," 221; a helpful discussion is Tracy, "Patriarchy and Domestic Violence," 573–594).

94. Our exegetical analysis of Gen 1:26–28 does not simply allow a "grab bag" of all the above options. This serves neither biblical theology nor ethics. Goldingay stresses a similar concern: "The narrative hardly suggests that God combines male and female, nor is there anything in the context to point to a stress on relationality . . . Male and female is a *biological* distinction" (*Old Testament Theology*, 1:104; emphasis added).

95. Goldingay, *Old Testament Theology*, 1:102.

96. Miller, "Man and Woman," 317.

97. The otherwise helpful work of theologian Stanley J. Grenz also illustrates, I believe, a minimizing of embodied personhood for interpersonal communion in *The Social God and the Relational Self*. More recently, Leupp, *The Renewal of Trinitarian Theology*.

identity is more fluid, it nonetheless "stands in marked contrast to the stable difference of *sexed bodies*."[98] Both representing (via relationship) and resembling (via corporality) are vital to a theology of image. Those who would minister to the sexually traumatized must include the *somatic referent* in their definition of imaged personhood, corporality with equality.[99] It is the body, not the soul, that is the temple of the Holy Spirit (1 Cor 6:19–20). But re-dignifying the body can be difficult for survivors whose personal bodies can feel like "crime scenes," bodies prone to *dissociation. The somatic referent is the warrant, both for the victim's *complex PTSD (*post-traumatic stress disorder) as well as the sophisticated care of the trauma counselor, a child's *play therapist, and the victim's healing journey through constructive means of *self-soothing (e.g., a craft, gardening, dance).

Finally, regarding personhood and *eschatology. A strong argument can be made that heaven for the believer will still be realized as a *gendered* reality, since gender is part of personhood. The role of sexuality may be different (cf. Matt 22:30), but as Volf explains:

> Paul's claim that in Christ there is "no longer male and female" entails no eschatological denial of gender dimorphism. What has been erased in Christ is not the sexed body, but some important culturally coded norms attached to sexed bodies . . . The oneness in Christ is a community of people with sexed bodies and distinct gender identities, *not some abstract unity of pure spirits or de-gendered persons.*[100]

Similarly, Joel B. Green refers to life-after-death as "re-embodiment . . . provid[ing] the basis for relational and narrative continuity of the self."[101] Paul's descriptions of being "with Christ" and "in Christ" (Phil 1:23; 1 Thess 4:16) elevates simple prepositions to profound *relational* realities.[102] But this continuity of personhood may be both frightening and liberating for abuse survivors. Competent spiritual guidance is needed as survivors work through these eschatological implications of personhood. In this life and the next, our relationship with God is realized through gendered expression, even if it is a heavenly version. Thus, heaven as *The Great Healing* is not a release from the material body into "nakedness"—just the opposite!—it is into the "clothing" of a new *soma*, an unmolested body (2 Cor 5:1–3, 8).[103] In light of this eschatological reality, a reminder of what nakedness can mean is helpful. So we briefly return to the Eden narrative of Genesis 2.

NUDITY AND INNOCENCE VS. NAKEDNESS AND EXPLOITATION

When we contemplate the relational innocence and safety of Eden, the narrator has succeeded in the use of *implied contrasts*—nudity and safety don't compute this side of Eden![104] The beauty and fertility of the garden sanctuary (2:10–14) matches the innocence and fecundity of the garden's keepers (2:15). Nudity is a powerful concept biblically (2:25);

98. Volf, *Exclusion and Embrace*, 174; emphasis added.

99. Boyarin, *Paul and the Politics of Identity*, 239.

100. Volf, *Exclusion and Embrace*, 184; emphasis added.

101. Green, *Body, Soul, and Human Life*, 179.

102. Ibid., 178.

103. E. Schweizer, "*soma*," *EDNT* 3:323.

104. Though lost in English translation, the narrator employs a word play: the couple are "nude" (ʿārûmmîm, 2:25) and the snake is "shrewd" (ʿārûm, 3:1)—they're in trouble! (cf. 3:7, 10–11, 21).

it speaks of vulnerability (cf. Gen 9:22; Isah 47:1–3). Some of humankind's deepest relational dignities and social boundaries are at stake, so stripping someone was intentionally degrading and profoundly humiliating (2 Sam 10:4–5; Isah 20:4).

> Clothing is also such a boundary for the physical body, which is a microcosm of the social system. Nudity means the complete absence of boundaries; the body is accessible to any and everyone, thus destroying its exclusivity as something "set apart." [In the Old Testament] nudity erases social clues and so is unclean.[105]

To aggressively expose someone is to shame them (cf. Matt 27:28, 31). "Shame" implies physical exploitation and humiliation—"to be ashamed before one another,"[106] so the absence of shame for the garden couple is simply unimaginable for all who have grown up outside Eden (cf. Deut 28:48; Isah 58:7).[107] For the sexually abused and raped, however, shame, exploitation, and humiliation are not some sectarian custom or ancient Bible story—it is their story! It is the couple's rebellion that will dismantle their naked vulnerability (3:7, 10). First, we hear a significant celebration.

SEXUALITY IN CELEBRATION: GENESIS 2:23

Heralding a perfect complement, speech and celebration precede sex and preclude self-absorption: "This one finally, is bone of my bone, flesh of my flesh"—"They are *one*! That is, in covenant (2:24). The garden exists as a context for the human community."[108] Using "bone and flesh" means that the other person "is as close as one's own body."[109] This bonding, including sexually, means that what affects one, affects the other. Hurting one will hurt both (Eph 5:28–29).[110] Through the instrument and affirmation of speech, the image of God (1:26) is, to some degree, now *illustrated* in the man's poetic celebration (2:23).[111]

> "This one [zō't] is finally bone of [min] my bone,
> and flesh of [min] my flesh;
> this one [zō't] shall be called 'woman' ['iššâ],
> for from man [min 'îš] was taken this one [zō't]." (AT)

The man's words function as a testimony, an exuberant announcement in the very presence of his attending Creator. With punning poetry, the man's declaration sets human

105. Neyrey, "Nudity," 140. In Western culture, nudity is a form of self-expression, protected under the constitutional right of free speech (Ibid., 141).

106. The force of *Hitpolel* imperfect form of Gen 2:25, F. Stolz, "שׁוב," *TLOT*, 1:206. Nakedness can also function metaphorically for moral shame (e.g., Isah 20:2–4; 47:3; Ezek 23:28–29; Matt 22:11; Rev 16:15).

107. *Voyeurism and exploitation are vividly portrayed in Hab 2:15–16: "Woe to him who gives drink to his neighbors, pouring it from the wineskin till they are drunk, so that he can gaze on their naked bodies! You will be filled with shame instead of glory. Now it is your turn! Drink and let your nakedness be exposed!" The Scripture is clear, however, Israel was to clothe the naked (Isah 58:6–7; Job 22:6; 24:7, 10); and following Jesus, Christians are still to intervene for the naked and exploited (cf. Matt 25:36, 38, 43; 2 Cor 5:1–5; Jam 2:15; Rev 3:18).

108. Brueggemann, *Genesis*, 47.

109. Davidson, *Flame of Yahweh*, 31.

110. Waltke, *Genesis*, 89 n.39.

111. For further discussion see my "A Theology of Sexual Abuse," 797–99.

sexuality apart. The first time we hear the man speak is when he meets the woman who is truly another "suitable for him."[112] Sharing and receiving someone's voice forms a special connection (Song 2:14; John 10:27). The man "is saying yes to God in recognition of his own sexual nature and welcoming woman as the equal counterpart to his sexuality."[113] In short, the man illustrates how "words are rooted in reality because speech arises out of experience."[114] *What the reader hears is the sacrament of surprise, "this one"—definiteness so vital to healthy sexuality in marriage.* Genesis 2:23 is a benchmark of relational celebration—the "man" (*'îš*) for the visible presence of the "woman" (*'iššâ*).[115]

In the Old Testament, the face (*pānîm*) could be the most important part of a person's body, face being a relational concept referring to the entire person.[116] So one hears the "lover" declare in the Song of Songs, "Show me your face, let me hear your voice" (2:14). Intimacy has been stirred in these gardens (cf. 4:14; 6:2). Here is the "I–Thou–We" dynamic, initiated in divine declaration (1:26) and now matched in human celebration (2:23). Uniqueness of personhood (from the narrator, 1:27) has flowered in unity of relationship (from the man, 2:23). This unity was creation's design, the paring of one "male and female" that Jesus refers to as the original plan (Mark 10:6–9). We now take a closer look at sin and its consequences.

THE RELATIONAL ECOSYSTEM: SEXUALITY AMID CONSEQUENCES

Christian theology has historically separated culture from nature and nature from theology, which unfortunately has dichotomized the temporal from eternal, material from the spiritual, and so creation from redemption.[117] "Science has now stepped in as lord of the

---

112. Departing from the Hebrew MT ("I will make"), LXX-Gen reemploys the plural pronoun in Gen 2:18 ("let us"), an intentional connection to the plural usage in Gen 1:26. The Vulgate's plural (*faciamus*) reflects Trinitarian sympathies of Christians, not a different *Vorlage*, but, would have been problematic "for Jewish monotheistic readers" (van der Louw, *Transformations in the Septuagint*, 133).

113. Davidson, *Flame of Yahweh*, 34.

114. Wood, *The Gospel According to Tolkien*, 33. The implications for validating the experience of survivors by listening to various expressions of their stories, is quite evident, both inside and outside the church (e.g.,*narrative therapy, confrontations, drama, victim impact statements, letters, testimonies, prayers, poetry, etc.).

115. For a discussion of how sexual abuse disfigures the "face identity" of others, see my, "A Theology of Sexual Abuse," 797–99.

116. van der Woude, "*pānîm*," *TLOT* 2:1001.

117. Of early Christian exegesis surrounding sexuality, marriage and Christ, Elizabeth A. Clark writes:
[T]he metaphor of 'celibate Bridegroom' enabled Christians simultaneously to valorize the institution of marriage while lauding (in a titillating manner) sexual continence . . . Tertullian had instructed his wife that in their heavenly reunion there would be no resumption of 'voluptuous disgrace between us' . . . the Church Fathers understood metaphor all too well: sexual associations continued to 'hover over' the metaphor of the 'celibate Bridegroom,' keeping sexual renunciation as an object of erotic desire, while prompting patristic writers to keep on theologizing ("The Celibate Bride Groom," 1, 24, 25; quoting Tertullian, *Ad uxorem* 1.1).

domain which man used to refer to Creation."[118] All this has left a *fragmented* universe[119] and a truncated salvation that lacks holism and *restoration* (cf. Rom 8:19–22).[120] This is disconcerting at several levels.

As God's vice-regents, people live and interact within a *relational ecosystem* of dynamic proportion.[121] In the garden-sanctuary, foundational bonds are established between: the human and God, humankind and the ground, human and animal, and between humans. Though somewhat distasteful to contemporary readers, in the theology of Genesis, one's place of origin and the nature of their birth determine the core characteristics and purpose in life.[122] In addition to humankind made in the image of God (1:26, discussed above), other significant "bindings" include: the "human" (*ʾādām*) extracted from the "humus" (*ʾădāmâ*, 2:7) and the "woman" (*ʾiššâ*) extracted from the "man" (*ʾîš*, 2:22). So Adam is uniquely bound to the fertility of the soil as Eve is uniquely bound to the fertility of the body.[123] The animals are also "formed out of the ground" (2:19) as "creatures that move on the ground" (1:30). Thus, *the biblical notion of self is a relationally "embedded" self, rooted in a web of extended relationships.*[124] This contrasts with the Western value of the individual as an *unembedded* self. It's important to observe then, how the relational ecosystem is shattered in Genesis 3. The mistrust of rebellion breaks this web of relationships (3:5).

The "Bindings" Break Apart

Both functional and relational,[125] the *compensatory judgments* of 3:14–19 follow the order of transgression (serpent → woman → man; cf. 3:1–7).[126] Naham M. Sarna helpfully observes that the judgment for each party not only: (1) affects what is of central concern

---

118. Westermann, "Biblical Reflection on Creator-Creation," 92. First written in 1971, his modernist concerns still apply to a postmodern church culture now struggling with finality in suffering and redemption.

119. Hiebert, "Creation," 1:780.

120. "We know that the whole creation has been groaning as in the pains of childbirth right up to the present time" (Rom 8:22). The Greek prepositions used here stress all the parts of which creation is comprised, together "groaning" and "travailing."

121. The insightful language of McFadyen, *Bound to Sin*, 79, 233; and Biddle, *Missing the Mark*, esp. 115–139.

122. Levenson, "Genesis," 8. Cf. Gen 18:10–15 with 21:1–3, 6; 19:36–38; 25:22–27; 38:27–29, 41:50–52.

123. In the ancient Near East world, the woman defined "barrenness" since procreation was viewed in agricultural terms—he as farmer, she as arable land. His "seed" was sown in the "empty soil" where it was nurtured to "maturity" as the "fruit of the womb" (cf. Deut 7:13; 28:4). Rather than biologically caused, childlessness was a theological issue for prayer (Gen 25:21; 1 Sam 1:11), and supervised by the Creator who could always perform another act of creation (Gen 30:2, 23; 1 Sam 1:6, 27; Luke 1:7, 36; cf. Gen 12:17; 20:17–18; Eccl 11:5).

124. Di Vito, "Old Testament Anthropology and the Construction of Personal Identity," 217–238. Again, this solidarity is well illustrated in Gen 3:15 with "you . . . woman; your seed . . . her seed" (cf. Gen 28:14, "Your descendants will be like the dust of the earth, and you [sg.] will spread out").

125. Arnold, *Genesis*, 60.

126. It is interesting to note that after the transgression (3:1–7), even the plural forms (verbs and pronouns) disappear; twenty some plural uses now fall silent in 3:8–19. One more clue to community now shattered.

in the life of that entity, (2) but also regulates an external relationship.[127] Thus, there is some measure of correspondence between the offense and the judgment, point of origin, and future orientation. Relational hostility will exist between humans and the serpent (3:15).[128] The woman will pursue fertility amid relational antagonism with the man (3:16b).[129] Similarly, the man pursues the soil's fertility amid its antagonism (3:17–18). Their points of origin no longer offer security or fulfillment. While the Creation Mandate remains, it is pain and alienation that bind relationships now (Gen 5:29; Eccl 2:23). The man's "painful toil" (*ṣābôn*, 3:17) working the ground repeats her "pains" (*etseb*) enduring childbirth (3:16).[130] A final bond is ruptured when the couple is "banished" from the presence of the LORD (3:23). Once Abel's blood soaks into "the ground" (4:10), it "will no longer yield its crops" for Cain (4:12), and ultimately a pervasive "wickedness" reigns in "the human heart" (6:6), stunningly matched by the "pain" (*atsab*) of the LORD's grieving "heart" (6:6).[131] Sin has ecological and cosmic effects—from creature to Creator, the entire relational ecosystem now suffers (6:7; Deut 11:13–17; Rom 8:22).

When theology is severed from the foundational Creator-creature relationship, then a veneer of anthropology is all that remains. The practical outcome is both a shallow theology of sexuality and a minimizing of the holistic needs of victims who may simply be told that "all things God works for the good" (Rom 8:28a).[132] So Claus Westermann prophetically warns:

> When the theology and the preaching of the Church are concerned only with salvation, when God's dealings with man is limited to the *forgiveness of sins or to justification, the necessary consequence is that it is only in this context that man has to deal with God and God with man . . . what sort of God is he who does everything for the salvation of man but clearly has nothing at all to do with man in his life situation?[133]

127. Sarna, *Genesis*, 27.

128. I take the imperfect forms of the same Hebrew verb (*šûp*) in 3:15b as *iterative*, stressing reciprocal and persistent hostility from both parties (so "strike" used of both parties, NRSV, Tanak, HCSB; similarly ESV ["bruise"]).

129. Much discussion surrounds the woman's "desire" and the man's "rule" in 3:16b (see the recent survey of views in Davidson, *Flame of Yahweh*, 58–80). Suffice to say that framing the issue as *prescriptive* verses *descriptive* largely isolates a (Western) concern with personal fairness and ethics, but offers limited resolution to the issue, contextually. It may be better to view the nature of the oracle as *life-illustrative* verses *life-stipulative*; that is, what *does* happen, not what *should* happen. It goes without saying that this is no warrant for any abusive action or avoiding any measures that would alleviate suffering for any party.

130. Rhetorically, the compensatory judgments of the serpent and man *encloses* the woman within one divine discourse (e.g., "you will eat" [14b, 17b], "all the days of your life" [14b, 17b]), etc., and also move *through* her—she is the only party mentioned in all three oracles (15a, 16a, 17a). That 3:16 cannot be read in isolation from the serpent and the man, is also evident in the *asyndetic* syntax (without a conjunction) of v.16, connecting 3:14–19, making the woman's oracle appositional to the others (i.e., "to the serpent [v.14] . . . to the woman [v.16]").

131. Arnold, *Genesis*, 91.

132. More deserves to be said on this *reductionism, often cited by the non-abused. Suffice to say that the insensitive application of Rom 8:28 in the face of a victim's traumatic experience comes horrifyingly close to divine *collusion with evil (i.e., "Omelets come from broken eggs, so you will be such a showcase of God's grace!").

133. Westermann, "Biblical Reflection on Creator-Creation," 92.

The biblical creation account, however, does not distinguish between nature, culture, and community. "For," as William P. Brown explains, "every text in which creation is its context, the moral life of the community is a significant subtext."[134]

SIN, ABUSE AND ITS ENVIRONMENT: "IT'S WORSE THAN WE THOUGHT"

In order to better address the brokenness to the relational ecosystem reflected in sexual abuse, we must move beyond such notions as an isolated "event," the autonomous self, and the legal equation of "sin-as-crime." "Sin is disruption of created harmony and then resistance to divine restoration of that harmony."[135] The problem is that standard notions of "sin-justification," "culpability-innocence," and "offense-forgiveness" are synthetic and binary, and therefore an inadequate diagnostic framework to identify, protect, purge, and bring healing to the individual lodged within a particular socalized context. *To understand and address sexual abuse, a fuller spectrum of sin's afterlife must be dealt with that explains the social embeddedness, *intrafamilial customs, trans-generational patterns, and *internalized beliefs.*

EVIL AND POLLUTION IN THE SIN-PORTFOLIO

Sexual abuse has a complex sin-portfolio, which helps explain the phenomenon of trans-generational victimization (cf. Matt 23:36; Luke 11:51). Sexual abuse-type sin occurs in organic systems of families, societies, and traditions, often going back generations. Sin has its own life cycle, its own environmental logic that moves from: (1) the *act*, (2) through the resulting *guilt*, (3) to the perversion that is brought to others as *consequence*.[136] Not all sin is equally devastating.[137] But sexually violating a dependent child, for example, is a profound betrayal of trust, an affront to their Creator, a toxin to their psyche, and the vandalism of community *shalom. Understanding the sexually abused means recognizing that any "act" is embedded in the tissues of relationships.

Evil is the resulting corruption of that environment, the exploding and imploding of creation that follows a despoiling act.[138] Cornelius Plantinga states it well: "[M]oral evil is *social and structural as well as personal*: it comprises a vast historical and cultural matrix" of derived effects—"we both discover evil and invent it; *we both ratify and extend it*."[139] Other chapters address the tenacity of such *family dysfunction. Sadly, the sin of sexual abuse illustrates how "evil often springs from the best of things rather than the worst."[140] This only complicates matters. Especially in a child's developmental years, such fine moral nuances are easily confused and perverted. Pollution follows from corruption.

134. Brown, "Creation," 293.

135. Plantinga, *Not the Way It's Supposed to Be*, 5.

136. Biddle, *Missing the Mark*, xviii.

137. A distinction recognized in both Protestant and Catholic traditions. So the *Second Helvetic Confession* (chap. 8): "We . . . confess that sins are not equal; although they arise from the same fountain of corruption and unbelief, some are more serious than others. As the Lord said, it will be more tolerable for Sodom than for the city that rejects the word of the Gospel (Matt 10:15; 11:20–24)."

138. Plantinga, *Not the Way*, 30.

139. Ibid., 25, 26; emphasis added.

140. Wood, *The Gospel*, 53.

For example, *a father's incest not only damages his child, it also pollutes his marriage—perverting the gift of sex at several levels.*[141] Those ministering to the sexually abused must be cognizant of the larger field of pollution within the relational ecosystem.

THE DISTORTION OF WORSHIP

Pollution corrupts by *addition*, combining what should be kept apart.[142] This polluting effect of sin inhibits worship through idolatry. "In idolatry a third party gets in between God and the human persons, adulterating an exclusive loyalty."[143] By God's design, intact families require sexual fidelity, so an incested child naturally begins to wonder if their abusing mother or father is their guardian or lover. The new abusive dynamic compromises the intended relationships by contaminating individuals, severing communities, and *so defiling the victim's proper orientation to God.*[144] Third parties are always wedge-shaped.[145] Throughout Scripture, idolatry and adultery are mirror images, theologically (Ezek 6:9; Mark 8:38). When personhood is misplaced, the symphony of doxology is muted. Exploring sexual abuse, Alistair McFadyen also notes this distorting effect on worship:

> Sin is hence, not so much free choice, as spiritual disorientation of the whole person at the most fundamental level of life-intentionality and desire . . . In all our relations, we live out an active relation or misrelation to God, we enter the dynamic of worshipping God or other forces and realities. Sin is therefore living out an active misrelation to God . . . Genuine transcendence, and so the grounds for genuine joy, are blocked.[146]

Understanding how worship can be disoriented for victims of abuse means helping them wade through the contaminating and dividing effects of sin—whether as self-idolatry or other-idolatry. Caring for the abused requires us to bring *counter-dynamics* into their relational ecosystem. Healing may take time, even a lifetime. But between the forgiveness of the *good Pardoner* and the healing of the *Great Physician*,[147] a survivor's worship can be renewed and even strengthened. That said, healing from abuse cannot be scripted. Restoring worship, however, may be the most precarious stretch of the journey home. Many wounded leave the path right here, at the juncture of joy.

FACING SIN'S ORGANIC CONTINUUM

Long after the sin may have been forgiven, the consequences can live on as part of the organic continuum of sin. This points-up the shortsightedness of the "blame-justification" model to address the multidimensional nature of evil surrounding SA.[148] As Mark Biddle explains:

141. Plantinga, *Not the Way*, 43.

142. Ibid., 45.

143. Ibid., 44.

144. For related discussion, see Beale, *We Become What We Worship*, esp. 268–282.

145. Plantinga, *Not the Way*, 44, 45. For examples of "putting away gods," cf. Gen 35:2; Josh 5:1–9; 24:14–15; Judg 10:6–16.

146. Alistair McFadyen, *Bound to Sin*, 221, 223, 237.

147. Plantinga, *Not the Way*, 149.

148. Biddle, *Missing the Mark*, 95, using the phrase of Ellens, "Sin or Sickness," 454.

[T]he biblical notion of sin as a mishandling of the uniquely human calling to bear the image of God in creation implies responsibility not only to God—first and foremost, of course—but also, in fulfillment of the call, to other people and to the created order. *Forgiveness must, therefore, include remedy and healing . . . [for] the real injury that outlives the act of wrongdoing.*[149]

Helping victims move toward remedy and healing brings real-time dignity to real injuries. These are the raw, if not fresh moments, for the scripted certainties of juridical claims tend to slip out the back when the ambiguities of sin show up. But the subtler and more pervasive danger of modernity's "turn to the subject" (noted earlier) runs aground here as well. When the autonomous self remains unaccountable or some consequences of evil are minimized because the harm was "unintentional"—then that act is placed beyond the realm of redemption.[150] Increasingly, "[T]he nexus of sin and its consequences—its afterlife in the everyday world—has no place in the popular Christian mind."[151]

The organic continuum of sin works with *antecedent condition* in its socio-religious environment as: cause → effect → further cause.[152] Stories such as the rape of Tamar (2 Samuel 13) show that, unless sin is checked, the continuum naturally "matures" into further results (Gen 15:16; Rom 1:18–32).[153] Evil's corrupting effects twist and pervert reality. Thus the dynamic of intergenerational transmission reflects: (1) children impacted by their parents' sins, (2) creating conditions that negatively affect the options available to the children, (3) predispose the children toward certain choices, (4) that contribute destructively to their present identities.[154] Sin is inherited not as legal guilt, but as the tendency to perpetuate parental behavior.[155]

In summary, while God is eager to forgive and heal, he does not alter the moral and physical principles that structure his creation. "Sin, as a continuum, twists reality and passes on this contorted system as an antecedent reality to those who come after, limiting their freedom to perceive reality properly and, thus, also their freedom to choose rightly."[156] From these factors, sexual violence can live on in families and social structures of society. Environment is not destiny, but environment is a predisposing factor.[157] The complex actions of biblical characters validate precisely this. In several biblical stories one

149. Ibid., 96; emphasis added.

150. Ibid., 97.

151. Ibid., 117.

152. Ibid., 131.

153. The way Paul emphasizes God's role as "Creator" (1:25) and his argument based on "nature" (1:19–20, 26–27) employs many elements taken from the image of God (Gen 1:26–27). Robert A. J. Gagnon states, "Paul's main problem with *homosexual practice was not that it was typically exploitative or promiscuous. . . . but that it was *a violation of God's will for male–female pairing established in creation*" ("Article Review of Stacy Johnson, *A Time to Embrace*," 71; emphasis added); for a helpful chart paralleling eight points of correspondence between Gen 1:26–27 and Rom 1:23, 26–27, see p. 71 of Gagnon's article. Also Gagnon's major study, *The Bible and Homosexual Practice*.

154. Biddle, *Missing the Mark*, 120; cf. Exod 20:5; 34:7; Num 14:18; Deut 5:9–10; Jer 32:18.

155. Ibid., 121; cf. Isah 65:6–7; Jer 11:10; 36:31.

156. Ibid., 128.

157. Ibid., 135.

sees heinous sexual acts whose actions in turn reverberate far beyond their own lives to warp the realities in which others act. Again, "*One sees sin lingering in the world, distorting perceptions, offering inauthentic possibilities, skewing the system, perpetuating itself . . .* forgiveness granted the first sinner in the chain of causation is sometimes, sadly, unable to interrupt the sequence if the seeds sown in the environment have already taken root in the lives of others."[158] We can demonstrate this continuum of sin by noting significant similarities in four Old Testament narratives.

ESCALATING VIOLENCE IN OLD TESTAMENT STORIES OF RAPE

Some familiar biblical stories of sexual violence illustrate how evil progressively shapes reality, colonizing itself through destructive social interactions that *increasingly tear apart the relational ecosystem*. In a stimulating study of Old Testament rape narratives, Frank M. Yamada uses a literary and rhetorical method to analyze the narratives of Genesis 34, Judges 19, and 2 Samuel 13, stories that reveal "explicit thematic or functional connections between them" when read alongside each other.[159] He finds that these "stories betray similar elements, development, and outcome," namely: (1) rape (2) that leads to excessive male violence (3) and culminates in social fragmentation (see table below).[160]

Yamada's findings supply further biblical demonstration for the organic spread of sin within the relational ecosystem. In fact, I would argue that eight to ten elements are so consistent in biblical stories of sexual violence that they form a *type-scene*, a programmatic sequence of familiar motifs.[161] This literary observation is achieved by reading these stories collectively, not just as individual accounts. In the following table, I place Yamada's three thematic observations within nine *additional* themes I've collected.[162] Adding Genesis 19 as a fourth text only confirms the profile and intensification of these themes.[163] Observe the table below.

158. Ibid., 130; emphasis added.

159. Yamada, *Configurations of Rape in the Hebrew Bible*, 11.

160. Ibid., 6, 2.

161. On type-scene, see Savran, *Telling and Retelling*, 7; a classic treatment is Alter, *The Art of Biblical Narrative*, 47–62.

162. This analysis also draws from the following literature: Hendel et al., "Gender and Sexuality," 71–91; Fields, *Sodom and Gomorrah*; Boda, *A Severe Mercy*; Younger, *Judges/Ruth*, 30–40, 349–66; Yamada, *Configurations of Rape*, 133–40; Bergen, *1, 2 Samuel*, 378–83; Arnold, *Genesis*; Matthews, *Judges & Ruth*.

163. I agree with K. Jeffrey Kuan that 2 Samuel 11 could also be considered as an additional rape narrative, especially since the organic continuum of sin evident in 2 Samuel 13 really begins with David's prior actions in 2 Samuel 11 ("Configurations of Rape," 257). However, space does not allow us to develop this powerful biblical account that includes deceit, male violence, death of a child, rape of a half-sister, murder of a half-brother, political rebellion, internal Israelite warfare, social fragmentation, etc. For our purposes, I only wish to isolate reoccurring themes shared by these narrative stories that construct a *type-scene*. Further study of the shared Hebrew vocabulary between these 4–5 texts is clearly needed. I want to thank my Hebrew students, George Quarles and Melissa Smith, for their assistance in developing this table.

SEXUAL VIOLENCE AND THEMATIC CONNECTIONS
WITHIN THE RELATIONAL ECOSYSTEM

Reoccurring Themes	Gen 19	Gen 34	Judg 19–20	2 Sam 13
1) Traveling Guest(s) in a City	1–3	1	15	
2) Violation of Hospitality Code		2, 7	15	8–11
3) Hostile City Residents	4–11	2, 23	22	
4) Night Evoking Danger	2–4		15–16, 20	
5) Threatened Male Gang Rape	5		22	
6) Door as Symbol of Personal Space	6, 9–11		22, 25–26	17–18
7) Rape of Female		2	24–25	14
8) Male-Male Violence	9, 11	25–26	Chap 20	28–29
9) Political Turmoil	13–28	13, 30	20:1	20, 30–36
10) Social Fragmentation	31–38	30	20:20	20, 22, 37–39
11) Absence of God		1–31	19:1–30	1–39
12) Narrator's Moral Assessment	16, 29	7	19:23, 30	(13:12; cf. 12:9)

Other chapters explore these narratives; here, I merely collate the reoccurring themes and highlight their progressive profile that reverberates between these texts. It is not surprising that numbers 1–6 reveal some *antecedent moral, domestic, and cultural patterns that lead up to* the female rape, excessive male violence, and social fragmentation—Yamada's core three (numbers 7, 8, 10). Collective shame and honor are very evident here. What begins with traveling strangers ends with people sexually violated, entire communities socially estranged or physically destroyed. I will comment briefly on themes 1, 6, 11, and 12, largely through the Lot narrative that Yamada does not address (Genesis 19).

The way travelers encounter the city "gate," whether welcoming or ominous, sets a *judicial tone for the entire narrative; stories that use menacing meetings of various kinds (Gen 19:1–2; cf. Judg 19:15).[164] Further, the "door" signals a deeper threshold. In the case of Lot, he is a keeper of both boundaries (e.g., gate, door), vital protection for vulnerable

---

164. When "gate" is used in Gen 34:24 (2x), the idiom ("going out of the gate") supports a military collocation in which the narrator humanizes a catastrophe of wholesale slaughter for the circumcised men functioning as the standing army; see Schmutzer, "All Those Going Out of the Gate of His City,'" 37–52.

strangers. The door functions as "personal space," a gateway to a far more private world (cf. Song 7:13; 8:9). Thus in these stories, movement itself is thematized with a threefold analogy: (1) entering the city gate, (2) passing through the door of a house, (3) and the threat of sexually penetrating the male or female body.[165] Sexual violence threatens every group, from male bodies to Lot's daughters, and finally Lot himself (19:5, 8, 9; cf. v. 36)! Breaching so many boundaries is not only hostility, but festers into greater violence, social disintegration, and vandalism of community shalom for all.

> The attempted violation of the house by the men of Sodom is the very image of rape . . . *In all narratives of sexual violence in the Bible, doors and entryways are central concepts in establishing narrative space*—marking a clear boundary between inside and outside—and *the site of violation is always on the rapist's own territory*.[166]

In these stories, rape—an abhorrent misuse of power—is both crime and catalyst, enflaming further brutalities. What happens to aliens and strangers is the antithesis of the command to "love them as yourself" (Lev 19:34). *Rape is the symmetrical opposite of hospitality*.[167] Not surprisingly, hospitality is implicitly tied to sexual danger.[168] Like a grotesque meal, "the host in Judges 19 offers the Gibeahites the concubine and his daughter as alternatives" to his male guest.[169] The rape of the concubine (Judges 19) is literally situated in a context of "religious, social, and moral decline,"[170]—"In those days there was no king in Israel; every man did what was right in his own eyes" (Judg 17:6 [chap. 19]; 21:25 RSV). How true: the concubine dies "with her hands on the threshold" of the door, what should have been a "safe zone" (19:26). The host shockingly spoke out of his moral conditioning, "do to them what is good in your own eyes!" (19:24 AT).

For Tamar, Amnon uses the door first to *isolate* a nurse, then *exclude* the shamed (2 Sam 13:17, 18). By contrast, the well-ordered Hebrew home was to be God-fearing, the very doors themselves testified of God's law and family shalom (Deut 6:9; cf. Exod 13:9; Matt 23:5).

165. Hendel et al., "Gender and Sexuality," 78.

166. Ibid., 80; emphasis added, citing Shemesh, "Biblical Stories of Rape Narratives," 315–344. The use of "inside vs. outside" boundaries is *constructively* used of marital exclusivity in Prov 5:15–23; a private vs. public motif that deserves further study in that text.

167. It is tempting to include the Lot narrative as a violation of hospitality code (shifting culpability from attempted gang rape), but this story is not that simple. First, the narrator has already hinted at the city's destruction (Gen 13:10) as well as their on-going wickedness (13:13). Further, God is aware of the "outcry" *against* Sodom, "cries for help from those who have been abused" (18:20–21; Boda, *A Severe Mercy*, 26, n.26). Clearly, the welcome of the *male* populous left much to be desired, but the men's express purpose "to know" (idiom for sexual intercourse/intimacy, 19:5, 8, 9; cf. 24:16) Lot's "guests," pushes the moral compass of this text beyond a breach of hospitality laws as "the wrong," which Lot also understood by offering his daughters "who have not known a man" (v. 8). In fact, S. Lasine argues that Judges 19 employs the Genesis 19 text ("Guest and Host in Judges 19," 40). I agree with Bill T. Arnold that arguments focused on poor hospitality have more to do with contemporary sexual politics (*Genesis*, 184; similarly, Levenson, "Genesis," 41; contra Carr, "Genesis," 36).

168. Hendel et al., 79. How serious must Jerusalem's sin be when her transgressions merit the punishment of Sodom (Isah 1:9; Jer 23:14; Ezek 16:48–49; Matt 10:15; Luke 10:12).

169. Younger, *Judges/Ruth*, 359.

170. Yamada, *Configurations of Rape*, 134.

Such stories can bring a rare expression of what Robert Alter calls "narrated monologue,"[171] the narrator's moral assessment or judgment—"They were shocked and furious, because Shechem had done an outrageous thing against Israel by sleeping with Jacob's daughter—a thing that should not be done" (Gen 34:7b; cf. Judg 19:23; 2 Sam 13:12). A thematic profile is also evident in God's absence or silence. So it is significant, I believe, when God's name is entirely withheld from a chapter of rape, deceit, and gruesome murder (Dinah, chap. 34), only to reappear in chapter 35 with "God" [10x], "El Bethel" [1x], "El-Shaddai" [1x], a divine audience (35:13) and eight occurrences of the names "Bethel" and "Israel."

THE NEW ORDER FOR THE REDEEMED

Moral order in sexuality has always been required of God's people, in any age. So it is significant to see how tightly Paul connects the Thessalonians' sexual ethics (1 Thess 4:3–8) with Christian love (4:9–12), and their future hope (4:13–5:11). The Dionysiac *fertility cult of their day was not their hope for a sure afterlife. Why should the Thessalonian Christians not participate in the sexual mores of their culture, because Paul claims that the Christians "are part of the eschatologically restored people of God,"[172] the fulfillment of Jer 31:31–34, with God's law now written on their hearts. Inscribed hearts is an upgrade from decorated doorways.

God's law that set his people apart in Moses' time still requires the Christians of Paul's day to distinguish themselves in their sexual behavior. Drawing on established texts of sexual conduct (Lev 18:1–30; cf. Ezek 22:9b–11), Paul exhorts a largely Gentile audience to "a holy life" (1 Thess 4:7).[173] Holiness is more prominent in 1 Thessalonians than anywhere else in Paul and, empowered by the Holy Spirit (4:8), practically embraces all of one's life (5:23).[174] They must stand apart from their society in their sexual activity, controlling their sexual urges.[175] Believers recognize that the body is "a gift from God through which we can manifest our Christian discipleship and obedience to the Lordship of Christ

171. Alter, *The Five Books of Moses*, 190. Alter comments:
This entire clause is a rare instance in biblical narrative . . . the narrator conveys the tenor of Jacob's sons' anger by reporting in the third person the kind of language they would have spoken silently, or to each other. It is a technical means for strongly imprinting the rage of Jacob's sons in the presence of their father who has kept silent and, even now, gives no voice to his feelings about the violation of his daughter (Ibid).

172. Thielman, *Theology of the New Testament*, 243, 244.

173. The prohibited sexual unions of Lev 18:7–23 are summarized for Gentile converts in Acts 21:25 under the term *porneia*. That these are not "Jewish rules" being placed on Gentiles is confirmed by noting that Acts 21:25 is merely honoring what had already been stipulated in 15:22–29. The *Didache* (known as the teaching of the apostles to the nations) has similar language and instructions for Gentile converts (*Did.* 2.2; see Milavec, *The Didache*, 170).

174. Marshall, *New Testament Theology*, 243; cf. 1 Thess 3:13; 4:3–4, 7; 5:23; 2 Thess 2:13; of the Holy Spirit's enablement, Ezek 36:27; Rom 8:1–4; Gal 5:16; 1 John 3:24.

175. Whether translated "wife" or "body" (so NRSV, TNIV, cf. 2 Cor 4:7), *skeuos* in 4:4 is lit. "vessel" and likely refers to the male sexual organ; see Smith, "Another Look at 4Q416 2ii.21," 499–504. On incest in the early church, see Koskenniemi, *The Exposure of Infants among Jews and Christians in Antiquity*, 53, 95, 97, 98, 100, 102, 131, 133, 145, 157.

in the public, visible world. Thereby accepting Christ as Lord becomes communicable and credible, which it would not be if it were merely an 'inner' or 'private' matter."[176] This critiques "my sex life" mentality. So Paul warns them that "no one should wrong or take advantage of a brother or sister" (4:6a). Because sin still pollutes communities, holiness is still required and "evidenced in sexual purity."[177]

The foundation for sexual ethics is doing God's will (Rom 12:1–2; 1 Cor 6:20; Eph 6:6). The ground for sexual conduct "is their status as part of the eschatologically restored people of God predicted by the prophets."[178] The believer's new identity stems from their "new humanity 'in Christ' [that] provides new creation and new corporate solidarity. Thus *evil forces in the world are more powerful than isolated individuals.*"[179] The Christian community is to be morally preserving. As Thielman states, "*Their relationships should not be characterized by exploitative sex but by a quality of love that signifies the eschatological work of God in their hearts . . .* God has chosen them to belong to his society."[180] So for the believer, the body is to be used to communicate what Christian service and futurity means.[181] Moral order is necessary for believers who are awaiting the full arrival of their new creation.

CONCLUSION

Among other things, understanding biblical sexuality means our expectations are not only rooted in the Creator's designs but we are also deeply aware of the fractured portrait of sexuality. We must acknowledge that Scripture's intention contrasts sharply with lived-experience, but biblical guidance is also given because of sexual corruption. To minister to the sexually abused, it is not enough to affirm "original sin" as some kind of theological escape clause. Instead, we must actively engage the "actual sin" of their violation. Solidarity with the abused requires a vulnerable empathy.

Speaking out is important, but so is writing down. Locally, we need leaders in the faith communities to draw up comprehensive policies against sexual abuse—for the healing of this generation and the protection of the next. It is hoped that our analysis fosters a redemptive grief for the abused who need the informed understanding of their Christian brothers and sisters in order to heal—their spiritual family. At one level, I look for a day when collective restitution, in a *sacramental declaration*, can be made on an inter-faith and international scale.

We also considered the profound "fall-out" of sexual abuse, largely by noting the dynamic nature of the relational ecosystem. Victims, infant and elderly; the sexually broken among the abused and abuser—all share the dignity of the image of God that connects us

---

176. Thiselton, *The Living Paul*, 70; emphasis original, citing Käsemann, *New Testament Questions of Today*, 135, cf. 108–37.

177. Marshall, *New Testament Theology*, 243.

178. Thielman, *Theology of the New Testament*, 245.

179. Thiselton, *The Living Paul*, 79; emphasis original.

180. Thielman, *Theology of the New Testament*, 245; emphasis added.

181. Thiselton, *The Living Paul*, 73.

to all realms of God's creation. This not only shapes the spectrum of relational trauma, it also highlights the relational contexts of healing. Creation theology shows us the male-female prerequisite for sexuality, affirmed throughout Scripture. Theologically, personhood is found in royal community for an ethical mission, making sexual abuse—the plundering of a fellow-image bearer—an inverted mission capable of intergenerational pollution. In the ministry of healing the sexually abused, it is vital to affirm the embodied realities of life, rather than isolating the nature of the image in the *interiority* of the person.

Those seeking to help the sexually violated must face the colonizing effects of sin that surround abusive relationships. "Sin-as-act" must also be viewed within the larger "neighborhood" of evil. This is the trans-generational nature of sexual abuse that must be addressed by pastor, counselor, and community alike. The vandalism of community shalom often results from the *antecedent* effects of sin. This needs more open and honest address in believing communities. Christian leaders must understand sin's *afterlife*, the polluting effects of abuse to sexuality. The way abuse disorients the survivor's relationship to God is devastating. This needs more holistic address from therapists and pastors. The community of the redeemed can truly be the healing family for the sexually broken. The moral order among God's citizens is to be a foretaste of mystery restored.

QUESTIONS FOR DISCUSSION

1. This chapter discusses how sexuality is both: (a) an embodied reality (b) and functions within a *relational ecosystem*. Whether you are a counselor, pastor, or abuse survivor, how does this fact impact your practice, ministry, and care for survivors? What have you experienced that illustrates the beauty, complexity, and fragility of this dual reality (both a, b)? When it comes to working with the abused, how does the *revealed truth* of Scripture work alongside *observed truth* of the sciences and the victim's lived-experience? In your practice, teaching, and ministry, how have you personally balanced these?

2. The author stated that there is a "need for collective restitution and healing on an international and inter-faith scale"; do you agree? Why or why not? From the perspective of survivors, why might this be meaningful? From the perspective of the Christian Gospel and social justice ministries? What might restitution look like on this scale? What could local churches do to contribute toward greater collective naming and healing of sexual abuse? What do you think is keeping this from happening?

3. How does a fuller understanding of creation theology bring dignity to sexuality? Explain the significance of sexuality being rooted in *doxology*? What is both dignifying and dangerous about personhood as "being-in-relation," the *I-Thou-We* of life? As discussed, what are the implications of sexuality serving as an "envelope" theme around Genesis 1 and 2 (see chart)? How do God's initial instructions to humankind actually *foster* life? Establish boundaries? Democratize dignity? Explain the significance of human sexuality being defined within community? What does this mean for therapy and healing rituals? How can preaching better communicate this?

4. The author argues that the image of God includes both *representation* and *resemblance*, a stewardship for God and ethical mission from God. How does this view of image relate to the forms of trauma survivors face? More holistic views of healing? How can one's view of the image of God create a *disembodied* victim? How is the danger of "disembodied" victims addressed in your practice or teaching ministry? Explain how reproduction and governance relate to the image of God and the Creation Mandate. In your opinion, what are the implications of this for a theology of sexuality? When the creation story consistently speaks of the human person in the plural, what are the implications of this?

5. Discuss the results of defining identity through subject–object opposition (i.e., oppositional logic). What are the pros and cons of using *paradigms of exclusion* when working with abuse survivors? Discuss Volf's preference for defining gender identity as "not-without-the-other," rather than *neutralizing* or *synthesizing* gender. How does this biblical-theological discussion help shape your approach in working with survivors?

6. What is the *organic continuum* of sin? Based on this chapter discussion, how does sexual abuse "live on" in systems of families, societies, and traditions? Explain the role of *antecedent sin* in Old Testament stories of rape and social fragmentation. Why is it important to understand the *afterlife* of sin when working with survivors? How do these theological and sociological truths overlap with *best practices in counseling? How can preaching and theological education more fully address the social, structural, and personal aspects of evil? Explain how evil corrupts a child's environment and sense of personal options, often perpetuating that evil?

7. Based on the discussion, how does the sin of sexual abuse stifle a survivor's worship by "defiling the victim's proper orientation to God?" What are the processes operating here? If you are a survivor, did you find this true in your life? As a Christian leader or therapist, how have you seen this play out among survivors you've worked with? How can modernity's "turn to the subject" actually hinder healing? Explain. Why is the nexus of sin and its consequences such a difficult notion for popular Christianity to accept? What are the implications of this for healing ministries in churches? What are some false messages that survivors may be entertaining about their own healing?

8. Explain the significance of Paul connecting the Thessalonians' sexual ethics (1 Thess 4:3–8) with their future hope (4:13–5:11). In what ways are the sexual ethics of believers related to eschatology? How does sexual sin "pollute" communities? From a biblical perspective, explain how our bodies are an integral part of Christian discipleship. Why is any exploitative sexuality incompatible with the Gospel and Christ-like character?

FOR FURTHER READING

Ash, Christopher. *Marriage: Sex in the Service of God*. Leicester: IVP, 2003.

Barnes Lampman, Lisa. Ed. *God and the Victim: Theological Reflections on Evil, Victimization, Justice, and Forgiveness*. Grand Rapids: Eerdmans, 1999.

Biddle, Mark E. *Missing the Mark: Sin and Its Consequences in Biblical Theology*. Nashville, TN: Abingdon, 2005.

Davidson, Richard M. *Flame of Yahweh: Sexuality in the Old Testament*. Peabody, MA: Hendrickson, 2007.

Hollinger, Dennis P. *The Meaning of Sex: Christian Ethics and the Moral Life*. Grand Rapids: Baker, 2009.

McFadyen, Alistair. *Bound to Sin: Abuse, Holocaust and the Christian Doctrine of Sin*. Cambridge: Cambridge University Press, 2000.

Plantinga, Cornelius Jr. *Not the Way It's Supposed to Be: A Breviary of Sin*. Grand Rapids: Eerdmans, 1995.

Schmutzer, Andrew J. "Spiritual Formation and Sexual Abuse: Embodiment, Community, and Healing." *Journal of Spiritual Formation and Soul Care* 2 (2009): 67–86.

———. "A Theology of Sexual Abuse: A Reflection on Creation and Devastation." *Journal of the Evangelical Theological Society* 51 (2008): 785–812.

Volf, Miroslav. *The End of Memory: Remembering Rightly in a Violent World*. Grand Rapids: Eerdmans, 2006.

9

Sexual Abuse in the Old Testament

An Overview of Laws, Narratives, and Oracles

RICHARD M. DAVIDSON, PhD

IN THE CONTEXT OF the Old Testament, *sexual abuse (SA) may be defined as "the violation of another physically, psychologically, and/or emotionally through the commission of a non-consensual sexual act that is imposed by the use of domination, force, and/or violence."[1] In this chapter we will examine Old Testament laws, narratives, and prophetic oracles that relate to sexual abuse.[2]

OLD TESTAMENT LEGISLATION CONCERNING SEXUAL ABUSE

Exod 22:16–17 [Heb 15–16] and Deut 22:28–29: Seduction of a Single Woman

Exodus 22:16–17 [Heb 15–16] contains a case law regarding the seduction of a single (unbetrothed) woman: "When a man seduces [*pātâ*] a virgin who is not engaged to be married, and lies with her, he shall give the bride-price for her and make her his wife. But if her father refuses to give her to him, he shall pay an amount equal to the bride-price for virgins."[3] Deuteronomy 22:28–29 presents similar legislation: "If a man meets a virgin who is not engaged, and he seizes her [*tāpaś*] and lies with her, and they are caught in the act, the man who lay with her shall give fifty shekels of silver to the young woman's father, and she shall become his wife. Because he violated [*'ānâ, pi'el*] her, he shall not be permitted to divorce her as long as he lives." The law in Exod 22:16–17 [Heb 15–16] is clearly a situation of verbal persuasion or seduction (the meaning of *pātâ*), but commentators differ on whether Deut 22:28–29 describes a case of forcible *rape or seduction (*statutory

---

1. Lipka, *Sexual Transgression in the Hebrew Bible*, 21. Lipka calls this kind of sexual act a "sexual transgression against personal boundaries," as opposed to sexual transgression against religious and/or communal boundaries.

2. For more complete discussion (with bibliography) of this biblical material, see Davidson, *Flame of Yahweh*, passim.

3. NRSV here and elsewhere, unless otherwise noted.

rape). This latter passage indicates that the man "seizes" (*tāpaś*) and "violates" (*ʿānâ*, *pi'el*) the woman. The verb *tāpaś* usually implies taking hold with force, and the verb *ʿānâ* in the *pi'el* ("mishandle, afflict, violate") is used several times elsewhere in the Old Testament to describe clear cases of forcible rape.[4] However, this passage in Deuteronomy 22 also seems to indicate that the woman had acquiesced and was a willing partner in the sexual encounter, when it notes that "*they* [not just he] are caught in the act [*wĕnimsāʾû*]" (v. 28).

Both of these laws are probably speaking of similar (but perhaps not identical) situations of sexual seduction (statutory rape) of a virgin who is not betrothed, the former involving or emphasizing more the psychological pressure (he "seduces" [*pātâ*] her) and the latter the physical pressure (he "catches, takes, seizes" [*tāpaś*] her).[5] The two laws are complimentary, the Deuteronomy passage being an extension of the Exodus law, and together they give the whole picture of circumstances and legal consequences.

These two Pentateuchal passages are best regarded as dealing with statutory, not forcible, rape (with the woman voluntarily submitting to the man's pressure to have sexual intercourse), *but even though the woman apparently consents to engage in sexual intercourse with the man in these situations, the man nonetheless has "afflicted/humbled/violated her"* (*ʿinnāh*). The Edenic divine design that a woman's purity be respected and protected has been violated. The penalty imposed is that either the rapist had to marry the one he had seduced and support her financially all her life (without possibility of divorce), or else the girl's father (as legal guardian) could on her behalf exercise the right of refusal and demand monetary payment equivalent to the dowry even though the seducer did not marry her.

Even though the woman may have acquiesced to her seducer, *nonetheless according to the law, the dowry is "equal to the bridewealth for virgins"* (Exod 22:16 [Eng 17]): *she is treated financially as a virgin would be!* Such treatment upholds the value of a woman against a man taking unfair advantage of her, and at the same time discourages sexual abuse.

Deuteronomy 22:25–27: Forcible Rape

Deuteronomy 22:25–27 gives legislation that clearly refers to forcible rape: "But if a man finds a betrothed young woman in the countryside, and the man forces [*āzaq*] her and lies with her [*šākab ʿimmāh*], then only the man who lay with her shall die" (v. 25 NKJV). In the context of this passage the verb *hāzaq* (*hip'il* with the *bĕ* preposition), "force," denotes the overpowering of a weaker by the stronger.[6] Verses 26–27 verify that this is the case: the young woman was not guilty, since she was forced against her will, like a victim in a murder, and since she was presumed to have cried out in the countryside but there was no one to hear.

---

4. See Gen 34:2 (Shechem's rape of Dinah); Judg 19:24; 20:5 (the men of Gibeah's rape of the Levite's concubine); and 2 Sam 13:12, 14, 22, 32 (Amnon's rape of Tamar).

5. That these two laws are variants of the same case is recognized by a number of scholars. See especially Pressler, *The View of Women Found in the Deuteronomic Family Laws*, 35–41.

6. Cf. Gen 19:16; Judg 19:25; 1 Sam 15:27; 17:35; 2 Sam 2:16; 13:11; Dan 11:7, 21. See BDB, 304; *HALOT* 303–304.

It is important to note that here the "biblical law assumes her innocence without requiring witnesses [22:27]; she does not bear the burden of proof to argue that she did not consent. . . . [I]f the woman *might* have been innocent, her innocence must be assumed."[7] But the man who violates the woman in this way receives the death penalty. *Thus the Mosaic Law protects the sexual purity of a betrothed woman (and protects the one to whom she is betrothed) and prescribing the severest penalty to the man who dares to sexually violate her.*

Leviticus 21:7, 14: The Rape Victim's Ineligibility as a Priest's Marriage Partner

Leviticus 21:7–9 lists prohibitions concerning marriage for priests, and vv. 10–15 enumerate prohibitions for the high priest. According to v. 7, "They [the common priests] shall not marry a prostitute [or promiscuous woman, *zōnâ*] or a woman who has been defiled [*wahălālâ*]; neither shall they marry a woman divorced from her husband. For they are holy to their God." According to v. 14, "A widow, or a divorced woman, or a woman who has been defiled [*wahălālâ*], a prostitute [*zōnâ*]—these he [the high priest] shall not marry; he shall marry a virgin of his own kin." Some commentators have taken *wahălālâ* as a reference to a woman's defilement by (cultic) prostitution, but Jacob Milgrom, after critiquing this and other interpretations, has made a strong case for translating this term as "one who was raped."[8] Though a rape victim was not stigmatized in ancient Israel with reference to being an appropriate marriage partner for a lay person, this passage indicates a *progression* in holiness, from a common person, who could presumably marry any of the aforementioned classes of women denied to the priests; to the common priest, who could not marry a prostitute or a divorcee but could marry a widow; to the high priest, who must only marry a virgin of his own house who has never been married. Significantly, as Milgrom demonstrates, these prohibitions focus on *reputation*, not on virginity.[9] There is simply a higher standard of purity (of reputation) demanded of a priest's bride than of the bride of a common person.

PENTATEUCHAL NARRATIVES INVOLVING SEXUAL ABUSE

Genesis 19: Sodom and Lot's Daughters

The well-known story of Lot and his daughters in Sodom (Gen 19:1–11) need not be repeated in detail here; the term *"sodomy" as a reference to male *homosexuality is taken from this story. There is strong biblical evidence that this account, as well as the parallel narrative describing the homosexual advances of the men of Gibeah (Judges 19), tacitly condemns homosexual practice in general, and in particular, expresses revulsion at the violent male homosexual *gang rape that was initially contemplated.[10] The story also al-

7. Keener, "Some Biblical Reflections on Justice, Rape, and an Insensitive Society," 126; emphasis original.

8. Milgrom, *Leviticus 17–22*, 1806–1808, 1819.

9. Ibid., 1808.

10. See esp., Gagnon, *The Bible and Homosexual Practice*, 71–100; cf. the later biblical interpretation of

ludes to the rape of women, as Lot offers the men of Sodom his two virgin daughters to rape instead of his (angelic) visitors (Gen 19:8), an offer that might have been carried out were it not for the angelic intervention. The narrator's depiction of these stories clearly underscores the violence, vileness, and horror of the sexual abuse of rape.

Genesis 34: Dinah

A forceful example of sexual abuse in the form of rape that was actually carried out appears in the narrative of Genesis 34. The narrator records the incident succinctly (vv. 1–2): "Now Dinah the daughter of Leah, whom she had borne to Jacob, went out to visit the women of the region. When Shechem son of Hamor the Hivite, prince of the region, saw her [*wayyar' ōtāh*], he seized her [*wayyiqqaḥ ōtāh*] and lay with her by force [*wayyiškab ōtāh way'anneḥā*, lit., 'and he lay her and he violated/raped her']." The steps in the rape are described in swift succession: Dinah ventures into association with pagan women, Shechem lusts after her, in the heat of his desire he takes her and lies with her, thus violating her person.

Is this really a case of rape? Some commentators argue that Dinah probably consented to the illicit sexual union.[11] But a closer look at the grammar of this narrative—especially the exact use of terminology in comparison with the rape narrative of Tamar and Amnon (2 Samuel 13)—has led me to a different conclusion. The narrator in Gen 34:2 says that Shechem (literally) "lay her," (using the verb *šākab* in its *transitive sense plus the direct object *ōtāh*, rather than the usual intransitive sense of *šākab* plus prepositional phrase *'immāh*, "lay *with* her"), thus emphasizing the use of force in the sexual crime.[12] The preposition *'im* ("with") often implies *permission*. So, for example, in the narrative of the rape of Tamar, Amnon first asks Tamar's permission when he says, "come, lie with me ['*immî*]" (2 Sam 13:11), but after she refused, Amnon "forced her and lay her [*ōtāh*]" (v. 14). This clear distinction in usage in the parallel rape narrative, coupled with the contextual clues within the narrative itself, point toward the conclusion that force was employed by Shechem in his sexual encounter with Dinah. Several modern translations have captured this nuance by rendering this phrase in Gen 34:2 as "he lay with her *by*

---

the Sodom narrative as involving a sexual sin: Ezek 16:43, 48–50; Jude 6–7; 2 Pet 2:4, 6–8.

11. See, e.g., Bechtel, "What if Dinah Is Not Raped? (Genesis 34)," 19–36; Gruber, "A Re-examination of the Charges against Shechem Son of Hamor," 119–127; Lipka, *Sexual Transgression*, 184–198; Visotzky, *The Genesis of Ethics*, 197; Wolde, "The Dinah Story," 225–239; and Wyatt, "The Story of Dinah and Shechem," 433–458.

12. This crucial grammatical detail is highlighted by, e.g., Caspi, "The Story of the Rape of Dinah," 32; and Sternberg, *The Poetics of Biblical Narrative*, 446. Van Wolde ("The Dinah Story," 228) seeks to counter this interpretation by citing results of the study by Orlinsky, "The Hebrew Root ŠKB," 19–22, who concludes that "there is no semantic difference" between *škb ēt* and *škb 'im*. This may be true when *ēt* is used as a preposition (in parallel with the preposition *'im*), but contra Orlinsky (Ibid., 23–27), who claims that all suffix forms vocalized as *ōt-* refer back to the preposition and not to the sign of the direct object. In my view Sternberg and others have correctly recognized that in Gen 34:2, *škb ēt* occurs in precise parallelism with (and flanked on each side by) two other verbs unmistakably followed by the direct object marker, and thus the narrator's intent here (as in the parallel rape story in 2 Samuel 13) is for *ōtāh* to be taken as the direct object marker (plus the feminine singular accusative suffix) indicating the use of force and not as the preposition "with" (plus feminine suffix).

force."[13] *This deliberate use of precise terminology seems to imply that Dinah was a victim of forcible (and not just statutory) rape.* Perhaps what is involved is a situation which today we would call *"date rape."

The verb *'innâ* (*pi'el*), "violate," refers to the illegitimate sex act (or its consequences), but does not by itself indicate whether or not the woman gave her consent. However, in a number of other Old Testament passages this verb is used in a setting of forcible rape[14] and probably is best translated as "violate" or "rape." In the context of Genesis 34—especially in light of the grammatical construction in v. 2 discussed above and the fact that *at no point in the chapter is Dinah blamed for what has happened*—I conclude that Dinah did not consent. Thus the violation of Dinah as a result of forcible rape is in view.

The rapid succession of the three verbs—he "took" her, he "laid" her, and he "violated/raped" her—probably serves as a *hendiadys to "express the single action of rape. The use of this device underscores the act. On another level the three words also suggest a *progressive* severity. They emphasize Shechem's increasing use of violence against Dinah in v. 2b."[15]

After the rape, Shechem apparently abducted Dinah, brought her to his own house (v. 26) and tried to woo her (v. 3): "his soul was drawn [lit., "clung," *watidbaq*] to Dinah daughter of Jacob; he loved [*wayyĕ hab*] the girl and spoke tenderly [lit., "to/upon the heart," *'al-lēb*] to her." The same word "to cleave/cling" (*dābaq*) is used here as in Gen 2:24, where it describes the covenant bond of marriage, but the meaning is significantly changed: here the cleaving comes *after* sexual intercourse but outside the marriage covenant. The phrase "to speak upon the heart" is used ten times in the Hebrew Bible, and always "in less than ideal situations, where there is a sense of guilt or repentance, where A attempts to persuade B of his feelings."[16] The subsequent attempts on the part of Shechem to woo Dinah, the offers of his father to Jacob to arrange for a marriage between Shechem and Dinah, even the character assessment that Shechem "was more honorable than all the household of his father" (Gen 34:19 NKJV)—none of these facts lessen the heinousness of the sexual abuse that took place.

While in my reading of the narrative the evidence points toward forcible rape on the part of Shechem, I acknowledge that this evidence is not conclusive. But even if Dinah did consent to have sex with Shechem, it still would constitute (in today's terminology) "statutory" or "power rape." If Shechem did not physically force Dinah, his position of power as "son of Hamor the Hivite, the prince of the country" (Gen 34:2); should be regarded as a psychological forcing of Dinah, a case of sexual violence.[17]

13. So the NRSV, the JPSV, and the NASB; emphasis added.

14. See Judg 19:24; 2 Sam 13:12, 14, 22, 32; Ezek 22:11; Lam 5:11.

15. Scholz, *Rape Plots*, 138. Cf. Sternberg, *Poetics of Biblical Narrative*, 446.

16. Hamilton, *The Book of Genesis: Chapters 1–17*, 355. Besides this passage, see Gen 50:21; Judg 19:3; Ruth 2:13; 1 Sam 1:13; 2 Sam 19:8; 2 Chr 30:22; 32:6; Isah 40:2; Hos 2:16.

17. See below for further discussion of "power rape," in connection with David's sin against Bathsheba. Those who deny that Genesis 34 constitutes rape define "rape" more narrowly than I do. For example, Lipka (*Sexual Transgression*, 180) defines "rape" as having two essential elements: (1) the sexual act is forced against someone's will; and (2) the sexual act violates the victim on a personal level (i.e., psychological effects). I argue that the coercion may be psychological ("power rape") as well as (or instead of) physical, and the

Susanne Scholz's articles on Genesis 34 and published dissertation[18] reveal that many, if not most, modern interpretations of Genesis 34, even if they agree that it was forcible rape that is in view, nonetheless "contain numerous assumptions complicit with a contemporary belittlement of rape."[19] But a *close reading of the narrative brings us face to face with the horrible nature of the rape crime. The narrator calls the violation of Dinah "a wanton sin" (NKJV) or "outrage" (*nĕbālâ*, v. 7), a term often used elsewhere in the Old Testament to describe various wanton sexual crimes or other kind. of "serious disorderly and unruly action resulting in the breakup of an existing relationship whether between tribes, within the family, in a business arrangement, in marriage or with God."[20] It is "the worst kind [of crime]—something absolutely unthinkable in Israel."[21] The narrator also implies that—at least in the minds of Dinah's brothers—the whole city was corporately guilty for the defiling of their sister. The Hebrew of v. 27 reads literally, "The sons of Jacob came upon the slain, and plundered the city, because *they* [i.e., the city] had defiled (*timm'û*) their sister." Although Dinah's brothers were not justified in the slaughter of the inhabitants of Shechem in *retribution for this terrible act—one violent act does not justify another—nonetheless, *their reaction correctly assesses the reprehensibleness of the violating rape, and the sense of moral outrage at an act that disrupted the whole social order.*[22]

The account of Dinah's violation not only decries her rape by Shechem, but the carefully crafted narration perhaps emphasizes *by its silence* the denigration and oppression of the woman in the story.[23] Dinah never speaks! Even though she is sexually abused, *feminist interpreters point out, she is given no voice to protest. Even in the brother's retaliation for the heinous crime done against their sister, Dinah is apparently not given the full respect of her personhood.

As a sequel to the story, Jacob chides his sons for having made him and his household "obnoxious among the inhabitants of the land" (Gen 34:30 NKJV) by slaughtering the men of the city of Shechem in revenge for their sister's victimization. The sons respond with the rhetorical question: "Should our sister be treated like a whore [harlot]?" (v. 31). The text does not say that the violation of Dinah's sexuality had made her the equivalent of a harlot, as some commentators maintain. Rather, "the sons are asserting that *their failure to defend their sister's honor* would be tantamount to regarding her as if she were a harlot . . . The sons see very clearly that *in rape—a man, or a community, treats a woman the way a harlot treats*

---

psychological effects on the victim need not be explicitly spelled out by the narrator, in order for the sexual act to be identified as rape.

18. Scholz, "Was it Rape in Genesis 34?," 183–198; idem, *Rape Plots*, 105–147; and idem, "Through Whose Eyes?," 150–171.

19. Scholz, "Was it Really Rape in Genesis 34?" 195.

20. See Phillips, "Nebalah—A Term for Serious Disorderly and Unruly Conduct," 241. For the other sex-related crimes described using this term, see Deut 22:21; Judg 19:23, 24; 20:6, 10; 2 Sam 13:12; Jer 29:23.

21. Freedman, "Dinah and Tamar," 62.

22. See Scholz, *Rape Plots*, 160, 168.

23. This point is made by a number of feminist interpreters of this story. See, e.g., van Wolde, "The Dinah Story," 237 and *passim*; and Visotzky, *Genesis of Ethics*, 197.

herself."[24] That is, the sexual abuse of rape denigrates and violates a woman's whole being—body, mind, and spirit.[25]

SEXUAL ABUSE IN THE PROPHETS/WRITINGS

Outside the Pentateuch there are several passages in which the prophet predicts (or records) a foreign army conquering a nation (Judah, Babylon) and "ravishing" or raping the women.[26] In the Song of Deborah and Barak, King Sisera's mother, waiting at the window for her son to return from battle with the spoils of victory, muses:

> Have they not found and divided the spoil? —
> A womb [*raham*] or two for every man . . . ? (Judg 5:30 ESV)

As Roy Gane comments, "Sisera's mother callously and crudely refers to Israelite girls as 'wombs,' that is, physical objects to be raped by Sisera and his Canaanite soldiers."[27]

In the time of the divided monarchy, the punishment for adultery also included the husband's public (physical) exposure of his unfaithful wife, as illustrated in ancient Near East (ANE) parallels,[28] and this imagery is also employed by several of the prophets to express divine judgment of unfaithful Israel.[29] A number of feminist scholars have in recent years deconstructed these and other prophetic portrayals of Israel's spiritual adultery, and using the *"hermeneutic of suspicion" have concluded that in these passages Yahweh is to be regarded as a battering husband subjecting his wife to all manner of physical and psychological abuse.[30] Special anger is vented against the Yahweh of Ezekiel 16 and 23 for his subordination and public sexual abuse of his wife, which is regarded as an implicit sanctioning for human husbands to treat their wives in the same way.

In response to this feminist *deconstruction of the materials in the Prophets on spiritual adultery, and Ezekiel 23 in particular, Corrine Patton has provided a thoughtful response to the feminist critiques of Ezekiel 23 and its parallel biblical passages dealing with the divine judgment upon Israel's spiritual adultery.[31] After examining the historical

24. Kass, "Regarding Daughters and Sisters," 36; emphasis original.

25. For further emphasis upon rape as sexual violence in this narrative, see Scholz, "Through Whose Eyes?" 150–171.

26. Regarding Babylonian wives being raped, see Isah 13:15. For women of Judah being raped by Babylonian soldiers, see Jer 13:22 (cf. 26); Lam 5:11 (cf. 1:1–22); and perhaps Mic 4:11. For women of Judah being raped in the eschatological battle against the nations, see Zech 14:2. For discussion of the motif of rape in Lamentations, see Dobbs-Allsopp and Linafelt, "The Rape of Zion in Thr 1, 10," 77–81. Lipka, *Sexual Transgression*, 223–240, also suggests that the divine punishment of Judah at the hands of Babylon (Ezek 23:29) implies that Judah will be raped, but this is not explicit and far from certain.

27. Gane, *God's Faulty Heroes*, 56. Robert Alter points out that the twice-repeated description in the previous verse of Sisera falling (literally) "between her [Jael's] feet" (Judg 5:27) is "a hideous parody of soldierly sexual assault on the woman of a defeated foe" (*The Art of Biblical Poetry*, 46).

28. For ANE parallels to the punishment of stripping a woman naked and publicly exposing her, see Greenberg, *Ezekiel 1–20: A New Translation with Introduction and Commentary*, 287. Greenberg also notes that this punishment in the context of Ezekiel 16 "echoes the childhood nakedness of the woman in vs. 7" (ibid.).

29. See Ezek 16:35–42; 23:10, 22–35. Cf. Isah 20:2; 32:11; Nah 3:5, etc.

30. For bibliography, see Davidson, *Flame*, 365, n.108.

31. Patton, "'Should Our Sister Be Treated Like a Whore?'" 221–227.

setting of Ezekiel 23 in particular, Patton shows how "this text does not substantiate *domestic abuse; and scholars, teachers, and preachers must continue to remind uninformed readers that such an interpretation is actually a misreading." Rather, "the theological aim of the passage is to save Yahweh from the scandal of being a cuckolded husband, i.e. a defeated, powerless, or ineffective god . . . [I]t is a view of a God for whom no experience, not even rape and mutilation in wartime, is beyond hope for healing and redemption."[32]

Aside from these general references to rape, three episodes are recorded in detail where the sexual abuse of a specific woman is a key event in the narrative: the gang rape of the Levite's unnamed concubine (Judges 19); the power rape of Bathsheba by David (2 Samuel 11); and the incestuous rape of Tamar, daughter of David, by her half-brother Amnon (2 Samuel 13). I will take up each episode briefly in turn.

Judges 19: The Levite's Concubine

I will not recount this "text of terror" in detail, but rather focus on the horror of the violent act itself and the equal horror in the calloused indifference of the men who abetted the violence.[33] The laws of hospitality clearly do not pertain to the concubine: the lord of the house offers the guest's concubine and even his own virgin daughter to the mob outside, and gives them permission to ravish the women: "Ravish them and do whatever you want to them" (v. 24). The narrator captures the unfeeling violence already in the actions of the Levite as he "seized (*āzaq*) his concubine and pushed to them outside" (v. 25b).[34] When the Levite brought out his concubine to the waiting mob, "they wantonly raped her, and abused her all through the night until the morning; then let her go at the approach of dawn" (v. 25). By the combination of the verbs "know sexually [*yāda*]" and "abuse/torture [*hitpa'el* of *'ālal*]" the ghastly reality of gang rape is described, and by the reference to "all through the night until the morning" the multiple acts of unrelenting terror in this situation are indicated.

But the strong Hebrew terminology for gang rape is not forceful enough for the narrator to drive home the shock he wishes to elicit from his readers. The last desperate attempts of the raped woman to secure help are vividly recorded: "As the morning appeared, the woman came and fell down at the door of the man's house where her master was, until it was light" (v. 26). Here is a:

> [P]ost-rape portrait of a devastated, nearly dead woman, that leaves no room for any commentator to imagine that she might secretly have enjoyed her evening with the mob . . . Lying there, 'with her hands on the threshold' (Judg 19:27), she seeks refuge with her last bit of strength. She has no voice, but the description is heavy with the violence she has endured.[35]

32. Ibid., 238.

33. For analysis of this narrative with particular attention to the rape, see esp. Trible, *Texts of Terror*, 65–92; and Bach, "Rereading the Body Politic," 143–159.

34. This translation by Trible, *Texts of Terror*, 76, captures the hurried and calloused roughness of the Levite denoted by the Hebrew word *hzq* in the *hip'il*, and of the lack of direct object "her" after the verb.

35. Keefe, "Rapes of Women/Wars of Men," 90. Cf. Coetzee, "'Outcry' of the Dissected Woman," 55–60 (although I cannot agree with Coetzee's implicating of the narrator as well as the male participants in the

Shocking as this scene appears, perhaps even more shocking is the callousness of the Levite, who casually wakes up the next morning, opens the door as if to leave alone without regard for his concubine, and upon seeing her with her hands on the threshold, barks the two-word (in Hebrew) order: "Get-up and-let's-get-going!" (v. 28). No bending down to see if she is alive. No "words to speak to her heart" as he had earlier intended to give (Judg 19:3). When she doesn't respond—is she dead or exhausted? the Hebrew ambiguity doesn't indicate which—she is flung onto his donkey's back like a sack of flour, taken home, and dismembered into twelve pieces.[36] No mourning for the man; no burial for the woman. She is distributed among the tribes of Israel like pieces of an animal—as the pieces of oxen that Saul later would similarly send out as a *call to war* (1 Sam 11:7). We see that:

> Of all the characters in Scripture, she is the least . . . She is property, object, tool . . . Without name, speech, or power, she has no friends to aid her in life or mourn her in death . . . Captured, betrayed, raped, tortured, murdered, dismembered, and scattered—this woman is the most sinned against.[37]

The narrator preserves the commentary of the people of Israel who witnessed this deed, and serves as a timeless response both to the "vile outrage" (Judg 20:6) of gang rape and the male insensitivity to women's suffering: "Consider it, take counsel, and speak out!" (Judg 19:30).

2 Samuel 11: Bathsheba

The next incidence of rape in the Former Prophets is found in David's act of adultery with Bathsheba, the wife of Uriah the Hittite. The historical narrative of David's adultery involving Bathsheba (2 Samuel 11) comprises one of the prime biblical examples of a sophisticated and intricately written literary masterpiece. Numerous lines of evidence have convinced me, contrary to a surprisingly common scholarly interpretation implicating Bathsheba as a co-conspirator,[38] that Bathsheba was a victim of "power rape" on the part of David and that the narrative indicts David, not Bathsheba.[39] Here I do not repeat the full array of evidence set forth elsewhere, which substantiates that it is a case of power rape, but only highlight the verses that characterize this sexual abuse.

According to vv. 1–2, at the time of year when kings normally go forth to war, David's general and his army, indeed "all Israel" are risking their lives on the battlefield, but King David himself stays at home in relative isolation, "leading a life of idleness in Jerusalem,

---

rape for reflecting the contemporary societal attitude of "silencing all women completely" [55]).

36. The Hebrew here is written for maximum shock value to get the attention of the readers.

37. Trible, *Texts of Terror*, 80–81.

38. Representative scholarly proponents of the conspiracy theory include, e.g., Bailey, *David in Love and War*, 86; Kirk-Duggan, "Slingshots, Ships, and Personal Psychosis," 59; and Klein, "Bathsheba Revealed," 47–64.

39. See esp. Davidson, "Did King David Rape Bathsheba?," 81–95; Dennis, *Sarah Laughed*, 144–155; and Garsiel, "The Story of David and Bathsheba," 244–262.

taking his leisurely siesta, getting up in the evening, and strolling about on his roof."[40] From the elevated placement of his royal palace, he had a commanding view over the dwellings in the Kidron Valley directly below. The narrator's description of David's walking about on the rooftop of his palace, by sight invading the privacy of his subjects below, has the effect of putting him "in the position of a despot who is able to survey and choose as he pleases."[41] He sees a beautiful woman engaging in a ritual washing, purifying herself from ritual impurity incurred during her monthly period (v. 4; cf. Lev 15:19, 28). While Bathsheba was seeking to faithfully discharge the requirements of Torah regarding prescribed ceremonial cleansing from ritual uncleanness, David was lustfully watching her.

When David enquires as to the identity of the one he is lusting after, he is told by someone, "Is this not Bathsheba, the daughter of Eliam, the wife of Uriah the Hittite?" (2 Sam 11:3 NKJV). Both Bathsheba's father (Eliam) and husband (Uriah) are listed among the select group of soldiers called David's "Thirty Mighty Men" (2 Sam 23:13, 34, 39). These men were David's close comrades, "trench-buddies" who had fought together before David was king! Furthermore, Eliam was the son of Ahithophel, David's personal counselor (2 Sam 15:12; 1 Chr 27:33). Recognizing such intimate ties between David and Bathsheba's husband and father and grandfather makes the sexual sin of David against Bathsheba all the more audacious and appalling. He "took" the wife/daughter/granddaughter of his close friends!

The fast narrative flow of 2 Sam 11:4 depicts David's impulsive succumbing to lust as he "sent messengers, and took her; and she came to him, and he lay with her" (NKJV). The string of verbs in this narrative sequence ("saw . . . sent . . . inquired . . . sent . . . took her . . . lay with her") indicates that it is David's initiative throughout, not Bathsheba's. These verbs, as Trevor Dennis puts it:

> [S]peak his power, and tell, surely, of his abuse of that and of Bathsheba herself. There is a terrible abruptness and stark quality to his actions. There is no time for speech or conversation, no time for care, and certainly none for love, no time for even courtly etiquette . . . Bathsheba's verbs in v. 4, by way of contrast, merely describe the setting for those actions of David, and their immediate prelude and aftermath.[42]

In particular, her action of coming to David (v. 4, "she came to him") is in obedient response to the explicit command of her sovereign lord, the king. "Summoned by the king, she must obey."[43] This interpretation is later confirmed by the use of the same expression with reference to her husband Uriah, who after being summoned by David, obediently "came to him" (2 Sam 11:7). That the authority of David's command was not to be trifled with is also confirmed in the later experience of Uriah: "Uriah's noncompliance with David's suggestions, commands, and manipulations cost him his life."[44] Bathsheba is

---

40. Ibid., 197.

41. Fokkelman, *King David (2 Sam 9–20 & 1 Kings 1–2)*, 51.

42. Dennis, *Sarah Laughed*, 148.

43. Ibid., 149.

44. Hyun Chul Paul Kim and Nyengele, "Murder S/He Wrote? A Culture and Psychological Reading of 2 Samuel 11–12," 114.

portrayed as "a powerless woman who was victimized by the conglomeration of David's power, gender, and violence."[45]

Two verbs found at the heart of this action-packed scene have David as their subject: David "takes her" and he "lies with her." The word "take" (lāqaḥ) here clearly implies coercion (at least psychological, if not physical) and not voluntary *collusion on the part of Bathsheba. Note that according to the text David sends "messengers" (plural), but the verb "to take" has a singular masculine subject ("he took her"). While many modern versions are ambiguous at this point, giving the impression that it was the messengers who "took" Bathsheba to the palace, the Hebrew unambiguously indicates that "he," i.e., David himself (by means of the messengers, to be sure), "took" Bathsheba. Bathsheba was "fetched" (one meaning of lāqaḥ) to the palace by the king's orders. By using the term lāqaḥ "took," the narrator clearly implies that "the primary emphasis is on the responsibility of the subject for that act."[46] David's "taking" Bathsheba makes him responsible for her coming to him. The whole narrative flow here suggests Bathsheba's vulnerability once she is inside the palace, yes, even before. As Dennis asks, "Who is there who might protect her from the designs of the king? We are made to feel there is no one."[47]

The expression "lay with" (šākab 'im) used for the sexual intercourse between David and Bathsheba does not stress the use of overpowering physical brutality on the part of David, as in the case of the terminology used for the rape of Dinah (Genesis 34) and Tamar (2 Samuel 13). However, as evidenced in the Pentateuchal legal material (Deut 22:25–27), the term "lay with" employed here can indeed imply rape if the context indicates such. Given the context of (at least psychological) coercion in this passage, *the best term to describe David's action is probably "power rape," in which a person in a position of authority abuses that power to victimize a subservient and vulnerable person sexually, whether or not the victim appears to give consent.* David, the king, who was appointed by God to defend the helpless and vulnerable (2 Sam 23:3; Pss 41:1; 72:2–4, 12–14; 78:71–72; cf. Prov 29:14), becomes a victimizer of the vulnerable! Just as intercourse between an adult and a minor, even a "consenting" minor, is today termed "statutory rape," so the intercourse between David and his subject Bathsheba (even if Bathsheba, under the psychological pressure of one in power over her, acquiesced to the intercourse) is understood in biblical law, and so presented in this narrative, to be a case of rape—what today would be called "power rape," and the victimizer, not the victim, is held accountable.[48]

---

45. Ibid., 115.

46. Douglas W. Stolt, "lāqaḥ," TDOT 8:17.

47. Dennis, Sarah Laughed, 5.

48. For helpful discussion of sexual abuse of power in the case of David with Bathsheba, and modern counterparts, see Spielman, "David's Abuse of Power," 251–259. Cf. Rutter, Sex in the Forbidden Zone, 21 (brackets 25): "*any sexual behavior by a man in power within what I define as the forbidden zone* [= 'a condition of relationship in which sexual behavior is prohibited because a man holds in trust the . . . woman'] is inherently exploitive of a woman's trust. Because he is keeper of that trust, it is the man's responsibility, *no matter what level of provocation or apparent consent by the woman*" (emphasis original). See also Deut 22:25–26, for a parallel situation to that of David with Bathsheba: "But if a man finds a betrothed young woman in the countryside, and the man forces her and lies with her [verb šākab plus prep. phrase indirect ob. 'immāh, just as in 2 Sam 11:4], then only the man who lay with her shall die. But you shall do nothing

The narrator stresses that, after the sexual intercourse, Bathsheba on her own initiative returned to her house and did not try to stay in the palace (v. 4b); she desired to go back to her status as Uriah's wife. Her response to David after she knows she is pregnant is a mirror image of what David had done to her: as he sent messengers to fetch her, so now she sends a message to him that she is pregnant. Dennis shows how *by this means the narrator gives to Bathsheba some dignity of her own:*

> She is doing what David did. She is sending him a message. She is answering his show of power with hers. He asserted her power over her by raping her. She asserts her power over him by conveying to him the words: 'I am pregnant.' . . . To David they [these two words in Hebrew] are devastating. He will never be the same again. On them the plot of his whole story, from 1 Samuel 16 to 1 Kings 2, turns. They are not the triumphant cry of a woman who knows she bears the probable heir to the throne. They are the plain speaking of a woman who has been raped and discarded, and who wishes most courageously to make clear to her rapist the consequences of his act.[49]

Verse 6 contains only one verb, "to send" (*šalah*), and this verb is utilized three times in the verse to describe David's use of kingly power to summon Uriah: "So David sent (*šalah*) word to Joab . . . Send (*šalah*) me Uriah the Hittite . . . And Joab sent (*šalah*) Uriah to David." The parallel between David's action toward Bathsheba and his actions toward her husband in this same paragraph of the narrative cannot be overlooked. Just as Uriah's wife was sent for, so he is sent for. *Just as Uriah is helpless and must do what the king orders, so Bathsheba was constrained by the same power pressure of the king's orders. David's power rape of Bathsheba is paired with his "power murder" of Uriah.*

The strong emotive language used to describe Bathsheba's grieving for Uriah when she heard he was killed assures us that she was by no means a co-conspirator with David: she doesn't just mourn (*ābal*, v. 27) but wails/laments with loud cries (*sāpad*, v. 26). The fact that the narrator still here calls her "the wife of Uriah" implies her continued fidelity to her husband, as does the reference to Uriah as "her lord/husband." By using the term "lord" (*ba'al*) to denote her husband, the narrator intimates that "if Uriah is her 'lord,' then David is not."[50] Furthermore, it is important to notice that the narrator carefully avoids using the name of Bathsheba throughout the entire episode of David's sinning, making her character more impersonal, and thus perhaps further conveying the narrator's intent that Bathsheba wasn't personally responsible.

After her mourning rites were passed, according to v. 27, David again sent for Bathsheba and "harvested" her: the Hebrew word *āsap*, usually used for harvesting a crop or mustering an army,[51] further implies King David's brutality and ruthlessness. In this

---

to the young woman; there is in the young woman no sin worthy of death . . . there was no one to save her." Deuteronomy 22:25–27 speaks of no one to save the woman who (presumably) cried out in the countryside; the narrative of David and Bathsheba presents a similar situation in which "all Israel" is gone off to war, and Bathsheba, alone without her husband, finds herself coerced by the psychological power of the king, with "no one to save her."

49. Dennis, *Sarah Laughed*, 149.

50. Ibid., 152.

51. BDB, 62; *HALOT*, 74.

same verse is a crucial statement of culpability: "But the thing that David had done—[not what David and Bathsheba had done]—displeased the Lord." As Dennis pointedly remarks, "David is here condemned by God, but Bathsheba is not. The most natural way to interpret that is to suppose that Bathsheba has indeed been the innocent party all along, and David's victim, not his co-conspirator."[52] Those who set forth arguments such as, "She could/should have said no!" are simply not hearing the overriding theological message of the narrative!

The parable told by the prophet Nathan to David in the next chapter confirms the conclusion that it is David who is indicted for his victimization of both Bathsheba and Uriah. Nathan equates the "little ewe lamb" with Bathsheba, who had (like the lamb) "lain in the bosom." Dennis rightly draws the implication: "Now there can be no doubt left. The lamb in Nathan's parable is an innocent victim. Nothing could be clearer. And that means Bathsheba in chapter 11 was also an innocent victim. Unless, of course both Nathan and God have seriously misjudged the events!"[53]

Finally, Nathan announces the death of the child conceived from David's intercourse with Bathsheba as divine judgment upon David's sin, not upon the sin of both David and Bathsheba (2 Sam 12:13–14).

2 Samuel 13: Tamar

The last incident with sexual abuse (rape) as the focus of the narrative is the incestuous rape of Tamar by Amnon, recorded in 2 Samuel 13.[54] In this account Amnon, David's eldest son, became lovesick over his beautiful virgin stepsister, Tamar, sister of Absalom, and, following the advice of his crafty friend Jonadab, he feigned sick and arranged with his father, David, that she care for and be alone with him. She prepared and served food "in his sight" (v. 8, lit., "before his eyes"). *"Voyeurism prevails."[55] But he was not satisfied with the illicit lustful look; he "took hold of [ḥzq, "seized"] her and said to her, 'Come, lie with me, my sister'" (v. 11). She answered, "No, my brother, do not force ['innāh, "violate/ rape"] me, for such a thing is not done in Israel. Do not do anything so vile [něbālâ]" (v. 13). Tamar, like Joseph, "tries to speak from the high moral ground."[56] She appeals to her would-be assailant that his doing such an act would be a moral outrage in Israel.

Tamar also speaks of the personal "reproach" or "shame" (herpâ) that would be hers and the reputation of being an "impious and presumptuous fool" (nābāl)[57] that would be his. Then she tried to talk Amnon into delaying the gratification of his sexual desire by suggesting that he speak to the king, their father, "for he will not withhold me from

52. Dennis, *Sarah Laughed*, 152–153.

53. Ibid., 155.

54. For discussion of this incident, see esp. Bar-Efrat, *Narrative Art in the Bible*, 239–282; Frymer-Kensky, *Reading the Women of the Bible*, 157–169; Keefe, "Rapes of Women/Wars of Men," 79–97; Matthews and Benjamin, *The Social World of Ancient Israel 1250–587 B.C.E.*, 182–186; Smith, "Stories of Incest in the Hebrew Bible," 227–242; and Trible, *Texts of Terror*, 37–63.

55. Trible, *Texts of Terror*, 43.

56. Frymer-Kensky, *Reading the Women of the Bible*, 160.

57. BDB, 614. Cf. *HALOT*, 663, referring to "infamous people in a misdirected profession."

you" (v. 13). But Amnon would not be dissuaded, and in the heat of his lustful passion, "being stronger than she, he forced ['innāh] her and lay with her [lit., "lay her," without the preposition, to stress the brutality]" (v. 14). Then his so-called love—which was really lust—turned to spiteful hate. "The crime is despicable; the aftermath, ominous."[58] He said (in effect) "Get up and get out!" Over Tamar's futile protestations, despite her pleading in broken sentences of shock and anguish not to be stripped of her last vestige of dignity,[59] Amnon tells his servant to "put *this* [no mention of "woman"] out, away from me, and bolt the door behind her" (v. 17, lit.). "She has become for him solely a disposable object."[60]

In this passage, narrative space is given not only to the violent act *but also to the woman's psychological experience of her sexual abuse.* Several authors have pointed out how the narrative is carefully crafted in a *chiastic structure with the central focal point drawing attention to the brutality and violation inflicted upon Tamar and showing how this tragedy was the turning point in her life.[61] The story, with its revelation of the *multidimensional* violence on the part of Amnon—physical, emotional, and social—serves to call forth from the reader a sense of outrage against such violence and sympathy for Tamar the victim. In this account, unlike the other rape cases, space is devoted to Tamar's personal torment after the rape and brutal ejection from the rapist's presence like a piece of unwanted trash (see vv. 15–18): "Then Tamar put ashes on her head, and tore her robe of many colors that was on her, and laid her hand on her head and went away crying bitterly" (v. 19 NKJV).[62]

Her full brother Absalom was no comfort. As too often in cases of domestic rape and *incest where the family tries to belittle the seriousness of the sexual violation and cover up the crime, Absalom, apparently for political motivation, minimizes what happened to her by not identifying the offense as rape ("Has Amnon your brother been with you?"), and then tries to silence her: "But now keep silent, my sister, he is your brother; do not take this matter to heart" (2 Sam 13:20). "Like so many other victims of domestic rape, she joins the *conspiracy of silence that dooms her"[63]—for two years she "remained desolate in her brother Absalom's house" (v. 20). The word for "desolate" (*šmm*) when used for people elsewhere in Scripture refers to those who have been destroyed by an enemy or torn to pieces by an animal (Lam 1:16; 3:11; Isah 54:1). Tamar is a broken woman. "*She lives*

---

58. Trible, *Texts of Terror*, 47.

59. Frymer-Kensky translates literally with the added words to make sense in brackets: "Don't [do this]! Concerning this great evil—[it is greater] than the one which you did to me.—Sending me away [is worse than the other evil you did by raping me]" (*Reading the Women of the Bible*, 164).

60. See Ridout, "The Rape of Tamar," 81–83; Trible, *Texts of Terror*, 43–44; cf. Keefe, "Rapes of Women/ Wars of Men," 91.

61. See Trible, *Texts of Terror*, 43–44; cf. Keefe, "Rapes of Women/Wars of Men," 91.

62. Frymer-Kensky, *Reading the Women of the Bible*, 185, points out that this public spectacle may be understood in light of a Middle Assyrian Law (MAL A §23; *The Context of Scripture*, 2.132:355–356) which indicated that if a woman was tricked into adulterous sex, she must make public declaration immediately that she was victimized or she would be treated as an adulteress. Perhaps in a parallel situation, by crying out, Tamar made public declaration of her innocence, as well as expressing her personal torment after the rape. Lipka ("Construction of Sexual Transgression," 295) suggests that Tamar's robe of many colors symbolized her special status of virgin princess, and her tearing of the robe signaled her loss of virginity.

63. Frymer-Kensky, *Reading the Women of the Bible*, 167.

out the rest of her life in social, psychological, and moral isolation."[64] In this narrative "the author depicts what transpires as a deeply traumatizing experience for Tamar from which she never recovers, illuminating for his audience the terrible emotional consequences of such acts for the victim."[65] The consequences depicted cover virtually the whole gamut of what recent social scientists have observed in the *emotional *trauma* of sexual abuse victims: "a sense of helplessness, loss, vulnerability, shame, humiliation, and degradation."[66]

King David, her father, paralyzed by his own moral indiscretions, allows the shameful crime of Amnon to pass unrebuked and unpunished. But the rape ultimately leads to murder—Absalom kills his brother Amnon to avenge his sister's rape (2 Sam 13:23–34)—thus partially fulfilling David's unwitting sentence upon himself that "he shall restore fourfold" (2 Sam 12:6) after hearing Nathan's parable.[67]

As if to pay tribute to this violated daughter, the narrator provides information about Absalom's children—three sons and one daughter—and only the daughter is named: "one daughter whose name was Tamar. She was a woman of beautiful appearance" (2 Sam 14:27). *The narrator records how a living memorial has been raised for Absalom's raped sister.*

These stories reveal sexual abuse, especially in the form of rape, to be, both then and now, "a particular kind of human violence . . . in which women's bodies, always implicitly subject to male possession, are objectified, fetishized, and freely violated. The threat of rape appears for us as a perpetual assault upon woman's autonomy, power and personhood."[68] In the face of such violation of the dignity and personhood of woman, what should be our reaction? *Contrary to many scholarly warnings to remain "objective" and emotionally detached and avoid terminology like "revolting" to describe these incidents, the text insists that we respond in shock and horror against the crime and in sympathy for the victim!* Truly:

> If the reader is not moved to some sort of emotion—whether it is horror, sympathy, or anger—one can only feel that the biblical writer has failed in what he intended to do . . . Surely we are meant to see that the behavior of Amnon was as totally and utterly repugnant then as it is now (Absalom certainly regarded is [sic] as repugnant). Why else include the episode at all?[69]

Trible concludes her discussion of the Tamar narrative with a rhetorical question: "Who will preserve sister wisdom from the adventurer, the rapist with his smooth words, lecherous eyes, and grasping hands? In answering this question, Israel is found wanting—*and so are we.*"[70]

---

64. Lipka, *Sexual Transgression*, 218; emphasis added.

65. Ibid., 222.

66. Ibid., 23; emphasis added.

67. The first was the child of the adulterous affair with Bathsheba (as noted in ch. 8); Amnon was the second to die, Absalom the third (2 Samuel 18), and Adonijah the fourth (1 Kings 2). See Rudman, "Reliving the Rape of Tamar," 326–339, for evidence that "Absalom's murder of his brother is in fact a replaying of the circumstances surrounding Tamar's rape, with Amnon as the principle victim." (327).

68. Keefe, "Rapes of Women/Wars of Men," 79.

69. Smith, "Stories of Incest," 238, 241.

70. Trible, *Texts of Terror*, 57.

DISTORTED SEXUALITY AS ABUSE:
A RECAP OF OLD TESTAMENT TEXTS

Besides the clear and unmixed ugliness of rape, one may argue that, in a sense, *all of* the distortions of sexuality found in the Hebrew Bible are ultimately attacks upon the wholesomeness, beauty, and goodness of sexuality as presented in the Edenic ideal and may involve some kind of sexual abuse.

The recital of sexual misconduct as recorded in the Pentateuchal narratives serves to point up the explosive and potentially disruptive force of human sexuality after the *Fall. Detailed legislation is provided at Mt. Sinai (Exodus and Leviticus) and at the borders of the Promised Land (Deuteronomy) to protect against various kinds of sexual abuse, such as parents giving over their daughters to ritual sex or prostitution (e.g., Lev 19:29),[71] betrayals of trust through incest (Lev 18:6–17), robbing a woman of her dignity and self-respect in divorce (Deut 24:1–4),[72] various other kinds of denigration of women,[73] and the ultimate abuse of children through child sacrifice (Lev 18:21; Deut 12:31; 18:10).[74]

The narratives of the Former Prophets depict in grim detail the distortion of sexuality from the wholesome beauty that God intended. The Samson narratives largely revolve around various erotic attachments formed in the indulgence of unrestrained or unlawful sexual passions.[75] Woman is no longer the helper/benefactor in a loving relationship, but a traitor, a harlot, a temptress. The husband no longer considers his wife as an equal partner but as *chattel, like cattle: "If you had not *plowed with my heifer*, you would not have found out my riddle" (Judg 14:18). The multifaceted loving and lasting relationship between husband and wife has evaporated in the fires of lust, distrust, and abuse.

The period of the Monarchy and Divided Kingdoms reveal wholesome sexuality gone awry. David and Solomon fall prey to the prevailing customs of *bigamy, *polygamy, or *concubinage. The author faithfully records the anguish, disharmony, and abuse involved in having a "rival wife" and the disastrous personal and national results of kings "multiplying wives" for themselves—they abandoned Torah instructions for kings (Deut 17:17). Within the context of these distorted sexual relationships, invariably the woman suffers greatly—in loss of status, freedom, and respect. The multiple female partners are robbed of the exclusive affections of their husband: think of the seven hundred wives and three hundred concubines of Solomon (1 Kgs 11:3)! Solomon's political alliances sealed by marriage to foreign women later in his life bespeak a degradation and abuse of women.

---

71. See the discussion of ritual sex and common prostitution (sex for hire) in Davidson, *Flame of Yahweh*, 97–113, 305–315.

72. See Ibid., 389–405, esp. 404.

73. For discussion of the high valuation of women in the Pentateuch, as elsewhere in the Old Testament, and legislation designed to protect women against various kinds of abuse, see Ibid., 213–295.

74. See Ibid., 489–490, which includes references to child sacrifice elsewhere in the Old Testament.

75. See Crenshaw, *Samson*, 65–98, for the identification and analysis of these three kinds of erotic attachments in Samson's career.

Throughout this whole period, sexuality is distorted as it is juxtaposed with violence,[76] and as it becomes a manipulative political tool in the hand of powerful men.[77]

In the Latter as well as the Former Prophets, God's original design for sexuality as a beautiful creation ordinance has also been distorted in the divinized sex of the *fertility cult *orgies. Those who were enticed into engaging in the sexual orgies of the fertility cult, either the temple prostitutes or the lay participants, experienced a form of institutionalized sexual abuse. Their conceptions of what constituted the divine design for sexuality were distorted: the divine plan that sexual intercourse be shared in private between a married man and his wife gave way to licentious sex orgies conducted as the high point of public worship. Israel's departure from a wholesome, beautiful relationship with God is compared by the prophets to sexual infidelity, the prophets even utilizing the vulgar terminology of the brothel (see especially Ezekiel 16 and 23) to portray the vile distortion of the divine ideal. Beautiful sexuality is twisted into heinous distortions of God's character and the divine-human relationship, and strewn with victims of sexual abuse.

SEXUAL ABUSE AND THE GRACE OF GOD

In the Hebrew Bible God is portrayed as the defender of the oppressed, including victims of rape and other forms of sexual abuse. Never is there any hint in Scripture that the victim of rape is assigned guilt. As Keener puts it, "Anyone who attributes to the rapist anything less than *all* the blame is making up his or her own ideas, not reflecting those of the Bible."[78] *According to the biblical witness, God is always on the side of the rape victim.* Although judgment is sometimes delayed against the *perpetrators of rape and other kinds of sexual abuse, God promises that ultimately those who have suffered unjustly will be vindicated.[79] Scripture "also offers a deeper hope to victims of rape and other major traumas: If they continue to cultivate their relationship with God, *God can turn their pain into healing for themselves and for others.*"[80]

While the severe legal penalty for rape and other forms of sexual abuse reveals God's revulsion for this distortion of sexuality, those who have committed these transgressions are proffered the same word of divine grace and *forgiveness and empowerment for purity as to those who have committed other sexual sins. Scripture is explicit that God offers forgiveness for the repentant rapist. Note the prophetic word to David after he repented of his power rape of Bathsheba: "The Lord also has put away your sin; you shall not die"

76. For the exploration of this juxtaposition of sex and violence throughout Scripture, see, e.g., Kirk-Duggan, *Pregnant Passion*.

77. Among the many studies of "sexual politics" in the Hebrew Bible, see, e.g., Fewell and Gunn, *Gender, Power, and Promise*; Fuchs, *Sexual Politics in the Biblical Narrative*; Kessler, "Sexuality and Politics," 409–423; Levenson and Halpern, "The Political Import of David's Marriages," 507–518; Spielman, "David's Abuse of Power," 251–259; Sternberg, "Biblical Poetics and Sexual Politics," 463–488; and Yaron, "The Politics of Sex—Woman's Body as an Instrument for Achieving Man's Aims," 269–292.

78. Keener, "Biblical Reflections," 129.

79. Keener (Ibid.) provides the following biblical passages to support the concept of divine vindication of the oppressed: Deut 32:43; 2 Kgs 9:7; Ps 79:10; cf. Rev 6:10; 16:6; 19:2.

80. Ibid., 130; emphasis original.

(2 Sam 12:13). But forgiveness did not mitigate divine justice: in the case of David, his son born out of the illegitimate sexual encounter died as judgment for David's sin (2 Sam 12:14).

The Old Testament presents a balanced picture of mercy and justice in God's dealings with sexual abusers, *while at the same time consistently portraying God as the defender, comforter, healer, and vindicator of the abuse victims.* There is an implicit call in the OT for God's people to actively join him in standing on the side of those who have been sexually abused.

QUESTIONS FOR DISCUSSION

1. What different kinds of sexual abuse are dealt with in the Old Testament? List some examples of Old Testament texts that increasingly develop the rights of the sexually violated. What are some cultural perspectives of society (both in and outside the church) that complicate the study and interpretation of these texts? From a more integrative perspective, how has this chapter helped your understanding Old Testament, anthropology, emotional trauma, social solidarity, and structural evil?

2. How do the Old Testament narratives describing sexual abuse reveal the devastating effects of such abuse upon the victim? Carefully reread the story of Tamar in 2 Samuel 13; list the various aspects of trauma that the narrative describes (this illustrates personal trauma rather well since it portrays Tamar's point of view). As a therapist, how can this biblical text be used to validate the experience of rape victims and "explain" the kinds of pain they've experienced. As a pastor, brainstorm about various ways this passage can be taught and preached: (a) to sensitively name the evil of sexual violence for those who've experienced it in your audience; and (b) to instruct others how to think of sexual violence from a biblical perspective? List some standard misconceptions of God's forgiveness and how you might better explain what these Old Testament narratives are saying.

3. In what ways did Old Testament legislation provide protection from sexual abuse for the vulnerable members of Old Testament Israelite society?

4. How does the Old Testament blend divine justice and mercy in dealing with the sexual abuser and the victim of sexual abuse? What is the relationship of God's forgiveness to on-going consequences? How is this illustrated in these Old Testament stories?

5. What are the ways in which Old Testament laws, narratives, and oracles that relate to sexual abuse prove helpful in dealing with contemporary issues of sexual abuse? How do contemporary definitions of sexual violation and individual will differ from ANE views of sexuality, personhood, and sexual violation? What misconceptions or *stereotypes of Old Testament laws and *sexual ethics has this chapter helped dispel?

FOR FURTHER READING

Davidson, Richard M. *Flame of Yahweh: Sexuality in the Old Testament.* Peabody, MA: Hendrickson, 2007.

Kirk-Duggan, Cheryl A., ed. *Pregnant Passion: Gender, Sex, and Violence in the Bible.* Semeia Studies 44. Atlanta, GA: Society of Biblical Literature, 2003.

Kroeger, Catherine Clark, and James R. Beck, ed. *Women, Abuse, and the Bible: How the Scripture Can Be Used To Hurt or To Heal.* Grand Rapids: Baker, 1996.

Lipka, Hilary B. *Sexual Transgression in the Hebrew Bible.* Sheffield: Sheffield Phoenix Press, 2006.

Scholz, Susanne. "Was it Rape in Genesis 34? Biblical Scholarship as a Reflection of Cultural Assumptions." In *Escaping Eden: New Feminist Perspectives on the Bible.* Edited by Harold C. Washington et al., 183–198. Sheffield: Sheffield Academic Press, 1998.

_____. *Rape Plots: A Feminist Cultural Study of Genesis 34.* New York, NY: Peter Lang, 2000.

Spielman, Larry W. "David's Abuse of Power." *Word and World* 19 (1999): 251–259.

Trible, Phyllis. *Texts of Terror: Literary-Feminist Readings of Biblical Narratives.* Overtures to Biblical Theology. Philadelphia, PA: Fortress, 1984.

Yamada, Frank M. *Configurations of Rape in the Hebrew Bible: A Literary Analysis of Three Rape Narratives.* Studies in Biblical Literature 109. New York, NY: Peter Lang, 2008.

10

Experiencing God's Healing Power

A New Testament Perspective on Sexual Abuse

J. Edward Ellis, PhD

"Therefore be imitators of God, as beloved children, and live in love, as Christ loved us and gave himself up for us, a fragrant offering and sacrifice to God. But fornication and impurity of any kind, or greed, must not even be mentioned among you, as is proper among saints. Entirely out of place is obscene, silly, and vulgar talk; but instead, let there be thanksgiving. Be sure of this, that no fornicator or impure person, or one who is greedy (that is, an idolater), has any inheritance in the kingdom of Christ and of God" (Eph 5:1–5).[1]

NAMING THE FOE

THE AUTHOR OF EPHESIANS draws a stark contrast between two ways of living: that of the person who belongs to Christ and that of the person who does not. The Christian's life, he says, should be lived in *imitation* of God and characterized by love. Vices such as *fornication and greed, which mark the lives of those who do not belong to Christ, have no part in the Christian's life. Indeed, such vices should not even be mentioned among Christians,[2] yet the author of this letter mentions them. Apparently, he sees them as a significant threat to the health of the Christian community in Ephesus. They clearly exist in the non-Christian world, among those with whom the Ephesian Christians interact daily, and, if the experience of the Ephesian Christians is similar to that of their brothers and sisters in Corinth, such vices present a serious problem within the Ephesian Christian community. So they must be mentioned. The author names them and warns against them. So it is with *sexual abuse (SA). It has no place in the Christian community, among those who claim the name of Christ, and yet we cannot escape it. It occurs in the world around us, scarring those to whom we seek to minister. It invades us from without, claiming our own as its victims. It even springs up among us, committed by church folk against church folk. So, we must speak of it. *If we, the Christian community, are to be a community of justice, *forgiveness, and*

---

1. All Scriptural quotes in English in this chapter, unless otherwise labeled, are from New Revised Standard Version (NRSV).

2. Collins, *Sexual Ethics and the New Testament*, 149.

healing, we must name sexual abuse and bring it into the light. This chapter will seek to bring the New Testament to bear on that endeavor.

NEW TESTAMENT TEACHINGS
RELEVANT TO THE ISSUE OF SEXUAL ABUSE

The New Testament, as understood here, says little, if anything, that relates directly to the topic of sexual abuse. What it says more generally about *sexual ethics, however, can be applied quite powerfully to our discussion. At least twenty-one of the twenty-seven books of the New Testament contain material relevant to a discussion of sexual ethics.[3] Since space limitations do not allow a discussion of the teachings of twenty-one books here, this study must proceed selectively. Numerous scholars have argued that Paul views sex negatively[4]; some have gone so far as to suggest, or even to argue outright, that his writings offer no help in the construction of a healthy sexual ethic.[5] I have argued elsewhere, however, that Paul sees sex in the proper venue—for him, heterosexual marriage—as godly.[6] This study will rely mostly upon the Pauline corpus[7] and draw on some material from the Gospels.[8]

What the New Testament Does Condemn

Obviously, sexual abuse takes a variety of forms. None of those forms is clearly singled out for condemnation in the New Testament. Some have seen references to *pederasty in Romans 1 and 1 Corinthians 6. Careful *exegesis, however, shows that the object of condemnation in those passages is more general. Romans 1 condemns *homosexual activity, both among men and among women, and 1 Corinthians 6 condemns homosexual activity among men.[9] In both passages, then, the condemned activity may include, but is not limited to, pederasty. In Rom 1:18–32, Paul's point is that all people, Jews and Gentiles, stand before God condemned and in need of salvation. He treats homosexual activity not as the *cause* of condemnation but as the *result* of a fundamental refusal to honor God properly, a refusal of which all humanity is ultimately guilty.[10] In 1 Cor 6:9–11, homosexual activity is seen as one of many sins that formerly characterized the lives of some of the Corinthian

---

3. Philippians, 2 Thessalonians, Philemon, and the Johannine epistles contain no relevant material for sexual ethics (Collins, *Sexual Ethics*, 22).

4. Bornkamm, *Paul*, 208; Weiss, *Earliest Christianity*, 582; Grant, *Saint Paul*, 25.

5. Fredrickson, "Passionless Sex in 1 Thessalonians 4:4–5," 23–30; Martin, "Paul without Passion," 201–215.

6. Ellis, *Paul and Ancient Views of Sexual Desire*, 147–159.

7. I use the term "Pauline corpus" to refer to the group of letters that bear Paul's name, though his authorship of some letters is disputed.

8. For treatments of New Testament sexual ethics, see Gagnon, *The Bible and Homosexual Practice*; Countryman, *Dirt, Greed, and Sex*; Collins, *Sexual Ethics and the New Testament*.

9. Hays, *The Moral Vision of the New Testament*, 382–383; Gagnon, *Bible and Homosexual Practice*, 306–308.

10. Hays, *Moral Vision*, 382–389.

Christians. Paul's point there is that the Corinthian Christians have been transformed and are no longer the people they once were.

THE OBLIGATION OF RELATIONAL RESPONSIBILITY

Both Will Deming and Ray Collins have suggested that a teaching against sexual *mo-lestation of children ("little ones") lies behind Jesus' teaching in Mark 9:42–48. Neither Deming nor Collins, however, argues that Jesus' words, in their present context in the Gospel, are meant to refer to child molestation. Rather, both scholars argue that, in Jesus' saying, the "little ones" are Jesus' disciples, not necessarily children.[11] In its present form and context, the saying warns disciples about the dangers of temptation.[12]

The Importance of the Body in the New Testament

While the New Testament does not speak specifically of sexual abuse, it does offer important contributions to the discussion. Perhaps one of the New Testament's most important contributions to the discussion of sexual abuse lies in Paul's high view of the human body. While Paul does in places (e.g., Gal 5:17) speak negatively of "the flesh" (*sarx*), which he sees as opposed to "the Spirit" (*pneuma*), this should not be taken as an indication that Paul sees the body as evil. One can readily see this by noting, for instance, that of the fifteen "works of the flesh" listed in Gal 5:19–21, no more than five seem to spring from physical appetites.[13] "The flesh," therefore, must represent something other than simply the physical body. *It seems that when Paul speaks negatively of "the flesh," he has in mind an approach to life that seeks self-gratification and absolutizes something other than God.*[14]

THE SOMA IN 1 CORINTHIANS

In 1 Corinthians, Paul speaks at length of the importance of the body (*soma*). In chapter 6, Paul deals with the Corinthian Christians' "over-realized *eschatology." The Corinthians apparently believe that they, having attained an advanced state of spiritual existence, have transcended their physical bodies. On this basis, they have concluded that their bodies do not matter—what they do physically is not important. Thus, in their minds, it is legitimate for one of their number to have a sexual relationship with his father's wife (5:1–2).[15] Their approval of the situation, they believe, is a sign of their spiritual advancement. Paul's response, however, emphasizes the importance of the physical body as God's creation. First Cor 6:13–14 is relevant to our discussion. Verse 13a quotes a Corinthian slogan: "'Food is meant for the stomach and the stomach for food, and God will destroy both one and the other.'"[16] This popular claim gives voice to the Corinthians' over-realized eschatol-

---

11. Deming, "Mark 9:42—10:12, Matthew 5:27–32, and *B. Nid.* 13b: A First Century Discussion of Male Sexuality," 70.

12. Collins, *Sexual Ethics and the New Testament*, 70.

13. Hays, "The Letter to the Galatians: Introduction, Commentary, and Reflections," 326.

14. Talbert, "Freedom and Law in Galatians," 17–28.

15. Talbert, *Reading Corinthians*, 28–30. Thus, "And you are arrogant!" (v. 2a ESV).

16. Here, the NRSV reads: "'Food for the stomach and the stomach for food,' and God will destroy both one and the other." This makes the first clause of the sentence a Corinthian claim and the second clause Paul's

ogy. For the Corinthians, sexual intercourse, like eating, is simply a biological function, a satisfaction of a physical appetite. Since the physical body is part of the present world, which God will destroy, the satisfaction of bodily appetites carries no moral significance. But in vv. 13b–14, Paul responds, stating: "The body is meant not for fornication but for the Lord, and the Lord for the body. And God raised the Lord and will also raise us by his power." Here, Paul *personifies* fornication and pictures it as a rival to the Lord. The body, he says, is meant for intimate union with the Lord, not for fornication. "'Body' here is used in parallelism with the personal pronoun in v. 14 ("us") and so stands for the entire person or self."[17] Verse 14 gives the basis for Paul's claim in v. 13b: though the body will be destroyed, God will raise it. The body, Paul believes, is important to God; therefore what one does with one's own body or to the body of another is important. Verse 15 drives home the point. "Do you not know that your bodies are members of Christ? Should I therefore take the members of Christ and make them members of a prostitute? Never!" Paul thoroughly rejects any *dualistic notion that would separate body from soul and diminish the importance of the former.[18] Clearly, Paul sees the body as an integral part of the person. Rudolph Bultmann goes so far as to say that, for Paul, "man does not *have a soma*; he *is soma*."[19]

The idea of the importance of the physical body finds further expression in the Gospel of John. The fourth Gospel teaches that "the Word *became* flesh" (John 1:14) and clearly portrays Jesus' post-resurrection existence as bodily (John 20:24–29).[20] Clearly, in the New Testament, the body is important. *Sexual abuse invades the body, using it and perhaps even claiming ownership over it. In so doing, it invades and injures the entire person at a very deep level.* If we are to appreciate the profundity of the offense of sexual abuse, we must understand the importance and value of the body.

Man and Woman as Equals before God: The Ethics of Mutuality

A further contribution to the discussion of sexual abuse lies in the New Testament emphasis on the equality of man and woman before God. This is an emphasis that many readers of the New Testament have failed to see. Such failure has encouraged many men to see women as inferior and, often, to treat them as property. Undoubtedly, this sort of errant thinking and acting has in turn contributed significantly to sexual abuse of women. Properly understood, the New Testament clearly portrays men and women as equals. A key passage in the discussion of this equality is Eph 5:21–33. Verses 21–23 command: "Be subject to one another out of reverence for Christ. Wives, be subject to your husbands as you are to the Lord. For the husband is the head of the wife just as Christ is the head of the church, the body of which he is the Savior." These three verses might easily be taken

---

response. Following Talbert (*Reading Corinthians*, 46), I have moved the closing quotation mark, making the entire sentence a quote of a Corinthian claim. Other translations take both clauses as part of the same Corinthian slogan (so TNIV).

17. Talbert, *Reading Corinthians*, 46.

18. Ibid., 46–50.

19. Bultmann, *Theology of the New Testament*, 1:194; emphasis original.

20. Harrington and Keenan, *Jesus and Virtue Ethics*, 135.

as establishing the authority of the husband over the wife, but such a reading is open to serious question. If we are to understand the argument of this passage, we must consider both its syntax and its use of the image of Christ as Head. First, we examine the syntax. The verb *hypotassō*, translated "be subject," occurs in the Greek text only in verse 21. It is not repeated in verse 22. A more literal rendering of the Greek would read, "Be subject to one another[21] in reverence for Christ, the wives to their own husbands as to the Lord." This suggests that the submission that this passage calls wives to show toward their husbands is similar to the submission that all believers are called to show toward one another. Thus the passage does not prescribe "*authoritarian dominance and submission. Clearly, it teaches mutuality and sharing."[22]

This conclusion finds further support in an analysis of the syntax and rhetoric of the larger passage of Eph 5:15–6:9. In 5:18, the Ephesian Christians are told to "be filled with the Spirit." In 5:19–21 *this filling with the Spirit is seen as facilitating a community life characterized by praise, thanksgiving, and mutual submission.*[23] The exhortation to this community life is articulated in a series of five participles (italicized in the following translation): "*speaking* to one another in psalms and hymns and spiritual songs, *singing* and *making music* with your heart to the Lord; always *giving thanks* for all things in the name of our Lord Jesus Christ to God the Father. *Being subject* to one another in reverence for Christ . . ." The emphasis on community is strengthened in verse 19 by the use of the singular noun *kardia* ("heart") modified by the plural second person pronoun *humōn* ("your"). In other words, the Ephesian Christians are told to praise God with their collective heart. *A Spirit-enlivened community that praises God with one heart would seem to have no room for the authoritarian domination of some members by others.*

Verse 21 seems to act as a sort of hinge transition, both concluding the preceding section, which exhorts the Ephesian Christians to Spirit-enlivened community life, and opening a new section in which the author shows how three types of relationship—husband-wife, parent-child, and master-slave—will look in this community. It is linked to the preceding material by *hupotassomenoi* (i.e., "being subject"), the fifth in the series of participles, and to the following material by its admonition to husbands and wives, the first of the three relational pairs discussed in the new section.[24] The new section contains three smaller sections, each of which addresses one of the three relational pairs. Observe that: (1) husbands are told to love their wives sacrificially (5:25–33), (2) parents are told not to provoke their children (6:4), and (3) masters are told to stop threatening their slaves, bearing in mind that they will answer to the "Master in heaven," who shows no partiality (6:9). This Christian *household code, then, insists on mutual respect and places limits on the exercise of power.

---

21. Pheme Perkins sees "mutual instruction and encouragement here" (Perkins, "The Letter to the Ephesians," 349–466 [443]). For a fuller discussion of mutuality in Eph 5:21–33, see Marshall, "Mutual Love and Submission in Marriage," 186–204 [197–204].

22. Kroeger, "Let's Look Again at the Biblical Concept of Submission," 139 [135–140].

23. See Marshall, "Mutual Love and Submission in Marriage," 196, n.30.

24. Barth, *Ephesians*, 608.

"Head" as Agent of Nurture and Sustaining

Having considered the structure and argument of Eph 5:15–6:9, we now turn to the image of Christ as head of the church. In 5:23, this image qualifies the statement that the husband is the head of the wife: "For the husband is the head of the wife just as Christ is the head of the church." A look at other New Testament passages that speak of Christ as *kephalē* of the church, then, will assist us in understanding the role that Eph 5:23 gives to the husband.[25] Two New Testament books, Ephesians and Colossians, speak of Christ as head of the church. In Ephesians, the idea occurs in one passage aside from the passage in question. In Eph 4:15–16, the author states, "But speaking the truth in love, we must grow up in every way into him who is the head, into Christ, from whom the whole body, joined and knit together by every ligament with which it is equipped, as each part is working properly, promotes the body's growth in building itself up in love." Here Christ, as head of the church, is portrayed as enabling the church to grow and thrive. The author of Colossians[26] presents Christ as head of the church in two passages, 1:18–20 and 2:18–19. In Col 1:18–20, he states:

> "[Christ] is the head of the body, the church; he is the beginning, the firstborn from the dead, so that he might come to have first place in everything. For in him all the fullness of God was pleased to dwell, and through him God was pleased to reconcile to himself all things, whether on earth or in heaven, by making peace through the blood of his cross."

Here, the image of Christ as head seems to convey the idea that Christ is God's appointed *agent* of *reconciliation and thus the one through whom the church has come into being and from whom the church receives its life. In Col 2:18–19, the author instructs his readers:

> "Do not let anyone disqualify you, insisting on self-abasement and worship of angels, dwelling on visions, puffed up without cause by a human way of thinking, and not holding fast to the head, from whom the whole body, nourished and held together by its ligaments and sinews, grows with a growth that is from God."

Here, perhaps even more clearly than in Eph 4:15–16, to call Christ the head of the church is to say that Christ nourishes the church and enables it to grow.

In light of all of these passages, it seems fair to conclude that Christ's role as the head of the church is more a life-giving, nurturing, sustaining role than a role of dominance and authority.[27] It would seem, then, that when the author of Ephesians states that "the husband is the head of the wife just as Christ is the head of the church," he does not mean that the husband should rule over the wife. Rather, he means that the husband should conduct himself in such a way as to nurture her, to help her to grow and thrive, perhaps both

---

25. See Fee, "Hermeneutics and the Gender Debate," 376, n.15 [364–381].

26. The authorship of Colossians has been a matter of considerable debate. According to Stephen Harris, those who believe that Paul wrote the letter constitute "a large minority" of New Testament scholars (Harris, *The New Testament*, 376).

27. I am not arguing that Christ does not have authority over the Church. I am simply suggesting that such authority is not what is emphasized when he is called the "head of the church."

as a member of the family unit and as part of the body of Christ. This conclusion finds further support in verse 25, which commands husbands: "Love your wives, as Christ loved the church and gave himself up for her . . ." *The husband is commanded to show his wife the same self-emptying love that Christ has shown for the church.* This sort of love seems not far removed from the submission prescribed in verse 21. So properly understood, Eph 5:21–33 does not establish the husband as a ruler over the wife. *Instead, it teaches that the husband and wife are to submit to each other, each seeking the other's good.*

EQUALITY IN THEIR SEXUAL RELATIONSHIP

Especially relevant to this discussion is 1 Corinthians 7, where Paul clearly states that *the equality between the man and woman extends to their sexual relationship.* In verses 3–4, he states, "The husband should give to his wife her *conjugal rights, and likewise the wife to the husband. For the wife does not have authority over her own body, but the husband does; likewise the husband does not have authority over his own body, but the wife does." So for Paul, the relationship is characterized not by any authoritarian rule, much less oppression, but by mutuality. Such mutuality, coupled with the love and submission required by Ephesians, would certainly preclude a sense of authority or ownership that might be used to justify sexual violence of any kind.

Parental Power and Children's Obedience

The limiting of the exercise of power is in Eph 5:21–6:9 is helpful in our discussion of sexual abuse, not only with regard to the husband-wife relationship, but also with regard to the parent-child relationship. It need not be said, of course, that the admonition to children to obey their parents in Eph 6:1–3 does not authorize sexual exploitation of children on the part of parents. Still, some children who are sexually abused by their parents may feel (or be told) that this passage forbids them to speak out about the abuse or to seek help. It is difficult to imagine, however, that the Spirit-enlivened community prescribed in Ephesians, a community that limits the exercise of power and shows concern for the well-being of traditionally subservient parties, will expect children to endure sexual abuse. *Indeed, by speaking out and setting in motion the chain of events that can lead to the abuser's repentance, those who are abused can help to move both individuals and the community toward spiritual wholeness.* Likewise, the Christian community, following the admonitions in Ephesians, should come to the aid of those who are abused when the cries of the violated are heard.

Healing for the Victim: The Role of Forgiveness

Where sexual abuse has occurred, healing is needed, both for the victim and for the abuser. *For both parties, this healing can involve a complex and difficult process.* Other chapters in this book deal ably with the intricacies of that process.[28] Here, it must suffice to bring some relevant New Testament data to bear on the matter. For the victim, a vital

---

28. Additionally, see "For Further Reading" at the end of the chapter.

step in the healing process is forgiving the abuser. The New Testament has much to say about *forgiveness.[29] Frederick W. Keene has argued that:

> [F]rom the point of view of the New Testament, interpersonal forgiveness is possible only when, within the context of the interaction in which the question of forgiveness arises, the putative forgiver is more powerful than, or at least an equal of, the person being forgiven . . . It is not possible from the point of view of the NT for one person to forgive another person of greater power.[30]

Keene argues mainly on two grounds. First, he states that, in the Mediterranean world of the first-century, "an offer of forgiveness" from an inferior to a superior was an insult to the honor of the superior.[31] Second, Keene argues that New Testament statements about forgiveness seem to reflect first-century Mediterranean assumptions about power relationships and forgiveness. The bulk of New Testament references to forgiveness, he notes, concern God's or Jesus' forgiveness of human sin. Clearly, in these references, the superior forgives the inferior.[32] An important text in Keene's treatment of forgiveness among humans is Luke 11:4,[33] where Jesus instructs, "And forgive [aphiēmi] us our sins [hamartia], for we ourselves forgive [aphiēmi] everyone who owes [opheilō] us."[34] As Keene correctly notes, the verb aphiēmi, here translated, "forgive," carries two basic and related meanings: (1) "to leave" or "to release," and (2) "to remit or forgive, especially a debt."[35] Clearly, in this passage, an analogy is drawn between forgiving sin and cancelling a debt. Keene argues,

> To be indebted in a commercial transaction is to be in the inferior position; the creditor is in the position of power. Thus the *hierarchy is that we forgive those over whom we have power; therefore we can ask God, who has infinite power, to forgive us. Nothing is said about those who have power over us and against whom we might have a grievance. In this situation, forgiveness flows down, from the more powerful to the less powerful.[36]

OFFENCE, SOCIAL POWER, AND FORGIVENESS

After discussing several more New Testament passages, Keene goes so far as to suggest that it is, in fact, impossible for the less powerful to forgive the more powerful. Noting that Jesus, having become powerless on the cross, asked his Father to forgive his tormenters rather than forgive them himself (Luke 23:34), he argues, "If he could, he would forgive. But he did

29. See, for instance: Matt 6:9–15, 18:21–35; Mark 11:25; Luke 6:37, 11:1–4, 17:1–4; Eph 4:29–32; and Col 3:12–14.

30. Keene, "Structures of Forgiveness in the New Testament," 122–23 [121–134].

31. Ibid., 122.

32. Ibid., 125.

33. Ibid.

34. NRSV, modified.

35. Keene, "Structures," 123. Sin viewed as "debt" is not unusual (cf. 1 Pet 3:7).

36. Ibid., 125.

not, and thus no one should be asked or expected to forgive those who retain the power in a relationship where forgiveness might be applicable."[37]

Keene notes that sexual abuse often occurs within relationships in which the abuser has power or authority over the victim. For forgiveness to occur in such cases, he argues, the abuser must relinquish power. A minister or priest who has sexually abused a layperson must be stripped of ordination in order for forgiveness to occur. A daughter who has been abused by her father typically cannot forgive him until she has become an adult and he has grown old. With regard to the latter case, Keene states, "This may or may not be a psychological requirement, but the New Testament model of forgiveness explored here would indicate that it definitely is a theological and biblical requirement. Only when the patterns of power are reversed can the act of forgiveness be considered."[38]

Keene's interpretation, however, seems to *imprison* the New Testament within its cultural environment rather than allowing it to *challenge* that environment. While Keene's reversal of patterns of power is desirable, his claim that it is a theological and biblical requirement for forgiveness is not supported by the New Testament. A return to the discussion of Jesus' prayer in Luke 11 makes this clear. As stated above, the language of that prayer draws an analogy between the forgiveness of sin and the cancellation of a debt. As Keene himself notes, "The creditor is in the position of power."[39] If sin equals debt, the creditor equals the offended party. When one person has sinned against another, it would seem, the offender is indebted to the offended, placed in the inferior position. Regardless of what relationship may exist between the two outside the context of the sin, *as regards the sin, the offended party is in the superior position and holds the power to forgive. Thus Jesus' ethic of forgiveness empowers the powerless and overthrows social structures based on power.*

Forgiveness and the "Grammar of Release"

What does it mean for a victim to forgive an abuser? While this chapter will not attempt to exhaust the meaning of forgiveness or *remission of sin, one element of forgiveness seems especially relevant to the topic of sexual abuse: *the element of letting go*. As noted above, the Greek word *aphiēmi*, the most prominent verb for "forgive" in the Gospels, carries the idea of "leaving" or "releasing." When the New Testament uses it to speak of forgiving a person's sin, the syntax indicates that *the sin, not the person, is the object of the act of forgiving*. When the verb is passive, the word for sin is its subject. Thus, for example, in Mark 2:5, Jesus says not, "You are forgiven," but, "Your *sins* are forgiven."[40] When the verb is active, the word for sin occurs in the *accusative case, the case of direct object, while the word naming the offender occurs in the *dative case, which, while it has many uses, can be used to point out "the person . . . *for* whose benefit something is done."[41] In Luke 11:4a,

37. Ibid., 129.

38. Ibid., 132–33.

39. Ibid., 125.

40. The passive voice used here is an example of a *divine passive*; God clearly does the forgiving (Wallace, *Greek Grammar Beyond the Basics*, 437); emphasis added.

41. Ibid., 139.

which reads: "And forgive us our sins," the word for "sins," *hamartia*, is in the accusative case, while the pronoun "us" is in the dative case. Luke 11:4a, then, might be translated, "And forgive our sins for our benefit."

Luke 12:10 reads, "And everyone who speaks a word against the Son of Man will be forgiven; but whoever blasphemes against the Son of Man will not be forgiven." A more literal (and slightly awkward) translation, however, would read, "And everyone who speaks a word against the Son of Man, it shall be forgiven for his benefit, but for the benefit of the one who blasphemes against the Holy Spirit it shall not be forgiven." Even when no term for sin is present, the word naming the person whose sin is forgiven occurs in the dative case. In Matt 18:35, for instance, Jesus says, "So my heavenly Father will also do to every one of you, if you do not forgive your brother or sister from your heart." In the Greek, *adelphos*, the word for "brother" (i.e., "fellow Christian," male or female) occurs in the dative case. While some Greek words take direct objects in the dative case, *aphiēmi* does not seem to be such a word. When *aphiēmi* is used to refer to "leaving" or "releasing" something other than sin, the word naming the thing left or released occurs in the accusative case (e.g., Mark 1:31; Matt 4:20, Luke 17:34). Clearly, the Gospels portray the sin, rather than the sinner, as the object of forgiveness when the verb *aphiēmi* is used. *For the Gospels, to forgive is to let go of an offense; the offender is presented as benefitting from that act of letting go.* In the context of a discussion of sexual abuse, this suggests that for the victim to forgive means to "let go" of the abuse. To refuse to do so is to continue living in the pain the abuse has caused. This kind of "letting go" is not rooted in pop culture. Forgiving, letting go, is necessary for healing.

The Agency of the Victim to Forgive
The New Testament seems to teach that this forgiveness is possible, even necessary, whether or not the offender repents. In Luke 17:3 Jesus says, "If another disciple sins, you must rebuke the offender, and *if there is repentance*, you must forgive." This would seem to make repentance a *condition* for forgiveness. In the next verse, however, Jesus says, "And if the same person sins against you seven times a day, and turns back to you seven times and says, 'I repent,' you must forgive" (17:4). In such a case, the genuineness of the repentance would seem quite doubtful, yet Jesus commands forgiveness. In Matt 18:21–22, Peter asks Jesus, "If another member of the church sins against me, how often should I forgive? As many as seven times?"[42] Jesus answers, ". . . Not seven times, but . . . seventy-seven times." Here, we see no mention of repentance. I would argue that forgiveness can occur with or without the offender's repentance or penitence. I am not arguing that in the case of sexual abuse justice should not be sought. It *should* be sought. *Further, no relationship destroyed by the abuse can be healed without genuine repentance.* Still, lack of repentance does not stop the offended party from forgiving, "letting go" of, the sin.

From a New Testament perspective, this forgiveness is made possible by the work of Jesus Christ. In Matt 26:28, Jesus says, "This is my blood of the covenant, poured out for many for the forgiveness of sins." In Rom 3:25, Paul states that God publically displayed Christ as a "sacrifice of atonement." According to Heb 9:26, Christ "has appeared once for

42. Lit. "If my brother" is again, male or female fellow Christian (so RSV, NIV) "someone" (TNIV).

all at the end of the age to remove sin by the sacrifice of himself." Discussions of particular theories of *atonement or the correct translation of *hilastērion* in Rom 3:25[43] aside, the New Testament clearly teaches that Jesus Christ has dealt with sin. What can and must be done about sin in an ultimate sense has been done. *This, I would argue, leaves the victim of abuse free to forgive and thus to remove a major obstacle to the process of healing.* I am not suggesting that such forgiveness will come easily, quickly, or cheaply. The discussion of the *process* involved is covered in other chapters. I argue only that the New Testament calls for it, that the work of Christ makes it possible, and that it facilitates the victim's healing.

Healing for the Victim: Jesus as Bearer of Burdens

Like the forgiveness that facilitates it, this healing will not come easily or simply; it will likely involve a process better discussed in depth elsewhere. That process will require time and work, and it will likely facilitate a deeper experience of God's presence, power, and grace than would be possible in an instantaneous healing. The victim seeking healing may find strength and reassurance in the New Testament's image of Christ as the bearer of burdens: "Come to me, all you that are weary and are carrying heavy burdens, and I will give you rest. Take my yoke upon you and learn from me; . . . and you will find rest for your souls" (Matt 11:28–29). The invitation *to take the yoke is an invitation to be bound to Jesus,* to walk beside him through the pain and struggle of human existence, and to receive rest and healing through the journey. The journey may be difficult, but it leads to what Paul calls "the peace of God, which surpasses all understanding" (Phil 4:7).

Healing for the Abuser: Deliverance and Transformation

This peace, the New Testament teaches, can come to the abuser as well as to the victim. As stated above, the New Testament teaches that Jesus Christ has dealt with sin. In Romans 5, Paul discusses in-depth the *results* of Christ's work:

> "Therefore, since we have been justified by faith, we have peace with God through our Lord Jesus Christ . . . but God shows his love for us in that while we were sinners Christ died for us . . . For if while we were enemies, we were reconciled to God through the death of his Son, much more surely, having been reconciled, will we be saved by his life." (vv. 1, 8, 10)

Through the death of Jesus Christ, Paul says, the sinner can be saved from the wrath of God and reconciled to, brought into a right relationship with, God. Further, in Rom 6:17–18, Paul teaches that the abuser, having been reconciled to God, need not remain an abuser: "Thanks be to God that you, having once been slaves of sin, have become obedient from the heart to the form of teaching to which you were entrusted, and that you, having been set free from sin, have become slaves of righteousness." Similarly, in 1 Cor 6:11, after reciting a list of offenders who he says will not inherit the *kingdom of God, Paul says to the Corinthians, "And this is what some of you used to be. But you were washed,

---

43. The term (*hilastērion*) is only used again in Heb 9:5, where it is translated "mercy seat" (cf. Exod 25:17–22; Lev 16:15). For further discussion see, Talbert, *Romans*, 106–115; Bailey, "Jesus As the Mercy Seat."

you were sanctified, you were justified in the name of the Lord Jesus Christ and in the Spirit of our God." While Paul's list does not name all categories of sexual abusers (though "sodomites"[44] would include pederasts), the relevant point here is that, *by God's grace, offenders can be transformed.* Clearly, Paul teaches that Christ brings freedom from sin.[45]

While, for Paul, all those who do not know Christ are slaves to sin, most are not aware of their slavery. The sexual abuser, by contrast, may be very much aware of that slavery. The abusive behavior may in fact be behavior that the abuser hates but feels driven to commit. Like healing for the victim, the freedom of which Paul speaks likely will not come easily and will involve a process better discussed in other chapters. Here it must suffice to say that such freedom, according to the New Testament, is possible. *It may be that, in this life, freedom from the behavior will not mean freedom from temptation or struggle.* That level of freedom may come only when God brings about the work that Paul foresees in Romans 8:

> "I consider that the sufferings of this present time are not worth comparing with the glory about to be revealed to us . . . We know that the whole creation has been groaning in labor pains until now; and not only the creation, but we ourselves, who have the first fruits of the Spirit, groan inwardly while we wait for adoption, the redemption of our bodies." (vv. 18, 22–23)

The New Testament bears witness both to the "now" and to the "yet to come" of Christian existence. While both are glorious, the "now" is also difficult and painful. Neither is more real than the other.

God's Healing Power

Sexual abuse presents a great challenge to the Christian community. It touches us, hurts us, and involves us in the destruction it wreaks. Despite the difficulty and the pain of facing it, we must not, indeed need not, hide from it. When we drag it into the light and expose it to the truth of Scripture, we can see it for what it is: a dreadful yet conquerable foe. The New Testament promises healing, both for the abused and the abuser, and calls us to look forward to the day pictured in Revelation 21, when the "sea"—representing rebellion against God—is gone,[46] all tears are wiped away, and all things are made new.

---

44. The NRSV's "sodomites" (1 Cor 6:9) translates the Greek *arsenokoitēs*, which, I would argue, refers to the *active* partner in male homosexual activity. See Gagnon, *The Bible and Homosexual Practice*, 316; cf. "practicing homosexuals" (TNIV), "sexual perversion" (ESB), "homosexual offenders" (NIV).

45. While Paul seems to say in Romans 7 that he finds that he repeatedly does things he does not want to do and does not do what he wants to do, I hold, along with several other commentators, that in that chapter Paul is using something like a dramatic monologue to portray the person who has not come to Christ. See, for example, Talbert, *Romans* 186–189; Wright, "The Letter to the Romans: Introduction, Commentary, and Reflections," 551–553.

46. Mulholland, *Revelation*, 314–315.

QUESTIONS FOR DISCUSSION

1. How does the New Testament portray the relationship between husband and wife? Is the view presented in this chapter accurate and/or practicable? How can a married couple make sure each spouse's needs, thoughts, and feelings are fully respected and valued? When practiced in a marriage, how will mutual submission manifest itself in the couple's decision making? In the couple's sexual relationship? Can a sexual relationship be unintentionally abusive? How? How can the church promote healthy mutual submission in marriages? What sort of marital relationship do the teachings and/or polity of your church promote?

2. What role should forgiving the sexual abuser play in the victim's recovery? Can a victim really forgive? How? How should victims of abuse deal with their anger toward their abusers? Can/should a relationship be restored between abuser and abused? Assuming that forgiveness is possible and appropriate, how can pastors and counselors specifically help to bring it about?

3. When sexual abuse is discovered within the Christian community, how should the problem be handled? Should it be handled privately or made public? Who decides? Which is more important in dealing with the abuser: redemption or calling to account? Can one happen without the other? What is the role of the leaders of the Christian community? Should churches have "wounded leaders," men and women in leadership who've been abused themselves and can extend an experiential empathy? Why or why not? What is the role of law enforcement? Does your church have a policy regarding sexual abuse?

4. How should Christians view sexual abusers? Should they be fully welcomed? Welcomed but eyed with suspicion? Shunned? Should acceptance in the Christian community be *unconditional* or contingent? If contingent, upon what? How can Christian leaders help to foster the correct response to sexual abusers? Discuss this with an abuse survivor to get their insights.

5. This chapter stated that the offended party (i.e., abused person) is actually in a position of superior power that overthrows social structures. Discuss the theological reality of that; including the psychological and cultural realities. Do abuse victims view the social system this way? What is the greatest contribution the New Testament can make to the discussion of sexual abuse? Can it contribute to the problem? If so, how? Can it foster healing? If so, how? How does Jesus' ethic of forgiveness empower the powerless?

FOR FURTHER READING

Bromley, Nicole Braddock. *Hush: Moving from Silence to Healing after Childhood Sexual Abuse*. Chicago: Moody Publishers, 2007.

Fortune, Marie M. "Violence against Women: The Way Things Are Is Not the Way They Have To Be." In *Sexuality and the Sacred: Sources for Theological Reflection*, edited by James B. Nelson and Sandra P. Longfellow, 326–334. Louisville, KY: Westminster/ John Knox, 1994.

_____. "Forgiveness: The Last Step." *Violence against Women and Children: A Christian Theological Sourcebook*, edited by Carol J. Adams and Marie M. Fortune, 201–206. New York, NY: Continuum, 1995.

Gagnon, Robert A. J. *The Bible and Homosexual Practice: Texts and Hermeneutics*. Nashville, TN: Abingdon, 2001.

Hays, Richard. *The Moral Vision of the New Testament: A Contemporary Introduction to New Testament Ethics*. San Francisco, CA: HarperSanFrancisco, 1996.

Heitritter, Lynn, and Jeanette Vought. *Helping Victims of Sexual Abuse: A Sensitive Biblical Guide for Counselors, Victims, and Families*. Rev. ed. Minneapolis, MN: Bethany House, 2006.

Horsfield, Peter. "The Gerasene Demoniac and the Sexually Violated." In *Violence against Women and Children: A Christian Theological Sourcebook*, edited by Carol J. Adams and Marie M. Fortune, 141–150. New York, NY: Continuum, 1995.

11

Forgiveness in Sexual Abuse

Defining Our Identity in the Journey Toward Wholeness

JIM SELLS, PhD,
AND EMILY G. HERVEY, MA

T HE VIEWS OF *FORGIVENESS and *sexual abuse (SA) can polarize us into the extremes. In one extreme, forgiveness as an *intervention for sexual abuse is a formula for clinical abuse—as in *re-victimizing the victim by requiring the acceptance of the violator who has caused such great suffering. In the other extreme, it is the most promising source of individual healing and family *reconciliation. Forgiveness may provide a means for *self-care and a potential for restoration of relationships in spite of the destructive experiences in the past.

To some, it is a dangerous threat in which the victim is expected to implement a *denial and an acceptance of immoral, maybe even criminal actions of another. For example, in their classic book on sexual abuse recovery, *The Courage to Heal*, Bass and Davis write: "Trying to forgive is *a futile short-cut* to the healing process . . . Forgiveness is not the grand prize, it is only a by-product. And *it is not even a very important one*."[1]

To others, forgiveness is described in absolute terms—something clients *must* do in order to be whole or healed. McAlister views forgiveness as an imperative, stating that "the client may not initially be able to forget, *but the client must forgive* because we have a need not only to be forgiven but also to forgive."[2]

Most of us are somewhere in the middle of these extremes. We are left to read through the rhetoric and determine how forgiveness is to be used as a tool for our own healing. We must understand how best to aid in the healing of others who have been victimized with sexual invasion as children or young adults by those who were trusted to provide protection. And we must sensitively guide individuals and families who seek healing through repentance and restoration to those who have violated the integrity of personhood through *coercive use of power for personal pleasure.

---

1. Bass and Davis, *The Courage To Heal*, 162; emphasis added. Sounding conflicted on the issue, Judith L. Herman has very little to say about forgiveness—and that in a classic book on *recovery* (*Trauma and Recovery*, esp. 189–190).

2. McAlister, "Christian Counseling and Human Need," 55; emphasis added.

FORGIVENESS: A MULTIVALENT PROCESS

To us, *forgiveness is defined as a gradual healing and restoration process that takes place simultaneously on three levels: psychologically, spiritually, and relationally*. Psychologically, forgiveness includes releasing or overcoming negative and/or detrimental cognitions about and emotions toward the *perpetrator and toward oneself, such as anger, shame, guilt, and bitterness. Spiritually, it is the acceptance of the reality of injury and the commitment to have one's identity defined by the journey toward wholeness through the grace of God rather than allowing one's identity to be defined by the past sinful actions of others and/or oneself. Finally, while it may not include an immediate renewal of a negative relationship, the restoration process also reshapes one's *perception* of the perpetrator, resulting in release from related burdens.

In this chapter we seek to inform the reader of research and theory that addresses sexual abuse recovery with the inclusion of forgiveness and its relationship to reconciliation. We will do so by contemplating four key questions:

- What is the historical use of forgiveness as a tool for healing sexual abuse victimization?

- What is the current practice of forgiveness within the church and the mental health profession regarding sexual abuse?

- Given the findings from historical and current practices, can forgiveness as defined by Christian theology and conducted in Christ-centered contexts speak to the broader mental-health field?

- What are the future trends and unresolved issues related to the practice of forgiveness within the context of the sexually abused?

GAINING HISTORICAL PERSPECTIVE:
SEXUAL ABUSE, FORGIVENESS, AND HEALING

John Beckenbach summarizes the historical use of forgiveness by mental health professionals: "Forgiveness has been, at best, reluctantly considered by the sexual abuse theorists, mostly discouraged and usually ignored."[3] To test the reality of Beckenbach's claim, a computer database search was conducted in November 2009 using *sexual abuse* as the lone query. The search received 6,455 hits, suggesting an abundant volume of empirical and theoretical literature addressing sexual abuse. However, when "forgiveness" was added as a second search word (sexual abuse + forgiveness)—only twenty hits were found. Of those twenty hits, thirteen were written since 2000. With only 0.31 percent of the academic citations addressing sexual abuse including forgiveness as a component of treatment, certainly Beckenbach's claim of exclusion is supported. Beckenbach's assertion suggests an obvious problem—while the public, particularly the Christian culture who deal daily with the reality of sexual abuse and its effects on individual well-being and family functioning consider forgiveness as a means of coping and healing, *the community*

---

3. Beckenbach, *Sexual Abuse and Forgiveness*, 56.

of scholars and therapists are ignorant as to when and how forgiveness might be effectively used as an agent of healing.

Models of Forgiveness in Flux

While minor compared to other perspectives, forgiveness is present in the literature on sexual abuse recovery. Christine Courtois, who has authored groundbreaking insights into sexual abuse research and intervention, discussed it, with appropriate caution, as a beneficial step for some in the advanced stage of recovery.[4] Other significant theorists writing in the last two decades of the twentieth century do not even include forgiveness in their model of recovery.[5] It is doubtful that this lack of inclusion has occurred as a result of intentional antagonism toward forgiveness. *Rather, forgiveness is simply not a concept consistent with their mental framework. Because it doesn't fit with their assumptions, it can be overlooked, minimized, or just discarded.* The majority of those involved in sexual abuse intervention were theorized through *feminist paradigms. A central tenet held by the majority of these thinkers was the need to redistribute *power* from the perpetrator to the victim. Early theorists and many current thinkers, who do not understand the complexity of forgiveness, misconstrue it with allowing sexual *predators to continue perpetrating injury or with demanding that victims must re-victimize themselves by condoning the immoral or illegal actions of those who cause great harm.

In the mid-1990s forgiveness research and interventions became popular among mental health scholars. These interventions varied, some emphasizing *cognitive-behavioral perspectives, such as the research by Robert Enright, while others emphasized *empathy based interventions,[6] and some were drawn from *systemic family theories.[7] With the emergence of *forgiveness interventions, a plurality of researchers found that victims of sexual abuse who include components of forgiveness as part of their treatment demonstrated meaningful benefits.[8] Freedman and Enright[9] were the first to focus specifically on forgiveness as a *therapeutic* tool for victims of sexual abuse. Using Enright's process model, they found that women participating in a childhood *incest survivors group showed higher levels of improved psychological health compared to the control group consisting of traditional *group therapy experiences. In addition, participants showed lower levels of *depression, anxiety, and higher levels of self-esteem. This study opened the door for new paradigms to emerge for forgiveness and sexual abuse.

Initial criticisms that a forgiveness focus would further harm victims who have already suffered childhood/adolescent sexual *trauma were not founded in the empirical

---

4. Courtios, *Healing the Incest Wound*; idem, *Theory, Sequencing and Strategy in Treating Adult Survivors*, 47–60.

5. This list of scholars includes Lew, *Victims No Longer*; Crowder, *Opening the Door*; Briere, "Treating Adults Severely Abused as Children: The Self Trauma Model," 177–204; Gartner, *Betrayed as Boys*.

6. Worthington, *Dimensions of Forgiveness*.

7. Hargrave, *Families and Forgiveness*.

8. Holeman and Myers, "Effects of Forgiveness of Perpetrators on Marital Adjustment for Survivors of Sexual Abuse," 182–188.

9. Freedman and Enright, "Forgiveness as an Intervention Goal with Incest Survivors," 983–992.

research. Conversely, research has indicated that all forgiveness interventions are not beneficial for all participants. Some victims feel forced, compelled, or obligated to "forgive."

CURRENT PRACTICE OF FORGIVENESS IN MENTAL HEALTH AND THE CHURCH

Through the innovative work of serious scholarship, *forgiveness is now recognized as a legitimate mental health intervention and its limitations and applications are becoming more clearly understood.* Current practices include complex definitions of forgiveness that reflect many dimensions and approaches to understanding and addressing healing. Models of forgiveness serve to guide pastors and counselors in understanding contexts *where* forgiveness is advised, *when* in the recovery process it should be introduced, and *what* attitudes and actions need to be applied.

Forgiveness Defined: The Struggle for Definition and Application

Initial definitions of forgiveness centered on the act of "letting go." Pingleton amplified this idea by stating that forgiveness:

> Recognizes, anticipates and attempts to mitigate against the *lex talionis*, or law of the talon—the human organism's universal, almost reflexive propensity for retaliation and *retribution in the face of hurt and pain at the hand of another. Thus, forgiveness can be understood as comprising the antithesis of the individual's natural and predicable response to violation and victimization.[10]

This release could include negative emotions such as: rage, anger, or fury[11]; retaliation, revenge, or record of wrongs;[12] shame;[13] and/or bitterness or resentment.[14] Scholars who have advised a more cautious or contradictory approach to forgiveness would emphasize different aspects in their definition.[15] As Walton notes, common in these perspectives is the concern that "forgiveness [could be] using an interpersonal framework that may include inappropriate condoning and pardoning or contentment with one's victim role. Hence, they argue that forgiveness might function as an opiate perpetuating slavery and oppression and making further victimization more likely."[16]

---

10. Pingleton, "The Role and Function of Forgiveness in the Psychotherapeutic Process," 27.

11. Davenport, "The Function of Anger and Forgiveness," 130–143; Fitzgibbons, "The Cognitive and Emotive Uses of Forgiveness in the Treatment of Anger," 629–633.

12. Cloke, "Revenge, Forgiveness, and the Magic of Mediation," 67–78; DiBlasio, "Practitioners, Religion and the Use of Forgiveness in the Clinical Setting," 181–187.

13. Halling, "Shame and Forgiveness," 74–87.

14. Enright and the Human Development Study Group, "Counseling Within the Forgiveness Triad," 107–126. The Human Development Study Group consists of a community of scholars, faculty and graduate students who collaborate in the study of forgiveness. They meet regularly at the University of Wisconsin—Madison.

15. See Bass and Davis, *The Courage to Heal*; Engel, *Families in Recovery*; and Murphy, *Getting Even*.

16. Walton, "Therapeutic Forgiveness," 195.

Most forgiveness definitions include the fundamental concepts articulated by North[17] and Enright and the Human Development Study Group in which forgiveness is:

> Defined as an unjustly hurt person's act of deliberately giving up resentment toward an offender while fostering the underserved qualities of beneficence and compassion toward the offender . . . There is a decided paradoxical quality to forgiveness as the forgiver gives up the resentment, to which he or she has right, and gives the gift of compassion, to which the offender has no right.[18]

Finally, there is some difference of views as to whether forgiveness is an individual act focusing exclusively on cognitive/*affective processes;[19] or whether forgiveness is an act that combines individual development with relational processes, in which "the work of forgiveness . . . is defined as the effort in restoring love and trustworthiness to relationships so that victims and victimizers can put an end to destructive *entitlement."[20] This disagreement as to whether forgiveness is an *internal cognitive* process or an *external relational* process demonstrates the complexity of forgiveness and the required components of internal cognition and external relational healing that are unique to every injury.

We have declared that forgiveness is an individual and internal process reordering the view of self from the self-definition of being victimized, damaged, destroyed, or marginalized to one who, by the grace of God and the power of the Holy Spirit, is made whole. Forgiveness is first and foremost the reformulation of the way we see ourselves, no longer using the events of trauma, tragedy, or sin as the primary source of definition and identity. It becomes possible to let go of the right to retaliate because it no longer is seen as the essential means by which one maintains protection from future harm, or organizes an understanding of self through past events. The self definition of the victim *as victim* is replaced by the experience of restoring love. Gregory Jones states that, "Those who embody forgiveness discover that one of the chief obstacles to overcome is the tendency to see one's own life as something to be either possessed or simply given over to another's possession; *too often, the result is that people cling to their power or even their powerlessness.*"[21]

Integrating Biblical Perspectives on Forgiveness

In a very useful essay, Steven Tracy describes the complexity of forgiveness within the biblical narrative.[22] He argues that the "letting go" concept is one of a plurality of definitions of forgiveness within Scripture. Tracy argues that this definition of forgiveness is used in a simplistic manner to mean that evil actions, along with the host of ways we can confront *depravity, are to be "let go" or brushed aside. He further argues that forgiveness is a *complex process* involving God, humanity, cognitive, behavioral, affective, and relational components that must be carefully parsed within a comprehensive theology. He identifies key compo-

17. North, "Wrongdoing and Forgiveness," 499–508.
18. Freedman and Enright, "Forgiveness as an Intervention Goal," 983.
19. Baskin and Enright, "Intervention Studies on Forgiveness," 79–90.
20. Hargrave and Sells, "The Development of a Forgiveness Scale," 43.
21. Jones, *Embodying Forgiveness*, 6; emphasis added.
22. Tracy, "Sexual Abuse and Forgiveness," 219–229.

nents in the common definition of forgiveness which, when considered independently, makes forgiveness potentially harmful and theologically naïve. For example, does "let it go" apply to the child who musters the courage to tell his or her unsuspecting parents that a Sunday school teacher, or coach, or a neighbor, or a family member is repeatedly *molesting him or her? No reasoned person and no responsible biblical scholar would agree. Tracy argues that forgiveness operates in three contexts—*judicial, psychological,* and *relational.* A fuller understanding and application of these three are essential when working with sexually abused people.

Judicial Forgiveness

Judicial forgiveness refers to divine pardon and *remission of sin:

> It involves a complete removal of the guilt of one's sin (Ps 51:1–9) and is available to sex offenders, as well as all other categories of sinners (Ps 32:1–5; 1 Cor 6:10–11). The judicial forgiveness of sin by God lies at the very heart of Christianity and the salvation experience. God's desire is unequivocally to forgive and to heal those labeled by society as the worst, most hopeless and worthless sinners, a prospect which was as odious in the first century (Matt 9:9–13) as it is today.[23]

Only God has the judicial authority and freedom to forgive the sin of all, including the victim, victimizer, counselor, friend, and distant bystander. Furthermore, *judicial forgiveness is an act of God to be accepted as a fact*—based on the character of God and his declared commitment to creation through the work of Christ on the cross. This forgiveness is contingent upon confession and repentance (Ps 32:5; 1 John 1:9).[24]

Biblically, forgiveness of sin does not pardon the offender from punishment as part of God's judgment. Moses, while forgiven, was not permitted to enter the Promised Land. David, though forgiven, was not exempted from political turmoil. Jesus draws parallels to both forgiveness (Matt 18:15–18) and divine judgment to those who bring harm to children (Matt 18:1–6). The idea of God's judgment is that he alone has the right to retribution for sin. *Vengeance for evil is a divine activity (Rom 12:19).

Psychological Forgiveness

Psychological forgiveness refers to an internal cognitive process that involves the releasing of negative, corrosive emotions such as hate, resentment, bitterness, and spite and the holding of positive emotions such as peace, joy, patience, and hope. The prevailing emphasis in forgiveness research is to reveal the psychological and physical benefits that come from "letting go" and "holding on." Worthington and his associates have produced a large and methodically respected body of research that demonstrates the positive effects of letting go of "unforgiveness,"[25] as well as the benefits for building the emotions of love, empathy, compassion, and care in the space once occupied by unforgiveness.[26]

23. Tracy, "Sexual Abuse and Forgiveness," 221.

24. Cf. John 24:47; Acts 2:38.

25. McCullough et al., *To Forgive is Human*; Worthington, *Handbook of Forgiveness.*

26. McCullough et al., "Interpersonal Forgiving in Close Relationships," 321–336; Worthington and Wade, "The Psychology of Unforgiveness and Forgiveness and Implications for Clinical Practice," 385–418;

Psychological forgiveness for the victim of sexual abuse is an internal process in which the person *relinquishes the right to retaliate* for the hurt, damage, and injury done to him or her. This "letting go" is not to pardon, excuse, minimize, justify, or silence the trauma; nor to deny the experiences. That which is released is the "emotion of corrosion" that is self-destructive, along with the thought process that destroys the person by declaring that the victim is responsible, guilty, shameful, or devalued. Psychological forgiveness can be accomplished through the actions of faith in God's promise of love, care, presence amidst suffering, and God's own character as loving and purposeful.

RELATIONAL FORGIVENESS

Relational forgiveness is distinct from psychological or judicial forgiveness. *It occurs in the space between people rather than as a cognitive process within a person.* It refers to the potential for restoration of relationship subsequent to confession and repentance. *Relational forgiveness is synonymous with reconciliation.* Biblically, it is the desirable goal for humanity, although it is not always possible, wise, or prudent. A clear emphasis in the New Testament is that of reconciliation between God and humanity (2 Cor 5:18–21) and between persons (Eph 2:11–14). But relational forgiveness requires repentance on the part of the wrongdoer. Jesus taught relational forgiveness by using the powerful condition of *if*, as in "if he repents, forgive him" (Luke 17:3).

The Need for Time in the Forgiving Process
In sexual abuse, repentance by the one who has caused the injury must include: (1) the cessation of harm, (2) and the assumption of responsibility for that harm. Repentance is not a one-act *declaration* of intention or request for forgiveness. It is a change or an "about face." It must be understood that repentance is not a mere act of saying "I am sorry" or offering an apology, just as forgiveness is not a mere act of saying "I forgive you." Both victim and victimizer need time. *Relational forgiveness demands time so that responsibility for one's actions can be demonstrated and so that trustworthiness can be evidenced.* For the perpetrator, there must be genuine "fruit," evident over time. The perpetrator needs to understand that the one harmed also needs time to heal, rather than expecting immediate *absolution. Along with time includes a commitment to the gradual rebuilding of trustworthiness. *It is vital that those working with the abused understand that time is needed in the process of forgiving.*

FORGIVENESS, SEXUAL ABUSE, AND THE CHRISTIAN FAITH

Historically, theological tradition supported the idea of forgiveness as essential to well-being,[27] but professional counselors and psychologists have been resistant to integrating models of forgiveness lest they inadvertently *collude with the abuser in promoting injury. However, the question as to whether forgiveness is a legitimate path for healing is settled,

---

Ripley and Worthington, "Comparison of Hope-focused Communication and Empathy-based Forgiveness Group Interventions to Promote Marital Enrichment," 452–463.

27. Smedes, *Forgive and Forget.*

both empirically and theologically, meaning that our science and our theology indicate that forgiveness can contribute to healing. That it is "settled," however, does not mean that it is simple. Indeed the body of social science literature and theological discourse suggests that the application of forgiveness in all contexts, and especially the context of sexual abuse, requires wisdom and discretion. Research is conclusive that:

> Forgiveness counseling is an *addition* to the repertoire of applications for the professional counseling community . . . Although it should not be seen as a cure for all psychological concerns, there are certain emotional health issues for which it is particularly well suited, such as incest survivors, adolescents hurt by emotionally distant parents, and men hurt by the abortion decision of a partner.[28]

The Christian tradition has and continues to have significant influence as to how forgiveness is understood and how it might be used to address the trauma of sexual abuse and exploitation. While there has been some attention from Christian scholars and clergy that addresses the treatment of sexual abuse within a Christian paradigm,[29] there is little empirical evidence within the Christian culture that addresses sexual abuse and forgiveness (hence the reason for addressing this topic in this book). Tracy also admits: "Although some fine academic work has been done on the general nature of Christian forgiveness, there is a need for additional application of this doctrine to the specific issue of sexual abuse."[30]

Facilitating Forgiveness

Having established that forgiveness is beneficial psychologically and relationally, and is essential theologically, the question becomes *how* it should be addressed and integrated into work with survivors of sexual abuse. Clearly the judicial form of forgiveness is outside of our influence, but the significance of divine forgiveness for humankind serves as bedrock for the biblical call to forgive others (cf. Matt 6:12, 14). Relational and psychological forgiveness may fall closer to the pastor or therapist's realm of influence, but these overlapping boundaries must be approached with care. It is highly unlikely that the abuser will come in humble repentance seeking reconciliation with the abused. Instead, it can at times be critical to ensure that unhealthy relationships that foster such abuse do not continue. *Nevertheless, the trauma of abuse can easily affect other relationships through patterns of mistrust and long-held bitterness—precisely where the work of forgiveness is necessary.*

Different practical approaches to facilitating forgiveness correspond to the variation in psychological and relational models of forgiveness. Three published models fall on a continuum of internal to external goals of forgiveness. Enright[31] focuses predominantly

---

28. Baskin and Enright, "Intervention Studies on Forgiveness," 89; emphasis added.

29. See Holderread-Heggen, *Sexual Abuse in Christian Homes and Churches*; Allender, *The Wounded Heart*; Schmutzer, "A Theology of Sexual Abuse," 785–812.

30. Tracy, "Sexual Abuse and Forgiveness," 219.

31. Enright, *Forgiveness is a Choice*.

on psychological outcomes, while Worthington[32] incorporates a combination of psychological and relational aspects, and Hargrave's[33] emphasis is predominantly relational.

Enright's Guideposts to Forgiveness

Robert Enright has articulated a model of forgiveness that draws from *cognitive development theory. The model has four phases: (1) *Uncovering Anger*, (2) *Deciding to Forgive*, (3) *Working on Forgiveness*, (4) and *Discovery and Release from Emotional Pain.*

(1) Phase #1: Uncovering Anger

This is the process of self examination in which anger surfaces because of the injustice caused by another. The purpose of Phase 1 is to avoid any tendencies toward denial or *avoidance of the difficult appraisal of injury and suffering.

(2) Phase #2: Deciding to Forgive

This is the volitional commitment to focus and remain in the present rather than be manipulated by the pain-filled emotions from the past. This is an internal process in which the person dedicates oneself to the value of forgiveness by: (a) turning away from being controlled by one's past, (b) focusing on the present and future, (c) and choosing a path of forgiveness. Forgiveness at this stage is to win the struggle to "stay in the fight." A frequent repetitive thought process could be, "Yes, I was hurt, but that was then. That is not today." *Before one moves to work on the experience of forgiveness, one has to be committed to staying in the present time frame.*

(3) Phase #3: Working on Forgiveness

This phase permits the injured to gain perspective toward the other who has caused pain. It includes *narratives and journaling that permit the formation of empathy and perspective building so that the victim may learn the aspects of the past that have preceded the experiences of injury. In addition, the individuals are encouraged to think toward compassion of the other, the acceptance of pain, and *offering a gift to the offender* that symbolizes that the injured is no longer controlled by the presence of injury. During this phase Enright encourages the injured party to enter the world of the injurer by learning and recording his or her story. The potential result is empathy and separation. The experience opens the injured to the realization of compassion and *it aids in the creation of boundary* through the discovery that the perpetrator's' actions were likely less about the injured and more about the inadequacies of the perpetrator.

(4) Phase #4: Discovery and Release from Emotional Prison

The process of forgiveness can culminate in tying it to a greater context. The injured must make sense of their suffering. *It must be placed in a frame of meaning.* Enright appeals to psychiatrist and Holocaust survivor Victor Frankl's idea of a "supra-meaning."[34] Forgiveness changes people: in their view of suffering, in their view of the complexity of emotions from

32. Worthington, *Forgiveness and Reconciliation.*
33. See Hargrave, *Families and Forgiveness.*
34. Enright, *Forgiveness is a Choice*, 174.

injury by and to others, in the embrace of community, in identifying renewed purpose, and in experiencing the freedom from the weight of injury/revengefulness.

Worthington's REACH Model

Everett Worthington's[35] approach incorporates five components to facilitate relational forgiveness.

(1) *Recall the Hurt:* This is an opportunity for emotional expression and assessment. While formal assessment may not be required, it provides a means of measuring changes over time. Recalling the event(s) may aid overall processing, which is helpful in most traumatic situations. Other exercises can promote a more objective or compassionate view, such as asking the client to imagine it from the perpetrator's perspective.

(2) *Empathy:* Worthington suggests this is a period of replacing unforgiving emotions with empathy, sympathy, compassion, and love toward the perpetrator, through activities such as considering the perpetrator's own problems. This process is, in essence, "hate replacement." Emotions of unforgiveness are replaced, carefully and compassionately, with emotions of forgiveness. The client is not expected to "become buddies" with the one who caused hurt. Rather the expectation is to "reconsider." That is, to think along a new path the story and circumstances of the one who caused harm.

(3) *Altruistic Gift of Forgiveness:* While forgiveness is beneficial to the individual, this step also seeks to develop altruistic attitudes toward the perpetrator. Drawn from the concept of "love your enemies," it seeks to implement a love for the one who has caused hurt without placing the injured in the position to become traumatized by additional injury. The client may be asked to remember an incident of offending another, being forgiven, and the resulting gratitude.

(4) *Commitment to the Forgiveness Experienced:* This is a *public* commitment, even if only with the pastor or therapist, to continue in the progress being made. It is important to offer continuing encouragement to the *survivor as the individual moves from *decisional* forgiveness to *emotional* forgiveness.

(5) *Hold on to the Forgiveness:* It is common for survivors to later doubt the forgiveness given, particularly when other negative emotions arise, often in a form of *defenses or protections. Fears that some former ways of the relationship will return are central in remaining guarded from further harm. *The forgiveness journey requires that those seeking to forgive are talking through the emotions with trusted confidants.* Emotions fire off in multiple directions. Misreading the actions and intentions of others is common. The individual must learn to interrupt negative *ruminations and emotions, reconsider snap judgements, and think more positively to maintain emotional forgiveness.

Worthington's model of forgiveness is thoughtful, grounded in sound theology. A significant body of research has guided its method and demonstrated its effectiveness. It works, but it works best with a carefully designed environment with a counselor or informed support system that can assist in the healing process. Forgiveness does not hap-

---

35. See Worthington, *Forgiveness and Reconciliation.*

pen because a book is read or a seminar attended. In this model it occurs through careful intention to learn to grow and to heal.

HARGRAVE'S FOUR STATIONS OF FORGIVENESS

T. D. Hargrave[36] proposes four stations in the forgiveness process. Rather than progressive stages addressed in the other theories, he proposes "stations." Hargrave writes that "it is inappropriate to assume that people move through them sequentially or that they do not oscillate between stations many times in the course of the same relationship. The stations of forgiveness are simply constructs for us to better understand the work of forgiveness."[37] The four stations are divided into two divisions—**Exonerating**, which contains the stations of *Insight* and *Understanding*, and **Forgiving**, which includes *Giving Opportunity for Compensation* and the *Overt Act of Forgiving*.

Division I: Exonerating

(1) The station of *Insight*—the victim becomes aware of the steps and processes that lead to the perpetuation of injury, then intentionally blocks that process in order to cease further harm. "Insight allows persons to see the mechanisms that have caused the damage and hurt, and this perspective then provides them with the means to protect themselves from further hurt and damage."[38] An important area of growth for the victim is to discover that he or she does possess power in self-protection. Insuring such immediate safety not only secures the person from historical harm, it also provides an initial foray into the experience of autonomy.

(2) The station of *Understanding*—permits the injured to comprehend the motives, sources, and causes of the perpetrator's actions. By understanding the experiences of the other, the injured realizes that: (a) their injuries received at the hand of the injurer had less to do with the injured and *more to do with the prior transmission of family injury occurring over generations*; (b) and the injury can become *depersonalized by the injured, allowing the injured to let go of self-condemnation and *self-loathing.

For abuse victims, it is common for the journey of forgiveness to pause or even stop at understanding—thereby *avoiding interactions far more vulnerable*. Yet often, and counter-intuitively, the injured and injurer are capable of deeper and fuller experiences of forgiveness.

Division II: Forgiving

(3) The station of *Giving Opportunity for Compensation*—provides specific steps toward relational repair on the part of the injurer toward the one who is injured. This station permits trust to gradually be reconstructed. Through specific acts of goodness, wrongdoing is acknowledged and a commitment to repair the injuries is formally made.

---

36. Hargrave, *Families and Forgiveness*, 15.

37. Ibid.

38. Ibid., 22

(4) The station of *Overt Act of Forgiveness*—is achieved "by the positioning of the victim and victimizer in an immediate alignment of love and trust."[39] This is their mutual declaration to live in a relationship different from the one defined previously. Their relational dynamic is now characterized by a new limitation, that of Buber's I–Thou. There is a demonstration of disciplined mutual respect. Such a boundary serves as a protection to assure that the past will not invade and destroy the fragile ongoing relationship. *Significantly, the past is not erased and, in fact, can be an important continued conversation, but it is not to be used to extract additional payment or to cause further injury.*

Some Contingencies and Complexities in Sexual Abuse and Forgiveness

Robert Roberts[40] also recognizes the limitations of forgiveness, including: (1) the severity of the offense, (2) a lack of repentance, (3) the absence of suffering or remorse by the offender, (4) moral distance, (5) and a lack of relationship with the offender. These factors may be prominent in a scenario of sexual abuse, which is a severe offense and very likely may be in the context of a relationship that cannot or should not be maintained due to the danger of future abuse. *This is often a key concern, as the majority of sexual abuse incidents take place with someone known by the victim, only 4 percent of abusers being strangers.*[41] In addition, abusive relationships are often ongoing rather than a single episode of abuse. It is in these circumstances that the importance of reconciliation may be trumped by safety. This may seem simple if the perpetrator was a stranger, as no one would expect the victim to ever talk with their victimizer again, much less seek reconciliation. But when it occurs in one's immediate circle of family and friends, reconciliation is more likely to be encouraged, whether for the sake of outward appearance or genuinely good intentions. In such a context, it is critical to conduct a careful *risk assessment before supporting renewed relationships.

THE REALITY OF ANGER IN FORGIVENESS: THE ROLE OF THE COUNSELOR AND PASTOR

While Roberts'[42] emphasis is on the restoration of relationships, his discussion of overcoming the emotion of anger can also be applied on an *internal* basis. The survivor may still be able to view the abuser's perspective or to become aware of the commonality of sin across humanity and the subsequent need for forgiveness that all people have. These perspectives help overcome the anger, even in the absence of the offender. Addressing feelings of anger and hate toward the abuser requires *both cognitive and emotional attention.* This may include identifying what *triggers the negative thoughts and feelings, processing internal and external responses, and developing alternative means of response.

---

39. Ibid., 90.

40. Roberts, "Forgivingness," 289–306.

41. Langan and Harlow, "Child Rape Victims," 1992.

42. Roberts, "Forgivingness."

Here meaningful Scriptures, such as reminders of God's grace (Eph 2:7), forgiveness (Ps 65:3; 1 John 1:9), and prayer (Ps 34:6; Phil 4:6) can serve as helpful tools.

When seeing forgiveness as centered on overcoming emotions of anger, the problem of anger should be acknowledged as greater than solely what is felt toward the perpetrator. First, individuals who have been sexually abused commonly hold anger toward themselves. This may be in a form of *self-blame, whether in their initial desire to be with the offender or guilt from any physical pleasure they felt during sexual interaction.[43] This goes hand in hand with a lower self-esteem, as they feel the experience of abuse become part of their identity. To address these negative feelings toward the self, the counselor or pastor needs to assess the survivor's level of shame, *normalize these reactions and emotions vis-à-vis the trauma, and use biblical truths to counter the warped thoughts from a Christian perspective. God's forgiveness and unconditional love toward them are always present. Survivors of abuse need to be reminded that they are guilt-free through Christ's *atonement and they can find their true, purified identity in him.

However, for some victims these truths can be very difficult to accept and internalize, *particularly if they also feel anger toward God for allowing the abuse to occur.* Almost any form of suffering is followed by the "why?" cry, the struggle to understand whether the occurrence was some form of testing, punishment, or simply abandonment by God. Examples of suffering and the resulting questions in the mind of the afflicted are present throughout Scripture: from Job's extensive monologues to Jesus Christ's own cry, "My God, My God, why have you forsaken me?" (Mark 15:34). *In the midst of deep pain and guilt it may be a challenge for the abused to even acknowledge their anger toward God,* while others might express it openly. Susan Turrell and Cassandra Thomas suggest that it is better to express anger toward God, who already knows the emotions present and can handle that anger, than for the victim to hide it and live hypocritically, feeling guilty for that anger. God does not need judicial forgiveness but wants the individual to find the psychological forgiveness for their own well-being and relational forgiveness so as to accept God's love fully.

Forgiveness as a Christian Disposition

Appropriately, Roberts takes forgiveness a step beyond a specific *act* and presents "forgivingness" as a virtue, or the disposition to go through the process of forgiveness. An individual applying greater forgiveness seeks harmonious relationships with others and has the capacity to control their emotions of anger. *Forgivingness* is the ability to allow empathy to reduce the feelings of anger stemming from the consideration of the perpetrator's own suffering and their commonality of sin.

This forgiveness is first and foremost an *internal* process. It is a product of a cognitive maturation in which the forgiver first embodies forgiveness as a way of being. Secondarily, forgiveness can engage the perpetrator in stages of restoration, if circumstances such as safety, trust, and repentance are evident. From this standpoint, overall growth as an indi-

---

43. Turrel and Thomas, "Where Was God? Utilizing Spirituality with Christian Survivors of Sexual Abuse," 133–147.

vidual—just as someone could become more patient or kind—would precede the ability to address a specific situation with an attitude of forgiveness. From a Christian perspective, such a virtue may stem from growth in the individual's relationship with God, being made in his *image (Gen 1:26; Jam 3:9) and reflecting his forgiving nature.

From a theological perspective, forgiveness is crucial. Numerous times Jesus calls for us to offer forgiveness, and at the same time, receive forgiveness—it flows both ways: "For if you forgive other people when they sin against you, your heavenly Father will also forgive you. But if you do not forgive others their sins, your Father will not forgive your sins" (Matt 6:14–15). While this may sound like an *ultimatum*, a prerequisite to receiving forgiveness, it does not necessarily refer to a specific act that one must complete to acquire God's forgiveness. Rather, it may be seen as a process, or a means of placing oneself in a position of being able to receive God's forgiveness. Ultimately, *forgiven by God, one is then freed to forgive.*[44] By Tracy's model, this may be predominantly in the psychological context of forgiveness, but rather than being purely cognitive and emotional, the *process* itself may be seen on a spiritual level, relinquishing the resentment and receiving God's grace.[45] Helping both the abused and perpetrator cultivate humility is vital in this process of forgiveness.[46]

Forgiveness and Reconciliation: Learning a Lifestyle

L. Gregory Jones takes the model of Tracy further in his presentation of "embodying forgiveness."[47] He claims: "forgiveness is not primarily a *word* that is spoken or an *action* that is performed or a *feeling* that is felt. It is a *way of life* appropriate to friendship with the Triune God. As such, it includes within it appropriate words, actions, and feelings."[48] Jones presents forgiveness as a lifelong learning experience as an apprentice under the tutelage of the Giver of perfect forgiveness, including both transformation as an individual as well as learning to use forgiveness in the daily context. From this perspective, *Christian forgiveness is based on commitment to a way of life that reflects God's holiness, both through "unlearning" sin and replacing it with life in communion with God, one another, and the rest of creation.*

Such communion is also the basis for reconciliation, particularly among believers. Forgiveness as communion with God is important for all, but it can be a special source of comfort for those who experience the continued effects of physical and psychological trauma through such things as: *panic attacks, *body memory, *flashbacks, *intrusive thoughts or reoccurring images. *To embody this forgiveness is to define one's life by who we love, and who loves us, rather than by who we hate* (or by whom we have been hurt) and who hates us (or who has hurt us). When one's identity is intimately tied to Christ and we

---

44. Cf. Matt 9:2, 5, 6; 12:31–32; 18:32; Eph 4:31–5:2; Col 3:13.

45. Tracy, "Sexual Abuse and Forgiveness," 219.

46. Regarding humility and forgiveness, see the helpful analysis of Worthington, *A Just Forgiveness*, esp. 47–53, 80–85, 98–101, 167–69, 223–30; idem, *Forgiveness and Reconciliation*.

47. See Jones, *Embodying Forgiveness*.

48. Ibid., 218; emphasis added.

embody forgiveness as indeed he has forgiven us, it becomes possible to understand pain, suffering, and its lasting residual effects through that experience. The alternative, seeking to understand forgiveness through a perpetrator's depravity, will lead one to despair and rage.

The outgrowth of forgiveness from a lifestyle of holiness may sound idealistic or unrealistic in today's world of atrocities, including that of sexual abuse. However, Jones also recognizes the presence of "enemies," even as part of Christ's command to love our enemies (Matt 5:44; Luke 6:27), and does not expect an immediate reconciliation, instead holding such forgiveness as part of the life-long process. His emphasis on the communion that depends on reconciliation remains within the Christian community; injustice and hostility cannot be eradicated in the present age, and therefore repentance and reconciliation is not always possible. Instead, the challenge may be to maintain a *willingness* to reconcile if the offender were to fully repent.

In addition, God's mercy does not replace judgment; nor is forgiveness a substitute for accountability and punishment, which precede repentance. But regardless of the outcomes in the life of the offender, the call remains to show love, which stems from the *embodiment of forgiveness. The community of the cross plays a vital role in providing a redemptive context for this love to occur through the direct confrontation of two stories: the reality of our mutual brokenness/sinfulness and the reality of healing forgiveness. So Jones writes:

> We cannot afford to fail to acknowledge these pains and struggles, and even if we proclaim—albeit, at the least in some circumstances, cautiously or even silently— that God's forgiveness bears no limits, we will do so authentically *only* if we confront the profound pain that many of our brothers and sisters (and perhaps we ourselves) have suffered and continue to suffer *as a result of our pervasive brokenness*, the ways in which *we diminish and destroy one another and ourselves*. That is, we cannot afford to "pass" on these stories; we need to confront them.[49]

CONCLUSION: SOME FUTURE DIRECTIONS AND UNRESOLVED NEEDS

Forgiveness should not be seen as a single task or goal to be reached by the survivor of sexual abuse. Rather, it is an integral part of a long period of growth and restoration. In some ways it is both a *factor* facilitating healing and an *outcome* of that healing process. This may be seen in a circular pattern, as the survivor draws near to God, receiving his forgiveness, and begins to replace feelings of anger and bitterness with God's love. The more restoration that takes place, the more forgiveness can overcome anger. The more forgiveness is present, the more healing will follow. Thus, in counseling, forgiveness may not be a single item to address but rather an ongoing *theme*, inseparable from spiritual growth and emotional renewal.

As evident throughout this chapter, many different models and approaches to the concept of forgiveness have been suggested. The research on the subject of forgiveness and

---

49. Jones, *Embodying Forgiveness*, 297; emphasis added.

sexual abuse is lacking both in quantity and in quality, as vague definitions and pragmatic goals make it difficult to draw conclusions from multiple studies that may be exploring different components of forgiveness. There is an even greater void in quality research exploring the relationship between spirituality and forgiveness in the context of sexual abuse. While quantifying forgiveness may be difficult, particularly when viewed as a way of life, research is still beneficial in identifying effective means of therapy and reducing unhelpful practices while endeavoring to include forgiveness in the healing process.

There is no easy path to follow to reach a point of complete forgiveness. Instead it is a long, challenging, and unique journey for each individual. However, it is critical that we as mental health professionals, pastors, and spiritual mentors seek effective means of facilitating this process. This includes grappling with the *significance* and *means* of incorporating forgiveness into the healing process for abuse survivors, both from an empirical and theological perspective. Concrete conclusions may remain illusive, but room for growth is abundant.

QUESTIONS FOR DISCUSSION

1. In this chapter, forgiveness was defined as a gradual healing, a process of restoration that takes place simultaneously on three levels: psychologically, spiritually, and relationally. Compare and contrast this process definition with the idea that forgiveness is a *declaration* or a one-time act. What is the role of *non-abused* family members and/or church leadership who grow impatient, not adequately understanding why a sexually abused man or woman is unable to "find victory" and forgiveness (as they believe it should be)? Discuss a scenario or two where this has happened? What did the survivor end up doing?

2. With ideas found in this and the other chapters in this book, consider how sexual violation alters the general dialogue and application of forgiveness. Why is forgiveness not the first or main objective? Talk to a survivor about this. How do they see forgiveness operating in their healing journey? Where is this person in their healing process? Why? What are the competing "voices" they hear, pulling them in various directions (i.e., the therapists, family members, spiritual leaders, etc.)?

3. How should pastors and counselors modify their counsel based on the age of the victim, nature of abuse, and circumstances surrounding the violation and the recovery? If you are teaching in an academic setting, how do you teach the issue of forgiveness? How is forgiveness taught and applied to cases of abuse in your church? How does your church policy on sexual abuse need to change?

4. List some obstacles that individuals who have been abused must face on their journey toward forgiveness? How should those obstacles best be addressed? As a counselor or educator, how would you describe the *spiritual* component of your definition of forgiveness? What does forgiveness mean without a biblical God? As a pastor or church leader, when was the last time you heard an abuse survivor tell their "story" about their journey toward forgiveness and reconciliation?

5. In this chapter, forgiveness is understood as an internal healing process that can lead to the potential of relationship restoration. How might the *intergenerational transmission (i.e., over generations) of family injury affect a present abuse survivor's context of healing? What are the dangers that must be considered if the forgiveness process moves too quickly toward reconciliation or if reconciliation is seen as the primary objective?

6. Discuss the ideas of "decisional forgiveness" and "emotional forgiveness." How is the healing process enhanced by the separation of forgiveness into these two themes? What are the potential outcomes of both in one's journey toward healing?

7. If you are a survivor, how in particular has this chapter helped you? If you are a pastor, what do you see differently about sexual abuse and forgiveness? If you are a counselor, what part of this discussion on forgiveness could you integrate more into your practice? If you are a spouse of a survivor, what hope does this chapter give you?

FOR FURTHER READING

Couenhoven, Jesse. "Forgiveness and Restoration: A Theological Exploration." *The Journal of Religion* 90 (2010): 148–155.

Enright, R. D. *Forgiveness Is a Choice: A Step by Step Process for Resolving Anger and Restoring Hope.* Washington, DC: American Psychological Association, 2001.

Hargrave, T. D. *Families and Forgiveness: Healing Wounds in the Intergenerational Family.* New York, NY: Brunner/Mazel, 1994.

Jones, L. Gregory. *Embodying Forgiveness: A Theological Analysis.* Grand Rapids, MI: Eerdmanns Press, 1995.

Journal of Psychology & Christianity. Studies in Forgiveness (Special Issue). ed. Everette L. Worthington, Jr. 27 (2008): 293–370.

Lampman, Lisa B., ed. *God and the Victim: Theological Reflections on Evil, Victimization, Justice, and Forgiveness.* Grand Rapids: Eerdmans, 1999.

Schimmel, Solomon. *Wounds Not Healed by Time: The Power of Repentance and Forgiveness.* Oxford: Oxford University Press, 2002.

Schmutzer, Andrew J. "Spiritual Formation and Sexual Abuse: Embodiment, Community, and Healing." *Journal of Spiritual Formation & Soul Care* 2 (2009): 67–86.

Worthington, Everett L. Jr. *A Just Forgiveness: Responsible Healing without Excusing Injustice.* Downers Grove, IL: IVP, 2009.

_____. *Forgiveness and Reconciliation: Theory and Application.* New York, NY: Routledge, 2006.

12

Sexual Abuse and a Theology of Embodiment

Incarnating Healing

JOY A. SCHROEDER, PhD

✷ S EXUAL ABUSE (SA) IS a profound violation of a person's body, with devastating effects on one's psyche. It causes *survivors to experience their own bodies as sites of violence and *trauma, frequently altering victims' views of their bodies. According to one survivor, "I was no longer the same person I had been before the assault, and one of the ways in which I seemed changed was that I had a different relationship with my body. *My body was now perceived as an enemy . . . and as a site of increased vulnerability.*"[1] Sometimes sexual abuse causes survivors to experience a sense of alienation and detachment from their bodies. A survivor of childhood *incest reports: "My body doesn't belong to me—it's as if because he possessed it, he owns it. It feels like a house I can be thrown out of at any time."[2] Some victims even regard their bodies as something to be despised.

Given the *corporeality of sexual abuse, it is vital for pastoral caregivers to reflect theologically on what it means to be "embodied."[3] In the past three decades, a growing number of theologians have tried to recover the wisdom of the biblical teachings about the body. Theologies of *embodiment resist a body-soul *dualism that pits body against soul, denigrating the body as something inferior or unworthy. The soul is not a detachable entity that, at death, discards the body as if it were a shell or packaging. Embodiment theologies assert that we don't *possess* bodies in the manner that someone owns a coat or automobile. Rather, *the body is integral to one's identity*. J. Philip Newell writes: "We are rooted in our bodies. At birth, in our play and work together, in our love-making and at our death, it is not simply that we *have* bodies. It is more that we *are* bodies."[4] At the same time, we cannot be reduced to our bodies and sexual organs. With profound reverence for the body, *embodiment theology condemns violence that treats people's bodies as objects or commodities to be abused and exploited.

---

1. Brison, *Aftermath*, 44; emphasis added.
2. Westerlund, *Women's Sexuality After Childhood Incest*, 53.
3. For the language of "corporeality" of sexual violence, I am indebted to Blyth, "Terrible Silence, Eternal Silence," 67–71.
4. Newell, *Echo of the Soul*, ix.

Christian embodiment theology does not offer new, innovative doctrines that diverge from church teachings. Rather, it *reclaims* a neglected aspect of Christian tradition. Elisabeth Moltmann-Wendell writes: "A theology of embodiment does not seek to outline a new theology, but it does seek to open up a forgotten place which is important today, from which there can be theological thought and action: the human body."[5] Embodiment theology affirms the goodness of the flesh, created by a gracious God who loves our bodies.[6] It ponders the meaning of Christ's *incarnation. It considers Jesus' ministry of healing, his bodily suffering, death, and resurrection, as well as his promise that we ourselves will experience bodily resurrection. The central Christian doctrines related to embodiment have relevance for the pastoral care and healing of survivors of sexual abuse.

HISTORICAL AND CONTEMPORARY CHRISTIAN THEOLOGIES OF EMBODIMENT

Though "embodiment theology" is a recent term, popularized in the 1970s and 1980s by works such as James Nelson's *Embodiment: An Approach to Sexuality and Christian Theology*, its principles have roots in the Bible and early Christian teachings.[7] In John 1:14, we read: "And the Word became flesh and lived among us."[8] The church rejected *Docetism, the teaching that Jesus came as an apparition, only *appearing* to be human. Likewise, the church condemned *Gnosticism and *Catharism, movements which denied the reality of the created goodness of human bodies. Despite suspicion of embodiment, which subjects humans to "the ravages of time, decay, spatial limitation, and ethical imperfection,"[9] Christian tradition has repeatedly professed that the body is a noble and worthy creation. Furthermore, Christians have insisted that bodies will be raised from death. Beth Felker Jones asserts: "Orthodox understandings of the body were formulated in careful response to Gnostic alternatives."[10] Even at times when some Christians advocated extreme fasting and self-inflicted punishments, the church never denied the reality of the incarnation or the resurrection.[11]

Through the centuries, however, Christians have been ambivalent about human flesh. Despite the centrality of teachings that honor creation, Jesus' incarnation, and bodily resurrection, Christianity has been influenced by *dualistic philosophies that emphasize the soul's flight from the body and rejection of the material world. Plato had commended philosophers for "despising the body" as an "an impediment which by its presence pre-

---

5. Moltmann-Wendel, *I Am My Body*, 103.

6. "Flesh" here refers to the physical, embodied nature of humans. In the New Testament, "flesh" sometimes has a neutral or positive meaning. John 1:14 says that "the Word (i.e., God the Son) became flesh and dwelt with humans," an event which was deep affirmation of flesh. Elsewhere in the New Testament, especially the writings of St. Paul, "flesh" does not refer to the physical body *per se*. Rather, the term is used as a way to refer to sin and disorder. Sinful impulses are said to arise from "the flesh" (cf. Romans 8).

7. Nelson, *Embodiment*.

8. Scripture quotations are from the New Revised Standard Version (NRSV).

9. Cox Miller, *The Corporeal Imagination*, 5.

10. Felker Jones, *Marks of His Wounds*, 12.

11. See Walker Bynum, *The Resurrection of the Body in Western Christianity, 200–1336*, 59–113.

vents the soul from attaining to truth."[12] Unfortunately, many Christians appropriated such dualism by adapting it and *stressing the importance of the body's subjection to the soul.* Furthermore, traditional western Christian theology has often regarded bodies—especially the bodies of women—with deep suspicion. The flesh was often considered a site of lust, sin, corruption, and decay. In fact, numerous Christians believed that sexual abuse was provoked by the body of the victim (for instance, by a woman's beauty, demeanor, or presence to outdoors).[13] Thomas Ryan claims: "On the one hand, [Christianity] has the highest theological evaluation of the body among all the religions of the world, and on the other hand, it has given little attention to the body's role in the spiritual life in *positive* terms."[14]

In the last quarter of the twentieth century, theologians and ethicists worked to counteract teachings that denigrate the body. Wishing to heal the body-soul split often found in Christian thought, they reclaimed a biblical "theology of the body" or embodiment theology, which celebrates the body and sexuality as a gracious gift from God. Writing in 1978, James Nelson said that many people experienced a sexual shame, *repression, alienation, and *"dissociation of self from body" brought about by body-soul dualism. Affirming the goodness of the body and sexuality, Nelson exhorted his readers to think of the body *as* self.[15] Pope John Paul II also wrote on the "theology of the body" in the 1970s and 1980s, urging Christians to celebrate bodies and sexuality as gifts from God, to be used in ways that were loving and life-giving rather than exploitative.[16]

A number of these seminal books were written before it became common to talk openly about sexual abuse in the media, schools, daytime talk shows, or theological writings. Thus, while a few late twentieth-century "embodiment theologians" offered a sensitive acknowledgement of sexual abuse, in most cases references to sexual violation were far too brief or absent altogether.[17] In many cases, the desire (however worthy) to *celebrate* embodiment kept the focus away from the ways the body has been a site of violence. There is now a growing awareness that *embodiment theology needs to deal more fully with the issues of bodily abuse.* Jones writes: "The theology of the body is important because real bodies are broken, beaten, *raped, tortured, and killed."[18] Nevertheless, while some recent works have argued that theological reflection on embodiment has implications for discussions of abuse, most authors have simply left it for others to develop these ideas.[19] But this discussion is needed now.

---

12. Plato, *Phaedo*, 48–49.

13. Schroeder, *Dinah's Lament*, 14–29, 162–64.

14. Ryan, *Reclaiming the Body in Christian Spirituality*, xi; emphasis added.

15. Nelson, *Embodiment*, 20.

16. John Paul II, *Man and Woman He Created Them*, 297–99.

17. For instance, James B. Nelson only briefly mentions sexual violence in *Body Theology*, 17, 89.

18. Jones, *Marks of His Wounds*, 11.

19. Moltmann-Wendel (*I Am My Body*, 13–15, 103) mentions the importance of considering the experience of sexual violation. However, she does not explore sexual abuse at any length. She says that "topics like handicap, incest, rape, which are only alluded to here, need a separate investigation" (xiv).

In responding to sexual abuse, embodiment theology is a resource whose potential has been largely untapped. This chapter is a preliminary attempt to consider embodiment theology through the lens of sexual abuse, bringing Christian theology into conversation with the words and experiences of survivors. A theology of the body must speak to the bodies and spirits of those broken by sexual abuse, asking questions such as: "What might 'embodiment theology' mean to a boy who was molested by his minister?" "How is it possible to affirm and celebrate the goodness of the body when one's body has been harmed and violated in profound ways?" So we now turn to the central Christian teachings about the body, examining ways that a theology of embodiment can serve as a resource for those who care for and respond to survivors.

EMBODIMENT, CREATION,
AND THE SIN OF SEXUAL ABUSE

Scripture and Christian teachings affirm the goodness of embodied humanity. After creating humans in the divine *image (Gen 1:27), God views all of creation as "very good" (Gen 1:31). Genesis 2 celebrates the creation of Adam from the earth (Gen 2:7). His response when he sees the woman taken from his side is an exultant cry: "This at last is bone of my bone of my bones and flesh of my flesh" (Gen 2:23). The psalmist praises the mysterious, creative power of God: "For it was you who formed my inward parts, you knit me together in my mother's womb. I praise you, for I am fearfully and wonderfully made" (Ps 139:13–14). Compare this to the *self-hatred of an assault victim, attacked at knifepoint by a man who entered her bedroom at night: "Never having liked my body, I've carried a particular disdain for it since my assault. I especially hate my breasts and think of them as beaten and bruised, as they were during the assault."[20] Scripture offers an alternative perspective, asserting the goodness of human bodies, including *victimized* bodies.

A theology of embodiment *celebrates the enfleshed body as wonderfully and beautifully made*. Sexual abuse should be regarded as a grotesque mistreatment and abuse of this gift. Whenever a body is threatened or harmed by sexual assault, incest, *childhood sexual abuse (CSA), *human trafficking, or any other form of sexual abuse, the abuser has harmed someone who was lovingly made by a gracious God. In all too many cases, in a horrific misuse and violation of our human calling to care for one another, sexual abuse is perpetrated by someone who has a special responsibility to *protect* the victim: a parent, spouse, relative, teacher, athletic coach, daycare worker, babysitter, or minister. It is vital that we name sexual abuse and violence as *sin*. *Abuse perpetrated upon the victim's body is experienced as an attack upon the self.* One survivor writes that sexual abuse "felt like a sword had pierced through every layer of my skin, flesh, and bone and on to my core, leaving a virulent solution that seeped into my soul."[21]

Theologians of embodiment insist on the intimate relationship between the person and his or her body. This is borne out in the words of survivors who describe the intensely *corporeal* experience of sexual abuse *with profoundly harmful effects upon the psyche*. A

---

20. Quoted in Carosella, *Who's Afraid of the Dark?*, 36.
21. Ibid., 41.

survivor of incestuous childhood sexual abuse says: "Something has broken in me and I do not know if I will ever be whole again."[22] One individual assaulted at gunpoint writes: "The rape was in my body, my heart, my relationships, my perceptions of the world and my reactions to the world."[23] An abuse survivor says: "The soreness of my physical wounds penetrated to every bone in my body. As my body was broken, so too was my spirit."[24] Reflecting on her recovery from sexual assault, Susan Brison writes: "The intermingling of mind and body is also apparent in traumatic memories that remain in the body, in each of the senses, in the heart that races and skin that crawls whenever something resurrects the only slightly buried terror."[25] Rhonda Copelon observes that sexual violence renders a victim "homeless" in one's own body.[26]

The close connection between bodily and emotional experience causes many victims to attempt to escape *from* their bodies, the very site of pain and shame. Victims of sexual abuse may experience dissociation, a sense of detachment from their own bodies. Separating oneself from the body that is being abused is a way for a victim to cope (at least temporarily) with the profound corporeality of the abuse. One survivor writes: "I was just really aware that it wasn't my body, it was me and my brain was somewhere else, just staring down at what was happening—it just wasn't real, like it isn't me, it isn't me!"[27] Another abuse victim says, "In that moment, I detached my mind from my body."[28] An adult survivor of childhood incest reports: "I think I used to shut my mind off to it."[29] A woman abused as a teenager by an acquaintance recalls: "Part of me watched and made narrative comments: 'His hand is on your breast' and 'you cannot move.'"[30] As noted in other chapters of this book, this sense of dissociation can endure long after the abuse has ended. One childhood incest survivor says: "My body is like a stranger to me, somehow disconnected from the real me."[31]

Some cultures regard a victim's body as tainted or polluted by the sexual abuse he or she endured.[32] Often victims internalize the sense of being polluted by sexual abuse. In her study of survivors of sexual violation, Sue Lees reports that victims often have "feelings of being dirty, defiled, contaminated"[33] and "cannot stop scrubbing themselves afterward."[34] We need a more accurate and sensitive framing of sexual abuse as sin in

22. Ibid., 176.
23. Ibid., 130.
24. Ibid., 59.
25. Brison, *Aftermath*, 44.
26. Copelon, "Gendered War Crimes," 202.
27. Quoted in Kelly, *Surviving Sexual Violence*, 171.
28. Carosella, *Who's Afraid*, 58.
29. Kelly, *Surviving Sexual Violence*, 175.
30. Carosella, *Who's Afraid*, 24. In the report, notice the third person perspective ("his"), maintained to distance the victim from victimizer and process the trauma.
31. Westerlund, *Women's Sexuality*, 54.
32. Lees, *Carnal Knowledge*, 1–2.
33. Ibid., 19.
34. Ibid., 2.

which guilt attaches only to the *perpetrator. Sometimes sexual abuse is treated chiefly as a sexual infraction—as though it were chiefly a form of *fornication or adultery—rather than the bodily abuse of persons whom God created, blessed, and pronounced as "good" (Gen 1:28, 31). Sin has often been seen as succumbing to carnality, lust, and "the flesh." But in the case of sexual abuse, it is better to regard a perpetrator's actions as a heinous offense against the body and integrity of someone who is God's beloved handiwork. Nancy J. Ramsey emphasizes that *sexual abuse survivors need "images of God's power and love that unequivocally disclose God's righteous anger in response to their abuse, fierce commitment to their healing and empowerment, and tender compassion for their wounded bodies and spirits."*[35]

AN EMBODIED SAVIOR: THE INCARNATION, MINISTRY, AND SUFFERING OF JESUS

At the incarnation, God the Son became flesh, assumed human nature, and joined the company of embodied beings. Thomas Ryan writes: "In the birth-event at Bethlehem, the Eternal Word of God took on the world as part of himself in the body of Jesus of Nazareth. The stuff of material creation quite literally became the body of God."[36] His birth has profound implications. Beth Felker Jones asserts: "Because the Word was made flesh, our thinking about our own flesh must be irrevocably altered."[37] Both intended embodied living, and especially those in broken and violated bodies deserve *empathy and special care. This is also necessary if violence is to be adequately addressed.

A central part of Jesus' ministry was the healing of people's bodies. Scripture asserts that this was an integral part of his self-understanding as "Messiah" (Matt 11:2–5). Jesus directed his followers to tend to the bodily afflictions of others (Matt 25:31–46; Luke 9:1–2; 10:9). A particularly pertinent account in Jesus' ministry was his healing of the woman with "the flow of blood" when she touched the hem of his robe (Mark 5:24–34). Moltmann-Wendell recommends that Christians use this story as the starting point for a theology of embodiment, for "more than any other, this healing story, the story of the woman with a flow of blood, plunges us deeply into the dimensions of the body . . ."[38] Vaginal hemorrhaging might seem an unseemly topic for religious literature, yet this account is included in Scripture. Jesus' ministry of healing included even the most intimate of bodily afflictions—"she felt in her body that she was healed" (Mark 5:29). New Testament authors were willing to write about suffering and disorder in the vagina, a location that, for too many women, has been a site of violence. Might it be possible to place this story of suffering and healing alongside a sensitive reading of the graphic accounts of Rwandan survivors of genocidal *gang-rape? One victimized woman recounts: "After the rape, I was torn and bleeding for almost a month."[39] Another survivor recalls: "When I

---

35. Ramsey, "Preaching to Survivors of Child Sexual Abuse," 58; emphasis added.

36. Ryan, *Reclaiming the Body*, 23.

37. Jones, *Marks of His Wounds*, 14.

38. Moltmann-Wendel, *I Am My Body*, viii.

39. Quoted in Nowrojee, *Shattered Lives*, 52.

urinated, it came out like blood. Black, coagulated blood kept coming out of my vagina."[40] Very meaningfully then, Moltmann-Wendel says Jesus' response to the hemorrhaging woman (Mark 5:34) was literally, "Go in wholeness—*shalom*."[41] Such caring words can offer promise and hope to survivors of sexual abuse.

The incarnation rendered Jesus himself vulnerable to violence and abuse (Phil 2:5–8). Crucifixion entailed *real* suffering of a *real* body. *We have a Savior who can understand suffering not only in an abstract way as an omniscient spiritual being, but as one who has experienced pain, battering, and humiliation* (Mark 15:16–39; John 19:1–3). As a victim of violence, Jesus' suffering makes him able to identify with victims in deep and profound ways. We may even see Jesus as a victim of sexual *shaming. Though most depictions of the crucifixion show Jesus covered with a loincloth, in actual Roman practice, individuals being crucified were normally completely stripped so that they would be naked and shamed as part of the ordeal.[42] Quoting Psalm 22, John 19:24 speaks of the soldiers' treatment of Jesus: "They divided my clothes among themselves, and for my clothing they cast lots." It is appropriate to juxtapose these words against the poignant narrative of a victim of genocidal rape who recounts: "They stripped us of all our clothes. At that time, I do not even think I could call myself a person."[43] *Christian reverence and compassion for the body of Jesus, a victim of violence and abuse, ought to extend to all victims of violence.*

THE RESURRECTION OF THE BODY

Perhaps the greatest affirmation of human embodiment is found in the doctrine of the resurrection. Gospel writers take pains to emphasize that the resurrected Jesus had a real body (Luke 24:36–43; John 20:27). Jesus was not raised as some disembodied spirit, but as flesh. Beth Felker Jones suggests that the doctrine of the resurrection is the best lens through which to consider embodiment theology: "The concept of the resurrection of the body, essential to the earliest Christian confessions of faith, includes the expectation that not only was Jesus of Nazareth raised from the grave, but all of humanity will also someday so arise. This hope is determinative of any Christian theology of the body."[44] However, she laments that we "are conditioned to think of salvation as being about anything but the body," and adds: "When pressed, many members of Christian congregations deny the resurrection of the body in favor of some version of immortality only for the soul."[45] The doctrine of the resurrection is both affirmation of the goodness of the body and the promise that our own bodies will be healed and restored (Phil 3:20–21).

An orthodox doctrine of the resurrection does not claim that humans receive "replacement" bodies. This body will not be discarded like a shell or wrapper. *Christian*

---

40. Ibid., 45.

41. Moltmann-Wendel, *I Am My Body*, xi.

42. Ancient sources say that criminals were crucified naked (see Hengel, *Crucifixion in the Ancient World and the Folly of the Message of the Cross*, 21, 29).

43. Nowrojee, *Shattered Lives*, 52.

44. Jones, *Marks of His Wounds*, 4.

45. Ibid., 3.

eschatology is not a flight out of embodiment but a celebration of it. The doctrine of the resurrection is a promise for *this* body. Bodies which have been assaulted and abused are loved by Christ, anticipated in his death, redeemed through his incarnation and resurrection, and will be healed and restored in God's own time. Such a teaching insists upon God's own reverence for the flesh. The body remains precious despite the injury done to it.

Though the doctrine of the resurrection is a hope-filled promise, it continues to acknowledge the reality of suffering and victimization. It does not divert attention or minimize the horrific experiences of the children, women, and men who have endured sexual violence. Affirmation of the resurrection should not engender inappropriate cheeriness. *Eschatology must not be misapplied to deny victims' present suffering or substitute for the protection and healing survivors need now*. Rather, the hope inspired by the promise of the resurrection resonates with Paul's words that "we ourselves . . . groan inwardly while we wait for adoption, the redemption of our bodies" (Rom 8:23).

The promise of future resurrection has implications for the present: "Resurrection doctrine is indicative *not only of final hopes, but also of present attitudes* toward the bodies of the living."[46] Christians are called to honor and protect bodies *now* and align themselves with "the politics of God's *kingdom . . . where the bodies of some are no longer targeted for abuse."[47] Thus, embodiment theology acutely shapes Christian ethics. For centuries, Christian tradition urged its adherents to practice acts of "corporal mercy," including care for people's bodily afflictions. By extension, we should have a high estimation of those who work to heal and protect survivors: therapists, social workers, doctors, trauma nurses, police, UN observers, ministers, and even third-grade teachers (i.e., *mandated reporting). *We can invite parishioners to see that the care and protection of the abused is part of a holy vocation, in imitation of and union with Christ's ministry of healing*. Our care for victims' bodies does not stop with medical and therapeutic responses to their suffering. It must also include *advocacy and prevention. Christians will work to create *safety plans, *protective services, influencing justice systems to provide safety for current and future possible victims of sexual abuse.

EMBODIED MEMORY, HEALING, AND THE SCARS OF JESUS

At the crucifixion, Roman enemies inscribed their violence and hostility onto Jesus' body. After the resurrection, the "marks" of Jesus' wounds remained in his body (John 20:19–27). His flesh wore the memory of his physical abuse and degradation. Therapists say that memories of sexual abuse can be integrally bound up with the body. Some victims have visible scars, permanent injuries, chronic pain, sexually transmitted diseases, and pregnancy. For others, the scars are not visible, but memory of the abuse remains lodged in the psyche and as *body memory. Susan Brison says that "traumatic memories . . . are more tied to the body than memories are typically considered to be."[48] Writing about her own

---

46. Jones, *Marks of His Wounds*, 4; emphasis added.
47. Ibid., 18.
48. Brison, *Aftermath*, 45.

experience, she reports that "trauma not only haunts the conscious and unconscious mind, but also remains in the body, in each of the senses, ready to resurface whenever something *triggers a reliving of the traumatic event."[49] Some survivors report ongoing psychosomatic pain: "The pain in my body is pretty constant. It is hard to describe, but it is on both an emotional and physical level. I relive the pain. I feel it in my vagina. The pain in my heart sometimes feels like heat and tightness, and it is difficult to breathe."[50] In her study of the relationship between childhood incest and eating disorders, Jennifer Manlowe says that many survivors *"'wear' the struggle* to regain self-respect on their bodies . . ."[51]

A Christian theology of embodiment takes wounds and scars seriously. New Testament accounts of Jesus' resurrection do not deny the violence that he had endured (cf. Rev 5:6). *Rather, the resurrected Christ and his followers refused to accept the meaning of the violence intended by the perpetrators.* Jesus' abusers mocked and shamed him, but he refused to be defined according to their terms.

Even as Christian teachings affirm the *future* resurrection of the body, sexual abuse survivors also voice the possibility of a process of healing *in this lifetime*. Speaking from her own experience, Brison writes: "As devastating as sexual violence is, however, I want to stress that it is possible to survive it, and even to flourish after it, although it doesn't seem that way at the time."[52] The ongoing journey of healing from sexual trauma in this present age anticipates the future, complete healing promised in Scripture.

In addition to counseling, some survivors are aided by experiences of entering more fully into their bodies, "reclaiming" what had been taken from them. *Many survivors report that emotional healing involves affirming their physicality and strengthening their bodies.* One individual, as part of her *self-care, took a three-day hike in the Grand Canyon where she found herself "reclaiming my physical power" and "filled with joy and hope." She adds: "It was the first time I let out a full belly laugh since the rape."[53] Another survivor found it empowering to take a self-defense class—though harboring no illusions that it would make her invulnerable to future violence.[54] Laura Levitt talks about the healing effects of immersion in the ritual bath used by observant Jewish women following their menstrual periods. Levitt writes: "My body was violated by rape. The *mikvah offered me a place to acknowledge both that violation and my desire to heal. My need for *ritual was very real. I needed to do something concrete to express my *psychic and physical pain . . ."[55] Randy, a truck driver who contracted AIDS when he was sexually assaulted by two men, found hope through the physicality of communal singing and marching at an AIDS awareness gathering:

49. Ibid., x.

50. Carosella, *Who's Afraid*, 177.

51. Manlowe, "Seduced by Faith," 328; emphasis added.

52. Brison, *Aftermath*, 19.

53. Carosella, *Who's Afraid*, 62.

54. Brison, *Aftermath*, 14.

55. Levitt and Wasserman, "*Mikvah* Ceremony for Laura," 26.

It was incredible to be surrounded by so many people who understand how I feel. We were all singing and waving banners. This was the first time since knowing that I have AIDS that I have felt like there is hope. I now know the strong connection between how my mind feels and how my body feels. I really take care of myself now. In fact I'm doing much better than I was when those doctors gave me my death sentence. I hung my banner from the march up on the wall. Now my goal is to live, so that I can be singing right along with everyone else when the march happens again next year.[56]

Just as physical empowerment can be emotionally therapeutic, healing in the mind and emotions may also lead to bodily joy. Recovering from the ongoing physical sensation of "painful, horrible memories" trapped in her body for years after experiencing abuse, one survivor reports: "Many therapy sessions later, normal movement is returning. Movement is freer. Running, dancing, playing, and sex are joyfully spontaneous. My mind and heart are also returning to joy."[57]

CONCLUSION: INCARNATING WHOLENESS

Christianity affirms the physicality of God's repair work. Baptism and the Lord's Supper, the ritual actions commanded by Jesus, are powerful *bodily* events—washing, eating, and drinking—involving earthy elements: water, bread, and the fruit of the vine. Moltmann-Wendel writes: "Eternal life begins here in us with our bodies . . ."[58] Parish leaders and others who care for victims must challenge congregations to view the issue of sexual abuse through the lens of Jesus' incarnation and resurrection. We see that God's intent for us is healing and wholeness. *Christ entered into the suffering of the world, sharing the journey of all who have experienced unspeakable violation.* In turn, congregations and parish caregivers are called to accompany survivors on their journey of healing. Sharing in God's solidarity with victims, Christians are charged to be advocates, healers, and protectors of the vulnerable. With compassionate support from others, survivors may learn to value and cherish their own bodies, recognizing that God's loving intent for their bodies is safety, wholeness, and joy.

QUESTIONS FOR DISCUSSION

1. What does it mean that we *are* our bodies but cannot be *reduced* to our bodies? As you reflect on your faith community, what has contributed to the minimizing of embodied life? How do you see a clearer biblical *anthropology taught in your church helping the sexually violated? The author spoke of practicing "corporal mercy." Discuss specific ways this needs to be implemented where you work.

2. How does the incarnation, death, and resurrection of Jesus' body change the way we view our own bodies? How do Christian teachings about Jesus' experience of suffering, violence, and resurrection affect the way we view the bodies of sexual abuse

---

56. Carosella, *Who's Afraid*, 15.

57. Ibid., 133.

58. Moltmann-Wendell, *I Am My Body*, 78.

victims? A victim of sexual abuse states that there is simply no way God can understand physical violation; write out an answer to this common claim of victims.

3. Scripture says that when Jesus was raised from the dead, he still bore the marks of his wounds (John 20:26–28). What does it mean to be both wounded and healed? How does embodiment theology help us to: (a) avoid certain views of SA healing, (b) emphasize key elements in counseling, teaching, or plain encouragement to victims, and (c) equip care givers to be more hopeful and sensitive toward struggling victims?

4. In our culture today, what kind of dualisms function in a way that is destructive to the healing of abuse survivors in the church? Make a list of these, then contemplate their relationship to victims of: (a) childhood sexual abuse, (b) *date rape, and (c) *marital rape. What are you going to emphasize differently next time you have the privilege of walking with an abuse survivor?

FOR FURTHER READING

Copeland, M. Shawn. *Enfleshing Freedom: Body, Race, and Being.* Minneapolis, MN: Fortress, 2010.

Gottschall, Marilyn. "Embodiment." In *New and Enlarged Handbook of Christian Theology*, ed. Donald W. Musser and Joseph L. Price, 155-57. Nashville, TN: Abingdon, 2003.

Schroeder, Joy A. "The Woman and the Dragon: Feminist Reflections on Sexual Violence, Evil, and Bodily Resurrection." *dialog* 33 (1994): 135–41.

Thiselton, Anthony C. "Paul's View of Humanity." In *The Living Paul: An Introduction to the Apostle's Life and Thought*, 67–74. Downers Grove, IL: IVP, 2009.

13

The Nature of Evil in Child Sexual Abuse

Theological Consideration of Oppression and its Consequences

Philip G. Monroe, PsyD

Christians use a variety of words to describe acts and attitudes opposing God's design for human living: *wickedness, sin, bad, wrong, unrighteousness,* and *moral evil.* While some words provide labels (e.g., right and wrong), other words, such as moral evil, describe the *power* and *direction* behind acts that violate God's plans and purposes for creation.[1] These evil acts produce far-reaching and often unintended consequences for both victim and offender. Adam and Eve's first act of disobedience resulted in loss of home, exposure to hardships, and alienation from God (Gen 3:12–24; Col 1:21) for all subsequent humankind. The Israelite spies' refusal to trust God left an entire generation of Israelites to die in the desert (1 Cor 10:5). Those who follow sinful lusts later find themselves enslaved to their desires (e.g., Prov 11:6; Rom 6:12; 2 Pet 1:4). Even though grace, mercy, and *forgiveness of sins have been granted to those who follow Jesus, evil acts by Christians do not result in good consequences (Rom 3:8). And yet, these corruptive consequences of moral evil provide us with some insight into the nature and impact of specific *kinds* of evil. In this chapter we consider a specific, corrupting evil act—*child sexual abuse (CSA).

Child sexual abuse is an evil that corrupts both abuser and abused. A young boy questions his sexuality after repeated *sexual abuse by a male neighbor. A girl, *molested by her youth leader, comes to believe she only has value when adults take a sexual interest in her. An adult female, abused by her father and grandfather, struggles to relate to male leaders in her church—feeling both rebellious and yet in constant danger of further abuse.

There is a growing body of literature that explores both anecdotal and empirical psychological data illustrating the corruptive nature of such abuse. While this chapter begins with a brief review of key *psychological sequelae stemming from CSA, its primary focus is to view such evil through a biblical-theological lens in order to understand the spiritual and community implications of abuse.

---

1. Moral evil, as opposed to natural evil, requires *agency* and *volition.* See Wismer, "Evil," 186–88.

BRIEF REVIEW OF PSYCHOLOGICAL DATA
REGARDING CHILD SEXUAL ABUSE

Common sense suggests that the evil act of CSA disturbs a victim's perception of love, intimacy, sexuality, safety, proper boundaries, identity, and sense of self in relationship to others. These disturbances are known to last into adulthood. *Trauma clinicians provide ample evidence that CSA victims—especially those having experienced particularly early, brutal, and/or prolonged abuse—often exhibit a common constellation of psychological and relational symptoms. They include distorted self-perceptions, chronic guilt and shame feelings, relational *hyper-vigilance, difficulties *modulating emotions, repetitive experiences of *depersonalization, and other forms of confusion.[2]

Child-Specific Trauma: A Unique Form of Post-traumatic Stress

Frequently, adult survivors of CSA receive diagnoses of *post-traumatic stress disorder (PTSD).[3] This diagnosis highlights the survivor's common struggle with *intrusive, painful memories or imagery from past trauma, unproductive attempts to avoid such experiences via *numbing or *impulsive actions, and yet a persistent heightened anticipatory anxiety despite *avoidance efforts. However, researchers like Judith Herman now recognize significant differences between trauma experienced by adults (e.g., *rape, a car accident, or war) and trauma responses in adults originating from CSA. These differences include: (1) difficulties with modulating *affective experiences and impulses, (2) staying in the present, (3) maintaining accurate self-perception, (4) building trust relationships with others, (5) *somatic expressions of the stress, and (6) sustaining an overarching system of meaning in the face of hopelessness.[4] Such an experience of trauma can leave an individual in a chronic state of panic, voiceless, full of *self-loathing, and running from the past without hope of emotional safety or rest in the future. While all forms of PTSD produce distress, *CSA traumas differ in the pervasiveness of their impact on the victim.*

Of significant note is the impact of CSA on *relational* and *trust* capacities of the victim. It stands to reason that if withholding relational and intellectual stimulation from an infant leads to *cognitive deficits such as mental retardation, then children subjected to CSA may also experience lasting deficits in relational and trust capacities.[5] Gobin and Freyd found evidence suggesting that victims of CSA have significantly greater difficulty forming trust relationships, experience higher incidences of betrayal in adult life *and yet* are less likely to withdraw from relationships where betrayal occurs.[6] This may be due to

---

2. Herman, *Trauma and Recovery*; Langberg, *Counseling Survivors of Sexual Abuse*; Luxenberg et al., "Complex Trauma and Disorders of Extreme Stress (DESNOS) Diagnosis, Part One: Assessment," 373–394.

3. American Psychiatric Association, *Diagnostic and Statistical Manual of Mental Disorders, 4th Edition* [*DSM-IV-TR*], 463–468.

4. Luxenberg et al., suggest a new diagnostic term for this constellation of symptoms: *Disorder of Extreme Stress, Not Otherwise Specified (DESNOS).

5. Cicchetti, "The Impact of Child Maltreatment and Psychopathology on Neuroendocrine Functioning," 783–804.

6. Gobin and Freyd, "Betrayal and Revictimization: Preliminary Findings," 242–257.

chronic patterns of self-doubt and perceptions of interpersonal powerlessness. Further, many married adult victims of CSA struggle to identify positive feelings about their sexuality and passions.[7] Not surprisingly, many couples report decreased marital satisfaction when one partner has experienced childhood maltreatment.[8]

With advances in *cerebral imaging technologies, researchers now have some evidence of the physiological damage caused by CSA. *It appears that sexual abuse victims have greater likelihood of abnormalities in the *limbic and *adrenal systems*[9] *along with overactive stress hormone production and underproduction of *serotonin.*[10] Stress hormone production has been associated with the making of memories and may be a factor in the creation of intrusive and repetitive re-experiencing of trauma long after CSA.[11] While the correlation of cerebral activity differences in victims of CSA does not determine a causal relationship with abuse, the differences in CSA victim brains suggests that real damage occurs that cannot be ignored.

The ample medical and psychological literature detailing the corruptive effects of CSA on victims stands in stark contrast to the paucity of literature on the *effect* of abuse on the victimizer. However, interested readers may wish to explore Anna Salter's interviews with confessed child abusers. They reveal the tendency to deceive self and others via *blame-shifting tactics that put the responsibility for the abuse back on the victim (e.g., white lies, focusing on the victim's failure to keep promises of secrecy) and *grooming techniques (e.g., attention, gift-giving, false intimacy, and minor demands) respectively.[12] It appears that while both blame-shifting and grooming behaviors make abuse possible, *repetitive abusive actions lead the victimizer to be less and less able to take personal responsibility for actions or to respect another's rights.* Readers may also find journalist Jan Hatzfeld's *empathetic and objective interviews with Rwandan *genocidaires* illustrative of the human capacity to deny first person responsibility for violent atrocities while admitting participation in mass killings when speaking in the third person.[13]

THEOLOGICAL CONSIDERATIONS OF EVIL AND CHILD SEXUAL ABUSE

While psychological data offers *descriptions* of common symptoms resulting from CSA, it is helpful to consider the nature of the evil behind such abuse from a theological vantage point.[14] Such theological work also bears witness to the fact that CSA not only is an in-

---

7. Messton et al., "Women's History of Sexual Abuse, Their Sexuality, and Sexual Self-Schemas," 229–236.

8. DiLillo et al., "Child Maltreatment History Among Newlywed Couples," 680–692.

9. Stein et al., "Hippocampal Volume in Women Victimized by Child Sexual Abuse," 951–959.

10. Heim et al., "Pituitary-Adrenal and Autonomic Responses to Stress in Women After Sexual and Physical Abuse in Childhood," 592–597.

11. Roozendaal et al., "Stress, Memory and the Amygdala," 423–433.

12. Salter, *Predators: Pedophiles, Rapists, and Other Sex Offenders.*

13. Hatzfeld, *Machete Season.*

14. *Biblical theology differs from other theological disciplines in that it "seeks to analyze and synthesize the Bible's teaching about God and his relations to the world on its own terms, maintaining sight of the Bible's overarching narrative and Christocentric focus" (Rosner, "Biblical Theology," 10).

stance of law-breaking but also a destructive and corrupting force against the individual and communal reflection of the *imago Dei*.

The Core of Christian Living: Loving Protection of Others

It may help to consider the core of Christian living prior to exploring its opposite—the evil behind CSA. Jesus sums up the entirety of the Christian life with his call to love God and neighbor (Matt 22:37–40; cf. Lev 19:18; Deut 6:5).[15] Identifying as a Christ follower requires one to accept the ethical mandate—to care for *the other*, whether a near or far neighbor (Luke 10:36; cf. Lev 19:34; Deut 10:19). Lest anyone think that it is possible to separate love of God from love of neighbor, to dutifully keep one while dismissing the other, Matthew records Jesus' curse of the Pharisees for tithing even down to their herbs but failing to love others via acts of justice and mercy (Matt 23:23).[16] Failure to love others means a failure to love God. In similar fashion, James reminds listeners that true religion consists of caring for the needs of widows and orphans (i.e., those who can never repay) as well as remaining free from the pollution of the world (Jam 1:27; 1 Tim 5:3–16). Without a doubt, the *kingdom of God is one marked by love toward others, especially those who are weak and unable to protect themselves.

GOD AS PROTECTOR

It is no surprise then that a key theme throughout Scripture is that of God's protection of his people facing hardships in a fallen world. The Old Testament narratives are full of examples of God's protecting acts of love—from provision for Adam and Eve and even their murderous son, Cain, to rescues of Noah, Sarah, Lot, Joseph, David, Daniel, and more.[17] The Psalms offer additional images of God's protection. He answers those in distress (Ps 20:1). He hides his people from trouble (Ps 32:7). He consumes and destroys enemies (Psalms 59, 64). He protects the persecuted (Ps 69:29). He provides justice for the wrongly accused (Psalm 140). Such imagery is not only found among the Old Testament poets but also in the New Testament. Jesus himself reminds us of God's protection. He comforts the disciples by telling them he will not leave them as orphans but will send the Spirit after his ascension (John 14:18). Later in John, Jesus asks the Father for spiritual protection for the disciples—the fulfillment of the promise to Jesus that none of his children would be lost (John 17:11). One can argue that God's provision of physical care and healing points to his ultimate concern for the spiritual redemption (protection) of his people.[18]

---

15. Cf. Rom 13:9; Gal 5:6, 14; Jam 2:8.

16. Cf. Isah 1:16–17; Jer 22:3; Hos 6:6; Mic 6:8; Zech 7:9.

17. Consider the book of Judges as example of God's relentless pursuit of rescue and protection for Israel despite their wandering ways. The book reveals *cycles* of: (1) peace under the protective watch of a judge (ruler) followed by (2) periods where Israel "forgets" the Lord leading to (3) a period where Israel again falls victim to neighboring marauders. Israel then (4) cries out for help to the Lord. He hears and (5) provides another judge to rescue them from their oppressors.

18. Monroe and Schwab, "God as Healer," 121–129.

GOD'S SPECIAL PROTECTIONS FOR THE WEAK

While God cares for all of his children, he provides an extra portion of care for the most needy, especially those orphaned or living as aliens in a strange land. Throughout the Old Testament, some thirty-one verses direct the Israelites to treat the *alien* justly (e.g., Deut 24:17; Jer 22:3). For example, in Genesis we see Lot protected by angels when vulnerable in Sodom (19:8). The foreigner was to receive the same kindness shown to fellow Israelites. God's people were not to take advantage of widows, orphans, or strangers in their midst (Deut 10:18). But godly treatment of the weak did not end with the *absence* of harm. Israel was expected to make *extra* provision for those in need. Farmers were to bless the poor by leaving ripened crops in their fields for those who had no means to purchase food (Deut 24:19–22). Even those who loaned to the poor were required to forgive debts every seven years (Deut 15:1).

GOD PROVIDES HUMAN PROTECTORS

In God's providence, he supplies special human leaders to protect and serve his people. Early Old Testament examples of such leaders include Noah's building of the ark, Abraham's protection of Lot, Joseph's famine relief, and Moses' guidance of Israel through the desert. Later, God sends a variety of judges to rescue Israel from the hands of their enemies. When Israel demanded a human king, God installed kings who were to lead and care for all Israel. Today we may not look to human kings for aid and protection, yet we recognize God's providential supply of parents and government leaders for our protection and safety.

LOVE AS A HALLMARK OF KINGDOM LIVING

In the New Testament, both Jesus and the Apostle Paul emphasize the call to love one another as a key ethic of the *new covenant. Building on Jesus' summation of the Gospel, Paul also connects the keeping of the Law with love of neighbor (Romans 13). In this regard, love is the fulfillment of the Ten Commandments and the debt all owe to others. This love not only counters self-interest, impatience, and demandingness but goes a step further in that it "always protects, always trusts, always hopes, always perseveres" (1 Cor 13:7 TNIV).

One such form of protection of others is the willingness to give up personal rights for the good of another. Paul implores readers to follow the loving act of Christ by not demanding rights but rather humbly providing sacrificial love to others (Phil 2:1–8; Eph 5:22).[19] In doing so, humans emulate God's loving protection of those unable to save themselves (Titus 3:4).

---

19. Notice that sacrificial love is a *choice*, freely made, to forgo personal rights for the sake of another. This kind of sacrifice is never the result of a demand (e.g., "You will give me what I want or else." Or "You must continue to live with your abuser for the sake of love"). Nor, however, does sacrificial love negate the biblical license to seek justice.

Behind the Value of Loving Protection: Identity within Community

Why do the biblical writers go to such lengths to command human beings to love and protect all—especially the most vulnerable? Why is it reprehensible to use one's power to take something (object or identity) that rightfully belongs to another? One likely answer is that such activity violates and disturbs the *imago Dei* in both victim and victimizer. Stanley Grenz argues that *imago Dei*, or the image of God breathed into human beings (Gen 2:7), is not a particular structure or substance (e.g., logic, functional role, etc.) but something social and *inter-relational* in nature, forming the core of human agency and contextual identity.[20] Human beings reflect the character and essence of God when they relate to each other as fellow members of a covenant community—one founded on unity, diversity, and sacrificial love.[21] In turn, community members develop personal identity through interwoven relationships with other members and with God—a reflection of the perfect communion within and between the members of the *Godhead.[22] Thus, any evil done by one community member against another violates the true picture of communion—especially peace, trust, and safety—as expressed in the *Trinity.

But the evil of abuse does more than dishonor relations between members of the Trinity. It also confuses and distorts functional roles and relationships among image bearers. God the Father has functional authority over Son and Spirit, even as all three of the Trinity are equal in value. So also, some image bearers are given functional, delegated positions of authority over others (e.g., Rom 13:1–5; Eph 5:21).[23] Children submit to parents as parents submit to the Lord (Col 3:20); parishioners submit to pastors as pastors submit to Christ (Eph 5:24a). Yet it is in distorted functional role differences where CSA flourishes. Abusers often hold functional power (authority) over another and use that power to violate their victim. *CSA is not merely a sin against another person but something that both distorts the reflection of God's character and disturbs the imago Dei in the child* as he or she is a developing member of the same community of Christ. Limiting abuse of delegated power seems to be one of the reasons why God makes specific prohibitions against both sexual relations between family members and child-sacrifice (Lev 18:6–21). Significantly, if the image of God is best reflected through covenanted "humans in community," then whole communities (e.g., families, churches, etc.) should expect to struggle with *identity confusion and relational turmoil as a result of familial CSA or child murder.

Thus we see the command to protect weaker members of the community tied directly to the very nature, character, and mission of God. The evil behind this failure to reflect the love the Father, Son, and Spirit have for each other also leads to lasting and potentially unforeseen consequences for victim, victimizer, and community. Considering John Calvin's assertion that one cannot understand self without also understanding God (and vice versa), then it stands to reason that the victim of CSA experiences a disruption

20. Grenz, "The Social Imago," 57.

21. Grenz, *The Social God and the Relational Self*, 303.

22. As seen in Jesus' prayer in John 17. See Piper (*The Pleasures of God*, esp. 38), for more on the delight between the members of the Trinity.

23. See Schmutzer, "A Theology of Sexual Abuse," esp. 796–97, for a discussion on how sexual abuse distorts *delegated* authority.

of the understanding of God and self resulting in *systemic disruption of their ability to reflect the *imago Dei*.[24]

Oppression as the Opposite of Protection

Having explored loving protection as a central feature of Christian living and the character of the Trinity, we now turn to its opposite. In today's language, we often consider hate to be the opposite of love. In actuality, oppression better describes the opposite of protection. *Oppression, the active subjugation or using of another for one's own pleasure, is at the heart of the evil of CSA.*

The Scriptures make clear that violating another for one's own pleasure is an act against God himself (Prov 14:31) and one that deserves His wrath (Matt 18:32-35). Oppressive acts toward the poor, alien, and fatherless are clearly condemned (e.g., Exod 22:2; Zech 7:10). Ezekiel concludes that Sodom's detestable practices and attempt to sexually assault a stranger in their community stemmed from a lack of concern for the needy (Ezek 16:49–50).

God condemns delegated leaders who violate their subjects: leaders who tear flesh from bone (Mic 3:1–3), wealthy women who exploit the needy (Amos 4:1), and shepherds who feed on the very sheep they should protect (Ezek 34:10). The promised Messiah comes to end oppressions such as these (Luke 4:18).

OPPRESSION AS THE PRIMARY EVIL BEHIND CHILD SEXUAL ABUSE

Oppressive subjugation provides a descriptive "lens" to best understand the nature and consequences of the evil behind CSA. The following five facets of oppression illustrate the *depth* and *toxicity* of the evil of CSA—blatant opposition to the call to love and protect weaker members of the covenant community: (1) abuse of power, (2) deception and false teaching, (3) failure to lead and protect, (4) *objectification, (5) and forced false worship.

Abuse of Power: Causing Fear and Bodily Harm

By definition, all oppressors *take*, by force or manipulation, something rightly belonging to another. The one committing CSA uses physical and positional power to take another's genitalia, virginity, innocence, and security for personal pleasure. One of the best biblical illustrations of sexual abuse of power is found in the story of Amnon's rape of Tamar (2 Samuel 13). Despite Tamar's plea to be spared from a sexual assault and willingness to have Amnon marry her so he would not commit a crime, Amnon uses force to take his half-sister's virginity and social honor (v. 14). Amnon's actions follow that of his father—the murder of Uriah to take Bathsheba to be his wife (2 Sam 11:15). *In both of these cases the one who was weaker had an expectation of protection and safety* and had given no cause for the harm suffered.

---

24. Calvin, *Institutes of the Christian Religion*, 35–39.

The experience of abuse of power (e.g., forced enslavement, rape, denial of rights) leaves the victim in a state of bodily harm and helpless fear. Tamar reacts with fear and is left "desolate" for the remainder of her life (2 Sam 13:20). The writer here uses a Hebrew word, *shamem* ("desolate" [TNIV], "forlorn" [Tanak]), which conveys both physical and psychological destruction.[25] Such is common when one is harmed by a presumed protector. Similar abuse is described elsewhere using the language of "gleaning" or "stripping" another bare (Jer 6:9). One of the more horrific abuses can be found in Judges 19, where a concubine is not protected but raped and abused all night, ending in her death. Even when life is spared, the devastation from abuse induces persistent helpless fear (Ps 38:13) and an inability to save oneself (cf. Exod 3:7).

When a developing child is unable to prevent abuse and violence from happening, that child often enters a state of immobilizing fear. If this fear is not reversed through experiences of *effective personal agency* (e.g., asking for and receiving protection), the perception of helplessness continues and expands with each re-experiencing of ineffectiveness. Even adult memories of CSA often *trigger perceptions of helplessness and fear, thereby making them less effective in appropriate help or comfort seeking.[26]

Along with paralyzing fears about safety and the future, the victim of CSA experiences numerous questions that have no satisfying answer: "What will become of me? Why does this one who says he/she loves me hurt me this way? Will anyone believe me?" We see hints of such questions in the life of David as he runs from King Saul in fear of his life. David wonders what he did wrong (1 Sam 20:1, 26:18, 29:8). He is distressed (Psalms 18, 38, 63) to the point of being totally overwhelmed (Ps 55:1–5). Thus, we see that abuse of power not only hurts *during* the abuse but often continues *long after* the abuse has ended.[27]

Deception and False Teaching: Moral and Relational Confusion

Oppressive acts almost always include some form of deception and distortion of the truth. While one may abuse by sheer violence, most forms of harm are shrouded in deceptive acts intended to break down the victim's resistance. The child can be told any number of messages: (1) they are deserving of their abuse, (2) they are being punished for wrongdoing, (3) what is happening to them is not really abuse at all but special or even necessary attention, (4) even that God approves of the abuse or has abandoned them. For victims, this is also *spiritual incest. The message need not be logical—merely plausible to a child—as confusion reigns when one in a protector role attacks. Because deception is difficult to grasp (at first), the Scriptures warn of those who use it to oppress the weak, vulnerable, and naïve in order to lead them astray (e.g., Lev 6:2; Mal 3:5).[28]

25. Davidson, *The Analytical Hebrew and Chaldean Lexicon*, 725.

26. van der Kolk, "Clinical Implications of Neuroscience Research in PTSD," 277–93.

27. See Volf, *The End of Memory* for an excellent treatise on the ongoing struggle to remember rightly and forgive after experiencing the abuse of power, in its various forms.

28. Cf. Isah 9:6; Jer 23:32; and Ezek 13:10.

Such use of deception creates opportunity for confusion in the mind of the victim. *Confusion, in turn, encourages distortion of the truth and inhibits image bearers from carrying out their mandate to name things as they appear* (Gen 2:20). In Genesis 2, God installs Adam in Eden to "care" and "guard" it (2:15; cf. 3:23). This includes naming the animals—an act reflecting God's prior activity in identifying both good and evil in the garden. The serpent deceives Adam and Eve by providing a false name (i.e., seeking knowledge) for an act that is more accurately called rebellion. In CSA, the victim is deceived by being offered false names for their experiences. They are led to believe that: (1) *they are responsible for their victimhood*, (2) *unwanted pleasurable feelings indicate a desire to be abused*, and (3) *the only attention they are worthy of is that obtained through abuse*, etc.

While these lies have little power for non-abused adults, among CSA victims it is common to find those who refuse to lay blame at the feet of their offender. Instead, they seem to find some comfort in accepting full blame for any abuse while denying characterological flaws in their abuser. We've suggested that this confusion is rooted in the deceptive practices of the abuser. And yet, another explanation suggests that danger (i.e., abuse) triggers human desires for *attachment and comfort from other community members. According to some, "When there is no access to ordinary sources of comfort, people may turn toward their tormentors."[29]

Failure to Lead and Protect: Chaotic Choices

Oppressive leaders not only ignore the welfare of their charges but use them as "food" (Ezek 22:26–29). When leaders oppress, they no longer act in accord with their divinely delegated leadership. Subsequently, the weaker person cannot place any trust in this leader who uses others for his or her own purposes but will scatter, searching for their own path (cf. Jer 23:2; Zech 11:17).

The oppression of CSA leaves many victims fending for themselves against "lions" and "wild animals" (cf. Jer 50:17; Ezek 34:5). They do not know *how* to trust, *who* to follow, or *where* to find safety. In the absence of clear lines between safe and dangerous leadership, victims may find themselves forever searching for a protector but always fearful of recurring abuse. Isolation may bring a modicum of safety but reinforces the perception that no one, including God, looks out for them. Submitting to another may also offer a distant promise of safety. *But human failings (i.e., broken promises) and the fear of more abuse create oscillations between unhealthy dependence and overreactive resistance responses to those in leadership.*

Objectification: Distortion of Self-Perception and Purpose of Genitalia

God created humans as sexual beings with sexual organs, feelings, functions, and gendered identities.[30] Sexual facets of human existence are not to be viewed as unnecessary or incidental to personhood. Rather, they are integral to the meaning of male and female. Not only does a person's sexuality form an integral part of the self, it also is expressed in

---

29. van der Kolk, "The Compulsion to Repeat Trauma," 389–411.

30. For further discussion of gendered identity, see Schmutzer, "A Theology of Sexual Abuse," 791–92.

interactions with every other engendered person. Further, God designed highly sensitive genitalia for the express purpose of pleasure for both the self and spouse during covenantal intercourse.

CSA disembodies sexual beings by objectifying sexual parts apart from the person. A person becomes a receptacle for sexual activity of an abuser. Females are treated as if they are the sole *cause* of lust. Similarly, children become containers for an abusive parent's anger.

Sexual objectification destroys and distorts several facets of sexuality: identity, agency, and pleasure. What was intended for good is now contorted, by the abuse, into something ugly and distasteful. For example, genital feelings, once designed for pleasure, now elicit fear, disgust, and *self-hatred.[31] Or sexual identity, intended to form part of the self, becomes a dominant, all-consuming "tagline" of the person. CSA victims may fall into one of two extremes of sexual expression. Either they are inclined to deny their sexuality or engage in compulsive *sexualized behavior.

Forced False Worship: Enslavement to "False Gods"

When God's people follow idols they exchange their glory (cf. Rom 1:23 TNIV)—shame themselves—and dishonor the Lord (Jer 2:11), forfeiting his grace (Jonah 2:8). However, when the leaders of the people encourage false worship, they cause those who follow them to stumble into evil practices (cf. Ezek 14:1–5). Such leading of others into sin is so detestable that God judges repentant leaders as *permanently* unworthy to speak for him; they are only worthy of servant-like work (cf. Ezek 44:10–14). The worship of idols not only dishonors the Lord but makes all vulnerable to deception (Zech 10:2) as they introduce their lies (2 Pet 2:1–3). Perceiving that their oppressors speak for God, those who are vulnerable may be more easily led astray and burdened with sinful behavior (1 Cor 8:12; 2 Tim 3:6).

Sexual abuse victims often react to their abuse in a variety of ways. Some become overly self-protective, committed to a life of avoidance of community relations, while others seek power over others through their own deceptive practices.[32] The power of these early experiences of oppressive deception makes it difficult for the CSA victim to know which voices in their community are speaking the truth. Left to themselves, they listen only to their own fearful thoughts and conflicting emotions. Patterns such as these often develop into fixed demands: "I must be safe," "I must never trust another person," "I must never be weak," "I must never experience any passion," etc. These perspectives illustrate how the oppression behind the abuse has lingering effects.

---

31. CSA victims sometimes report feeling betrayed by their own body when they experienced pleasure during the abuse. This feeling only exacerbates their sense of confusion, shame, and self-loathing.

32. Allender, *The Wounded Heart*, 120.

CONCLUSION: THE NECESSITY OF DIVINE
AND HUMAN PROTECTION

Having explored how the evil of CSA and its consequences are best understood through the theological lens of oppression, we conclude this chapter with some comments on God's care for the oppressed and his provision of a Savior who rescues victims.

With the *Fall, God's people fail to love God and fellow covenant community members. One of the consequences of this failure is the opportunity for oppression. Psalm 44:11 reminds us that God scatters his people and allows oppression to flourish. But his *master plan* is one of rescue. God acts to respond to the oppression of the weak and needy (Ps 12:5; Jer 49:11). He provides gifts for the poor (Ps 112:9) and is working his will to bring the oppressed to a place of safety and security as well as judge those who supported the oppression (Ezek 28:26; Zeph 3:19–20). At the consummation of all things, those oppressed will no longer live in fear (Jer 23:2–6) of abuse of power. But God's rescue is not merely something that happens in heaven; he provides opportunities to flourish even now while oppression continues.

One such sign of flourishing is the capacity to speak the truth with confidence. The book of Acts details the scattering of the disciples due to the attack of both Greeks and unbelieving Jews. Despite the persecution, they joyfully speak the truth to their hearers—even as they face martyrdom (Acts 8:4; 11:19). *When victims of CSA show signs of recovery, they speak the truth, restoring proper names for the wrongs done to them.* How is this possible? God provides a Savior who seeks and gathers his children with justice (Ezek 34:16). Jesus, God in the flesh, defeats evil and frees those enslaved to fear (Heb 2:15).

Since Jesus' victory over death and his ascension, the church functions as the human agent of God's protection of the community of believers. Paul admonishes church leaders to guard the sheep so that "wolves" will not destroy them with false doctrine (Acts 20:28–31). May we take seriously God's charge to care for "the least of these" so that we do not face his judgment and wrath (Matt 25:40–45).

QUESTIONS FOR DISCUSSION

1. How might the theological lens of oppression help us appreciate the extent of the consequences of the evil of child sexual abuse? How might this enhance our understanding and influence with ministries to both the oppressed and oppressor? Where does your community discuss concepts such as deception, abuse of power, false teaching, and so on as dangers within the community? What other theological concepts or Christian values may draw (or appear to draw) attention *away* from the serious consequences of CSA?

2. How might churches and theological institutions better educate leaders regarding the nature of abuse and oppression? How might we discuss the long-lasting effects of CSA while also giving hope for ongoing healing and maturity? How might *spiritual formation programs better account for the ongoing experiences of CSA without under- or over-promising freedom from suffering?

3. Given the consequences of CSA, how might the church practically respond to victims? What protections might your church enact to add further protection against CSA? What denominational beliefs, fears, cultural thought patterns, and legal concerns encourage silence on the matter of CSA? Based on this chapter discussion, explain how re-victimization occurs.

4. Victims of CSA often display conflicting relational responses that appear to be willful and frustrate their helpers. How might we better interpret their responses in light of the consequences of oppression? Think of an example of a survivor's overactive resistance to leadership; how was it handled and how might such situations be addressed in the future? What CSA experts might you seek to help discern the boundaries between responsibility and victimhood?

5. Central to human agency is the power to name things rightly (Gen 2:19–20). CSA provides false names for abuse in order to deceive victims. What pastoral and professional practices best encourage victims to regain their lost voice and power? What current helping practices might actually (and unintentionally) continue to encourage victims to remain voiceless and passive regarding their mandate to name things rightly? What temptations do the non-abused face when the victim's first use of their "voice" is not as well nuanced as we would hope?

FOR FURTHER READING

Barker, Megan. "The Evil That Men, Women and Children Do." *The Psychologist* 15 (2002): 568–571.

Haugen, Gary A. *The Good News About Injustice.* Downers Grove, IL: InterVarsity Press, 1999.

Mason, T., J. Richman, and D. Mercer. "The Influence of Evil on Forensic Clinical Practice." *International Journal of Mental Health Nursing* 11 (2002): 80–93.

McFadyen, Alistair. *Bound to Sin: Abuse Holocaust, and the Christian Doctrine of Sin.* London: Cambridge University Press, 2000.

Nelson, S. "Facing Evil: Evil's Many Faces; Five Paradigms for Understanding Evil." *Interpretation* 5 (2003): 398–413.

Salter, Anna. *Predators.* New York, NY: Basic Books, 2003.

Swinton, John. *Raging with Compassion: Pastoral Responses to the Problem of Evil.* Grand Rapids, MI: Eerdmans, 2007.

Volf, Miroslav. *The End of Memory: Remembering Rightly in a Violent World.* Grand Rapids, MI: Eerdmans, 2006.

PART THREE

Addressing Sexual Abuse through Pastoral Care

14

A Charge for Church Leadership

*Speaking Out Against Sexual Abuse
and Ministering to Survivors*

NANCY NASON-CLARK, PhD,
AND STEPHEN MCMULLIN, PhD

TIMID AT FIRST, TENTATIVE *as it were, he began the long journey down the aisle toward the altar rail. I, too, began to walk, slowly, watching each step as I descended the stairs that led from the chancel to the nave and down the aisle. He was large-framed, older, with a look that I took as anger etched across his face. I was younger, rather inexperienced, and nervous. Yet, passion forced the powerful words from my mouth as I brought the homily that Sunday morning. We walked toward each other as the crowded cathedral filled with the sound of music. The notes and the melody engulfed each parishioner who stood to sing, rendering them unaware of our movements. They saw neither my fear nor his angst. As if the sun stood still, we moved in slow motion, the moment quickly approaching when we would stand face to face. My heart was racing. I felt afraid. Perhaps I had overstepped my bounds— suggesting that houses of worship be safe places to disclose the secrecy of abuse. And then it happened. He fell into my arms—no angry fist had he—and he wept and wept and wept. It was as if we were dancing—this man and I—as we shuffled together out into the vestry area. With an usher as our guide, we found a quiet space downstairs in a classroom. The lines in his aboriginal brow were deep, and at once I knew that they held the story of pain—of terror—from the days of his childhood. "I have never told anyone," he began. "This is the first time I heard someone in God's house say it was wrong!"*[1]

Spiritual shepherds have the potential to enhance the healing journey of a man or a woman of faith whose life has been impacted by the *trauma of *sexual abuse (SA). Often, however, pastors, priests, and other religious leaders have neither ears to hear the cries for help nor eyes to see their suffering. As a result, they become an obstacle, rather than a resource, on the road to recovery. Clerical silence is taken as complicity with the acts of terror; their dismissal of the pain and despair perceived as one more indicator of rejection. *God's rejection.*

---

1. Based on an experience of Nancy Nason-Clark several years ago in Calgary, Alberta.

In this chapter, we consider the powerful opportunity that clergy have to speak out against sexual abuse and to minister with compassion and *best practices to those who have been impacted by it. Drawing on our joint experiences, Nancy's extensive research program on abuse in families of faith and Steve's years of pastoral ministry, we weave together what we believe is an evidence-based charge to church leaders. Offering God's care to those who are hurting—*a cup of cold water in the name of Jesus*—should be natural to the followers of Christ. Sometimes, though, we need to be reminded that our actions and our words bring forth God's healing power in the lives of others. As church leaders, we need to learn to pair the *practical act* (i.e., cold water) with our *mission* (i.e., in the name of Jesus).

THE LANGUAGE OF THE SPIRIT AND THE LANGUAGE OF CONTEMPORARY CULTURE

The truth expounded in the sacred Scriptures is clear—*we are to expose the deeds of darkness* (cf. 1 Cor 4:5; 2 Cor 6:14). Reading in Psalm 9, beginning at verse 8, we see that "He rules the world in righteousness and judges the peoples with equity." For "The LORD is a refuge for the oppressed," the psalmist continues, "a stronghold in times of trouble" (TNIV). The prophetic voice, grounded in the twin pillars of *justice* and *mercy*, calls out for evil to be overcome and compassion to be offered as the healing balm of Gilead to wounds sustained at the hands of the powerful (Isah 58:6–7; Jer 22:3). And yet, even as the voices of religious leaders speak out to condemn sexual abuse, their hands must be ready to attend to the needs of those who suffer. In contexts where those impacted by sexual abuse look for help, the language of the Spirit must be accompanied by the language of contemporary culture. While the language of the Spirit includes religious words, *rituals, and practices that invoke the spiritual traditions endowed with sacred significance, the language of contemporary culture encapsulates issues of safety, legal processing, therapeutic respite, and material provisions.[2]

The Care and Assistance of Spiritual Leadership

Pastoral care—as we understand it—involves both. *Proclamation and practical assistance are two of the core components of pastoral care.* The language of the Spirit brings peace and healing—a vital supplement to the needs of daily life—breathing hope into dark, fearful places. Proclamation, or speaking out against the *prevalence and severity of abuse, is a necessary first step in offering a *sacred space* safe for a victim to disclose the horror of what has occurred to them. When religious leaders stand behind the pulpit they are in a position of authority—moral authority—and here their words, however inadequate, become anointed, powerful, rendering problems on earth of heavenly concern. *God's voice to the people.*

Practical assistance, which involves such activities as sustained listening, counseling, referral information, and attention to the necessities of life—like food, shelter, and

2. For elaboration, see Nason-Clark, "When Terror Strikes at Home," 303–310; idem, "Christianity and Domestic Violence," 161–66.

fiscal resources, is infused with a therapeutic *empathy offering hope. Who better to give hope and the language of a new start than religious leaders? Translated in this way—and through practical means—God's message becomes one of peace, accountability, provision, justice, and even *forgiveness. The story of the Good Samaritan (Luke 10:25–37) reminds us that when we are bleeding and left for dead, temporary bandages to thwart the loss of blood and transportation to a place that has the potential to sustain us trumps fancy words, advanced degrees or clerical robes. In other words, practical care is so much more impactful than great intentions and superficial sympathy. The story teaches as well that: practical care has boundaries, can exact a cost, disregards *stereotypes, may require many caregivers, and that those prepared to help in one way may not be equipped to help in other ways. To be sure, the parable of the Good Samaritan reinforces contemporary professional best practices including referrals (*referring agencies), client boundaries, cross disciplinary cooperation, and *interdisciplinary triage*, to name but a few.

The pairing of practical assistance with spiritual resources empowers the *survivor, makes the offender accountable, and paves the pathway for safety, security, and *a life where the pain and vulnerability of the past no longer controls the present*. As a result, spiritual leaders have a very important and unique role to play in ministering to those whose lives have been impacted by various forms of violence and sexual assault. But this is neither straightforward nor easy. The message is difficult to translate whether one is a religious leader serving the flock or a professional in a community-based agency serving a diverse population. The charge for church leadership has implications for those who work in both sacred and secular contexts. Working together involves bridge building. It involves trust, respect, negotiation and sometimes compromise. Through collaborative efforts, churches, their leaders, and the people who support them have the power and potential to reach those who are vulnerable, those impacted by evil deeds, and communities everywhere. This we can say with confidence because it is based on more than twenty years of research attempting to understand the story of what happens when women, men, teens, and children who have been impacted by forms of abuse look to their faith communities for help in its aftermath.

CLERGY ADDRESSING ISSUES OF SEXUAL ABUSE

By and large a "holy hush" permeates religious congregations and their leadership when it comes to the issue of violence in general in the domestic setting. For many years, our research team has claimed that Christian family life can be dangerous to the physical, emotional, or sexual well-being of its members.[3] So much can happen behind the closed doors of the family home. There are often tears held back behind the sweet Sunday smiles of parishioners. While it may be sacred, Christian family life is hardly safe at times. It is time for the faith community to wake up from its slumber and for pastors and religious leaders to sound out a call for action. But, like the priest and the Levite in the story of the Good Samaritan, it is so much easier to look the other way. Biblical love, however, looks past social class, ethnicity, and professional image.

---

3. Kroeger and Nason-Clark, *No Place for Abuse*.

Employing a variety of research strategies over the years—including questionnaires, interviews, *focus groups, and *community consultations—with pastors and church people from a variety of denominational affiliations, we have learned a great deal about *domestic violence in families of faith.[4] We have heard of the desire of victims and survivors that their faith leaders address these issues head on—*learning themselves, and then teaching others, to recognize its prevalence and severity in their midst.* We have also documented the disappointment of those who look to the church for help only to have their pain dismissed, minimized or handled with disregard by well-meaning but poorly prepared spiritual leaders. While our focus has been firmly rooted in the broad area of domestic violence, there is much overlap in what we have learned about the "sacred silence" that pertains as well to sexual abuse.

Lessons Learned Along the Way

Below, we have identified some of the key findings to emerge from our studies. These provide a context for us to discuss why we believe pastors are a central component in any community-based response to sexual abuse. Observe the following.

- The majority of clergy are called upon several times a year to respond to a man or a woman who is coping with issues of abuse from their childhood;[5]

- Victims of abuse who look to their pastors for assistance are often unhappy with the help they receive. In particular, they are disappointed to find that there is limited awareness and understanding of the issues surrounding abuse and often a reluctance to provide help of an explicitly spiritual nature (such as prayer, Bible readings, or spiritual counsel);[6]

- Less than one in ten pastors report that they feel well equipped to assist victims and *perpetrators in the aftermath of abuse in the home;[7]

- Many clergy are reluctant to refer those who come to them for help to other professionals in the community or to community-based agencies where the therapists and advocates are employed. Where referrals are most urgently needed (among those religious leaders with little or no training) they are least likely to occur;[8]

- The informal support network that operates in many faith communities—especially where women reach out to other women in need—is one way that congregations

---

4. See Nason-Clark et al., "The RAVE Project," available online at www.uwindsor.ca/units.socialwork/critical.nsf/.

5. Nason-Clark, *The Battered Wife.* Chapter 4, in particular, highlights some of the data surrounding clergy experience in responding to the needs of victims and *perpetrators of abuse. A total of 41.4 percent of religious leaders in a study of *evangelical clergy reported that they were called upon at least twice a year by "a woman who was abused in childhood by a parent," and 20.9 percent were called upon at least twice a year by a man in similar circumstances.

6. Nason-Clark and Kroeger, *Refuge from Abuse.*

7. Kroeger and Nason-Clark, *No Place for Abuse.*

8. Ibid.

put into practice the notion that "they will know we are believers by our love for one another;"[9]

- Mistrust between churches and community agencies poses a real challenge for those workers who desire cooperation and collaboration between congregations and the neighborhoods where they feel called to minister. Yet, there is evidence that initiatives to foster collaboration can be successful;[10]

- When clergy take seriously their responsibility to speak out against violence in all its many manifestations, offer support and referral suggestions, and hold those who act abusively accountable for their actions, the impact can be profound.[11]

The message for clergy is three-fold: (1) the need is great, (2) many men and women look to religious leaders for help in the aftermath of violence or sexual abuse, (3) and it is imperative to pair spiritual resources with practical help.

Christian churches and their leaders across this nation and indeed worldwide must provide resources for victims of sexual abuse. Those who have acted abusively must be called to account and the needed help must be found for them. Cooperation and collaboration with community-based resources, such as shelters, therapists, police, and legal aid must be encouraged. Churches, and those who lead them, must encourage all of us to condemn abuse, including sexual abuse, and seek our place as part of a broader collaborative community response. Without such initiatives, the pain often goes unrecognized and grows more severe, and the potential for healing is sacrificed to a *conspiracy of silence. When we feed, clothe, and weep with those who are suffering, we serve our communities like our mission statements promise. Our voices—both prophetic and priestly—apply God's healing power to those who have been impacted by shameful acts of sexual aggression.

Some Intentional Pastoral Steps

Pastoral care can shatter the silence on this issue through intentional words and actions. Here are some steps every pastor can take:[12]

1. Every pastor and every congregation acknowledge that sexual abuse is a serious problem in society and affirm in the strongest terms possible that there is no biblical justification for it inside or outside families of faith;

2. Every pastor and every congregation affirm its intention to shatter the silence on sexual abuse by intentional words and actions concerning abuse and offering support—emotional, practical, and spiritual—to victims, abusers, and their families,

---

9. Nason-Clark and Kroeger, *Refuge from Abuse.*

10. Nason-Clark et al., "The RAVE Project," 11:1.

11. Fisher-Townsend et al., "I am Not Violent," 78–99; Nason-Clark et al., "An Overview of the Characteristics of the Clients at a Faith-Based Batterers' Intervention Program," 51–72.

12. Based loosely on some recommendations that Dr. Nancy Nason-Clark prepared on domestic violence for the General Board of Administration of the Wesleyan Church International in 2007, which were later adopted by its general assembly.

especially those who seek out pastors and church leadership for support in the aftermath of crisis;

3. Every pastor undertake training opportunities to prepare themselves for offering help to those who suffer abuse in its many and varied forms. These may include print resources, attending training sessions, or visiting proven websites;[13]

4. Every pastor foster and support community-based policies, programs, and services that protect victims and hold offenders accountable;

5. Every pastor should consider how to make information available about sexual abuse to congregants in a way that is accessible but appropriately confidential (such as brochures in the church washroom, material on the church website that can be downloaded and printed at home, books in the church library, etc.);

6. Every congregation, with help from its administrative leadership, develop a protocol for dealing with pastors and other church leaders accused of abusing their own family members or other individuals with whom they are in relationship.

Even small steps toward the goal of speaking out and responding compassionately and with best practices to those who have been impacted by sexual abuse is very powerful. May we challenge each pastor to think creatively and to respond with courage.

A PASTORAL PERSPECTIVE: PASTOR-TO-PASTOR

One of the unfortunate lessons of the past few decades is that although sexual abuse within churches and church families has been well hidden, it is nevertheless a serious problem that needs to be addressed. Pastors and other church leaders (e.g., Sunday school teachers, youth leaders, women's ministry coordinators) need to be prepared to respond to sexual abuse both *proactively*—by clearly addressing the problem, condemning the practice, encouraging victims to seek help and healing, and providing guidance, resources, and accountability for those who are at risk for abusing others—and *reactively*—by being ready to respond appropriately, helpfully, and scripturally to victims who come to the church for help. So how can we do that? Where can we turn? And what are some of the challenges along the way?

Some Serious Recommendations for Serious Realities

One of the important lessons learned by the Religion and Violence e-Learning (RAVE) team at the University of New Brunswick is that pastors feel unprepared to respond to those who have been victims of abuse. Our studies among hundreds of pastors have shown that only 8 percent believe that they are well-prepared to respond.[14] In our research at seminaries, we have found that the rate among seminary students preparing to graduate is even lower. Additionally, we know that many pastors never address the issue

13. Such as the RAVE Project www.theraveproject.org; see further listing of websites under Web-based Resources in Appendix C of this book.
14. Nason-Clark, *The Battered Wife*, esp. chapter 4.

of abuse from the pulpit, and our seminary research suggests that one of the reasons is the fear that if the issue is addressed publicly from the pulpit, victims will come forward and the pastor will be unprepared to deal with the aftermath. This current state has many implications. For example, if abuse is not addressed effectively from the pulpit and in men's and women's ministries, in youth groups and appropriately among children, there is the very real danger that victims will simply remain silent while they continue to be victimized or not receive needed care. Such silence will often be interpreted by both the victim/survivor and the broader community as complicity with the acts of violence—or at least an inability or unwillingness to confront the problem of sexual abuse head-on.

Since sexual abuse is closely related to issues of power and authority, the abuser may be able to enforce a "code of silence" that keeps the victim from speaking out. If the abuser is a church leader, the victim may feel that they have a responsibility to protect the church by keeping the abuse a secret. If the abuser is a family member, the victim may feel that to disclose the abuse would be to destroy the sacredness of a marriage or a family unit. *Defining, effectively addressing, and condemning sexual abuse by naming it publicly in a sermon are important ways of disempowering the abuser and providing the victim or survivor with the permission they may feel they need to seek help and safety.*

Pastors are probably right in the belief that if they address the issue of sexual abuse from the pulpit, they will need to be ready to respond to victims who feel that the sermon has given them permission to seek help. Since most pastors feel unprepared to respond, they mistakenly decide it is better not to address the issue at all and hope that it isn't happening in their congregation. Indeed, victims or concerned families can be desperate to find help when the issue is brought into the open, but these leaders often have the wrong strategy. Instead of deciding to keep the issue hidden, pastors need to prepare themselves to respond.

Many pastors seem to have the mistaken impression that being prepared to respond to victims of sexual abuse means fulfilling the role of a qualified family therapist. That is not the case. In fact, it is those pastors who are least prepared to respond who are most likely to attempt to "fix" the problem by counseling or advising the victim and/or the abuser. Such attempts by unqualified pastors can cause great harm. Pastors who know how to respond when a victim comes seeking help understand two things.

First, as trained shepherds, they are qualified to provide spiritual care, guidance, and support to the victim of the abuse. Victims of sexual abuse who are part of the faith community will have many questions about God, about themselves, and about the abuse that has happened—*or is still happening.* Throughout that difficult process, pastors can provide the biblical guidance, spiritual care, and prayer that is so essential to the healing process. Pastors are qualified to address the issue of sin in the life of the abuser. They are also able to mobilize the church community to respond in love and in grace to provide practical support for the victim and offer various kinds of accountability structures for the abuser.

Second, well-prepared pastors also understand that they are not qualified to provide more technical counseling or therapy, legal opinions, or law enforcement. For these important aspects of the response to a victim of abuse or assault, pastors need to be familiar with and be ready to refer to other qualified resources in their wider community—resources that may include people within their congregation and also resources in the wider community. When a member of the congregation discloses to the pastor or to another church leader that they are being sexually abused, the pastor needs not only to know who to contact but also needs to have built good working relationships with those people so that referrals may be made with confidence.

For example, when a female victim of sexual abuse needs to go to a women's shelter so that they are safe from the abuse, it is important that the pastor be able to do more than look in the Yellow Pages to see who to call. A wise pastor will have already visited the nearest women's shelter and built a relationship with some of the staff members so that the pastor and the shelter workers can work together in the interests of the victim—the pastor providing spiritual guidance and support, while the staff members deal with the practical issues of keeping the woman safe from harm. Similar relationships can be built with law enforcement, with counselors and therapists, and with other community resources. It helps a victim a great deal when the pastor can confidently recommend a qualified counselor or therapist who will understand the victim's faith.

Ongoing Needs among the Wounded

Wise pastors have also learned to be sensitive to those in their congregations who have been victims of abuse. When describing marriage or family in teaching and sermons, it is important that biblical ideals be portrayed faithfully and honestly, but it is also important to relate that too often marriages and families are marred by sin and brokenness. When families are proclaimed from the pulpit as God's perfect plan and when families are praised as the ideal way for children to be raised, *pastors need to remember that many marriages and families—even in churches—are deeply marked by abuse.*

In light of the examples of family life that are included in the Scriptures, it seems surprising that so many pastors are tempted to preach the "perfect family" sermons that victims of abuse find so difficult to hear. When we look at the families in the Bible, it seems that God went out of his way to make it clear that even in homes of faith there can be terrible wrongs. God chose to include in Scripture many Old Testament stories of people—some of whom were kings and priests—who did terrible things to members of their own families as well as to others. Surely the biblical concept of the family needs to be portrayed with a clear understanding of how sin can affect that which is intended by God to be such a nurturing, loving relationship. Immediately, examples of the trafficking of Joseph (Genesis 37) or the rape of Tamar (2 Samuel 13) come to mind, but there are many others as well.

Pastors who decide that they would rather not address the issue of sexual abuse need to realize that when such serious problems are allowed to stay hidden in the church, *victims or survivors continue to endure physical and emotional pain even as their concept of God and his love for them becomes distorted.* A church where abuse is never addressed is a church where people are not safe from being victimized. Furthermore, such unaddressed behaviors can also do irreparable damage to the witness of the church. Additionally, when the abuser is a church leader and the abuse is allowed to continue unaddressed, it can destroy the very fabric of the congregation, possibly even separating families.

Ministering to the Reality of Shame

The issue of shame also needs to be considered by church leaders. Sexual abuse leads to shame on so many levels.[15] The abuser often uses shame to keep the victim silent, and the victim may feel ashamed to come to church, believing that if others knew what they were enduring they would be rejected or shunned or misunderstood. But another powerful aspect of shame is the desire of church leaders and members to maintain the illusion that abuse never happens in churches, or that it doesn't happen in *this* church or in *this* denomination. Such attitudes can keep a church from ministering to the hurting as Jesus would (Matt 20:34; Mark 1:41). By recognizing that sexual abuse is an important issue for churches and addressing it publicly, pastors have the opportunity to turn the shame into an opportunity to care for the hurting. By shattering the myth that "there are no victims here" and proclaiming that the church is a place where victims are welcomed and loved, the sin is named, the shame is broken, and the church is freed to begin reaching out with the love of Christ to care for its wounded by providing an atmosphere of grace and understanding and by providing acts of love that demonstrate in practical ways that the gospel is not limited to those who are from "ideal" families.

We have heard very troubled responses to talks about ministry to church members who are victims of abuse. Often the response is one of shame or *denial or embarrassment, that there would be such problems among God's people. Such shame and embarrassment shows a lack of understanding of who we are. We must remember that Jesus invited hurting people to come to him to find rest for their souls. Instead of feeling shame, we can rejoice that hurting people are in the pews of our churches. Maybe the very reason that they are in church is because they are seeking to respond to Jesus' invitation—they need rest for their souls. Instead of portraying the church as a place for perfect people, we can define the church as a place for those who are hurting and broken. When churches do that, we will no longer be ashamed of the issue in the church, nor will we be ashamed to have survivors in our midst. And victims will be able to worship with us without feeling shame. Realizing and acknowledging that there are victims in the church becomes an opportunity for ministry and healing, and shattering the silence will make the church an inviting place for victims to come to find spiritual strength and to experience God's grace at deeper levels. The church is a healing house.

The Fear Behind the Anger

Not only can being a victim of sexual abuse lead to shame, it can lead to anger. Anger can be a very appropriate and righteous reaction to the injustice and evil of our world (Mark 3:4–5; Eph 4:26a), so it should not be surprising that those who have been the victims of the injustice and evil of sexual abuse would feel anger. However, anger is intended as a short-term response to an evil circumstance (Eph 4:26b). *But the feelings of betrayal*

---

15. Tracy, *Mending the Soul*; also research by Diana Garland: www.baylor.edu/clergysexualmisconduct.

and pain experienced by survivors of sexual abuse are not short-term feelings, so for those who have been victimized, anger can become a way of life that affects all of their relationships in unhealthy ways and enables them to surround their bruised emotions with self-protective barriers that hide their feelings of vulnerability. What appears to others as hostility or obstinacy or an "unspiritual" attitude may actually be the outward manifestation of deep fears of being hurt or disappointed or victimized again. It will take time and trained help for victims to learn that although their trust has been terribly betrayed by an abuser, it does not mean they should never trust again. During that sometimes long process, religious leaders will need to show patience, compassion, and understanding in their response to angry survivors.

Our research has also shown that it is not only victims who are affected by fear. Our study among seminary students has shown that those preparing for pastoral ministry are also very fearful of responding to survivors of abuse. Students expressed to us a wide range of fears, from their concerns that they might "say the wrong thing" to a victim, to fears about dealing with their own personal issues (religious leaders may also struggle with abuse in their own past, which needs to be addressed), to fears that their ministry could be negatively and severely impacted by the discovery of abusive situations among church families. Such fears can lead to an unhealthy anger among church leaders toward the victims of sexual abuse. From our studies, it is clear that such fears among seminary students are related to a lack of preparedness to respond to victims. Those leaders who think they must by themselves "fix" the hurts caused by abuse are the most fearful. Those who realize that they can build good working relationships with therapists and advocates and other community resources are better able to respond in healthy and appropriate ways to calls for help from survivors.

Further Ideas and Recommendations

It is also important for leaders that we make as certain as we can that the church is a safe place, both to prevent victimization and to make those who have been victimized know they are emotionally and physically safe in our midst. Many churches have decided to address issues of safety in order to address liability concerns, but liability concerns should not be the church's primary motivation. *The primary reason for making certain that the church is a safe place is not to protect the church and its finances or to protect the church officers from lawsuits but to protect those who might be victimized from further harm.*

Leaders need to be aware of ways in which the church may be a place where people are particularly vulnerable: the ease with which volunteers may have access to children and adolescents, for example, or the ways in which abusers in positions of spiritual authority may twist the meaning of Scripture to demand cooperation and silence from their intended victims. When churches begin accepting volunteers without adequate screening or supervision, we can put children and youth in great danger. When churches presume that people can be trusted simply because they are faithful attendees, liked in the community, or willing volunteers, we put children in danger. When churches have no policies in place to respond to concerns or troubling signs, we put children in danger and the wounded in harm's reach. Moreover, when we do not explain to children and youth in the church how they should report inappropriate touch or inappropriate comments, we put them in danger.

The issue of screening church workers is an important one. In some churches, a "criminal record check" is the only requirement before volunteers are permitted to work with children or youth. Although the criminal record check should always be a part of the screening process, it is hardly adequate by itself. More important are interviews with the volunteers that explicitly address issues of sexual and physical abuse, and (especially if the volunteer is not well known) references from previous ministry situations that express unqualified confidence that the individual is not a risk to those with whom they work. But it should be remembered that even the best screening process is of little value without adequate and carefully enforced supervision policies and procedures. *Vulnerable persons in the church should never be alone with a paid or volunteer staff worker, and procedures should be in place for reporting and recording any reasons for concern.* Thus, background checks, references, interviews, and supervision must all become intentional practices in our churches. But there's more we can do.

Ministry workers need to be trained to know how to respond immediately when children or youth report concerns, and church leaders need to make sure such concerns are addressed quickly and properly. Churches also need to know how to respond when a known sexual abuser is part of the congregation and attending services—especially if his or her victims are *also* part of the congregation. Additionally, church leaders should know what to do when someone from their congregation who has been a sexual abuser decides to go to another congregation where people will not know of their past. *Churches have a moral obligation to protect those who have been victims and to make sure that others are not victimized because of the silence of the church.*

CONCLUDING THOUGHTS

Proclaiming that sexual abuse is wrong and never part of God's design for healthy sexuality or healthy family living is part of the responsibility of every pastor of every congregation. Offering pastoral assistance to those who have been impacted by abuse is integral to the call of God to care for those who are hurting. It is also imperative to hold offenders accountable and to protect children, youth, and adults in our congregations from *predators. Church leadership needs to take these responsibilities seriously and to act accordingly. This may include offering their facilities to local *support groups run by professionals and/or peer mentors. Yet, pastors cannot—and should not—act alone. *Rather, when clergy see themselves as part of a coordinated community response to victims, survivors, offenders, and those related to them, everyone will be better served.* An awareness of the prevalence and severity of abuse—accompanied by an awareness of the various community-based agencies poised to assist—will help a pastor feel better equipped and help to protect a religious leader from feeling overwhelmed. Moreover, as religious leaders cooperate and collaborate with professionals in the community on the issue of sexual abuse, it strengthens the bidirectional relationship of referrals (between churches and their communities), and it also serves those most impacted by the trauma of sexual abuse. Speaking out on this issue shatters the silence. Supporting victims reduces the shame even while it applies the healing balm of Gilead to their wounds.

QUESTIONS FOR DISCUSSION

1. Is my office a safe place for a victim of sexual abuse to disclose the pain he or she has suffered or is presently suffering? What would make it safer? What kind of official policies are in place to address sexual abuse? Do these policies reflect the current reality of abuse in the church and society?

2. Am I equipped as a pastor, or religious leader, to walk with a victim—or a perpetrator of sexual abuse—as they seek healing, justice, and wholeness in its aftermath? How might my skills be enhanced? What can be done to communicate to victims that this church is a "safe house?" Have I adequately educated parents with a *safety plan for their own families? What kind of *available* literature do we have that communicates we understand what victims are going through and are already planning for their needs?

3. In what ways might our congregation or our leadership team cooperate with other churches and community-based agencies to speak out against sexual abuse, responding compassionately and with professional best practices to those impacted by it? Are referring agencies known and spoken of, and is their contact information clearly available to all in leadership? What can be done in attitude, philosophy, and practice within the church leadership to create more effective "bridge-building" with other community-based agencies and interested area churches?

4. What are some current community resources and agencies in your area to help respond to sexual abuse? How have I learned to respond by employing the "language of the Spirit?" What kind of modeling have I done that balances condemnation of sexual abuse alongside the offer of grace and forgiveness? Are people in our congregation being trained, at various levels, to "walk with" the sexually broken in their midst?

5. How might our congregation take seriously the charge to be both prophetic and practical as it relates to the prevalence and severity of sexual abuse in church families and in the communities where we minister? Does our congregation adequately understand the danger of "conspiracies of silence" that can hide in their families, churches, and communities?

FOR FURTHER READING

Clergy Sexual Abuse Project, www.baylor.edu/clergysexualmisconduct.

Grant, Beth and Cindy Lopez Hudlin, eds. *Hands That Heal International Curriculum for Training Caregivers of Trafficking Survivors—Community-Based Editions—Part I; Part II.* Springfield, MO: Project Rescue International and FAAST, 2007.

Kroeger, Catherine and Nancy Nason-Clark. *No Place for Abuse: Biblical and Practical Resources To Counteract Domestic Violence.* Downers Grove, IL: InterVarsity Press, 2001.

Lile, Sherry, Debbie Tetsch, N. Nason-Clark, L. Ruff, and Christa Hayden Sharpe. "Counting the Cost: Caregiver Issues." In *Hands That Heal International Curriculum for Training Caregivers of Trafficking Survivors—Academic Edition*, edited by Beth Grant and Cindy Lopez Hudlin, 290–324. Springfield, MO: Project Rescue International and FAAST, 2007.

Steven R. Tracy *Mending the Soul: Understanding and Healing Abuse.* Grand Rapids: Zondervan, 2005.

The RAVE Project [Religion and Violence e-Learning], www.theraveproject.org.

15

What Every Minister Should Know about Sexual Abuse

A Counselor Shares Some Concerns

DIANE M. LANGBERG, PHD

THIS CHAPTER IS FOR you, dear shepherds of the sheep in the body of Christ. It is my hope that reading these words will help you to see more clearly who is sitting in the pews of your churches and understand more fully how to care for sheep wounded by *sexual abuse (SA). Too many in pastoral ministry do not know or believe that they have sheep that have been sexually abused. *Statistics reveal that these assumptions are illogical and dangerous.* *Childhood sexual abuse (CSA) occurs in the lives of one in four women and one in six men before the age of eighteen (1996).[1] According to the US Department of Justice, someone is sexually assaulted every two minutes in the United States.[2] In a September 2009 news release, Baylor University's School of Social Work reported that 3.1 percent of adult women who attend religious services at least once a month have been victims of clergy sexual abuse since turning eighteen. *That means you have men and women in your church who have experienced the *trauma of abuse and assault—some by previous shepherds.* Many victims have never spoken about their experience. Stop and think about the numbers in the context of the number of people in your church or in a youth group or in a Bible study, and you can begin to grasp something of the regularity of these crimes. Given the impact of sexual violence on an individual life and on society, and given the frequency of its occurrence, it is absolutely crucial that the church not be silent. Not only does God call us to intervene, he also calls his church to be a refuge and a place for hope and healing. Anything less is a failure to demonstrate his character in this world (Isah 61:1–4).

AN OFFENSE TO CHILDREN IS AN OFFENSE TO GOD

In this chapter we will be considering: (1) *how to think* about sexual abuse, (2) *how to respond* to a victim as pastor, and finally (3) *how to teach* your church to respond and care for those who have been abused. Matthew 18:5–7 contains a powerful warning:

1. ACE Study-Prevalence-Adverse Child Experiences, http://www.cdc.gov/needphp/aceprevalence.htm.
2. http://www.rainn.org/get-information/statistics/frequency-of-sexual-assault.

"And whoever welcomes one such child in my name welcomes me. If anyone causes one of these little ones—those who believe in me—to stumble, it would be better for them if a large millstone were hung around their neck and they were drowned in the depths of the sea . . . woe to the person through whom they come!" (TNIV)

Jesus says here that whoever offends—whoever among us is an impediment, trips up, or causes someone to distrust and desert the Father who ought to be trusted and obeyed, whoever does this to a "little one," a child—or one who is less in size, age, rank, power or influence, better for that person to incur the most imminent peril to their life (e.g., having a millstone turned by a donkey hung around his neck and be thrown into the sea).[3] In other words, *God is such a severe avenger of these offenses that it is better to suffer anything else, including death, than to offend the vulnerable in this way.* It is quite interesting to note that God speaks of putting a grinding, crushing, pulverizing instrument around the offender's neck. This is symbolic of what sexual abuse does to a human life—it crushes and pulverizes the victim.

If we take this Scripture at face value, then obviously God takes the abuse of a vulnerable human being very seriously. A vulnerable person is one who is easy to wound—a child, a person in a weakened state (e.g., physically, emotionally, spiritually). Someone who is being cared for by another who has power is vulnerable as well—a patient with a doctor, a parishioner with a pastor, a student with a teacher or coach, or a client with a counselor. Anyone who takes advantage of the dependent state of another in order to feed themselves in some way—their ego, their lust, or their wallet—is by definition a *predator, one who robs from another.

Offending anyone God calls "a little one" and causing them to stumble in their relationship to God is a very serious matter (cf. Mark 9:33–37). It is not just individuals who offend; institutions can offend corporately. *A church, a school, a mission board can be a stumbling block to a "little one" if they close ranks around the abuser and protect him or her rather than the victim.* It can happen when a victim is discredited or not helped when they disclose their abuse. It can happen when a church body does not want to deal with the mess and chooses to ignore the wrongdoing. *It happens when churches ignore the reality of sexual abuse and victims never hear any teaching from the Word of God about these issues.* Certainly the cross of Christ is sufficient for sex offenders and abusers, but at the same time our God is very clear about his response to such sin (Matt 18:7; Mark 9:42). He loves justice and truth and he abhors evil (Mic 6:8). His church is to look like he does, and where the church does not, it teaches the "little ones," those in a weakened state, lies about who God is.

UNDERSTANDING THE SEXUAL ABUSE VICTIM

If, as a pastor, you are to respond well to those who have been sexually abused, you must have some understanding of what abuse does to human beings. Victims of sexual abuse have experienced fear and helplessness. They may have been helpless due to force, au-

---

3. The word "little" does not simply mean a child in years. In view is a willingness to be dependent with a trusting spirit (cf. Matt 18:3–4).

thority, isolation, manipulation, or coercion. *They have experienced an abuse of power.*[4] That power may have been physical, emotional, relational, verbal, spiritual, and often a combination of these. Someone has used one or all of these means to have sexual access to them at a time when they were vulnerable—*little in size, rank, or influence.* What they thought or wanted or felt was irrelevant. Victims have been silenced; their voice did not matter. Relationship has become an unsafe, cruel, and frightening place. They have felt helpless and are afraid to be in that position again.

You have, sitting in your pews, many who have experienced these things. Some of them grew up with repeated experiences of abuse and violence in the home. Others have experienced these things in the terrifying moments of a *rape. Others have been in a vulnerable position and have been abused by those who had power, such as a doctor, counselor, or pastor. This abuse has impacted their view of themselves, their relationships, their faith, and their future. As pastor you are in a position of power and authority. *In the minds of many, you speak for God—the very God who allowed the abuse.* They are afraid of their *molester and you, even as they long to know that you are safe and that God is present and loves them.

The Victim's Faith is Damaged

Sexual abuse has a very profound impact spiritually. If the abuse occurred repeatedly throughout childhood, then the victim's thinking has been shaped by that abuse. The hideous lies that abuse teaches become the *control beliefs* for the rest of life. *It is common to find someone who fiercely believes that God is love, but that he does not love them.* When the abuser has been a pastor or a father, the hypocrisy makes God's truth seem empty as well. Victims have been treated as if they are worthless, trash, and even evil. How could God love such a one as that? Pastors often have the experience of trying to teach people with abuse histories about the love of God and yet realizing their instruction is not penetrating the heart at all. The person nods assent but it does not go in.

There are also those who *seem* to experientially know the truths of Scripture and apply them to themselves, but on closer look are found able to do so largely because *they have yet to face the truth of the abuse they endured.* They have so *compartmentalized* the abuse that they can receive the truths of our God without any apparent strain. Elie Wiesel, one of the foremost writers of the Holocaust, struggles again and again in his books with the apparent mutual exclusivity of God and trauma, God's commitment and human suffering. Throughout his books he tells the reader not to assume that it is a consolation to believe that God is still alive.[5] Rather than being the solution, saying "God is alive" simply states the problem.[6] He wrestles with what he describes as two irreconcilable realities: God and the reality of Auschwitz. Each seems to cancel out the other, yet neither will disappear. Either alone could be managed, Auschwitz and no God, or God and no Auschwitz. But together, how does one assimilate both Auschwitz *and* God?

---

4. Kroeger and Beck, *Women, Abuse, and the Bible*, 58–69.

5. Wiesel, *Night*.

6. McAfee Brown, *Elie Wiesel*.

For many *survivors of sexual abuse the same two irreconcilable realities exist: the reality of a God who says he loves and provides refuge for the weak (Ps 9:9), and the reality of the ongoing sexual violation of a child or a violent rape or abuse by a trusted caretaker such as a doctor or pastor. Each seems to cancel out the other, yet both exist. *Again, the human mind can manage either alternative: sexual abuse and no God, or God and protection from sexual abuse.* What is one to do with rape *and* the reality of God? Most victims will come down on one side or the other. They have faced the abuse or the rape and God is not to be trusted. Or they hang on tightly to God and the rape is "no big deal." This dilemma is not easily solved. *The damage is exacerbated whenever church leadership minimizes the evil by using timetables for healing, redefining the victim's story, or suggesting that the proper amount of faith will provide a quick and immediate fix for the devastation.*

I want to make sure that we grasp the profound impact of abuse to a person's understanding of God. Let us consider some specific examples, and as we do I would like you to imagine that these people with the following histories are sitting in your pews week after week. Try to imagine how they might be experiencing church, relating to the people around them, and hearing the preaching.

Case #1: Sarah

Sarah is five. Her parents drop her off at Sunday school every week. She has learned to sing, "Jesus loves me, this I know, for the Bible tells me so. Little ones to Him belong. They are weak, but He is strong." Sarah's daddy rapes her several times a week. Sometimes she gets a break because he rapes her eight-year-old sister instead. The song says that Jesus loves her. It says that He is strong. So she asks Jesus to stop her daddy from hurting her and her sister—nothing happens. Maybe Jesus isn't so strong after all, or at least not as strong as daddy. Nothing, not even Jesus, can stop daddy. The people who wrote the Bible must not have known about her daddy.

Case #2: Michael

Michael went away to a Christian overnight camp at age seven. He was scared and home-sick. His counselor paid him special attention. It made him feel important, but then it got strange and scary. The counselor would teach the Bible study at night and then take Michael for a walk and make him do things he didn't like.

Case #3: Susan

Susan dated the pastor of her previous church's singles group. He was a leader who was well liked. He treated her one way in public, but when they were alone he became demeaning and critical and began pressuring her for sex. He eventually raped her and then blamed her for seducing him. The church leadership did not believe her and supported him instead. She has not been in a church for several years.

Lessons from the "Seen and Unseen" for the Abused

Keep in mind as you think through these examples that not only do children think concretely and, therefore, learn about the abstract by way of the concrete, as adults, we continue to be taught about the unseen through the seen. We are of the earth, earthy. God often teaches us eternal truths through things in the natural world. One could say we grasp a bit of eternity by looking at the sea. We get a glimmer of infinity by staring into space. We learn about the shortness of time by the quick disappearance of a vapor (Jam 4:14). Jesus taught us eternal truths the same way. He said He was "living water," "bread," the "light," and the "vine" (cf. John 4:14; 6:35; 8:12; 15:1). *We look at the seen and learn about the unseen.* Consider the sacraments—water, bread, and wine. We are taught about the holiest of all through the diet of a peasant. This method of instruction is used throughout Scripture, including for our understanding of the character of God himself when God appears in the flesh (John 1:14). God explains himself to us through the temporal, the material, and the human.

What then are the lessons about the unseen when sexual abuse occurs? Think about hearing that God is a "refuge" or God is our "stronghold" (Ps 46:1). Think about hearing that God is a God of love and compassion (Lam 3:22). What does a child who is a victim of *incest do with the idea of God as father (Gal 4:6)? How does a traumatized and finite human mind reconcile the God of the Scriptures whom we worship and adore with the experience of sexual violence? How do victims process the biblical truths taught from the pulpit? And how should the church and its leadership respond to the victims sitting among them?

THE BODY OF CHRIST

In 1 Corinthians 12, Paul gives us a description of the body of Christ and some of the ways in which it functions. He makes it clear that those of us who are part of the body of Christ are connected in a vital way. Each part affects the others, and we are called to show a common concern for one another. Paul goes on to say two very relevant things. He says that the members of the body who seem to be "weaker" are necessary. "Those members of the body which seem to be more feeble are necessary" (1 Cor 12:22 ASV). How unlike us that is! We would typically hide or remove or try to change those who are weaker. We tend to see them as a hindrance to our goals.

Children and Survivors: Lessons of the "Weak"

There are two groups in the context of sexual abuse we might say are weaker. First, of course, are the children. They are little, vulnerable, and in need of constant protection. In order for a church to care for them, it has to slow down, bend down, speak simply, wait, and think protectively. In the context of sexual abuse, that means that the care and protection of children must be considered paramount. Their care should always be a central and governing principle and that should be evident in church policy, core value statements, and procedures. Background checks need to be done for those involved in childcare so that known *sex offenders are not allowed access to children. Training should also be given for how to treat children and keep them safe as well as information about state regulations on *mandated reporting. *Concern about the safety of children is also a gift to those who endured sexual abuse as children.* They then see that the church is indeed a refuge for children.

A second group that might be considered "weaker" is the group of those who have suffered sexual abuse in their own lives. *You cannot even discuss this topic without impacting them any more than you can discuss combat without affecting veterans.* Their memories get "yanked up" to the front of their minds, and their emotions take them on a roller coaster ride. To even consider this issue *costs* them! And they too are *necessary* to you. Both the children and the survivors will force you to think of and weigh carefully things you might not give thought to if they were not present. They are not a hindrance. Nor are they a nuisance. God says they are necessary. He put them in the body as he desired and for your sake. If the body does not allow their concerns and pain and protection to influence them, *or fails when appropriate to give them a redemptive role in the church*, then the body has failed to care for some in their midst. Pastors, in what ways does your church body reflect these concerns?

Paul also tells us that when one member of the body suffers, we all suffer (1 Cor 12:26). That means being part of the body of Christ inevitably brings us into contact with the suffering of others. If we are ignoring, minimizing, or *denying this suffering, we are not living out our calling as connected and caring for others' suffering. *To be part of a faith community that allows itself to be impacted by the suffering of others is to be willing to bend down and share their burdens with them, truly a supernatural and redemptive work.* It is redemptive to all parties, both those who suffer and those who care for them. It demonstrates the character of our God before a watching world—a world hungry for refuge, love, mercy, and compassion. Those individuals who sit in our congregations dragging a history of sexual violence around with them and living silent, isolated lives have been put there by our God, for their sakes and for ours as well.

HOW SHOULD THE CHURCH RESPOND?

How Others View Pastors: A Reality Check

Before we look specifically at the response of the church, let us take a reality check. To date, most pastors are male. That is especially true in the *evangelical world. The great majority of sex offenders of both male and female victims are also male. Pastors are in positions of power and authority. That power has nothing to do with *feeling* powerful; it has to do with position, theological knowledge, verbal ability, and authority. Sexual abuse of any kind causes the victim to experience profound helplessness and powerlessness. Much of church leadership is also male, such as elders or deacons or heads of denominations. Potentially, that means that *no matter how much integrity you have, how kind you are or even how approachable you feel, you are a frightening person to a victim.* You are also someone who represents God, who speaks for and about God, and so you are someone victims long to hear from even while they are afraid to hear. They want to hear that God loves them; they will not believe you. They want you to show yourself trustworthy; they will be afraid of you. They want to hear that God hates evil and that what was done to them has done violence to his character as well as theirs. They fear you will blame them for their abuse or sanction the *conspiracy of silence. Needless to say, a pastor, at best, produces ambivalence in a victim of sexual abuse.

Ready with Other Care Takers

It is critical to understand these issues so that when you have a female church member come to you about abuse you have particular women in the church who have read and studied the area and can walk alongside the victim as she seeks to heal and learn about God in the midst of her suffering. Obviously having some mature men in the church that can do this for male victims is critical as well. It is also wise to have a referral list of professional Christian psychologists or counselors with expertise in addressing sexual abuse. The work of dealing with abuse is often intense and long term, and while the role of pastor is crucial, it is different from that of counselor. Ideally, victims of abuse will see a trained professional, have several people in the church who will come alongside them as they struggle and do the work of healing, be taught by a pastor who speaks truth and shepherds safely and *empathetically those sheep who have been wounded.

The Role of the Shepherd for the Wounded

So we come again to our core question, "What should be the response of the pastor and the church?" The survivor is struggling with deep questions about God: "Who is he?" "What does he think?" "What does he think about me?" "Was it my fault?" "Am I evil?" "Does his patience run out?" "Why should I have hope?" The church becomes the representative of God to the victim. *The church is to teach in the seen that which is true in the unseen.* People's words, tone of voice, actions, body movements, and responses to rage, fear, and failure all become ways that the abuse victim learns about and reshapes their view of God. I believe that the very reputation of God himself is at stake in the people in the church. As the shepherd, you can shape a congregation's attitudes toward sexual abuse and help eradicate damaging assumptions and *stereotypes. We are called to represent Christ well. Our task becomes that of living out the character of *the* Shepherd before his wounded sheep.

INCARNATING GOD AND RESCUING VICTIMS' THEOLOGY

I first began to understand this early on in my work with victims. I was working with a woman who had been chronically abused and I longed for her to truly grasp the love of God for her. I tried telling her about it but realized at some point that she was politely tolerating what I was saying, but it was not "going in." I got down on my knees before God begging him to help her see what she so desperately needed to see—that he really loved her. What I understood him to say was, "You want to know how much I love her? Then you go love her in a way that *demonstrates* that. You want her to know that I am trustworthy and safe? Then you go be trustworthy and safe." In other words, pastors must demonstrate in the flesh the character of God over time so that who you are reveals the truth of who our God is to the one who has been abused. And that, of course, is the *incarnation: Jesus, in the flesh, explaining God to us; Jesus, bringing the unseen down into flesh-and-blood actualities.

Those who have been abused need Christ-like leadership to incarnate God for three reasons. First, all of us need that; humanity needs to see God in the flesh. Jesus came to explain God to us (John 1:18). Jesus knew that and used countless examples in the seen to teach his disciples about the unseen. Secondly, *this need is intensified for the victim because what has been taught in the seen is the antithesis of the truth of God.* She or he has learned about fathers, trust, love, and refuge from one who emulated the "father of lies" (John 8:44). That unseen, full of lies, has been lived out before her and she has learned her lessons well. If you want an abuse victim to understand that God is a refuge, then be one. If you want the betrayed to grasp the faithfulness of God, then be faithful. If you want the confused to understand the truthfulness of God, then do not lie. If you want victims to understand the infinite patience of God, then you must be patient. And where you are not a refuge, or are tired of being faithful, or squirm to tell the truth, or grow impatient with the necessary repetition of truth, then get down on your knees and ask God to give you more of him so that you might better represent him.

The second aspect of our response is to speak truth. *Victims carry deeply embedded and longstanding lies within. Such lies need to be exposed, gently and slowly, so the light of the truth of God can begin to take their place.* Working through the lies is arduous and slow. It requires tremendous patience. The rewards are wonderful, for over time you begin to see light dawn in a darkened and confused mind. It is quite different, however, from simply telling someone God loves them and having them believe it. You must speak it, live it, be it, then do it again!

The third aspect of the incarnation story is that there is tremendous healing for survivors as they begin to study and truly grasp the suffering and death of Jesus, for them and because of them. He *knows*—that is a phenomenal revelation. I recently had a woman come in to a session who was working through some of the Scripture on the crucifixion. I had suggested at her previous session that she go home and read John 19:23–25 over and over. She returned the next week and had barely sat down when she began saying over and over: "They took his clothes. I never saw it before. They took his clothes." This is a woman who had many perpetrators and has countless memories of standing naked as an adolescent in a group of men. Something way down deep in her soul was touched that day when she saw that *Jesus knew and understood the humiliation, exposure, and shame she had experienced.*

The cross of Christ demonstrates the extent of the evil. The cross of Christ demonstrates the infinite love of God. The cross of Christ covers any evil done by the victim. This is crucial, as many victims blame themselves for the abuse (a lie) but also believe they are beyond redemption because of some of their own choices rising out of their abuse (e.g., addictions, *sexualized behaviors, etc.). *Any inadequacy in the cross of Christ means that none of us is safe.* The cross of Christ is "God with us"—in our sin, our suffering, our grief, and our sorrows. In order to redeem, he became like us (John 1:14). In order to redeem, he bore our sorrows (Isah 53:4).

This work is not simply about teaching or instructing. I often direct people to a particular passage or raise a specific question, but I do not simply teach them about the crucifixion. I send them to learn and study, and then we dialogue together. The work has far more power when they wrestle with it themselves. This is not something I do early on in my relationship with them. *It happens after a significant relationship has been developed and after they have faced the memories of abuse that plague them.* I find they will grasp the profound truths of the cross far more readily and deeply if they have seen some representation of those truths in their relationship with me. They have been able to speak the unspeakable. They are known. They are loved. No matter what they tell, they remain safe. I can forgive. I have hope for them. They have hopefully found in their relationship with me an aroma of the person of Christ (2 Cor 2:15). Out of that experience in the seen, in flesh and blood, they can then safely turn to the person and work of Christ and his *identification* with them. I have without exception found it a powerful way of teaching truth and of bringing healing.

CONCLUSION

There are three elements that are necessary if the church is to care for victims well. This is a ministry the church has been called to do. *First, we must know about people and about trauma.* We must understand what trauma does to human beings. If we do not understand such things we will make wrong evaluations. We will prematurely expect change. We will give wrong answers. We will fail to hear because we think we know. Listen acutely. Study avidly. Hebrews 13:3 talks about remembering others "as if we" were in their place. We cannot do that without taking the time to listen, study, and understand. We need to study the issues so that we can respond "as if we" had been abused. This entire book is a resource to that end.

Second, we must know God and his Word. We are to be avid students of that Word. If we are going to serve as spiritual leaders in the *spiritual formation of others, we need to know him well. We are often so presumptuous and we speak for him where we do not really know him. We need to be so permeated by his Word that we learn to think his thoughts. George MacDonald said: "If you say, 'The opinions I hold and by which I represent Christianity, are those of the Bible,' I reply, 'that none can understand, still less represent, the opinions of another, but such as are of the same mind with Him.'" May we never forget that to know his Word, according to him, means it is so woven into our lives that we live obedient to it. Where we do not live according to his Word, where we fail to care for the abused, we do not truly know God.

Finally, do not do this work without utter dependence on the Spirit of God. Where else will we find wisdom? How will we know when to speak and when to be silent? How will we discern the lies from the truth? How else will we love when we are tired or be patient when we are weary? How can we know the mind of God apart from the Spirit of God? How can we possibly expect to live as a person who demonstrates the character of God apart from the Spirit of God? How can we think that the life-giving power of the work of Christ crucified will be released into other lives unless we have allowed that cross to do its work in our own lives? *To work with sexual abuse is to work with lies, darkness, and evil.* It is hell brought up from below to the earth's surface. You cannot fight the litter of hell in a life unless you walk dependent on the Spirit of God. You cannot bring life to the place of death unless you walk dependent on the Spirit of God.

This is a work that is a privilege to do. It is a work that is difficult to do. It is a work God has called his people to do. The task of serving as a representative of God in the seen so that the unseen can be grasped, understood, and believed, in some measure, is far beyond any capability of yours or of mine. It is a work, however, that if we will let it, will take us to our knees with a heart hungry for more of God so that we might in turn bring his presence in very concrete ways into places and lives where he has not yet been known. As a result, those in your church who have been victimized by sexual abuse will come to know our God as he truly is, and in turn they will be used by God to do his redemptive work in you as his shepherd and in your flock as well. Welcome them in his name.

QUESTIONS FOR DISCUSSION

1. On a practical level, what does it mean to minister to victims of sexual abuse in a way that reflects an understanding of both the greatness of the evil and the greatness of our God, as well as the terrible dilemma this is in the soul of the one who has been victimized? List several concrete steps that seminaries and spiritual formation programs can do to better prepare men and women to engage the problem of sexual abuse in ministry. Church leaders can attend a seminar on sexual abuse to fill in the "knowledge gap," but how do leaders develop empathy for the sexually traumatized? List the ways you can let abuse survivors help other victims in the various ministries of the church. Consider letting a survivor read a written *lament to God in an appropriate service. (See the Written Prayers for Survivors in Appendix B).

2. Can you articulate some of the lies about God that the experience of child sexual abuse might teach? Given those lies, what specific kinds of character traits will you need to demonstrate in your relationship with victims? Which traits will be most difficult for you and how will you manage that? Discuss the nature of spiritual damage that victims suffer. Compare the insights from this chapter with the spiritual struggle of a recent victim you know. What are the parallels?

3. This chapter discussed the significance of the "seen" and "unseen" operating in peoples' lives, including victims'. Explain how various approaches to church ministry can capitalize on this reality to help victims? Can you lay out some action steps for your congregation to take so that victims in your midst will be well cared for? Consider such things as: a reading list, training by a competent counselor, background checks for all staff (employees and volunteers), a referral list of counselors, a support group, and an understanding of mandated reporting laws in your state. Contact area churches to see what programs they have in place.

FOR FURTHER READING

G.R.A.C.E. Godly Response to Abuse in a Christian Environment, www.netgrace.org.

Herman, Judith. *Trauma and Recovery*. New York, NY: Basic Books, 1992.

Kroeger, Catherine Clark & Beck, James, *Women, Abuse and the Bible*. Grand Rapids: Baker Books, 1996.

Langberg, Diane Mandt. *Counseling Survivors of Sexual Abuse*. Xulon Press, 2003.

_____. *On the Threshold of Hope: Opening the Door to Healing for Survivors of Sexual Abuse*. Carol Stream, IL: Tyndale House, 1999.

Nouwen, Henri J. M. *The Living Reminder: Service and Prayer in Memory of Jesus Christ*. New York, NY: Seabury Press, 1981.

Tracy, Steven R. *Mending the Soul: Understanding and Healing Abuse*. Grand Rapids: Zondervan, 2008.

_____. *Mending the Soul Workbook: Understanding and Healing Abuse*. Global Hope Resources, 2009.

16

Spiritual Formation and the Sexually Abused

Redemptive Companionship

JoAnn A. Shade, DMin

HOW CAN THOSE WHO'VE suffered *sexual abuse (SA) be supported in their *spiritual formation by the church and by the academy? What understandings of sexual abuse and the formation process are vital to the pastor, spiritual director, or the community of believers as they walk with their brother or sister toward God? How can the ancient theological themes of *forgiveness, shame, trust, evil, restoration, and community so vital to spiritual formation speak to the pain and betrayal felt by one who has been sexually abused? And is it possible for the lay leader, seminary professor, or youth pastor to mediate the healing and restoring work of the Holy Spirit rather than meddle in areas that could damage the growth and development of the abuse victim?

SPIRITUAL DIRECTION AND SEXUAL ABUSE: FROM WHENCE WE'VE COME

Until at least the mid 1970s, sexual abuse was simply not a topic of discussion in public settings or within the church.[1] While it clearly existed prior to that, as evidenced by Tamar's rape at the hands of her own half-brother, Amnon (2 Samuel 13), her experience was descriptive of those ravaged in this way: "And Tamar lived in her brother Absalom's house, a desolate woman" (2 Sam 13:20b TNIV). *Like Tamar's narrative, sexual abuse was historically hidden within the home or held within the heart and memory of the abused, their desolation a private matter.*

As the subject of sexual abuse surfaced in the church, its initial response consisted of turning to the professional therapeutic community for the healing and development of the victims and to the legal system for justice and protection. In the ensuing years, the church has wrestled with its response to sexual abuse, and now it often offers growth or therapy groups for *survivors, provides some training for its clergy, and has a raised awareness of the dangers of clergy sexual abuse.

---

1. Davis, *Accounts of Innocence.*

Understanding Spiritual Formation

Spiritual formation is also a relatively new catch phrase among *evangelicals,[2] with a scope far broader than its predecessors of Christian education and discipleship training. Gerald May describes it as "a rather general term referring to all attempts, means, instructions, and disciplines intended toward deepening of faith and furtherance of spiritual growth. It includes educational endeavors as well as the more intimate and in-depth process of spiritual direction."[3] M. Robert Mulholland offers a definition that fits a contemporary understanding of spiritual formation: *a process of being conformed to the image of Christ for the sake of others.*[4] Spiritual wholeness is:

> [S]een to lie in an increasingly faithful response to the One whose purpose shapes our path, whose grace redeems our detours, whose power liberates us from crippling bondages of the prior journey and whose transforming presence meets us at each turn in the road . . . a pilgrimage of deepening responsiveness to God's control of our life and being.[5]

Over the past four decades, a contemporary view of spiritual formation has unfolded that incorporates the classic Christian journey, is holistic, and develops "in the midst of our emotional, psychological, physical, and mental conditions and emerges out of them."[6] In light of this description, it is evident that spiritual formation cannot take place in a vacuum and must take into consideration the various experiences of the individual that make up his or her story, including sexual abuse.

APPROACHES TO SPIRITUAL FORMATION

A holistic approach to spiritual formation welcomes many components and various approaches. First, there is the broad experience of church attendance and corporate worship that still may be the main avenue of spiritual formation experienced by the majority of those who call themselves Christian. Even as we design courses and plan retreats, it is essential to realize that many believers depend on our corporate gatherings for their growth in Christ.

A second component of spiritual formation is the church-based discipleship, growth and/or spiritual formation groups that dot the Christian landscape. Many function as adult Sunday school classes, while others take on the *adult Bible fellowship format or may have a therapeutic overtone.

Within the academy, the approach is both academic and interpersonal. Most seminaries are incorporating spiritual formation in their core values, such as Ashland Theological Seminary's "intentional commitment to grow, study, pray, and be held accountable for our life and witness, both before God and one another."[7] Spiritual formation

2. Willard, *The Great Omission.*

3. Gerald G. May, quoted in Willard, *The Great Omission*, 2006.

4. Mulholland, *Invitation to a Journey*, 12.

5. Ibid., 13.

6. Ibid.

7. Ashland Theological Seminary, www.ashland.edu/seminary; accessed November 2, 2009.

classes, small groups formed for accountability and growth, and mentoring relationships all contribute to the spiritual formation of the student and present conceptual approaches to spiritual formation.[8]

The ancient tradition of spiritual direction long used by Catholics has recently been discovered and/or appropriated by the wider church. Described by James Keegan, a Roman Catholic spiritual director, it is "the contemplative practice of helping another person or group to awaken to the mystery called God in all of life, and to respond to that discovery in a growing relationship of freedom and commitment."[9] As a proponent of spiritual formation, Richard Foster recognizes the solitary and interior nature of its work known only to God, a work of inner transformation.[10] Yet Foster also understands the needed support of others in our efforts:

> We are not alone in this work of the re-formation of the heart. It is imperative for us to help each other in every way we can. And in our day, the desperate need is for the emergence of a massive spiritual army of trained spiritual directors who can lovingly come alongside precious people and help them discern how to walk by faith in the circumstances of their own lives.[11]

A fifth approach is pastoral and licensed psychological counseling or therapy. When symptoms are severe or day-to-day functioning is compromised, the guidance of a wise and well-trained counselor is essential. Even when the individual seems to be functioning well, counseling directed at the sexual abuse experience supports the maturing of the heart.

In truth, spiritual formation can be framed by many or all of these opportunities. With a different starting point, each of these approaches may incorporate the practice of the classic *spiritual disciplines, time spent in prayer, individual or corporate prayer, retreats, directed Bible study, meditation, and intentional spiritual conversations.

WHEN SEXUAL ABUSE INVADES THE NARRATIVE

Understanding that spiritual formation takes place in a myriad of ways and is facilitated by people of various backgrounds and training, how can the director, teacher, or friend work effectively and respectfully with the person who has experienced sexual abuse, even if we are not aware of its existence? Many men and women who've suffered sexual abuse live relatively normal lives, and those early experiences may only surface in times of intense struggle or concentrated spiritual and emotional reflections. Whether fully aware of their abuse or not, a starting point is to recognize that sexual abuse is only one part of the

---

8. Formational literature is growing. See recently: Wilhoit, *Spiritual Formation as if the Church Mattered*; also *Journal of Spiritual Formation and Soul Care*.

9. Spiritual Directors International, www.sdiworld.org; accessed November 2, 2009.

10. Foster, "Spiritual Formation Agenda: Three Priorities for the Next 30 Years," http://www.christianity today.com/ct/2009/january/26.29.html.

11. Ibid.

person's story—it need not define who they are, nor does it excuse the individual's sinful response to the abuse and to life in general.[12]

The one who accompanies an abused seeker on the path of spiritual formation is wise to recognize the common areas of struggle. Research indicates that those who've suffered sexual abuse have been adversely impacted in three areas of spiritual functioning:

- a sense of being loved and accepted by God,

- developing a sense of community,

- trusting in God's plan.[13]

It is likely that an abuse victim sees themselves as too defiled to be loved by God, believing that there's no way a holy God could accept their life with its shameful past. Likewise, the boy who's been molested by an uncle imagines that every boy in the locker room knows his story and begins a pattern of *avoidance and isolation that lasts long into adulthood—extending into the small group at the church that his wife drags him to twenty years later.

For the abuse victim, an inability to trust in God's plan is painful. "If God is good and has a plan for me," the thinking goes, "then either I did something wrong or God made a mistake in my life." "How can I trust him, if he allowed this to happen to me?" Yet, as Allender explains, "[W]hen we fail to trust the real God we do not escape trusting someone or something . . . *We cannot fail to trust God without turning our trust to something that becomes a new god for us*."[14]

MEDIATING VS. MEDDLING

Trauma survivors' experiences of recovery . . . strongly suggest that God may have ordered creation and redemption in such a way that God depends upon the cooperation of other persons' free choices to love their neighbor for mediating divine grace.[15]

Having spent more than thirty years in the frontlines of pastoral, social service, and counseling work, I recognize the need for specifics that allow the guide to mediate God's grace and God's Spirit rather than simply meddle in the life of another. As my friend and former colleague Caroline Stanczak reminds me, these are people who have been traumatized, who have suffered genuine damage. We must use the utmost care to avoid causing further damage through our insensitivity or personal stories.

The Spiritual Guide: Caring and Cautions

Before considering the specific work of the one who *listens*, *directs*, and *speaks* God's healing word, it is essential to look to the heart and identity of the spiritual guide. The one who comes alongside must know himself or herself. He or she must do the hard work

12. See Allender, *The Wounded Heart*, for further discussion on the response of the abused.

13. Hall, "Spiritual Effects of Childhood Sexual Abuse in Adult Christian Women," 129–134; also Schmutzer, "Spiritual Formation and Sexual Abuse," 67–86.

14. Allender, *The Wounded Heart*, 25; emphasis added.

15. Beste, "Mediating God's Grace Within the Context of Trauma," 246; emphasis added.

of personal formation. As a mature believer, the spiritual guide has a store of resources within: love, truth, wisdom, and the ability to be compassionate and respectful. With such resources, it is possible to move without fear toward the one who has been wounded by abuse, validating their struggle.

This is not an easy journey for either party. *The one who listens and guides also suffers.* Hearing the stories of abuse and its aftermath can be devastating to the listener, yet it is ours to receive and hold gently and to pour out to God. Having worked for many years with those who've experienced sexual abuse, Diane Langberg recognizes this:

> One of the most difficult things for me was to learn how to enter into another's pain without being drowned by it. Because the despair was so deep, it was difficult not to let it engulf me. I kept returning to this truth: 'Greater is he who is in you than he who is in the world.'[16]

Langberg's chapter on suggestions for people walking alongside a survivor is an invaluable tool, providing practical and insightful direction for this entrance into the fellowship of another's sufferings.[17]

Our prayer must always be for *discernment*—when to validate and confirm, when to exhort or challenge. Be aware of the possibility of manipulation, and get some feedback from a supervisor or a more experienced colleague when confused or sucked into the drama. Don't work without a *safety plan/net. Often denominations and institutions have resources in place for supervision or consultation—don't do additional harm by failing to utilize available support.

Realize that the person you are working with deserves an expectation of confidentiality. Make that a point of discussion early on in the relationship. When working with a group, unless a participant gives permission, sensitive revelations should stay in the room at the end of the session.

A sincere, mature believer can support someone who's experienced sexual abuse, yet cautions must be heeded. First, don't underestimate the depths of evil—*this battle has been waged in the body, and the victim may suffer lifelong consequences.* Powerful, even explosive emotions can lie quietly for years, only to be disrupted by life passages such as the birth of a child or by the introspection that comes during a time of intense spiritual development. While the sexual abuse survivor may know cognitively that the abuse wasn't his or her fault, the body and emotions may bear an alternate message of blame and shame. Their trauma is real. This is war.

If you're serious about walking alongside, take a crash course in the impact of sexual abuse, including the possibility of long-term *depression, eating disorders, anxiety, and *post-traumatic stress disorder (PTSD). While not all victims encounter these serious consequences, it is wise to be aware of what can occur. In particular, the effects of PTSD are three-fold. First, the victim is often *hyper-vigilant, easily startled, and plagued with anxiety and sleeplessness. He or she may re-experience the abuse with *flashbacks and *intrusive thoughts and images. Other sufferers are more impacted by what is called *con-

---

16. Langberg, *On the Threshold of Hope*, 199.

17. Ibid., 197–205.

striction: *numbness, *detachment, and avoidance, making relationship development problematic.

It is essential to have an awareness of danger signs that could require professional *intervention. *Suicidal ideation cannot be ignored, and the emergency room must be utilized in those instances. Other *self-destructive behaviors need treatment as well. Watch, too, for overwhelming life stressors that strip the person of the resources they need to cope or for a decrease in basic life functions such as personal hygiene, care of children, etc. They also may *present as very needy, and have difficulty setting boundaries because of their deep desire to belong. Be aware of your own personal boundaries, and use caution.

Naïve but well-meaning "helpers" have the capability of re-offending the abuse victim by careless actions or touch, so one must be aware of such practical concerns. Those working in private situations must be cautious of closed doors. An appointment for spiritual direction at the church at 9:00 p.m., when everyone else has gone home, is not appropriate. One key rule of thumb: if your spouse knew where you were and who you were with, would he or she be concerned? Be aware as well of the use of physical touch. Touch intended to be comforting or compassionate can be uncomfortable or painful to one who has experienced abuse.

I've been writing with the assumption that those we work with have experienced sexual abuse in the past, *but it is possible that the abuse is current as an adult*. This can play out within an abusive marriage or could be occurring in another setting, such as work or even the church. Be sensitive to the words used, *the tense of verbs*.

A final note of caution must be sounded—that of clergy sexual abuse (abuse perpetuated by anyone in a position of power based on spiritual leadership). Care must be used to keep from crossing the line of inappropriate behavior, thinking, or emotion. Words and actions can be misunderstood, adding to the abuse rather than bringing healing.

Not all sexual abuse is premeditated by an adult *pedophile to a young child victim. Sexual abuse also occurs when a "religious leader disregards the damaging results of the relationship for the one over whom he has power. Because of his power, he can manipulate the victim not only psychologically but also morally, *inducing spiritual confusion and guilt*."[18] While a sexual relationship between a spiritual leader and a parishioner often gets labeled as adultery or consensual sex, "it is still the minister's responsibility to maintain professional boundaries and not pursue a sexual relationship; to do otherwise is to take advantage of a congregant's vulnerability."[19] While Diana Garland speaks specifically of helping women survive clergy sexual abuse, *it must be noted that both men and women can abuse and be abused*.

Borrowing the phrase from the TV program *Law and Order*, sexual abuse perpetrated by clergy is "particularly heinous." Consider the example of the sons of Eli in the Old Testament, when they misused their priestly position to engage in sexual relations with the women serving at the Tent of Meeting (1 Sam 2:12). As Garland so clearly un-

18. Garland, "When Wolves Wear Shepherds' Clothing," 3. See also *spiritual incest.
19. Ibid.

derstands, "because [the clergy abuser] has redefined what is right and holy based on his own needs, she [the victim] is left with a deep mistrust of her ability to distinguish right from wrong. Her sense of shame and willingness to take the blame are consequently exaggerated."[20]

When the abuse is perpetrated by clergy, a Sunday school teacher or Christian counselor, the damage caused is compounded—not only is there physical violation, but as one victim describes the experience, her very soul was raped. Depression and PTSD are common, and many experience a crisis of faith as a result of the abuse.[21]

THEOLOGY AND SCRIPTURE

While theology can be seen primarily as an intriguing subject for study and dialogue, what we believe does influence how we live. How does an abused man or woman think about shame? Is it a means to bring the heart to genuine repentance, or does it stain the soul with no possibility of redemption? What about the problem of evil in the world, the darkness that constantly threatens to overwhelm the light? How can a holy God just sit back and watch the evil that is done to the innocent? What of the role of suffering in the life of a believer? These questions inform *theodicy, an important theological issue. But theological questions don't stop here.

What is an abuse victim supposed to do in response to a sermon on forgiveness? Should he or she literally "turn the other cheek?" *All too often, friends, family, church, and community "urge forgiveness out of a desire to put the ugliness behind them, not out of an understanding of the damage that has been done."*[22] Forgiveness is a long road, not a quick fix.[23]

Then too are the questions of restoration, *reconciliation, and justice. How can trust be restored? Does God expect the one who has experienced abuse to reconcile with their abuser? Can the abuser be restored to the fellowship of the church? What needs to happen for that to occur? Are there justice issues that go beyond law enforcement?

The wise companion must be willing to engage such questions, for much of the work of spiritual formation, as in counseling, is to help form the right questions. Ultimately he or she must also be willing to answer, as does Diane Langberg: "I cannot give answers that will result in your feeling satisfied. I don't know anybody who can. I cannot answer the whys. I can only tell you *who*."[24]

The spiritual guide, whether in personal direction or in classroom instruction, has the privilege of opening new horizons of theology to the listener. The director can introduce new images of God and help the survivor claim new names for God. He or she wisely recognizes the difficulty with the words that connect to the abuser such as the word "father." Wendy Read offers a victim's perspective on the confusion: "If we can, we cope

---

20. Ibid., 11.

21. Ibid., 5.

22. Ibid., 15.

23. For a comprehensive treatment on forgiveness, see Enright and Clark, *Exploring Forgiveness*.

24. Langberg, *On the Threshold of Hope*, 179.

with the discrepancy by maintaining two separate meanings for the word father, one for in our prayers in church and the other for in our beds at home. But what if we can't?"[25]

*Instead of Father or Lord, potentially problematic or painful for the *incest victim or the one abused by a power figure,* God can also be seen as Mother, Rapha ("the God who heals," Exod 15:26), or El-Roi, Hagar's name for "the God who sees" (Gen 16:13). Isaiah's image of the shaking, smoke-filled temple (Isah 6:4) can be balanced with the image of Jesus gathering the lost sheep to his heart (Luke 15).

This can be time to consider the topics of gender and sexuality in light of the teaching of Scripture. What does it mean to be a man or a woman in light of the abuse that was experienced? How can sexuality be seen as a gift instead of a curse? A safe place to raise these questions can be invaluable to healing.[26]

A third theological consideration is *embodiment, as explained by Beth Crisp:

> [W]e do not limit our experience of God to our intellectual faculties, but allow ourselves to experience God in all things, including our bodies. If the body can be experienced as a source of limitation, a deepening spirituality which is inclusive of bodily experiences may also stimulate growth.[27]

The body is not separate from the mind and spirit, and a spirituality of embodiment "has to do with how we experience the vitality of God's spirit within us and within the creation in all that we do in Christian life."[28] The one who comes alongside has the privilege of embodying *agape* in the relationship. Simon Robinson explains: "The Christian doctrine of the *Incarnation confirms that agape is essentially embodied, with the love of God expressed in and through the practice and experience of Christ."[29]

It may be helpful to introduce *feminist and *womanist understandings of Scripture passages. While radical voices exist in these camps, when used carefully these perspectives offer what womanist Linda Thomas describes as the "empowering assertion of the black woman's voice."[30] Phyllis Trible suggests that a feminist approach "retells biblical stories of terror *in memoriam*, offering sympathetic readings of abused women, appropriating such evidence poetically and theologically. At the same time, it continues to look for the remnant in unlikely places."[31]

Seeing familiar (and unfamiliar) Scripture through new eyes can provide a sense of liberation for the reader. Women can recognize themselves in Hagar's oppression (Genesis 16, 21), Tamar's desolation (2 Samuel 13), Abigail's courage (1 Samuel 25), and Bathsheba's quandary (2 Samuel 11). They can appreciate Vashti's "no" (Esther 1) as well as Esther's "yes" (Esther 2–10). Through such approaches, "women can learn to imagine

25. Read, *A Conspiracy of Love*, 75.

26. Christians for Biblical Equality offers resources that can aid in the exploration of these topics. www.cbeinternational.org.

27. Crisp, "Spiritual Direction and Survivors of Sexual Abuse," 9.

28. Chopp, *The Power to Speak*, 68.

29. Robinson, "Agape and Moral Meaning in Pastoral Counseling," 150.

30. Thomas, "Womanist Theology, Epistemology, and a New Anthropological Paradigm," 1.

31. Trible, "Feminist Hermeneutics and Biblical Studies," 116.

themselves in the text . . . this type of imagining challenges traditional interpretations . . . and moves interpretation to a new level of engagement with the contemporary life of the church."[32]

As Diane Langberg understands, *Scripture speaks powerfully from the margins of the stories.* The death on the threshold experienced by the Levite's concubine (Judges 19) brings a familiar feeling to the abuse victim, but it can be remembered and redeemed through the healing and formation of the woman or man who experiences the healing touch of God. That same threshold of death can be transformed into the threshold of hope.[33]

THE CHURCH AND COMMUNITY

If the majority of church members receive the bulk of their spiritual formation through the corporate gatherings of the church, then the *liturgy and language used is important to this discussion. How is personal responsibility for sin and confession balanced with a call to justice? Does the use of or lack of *androcentric language within the worship service matter to victims? These issues are tied to core values and must be thought through.

How does the church speak to teenagers about sexual purity? Consider the message heard by the fifteen-year-old who's been sexually abused by a stepfather. How can the message of sexual purity and responsibility be spoken to her? If indeed true love waits, what if the waiting has been stripped from the child or teen by another? Can virginity be seen as something to be given away, not taken away?

The pastor also can speak to both the individual victim and the church. Dan Allender addresses the culture-changing ability of the leader who preaches and teaches, suggesting that the pulpit serve as a platform for educating and changing misconceptions on subjects such as forgiveness and grace.[34]

For many believers who don't have access to spiritual formation groups, integrative counseling, or time with a spiritual director, formation may very well come through the music of the faith. Consider what a child learns from the following Sunday school song:

> The devil is a sly old fox,
> If I had him I'd put him in a box.
> Lock the box and throw away the key,
> For all the tricks he's played on me.[35]

Is that truly how evil works? Does the child have the power to lock away the evil perpetuated on him or her? Is the abuse only "a trick of the devil"? Is the devil a "he"?

How does the abuse victim understand this one:

> O be careful little eyes what you see . . .
> O be careful little feet where you go . . .

---

32. Thistlethwaite, "Every Two Minutes: Battered Women and Feminist Interpretation," 104.

33. Langberg, *On the Threshold of Hope,* 12.

34. Allender, *The Wounded Heart,* 261.

35. Author unknown.

O be careful little ears what you hear . . .
For the Father up above is looking down in love,
So be careful little _____ what you do.[36]

Are these words applicable to adults too? What about those in authority who can permanently alter a child's life? The adult who sang these words forty years ago may still hear
their echo: if only I hadn't gone next door with the neighbor, if only I had been more
careful, maybe this wouldn't have happened. But their reaction to this message can also be
one of deep *betrayal*, because the God who was supposed to be keeping his eye on them
apparently was looking elsewhere when his or her abuse occurred.

As a teen struggling with my own abuse experience, I was drawn to music with a
contemplative, healing call such as these words sung by *Take 6*:

There is a quiet place, far from the rapid pace,
Where God can soothe my troubled mind.[37]

I also found myself claiming again and again the words of Marsha and Russ Stevens:

You said You'd come and share all my sorrows,
You said You'd be there for all my tomorrows;
I came so close to sending You away,
But just like You promised, You came there to stay;
I just had to pray!

And Jesus said, "Come to the water, stand by My side,
I know you are thirsty, you won't be denied;
I felt ev'ry teardrop when in darkness you cried,
And I strove to remind you that for those tears I died."[38]

As a final example, Cleland McAfee's words of strength bring a blessed assurance to
those who've been hurt so profoundly:

There is a place of quiet rest, near to the heart of God,
A place where sin cannot molest, near to the heart of God.
O Jesus, blest redeemer, sent from the heart of God,
Hold us, who wait before thee, near to the heart of God.[39]

The power of music to create new meaning and bring healing to the traumatized cannot
be overestimated, by survivors or their spiritual leaders.

INTERCESSION AND INTERVENTION

Just as the choice of language or music can be destructive or healing, so too can specific
intercession and intervention. Daily intercessory prayer for the circumstances and the
person is a precious gift, while inner healing prayer models can guide through a process

36. Author unknown.
37. Ralph Carmichael, "A Quiet Place" (Lexicon Music Inc, ASCAP, 1967).
38. Martha J. and Russ Stevens, "For Those Tears I Died" (Bud Johns Songs Inc, 1972).
39. Cleland McAfee, "Near to the Heart of God" (1903; Public Domain).

of imagery, prayer, forgiveness, release, etc. *Care must be used to avoid promises of healing if only certain steps are followed correctly in the prayer process, for the work of God cannot be predicted or manipulated through the actions of God's people, no matter how sincere, needy, or faithful.*

Spiritual intervention will likely include the use of the classic spiritual disciplines. *While some hold little difficulty for the abuse victim, the disciplines of silence, meditation, and solitude can be problematic.* Imagine being alone with a mind full of racing thoughts or terrifying flashbacks. These disciplines may have to be taken in very small doses, along with the introduction of what are known as *trauma "brakes," including time limits for meditation, a safety net of someone to call, a direct physical intervention.

The discipline of silence may also be difficult because of its meaning. All too often survivors have been silenced, both by their abuser and by the culture around them, and have felt unable to express their thoughts and emotions. *Silence is the familiar place, and finding voice may be a more necessary act of faith than keeping the discipline of silence.*

When in a one-on-one spiritual direction relationship, Beth Crisp offers a reflection on PTSD that is useful for the one listening, because one effect from suffering trauma is the loss of the ability to think quickly. An effective helper may be one who "does not insist on instant answers and invites the directee to think through an issue over the following days and weeks."[40] Trauma "brakes" are useful in these relationships as well. Should the person you are with begin to "come undone," it may be necessary to ask them to stop what they are doing, make eye contact with you, and speak *in the present tense.* They may need to take a break or get a drink. Some subjects may need to be approached slowly and referred to a trained mental health professional when they are too painful for the one who has been abused. If in doubt as to how to proceed, consultation with a supervisor or mental health professional can provide clarity to the director.

CONCLUSION

As we integrate our knowledge in the sexual abuse treatment field with spiritual formation, we can seek new metaphors for the journey toward God. I offer a few redemptive metaphors or images. I envision a campfire circle, where the darkness is banished by a roaring fire that gives off light and warmth. "Come by here, Lord, *kum bah yah.*" Someone's crying, someone's laughing, someone's trusting—come by here. We'll share a s'more or two, a foretaste of the sweetness of the *kingdom to come.

There'll be plenty of time for our stories to be told, speaking of the dignity and *depravity of each one, and of the redeeming power of Jesus. The tears shed will be carefully collected as the Psalmist promised: "You keep track of all my sorrows. You have collected all my tears in your bottle. You have recorded each one in your book" (Ps 56:8 NLT). Gazing around the circle, Jesus will gently receive the carefully spoken stories, the cherished tears, and the wounded hearts, to present them clean and without blemish into the hands of the Father.

---

40. Crisp, "Spiritual Direction," 11.

A second image is a whole loaf. All too often, those who've suffered abuse relate to the Syro-Phoenician woman who begged Jesus to heal her daughter, pleading with him of her willingness to accept even the children's crumbs (Mark 7:24–37). As Marjorie Procter-Smith tells us:

> We who are Christians, who have been formed by Christian rhetoric about humility and suffering, have few spiritual resources that enable us to claim the whole loaf of survival and well-being. Where is the model for Christians who need to ask for the whole loaf, for themselves and for their children? We need spiritual resources that empower us to ask for the whole loaf.[41]

Spiritual formation for the sexually abused begins at the same place as it does for all broken people, with a desire to become whole and holy in Christ. Those privileged to accompany the person with a history of abuse do so with the resources provided them by God, including their own walk of faith, their training, their life experiences, and the wisdom that develops through dependence on God. While caution is appropriate and necessary, the compassionate and respectful relationship that develops in the formation process allows for truth to be spoken with care and courage. As godly men and women speak into the lives of each other, the Tamars of our communities will be freed from their personal desolation and the confines of their brothers' houses.

QUESTIONS FOR DISCUSSION

1. How does the spiritual guide support the survivor of sexual abuse when he or she asks the "why" questions: Why did this happen to me? Why does a good God allow evil? Why are the most vulnerable people abused? Have you ever seen a spiritual leader address such questions in a *support group? If you are a survivor, what advice would you share with leaders who are trying to help?

2. What rituals might the spiritual guide use to ease the healing from abuse? What images or metaphors are you aware of that would be very healing (or frightening) to victims? List several ways in which churches can incorporate the "particularly heinous" evil of sexual abuse in their worship. Explain why some spiritual disciplines are difficult or even destructive for sexual abuse victims. What are some healing rituals proven meaningful for survivors in contexts of spiritual formation?

3. Where is the line between spiritual formation/spiritual direction and professional counseling for the abuse survivor? At what point do they overlap? Where are they most different? List several specific things seminary programs can do to help their graduates minister more intentionally to abuse survivors. How can worship leaders be more creative and intentional about ministering to the abused in their congregations? What kind of lyrics should be avoided in light of traumatic experiences?

4. How does the spiritual guide use the experience of his or her abuse in the spiritual direction relationship? Is there ever a time to disclose one's own history? How does your formation program or church worship service name the evil of abuse and ac-

41. Procter-Smith, "The Whole Loaf," 464–65.

knowledge the abused in their midst? Explain the significance of listening to the *verb tense* in victims' language. Give some illustrations. What are the implications of such language for the healing journey of victims? Give a survivor one of the written prayers in this book to read: (a) ask them what words they identify with, (b) have them characterize their "talk" with God, (c) encourage them write their own prayer to God, (d) then have them read it to a group or in a worship service.

FOR FURTHER READING

Allender, Dan. *The Wounded Heart: Hope for Adult Victims of Childhood Sexual Abuse.* Colorado Springs, CO: NavPress, 1995.

Fischer, Kathleen. *Women at the Well: Feminist Perspectives on Spiritual Direction.* Mahwah, NJ, Paulist Press, 1988.

Foote, Catherine. *Survivor Prayers: Talking with God about Childhood Sexual Abuse.* Louisville, KY: Westminster/John Knox Press, 1994.

Guenther, Margaret. *Holy Listening: The Art of Spiritual Direction.* Cambridge, MA: Cowley Publications, 1992.

Landberg, Diane Mandt. *On the Threshold of Hope: Opening the Door to Healing for Survivors of Sexual Abuse.* Wheaton, IL: Tyndale House, 1999.

Moon, Gary and David G. Benner, eds. *Spiritual Direction and the Care of Souls: A Guide to Christian Approaches and Practice.* Downers Grove, IL: InterVarsity Press, 2004.

Reed, Angela H. *Quest for Spiritual Community: Reclaiming Spiritual Guidance for Contemporary Congregations.* London: T&T Clark, 2011.

Schmutzer, Andrew J. "Spiritual Formation and Sexual Abuse: Embodiment, Community, and Healing," *Journal of Spiritual Formation & Soul Care* 2 (2009): 67–86.

Wolpert, Daniel. *Creating a Life with God: The Call of Ancient Prayer Practices.* Nashville, TN: Upper Room Books, 2003.

17

Counseling the Abuse Victim

Integrating Evidence-based Practice Guidelines with Spiritual Resources

TERRI S. WATSON, PSYD, ABPP

IT IS TRULY AN honor and privilege to be able to walk with the adult victim of *child sexual abuse (CSA) through the process of healing. Effective counseling requires both *clinical competence* and *spiritual sensitivity*. The counselor must be able to create a safe place for healing and recovery where the abuse victim can learn important skills, process traumatic experience, and integrate their experiences with a coherent sense of self, relationships, and with God. This can be a daunting task, as the counselor is called to bear witness to experiences of abuse and *trauma. However, the blessings far outweigh the risks, as the counselor has much to learn from the courage, *resilience, and faith demonstrated by adult victims of *sexual abuse (SA) as they seek wholeness and health.

This chapter will provide an overview of *evidence-based practice guidelines from contemporary psychology for the *assessment and treatment of adult victims of SA, with recommendations for incorporating the client's spiritual resources into the process of treatment. A core assumption is that effective Christian clinicians utilize counseling approaches to specific problems that are supported by scientific study, clinical experience, and biblical wisdom. Toward that end, the intent of this chapter is to incorporate current research on effective treatment of adult victims of SA into a comprehensive, holistic, *biopsychosocial, and spiritual approach to counseling. Topics covered will include an overview of the assessment and treatment process, introduction to specific techniques, discussion of *therapeutic modalities, and recommendations for counseling in a church setting. Counselor concerns will be addressed, including issues of competence, vicarious traumatization, and the need for training and education.

BEST PRACTICE GUIDELINES FOR COUNSELING

Need for Counseling

Do adult victims of child abuse always develop problems and symptoms in adulthood that require counseling? The impact of CSA depends on a number of factors, including: type of abuse, age when the abuse began, duration, relationship to the *perpetrator, perceptions of blame, individual psychological health and resilience, nature of termination, and social support.[1] Some victims of CSA are able to survive and even thrive in the aftermath of abuse, a phenomena described in the literature as *"post-traumatic growth"[2] or "adversarial growth."[3] However, roughly two-thirds of adult victims of CSA will experience symptoms of *post-traumatic stress disorder (PTSD) at some point in their lives. This is either as a direct result of CSA or as a consequence of *revictimization experiences.[4] These symptoms can be triggered by different developmental events of adulthood, including marriage and realities of parenting.

Overview of the Treatment Process

The growing body of theory and research on the treatment of trauma provides evidence-based practice recommendations for competent treatment of SA *survivors. *Effective approaches are multi-theoretical and multi-disciplinary, attending to the biopsychosocial and spiritual needs of the client.* While there are a variety of proposed treatments, most include the following practices: (1) emphasis on creating a safe and collaborative therapeutic relationship, (2) careful and accurate assessment of symptoms resulting in a collaboratively developed treatment plan, (3) psychoeducation and skills training with a focus on regulating and managing *affect to promote stabilization, social support, some type of gradual exposure to traumatic material in the form of remembering and reprocessing while utilizing *affect regulation skills, (4) and finally, reintegration of the trauma experience with a focus on growth and moving forward.

Creating Safety

Foundational to any treatment—particularly the treatment of individuals who have been harmed by those in positions of power and trust—is the establishment of a safe, secure, professional therapeutic environment for healing. *Informed consent and collaborative discussion of the therapeutic goals and process gives the client a sense of predictability and shared power. Therapist *empathy, respect, acceptance, and genuineness help the client

1. For a good summary of research on factors contributing to growth following SA, see Lev-Wiesel et al., "Posttraumatic Growth among Female Survivors of Childhood Abuse in Relation to the Perpetrator Identity," 7–17.

2. An excellent introduction to the theory and research on growth through trauma can be found in Tedeschi and Calhoun, *Trauma & Transformation*.

3. Linley and Joseph, "Positive Change Following Trauma and Adversity," 11–21.

4. Rodriguez et al., "Posttraumatic Stress Disorder in Survivors of Childhood Sexual and Physical Abuse," 17–45.

begin to feel understood and empowered as they share their concerns. Education about the process of therapy, length of sessions, therapist policies (including contact information, how crisis calls are handled, payment issues, cancellation policy) give the counseling experience predictability for the client, establish good boundaries, and facilitate trust. As clients feel secure in the counseling relationship, they can begin to take risks in sharing their difficult histories with the counselor, and thus begin their healing journey.

Assessment: Procedures and Challenges

Effective counseling is dependent on a thorough assessment of *presenting symptoms, which will inform therapeutic goals and techniques. *Often, SA victims seek counseling for problematic symptoms and interpersonal difficulties, and they may not disclose or even connect these symptoms to their trauma history.* Sexual abuse or assault increases lifetime risk for a variety of psychologically based problems, including eating disorders, substance abuse, *self-destructive and suicidal behaviors, *dissociative disorders, *sexual dysfunction, and anxiety disorders.[5] Other presenting problems for adult survivors include: anger difficulties, *emotional regulation problems, *self-blame, social withdrawal, *somatization, and trust impairment.[6] Counselors should not suggest to a client that they have been sexually abused based on a set of symptoms or patient characteristics. Rather, questions about childhood and family experiences that may contribute to the presenting problems are posed in an open-ended, non-leading manner.

If a client does disclose a history of child SA early in treatment, the counselor may or may not explore details about the event(s) based on the client's level of distress and current functioning. As noted, important information to explore includes such elements as: type of abuse, duration, relationship to perpetrator, and abuse related symptoms. For many clients, this specific information about traumatic history emerges over time as the therapeutic relationship strengthens. While it is helpful to gain a general understanding of the type of abuse the client has experienced, *it is of greater importance to wait until the client is able to share details without a high level of distress.* Most adult victims of SA will have memories of the abuse, but it is possible for experiences to be forgotten and later remembered.[7] Counselors should focus on helping the client weigh the evidence and develop their own conclusions about what really happened based on their *self report of memories, information from third parties (such as other family members), and written materials such as letters or journal entries.

Any time a history of childhood abuse is revealed or suspected, it is important to assess whether PTSD symptoms are present. Counselors should inquire about troubling thoughts or memories, *flashbacks, nightmares, *avoidance of people or places, sleep problems, and difficulty with concentration.[8] Psychological tests can be useful as well for

5. Finkelhor, "Early and Prolonged Effects of Child Sexual Abuse," 325–330.

6. Budrionis and Jongsma, *The Sexual Abuse Victim and Sexual Offender Treatment Planner*, 15–94.

7. A good discussion and clinical implications of the "false memory" debate in psychology can be found in Alpert et al., "Final Conclusions of the American Psychological Association Working Group on Investigation of Memories of Childhood Abuse," 933–940.

8. For a comprehensive list of symptoms see the American Psychiatric Association, *Diagnostic and*

accurate diagnosis of symptoms. While basic measures of personality may not pick up on trauma symptoms, numerous assessment tools have been developed to assess the impact of trauma, which can assist in diagnosis and treatment planning.[9]

In addition to PTSD symptoms, *adult victims of CSA often exhibit impairments in interpersonal functioning and *affect regulation.* Theorists speculate that the experience of sexual trauma during the formative developmental stages in childhood results in impairments in basic trust, self-perceptions, and emotional functioning. Adult victims of CSA, who manifest problematic symptoms in these areas, are often diagnosed with *borderline personality disorder (BPD). However, this diagnosis can also stigmatize clients, and does not adequately reflect the PTSD component of symptoms. Newer diagnostic categories have been recommended for the cluster of symptoms exhibited by adult trauma survivors including *complex PTSD and *disorders of extreme stress not otherwise specified (DESNOS).[10]

Determining Client Health and Resilience

Assessment of client strength, resilience, and spiritual resources is especially important when treating SA, as the client will need to draw on these resources throughout the treatment process. Many clients turn to God and their faith community for help and support in the aftermath of trauma; for others, *the trauma experience often results in a spiritual crisis and difficulties trusting both God and the Christian community.* Researchers have identified both "positive" and "negative" religious coping strategies that correspond with turning to God or away from God when coping with difficulties.[11]

Positive *coping strategies among trauma survivors lead to decreased PTSD symptoms and include drawing comfort from God and the religious community, working in cooperation with one's faith tradition and others to deal with the trauma, using such things as prayer to seek help from God with specific issues. Religious coping strategies that are *not* helpful, and in fact can exacerbate PTSD symptoms, include: viewing the trauma as God's punishment, believing one has been abandoned by God and others, and dissatisfaction or negative feelings toward God and clergy.[12] Counselors can assess religious coping with the goal of strengthening "positive" coping strategies and addressing "negative" beliefs and attitudes that may contribute to distress and distance the client from the much-needed support from God and others in Christian community. An assessment of spirituality and religious coping should include how the client understands God's role in suffering, current struggles and challenges, prayer life, practice of *spiritual disciplines, experience of God, church community, and history of involvement.

Statistical Manual of Mental Disorders IV-TR, 463–468.

9. An excellent overview of assessment tools and techniques can be found in Rodriguez-Srednicki and Twaite, *Understanding, Assessing, and Treating Adult Victims of Childhood Abuse*, 235–259; and also Courtois, "Complex Trauma, Complex Reactions," 86–100.

10. For a good description of this diagnostic debate, see Courtois, "Complex Trauma," 86–89.

11. Pargament et al., "Patterns of Positive and Negative Religious Coping with Major Life Stressors," 710–724.

12. Harris et al., "Christian Religious Functioning and Trauma Outcomes," 17–29.

Stages of Treatment and Specific Techniques

Most trauma specialists recommend thorough assessment and therapeutic relationship building followed by a three-stage model of *psychotherapy.[13]

- *Stage one* involves establishing safety, providing psychoeducation, and skill building to promote stability.

- *Stage two* focuses on reprocessing and resolution of traumatic experiences utilizing graduated exposure while managing affective responses.

- *Stage three*, and its emphasis, is reintegration with a focus on personal and relational growth and development. The following discussion will provide an overview of each treatment stage and offer specific techniques.

Psychoeducation, Stabilization, and Skills Training

The initial stage of treatment focuses on helping the client stabilize and prioritize personal safety. The counseling relationship is established as a place of safety where the client can begin to develop the personal and life skills necessary for improved functioning. Through psychoeducation and skill building, clients work on decreasing impulsive and self-destructive symptoms and improving their day-to-day functioning. Depending on the severity of presenting symptoms, this may be the most important part of treatment for some clients; in fact, not all clients will opt to continue treatment beyond this stage.[14]

Depending on the individual needs of the client, specific goals for this stage of therapy include: treatment and stabilization of self-destructive behaviors, improved regulation and tolerance of feelings, interpersonal and assertiveness skills to facilitate safe relationships, increased social support, understanding of the effects of trauma, improved *self-care and life skills, and decrease in faulty cognitions about self, others, and God.

Counselors create a safe, therapeutic relationship for clients by teaching skills, containing self-destructive behaviors, and attending to interpersonal dynamics in the therapy relationship. Through psychoeducation, counselors can provide information about the process of therapy, effects of trauma, and the relationship between emotions, behaviors, and cognitions. *Cognitive behavioral techniques are utilized at this stage to improve emotional regulation and to address, yet again, faulty views of self, others, and God. Self-destructive and injurious behaviors are addressed through helping clients identify *triggers, develop *coping skills, and seek support from others. *Behavioral contracting can be utilized to establish boundaries and provide containment of self-destructive impulses. Clients may need to learn interpersonal and assertiveness skills with the goal of establishing safe, supportive relationships with others that can provide an important social support network to rely on during the healing process. Education on healthy self-care and life skills help clients establish increased normalcy in their day-to-day lives.

---

13. Courtois, "Complex Trauma," 91–96; and Zerbe Enns et al., "Working with Adult Clients Who May Have Experienced Childhood Abuse," 248–251.

14. Courtois, "Complex Trauma," 93.

Clients who struggle with eating disorders or substance abuse should also receive symptom-specific treatment at this stage. Counselors should consider referring the client for specialized treatment if they are not knowledgeable and experienced in treating these disorders.[15] In addition, clients who experience symptoms of anxiety and/or depression that interfere with their ability to function can be referred to a psychiatrist for a medication evaluation. *The complex and multifaceted nature of treatment with many adult SA victims can require a multidisciplinary team of professionals for effective care.* As the primary caregiver, counselors can also serve as "case managers" to coordinate treatment planning and implementation.

One effective integrative approach to stabilization of complex PTSD symptoms is *Dialectic Behavioral Therapy (DBT).[16] DBT was developed to treat problems in emotional regulation and interpersonal functioning characteristic of clients diagnosed with borderline personality disorder. Using behavioral therapy techniques, skills training, and *mindfulness practices, clients synthesize "acceptance" and "change" strategies in therapy. DBT has received empirical support for decreasing hospitalizations and suicidal behaviors among clients, and for keeping clients engaged in treatment.[17] DBT is offered as both an individual and a *group therapy. Clients who struggle to manage suicidal and self-destructive behavior and/or exhibit problems in interpersonal functioning and emotional regulation may benefit from a referral to a DBT group concurrent with their individual counseling.

Spiritual teaching and *interventions can be particularly important for the Christian client during this stage. Spiritual practices including contemplative and intercessory prayer, daily devotions, regular worship, and fellowship with other believers help the adult CSA victim develop faithful practices that can contribute to spiritual and personal health and stability. Clients can be encouraged to practice self-care as a spiritual discipline, treating their bodies as "living temples" (1 Cor 3:16; 6:19–20).

Trauma Resolution and Reprocessing

As clients exhibit greater stability in their day-to-day functioning and improved skills for managing emotions, they demonstrate readiness to address the memories of the traumatic experience(s) more directly. The next phase of treatment involves a gentle, graduated exposure to the traumatic memories, helping the clients utilize their skills to cope with resulting thoughts and feelings. There is strong research support for the effectiveness of *exposure therapy for decreasing PTSD symptoms.[18] Researchers recommend that a combination of "imaginal" and *"in vivo" exposure therapy provides the best outcome.[19]

15. Treatment plans and interventions for eating disorders and substance abuse disorders can be found in Budrionis, "The Sexual Abuse Victim," 31–39 and 249–257.

16. A good introduction to DBT is found in Linehan, *Cognitive Behavioral Treatment of the Borderline Personality Disorder.*

17. Foa et al., *Effective Treatments for PTSD*, 549–558.

18. Bisson and Andrew, "Psychological Treatment of Post-traumatic Stress Disorder (PTSD)."

19. Foa, *Effective Treatments*, 557.

It is very important that the reprocessing of traumatic experiences proceed at the client's pace, not overwhelming the client and their coping skills or overprotecting the client and *colluding with the avoidance of painful material. Clients and therapists jointly decide on the best approach to process traumatic memories, with therapists providing guidance and education regarding various effective techniques while empowering the client to decide how they want to proceed. The following is a description of techniques and therapeutic approaches commonly utilized to help adult victims of SA reprocess their traumatic memories.

Some Proven Techniques and Therapeutic Approaches

Cognitive behavioral strategies facilitate a graduated processing of the thoughts, feelings, and memories of traumatic experiences while the client utilizes skills to manage intense affect, *self-soothe, and address negative thinking patterns. *Cognitive Processing Therapy (CPT)[20] provides a structured approach to dealing with traumatic memories through a verbal or written trauma narrative. *Stress Inoculation Training (SIT)[21] combines cognitive therapy techniques with relaxation training and helps clients anticipate and cope with triggers of stress reactions. In vivo exposure[22] involves exposing the client in a graduated way to low-risk people and situations that have been avoided or feared, while practicing cognitive, behavioral, and affect management skills. *Trauma-focused Cognitive Behavioral Therapy (TF-CBT)[23] is an integrative cognitive behavioral approach developed for children and adolescents that incorporates skills training with graduated exposure to traumatic material. This model has received strong research support,[24] and interested clinicians can pursue web-based instruction in this model. TF-CBT has also been applied to the treatment of adult trauma with good outcomes. In a recent review, individual and group TF-CBT, stress management treatment, and *Eye Movement Desensitization and Reprocessing training (EMDR, see discussion below)[25] were all found to yield significant outcomes in effective treatment of adult PTSD.[26]

Eye Movement Desensitization and Reprocessing training is an integrative approach to the treatment of post-traumatic stress disorder that combines psychotherapy with various eye movement stimulation techniques. This structured approach to reprocessing traumatic experiences has received empirical support for its ability to decrease PTSD symptoms.[27] Counselors can receive specialized training in the EMDR approach to treat-

---

20. Ibid., 550.

21. Ibid., 549.

22. Ibid.

23. For a comprehensive overview of this approach see Cohen et al., "Trauma-focused Cognitive-Behavioral Therapy for Sexually Abused Children," 1–2; also a Web-based instruction course in TF-CBT for children is available at: http://tfcbt.musc.edu.

24. Cohen et al., "A Multi-site, Randomized Controlled Trial for Children with Sexual Abuse-related PTSD Symptoms," 393–402.

25. An introductory text to EMDR is Shapiro, *EMDR as an Integrative Psychotherapy Approach*.

26. Bisson, "Psychological Treatment," 2.

27. Ibid.

ment of trauma[28] or refer their clients to an EMDR specialist as an adjunct to individual counseling.

Emotion focused and *gestalt techniques can also be utilized effectively to process traumatic events.[29] Clients recount and re-experience the emotional and cognitive aspects of the traumatic experiences in an empathic and supportive therapeutic environment. Counselors can help clients express and manage affect, explore thoughts and beliefs that arise, and construct new and adaptive meanings for past events. Clients become less overwhelmed by the feelings surrounding events and better able to utilize their emotional responses to current situations in an adaptive manner.

For clients who have difficulty verbally processing their traumatic memories, expressive therapy techniques utilize art, music, drama, and even dance to facilitate expression and understanding. Expressive therapies can provide an important "bridge" for some clients to the eventual verbal processing of memories and experiences. These techniques, while widely used and supported by clinical experience, do not have strong empirical support at this point, and should be used in combination with other evidence-based approaches.[30]

As traumatic material is processed using one or more of the above approaches, counselors help clients identify and explore their resulting emotions, beliefs, and impulses that arise. As noted, assumptions about self, others, and God are reevaluated, altered, and consolidated. Clients mourn losses and seek to find a sense of meaning and purpose in their suffering. It is important to note that the "therapeutic power" in this phase of treatment is not in the *catharsis of simply retelling the story of the abuse but rather in the remembering, re-experiencing, and processing of previously avoided memories, people, and situations in the here and now, while utilizing adaptive *coping skills.

Action steps such as real or imagined confrontation of significant others may be an outcome of this stage of the therapy (e.g., writing a letter to one's abuser). Clients may choose to pursue litigation as a means of seeking justice. Setting firm boundaries in harmful relationships is also a common outcome. Counselors can empower client actions and decisions, helping them assess their readiness to engage in action steps and implement coping strategies when actions trigger disruptive emotions or behaviors.

Spiritual resources can be an integral component of client growth and healing at this stage of treatment. Clients need the love and support of a Christian community during this often-difficult stage of treatment as they courageously face long-avoided memories. Pastoral care and Christian friendship provides ongoing prayer, consistent support, and accurate biblical teaching about God and relationships. Christian clients often struggle during this stage with questions about suffering, God's perceived presence or absence during abuse experiences, issues of justice, and a sense of self-blame and shame. Caring Christian support provides the opportunity for clients to wrestle with these important issues, and it sensitively offers spiritual resources as clients are ready to receive them. As

---

28. See www.EMDR.com for a description of education and training opportunities.

29. Elliott et al., "Process Experiential Therapy for Post-traumatic Stress Difficulties," 249–271.

30. Foa, *Effective Treatments*, 600–602.

clients are able to process their experiences of abuse, they may benefit from recounting their experiences to trusted, safe mentors or friends who can respond with acceptance and care.

Reintegration, Post-traumatic Growth, and Moving Forward

In the last stage of treatment, *clients integrate their new insights and behaviors into their day-to-day functioning as they seek to address the impact of the trauma on various areas of their lives and relationships.* Counselors help clients move forward in their lives with the new behaviors and insights they have gained. Clients may need to *renegotiate* relationships, forgive those who have harmed them, and consider how to find meaning and purpose in their suffering.

Healing from past relational trauma involves incorporating healthy behaviors and practices into current relationships. Clients may need to make changes in their relationships with spouses, parents, children, friends, and colleagues. Counselors can empower clients to incorporate newly learned relationship skills and attitudes into current relationships. At this point, issues of boundaries, trust, conflict resolution, and communication must be addressed. Many clients also seek to *redeem* the suffering they have experienced through service to others. The church can be an ideal place for the client to begin to shift their focus *outward* toward service as they begin to recognize and value their own abilities and insights.

Religious coping during this stage of treatment often involves helping clients find a sense of coherence, meaning, and purpose in the suffering they have experienced. Clients may continue to struggle with issues of justice, for example, trying to understand why God seems to allow the innocent to suffer and *perpetrators to go free.[31] Progress toward resolution of these often lifelong questions helps the client decide how they will move forward in their lives as they seek to transform their experience of trauma into hopes and dreams for the future. Often, survivors find rich meaning in treating others differently than they were treated, particularly in their own families, and thus stopping the generational patterns of abuse.

Resolution of traumatic experiences for many clients includes *the process of *forgiveness* of those who have harmed them, both as a spiritual discipline in obedience to God, and as a means of experiencing freedom and closure. The decision to focus on forgiveness at this stage of therapy should be made collaboratively, between the client and counselor. Clients can benefit from planning and implementing a formal *ritual of forgiveness, such as: writing and reading a letter, engaging in a "*liturgy of forgiveness," writing out personal prayers, and dramatizing key Scripture texts.

Counselor-Client Termination

The end of counseling deserves special consideration when treating adult victims of abuse. For many CSA victims, the therapeutic relationship is one of the few places where they

---

31. A thoughtful introduction to the *theodicy discussion can be found in Hall and Johnson, "Theodicy and Therapy," 5–17.

have experienced a sense of trust, validation, empowerment, and safety; for these reasons, it can be difficult to bring this professional relationship to a close. Counselors and clients should decide together when treatment goals have been met. Preparation for termination includes helping the client strengthen relationships with spouse, supportive friends, and family, and those who can offer ongoing spiritual support. The process of termination should include: (1) a review of skills gained, (2) progress made, (3) and anticipation of future challenges. Counselors affirm clients for their growth and courage, and they offer availability for follow-up sessions in the future as needed.

TREATMENT MODALITIES

What is the best treatment approach to accomplish all of the above? Do adult victims of SA benefit most from individual, group, or even couple therapy? Decisions about *therapeutic modality* should be made on an individual basis and in collaboration with the client. However, outcome research sheds light on the approaches that work best for most people, and therefore constitutes evidence-based practice for counselors. Reviews of CBT approaches to the treatment of PTSD concluded that there is the strongest research support for *exposure therapies* administered on a 1:1 basis with clients.[32] Other studies found that group administered TF-CBT was effective but evidenced a higher rate of drop-out than other therapies.[33] Based on outcome research, *best practice guidelines suggest that adult victims of SA with PTSD symptoms should be treated with individual trauma-focused therapy approaches incorporating stabilization and skills training with *exposure techniques.

Group Therapy

Group therapy is often used as an adjunct to individual therapy for adult survivors of CSA for the purposes of additional support, *normalizing symptoms and challenges, addressing interpersonal difficulties, and meaning making. Clients may benefit from group therapy during the first stage of treatment with a focus on skill building and stabilization, and to facilitate *reintegration and moving forward in the third stage.

Group treatment of adult CSA survivors includes psycho-educational and skills focused groups (such as DBT), structured process-oriented treatment groups where members *reprocess* traumatic material and work through the emotional response in the presence of supportive survivors who have also experienced abuse, CBT groups where clients learn and implement *cognitive strategies for processing trauma-related cognitions and emotions, and *support groups that facilitate healthy interpersonal functioning. Combined groups such as TF-CBT are growing in popularity, demonstrate good research support,[34] and show future promise as a treatment of choice for trauma symptoms.

As a primary modality of treatment of CSA, group therapy would be considered in cases where a client is unable to tolerate the intensity or *counter-transference issues

32. Foa, *Effective Treatments*, 556.
33. Bisson, "Psychological Treatment," 2.
34. Rodriguez-Srednicki, *Understanding, Assessing, and Treating*, 283–302.

that arise in individual therapy, or in cases where a client struggles with interpersonal difficulties and distortions as their primary treatment issue.[35] Clients should be carefully assessed for readiness for group therapy. Important considerations include: (1) the client's ability to manage the intense affect that may arise from hearing the trauma stories of others and telling one's own experience, (2) ability to function within group boundaries and guidelines, (3) and agreement with group goals. Additionally, clients who have only vague suspicions that they were abused as children, without clear memories, would not be appropriate for a group therapy for SA victims due the potential influence of other's stories on their own perceptions and memories.[36]

Couple and Family Therapy

For adult victims who are currently in a couple relationship, couple therapy can be an important and effective modality. *Emotion Focused Therapy (EFT) is an approach to couple therapy used with trauma survivors and their spouses that integrates experiential, *systemic, and *attachment theory to help couples identify problematic patterns of relating toward improving the couple's emotional connection and emotional responsiveness to each other. Trauma-focused EFT assumes that there is as much, if not more, healing power in helping the adult victim of CSA develop an emotionally close and safe relationship with their partner than with an individual therapist.[37] Outcome research on EFT with trauma survivors shows good promise.[38] Due to limited research on couple and family therapy as a primary intervention with PTSD clients, it is recommended that these modalities be utilized in conjunction with or following a course of individual therapy.[39] Future research may support use of some couple therapy approaches such as EFT as a primary modality.

COUNSELOR ISSUES AND CONCERNS

Competence

Counselors should evaluate whether they possess the necessary clinical skills for the often-complex treatment of the symptoms presented by the adult victims of SA. Providing effective counseling for abuse victims requires specialized knowledge, skills, and supervised experience in treatment of trauma and trauma-related symptoms. Counselors can seek out continuing education opportunities focusing on treatment of CSA and utilize supervision to gain the necessary skills. If a counselor determines that he or she does not possess the necessary skills, there are still many ways to provide care and counsel to the victim of SA, including pastoral care and support.

35. Zerbe Enns, "Working with Adult Clients," 250.

36. Ibid.

37. An excellent introduction to couple therapy with adult victims of CSA can be found in Johnson, *Emotionally Focused Couple Therapy with Trauma Survivors.*

38. MacIntosh and Johnson, "Emotion Focused Therapy for Couples and Childhood Sexual Abuse Survivors," 298–315.

39. Foa, *Effective Treatments,* 596–599.

Ethical Considerations

Informed consent, *limits of confidentiality, record keeping, and use of physical touch in therapy are each important ethical issues to address with adult victims of SA. Clients should be informed about the therapeutic goals and the specific techniques utilized so they can be true partners in the therapeutic process. Counselors should keep descriptive records about the content of sessions, homework, client's descriptions of traumatic material, and client progress to ensure documentation of the counseling experience. Clients should know the limits of confidentiality and in what situations the counselor would need to break confidentiality to protect the client from harm to self or others, or inform *child protective services about suspected abuse of children. Counselors should maintain good physical boundaries with clients and be cautious about use of touch. Even if the client initiates the physical contact (e.g., asking for a hug at the end of session), the *meaning* of physical touch for the client should be discussed and the purpose of therapeutic boundaries explained.[40]

Counter-transference and Vicarious Trauma

Working with victims of SA can stir up feelings in the therapist of helplessness, frustration, rescuing tendencies, anger, or over-protectiveness, to name just a few of the common counter-transference reactions. *If the counselor also has a history of childhood abuse, care must be taken to not over-identify with the client or take on too much responsibility for their care.* Counselors who work with CSA victims can experience "vicarious" or "*secondary" trauma symptoms if they are not diligent about practicing good self-care.[41]

CHURCH SUPPORT FOR COUNSELING THE ABUSE VICTIM

What is the role of the local church in providing care and counseling for the sexually abused? Many clients will seek out the help of a trusted pastor or priest *before* they will contact a mental health professional. Pastoral care can play an important role in restoring the SA victim to relational and spiritual health in particular, providing a safe place for healing, within a faith community. Educating clergy to recognize the signs and symptoms of PTSD will improve identification and referral of those who require professional counseling.[42] *Most adult victims of SA will require treatment from a mental health professional who can provide a thorough assessment and recommend the course of treatment that will be of greatest benefit.* It is important for pastors and church leadership to have trusted referral sources with expertise in this area. Counselors and pastors must work together to provide a support network for healing and help.

In many ways the church is an ideal setting to offer support groups for adult victims of SA, particularly those who have also received individual counseling and are relatively

40. Zerbe Enns, "Working with Adult Clients," 252.

41. For an introduction to therapist impact see Mcann and Pearlman, "Vicarious Traumatization," 131–149.

42. Good recommendations for clergy-mental health professional coordination can be found in Weaver et al., "Posttraumatic Stress, Mental Health Professionals, and the Clergy," 847–856.

stable in terms of their current functioning. It can be of great benefit for clients to both give and receive support in an atmosphere of shared values and beliefs. Church-based support groups can provide survivors with the opportunity to develop accurate views of God, self, and others; to seek prayer and support; and to realize they are not alone.[43]

Finally, the church can also play a significant role in prevention and education in the area of SA. Most churches now require anyone in a teaching role with children to receive training, education, and even a background check. Youth leaders and teachers can be taught to recognize the signs and symptoms of sexual violence and abuse, being appropriately educated about their role in reporting suspected abuse to church leadership.

CONCLUSION

The intent of this chapter is to contribute a contemporary psychology "voice" to the multidisciplinary conversation about caring for adult victims of SA with the hope of improving cooperation between Christian mental health professionals and the church. By incorporating evidence-based practices with biopsychosocial and spiritual approaches to healing, Christian counselors can provide clear direction and effective techniques for competent treatment. Incorporating church-based resources in the form of pastoral support counseling and group treatment modalities can increase the "power" of treatment and offer adult SA victims the opportunity to draw support from God and their Christian community.

QUESTIONS FOR DISCUSSION

1. What are some strategies for balancing psychological and spiritual interventions in counseling and ministering to SA victims? Which ones do you have personal experience with? When, in the healing process, do you think psychological resources are most important? Spiritual resources? How can professional counselors and pastors work together most effectively to provide the best care?

2. What counselor characteristics are important in creating a safe environment for clients to talk about difficult experiences? What characteristics would you like to see emphasized more in mental health training? Which ones have you found most helpful? Least helpful?

3. Do you think most churches have adequate understanding of the process of healing for adult victims of SA? Explain. Given the three-stage model discussed in this chapter, where do you see your current church resources making the greatest contribution to the healing process? Where are additional church resources needed?

4. Regardless of your profession, what has this chapter helped you understand about sexual trauma? What parallels are you aware of between soldiers' PTSD and survivors of SA? Why do you think "vicarious traumatization" occurs and what steps can

---

43. A support group ministry developed specifically for the treatment of women who have been sexually abused is "In the Wildflowers," a Christ-centered DVD curriculum and support group. Groups are led by Christian counselors and participants must be screened by a mental health therapist before beginning the group. The participants are encouraged to be in individual therapy while they are participating. See www .rthm.cc/wildflowers.

counselors and pastors take to prevent this? As a minister in the church, what key areas of training do you need in order to more holistically address sexual violence in your church?

5. What are some specific steps you can take through your church to be a part of preventing child abuse and supporting victims in their healing? What kind of contacts, collaboration, or general instruction do people need in your church? What do seminary programs need to do differently to better prepare men and women to face sexual trauma?

6. What new skills would equip you to work more effectively with adult victims of SA in your role as pastor, counselor, or friend? What steps might you take to develop these skills?

FOR FURTHER READING

Allender, Dan B. *The Wounded Heart: Hope for Adult Victims of Childhood Sexual Abuse*, rev. ed. Colorado Springs, CO: NavPress, 1995.

Budrionis, Rita and Arthur E. Jongsma, Jr. *The Sexual Abuse Victim and Sexual Offender Treatment Planner*. Hoboken, NJ: John Wiley & Sons, 2003.

Courtios, Christine and Julian D. Ford. *Treating Traumatic Complex Stress Disorders: An Evidence-based Guide*. New York, NY: The Guilford Press, 2009.

Foa, Edna B., Terence M. Keane, Matthew J. Friedman, and Judith Cohen. *Effective Treatments for PTSD: Practice Guidelines from the International Society for Traumatic Stress Studies*, Second Edition. New York, NY: The Guilford Press, 2008.

Herman, Judith. *Trauma and Recovery: The Aftermath of Violence—From Domestic Abuse to Political Terror*. New York, NY: Basic Books, 1997.

Johnson, Susan M. *Emotionally Focused Couple Therapy with Trauma Survivors: Strengthening Attachment Bonds*. New York, NY: The Guilford Press, 2002.

Langberg, Diane M. *Counseling Survivors of Sexual Abuse*. Wheaton, IL: Tyndale House Publishers, 1997.

McKay, Matthew, Jeffrey C. Wood, and Jeffrey Brantley. *Dialectical Behavior Therapy Skills Workbook: Practical DBT Exercises for Learning Mindfulness, Interpersonal Effectiveness, Emotion Regulation, and Distress Tolerance*. Oakland, CA: New Harbinger Publications, 2007.

Pellauer, Mary D., Barbara Chester, and Jane A. Boyajian. *Sexual Assault and Abuse: A Handbook for Clergy and Religious Professionals*. San Francisco, CA: Harper SanFrancisco, 1991.

Rodriguez-Srednicki, Ofelia and James A. Twaite. *Understanding, Assessing, and Treating Adult Victims of Childhood Abuse*. New York, NY: Jason Aronson, 2006.

18

Confronting Abuse

Fostering a Sense of Healthy Responsibility in the Abuser

KELVIN F. MUTTER, THD[1]

FEW THINGS STIR AS much anxiety and moral outrage within individuals and society as an account of *sexual abuse (SA) or a news report that a sexual offender is being released into the community. These expressions of anxiety and outrage reveal an understanding that *sexual abuse violates, not only the person and psyche of the abused, but also the bonds of trust on which social relationships are built,* and in the case of *intrafamilial sexual abuse, the natural order of familial relationships. While sexual offenders are frequently thought to be men, female sexual abuse perpetrators are not uncommon.[2] Many perceive the abuse *perpetrator as a predatory individual who lives for him or herself, lacking both social responsibility and a clear moral compass. Therefore, it is not surprising that the formal and informal sanctions society imposes on sexual abuse perpetrators place these individuals in the position of outlaws who are sometimes incapable of finding adequate work, housing, or even attending church.[3] While many view the use of sanctions,[4] which create a form of *ban, as a means of reminding abusers of their need to bear responsibility for their actions, there are at least two additional forms of responsibility-taking: self-examination[5] and developing *empathy for those who have suffered because of the abuser's actions.[6]

In addition, there is some indication that *an abuser's ability to acknowledge the pain caused by their actions and uncompromisingly take responsibility for these actions has the*

---

1. The author is thankful for the helpful feedback provided by fellow clinicians Carlton Brown, MSc, MDiv; Anita Diebel, MSW; Karen Ustrzycki, MDiv; and Mark Yantzi, MASc.

2. Jespersen et al., "Sexual Abuse History among Adult Sex Offenders and Non-Sex Offenders," 179–192. See also Female Sex Offenders, www.child-abuse-effects.com/female-sex-offenders.html.

3. Brannon et al., "Attitudes about Community Notification," 369–379; Ross, "Modern Day Lepers," 16; Spencer, "Sex Offender as *Homo Sacer*," 219–240.

4. E.g., electronic monitoring, restriction of activities, vigilante groups, sexual offender registries, etc.

5. Drapeau et al., "What Sex Abusers Say About Their Treatment," 93–94; Jenkins, *Invitations to Responsibility,* 132–167.

6. Drapeau et al., "What Sex Abusers Say About Their Treatment," 94; Jenkins, *Invitations to Responsibility,* 164–167.

power to release the abused party to more fully experience their own healing.[7] Hence the inclusion of a chapter on working with abusers in a book focused on understanding and ministering to the sexually abused. Because this work may be misunderstood, this chapter describes both a *mindset* with which a counselor and caretaker can approach this task as well as a *model* of *intervention that considers the theological, psychological, and relational context of the abuse and invites the abusers to renounce the victimization of others as the abusers consider the impact of their actions, accept responsibility for their behaviors, and submit to any sanctions which may be required.

PERSPECTIVES FOR INTERVENTION

Those who work with sexual abuse perpetrators need to consider the theological, ethical, and psychological contexts of their work. The following discussion highlights five important concepts, which apply to the work of both church leaders and Christian counselors.

Establishing Clear Counseling Boundaries

SAFETY FOR THE ABUSED

Those who counsel or provide support to sexual abuse perpetrators assume a critical role in the lives of both the abuser and the abused. It is, therefore, vital to establish clear working boundaries when working with persons who have committed acts of sexual abuse. Indeed, those who work with perpetrators need to remember that their first responsibility is the safety of those who have been sexually violated, even when the request for counseling is initiated by the perpetrator.[8] In situations involving a *minor, counselors and clergy are required to report all revelations of sexual abuse to the appropriate authorities (i.e., *mandated reporting) who will investigate and impose legal sanctions. The counselor or church worker must, therefore, *inform the abuser that confidentiality is limited by the need to ensure the safety of their victim(s), family, and community.*

ACKNOWLEDGING THE LIVED-EXPERIENCE

Counselors and clergy need to be sensitive to the experiences of those who have been abused, remembering that the provision of counseling and/or other services to the abuser may be perceived as a betrayal of those who have been sexually abused. In this regard, Isah 42:3 serves as a motif that invites a "pastoral style" in which those who minister do not exacerbate the pain and suffering of others: "A bruised reed He will not break and a dimly burning wick He will not extinguish; He will faithfully bring forth justice."[9]

---

7. Barcus and Bernstein, "Victim-Perpetrator Reconciliation," 515–532; Yantzi, *Sexual Offending and Restoration.*

8. Yantzi, *Sexual Offending and Restoration,* 139, 151.

9. Scripture citations are from the New American Standard Bible (NASB).

POTENTIAL CONFLICT OF INTEREST

Church workers and clergy need to understand why professional counselors believe it is unwise for the same person to attempt to counsel or provide support to both an abuser and the person they have abused. These reasons include the fact that the abused person cannot adequately express their feelings without placing themselves at emotional or physical risk, and additionally, that relational counseling can be used by the perpetrator to evade personal responsibility by blaming others for their actions.[10]

Abuse Is Sin

As society has become more serious about addressing the problems of sexual abuse and *domestic violence, it has sought to hold perpetrators accountable for their actions through the criminalization of these acts. While this shift may reflect secular sensibilities, the treatment of sexual abuse as a criminal act reflects neither the emotional and spiritual significance of the act(s) committed nor any aspect of the perpetrator's personal responsibility. *The sinfulness of sexual abuse is seen in its selfish and deceitful use of power.*[11] For example, the self-justified nature of sexual abuse contravenes the biblical commands that one "lay down his life for his friends" (John 15:13) and "not merely look out for your own personal interests, but also for the interests of others" (Phil 2:4). Similarly, the deceit of sexual abuse is seen in the way the perpetrator seeks to justify their actions,[12] sometimes even misappropriating Scripture.[13] The sinfulness of sexual abuse is also seen in its *effect*. Menninger writes:

> [T]he wrongness of the sinful act lies not merely in its nonconformity, its departure from the accepted appropriate way of behavior, but in an implicitly aggressive quality—a ruthlessness, a hurting, a breaking away from God and the rest of humanity, a partial alienation, or act of rebellion.[14]

Thus, the biblical story of the rape of Tamar (2 Samuel 13) reveals a violation of the prohibition against *incest (Leviticus 18), a violation of Tamar's trust in her brother, and a disruption in family relations. It is, therefore, essential that Christians be in the forefront of holding the abuser accountable for their actions. *Indeed, silence about the sinfulness of sexual abuse raises serious questions in the mind of the abused with respect to God's nature, God's presence in human history, and the relevance of the Gospel.*[15]

---

10. Remley and Herlihy, *Ethical, Legal, and Professional Issues*, 249.

11. Anderson, *Self Care*, describes the bent to sin as being located in the "instinct to use power over others and one's own life to gain fulfillment" (191).

12. Jenkins, *Invitations To Responsibility*, 120–131; Yantzi, *Sexual Offending and Restoration*, 167–174.

13. Margaret J. Rinck illustrates the misuse of Scripture in an example of spousal sexual abuse (*Christian Men Who Hate Women*, 73). For an overview of abuses of spiritual authority or *spiritual incest, see Johnson and VanVonderen, *The Subtle Power of Spiritual Abuse*.

14. Menninger, *Whatever Became of Sin?*, 19.

15. Gavrielides and Coker, "Restoring Faith," 345–365; Poling, *The Abuse of Power*.

*The Abuser Is Both a Sinner and Someone Created in *Imago Dei*

Neither the fact that abuse is a sin nor the deep sense of revulsion that these sinful acts stir within people's hearts nullify the core Christian belief that all humans are created in the *image of God and reflect some element of the personhood of the creator God (Gen 1:27; Jam 3:9). Although theologians may differ as to which element(s) of God's personhood are included in the statement of Gen 1:26–27 and the extent to which the divine image has been marred by the *Fall from grace (Genesis 3),[16] Christians affirm the biblical view that human dignity is rooted in the Creation act, that humans are the objects of God's love, and that God desires to relate on an intimate basis with humankind (cf. Gen 3:8–10; John 3:16–18; Rom 5:8). Thus, Christians who work with sexual abuse perpetrators are invited to recognize both the sinfulness of the abuser's actions and to treat them with the same dignity God shows to all people.

Engaging the Abuser Involves the Practice of Paraklēsis

The goal in counseling a sexual abuse perpetrator is to first elicit their acknowledgement of responsibility, and second to invite them to change. This level of engagement is seen in the Greek words *parakaleō* and *paraklēsis*, which are used in the New Testament with the sense of "beseeching" (Matt 8:5; Rom 12:1), "exhorting" (1 Tim 4:13), and "comforting" (Acts 9:31; 2 Cor 1:3–6).[17] This range of meaning suggests a way of being with persons such that *one can comfort and encourage the other while at the same time allowing for the possibility of confronting and summoning them to an alternate course of action.* Significantly, this pairing of characteristics—understanding and compassion combined with authority, leadership, and strength—was identified by inmates who had undergone a prison-based treatment program for sexual abuse as qualities they valued in their therapists.[18]

When *paraklēsis* is used with the sense of "comfort," it suggests a presence which, though not condoning the sin, is not anxious about the sins of the individual and conveys grace to the abuser in much the same way that Jesus both extends grace to the woman caught in adultery while at the same time identifying she was guilty of sin and challenging her to leave her life of sin (John 8:2–11).[19] *This demonstration of grace is not, however, a cheap grace that justifies the abuser's sins but rather a costly grace* that invites the abuser to move out of their entrenched thoughts and actions.[20] When *paraklēsis* is used with the sense of "exhort," it:

- *confronts* the abuser with their sin,

- *draws* the abuser to consider what keeps them in bondage to sin,

- *advises* the abuser to renounce their sin, and

16. Anderson, *On Being Human*, 69–103.

17. Braumann, "*parakaleō*," 569–571; Schmitz, "*parakaleō*," 773–799.

18. Drapeau et al., "What Sex Abusers Say About Their Treatment," 106; Levenson et al., "Perceptions of Sex Offenders about Treatment," 38.

19. Carson, *The Gospel According to John*.

20. Bonhoeffer, *The Cost of Discipleship*, 45–48.

- *invites* the abuser to take up a new way of being in relationship with others.

In this chapter the words "invite" and "invitation" reflect the meaning of *paraklēsis* in as much as they describe the process of drawing a person through a combination of grace and confrontation to take responsibility for their actions. Indeed, the practice of *paraklēsis* moves the abuser from a general sense of unease concerning their actions to the point where they are confronted with the need to assume responsibility for their actions. The significance of creating this grace-filled relationship is seen in the literature on confession where we find that *in order for there to be serious confession, there needs to be a relationship of trust between the confessant and the confessor.*[21] In Christian counseling, the goal of this relationship is to invite the abuser into acknowledgement of their actions such that they become self-conscious not only of their actions but of their guilt, shame, and loneliness and are moved to genuine repentance leading to union with God.[22] Thus the counseling relationship provides the context in which the abuser ceases to hide behind masks of minimization and rationalization and takes responsibility *for both the fact and the effects of their actions.*

Develop a Treatment Network

Because many abusers flourish within secretive relationships, care must be taken that they do not use their relationships with counselors and church leaders to justify their abusive behavior or to placate either their victims or the legal system. To safeguard against this, counselors and church leaders who work with sexual abusers need to consult with others who have contact with the abuser to verify the actions and choices they are reporting and to be informed of concerns they may have concerning the abuser's behavior. This *network* can include: the abuser's therapist, the leader of the abuser's sexual abuse *support group, the abuser's probation officer, persons from the faith community who provide counsel or support to the abuser, or someone who represents the concerns of the abused. In addition, churches are advised to develop protocols to safeguard children and vulnerable populations from sexual exploitation while they attend church activities. These protocols need to go beyond the use of background checks, defining protocols that will protect workers from being wrongly accused of sexual impropriety. In addition, churches need to develop protocols, as well as *safety plans for vulnerable families, that govern their response to the presence of accused and/or those convicted of a sexual offence, who desire to be a part of their church.[23]

INVITATIONS TO RESPONSIBILITY-TAKING

It's worth remembering that the treatment of sexual abuse can be highly specialized, requiring appropriate training and experience if it is to be done well. While many clergy may not be in a position to initiate these conversations with an abuser, clergy are in a posi-

21. Berggren, *The Psychology of Confession,* 36–49; Bonhoeffer, *Life Together,* 112; Fourez, *Sacraments and Passages,* 107.

22. Coe and Hall, *Psychology in the Spirit,* 263.

23. Ross, "Modern Day Lepers," 16.

tion to *reinforce* the value of these conversations and support the abuser as they undergo the counseling process.

Some Theoretical Foundations

The grace-filled confrontations or invitations presented in the following discussion are informed by *Narrative Therapy, employ commonly used interventions,[24] and are aimed at challenging the abuser's *cognitive frameworks rather than simply changing behavior. These invitations are more than just steps on a path. Rather, they address important aspects of the abuser's behavior, thought structures, and beliefs that need to be challenged and reshaped. It should be noted that these interventions apply primarily to the treatment of adults, since the treatment of youth who sexually offend requires the incorporation of a *developmental perspective.

Practical Considerations

One challenge confronting the treatment of sexual offenders is the question of *recidivism. Reported post-treatment[25] recidivism rates range from 13.4 percent (four- to five-year follow-up) up to the 40 percent range (fifteen- to twenty-year).[26] Furthermore, the highest rates of re-offense occur among those with *personality disorders,[27] *deviant sexual behavior, prior sexual offenses, deviant victim choices, and those who fail to complete treatment.[28] Thus, anyone counseling a sexual offender needs to recognize the real risks of re-offense, proceed with caution, and build in mechanisms for long-term accountability.

Another challenge related to treating sexual offenders is whether it is ever appropriate for the victim to confront their abuser. Embedded within this question is whether the victim will be *re-victimized or further traumatized by the confrontation session. As a result, the use of a confrontation depends on three factors: (1) Has the abuser undergone treatment and do they take responsibility for the impact of their actions on the life of the victim? (2) Has the victim undergone treatment and do they desire to confront the

---

24. Drapeau et al., "What Sex Abusers Say About Their Treatment," 93–94; Levenson et al., "Perceptions of Sex Offenders About Treatment," 35–56; Nezu "Social Problem-Solving Correlates of Sexual Deviancy and Aggression among Adult Child Molesters," 27–36.

25. It is necessary to differentiate between untreated and treated individuals as studies report significantly higher rates of re-offense (approximately double) for those who do not receive treatment (Hanson et al., "The Principles of Effective Correctional Treatment Also Apply to Sexual Offenders," 877).

26. Brannon et al., "Attitudes about Community Notification," 371; Hanson and Bussiere, "Predicting Relapse," 348–362; Wilson et al., "Circles of Support and Accountability," 5.

27. Caution needs to be exercised with respect to mental diagnoses as the diagnostic criteria of the *Diagnostic and Statistical Manual of Mental Disorders-4th Edition-Text Revision (DSM-IV-TR)* have not been demonstrated to be reliable when assessing sexual offenders (Marshall, "Diagnostic Issues, Multiple Paraphilias, and Co-Morbid Disorders in Sexual Offenders," 16–35); the DSM avoids the use of ethical language for behaviors Christians view as sin (Johnson, *Foundations for Soul Care*, 240–244); a Christian view of *psychopathology must take sin seriously (Coe and Hall, *Psychology in the Spirit*, 283–303), and "scientific classifications" can detract people from their available options, including responsibility-taking (White and Epston, *Narrative Means to Therapeutic Ends*, 53–54).

28. Hanson and Bussiere, "Predicting Relapse," 357.

perpetrator? (3) Are both the victim's and perpetrator's therapists in agreement as to the advisability of a confrontation session?[29] Such factors need to be worked out on a case-by-case basis.

INVITATION TO SUBMIT TO THE BAN

Acts of censure, such as arrest and restraining orders, serve to protect the abused from further harm resulting from contact with the abuser. This in turn, challenges the mindset of minimization, *denial, and justification that sustained the period of abusive behavior. Thus, *the first invitation to responsibility taking is to invite the abuser to set aside all attempts to minimize, deny, or justify their actions* and admit that their victims are in need of protection and to submit to all sanctions.[30]

INVITATION TO EXAMINE ONE'S CYCLE OF ABUSIVE BEHAVIOR

This phase begins by inviting the abuser to provide a detailed verbal description of their *cycle of violence* and abusive behavior (see diagram below). This information is retained in writing to guide further reflection and discussion. In reflecting on their cycle, the abuser describes their memory of the sequence of events for as many abuse cycles as possible. Because this process requires attention to detail, this discussion usually requires several counseling sessions (see list below of sample questions). This line of questioning can be extremely painful for most abusers. As a result, counselors need to ensure there is enough rapport in the therapeutic relationship to foster this line of questioning and the counselee has a safety plan[31] in place so they do not act out any anxiety that may be created by this process. In addition, the counselor needs to be careful not to rush this phase of the process as the goal is to begin challenging faulty beliefs such as "it was an accident."

---

29. Cf. DeMaio et al., "The Use of Clarification Sessions in the Treatment of Incest Victims and Their Families," 32; Yantzi, *Sexual Offending and Restoration*, 155–166.

30. Jenkins, *Invitations to Responsibility*, 145–149, 162–164.

31. "Safety planning" involves a commitment to: a healthy lifestyle, creating a support and accountability network, avoiding situations where they may reoffend or be accused of reoffending, engaging their support system when they experience stresses that may lead to reoffending, and avoiding the use of all sexually explicit material.

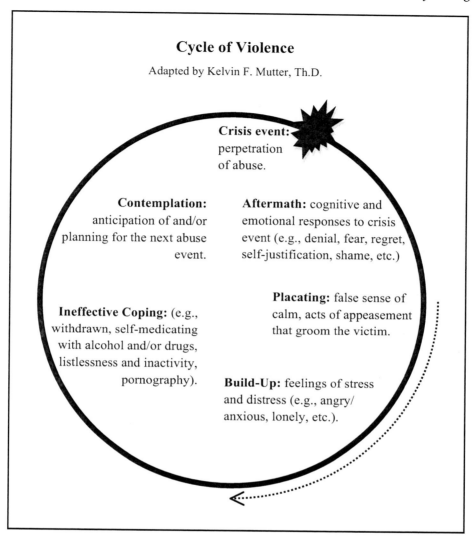

Cycle of Violence

Adapted by Kelvin F. Mutter, Th.D.

Crisis event: perpetration of abuse.

Contemplation: anticipation of and/or planning for the next abuse event.

Aftermath: cognitive and emotional responses to crisis event (e.g., denial, fear, regret, self-justification, shame, etc.)

Placating: false sense of calm, acts of appeasement that groom the victim.

Ineffective Coping: (e.g., withdrawn, self-medicating with alcohol and/or drugs, listlessness and inactivity, pornography).

Build-Up: feelings of stress and distress (e.g., angry/anxious, lonely, etc.).

Questions for Exploring the Cycle of Violence/Abuse

The cycle of abuse chart, along with the following questions, is designed to confront the counselee with the decisions and behaviors that resulted in the victimization of another person.

Aftermath: What was the previous act of sexual abuse? Following this act, what did you say to yourself about your actions? What did you say to [the victim]? What emotions do you remember feeling? What did you do to cope with these emotions? How did you feel about yourself?

Placating: How did you attempt to make peace following your previous abusive act? Did these actions lull [the victim] into a false sense of security or begin to *groom them for the next incident?

Build-up: Describe the stresses in your life. What emotions do these generate? How did you feel about yourself when you experienced these emotions? And the stressors?

Ineffective coping: Describe the things you do to try to cope with life's stresses (explore for the use of ineffective or *dysfunctional *coping mechanisms). Were any of these coping mechanisms of a sexual nature (e.g., fantasizing, pornography, prostitution)? How do these attempts to cope affect your level of stress?

Contemplation: What were the warning signs that you might abuse? In what ways did you contemplate, anticipate, or plan for the next encounter? How did you groom [the victim] to be sexually abused? What did [the victim] do or say? How did you respond?

Crisis event: What were the circumstances when the abuse took place? Where were you? Who did you abuse? How did you choose [the victim]? How did you trick/force/con [the victim] into sexual abuse? What did [the victim] do or say? How did you respond?

While this exploration focuses on the *cycle* of abuse and invites the abuser to take responsibility for their decisions and behaviors, a thorough understanding of the abuse cycle can also be used to invite the abuser to identify alternate decisions they can make that will result in health and safety for others. For maximum effect, the counselor proceeds around the cycle inviting the abuser to envision how they might act differently. For example, the abuser may choose to *cope with stress through exercise rather than self-medicate or engage in the use of pornography. Each alternate activity is evaluated to ensure it does not pose a risk to self or others and is discussed in detail to develop a plan for putting the new behavior into action.

INVITATION TO EXAMINE ONE'S FAULTY REASONING

*Abuse is maintained through the use of excuses or *cognitive distortions,*[32] which Jenkins describes as restraints to responsible action by which the abuser hides from responsibility.[33] Psychologically, an abuser's cognitive distortions are a complex set of beliefs that encompass a view of children as *sexualized beings, a misunderstanding of the nature of harm, a belief that the world is a hostile place, a sense of personal *entitlement, and a belief the abuser is unable to resist or control their urges.[34] Theologically, these cognitive distortions are a consequence of the *noetic* effects of sin and reside within faulty cognitive *schema that must be addressed if an abuse perpetrator is to assume responsibility for their actions[35] and may lie so buried one might consider it to be the hidden heart of the person, unknown to either themselves or others.[36] As a result, those who work with perpetrators do not merely invite the abuser to examine patterns of behavior and coping

---

32. Jenkins, *Invitations to Responsibility*, 120–131; Yantzi, *Sexual Offending and Restoration*, 167–174.

33. Jenkins, *Invitations to Responsibility*, 31–58, 168–181.

34. Gannon et al., "Cognitive Distortions in Child Molesters," 402–416.

35. McMinn, *Sin and Grace in Christian Counseling*, 135–147.

36. For discussion of the "hidden heart," see: Coe and Hall, *Psychology in the Spirit*, 297–303.

(e.g., cycle of violence, *offense cycle), they also challenge the abuser to critically examine the thought processes that undergirds and sustains these maladaptive behaviors.[37] Finally, the abuser needs to develop healthy cognitive structures that can support a *non*-abusive lifestyle.

Questions to Explore Cognitive Distortions[38]

These are examples of the types of questions that need to be asked of the abuser:

- Do you justify looking at sexually explicit material or fantasizing about someone?

- When did you last catch yourself masturbating to sexually explicit material or your fantasies?[39]

- How did you try to justify/explain away your behavior?

- When did you notice that the victim was distressed by what you were doing to him or her?

- How did you try to justify/explain away your abuse?

- What did you imagine, what stories did you tell yourself, that helped you ignore your awareness that sexually abusing others was wrong?

The purpose of asking these questions is to provide the counselor and abuser with a fuller understanding of the counselee's cognitive distortions so that both parties are able to recognize and confront this thinking whenever it emerges.

INVITATION TO ACKNOWLEDGE ONE'S OWN WOUNDEDNESS

A significant percentage of those who sexually abuse others have themselves experienced sexual abuse.[40] While it is in no one's interest to justify an abuser's actions on the basis that they also are a victim of abuse, neither is it helpful to ignore the impact this lived-experience may have on the person's thoughts and actions. *As a result, abusers who are also victims of abuse need to have permission to talk about this with a view to experiencing their own healing.*

---

37. While some counselors have used a polygraph (or a fake polygraph) to facilitate a greater level of honesty and disclosure on the part of the sexual abuser (e.g., Gannon et al., "Cognitive Distortions in Child Molesters"), the efficacy of this practice has been questioned as there is no way to differentiate between the effects of the treatment process, the use of a polygraph, or any other factor on the extent to which an abuser is honest in their disclosures (Gannon et al., "Does the Polygraph Lead to Better Risk Prediction for Sexual Offenders?" 40–41).

38. See Jenkins, *Invitations to Responsibility*, 211–221.

39. Use of inappropriate sexual material and the role it plays in the abuse and/or maintenance of unhealthy sexual thoughts need to be explored. While a sexual offender may report that they are no longer sexually interested in previous victims or additional children, an exploration of their continued attractions, behaviors and beliefs concerning sexuality is crucial as they may continue to fantasize about this behavior. These thoughts need to be challenged and support given to alter and/or replace them.

40. Jespersen et al., "Sexual Abuse History," 179–192. See also Coe and Hall's discussion of the connection between psychopathology and being sinned against (*Psychology in the Spirit*, 291–293).

INVITATION TO EMPATHIZE WITH THE ABUSED

Victim *empathy—that is, the abuser learning to have compassion for their victim—is considered by many to be an important dimension of responsibility-taking and long-term change on the part of the abuser.[41] One reason for this is the fact that the emergence of empathy means the abuser is now capable of looking at life through the eyes of the person they have abused. While this shift in perspective is important for all abusers, it is particularly significant when working with abusers diagnosed with personality disorders.[42] For many abusers, the experience of fear and shame can be so strong that it interferes with their ability to empathize with those they have abused. *Thus, a major step in breaking the impasse of the abuser's self-centeredness is their need to see the other as fully human.* This requires that the abuser no longer views the other as an object or a means for satisfying their own needs but rather as someone with feelings, aspirations, desires, and wishes whose life has been significantly affected by the actions of the abuser.[43] It is at this point when abusers who are responsive to this invitation begin to move from a generalized state of fear or shame to a particularized sense of guilt, one that sets the stage for taking ownership for their actions.[44]

INVITATION TO ACKNOWLEDGE THEIR ABUSE

Acknowledgement of abuse has much in common with the practice of confession (*exhomologeō*), which carries the ideas of "being in agreement with" in the classical Greek literature, and "to acknowledge" in the New Testament (e.g., Phil 2:11; Rev 3:5). In the New Testament *exhomologeō* also refers to a person's confession of sin as it occurs within the process of repentance and restoration (e.g., Acts 19:18; Jam 5:16).[45] Viewed from this perspective, *confession occurs when an individual agrees with the legal assessment of God (and others) on the matter and admits to their sin.* Thus the individual sets aside their attempt to minimize, deny, or justify their own actions and instead takes responsibility for them. The power of this intervention is highlighted by Hargrave:

> When the violation is kept *internal*, victims will many times question the validity of their feelings . . . [But] when victims have *the injustice confirmed overtly*, they experience the act as support for their identity . . . This support for the victims' perspective raises the victims' self-concept and allows them to be more confident.[46]

41. Davidson, "Victims Speak," 161; Drapeau et al., "What Sex Abusers Say About Their Treatment," 94; Levenson et al., "Perceptions of Sex Offenders about Treatment," 37.

42. Marshall, "Diagnostic Issues, Multiple Paraphilias," 29.

43. Mechanisms for developing victim empathy include: the use of victim's accounts to confront the abuser (Davidson, "Victims Speak," 172), the use of *role play (Levenson et al, "Perceptions of Sex Offenders about Treatment," 37), and the use of *victim panels in which the offender hears the stories of victims unknown to themselves (van Wormer, "Restorative Justice as Social Justice for Victims of Gendered Violence," 110).

44. Abusers who do not respond to this invitation remain stuck in their denial of the significance of their abuse and/or their feelings of shame.

45. See "*exhomologeō*," in Bauer et al., *A Greek-English Lexicon of the New Testament and Other Early Christian Literature*, 276; Fürst, "Confess," 344–347; Michel, "*homologeō*," 199–220.

46. Hargrave, *Families & Forgiveness*, 99; emphasis added.

For such an acknowledgement to occur, however, the abuser must move beyond denial, fear, and shame and experience guilt accompanied by a healthy sense of sorrow for their actions (2 Cor 7:10). Without guilt, any attempt to acknowledge one's wrong-doing is incomplete and rings hollow in the ears of their victims (see Types of Apology, below). To be done effectively, the abuser needs to consider their motivation for acknowledging the abuse. While it may take time and a lot of soul searching on the part of the abuser, clinical experience indicates that it is best for the abuser to admit to the wrongdoing, because this is itself the right thing to do, rather than as an attempt to repair the relationship with the other. *Indeed, the abuser needs to be prepared for the fact their acknowledgment of wrongdoing may not be accepted by the one who has abused.* Additionally, even if the abused can embrace *forgiveness, this does not imply relational restoration with the abuser. The abused have their own struggles to overcome, and their healing is also a process. Regardless, we must consider various forms of apology.

Types of Apology

The following types of apology can be identified.

Pseudo-apology: e.g., "If I have hurt you, I am sorry (= whatever you need to hear)." The subtext is that the abuser is maintaining their denial through a begrudging admission.

Fear-based apology: e.g., "I'm sorry (= please don't punish me)." The subtext is that the abuser is merely afraid of the consequences because of what they have done.

Shame-based apology: e.g., "Okay, I get it, I'm sorry (= please stop reminding me)." The subtext is that the abuser is ashamed of what they have done, resents what it is costing them, and does not want to be reminded of it.

Guilt-based apology: e.g., "When I think of what I have done, I recognize I have acted selfishly without considering your wants, needs, or feelings. I recognize I have caused you great suffering [may even identify how the person has suffered]. I deeply regret the pain I have caused. I recognize I have caused you to distrust and even despise me, and I recognize I deserve to be punished for my actions and will accept all punishment that is given." *The strength of the guilt-based apology is the fact it is other-centered.*

The process of arriving at a guilt-based apology involves persistence on the part of the counselor as the abuser needs to be repeatedly drawn to examine their cognitive distortions and reflect on how others experience them. Most abusers find this is a difficult process, especially in the early stages of treatment when any attempt to confront them with their actions can result in a retreat into denial, minimization, and self-pity. Other barriers to the development of healthy guilt include the abuser's manipulative tendencies and grandiosity on the part of the abuser. For these reasons, *abusers often need help apologizing*. While the process of arriving at a guilt-based apology is challenging, the results can be equally significant—as when the abused witnesses the abuser taking responsibility for their actions.

INVITATION TO ACCEPT THE CONSEQUENCES OF THEIR ACTIONS

Accountability arises from the abuser's willingness to take responsibility for their past actions *and the consequences of those actions*. Being accountable involves accepting punishment and censure, undergoing counseling, and making one's self answerable to a community-based circle of support that requires honesty and transparency from its participants with respect to their choices.[47] Accountability may also include acts of compensation or *restitution toward those whose lives have been impacted by sexual abuse (e.g., payment of legal fees, counseling costs, a written letter acknowledging responsibility for the abuse, etc.). It is worth noting that a key difference between an act of compensation and the abuser's past attempts to groom their victims is the fact that *a true act of compensation or restitution is given without any expectation of re-engaging with the abused individual(s) in a relationship* or influencing a *judicial process.

INVITATION TO HEAR THE VOICE OF THE ABUSED

Among the troubling questions raised by the problem of sexual abuse is the issue of promoting *reconciliation between the abuser and their victim(s). Given the depths of the emotional wounds that result from a sexually abusive relationship (e.g., violation of trust, abuse of power, etc.) reconciliation cannot be an assumed outcome.[48] While reconciliation may neither be possible nor desirable in many situations, some counselors find value in having at least one session in which the abusers hear from those they have abused.[49] *The purpose of these sessions is to confront the abuser with the words and emotions of those they have abused and to allow the abused individual an opportunity to witness the response of the abuser.* In other words, this is an opportunity for the abuser to listen to the abused rather than a commitment to restoring the relationship. As noted above, such a confrontation should only occur with a careful *risk assessment by the counselor and when both parties are ready. In the case of the abuser, a precondition to any clarification session is that they wrestle with, and experience grief over, their cycle of abuse, faulty reasoning, lack of empathy for the other, and responsibility both for the abuse as well as the impact of the abuse on the lives of others.

CONCLUSION

Acts of sexual abuse beget fear and shame as well as denial and self-justification in the heart of the abuser. Left alone the abuser will harden their heart to the pain they have caused and may continue to inflict on others. Those who work with abuse perpetrators choose to bear witness to this abuse in ways that confront the perpetrators with the reality of their actions. It is a role that requires the counselor to not only maintain their moral bearings but also *demonstrate the courageous compassion that calls the abuser to experience*

---

47. Brannon et al., "Attitudes about Community Notification," 377; Wilson et al., "Circles of Support and Accountability," 1–15.

48. Worthington, *Forgiving and Reconciling*, 178–79; Yantzi, *Sexual Offending and Restoration*, 129.

49. DeMaio et al., "The Use of Clarification Sessions," 27–39; Gavrielides and Coker, "Restoring Faith," 357; Yantzi, *Sexual Offending and Restoration*, 155–166.

costly grace. In so doing, the abuser is summoned to acknowledge that their actions are more than a violation of law, they are a violation of conscience and relationships, to see the damage their actions have caused others, and to commit to a life of accountability that is free of abuse.

The presence of a sexual offender within the community of faith is likely to challenge our assumptions about the nature of the church and its ministry. For example, while Christians view the church as a place where broken people experience grace and healing, the issue of sexual abuse confronts us with the brokenness of the abused, the need to protect those who are vulnerable, and *a realization that without grace the abuser is an outcast—from the grace they also need*. As a result, church leaders need to publicly address the issue of sexual abuse in ways that comfort the abused, identify and confront sexual abuse, and enact policies that protect the vulnerable. Next, clergy need to recognize the limits of their training,[50] expertise,[51] and time[52] and refer sexual abusers to qualified community-based programs and counselors. Finally, clergy must avoid cheap grace through practices that do not shield the offender from the consequences, including disciplinary and legal actions, of their behavior.[53] In this way the church informs the abuser of the seriousness of these sins and summons them to abandon their life of sin.

QUESTIONS FOR DISCUSSION

1. Called mandated reporting, the sexual abuse of children needs to be reported to the appropriate authorities. Construct an updated list of names and telephone numbers of the agencies in your area where you could report child sexual assault and/or refer people for treatment. How do you reconcile making this report with a client's desire for confidentiality? In your community, what kind of shared communication exists between therapists and clergy? List several ways this cooperation could be improved.

2. Explain why empathy is so vital for abusers. How do you account for an abuser's sense of grandiosity and entitlement? Four types of apology were described. Reflect on how someone who has been abused would receive each of these apologies. How would you invite the abuser to reflect on the message they give when they use these apologies? What methods do you think are (would be) most effective to help abusers communicate their apology? List some.

3. It was observed that the treatment of sexual abuse as a *criminal act* does not reflect the emotional and spiritual significance of that act committed by the perpetrator. Compare and contrast the contributions and concerns of the court to that of the local church regarding the abuser. Where do these concerns overlap? Where are different

---

50. Most MDiv programs only require *one* counseling course (Firmin and Tedford, "An Assessment of Pastoral Counseling Courses in Seminaries Serving Evangelical Baptist Students," 420–427).

51. McRay et al., "What Evangelical Pastors Want to Know About Psychology," 99–105.

52. Pastors can devote about five hours to any counseling situation (Benner, *Strategic Pastoral Counseling*, 44).

53. Ross, "Modern Day Lepers," 17.

emphases or worldviews represented between the court and church? As custodians of God's standards and the spiritual well-being of believers, what specific things can the church do to improve their ministry to the abused and abuser alike? The abuser needs to admit to the wrongfulness of their actions and commit to a life that is trustworthy even if they never receive forgiveness from, or are reconciled with, the individual(s) they have abused. Why do you think this is important? Consider the perspectives of both the abuser and the abused.

4. Costly grace is experienced when the abuser encounters someone who is gentle and yet resolutely calls them to account for their actions. Make a list of all the ways this type of grace "costs" the abuser. What are some ways in which an abuser might attempt to "cheapen grace?" In what ways is the failure to change also costly? What hurdles does the church still need to overcome to adequately address the needs of prior abusers worshiping in their midst? List some core elements that should be contained in a church policy of a congregation actively attempting to minister to abusers.

FOR FURTHER READING

Anderson, Ray S. *Self Care: A Theology of Personal Empowerment and Spiritual Healing*. Pasadena, CA: Fuller Seminary, 2000.

Jenkins, Alan. *Invitations To Responsibility: The Therapeutic Engagement of Men Who Are Violent and Abusive*. Adelaide, Australia: Dulwich Centre, 1990.

Lampman, Lisa B., ed. *God and the Victim: Theological Reflections on Evil, Victimization, Justice, and Forgiveness*. Grand Rapids: Eerdmans, 1999.

McMinn, Mark. *Sin and Grace in Christian Counseling*. Downers Grove, IL: InterVarsity, 2008.

Morin, J.W., and J. S. Levenson. *The Road to Freedom*. Oklahoma City, OK: Authors, 2002.

Rinck, Margaret J. *Christian Men Who Hate Women*. Grand Rapids: Zondervan, 1990.

Yantzi, Mark. *Sexual Offending and Restoration*. Eugene, OR: Wipf and Stock, 2009.

19

The Adult Survivor

What Healing Is and Is Not

Janelle Kwee, PsyD

O<small>NE WANTS DESPERATELY TO</small> forget, to erase a life chapter of *sexual abuse (SA), and to move forward with their lives. At the same time, the person who has been victimized by sexual abuse knows that the chapters they have lived cannot be erased; moving on today has to be built on the unchangeable realities of yesterday. Although there are a variety of legal, medical, and psychological definitions of sexual abuse, sexual abuse always implies nonconsensual sexual contact. This nonconsensual sexual contact includes a wide range of behaviors, including verbal sexual comments or threats, exposure to sexual material (*non*-contact), sexual touching, and penetration. In the case of *child sexual abuse (CSA), there is an inherent power differential between the child victim and the *perpetrator, who is typically an older child or adult. *In essence, to be sexually abused means to be victimized.* Although there is a greater *proportionality of male perpetrators and female victims, both victims and perpetrators of sexual abuse are male or female. When somebody is sexually abused, he or she has been taken advantage of. *This exploitative contact—often an ongoing relationship—results in varying degrees of spiritual, psychological, relational, and physical harm.* Because of the nature of sexual abuse, *survivors are also necessarily victims.

TERMS THAT SHAPE, DEFINE, AND HONOR

Terms like *victim* and *survivor*, however, are not synonymous, so it is worth asking what it means to be a survivor of sexual abuse rather than simply a victim. Does being a survivor imply that one has been healed, or does calling oneself a survivor begin to affirm the process of healing and wholeness? This is not meant to be a rhetorical question; a discussion on this can become rather complex. Preference for the term "survivor" versus "victim" is even disputed. For me, the language of "survivor" is important because it honors the *resilience already demonstrated by the person who has been abused. Working with survivors often reminds me of a person's reservoir of strength to affirm the God-given beauty and creative power of one's life in spite of the destruction caused by sexual abuse. The notion of a "survivor" seems to be able to capture this creative human resilience.

After several years of working in contexts of *domestic violence, *advocacy, and counseling, I became accustomed to a strong preference to refer to our clients as "survivors" and even an implicit admonition against the language of "victim." The drawback of saying "victim" appears to be that it implies helplessness or finality in the wounded state. A "victim" does not sound like a very powerful person. However, for me, the language of "victim" is equally important to hold on to. *Without it, we run the risk of minimizing the atrocity of malevolent, destructive acts that are perpetrated by some people against others, who are, by definition, victims.* For the same reason that the language of "victim" is sometimes avoided, it should be retained. Power differentials are usually part of victimization. While the possibilities for a person to be *em*powered are great and a state of victimhood is certainly not static or final, we cannot escape and should not deny that inappropriately wielded power does result in victimization.

SPEAKING AGAINST THE "UNSPEAKABLE"

Sexual abuse has an undeniably enormous capacity for devastation. Questions related to healing from sexual abuse do not lend themselves to simple, linear answers. However, the answers that point to healing need to be vigorously explored and continually talked about among survivors, faith communities, families, and trained professionals. Although sexual abuse could justifiably be described as an unspeakable tragedy, it is perhaps more true that one's experience of sexual abuse refuses to remain silent. It is a great social problem—the most antithetical to healing—that the "unspeakability" of sexual abuse often prevents communities of potential support from listening to the wounds of abuse, and consequently, from becoming places of healing for those who have survived the atrocities of abuse.

One of the most disconcerting realities pertaining to this topic is that sexually wounded people often suffer in silence. Locked in silence, their experiences of abuse speak a cryptic language, their wounds tirelessly seeking justice. But since the kind of pain they have experienced is socially unspeakable, their cryptic cries for help are not often heard or recognized. Moreover, the powerful desire for communities to deny that unspeakable exploitation has occurred in their midst often makes it impossible for its members to acknowledge these cries for help. This amounts to a *conspiracy of silence. To complicate matters, many who seek to help sexually wounded people are simply uninformed and lack knowledge or resources to properly care for them. *The very ideas that one has about healing can either get in the way or help to facilitate it*, hence the organization of this chapter into sections about what healing *is* and *is not*. Though the parameters of healing cannot be definitively presented, this chapter begins to address what we do know about healing from sexual abuse, the aid of "hearing" communities, and what it means to be a survivor.

SPEAKING OF HEALING: MYSTERY, MIRACLES, AND SCIENCE

There is an inherent paradox in addressing "healing" of sexual abuse from a *science-informed* perspective. In fact, the concept of healing is scarcely referenced in mental health and social science literature. Instead, one finds references to *"remission" and "recovery" from symptoms of *trauma. In a widely used Christian encyclopedia on Counseling and Psychology,[1] there are entries on "faith healing," "inner healing," and "psychic healing," but nothing that describes healing simply as an outcome or goal of recovery from emotional distress. Although it is generally accepted to speak of healing from a *faith-informed* perspective, the absence of science-informed literature referring to healing illustrates the aforementioned paradox of addressing it from my professional vantage point. Of course, operational definitions of concepts such as symptom remission are helpful. They even illuminate aspects of the holistic and spiritual notion of healing that is beyond our total understanding.

Healing, though related to remission and recovery, is not a measurable, practitioner-controlled outcome, and is essentially beyond psychological science. As a concept, though implied as a goal in medical and psychological treatment, it ultimately belongs in the sacred realm of faith. Healing ultimately belongs to God, our Jehovah-Rapha, "the Lord, your Healer" (Exod 15:26 ESV). To define either what healing *is* or *is not* is arguably beyond this author's authority as a mental health clinician. However, with a sense of mystery and reverence for God's supernatural role in healing, the following psychologically informed discussion about the adult survivor's healing is cautiously offered.

A HISTORY OF MIS-UNDERSTANDING

The historical literature on sexual abuse and recovery or healing from sexual abuse is surprisingly limited. Unlike facing the traumatic impact of disasters of the natural world, to look at psychological trauma *caused by human activity* requires us to confront two unsettling aspects of human nature: (1) the repulsive capacity for evil, (2) and our profound vulnerability to each other. These mirrors of human nature understandably provoke a deep ambivalence in the observer. In fact, the kind of conflict inherent to sexual abuse involves the power dynamic between a perpetrator and a victim. Psychiatrist Judith Herman insightfully observes that in the aftermath of a natural disaster, a witness naturally and automatically "sides" with the victim.[2] There is only one "who" to choose. *In contrast, a witness cannot be neutral to sexual abuse; either one sides with the victim or the perpetrator.* Moreover, people who are perpetrators of sexual abuse are often in positions of greater social influence. Too often, they are the "heads" of families, leaders in churches, and trusted relatives or community leaders. Frankly, *the narrative of the community that protects those in power does not afford space for the narratives of victims.*

The issue of "taking sides" becomes even more morally complicated when considering *intrafamilial abuse or *incest. The very foundations of a family identity are at risk if one faces the possibility of sexual abuse within their family. Perhaps these factors account for why some have claimed that the study of psychological trauma has a history of intermittent *amnesia; the field of study is vulnerable to being periodically forgotten due to the ambivalence it raises.[3]

---

1. Smith, "Faith Healing," 85.
2. Herman, *Trauma and Recovery*, 7.
3. Ibid.

Sigmund Freud and Sexual Abuse

Given his standing as the "Father of Clinical Psychology," it is fair to initiate a review of the field's conventional understanding of sexual abuse with Sigmund Freud. Early in his career, Freud came to the conclusion that his patient's *hysteria (i.e., physical symptoms with psychological origin) resulted from early childhood *molestation.[4] Although his patients did not initially remember or identify histories of sexual abuse, *repressed memories of abuse inevitably surfaced and relief was found through the "talking cure" in the validating and listening relationship between clinician and patient.[5]

Freud's clinical observations suggested that the symptoms of hysteria represented the refusal of sexual abuse wounds to stop "speaking." These symptoms were essentially the "cryptic language" of *experiences too unspeakable to remember or recount.* Through establishing a safe, believing, and trusting relationship with his patients, they eventually came to disclose repressed memories that had previously been spoken of only symbolically. He suggested that a patients' cure was found in bringing these unconscious memories to conscious awareness and speaking about them. After only two years (1895-1897), Freud abandoned the *seduction theory in favor of attributing infantile sexual experiences to unconscious fantasies of the child.[6]

Though controversial, *it has been suggested that Freud's switch of theories was actually a "cover up" of the unacceptable possibility of widespread intrafamilial sexual abuse, often perpetuated by the victims' fathers, among Freud's own upper-class Victorian community.*[7] Perhaps Freud—like many well-meaning helping professionals and clergy today—felt too uneasy about the radical social implications of the explanation of the seduction theory. In fact, what this theory would mean was that early experiences of sexual abuse were endemic, and this was intolerable. Freud's change of explanation represents a *dangerous shift of listening perspectives*: now, rather than believing the survivor's account of exploitation, victimization, and corresponding feelings of shame, he would focus on the patient's own sexual excitement in their account.

Regardless of whether Freud's early seduction theory adequately accounted for all of the symptoms he observed, his abrupt and dramatic shift of explanatory framework would have a long-term impact on the dynamics of sexual abuse disclosure. Now that the explanation for uncovered memories of early sexual abuse was found in the victim's own fantasies, *the account of anyone who may have been victimized by early sexual abuse lost credibility.* In fact, as Herman boldly states, "the most traumatic events of [the victim's] life take place outside the realm of socially validated reality."[8]

Although people continue to be silently victimized by sexual abuse in our families, churches, and communities, significant changes have taken place in the public sphere since Freud's groundbreaking work in this area. In the 1970s, events associated with

4. See Freud, "The Aetiology of Hysteria."

5. Freud's famous patient, "Anna O." coined the term "talking cure" to describe her work with Freud. See Breuer and Freud, "Studies on Hysteria," 35.

6. Esterson, "Seduction Theory," 518.

7. For a more detailed account, see Rush, *The Best Kept Secret.*

8. Herman, *Trauma and Recovery,* 8.

the women's movement would begin to facilitate this change. *Rape crisis centers were opened and research on the topic of sexual violence proliferated. Initially, rape crisis centers and hotlines were established to provide support and validation to victims of sexual assault. Sexual assault is often thought of as a random event between an innocent victim and an unknown perpetrator. One sees the perpetrator as an "other" and morally sides with the needs of the innocent victim. But when calls to these centers were increasingly represented by *incest victims*, it became necessary to acknowledge the possibility that the hypothesis of endemic sexual abuse, even within families and faith communities—which Freud retreated from—might be truer than we wish to admit.[9] And, the complexity of the relationship between the victim and perpetrator increased dramatically.

The relevance of this brief historical account to the question of healing is that it illustrates some of the requisites for a survivor to acknowledge their victimization and its reality. It was stated at the beginning of this chapter that insights pointing to healing from sexual abuse need to be vigorously explored and continually discussed. *This is the responsibility of families, neighborhood communities, and churches, not isolated experts and wounded patients.* By doing this, we create *healing spaces*—like the rape crisis centers and hotlines of the 70s in the U.S.—where the credibility of survivors' stories are affirmed, crimes are named, our consciousness is raised, and healing can begin.

EMBRACING HEALING: CHALLENGING MISCONCEPTIONS

A succinct and poignant description of healing is offered by Judith Herman, a specialist on trauma: "The core experiences of psychological trauma are disempowerment and disconnection with others. Recovery, therefore, is based upon the empowerment of the survivor and the creation of new connections."[10] Another author operationalizes the core "work" of the healing process in concrete terms: "In order to heal, the survivor must acknowledge the victimization and its reality, must understand it in the context of both the family and the larger culture, and must allow and experience the feelings associated with the trauma."[11]

Toward the healing goal of empowering the survivor and facilitating their life-giving connections with others, which includes *affective acknowledgment of the victimization that has taken place in a specific social context, the following elements of healing are offered. The discussion is organized around *safety, remembrance, reconnection, mourning,* and *hope.* These elements of healing are juxtaposed with *silence, forgetting, isolation, forced *reconciliation,* and *fear.* Perhaps deceptively straightforward, these principles should be considered with a willingness to confront some potential corresponding misconceptions.

9. Courtois, *Healing the Incest Wound*, xiii.

10. Herman, *Trauma and Recovery*, 133.

11. Courtois, *Healing the Incest Wound*, xvi.

Distinguishing the "Is" and "Is Not" of Healing

Survivors of sexual abuse too regularly face pressure from their own (even well-meaning) communities to pursue paths of so-called healing that are antithetical to recovery. Because of the essential role of one's community in fostering healing, community members' myths about healing are not benign or neutral misconceptions; they are toxic and disabling to an abuse survivor in their midst, who may otherwise have the opportunity to seek healing. Observe the following table of comparisons:

HEALING SEXUAL ABUSE: SOME VITAL COMPARISONS

What Healing *Is*	What Healing *Is Not*
Safety	Silence
Remembrance	Forgetting
Mourning/Lament	Forced Reconciliation
Reconnection	Disconnection/Isolation
Hope	Fear

The survivors I have worked with seem to always find a way to ask something like: "Will the effects of my experience of sexual abuse go away?" or "When will I be able to put this behind me?" Professionally, I frequently draw on the metaphor of physical wounds to explore what healing *is* and *is not* with clients who have been victimized by sexual abuse.[12]

SOME LESSONS FROM "FIRST AID"

When a wound is fresh, certain care is required to promote healing and minimize long-term consequences. A basic first aid response to a wound begins with cleansing, both with water and by respecting the natural cleansing process of bleeding, in order to prevent remaining dirt from causing an infection after the wound has been covered. Duct tape is not usually the bandage of choice; rather "breathable" materials like cotton cloth or gauze allow oxygen to get to the wound to promote healing. If a cut is deeper, it needs to be closed through stitches or staples after it has been cleansed. While a wound is healing, it requires continued care: cleaning, changing the bandage, and careful protection from further harm. In the initial period following an injury, the wound is acutely painful and runs certain risks, most notably the risk of becoming infected. The area of the wound is also more vulnerable to damage from re-injury.

Sensible first aid takes measures to reduce the possibility of infection and re-injury and to promote the path of fullest recovery. Sometimes, healing of minor traumas results in no permanent scar tissue. In many cases, however, *scars serve as long-term memorials*

12. Here, I draw on principles of first-aid from Werner, *Where There is No Doctor*.

to injuries. Scar tissue can be more sensitive to touch than unaffected skin. This tissue may also be uneven and pigmented differently, often leaving some kind of physical blemish. Scars, however, are very different than open wounds. While perhaps being more sensitive to touch, they are no longer acutely painful. They no longer serve as openings for foreign bacteria to take hold and cause infections or other secondary problems. They don't smell, and they don't need continued bandaging or any sort of special care. People with scars are people who laugh, run, and dance. While their scars carry painful reminders of being injured, the person can essentially move freely in restored functioning.

Although the process of healing for physical wounds is not exactly analogous to what we know about the journey of healing from sexual abuse, it is unquestionably useful and reflects common principles in the natural order. Perhaps this is especially true when considering *non*-healing. Imagine that it brings shame to have a flesh wound. *Imagine that the person in your family who dispenses materials from the first aid kit is also the one who wounded you.* Or, perhaps the person who wounded you or saw you get wounded told you that you would be punished for approaching the trusted person with the needed first aid kit. Shame hides. Fear submits. You don't want to experience further shame from having a flesh wound and you fear those in power over you. Naturally, you make efforts to hide the wound without tending to it. It festers, gets dirty, and becomes infected. As it gets worse, it consumes more of your attention. It refuses to stop speaking no matter how much effort you put toward silencing it. An infection may even spread to other parts of your body, causing increased danger, until you are finally forced to seek help. Or, maybe you take just good enough care of it to prevent spread of infection, but by not protecting it and allowing it to heal, the wound and ensuing scar becomes deeper.

Considering Phases of Healing

Reducing a complex process of healing into simple stages runs the risk of becoming formulaic and *reductionistic, especially because wounds from sexual abuse are uncommonly bound to specific, past episodes. *Often sexual abuse is ongoing and its ripples of impact are pervasive.* Nonetheless, there is a sequence of typical healing phases, which broadly include safety, remembering, mourning, and reconnecting. It is important, maybe even hope inspiring, both for survivors and their helping communities, to recognize and promote a survivor's journey into these vital aspects of healing. In order to resist thinking of them as discrete steps of a simple process, consider the phases of recovery as interrelated anchors of the healing process.

SAFETY VERSUS SILENCE

The first phase of healing could also be considered a *pre-condition* for healing to begin. It is safety, juxtaposed here with silence. The complexity of efforts to re-establish safety for a survivor of sexual abuse reflects the severity, chronicity, and circumstances (e.g., age of onset, relationship to perpetrator, etc.) of the abuse. Silence can be an omission of mention or an active attempt to conceal. In either case, silence upholds the *status quo.* A wound requires acknowledgement and attention, as soon as possible, to the time of injury. It requires immediate notice and protection from continued danger. Regrettably, silence around one's experience of sexual abuse is unfortunately, pervasive. This perpetuates the ill effects of abuse, vulnerability to continued abuse, and precludes seeking safety as silence always serves the interests of the abuser rather than the abused.

Pursuing safety is an intrapersonal, environmental, and interpersonal endeavor of empowerment. Survivors of trauma often experience prolonged physiological activation of the *"fight or flight" arousal mechanisms of the *sympathetic nervous system. *Their bodies can send ongoing indicators of danger, even when the source of the trauma has been removed.* To feel safe in his or her own body again, a survivor needs to establish life-affirming rhythms of sleep, eating, and exercise; after being in an ongoing state of *hyperarousal, it often feels foreign and even uncomfortable for a survivor to establish these rhythms. In fact, it is not uncommon for a trauma survivor to resist rhythms of *"normalization"; he or she has learned to appreciate the adaptive aspects of *hypervigilance.

At an extreme, attempting to restore natural rhythms may be resisted because it takes voice away from a trauma that is still calling out for justice. This is where the phases of safety and remembering begin to intermingle. *Part of remembering is converting an unspeakable story into one that has permission to be told and promise to be heard.* In addition to various therapeutic approaches, including *mindfulness training and *behavioral techniques aimed at relaxation and stress reduction, *psychotropic medications are often helpful in restoring a sense of safety within one's own body.

As an environmental and interpersonal endeavor, safety is the process of establishing healing contexts, including places and relationships. Establishing environmental and interpersonal safety requires one to assess whether one's home is a place of refuge or a place of potential (re)traumatization. It looks for new places of refuge. It honors the survivor's need for a unique combination of being alone and being together with certain others. *Paradoxically, because survivors of sexual abuse have become accustomed to unsafe circumstances, which are out of their control, they are more likely to resist environmental changes, even when these changes promote their safety.* This is because change itself introduces unpredictable threats. It is essential to respect a survivor's autonomy in deciding how fast and in what direction to move toward environmental safety.

As an interpersonal endeavor, safety establishes protective physical and emotional boundaries, including plans for future protection, between survivors and perpetrators. It is much easier to talk about safe boundaries between a survivor and perpetrator if we are addressing isolated incidents of assault. Understandably, this issue becomes incredibly complicated when a survivor is still in relationship with the perpetrator. In the experience of incest, this is not unlikely. Moreover, survivors often experience continued dependency on incest perpetrators because of financial realities, or pressures related to maintaining a family's "good social standing." Sometimes, survivors seek help in the context of family or couple's counseling. *Caregivers and friends need to be attuned to potential patterns of *coercive control between the perpetrator and adult survivor, not assuming that safety has been established.* Establishing protective boundaries between a survivor and perpetrator begins with increasing the survivor's range of autonomy. This includes, for example, building new social support networks and building increased financial autonomy, thereby reducing dependency of the survivor on the perpetrator.

Although it was stated that these phases of healing do not fall into a simple, linear model, *it is crucial to address a survivor's need for safety as a precondition for the other aspects of healing work.* A survivor needs to feel safe enough in their own body, in their environment, and in their relationship with others *before they have the emotional capacity to face the task of remembering.* There are two important caveats to this "order." First, as mentioned above, resistance to letting go of hyperarousal symptoms is complicated by their distinctive role in telling a story of trauma that is otherwise unspeakable, thus the promise of remembering and retelling in a way continues to facilitate this letting go. Second, feelings of *un-safety* are often *triggered through the subsequent phase of remembering, thus creating a cyclical need to re-explore and re-affirm conditions of safety.

Remembering versus Forgetting

There is no question that the phase of remembering is the most difficult part of the healing process; survivors and anyone in a position to help them face the enormous temptation to circumvent the remembering process. This part of the healing process is the most difficult because of the excruciating pain connected to one's experiences of sexual victimization. Memories of traumatic experiences are often *pre-narrative in nature; the survivor experiences *somatic symptoms and *"frozen" visual memories, but they are not able to connect them into a coherent and meaningful narrative.

In many ways, the disjointed pieces of traumatic memories are very similar to the survivor's experience of self: fragmented, sometimes *dissociative, and incomplete. In contrast, healing leads to restoration of one's wholeness. *There is a long history—significantly predating psychological practice and research—of understanding healing to mean wholeness.* For example, in the New Testament story of blind Bartimaeus (Mark 10:46–52), the Greek word *sózó* (v. 52) that Jesus uses to declare the blind man's healing is alternatively translated by the English words "heal," "make well," and "make whole." Because the man was not described as blind from birth (cf. John 9:1), his request to "see again" (v. 51) is indeed a healing restoration.

Freud would later begin to articulate the role of remembering in restoring a person's wholeness. Representing the most central part of the healing process, the word *remember* illustrates what healing is. Consider the core part of the word: *member.* Members of a body, or self, are each important parts, which create a whole person. Traumatic experiences destroy the unity of a person's members and *it is only through integrating these memories into one's life story (i.e., re-membering) that they can experience a whole, integrated sense of self again.*

Because of the atrocities revealed in traumatic memories, it may seem paradoxical that "recovering" and "working through" these stories serve one's wholeness. Wouldn't it serve a person better to banish traumatic memories from consciousness and only embrace the healthy parts of one's story? This perspective underlies the myth of healing that one should forget and move past the hurt—"forgetting what is behind" (Phil 3:13)—and just "forgive and forget." But ignored wounds don't heal themselves. This is where the analogy of the healing process of a physical wound may be particularly apt. The physical wound is inescapably a reality. Once it has happened, it simply *is*, like it or not. If one chooses to ignore or deny it, it still exists and finds ways to speak and cause pain. It must be cared for and protected. *If dealt with appropriately, the wound heals into a scar, which is incorporated into the new reality of the healed person.* It is only through facing the reality of the injury that it can properly heal. If a wound has been improperly dealt with or ignored, sometimes it needs to be re-opened and cleansed in order for adequate healing to take place. Though full of immense pain and grief, therapeutic remembering of past traumas is like touching a sensitive past wound *in order to re-set the conditions adequate for healing.*

Some Guidelines on Remembering

Since this chapter is dedicated to addressing what healing is and is not, it is far beyond its scope to adequately address therapeutic guidelines for the remembering work of sexual abuse survivors. Moreover, there are many helpful therapeutic methods designed to facilitate trauma survivors' ability to tell and *integrate* their story of abuse into their narrative of self. However, a few considerations should be noted. First, although safety is truly a precondition for remembering, the two "anchors" of healing continually go hand-in-hand. A survivor's sense of safety in their own body and environment needs to be continually re-assessed and established for the productive and healing work of remembering. For most people, this work of remembering produces an increase in *symptomatic distress; the survivor committed to healing must be prepared to tolerate this sense of "being-more-ill" for a time. As pieces come together, pain often increases, for there is more of the person's *re*-membered life to hurt now.

The remembering work takes effort and intentionality. It does not happen spontaneously or freely but requires planning and preparation by the survivor, therapist, and support community. Most people are able to engage in the tasks of remembering in the context of their everyday lives, provided that they are not experiencing major transitions or life crises. However, others benefit from significant modifications of their everyday lives (e.g., taking on less responsibilities, taking time off work, obtaining concrete support for things like childcare, and even planned hospital stays). Although specific treatments for specific traumas (e.g., combat stress and *post-traumatic stress disorder [PTSD]) have established timeframes within which the remembering work can occur, the experiences of sexual abuse survivors are rarely discrete traumatic events. Correspondingly, the work of remembering is significantly more complex.

MOURNING AND LAMENT VERSUS RECONCILIATION

Remembering sexual abuse introduces pain and awareness of the injustice of victimization. There are no words to describe the awful and devastating impact of sexual abuse on God's creation of sexual, spiritual, and relational persons. This is especially poignant when considering the impact to children who are in the most formative processes of discovering and building their selves, their sexuality, and their capacity for relationships, and who are, in many cases, dependent on the very people who have perpetrated sexual violence against them. *Because of the reprehensible realities faced in the work of remembering, mourning what has been damaged and lost is a natural and necessary response.*

When healing sexual abuse, it is likely an artificial distinction to discuss remembering apart from mourning. Mourning, as a psychological process, could be described as remembering *with *affect*. In the process of healing, the survivor remembers the traumatic events that took place and proceeds to mourn what that trauma has stolen. Among many elements, a survivor remembers the coercive relationship with a perpetrator of sexual trauma and experiences sorrow over the losses of protection, innocence, and meaningful relationship. *Mourning is a repetitive process, as the survivor remembers the trauma bit-by-bit and re-activates the emotions associated with mourning in its various phases.*[13]

Gradually, as the survivor comes face-to-face with the un-erasable reality of yesterday, they mourn the pieces of life that have been betrayed or destroyed—that, if it were in a benevolent person's control, would be re-written. But these pieces cannot be re-written, so mourning affords a person the necessary opportunity to imagine and contemplate the pieces of life that were lost, come to meaningfully describe the person they've become, *and gradually shift the energy from remembering what was lost into dreaming about who they are becoming in the process of healing.* The survivor is a person who has integrated their experience of victimization into the broader, whole reality as a healed person. It is somewhat paradoxical that focusing on what was lost allows the survivor the redemptive opportunity to release it and move forward with hope for creating a future. This only makes sense when considering the alternative, which is to unconsciously allow the devastation of the abuse to define and "win." *When childhood losses of things such as protection and innocence are not recognized, named, and mourned, one's self-concept and life-reality are overwhelmingly informed by the betrayal, violation, and shame associated with that abuse.* Such healing is neither simple nor quick.

Lament in Remembering and Mourning

Mourning is the most appropriate psychological experience to describe what accompanies remembering. However, it falls short of capturing the ancient Hebrew tradition of *lament, which arguably should be recovered in the work of survivors and communities of worship. Chapters of sexual abuse in many people's lives represent years that the "locusts have eaten."[14] The call back to the Lord with "fasting and weeping and mourning" (Joel 1:8–14) as the prophet Joel describes to Israel, is also an appropriate description of the opportunity and responsibility of survivors and their communities to acknowledge and cry out to God about the injustice of sexual abuse. South African theologian Denise Ackermann[15] describes lament as the language of not only victims, but of the penitent (cf. Pss 32, 57:1–4). It is simultaneously expectant of God to render mercy and compassion while complaining and accusing God of injustices (cf. Psalm 88). *Lament cries out to the Lord because it refuses to settle with the way things are; it calls on God to act* (cf. Psalm 44).

---

13. "Stages of grief" described by Elisabeth Kübler Ross include: *denial, anger, bargaining, *depression, and acceptance (Kübler Ross, *On Death and Dying*).

14. See the first few chapters of Joel (e.g., 1:4–7), particularly 2:25.

15. Ackermann, *After the Locusts*, 120.

Cries of lament, depicted especially well in the Psalms, navigate voices of anger and accusation, but also hope, trust, and praise (cf. Ps 13:1–4, 5–6). This is not a contradiction. One laments because one has a relationship with God. Thus, lament captures what Ackermann describes as:

> [A] profoundly serious understanding of the nature of relationship [between God and his people]. One can risk making honest statements about despair and grief at the same time one affirms all that is good and trustworthy about the relationship . . . [and this] acts as a safeguard against censoring our prayer.[16]

Echoing this, Walter Brueggemann argues that without a vocabulary of lament, God's covenantal relationship with his people is no longer genuine because the second party becomes voiceless, or at least restricted to praise and doxology.[17] He states that "celebrative, consenting silence does not square with reality" and that "covenant, minus lament is . . . a practice of denial, cover-up, and pretense, which sanctions social control."[18] The experiences of mourning and lament both suggest total acknowledgment and awareness of injustice. They do not let God, or perpetrators of violence, off the hook, *actively pursuing not only restoration but also justice.*

Forgiveness and Reconciliation

The role of *forgiveness and reconciliation between victims and perpetrators introduces a discussion that is beyond the purview of this chapter. These are complex and commonly misunderstood issues. For the purposes of this discussion, suffice it to say that *healing for the survivor of sexual abuse does not imply or require reconciliation with the perpetrator.* Reconciliation is liable to compromise the emotional, relational, or physical safety of the victim. There is a strong Christian ethic that brothers and sisters in the body of Christ must be reconciled to each other as we are reconciled to God through Christ Jesus (2 Cor 5:18–19). In practice, however, this ethic can be *mis*-applied in such a way that *victims are "bullied" into reconciliation with perpetrators who have not taken total responsibility for the effects of their abuse.* To let go of visions of *vengeance while lamenting the wrongdoing allows a victim to become a survivor, scar and all; reconciliation with the offending party, however, is not usually an appropriate part of the healing process.

RECONNECTING VERSUS ISOLATING

Although reconciliation with the offending party is not part of healing, reconnection to oneself, to others, and to life is essential to healing. This is a future-oriented aspect of healing, focused on creatively reaching into the depths of the survivor's own God-given beauty and power, and reaching out to sustaining and meaningful connections with others. The process of remembering and mourning in a context of therapeutic and community support allows a survivor to regain some capacity for trust. Slowly he or she learns

---

16. Ibid., 116.
17. Brueggemann, "The Costly Loss of Lament," 57–71.
18. Ibid., 60.

to engage this capacity in endeavors of reconnection with others. The survivor learns to reclaim and express his or her own sexuality and personhood.

Though no longer a victim beneath the power of others' violence, a survivor may feel like a foreigner in the world of freedom. Reconnection is a journey in this new world, a journey with moments of triumph, awkwardness, and risk-taking. *In the journey of inward and outward reconnection, the survivor faces a process of learning to be oneself while learning to be with others, and experience life-giving interdependence with others.* A survivor experiences a new "coming of age" through adolescence and into the adulthood of his or her self in the world.

A survivor of sexual abuse is not naïve to the potential for exploitation and victimization in human relationships. The tender scars that they carry serve as reminders of the precious vulnerabilities of life, a vulnerability that they are learning to honor and selectively entrust to others. The healing around the contours of the scar is a testament to the restoration that has taken place. The joy that survivors experience in re-discovering human relationships that protect, honor, and trust becomes less and less confusing and more real, more possible.

Healing is a dynamic process of reaching in and reaching out. Wholly committed to establishing safety, thus following the survivor's own pace and rhythm in experiences of aloneness and togetherness, healing finally allows the survivor to cautiously and hopefully engage risks of connection. But this experience of reconnection is a totally different experience than the perverted connections of dependency, manipulation, and exploitation that marked their abuse. Reconnection is guided by an inner compass of discernment; this inner compass gives one the power to say yes and no. Though fully guided by the survivor's inner compass, empowered reconnection with others is facilitated by a community ethic of "speakability," where acknowledgment of the devastating presence of sexual abuse is not hidden but *publically* lamented; answers are vigorously and continuously sought because of the precious importance of protecting and preventing sexual abuse wounds.

HOPE VERSUS FEAR

Finally, though not part of a sequential understanding of the tasks of sexual abuse, healing is marked by an encounter with hope, over and above the traumatic fear experienced in abuse. The discussion on hope versus fear is essentially a declaration of how the other healing components of safety, remembrance, mourning, and reconnection work to establish this hope for the survivor of sexual abuse. Embracing one's identity as a "survivor" rather than a "victim" resonates with this dynamic of hope. Fear is characteristic of the static, frozen, traumatic memories and *flashbacks that have not yet become a meaningful narrative of the survivor's life story. Fear is a hypervigilant and fearful self-protective state. The hyperarousal of the sympathetic nervous system is adaptive because it recognizes valid danger, but it is not a state of peace, wholeness, or healing.

Hope, on the other hand, should not be misunderstood as a naïve and undiscerning openness. The "anchors" of the healing process described in this chapter are anchors that convert generalized fear and hyperarousal from trauma into the wisdom of hope. Hope says yes to life with the wisdom accompanied by judicious awareness of the potential for evil and exploitation. Consistent with the language of lament, the psalmists capture the multidimensional poetry of hope in their simultaneous protest against evil and cry for justice with their enduring hope that reaching out to the Lord *will* be fruitful.

SOME FUTURE DIRECTIONS

The process of healing for the sexual abuse survivor cannot erase the destruction of yesterday's abuse; it is not possible to "undo" the harm committed. However, the devastating wounds of sexual abuse, when afforded the necessary conditions for healing, gradually give way to tender scars. Healing is about care, not cure. Healing takes place when the survivor's wound is seen, heard, believed, and cared for. The scars that remain are memorials to the violation of sexual abuse. They remind survivors of life's preciousness and vulnerability. The person with such a scar has learned to handle their vulnerabilities with care, to listen to their own voice of discernment, and to selectively trust others.

Moving forward, key areas to note include the need to rehabilitate lament, and for a holistic approach to forgiveness. McFarlane and van der Kolk state the apparent challenge that the church faces:

> [Although] external validation about the reality of a traumatic experience in a safe and supportive context is a vital aspect of preventing and treating posttraumatic stress . . . the creation of such a context of recovery can become very complicated when the psychological needs of victims and the needs of their social network conflict.[19]

If only praise and doxology are encouraged to fill the public life of the church, venues for healing are reduced to "underground" *support groups. The language of lament may allow the church to square with reality in such a way that space is created for the narratives of sexual abuse survivors and a two-way covenantal relationship with the living God is revived. Acknowledgment of the devastation caused by sexual abuse condemns abuse and honors the preciousness of God-given life.

There is growing literature on forgiveness (more recently within psychology). Generally, survivors of sexual trauma do not like the term forgiveness, except those steeped in a Christian tradition. If victimization is assumed, which reflects a power imbalance between the victim and perpetrator, the question of whether a victim even has the *power* to forgive could be raised. On the other hand, some sort of "letting go" is inevitably part of moving on from the pain of victimization and into the hope of healing. Mentioned in this chapter only in connection to *mis*-applications of reconciliation, forgiveness by survivors of sexual abuse, and the complexities involved, is appropriately explored in other chapters.

---

19. McFarlane and van der Kolk, "Trauma and Its Challenge to Society," 25.

QUESTIONS FOR DISCUSSION

1. The author argues that it is not possible to remain neutral in situations of sexual violence—one person against another—and that we unavoidably take "sides," *for* or *against* the abused. What are some reasons why people side with the perpetrator? What does this communicate to the abused? What does it look like to side with the abused? Consider the most recent example of sexual abuse you know of: what elements of this chapter help illuminate the struggle of that survivor to find safety and community understanding? If you are a survivor, what phase of the healing process do/did you most resonate with?

2. The point was raised in this chapter that there is no space for the narratives of victims in a community that protects individuals in power and their systems. What are some ways the church can facilitate the social accountability required to "call out" the powerful, thereby creating space for the stories of the wounded to be named, heard, believed, and acted upon? Considering some survivors you know, what were some complicating factors keeping their "voice" from being heard or appropriately respected? If you are a survivor, what elements of this chapter give you encouragement for your healing journey?

3. The author suggests that Freud shifted "listening perspectives" when he recanted his earlier position in which he had believed survivors' accounts of exploitation in favor of focusing on his patient's own sexual excitement and fantasy. What "listening perspectives" have you encountered in the faith community? What "listening perspectives" would be most conducive to healing for sexual abuse survivors? What "listening perspectives" can therapists and clergy uniquely create together?

4. It is suggested in this chapter that the work of remembering and mourning past traumas, though excruciating, is akin to touching or cleaning a sensitive past wound in order to "re-set" the conditions adequate for healing. List some spiritual or psychological myths about healing you have observed that get in the way of cleaning and setting necessary conditions for healing.

5. How could the faith community, by re-discovering the practice of lament, become a catalyst for fostering the healing of silent wounds in the church? Do some research: what types of "healing services" are already out there for survivors? What key elements could be included in a "healing service" for survivors of sexual abuse? Talk to some survivors about what healing practices they've found. Why don't we see more of these practices and services in our churches? What kinds of healing practices could therapists use more often or more effectively?

FOR FURTHER READING

Allender, Dan. *The Wounded Heart: Hope for Adult Victims of Childhood Sexual Abuse.* Colorado Springs, CO: NavPress, 2008.

Brueggemann, Walter. "The Costly Loss of Lament." *Journal for the Study of the Old Testament* 36 (1986): 57–71.

Herman, Judith. *Trauma and Recovery: The Aftermath of Violence—From Domestic Abuse to Political Terror.* New York, NY: Basic Books, 1997.

Kleber, Rolf, Charles Figley, Berthold Gersons, eds. *Beyond Trauma: Cultural and Societal Dynamics.* New York, NY: Plenum Press, 1995.

Langberg, Diane Mandt. *Counseling Survivors of Sexual Abuse.* NP: Xulon Press, 2003.

_____. *On the Threshold of Hope: Opening the Door to Healing for Survivors of Sexual Abuse.* Wheaton, IL: Tyndale, 1999.

Fuller Rogers, Daléne. *Pastoral Care for Post-Traumatic Stress Disorder: Healing the Shattered Soul.* New York, NY: The Haworth Pastoral Press, 2002.

van der Kolk, Bessel. *Psychological Trauma.* Washington, DC: American Psychiatric Publishing, 1987.

_____, et al. *Traumatic Stress: The Effects of Overwhelming Experience on Mind, Body, and Society.* New York, NY: Guilford, 2007.

Wolterstorff, Nicholas. "If God is Good and Sovereign, Why Lament?" *Calvin Theological Journal* (2001): 42–52.

20

Healing the Wounded Heart
through Ritual and Liturgy

Accompanying the Abused in their Healing

JAMES B. GOULD, MA

FIFTEEN YEARS LATER JENNA still talks about the service of healing held at her church. She was sexually abused as a child, and as an adult, spent several years in therapy. But the worship service had special significance in her recovery. "The humiliation and shame of abuse is incredible," Jenna says. "It's like wearing a scarlet letter—'A' for abused." *The power of the service, for her, was the public acknowledgment.* "I was no longer isolated. I no longer had to carry it all alone. There were others to say 'I'm sad with you. I'm angry with you.'"

This chapter explores how *liturgy and *ritual can be used to name, interpret, and heal the emotional and spiritual wounds of *sexual abuse (SA). I briefly identify *survivor needs—personal, social, and theological—that requires healing. I then explain the elements and purpose of liturgy and ritual. Finally, I review examples of rituals for public worship, small groups, and individual use. While healing liturgy cannot substitute for good *psychotherapy, both pastoral care and professional counseling are means of healing that God uses.

THE SURVIVOR'S BROKENNESS

In the beginning God created all things good. Psychologically, we are meant to experience inner harmony. Socially, we are meant to enjoy strong relationships. Spiritually, we are meant to know and love God. But, because of sin, the world is not the way it should be. Psychologically, the *Fall brings mental and emotional disintegration. Socially, the Fall causes alienation between people. Spiritually, the Fall breaks communion with God. Sin brings destruction to all aspects of human existence.

The Search for Self

The wounds of sexual abuse are emotional, relational, and spiritual.[1] First, recovery involves a *search for self*. Survivors often feel *self-loathing. They view themselves as unclean and dirty, as valueless and inadequate, as defective and flawed. Survivors also experience self-doubt. As victims, they were powerless and helpless. They may blame themselves for letting the abuse happen. This self-hatred and shame, the humiliation of thinking that they are worthless and unloveable, needs healing. Self-rejection must be replaced by self-respect—knowledge that they are a child of God's love, a person with value and rights.

The Search for Community

Second, recovery involves a *search for community*. Often as victims of someone they trusted, survivors learned to feel insecure rather than safe and to approach others with suspicion and anxiety. They became isolated, caught in a web of secrecy and silence. The result is "disenfranchised grief"—grief that "*is not or cannot be openly acknowledged, publicly mourned or socially supported*."[2] Abuse grief is socially disenfranchised; survivors feel alone, exiled from their families and faith communities. Healing means learning to trust which requires a welcoming, safe place where they experience connection rather than isolation.

The Search for God

Third, recovery involves a *search for God*. Believing in and connecting with God is difficult since the God who promised to be faithful did not stop the violence. In the "victory only" spirituality of many churches, *abuse grief is theologically disenfranchised since anger at and questioning of God are signs of spiritual weakness*.[3] To heal, survivors must learn the language of *lament and rethink simplistic views about God and evil. Three beliefs are necessary to address disappointment with God.[4] First, *God does not send us our pain*. God is not the source of evil, and abuse is not part of God's plan for anyone's life. Second, *God enters our pain and shares it with us*. God does not stand apart, indifferent and unconcerned. Instead, God's emotional life includes the suffering of creation—even the pain of sexual abuse. In clinical practice Rick Meyer has found that "only a God who is familiar with . . . sufferings will be allowed to come close . . . Only a God who knows pain . . . can provide healing."[5] Third, *God is able to bring deep healing and transformation from within*. Instead of willing or preventing evil, God works to restore wholeness and to bring good out of bad.

---

1. This outline of survivor needs draws on Poling, *The Abuse of Power*, and Schmutzer, "Spiritual Formation and Sexual Abuse: Embodiment, Community and Healing," 67–86.
2. Doka, "Disenfranchised Grief," 272; emphasis added.
3. The expression "victory only" comes from Manning, *Don't Take My Grief Away*, 78.
4. These three points come from Wuellner, *Heart of Healing, Heart of Light*, ch. 2.
5. Meyer, *Through the Fire*, 10, 13.

Sexual abuse wounds and misshapes the whole person. The survivor's healing requires finding a self that is valuable, a community that is trustworthy, and a God who is faithful.

THE HEALING POWER OF LITURGY AND RITUAL

Redemption is God's action to restore wholeness. The Hebrew Scripture proclaims God's desire for *shalom*—complete well-being within individuals, among people and with God. Holistic redemption was the focus of Jesus' mission (Luke 4:16–21), and his miracles brought healing—physical strength, emotional freedom, social reincorporation, and friendship with God. Throughout history the people of God have practiced liturgies and rituals that continue God's redemptive work. *Healing is a process of activities that enables recovery from wounding and moves a person toward the wholeness God intends.* Healing liturgies and rituals, then, are worship services and personal disciplines that acknowledge brokenness and move a person toward wholeness by bringing God's redemptive love to their needs.[6] James White says that "for centuries, the liturgy, actively celebrated, has been the most important form of pastoral care," the chief means of helping people in times of crisis.[7]

The Elements of Liturgy and Ritual

Liturgy consists of the forms and ceremonies that structure a worship service. The traditional four-fold pattern includes: (1) the gathering, (2) the proclamation of the Word, (3) Holy Communion, (2) and the dismissal. *Rituals*, on the other hand, are structured events that create and express meaning through the use of tangible symbols and physical actions.[8] Communication, in which people give themselves to each other, occurs in two ways—*verbally through words and non-verbally through symbols and actions*. God gives to us in the same ways, and so liturgy includes both speech acts and bodily acts.

Liturgy in the Verbal Element

Human beings have word-shaped psyches.[9] As intellectual beings we are shaped by linguistic acts. The ideas we believe form our understandings of self, others, and God. *Because abuse imprisons survivors in distorted beliefs, healing requires replacing lies with truth.* Kendra Hotz and Matthew Matthews point out that language has the power to shape reality: "language is a living, dynamic, creative force that organizes the world for us conceptually." Through immersion in the words of worship we "come to construe reality in particular ways . . . and to act in particular ways."[10]

God's word is powerful (Isah 55:10–11; Jer 23:29). Its truth sets us free from false ideas (John 8:32). It cuts to the center of our being, bringing wholeness to our identities

---

6. Evans, *Healing Liturgies for the Seasons of Life*, xv, and Peterman, *Speaking to Silence*, ch. 1 and 2.

7. White, *Sacraments as God's Self-Giving*, 117.

8. While liturgy and ritual are not identical, I will use the terms interchangeably.

9. This phrase comes from Roberts, *Taking the Word to Heart*, 293.

10. Hotz and Matthews, *Shaping the Christian Life*, 70–71.

(Heb 4:12). It corrects us by straightening and realigning crooked beliefs (2 Tim 3:16). In liturgy God communicates verbally in the reading of Scripture and in preaching, as well as through words of *forgiveness, assurance, and encouragement spoken to us in God's name by other people. Simon Chan notes that the reading of Scripture and preaching are sacramental events which are "permeated with God's saving presence . . . When the sacred scriptures are read in the church, God himself speaks to his people, and Christ, present in his own word, proclaims the gospel."[11] Through music, liturgy is also enhanced.[12] The words of worship are acts of interpretation that teach us essential truths about ourselves, others, and God, and let us see our lives in new ways—disrupting the competing narratives about who we are.[13]

Liturgy in the Non-Verbal Element

As *embodied beings, we also need material means of grace. "We are," Ronald Byars says, "whole persons who are formed not only by what we hear but also by what we experience—what we touch, what we feel, what we smell, what we eat, what we say, what we sing, what we do, how we move."[14] Images and gestures organize our understandings in ways that cannot be captured by literal propositions and abstract concepts. "The Bible is full of accounts of God's use of actions and physical objects as means of self-revelation. Jeremiah wears a yoke or smashes a clay pot. Jesus places a child in the midst of a crowd. Actions become means of God's coming to us."[15]

The Contribution of Symbols

God still becomes present to us and does things in our lives through symbolic objects and expressive actions—lit candles, holy oil, baptismal water, bread and wine. John Calvin says that rituals "impart spiritual things under visible ones."[16] Tilda Norberg and Robert Webber elaborate: "through prayer and the laying on of hands, through confession, anointing, the sacraments, and other means of grace, Jesus meets us in our brokenness and pain and there loves, transforms, forgives, redeems, resurrects, and heals."[17]

Tangible symbols are material objects and visual aids that express meaning. Symbols are complex, multidimensional, and packed with significance. *Icons, banners, and sacred art engage us emotionally and evoke meanings that cannot easily be put into words.* A cru-

11. Chan, *Liturgical Theology*, 134, 137.

12. Because it joins mind and heart, conscious and unconscious, music is an essential part of public worship. Many hymns, by affirming God's faithfulness, love, and healing presence in every moment, help survivors (e.g., "Breathe on me, Breathe of God"; "There is a Balm in Gilead"; "Precious Lord, Take My Hand"; "Healer of Our Every Ill"). But using only upbeat, happy music will inevitably alienate the abused by denying their feelings of doubt, anger, isolation, and abandonment. Songs like African-American spirituals, which weave together anguish and faith, are also necessary ("Kumbaya"; "Nobody Knows the Trouble I've Seen"; "When Israel Was in Egypt's Land"). See Epperly, *Healing Worship*, 66–68; Evans, *Healing Liturgies*, 9–11; Peterman, *Speaking to Silence*, 23–25.

13. Anderson and Foley, *Mighty Stories, Dangerous Rituals*, 5–7, 119–125.

14. Byars, *The Future of Protestant Worship*, 75.

15. White, *Sacraments*, 26.

16. Calvin, *Institutes of the Christian Religion*, 1361.

17. Norberg and Webber, *Stretch Out Your Hand*, 15.

cifix of Jesus, arms stretched open in wide embrace, reassures us of God's love. Burning candles remind us that the light of Christ, which no human pain or doubt can extinguish, shines in darkness. Consecrated oil soaks us with God's blessing.

Rituals also involve *physical actions* that we do. We sign ourselves with the cross, we kneel in humility, and we eat bread and drink wine. These bodily movements and physical gestures have deep meaning. In *passing the peace we do more than say "hello;" we offer God's *shalom* to our hurting neighbors. When we form a healing circle around someone and lay hands on them, we surround them with our care and the assurance that they are encircled by God's love. In anointing, "the touch of the hand, the saying of the name, the fragrance of the oil, remind each one that he or she is a precious child of God."[18] Smashing a plate, tearing a piece of fabric, or marking our bodies with ashes signify devastation and brokenness, while lighting a candle or planting a seed express hope in a new future and God's healing power. In addition to intellectual reflection and verbal expression, symbolic rituals help us express our feelings to God and to experience God's self-giving to us.

It is important to emphasize that *in liturgy God acts*. Ritual is more than remembering how God acted in the past. Rather, through word and sacrament, God comes to us in the present and does something to make us whole. As Nicholas Wolterstorff puts it, "to participate in the liturgy is to enter the sphere of God's action—not just the sphere of God's presence but the sphere of God's action, and not just God's past action but God's present action."[19] The concept of *anamnesis* captures this. When Jews reenact the Passover, they are taking part in what happened then, and in the Eucharist Christians are present at the cross and empty tomb, participating here and now in those saving events. As St. Thomas Aquinas says, ritual and the sacraments "not only signify, but also cause, grace."[20]

The Purposes of Liturgy and Ritual

Meaning is Created

Liturgy and rituals serve several important purposes.[21] First, they *create meaning*. Elaine Ramshaw says that through liturgy "we express the deepest meanings we know of, and often meanings deeper than we consciously know."[22] *This fundamental need to make meaning of experience is strongest in times of crisis and transition*; "the need for ritual expression and reinforcement of the symbolic worldview is intensified in situations which threaten meaning and coherence."[23] Emil Fackenheim makes a helpful distinction between root experiences and epoch-making experiences.[24] A *root experience* (such as the exodus or resurrection) is the key historical event of God's presence and action that creates a

18. Byars, *Future of Protestant Worship*, 112.

19. Wolterstorff, "The Remembrance of Things (not) Past," 153; also, White, *Sacraments*, 33, 43, 55.

20. St. Thomas Aquinas, *Summa Theologica*, 2356.

21. This section draws on Anderson and Foley, *Mighty Stories*, ch. 1, 2 and 3; Ramshaw, *Ritual and Pastoral Care*, ch. 1; and Peterman, *Speaking to Silence*, ch. 1.

22. Ramshaw, *Ritual*, 25.

23. Ibid.

24. Fackenheim, *God's Presence in History*.

people's foundational understanding. An *epoch-making experience* (such as the exile or crucifixion), by contrast, is a historical event that challenges and threatens to undermine those core beliefs.

In times of trouble, our experiences of pain threaten to completely define our stories. But for people of faith it is root experiences, not immediate traumas, that must shape our outlook on life. Scripture is the narrative of divine faithfulness in which hope is rooted. While the survivor's experience is real, it is not the source of their identity. Liturgy connects us to the narrative of God's faithfulness, and by "weaving together the human and the divine, enables us to hear our own stories retold with clarity and new possibility."[25]

EMOTION IS EXPRESSED

Second, liturgy and ritual *express emotion*. Janet Jacobs says that ritual, in a context of connection to others, *provides secure boundaries in which to acknowledge, express, and resolve emotional pain*.[26] In particular, liturgy allows dissonance and ambivalence. Janet Peterman suggests that "one of ritual's greatest strengths is its capacity to help us embrace powerful and even contradictory emotions . . . We may want both to cry out against injustice and to sing praises about God's presence with us through the most difficult days of our lives."[27] Ritual allows expression of anger and doubt while reinforcing a basic attitude of faith and trust. *It both displays emotion and structures it, thereby containing it and keeping us from being overwhelmed by it*.[28]

Those wounded by sexual abuse must express both grief and hope. In times of suffering and doubt, people of faith often adopt silence or pretense.[29] "In the Old Testament," however, "from beginning to end," Claus Westermann says, "the 'call of distress,' the 'cry out of the depths,' that is, the lament, is an inevitable part of what happens between God" and people.[30] Martin Marty observes that lament is not merely a "crying out" in pain, but is a "crying toward" a God who listens and cares. Lament is thus an act of faith, a movement toward God rather than an expression of unfaith and a turning away from God (e.g., Psalms 117, 131).[31]

Instead of retreating into silence or pretending that all is well, survivors whose lives are broken must speak their sadness and anger to the God *who knows their feelings anyway*. Rituals can contribute to emotional healing by promoting trust in God. Liturgy can bring psychological and spiritual strength and helps survivors live with hope and trust rather than anxiety and despair. Meaningful ritual must be both honest and hopeful. "It

25. Anderson and Foley, *Mighty Stories*, 18, 7.

26. Jacobs, "Religious Ritual and Mental Health," 291, 298.

27. Peterman, *Speaking to Silence*, 9–10; also Ramshaw, *Ritual*, 69, 33.

28. Driver, *The Magic of Ritual*, 156.

29. Brueggemann, *The Psalms and the Life of Faith*, 69.

30. Westermann, *Praise and Lament in the Psalms*, 261; also Billman and Migliore, *Rachel's Cry*, and Henderson, *Liturgies of Lament*.

31. Marty, *Cry of Absence*, 112.

makes room for the contradictory and painful in our lives, yet it generates a kind of hope and freedom that allow us to retell the story . . . in life-affirming ways."[32]

Transition and Transformation are Encouraged

Third, liturgy and ritual *enable transition* and *effect transformation*. In times of loss and life change, ritual helps us mark endings and beginnings. Rites of passage like graduation or marriage, for example, move people from one identity and life season to another. According to Tom Driver, a ritual is a *transformative* performance designed to change a situation.[33] The Christian sacraments, he suggests, are performances of freedom and healing. The message of the gospel is liberation (Luke 4:16–21) and Jesus' entire ministry displayed God's action in alleviating suffering and restoring wholeness. Liturgy and rituals:

> [A]re instruments for bringing nearer to fulfillment the freedom that God has promised to the world, which Christians see in the story of Jesus' life, message, death and resurrection. Hence a Christian sacrament may be defined as an action of God together with the people of God, ritually performed to celebrate freedom and to hasten the liberation of the whole world.[34]

Liturgy and ritual are also *confessional* performances.[35] To confess is to say where one stands and what one is and chooses to be. *By speaking truth, by bringing what is shameful and hidden into the light of personal and social recognition, survivors lose their old identity and adopt a new one.* For healing to occur, victims of abuse must speak truth.

Support is Provided

Fourth, liturgy and ritual *provide support*. Because we are relational beings, pain is acknowledged and hope is nurtured in community. White points out that "the presence of a community of faith in our [grief] is a strong statement of support and love . . . God's self-giving is experienced socially through the loving concern of others whose very presence in our affliction is a sign of divine love. God's love is made visible, not just in the words and actions . . . but in the assembly itself."[36] Instead of disenfranchising grief, the gathered community surrounding survivors with human love mediates God's presence to them.

Ritual provides *emotional support* of people who accept the survivor unconditionally.[37] "The psychological benefits of ritual," Jacobs says, "emerge out of the relational aspects of ceremonial acts that validate and give expression to the emotional reality of human experience."[38] Others hear and believe the survivor's story, embrace their pain, and commit to walking the path to recovery with them.

---

32. Anderson and Foley, *Mighty Stories*, 34.

33. Driver, *Magic of Ritual*, 190, 212; see *Performative Statement.

34. Ibid., 206–207.

35. Ibid., 109–119.

36. White, *Sacraments*, 89.

37. The distinction between emotional and cognitive support comes from Driver, *Magic of Ritual*, 152–153.

38. Jacobs, "Religious Ritual and Mental Health," 298.

Ritual also provides *cognitive support* from people with a shared worldview. When our personal faith falters, the corporate faith of others can carry us. As John Weborg says:

> [I]n times of crisis, ritual lets us say words of faith that we feel dishonest saying because we don't really believe them. "I can't believe it," we think. Say it anyway—it's not your faith, it's the church's faith. All these other people are believing for you. When the crippled man was lowered through the roof, the gospel says, Jesus saw his friends' faith and healed him (Matt 9:1–8).[39]

Healing is never individual but is always the result of connection with other people. For Jenna, having her story heard and believed, being joined in her suffering, and having her needs lifted in common prayer was a pivot point in her healing.

These are the purposes of ritual. When emotional and spiritual needs are under-ritualized, Kenneth Pargament says:

> [P]owerful negative events go relatively unrecognized, and people are left with un-resolved grief. Disconnected from rituals, people cannot participate in purposeful acts of transformation that propel them . . . from one place in life to another. Instead, they become stuck in particular emotions . . . or particular life conditions.[40]

In order to be a source of healing, ritual must enable survivors to speak their wound-edness and pain and to be reassured both of God's sustaining presence and of God's power to restore wholeness.

LITURGICAL AND RITUAL RESOURCES
FOR HEALING SEXUAL ABUSE

There are rituals for public worship that use regular service liturgies and are for the whole church; there are small group rituals—special, occasional liturgies for survivors; and there are personal rituals for private, devotional use.[41] While these liturgies focus on female survivors, it is increasingly clear that fresh liturgies, rituals, and prayers are also needed which are more inclusive, incorporating male survivors as well.

Liturgies for Public Worship

While special occasional liturgies for survivors have their place, they also, as Pamela Cooper-White observes, have the drawback of "taking abuse out of the mainstream of church life and worship."[42] Services of healing for sexual violence should be part of normal public worship. They can be of three types: general healing services, special abuse healing services, and the regular Sunday liturgy.

---

39. Weborg, Lecture Notes, North Park Theological Seminary.

40. Pargament, *Spiritually Integrated Psychotherapy*, 261.

41. For further discussion see Procter-Smith, "Review Article," 39–44. The entire issue is dedicated to ritual and liturgical materials for addressing sexual violence; also Duck, "Hospitality to Victims," 165–180.

42. Cooper-White, *The Cry of Tamar*, 250.

GENERAL HEALING SERVICES

Many Christian denominations have general healing orders of service in their worship books. These can either be anointing rites with prayer or entire services. For example, the Reformed Church in America has this *litany of healing prayer for regular Sunday worship:[43]

> O God the Father, whose will for us and for all your people is health and salvation, have mercy on us. O God the Son, who came that we might have life and have it in abundance, have mercy on us. O God the Holy Spirit, whose indwelling makes our bodies the temples of your presence, have mercy on us.

Those who wish to receive anointing with oil are invited and prayed over with the words: "May the hands of the Great Physician, Jesus Christ, rest upon you now in divine blessing and healing. May the cleansing stream of his pure life fill your whole being, body, mind and spirit, to strengthen and heal you." Intercessions and anointing, with healing stations set up around the sanctuary, can be integrated into any worship service.

There are also liturgies for entire healing services, such as this one written by Ruth Duck.[44] The *Call to Worship* uses Ps 103:1–5 to praise the God who renews our strength, heals our diseases, and saves our lives from despair. Confession of sin is replaced by prayer that acknowledges woundedness and proclaims assurance of God's healing love. Scriptures that tell the story of Jesus' healing ministry are read, and witness to God's healing power is given through a sermon and personal testimonies. General intercessions for healing are offered, and participants are invited for anointing, laying on of hands, and prayer. The Eucharistic prayer emphasizes God's desire to restore wholeness, and the prayer after communion thanks God for the miracle of new life. Additional general healing liturgies can be found in monographs and denominational service books.[45]

SPECIAL HEALING SERVICES FOR SEXUAL ABUSE

In addition to general healing worship, special services for the whole church that focus on sexual violence can be designed. The Church of the Brethren has a model liturgy emphasizing suffering, abandonment, and hope.[46] The call to worship is a series of questions:

> People of God, why are you gathered? . . . People of God, are you wounded? . . . People of God, what is your hope?

and answers:

> To worship the Lord who comforts us in our pain and distress, hears our cry for justice when we are wronged, and breaks the walls of silence that keeps the truth

---

43. Found at http://images.rca.org/docs/worship/healing.pdf.

44. Duck and Wilson-Kastner, *Praising God*, 165–171.

45. Epperly (*Healing Worship*), ch. 2–4 offers examples of healing Scriptures, homilies, confessions, prayers, anointing, and songs and describes *Taize services of wholeness, *Celtic blessing circles, healing light liturgies, imaginative prayer services, *lectio divina* practices and healing communion; also Evans, *Healing Liturgies*, 237–247; Wagner, *Healing Services*.

46. Church of the Brethren, Health Promotion Sunday Resources, authored by S. Douglas; also Mennonite Central Committee. *Lord Hear Our Prayers: Domestic Violence Worship Resources*.

> from being heard . . . Yes! We are wounded when children are neglected and abused. We are wounded when the weak are assaulted and oppressed . . . Our hope is in God who has promised to be with us in our suffering.

The biblical texts are healing stories from Jesus' life: the man born blind (John 9:1–7), the woman at the well (John 4:7–14), and the hemorrhaging woman (Luke 8:40–48). Prayers of confession acknowledge that both individuals and the church have tolerated violence and domination. A litany of compassion for victims of abuse names God's loving promise to share our burdens and bring comfort.

Another liturgy comes from the Christian Reformed Church. The congregation enters God's presence with a call to worship:

> God greets us as he did Israel, centuries ago. In Jeremiah, God says: "I have loved you with an everlasting love; I have drawn you with loving kindness. I will build you up again and you will be rebuilt (Jer 31:3–4a)." That God who loves us enough to rebuild our lives is here!

This is followed by: songs of praise, confession of need and pardon from sin, and passing God's peace to each other. Scripture and sermon focus on healing through forgiveness. A contemporary confession of faith proclaims that the church is a community of forgiven sinners dedicated to bringing healing to a broken world. Intercession, based on the Lord's Prayer, integrates petitions about sexual abuse. The service concludes with a hymn and blessing.[47]

A non-denominational liturgy opens with a litany of intense emotion: "Cursed be the violence of the strong . . . cursed be the evil power of secrecy . . . cursed be our *collusion and cowardice." After a greeting of love and the telling of the survivor's story, a written version of the abuse story is burned with these words, "may the evil and the harm wither away and be consumed." A candle, signifying God's light in dark places, is lit and a prayer of blessing offered. The survivor is anointed on various parts of the body with accompanying prayer: "from violence to your voice . . . body . . . feelings . . . mind . . . sexuality, be healed."[48]

The Reformed Church in America has an ecumenical service of healing for survivors of abuse which is held on *Holy Innocents Day and connects the weeping in Bethlehem to sexual violence. It begins with a call to worship, hymn, prayer of confession, the *Kyrie, and assurance of pardon. The Old Testament lesson (Jer 31:15–20) and Psalm 3 speak lament and hope, and the Epistle reading (Jam 5:7–11) challenges survivors to be patient

---

47. Evans, *Healing Liturgies*, 200–206 and at www.reformedworship.org/magazine/article/cfm?article_id=507. Any service that encourages forgiveness must be careful not to further wound survivors by reinforcing their shame and self-blame. As Cooper-White (*Cry of Tamar*, 253) says, "all too often, survivors of violence are retraumatized by pastors and other well-meaning helpers who press forgiveness upon them as if it were something which, if they tried hard enough, they could simply will into happening." In other words, when forgiveness is not the result of a *process* of grieving what was taken, working through pain and fear, claiming anger and rage, demanding justice and *restitution, and letting go of vengeance, then calls for instant forgiveness—especially when presented as a demand of Christian discipleship—will only produce guilt, confusion, and estrangement.

48. Evans, *Healing Liturgies*, 206–217.

in suffering. After the sermon, participants are invited to receive the laying on of hands with this prayer:

> In the name of the Lord I lay my hands on you. May God use my hands, which are caring and safe, to help you heal from the effects of other hands, which were uncaring and abusive. In the name of God our loving Creator, Christ our true redeemer, and the Holy Spirit our tender Comforter.

The service concludes with prayers of thanksgiving and intersession, a hymn and parting blessing.[49]

Finally, another Church of the Brethren service begins with a responsive call to worship and invocation that invites participants to bring their pain into God's healing presence.

Leader: Life is often not like we want it to be.

All: We have come here to God's house to find strength in time of need.

Leader: Sometimes life is worse than we ever thought it could be, because of what has happened to us or because of what someone has done to us.

All: We have come here to God's house to bring before God our pain and our questions, to find help with our pain and guidance in our questioning.

Leader: But life is also good. Even in times of trouble we see the light and goodness of God.

All: We have come here to God's house to reaffirm our faith, to be bathed in God's love, and be uplifted by the Holy Spirit.

Leader: O God, we thank you that you can feel our pain, know our anguish, and understand the questions we ask. In this time of worship may we find release from our pain, peace from our anguish and hope in our questioning. This we pray in the name of Jesus Christ who was no stranger to pain or anguish or questioning, yet put his trust in you, knowing that you would always be there for him. Amen.

Biblical texts include a psalm of lament (22) and prayers of trust in God (Psalm 27; Isah 25:4–5; Rom 8:31–39). The prayers of the people echo the Scripture readings and sermon theme:

Leader: O God of love, we cry out in our sufferings, sometimes of the body, sometimes of the mind, sometimes of the spirit.

All: O God, hear our prayer.

Leader: Sometimes, O God, we feel that you are nowhere to be found. Like the Psalmist, like our Lord, we cry out, "My God, my God, why have you forsaken me?" We long desperately for help but you do not seem to hear.

All: O God, hear our prayer.

49. Found at www.reformedworship.org/magazine/article.cfm?article_id=477.

Leader: In view of all this, what can we say?

All: If God is for us, who can be against us? Certainly not God, who did not even keep back his own son, but offered him for us all.

Leader: Who then can separate us from the love of Christ? Can trouble do it, or hardship or suffering?

All: No, in all these things we have complete victory through him who loved us. There is nothing in all creation that will be able to separate us from the love of God, which is ours through Jesus Christ our Lord.[50]

By publicly acknowledging the presence of survivors and *perpetrators, *by confessing the church's complicity with abuse,* and by committing the church to work against abuse, special healing services for public worship sensitize the congregation to issues of sexual violence. *By letting survivors tell their stories and name their wounds, and by providing gestures of embrace and validation, these services help rebuild the trust in community that was badly damaged in childhood.* Congregational preparation and education is necessary before conducting a public liturgy of healing, and pastoral after-care must be available following for those who need to process the experience.[51]

REGULAR SUNDAY WORSHIP: THE ROLE OF THE SACRAMENT

In addition to special healing worship, Cooper-White says:

> [T]he regular Sunday service of the Word, and the Eucharist itself, can be powerful liturgies of transformation and signs of promise and hope for survivors. It is here . . . in the central worship of the life of a congregation, and not for the most part in special liturgies, that the most effective healing . . . is accomplished.[52]

The *Evangelical Covenant Church hymnal has a gathering song for regular worship—"Each Man and Woman Raise Your Voice"—that intersperses readings between verses. It begins by affirming:

> This is a place where you are welcome. This is a place where you are safe. This is a place where no matter your background, no matter your lot in life, no matter your need or expectations you are welcome here for God is our gracious host.

One of the readings speaks of sexual abuse:

> Her childhood was taken away by her own father. He not only molested her body but raped her soul. It is no wonder that while sitting in this place she shudders at calling God "Heavenly Father." But God will be patient. Trust is something that takes time and the time will come when she will draw close without fear. That's why she's here.[53]

---

50. Church of the Brethren, Health Promotion Sunday Resources, authored by D. Shank. Also Mennonite Central Committee. *Lord, Hear Our Prayers: Domestic Violence Worship Resources.*

51. Evans, *Healing Liturgies*, 4–12. Additional abuse healing services for the whole church can be found at 206–217.

52. Cooper-White, *Cry of Tamar*, 251.

53. *Covenant Church Hymnal* (Chicago, IL: Covenant, 1996), Selections 505 and 867.

Notice that in this regular hymn, sexual violence is acknowledged and survivors are validated. Through Holy Communion in particular we experience God's self-giving. "One need which pervades our lives," Ramshaw asserts, "is the need for an assurance of God's love and our identity as children of that love. It is a strong . . . tradition of pastoral care to direct people to the sacraments as witness and guarantors of God's gracious love for them."[54] By connecting us to the roots of our faith, the Lord's Supper becomes the central act of Christian identity and self-definition.[55] In the first place, as the "sacrament of God's participation in our brokenness," the Eucharist expresses grief.[56] *Recalling Christ's death reminds us that God is not immune to pain, but has, in Jesus' wounds, taken on our sorrows and shares in our suffering.* From Christ's passion we learn how to confront suffering with hope, patience, faith, and courage.[57] As Hotz and Matthews put it:

> [W]hen we tear bread from the loaf, when we pour wine into the cup, when we taste the broken bread of Christ's broken body, when we drink the wine of his spilled blood, we come to participate mystically in the redemptive fragmentation of Christ that paradoxically brings new wholeness, harmony, and unity to the world.[58]

In the second place, the Eucharist expresses joy and hope. It reminds us that, while suffering is not good, good can come from it—that the horror of the cross is followed by the triumph of the resurrection. The Lord's Supper is an act of hope in which, by re-membering God's past saving acts, we experience God's saving power in the present. It is also an *eschatological event, an anticipation of the messianic banquet in the kingdom of heaven—a statement of trust in a God who triumphs over wrong.

Finally, the Holy Communion is a *koinonia, a communal meal that celebrates and builds oneness among God's people and heals the survivor's experience of isolation. Regular Sunday worship can heal survivors by bringing wholeness and peace with God, other people, and oneself.

---

54. Ramshaw, *Ritual*, 73.

55. Calvin, Luther and Wesley all believed that Holy Communion should be conducted weekly; see Byars, *Future of Protestant Worship*, 67.

56. Wolterstorff, *Lament For a Son*, 39.

57. There is a danger that asking survivors to "bear their cross" of grief and pain may further distance them from God. As Monica A. Coleman warns, "theories of redemptive suffering do not always account for the differences between *voluntary* and *involuntary* suffering. Whereas Jesus willingly suffered . . . sexual violence is always a situation of involuntary suffering" (*The Dinah Project*, 82; emphasis added). Poling (*Abuse of Power*, 168; cf. 173) agrees:

> [S]ome survivors have mixed feelings about Jesus. They say that the victimization of Jesus in the crucifixion seems to give implicit sanction to the victimization of women. By patterning their lives on that of Jesus, women are encouraged to accept their suffering as a sign of virtue rather than press their complaints toward justice and restitution.

See also Leehan, *Defiant Hope*, 96–97; Wilson-Kastner, "Theological Perspectives on Sexual Violence," 105–106.

58. Hotz and Matthews, *Shaping the Christian Life*, 153.

Liturgies for Small Groups of Survivors

Special rituals can be created for survivors and those who support them. Such liturgies, Mari Zimmerman says, "may be necessary to overcome the barriers of deep spiritual alienation before . . . survivors can be brought into active and beneficial celebration with [the] community of faith." Special prayer services "are not meant to create an exclusive or separate congregation for survivors but to be *a means for spiritual healing of that separateness*, a step toward assimilation into the existing community of faith."[59]

A service, designed by Jane Keene, begins with a greeting, Scripture reading, and a litany of mercy.[60] Three sets of prayers interspersed with psalms—for acknowledgement, forgiveness, and affirmation—honor each survivor's personal experience by allowing them to respond positively or negatively (since only they know what they feel and can truthfully say).

The question "Do you forgive your abuser?" has the alternative replies of: "With God's help, I forgive," or "I am not yet able to forgive."

The question "Do you believe that God loves you?" can be answered with: "I do" or "I do not."

The survivor reads a lament (from Psalms 22 and 88), and other participants offer prayers for deliverance (from Psalms 28 and 43 and Jeremiah 15). Those present surround the person as they indicate parts of the body—hands, mouth, breasts—that need healing, and they anoint them with oil. The service ends with scriptures and prayers of hope (from Isaiah 43 and 52). The survivor, still encircled, is blessed and dismissed with the sign of the cross.

Bonnie Summers has written a liturgy of thanksgiving for healing from sexual abuse.[61] The service begins, after a greeting and hymn, with the survivor's story. Each different memory of abuse is written on an index card and placed, together with various childhood objects, in a basket. The survivor lights a candle representing each year of abuse and hope for the years ahead. A responsive litany of confession and supplication is prayed, patterned as follows:

Survivor: God, I confess that I hide from myself and others, and try to hide from you.

Leader: God, help her/him not to fear your healing light. Help her/him to dare to approach you as she/he is, trusting your promised love for her/him.

Congregation: Have mercy on us, O God.

Scripture readings assure the survivor of God's love and care (Isah 41:10; Rev 21:4–5). Then a prayer of thanksgiving is offered:

Survivor: God, for wholeness, as much as I experience now, I am thankful.

Congregation: We also give thanks, O God.

59. Zimmerman, *Take and Make Holy*, 21; emphasis added.
60. Keene, *A Winter's Song*.
61. Summers, "A Service of Celebration and Thanksgiving for Healing," 13–25.

The survivor is anointed with oil as a sign of being released from the past and being given a fresh start. At the Eucharist, white wine signifies the healing Jesus brings. In closing, participants hold hands and offer spontaneous prayers of thanksgiving, followed by singing "Amazing Grace" and a benediction.

Other occasional services can be designed for specific needs. One liturgy uses water and prayer to cleanse a church sanctuary where the abuse occurred; participants are given gifts such as cleansing shower gel.[62] Another service is for a survivor upon the death of a perpetrator, an event which often reawakens grief.[63] The survivor renews their baptismal vows as a way of committing themselves to healing and of affirming that they are God's own dear child. Scripture lessons emphasize God's justice (Ps 119:137–144; Jer 31:29–34), God's love (Rom 8:35–39), and God's resurrection hope (Rev 21:1–4). The deceased is then committed to God: "Almighty God, into your hands we commend the soul of [*name*], in sure and certain trust in your justice and your grace." The service concludes with prayer for God's abiding presence in days of pain and grief.

In addition to single liturgies, series of services can be conducted—such as those Mari Zimmerman has written for different stages of recovery.[64] The first service acknowledges the difficulty of believing that wholeness is possible. Survivors state their desire for healing, name their doubts, express their anger and confusion to God, are assured that God loves and accepts them as they are, and receive support.

Another service lets survivors tell their stories and state feelings of being contaminated, unclean, and dirty. An act of cleansing—in which the survivor splashes water from a large bowl onto arms and back and face—signifies washing away undeserved shame. The celebrant dips a thumb in the water and makes the sign of the cross on the person's forehead as a proclamation of their innocence and of God's indwelling presence. The survivor wears white and the worship area is decorated with white flowers, creating a sense of purity.

A third service, which takes place outdoors, mourns the past and present losses of sexual abuse: a happy childhood, a loving and safe home, and estrangement from parents. Readings and prayers lament the fact that these things can never be restored. The survivor buries a symbol of lost childhood such as a photograph or a stuffed toy.

Another service, of thanksgiving for healing, uses plants (to symbolize new life and personal growth) or candles (to signify light overcoming darkness). Each participant is recognized for their redemptive presence in the survivor's life by being given a plant or candle.

A final service allows survivors to celebrate the choice of a new name (which some, like Jenna, change legally) or to invest their present name with new meaning. An Easter *paschal* candle is lit by the survivor as a symbol of resurrection life and of God bringing light to those in darkness. The survivor is anointed with oil as a sign of blessing and new life.

---

62. Read and Cashman, "Service of Acknowledgment of Organized Abuse and Cleansing of a Church Sanctuary," 7–12.

63. Vogel, "Creating Rituals that Speak to Us and for Us in the Winter-time of Life."

64. Zimmerman, *Take and Make Holy*.

Miriam Therese Winter has also designed various liturgies for survivors.[65] "Why Do You Weep?" recounts the stories of lamenting biblical women like Hannah and invites participants—through responsive readings, reflection and sharing, and silent and spoken prayers—to tell their own stories of weeping. Another ritual uses the symbol of living water in several ritual acts. Water is poured from pitcher to basin, its splashing a sign of God's abundant and overflowing grace. Participants are sprinkled in an act of blessing. Survivors wash their hands in a gesture of cleansing from shame. Participants pass and drink a shared cup of water with the words "This is living water; take and drink"—an act that symbolizes God relieving thirst in a dry land. A third ritual, "Out of Exile," offers release from bondage and deliverance from evil. The story of the exodus is read, followed by sharing of personal experiences. A litany is offered in remembrance of violated women from Scripture (Hagar, Dinah, Tamar, the woman accused of adultery) *and abuse victims*. After silence, a second litany celebrates liberated women in Scripture (Miriam, Esther, Elizabeth, Mary Magdalene) *and abuse survivors*. These prayers blend together grief and hope.

Janet Schaffran and Pat Kozk, as well as Rosemary Radford Reuther, have created general healing rituals for women that can be adapted for sexual abuse and to include men.[66] In general, these services follow the sequence of milestones in recovery, use psalms of lament and hope, symbolic acts, individual storytelling and Scripture readings.[67]

Rituals for Individual Use

Most public rituals, as well as specific devotional resources, can be used when praying alone. Personal meditation, prayer, and journaling "offer an opportunity for 'thinking about' abuse issues in ways that can heal and transform . . . [They] can be a forum for searching for meaning, exploring questions, stating newly discovered truth."[68] Catherine Foote has written a book of survivor prayers.[69] "Refusing to Move On" relates abuse to the violence experienced by Jesus:

> A scar is a scar. It doesn't go away. The broken bone may be set, but in the healing traces of injury remain. There it is. I was abused. I was hurt. And a scar is a scar . . . Jesus, I know that you remember your pain. You still carry those scars that Thomas touched with his doubting. You insist that there was a real cost when you were hurt. Stand with me in this place of remembering. Stand with me as I clarify: real injury means real pain. Stand with me in this truth: A scar is a scar.

Another meditation, "Prayer for Tenderness," in an echo of Psalm 131, reaches out to God as a young child reaching for nurture and care; "Jesus and the Children" imagines fearful youngsters resting in Jesus' lap, knowing they are safe. There is a prayer "To the Community of Faith" which asks how others will respond to stories of abuse: "will they

---

65. Winter, *Woman Prayer, Woman Song*; for contemporary psalms, see idem, *Woman Word*.

66. Schaffran and Kozak, *More Than Words*; Ruether, *Women-Church*; Pellauer, "Resources for Ritual," ch. 20.

67. See Zimmerman, *Take and Make Holy*.

68. Foote, *Survivor Prayers*, 3. See also, Leehan, *Defiant Hope*, ch. 8 and appendices.

69. Foote, *Survivor Prayers*.

turn their heads from me? . . . or will they make bandages and gently cover my wounds?" *Such prayers give survivors words and permission to speak honestly about anger, shame, fear, and isolation, and hopefully about acceptance, safety, healing, and God's faithful care.*

Sandra Flaherty has created devotional resources that focus on various dimensions of grief and recovery: remembering, sorrow, fear, anger, acceptance, forgiveness.[70] Each chapter has journal exercises and personal rituals for acknowledging feelings and connecting with God. She recommends physical exercise and relaxation (e.g., working in the garden or listening to music); imagining exercises (e.g., picturing oneself as a small child, holding her close and offering her love); writing letters of sadness and anger to God; praying with Scripture (e.g., imagining oneself as Mary Magdalene being asked by Jesus: "Why are you weeping?"); personal grieving rituals (e.g., collecting a few rocks, labeling each with a phrase about something missed during childhood, then burying them in the forest or throwing them in the river).

Flaherty also recommends the healing richness of traditional devotions like the *Stations of the Cross and the Rosary. Personalizing the misery of Jesus on his way to Calvary reminds survivors that God does understand our pain. They can pray the Stations in a church, can journal Jesus' pain and their feelings, or can draw each Station as a visual expression of their union with Jesus' suffering. Meditation on the cross reminds survivors that, instead of abandoning us, God shares *our* suffering. It also affirms the reverse, that our suffering is related to *Christ's* suffering, that we suffer in communion with the Lord (Col 1: 24). Liturgy and ritual, Vigen Guroian says, "help the faithful *map their suffering and grief onto the suffering and death of Christ.*"[71] Meditation on the "sorrowful mysteries" reminds survivors that Jesus, too, experienced great suffering. His agony in the garden, the scourging and crown of thorns, and carrying the cross speak to the sadness, fear, and shame they bear. The "joyful mysteries" can also be healing. The annunciation of Mary and her prayer—the *Magnificat—symbolize reversal and hope, while her visit to Elizabeth reminds survivors of those who support them in their journey. There are other valuable spiritual resources for healing abuse.[72]

Ann Weems' *Psalms of Lament* is a set of personal prayers, patterned after the biblical laments that voice both grief and hope:

70. Flaherty, *Woman, Why Do You Weep?*

71. Guroian, *Life's Living Toward Dying*, 93; emphasis added.

72. For example, Cummings, *Eyes Wide Open* follows the journey through discovery, honesty, grief and rage to trust, forgiveness, hope, and change. Each reflection has three parts: (1) personal storytelling, (2) reflection on "where is God in this experience?" (3) and "where is my faith community?" This book includes personal testimony, poems, songs, prayers, biblical meditations and suggestions for personal rituals. It has a reflection on Jer 31:15–17, which combines grief ("a voice is heard in Ramah, lamentation and bitter weeping") and hope ("there is hope for the future, says the Lord: your children shall come back to their own country") and on Ezek 37:1–14, where the valley of dry bones signifies a life put back together piece by piece. There is a ritual of hope using Psalm 126 in which each participant is given a few seeds to plant as a sign that healing will sprout and bloom, that God can bring new joy and strength. Cummings suggests an Epiphany party signifying new life and a ritual of renewing baptismal promises and reaffirming faith in the God who makes us loved children and releases us from the power of death and evil. See also, Jansen, *From the Darkest Night.* Prayers and meditations can be found at the end of Fortune, *Keeping the Faith*, idem, *Violence in the Family.*

I am *depressed, O God. I see no end to this cycle of sadness. People tell me: 'Everything will be all right,' but it isn't, and it won't be . . . What has happened can't be undone. What is done can't be prettied up. But you, O God, can stop the after-shocks. O God, tear through the night to rescue the one you have left too long.[73]

Another helpful resource is Joyce Rupp's *Praying Our Goodbyes*.[74] The prayers and journal exercises, which focus on change and transition, express both grief and hope. "Prayer of One Seeking Shelter in the Storms of Life" uses a burning candle in a globe to illustrate the sheltering love of God. A reflection on Jesus' calming the storm at sea (Matt 8:23–27) places the survivor in the boat and feeling the violence of wind and storm:

> Imagine Jesus in your boat. See how deeply he sleeps as the storm continues to rage. *How do you feel about Jesus being asleep during the distress that you are experiencing? Go over to Jesus and awaken him* . . . Tell him how you feel about the storm in your life right now.

"Prayer of One Who Feels Broken Apart" uses *ritual action* of tearing a piece of paper into shreds or breaking a china plate into pieces as a way of acknowledging and acting out the shattering of life and the feeling that things can never be put back together again:

> See your life broken apart. Look at all the pieces, harsh and jagged. Feel the broken-ness that is yours. Now gather the pieces together. See yourself taking them to Jesus. Have him hold the pieces in his hands. Listen to him tell you about his brokenness, how the Father raised him from the dead and brought him to a wonderful whole-ness. See the pieces of pottery in Jesus' hands come together into a beautiful jar.

The "Prayer of One Who Needs Inner Healing" involves putting on a bandage (to acknowledge hurts that need healing) and removing it (as a sign of God's healing love). "I shall bandage the wounded and make the weak strong" (Ezek 34:16). Most of the prayers in this book can help survivors deal with loss and move toward healing.

Constructing and Personalizing a Service: Some Key Reminders

Rituals can be used as published, adapted from existing materials, or developed from scratch. Janet Peterman outlines several steps for creating rituals.[75] First, name the need to be addressed. Each liturgy should have a specific focus and theme—community recognition, grief, forgiveness, healing, and so on. Second, identify biblical texts and worship resources—prayers, readings, ritual actions—which speak to that need. Third, select symbols—material objects and physical gestures—that express and represent both human experience and divine truth. Finally, plan the flow and structure of the service. Roy Oswald, as well as Anderson and Foley, also provide guidelines for designing rituals.[76]

---

73. Weems, *Psalms of Lament*, 99–100.

74. Rupp, *Praying Our Goodbyes*.

75. Peterman, *Speaking to Silence*, ch. 7. Additional ideas can be found in Coleman, *Dinah Project*, ch. 7; and Harris, *Creating Relevant Rituals*.

76. Oswald, *Transforming Rituals*, 106–110; Anderson and Foley, *Mighty Stories*, 128–130.

Services must be personalized and adapted to each survivor's unique situation, so talk with the participants about what words, symbols, and actions would be helpful or disturbing to them. Particular experiences lie behind the survivor's need for ritual, so allow them to tell their story *without rushing in with a theological resolution that suggests easy answers to complex life-crises.* Keep the ritual relatively simple; if it is overly complicated, meaning can be lost. Do not over explain the ritual; respect its ambiguity and let the symbolism speak for itself. Be creative and imaginative; *involve as many of the senses as possible,* and use non-verbal symbols and actions generously. Finally, make sure the ritual meets both the pastoral norm (of fitting the needs of the survivor) and the theological norm (of faithfully reflecting Christian truth).[77]

CONCLUSION

Rituals are acts of hope because they carry the power to change us. The Christian tradition has connected liturgy, belief, and behavior by the formula **lex orandi, lex credendi, lex agendi,* the rule of prayer)—or more generally, worship—is the rule of belief and the rule of action. Worship shapes the survivor's worldview, which in turn influences their way of life. By constructing new meanings, liturgy helps survivors make sense of their experience and live in new ways. Ritual lets them remember and mourn, reframe their stories, and reconnect to self, others, and God. In addition to liturgies of *treatment* (that bring healing to survivors), other rituals are needed—liturgies of *prevention* (that raise awareness of sexual violence), and liturgies of **reconciliation* (that offer repentant perpetrators a public declaration of forgiveness and **absolution*).

Like Jenna, Bonnie experienced a service of healing for sexual violence. The liturgy, she says:

> [H]ad many benefits. It helped me clarify my feelings and thoughts about my father, myself, the religious community, and God. It helped me open up to the love and support of my local church community, and to find a sense of belonging within the congregation and as a child of God . . . It help[ed] me change my experience from one of **denial and isolation to one of openness and community.[78]

Rituals of healing help survivors process inner feelings, find a community of supporting friends, and reestablish relationship with God.[79]

---

77. White, *Sacraments*, 121.

78. Summers, "A Service of Celebration," 15–16.

79. My thanks go to Kim Ebersole (Church of the Brethren), Marcia Friedman (Evangelical Covenant Church), Jane Schuyler (Reformed Church in America), and Beth Swagman (Christian Reformed Church) for suggesting resources and providing denominational materials. My attempt to gather resources from other denominations—Episcopal Church USA, Evangelical Lutheran Church in America, Lutheran Church Missouri Synod, Southern Baptist Convention, and Presbyterian Church USA—was not successful.

QUESTIONS FOR DISCUSSION

1. What is your experience with ritual and formal liturgy? If you attend a liturgical church, what do you find meaningful (or what would you change) about your tradition's rituals? If you attend a non-liturgical church, what might you find helpful about ritual and more formal liturgy? What makes you uncomfortable about ritual and liturgy?

2. Which of the purposes of ritual—creating meaning, expressing emotion, enabling transition and transformation, providing support—do you think is most important when it comes to healing sexual abuse? Why? If you are a survivor, are there additional purposes you believe should be added? If you are a leader who constructs worship services, what does this chapter help you understand about the needs of the sexually broken and the rituals available to address them? Talk with an abuse survivor and ask them how they would prioritize the purposes listed above.

3. Does your church regularly incorporate lament into public worship? If so, in what ways? If not, why not? What does the loss of lament mean for the sexually wounded (and other such needs)? In what ways might you incorporate lament into your service? Read this chapter with a group of survivors and ask them if or how they feel any *disenfranchised grief* in light of their abuse story and the church they attend (or once attended). Based on the survivors' suggestions, make a specific list of what worship services could do to incorporate the reality of so many sexually abused people.

4. Why do churches often not address sexual abuse—and other forms of brokenness—in public worship? What specifically makes us uncomfortable and afraid to do so? Why is addressing sexual violence and acknowledging the presence of survivors in public worship necessary?

5. Does your church publicly address sexual abuse? If not, why not? If so, in what ways? How might your church take it to the next level? What steps might your church take to acknowledge and heal the wounds of survivors? To the degree that other specific needs are publically named or acknowledged at your church (e.g., grieving widows), how do you suppose silence feels to the sexually abused (young and old) in the congregation?

6. What struck you—for good or bad—about the general healing services described in this chapter? About the special healing *services* for sexual abuse? About the personal devotional resources? How might these resources be modified for use in your church? What specific ideas came to your mind as you read these?

7. For counselors: How might counselors and psychotherapists more intentionally integrate ritual—both public and personal—into mental health care for survivors? What specific elements might be most helpful? How can engaging in ritual complement the therapy you use? What do you wish your therapy training would have addressed regarding healing services for people of faith?

8. For survivors: Have you experienced healing services for sexual abuse? If so, how were they helpful (or unhelpful)? If not, what would be most healing for you in a public healing service? What would you want included (or omitted) in a healing service? How have you used ritual in your own personal *spiritual formation?

9. For theologians: How are the themes of lament (Fall) and hope (redemption) expressed and balanced in Scripture? How can theologians bring their knowledge to inform pastoral care and worship practice in the local church? In what ways can the theology of a suffering God (see Bonhoeffer, Carson, Fretheim, Moltmann, Volf) be an antidote for survivors of sexual violence? How can theologians better address *involuntary* suffering, *embodied personhood, and the theology of the cross in light of contemporary expressions of evil?

10. For professors of various disciplines: How might you integrate hard issues, such as sexual violence, into classroom instruction? How would you handle the topic cognitively? Emotionally? How might you educate your students about the psychological and spiritual value of liturgy and ritual? How can you help reintegrate theology and religion back into the university setting, alongside study of the sciences? In your experience, what is lost (for the academy and students) when issues of faith are cordoned off in academic research and discussion?

FOR FURTHER READING

Anderson, Herbert and Edward Foley. *Mighty Stories, Dangerous Rituals.* San Francisco, CA: Jossey-Bass, 1998.

Billman, Kathleen D. and Daniel L. Migliore. *Rachel's Cry: Prayer of Lament and Rebirth of Hope.* Cleveland, OH: United Church, 1999.

Epperly, Bruce. *Healing Worship: Purpose and Practice.* Cleveland, OH: Pilgrim, 2006.

Evans, Abigail R. *Healing Liturgies for the Seasons of Life.* Louisville, KY: Westminster John Knox, 2004.

Moreland Jones, Doris. *God's Gift of Anger.* St. Louis, MO: Chalice, 2005.

Peterman, Janet. *Speaking to Silence: New Rites for Christian Worship and Healing.* Louisville, KY: Westminster John Knox, 2007.

Procter-Smith, Marjorie. "Review Article: Liturgical Responses to Sexual and Domestic Violence." *Journal of Religion and Abuse* 8 (2006): 39–44.

Ramshaw, Elaine. *Ritual and Pastoral Care.* Philadelphia, PA: Fortress, 1987.

Schmutzer, Andrew J. "Spiritual Formation and Sexual Abuse: Embodiment, Community and Healing." *Journal of Spiritual Formation and Soul Care* 2 (2009): 67–86.

Smith, Gordon T. *A Holy Meal: The Lord's Supper in the Life of the Church.* Grand Rapids: Baker, 2005.

Volf, Miroslav. *The End of Memory: Remembering Rightly in a Violent World.* Grand Rapids: Eerdmans, 2006.

21

The Effect of Sexual Abuse on a Woman's View of God

The Impact of Incest

MORVEN R. BAKER, DMIN, PCC-S, NCC

M OST MONDAY EVENINGS WILL find me huddled with a group of between eight to ten women in my small Victorian office. These dear souls all have one thing in common: they are the victims of *sexual abuse (SA) as children, many of them survivors of *incest.[1] Together in a group they learn that their perceived isolation is in reality a "sisterhood" of sorts, discovering that although their "shoes" were different, they had all walked on the same road of experience. Despite being afraid of having their feelings discounted and risking more rejection, the group members begin to share their tragic stories with one another. Eventually they feel safe enough to cry, learning that their tears are not shameful but healing. These women, who have experienced intrusion in touch, gently begin to reach out and comfort one another by holding a hand, patting a shoulder, or offering a tissue.

By the third week of our *support/therapy group experience, this cluster of kindred spirits is beginning to share in an emotional cacophony. They feel angry at and betrayed by their offenders and those who did not rescue them. They feel the confusion of both loving and hating those who hurt them. They both howl in pain and weep in silence. For some this small circle provides the first place they no longer feel alone, and they embrace the comfort of being understood as they process their shame. Only now is it safe to put into words the questions that could never before be asked: "Where was God for me when these things were happening?" "How could Scripture say God loves me, and yet he let my father rape me?" *Christian women, every one of them, yet not a single member of this group have a healthy view or image of God.* Yes, they "love" him, but they share that this

---

1. The most common form of *child sexual abuse (CSA), incest is any sexual contact between a child or adolescent and a person who is closely related or perceived to be related, such as a parent, sibling, cousin, uncle or aunt, grandparent, stepparent, or the live-in partner of a parent (Engel, *Partners in Recovery*, 8). This definition has also been extended to include sexual abuse by any person in a position of authority or responsibility over a child, such as a pastor, teacher, or babysitter (Blume, *Secret Survivors*, 4). For the purpose of this chapter, however, the definition shall be of sexual contact by anyone perceived to be related to the child.

is what they have been *taught* to feel. In reality, they often see God as distant, uncaring, judgmental, and cruel, believing his love for them is *conditional.*

A turning point comes at our fifth meeting when they all listen eagerly as I read them a story, each of them once again the small child that perhaps never had the experiences of safety and stories at bedtime. I tell them about a very *dysfunctional family, in which power has run amok. The father has a history of unhealthy marital relationships and affairs, and the children born from these relationships communicate with suspicion and jealousy. One of the sons *rapes his sister, another kills his brother, and their father does nothing in response to these atrocities. The women in the therapy group are outraged! They all feel the pain of the victimized daughter and, tragically, many of them fully understand what it is like to be part of a family where the incest was ignored or the victims were silenced when they tried to speak. When I tell them that this is the story of Tamar, daughter of King David, found in 2 Samuel, their jaws drop. With few exceptions, most of them have never heard of the existence of this story, and they are amazed that it is in the Bible. "Why does God have *this* story in Scripture?" I ask. They begin to respond, still trying to comprehend the wonder that *their* story is in the Bible. "To let us know that he understands our pain, that he knows what it was like for us, to let us know that he was angry." This, then, is the purpose of this chapter—to help those who care for the female incest *survivor to understand how sexual abuse, most specifically incest, can affect her view of God.

GOD'S IMAGE FROM SCRIPTURE

In Gen 1:26 we learn that God made people in the form of a divine plurality, what later would become understood as the *Trinity.[2] One definition states that an image is the visible representation of something and, if this is the case, this verse would suggest that God's image is reflected in the men and women he created.[3] Genesis 1 portrays God as speaking, looking, making, and creating, all human attributes.[4] Exodus 24:10 describes God as having feet, and other passages give examples of his having eyes, a nose, arms, hands, and a womb—everything but genitals.[5] Chapters 1 and 2 of Luke tell the story of how God became human in the form of a newborn baby, in need of nurture, protection, and instruction. Physically, God truly became one of us.

God's Female Roles

While the picture of God has been traditionally seen as having male roles,[6] such as father (Isah 63:16; Heb 12:9), warrior (Exod 15:3), defender, rock (Ps 18:2[3]), husband (Isah 62:5), and king (Ps 95:3), Scripture at times clearly defines God as having female roles:

2. Barth, *Church Dogmatics*, 191–192; Mathews, *Genesis 1–11:26*, 1:162–163; Collins, *Genesis 1–4*, 59–61.

3. Goldingay, *Old Testament Theology*, 1:102.

4. Ibid.

5. Sherwin, "The Human Body and the Image of God," 75–85.

6. Ezell, "Power, Patriarchy, and Abusive Marriages," 18.

housewife (Luke 15:8–10), knitter (Ps 139:13), midwife (Isah 66:7–9), and mother (Isah 42:14; 66:13).[7] The Hebrew word for "spirit," as in "Holy Spirit," is *ruah*, a grammatically feminine term.[8] The term *shekinah*, which means the presence of God among the people that is in the cloud of light and the burning bush during the post-biblical, rabbinic period,[9] is grammatically feminine.[10] The Hebrew for God's compassion, *rahum*, and the word for mercies, *rahamin*, literally means "womb love."[11] It is appropriate, therefore, when God is described as a woman in labor (Isah 42:14) and as a nursing mother (Isah 49:15), loving the child to whom she has given birth and whose name is forever written on her hand (Isah 49:16).[12] God is described as a bear robbed of her cubs (Hosea 13:8). God provides sanctuary, just as a mother who comforts her small child (Ps 131:2). God longs to protect his children, just as a mother hen gathers her chicks under her wings (Luke 13:34). When sinners repent, God is described as a celebrating "hostess," calling in all of her neighbors to rejoice with her for the lost is found (Luke 15:8–10).

It is suggested by one author that only when men and women are together, do we have God imaged (Gen 1:27).[13] God can thus be the loving father who carries the little child in his arms, and the strong mother who, like the mother eagle, pushes her offspring from the nest and teaches them how to fly.[14]

Seeing God through a Survivor's Eyes

She had that beautiful glow unique to pregnant women in the third trimester. Already a mother of two little girls, and just a few weeks away from delivering her third child, this young Christian woman had come to my office as an emergency intake referred by her pastor. She had recently been given the results of an ultrasound, had learned that she was carrying a son, and was becoming more anxious and afraid as her pregnancy approached full term. It did not take long to learn that she was an incest survivor, and that her father and brother were her *perpetrators.

This piece of information had exposed a hairline crack in my client's emotional foundation. *She was very fearful of history repeating itself, that her young daughters might be *molested by their brother.* As the session continued, I asked her to describe her relationship with God. She became slightly robotic and responded by saying all the "appropriate" words, such as "He's my father. He sent Jesus to earth to die for me, because he loves me." When I asked her what it felt like to say those things, without hesitation and with eyes flashing, she replied, "It makes me want to vomit." And then she began to weep.

---

7. See Fretheim, "God, OT View of," 2:603–618.

8. *HALOT*, 1197; Radford Ruether, "The Image of God's Goodness," 30.

9. Heschel, "The Mystical Element in Judaism," 288.

10. Bennett, "Overcoming the Biblical and Traditional Subordination of Women," 142.

11. Cooper-White, *The Cry of Tamar*, 40.

12. Scripture references are taken from the New Living Translation (NLT) unless otherwise noted.

13. Goldingay, *Old Testament Theology*, 1:106. His discussion on image of God, male and female, and gender is very helpful (98–109).

14. Radford Ruether, "The Image of God's Goodness," 31.

My years of working with both women and men who were molested as children has highlighted a serious issue. It has become apparent to me that most incest survivors who have been sexually abused by their fathers struggle with seeing God as "father." Those who have been molested by their brothers have issue with calling Jesus their "brother." Finally, those who have been abused by their mothers, or whose mothers did not protect them from the sexual abuses by male family members, tend to have difficulty with the whole concept of seeing the Holy Spirit as "comforter."[15] With this in mind, I began to share with my young client how Scripture describes the female characteristics of God—a woman in labor, a mother hen gathering her chicks under her wings, and a mother bear protecting her cubs. She could identify with the tenderness of a mother, as her own mother had been her protector when the abuses were brought to her attention. For her homework assignment, I encouraged her to journal how her picture of God might possibly change if she gave God female characteristics, and that every time she thought about holding her soon-to-be-born son to her breast to nurse, she should envision God as a nursing mother, gently holding her, gazing lovingly into her eyes. My client was eventually able to move beyond seeing God with only female characteristics and was able to embrace also the father and brother images of God.

THE VIEW OF GOD IN FAMILY AND HISTORY

In one of our family photograph albums, there is a picture that is very dear to my heart. It shows my husband as a toddler, standing right next to his daddy at a picnic area in a national park. In the photograph, my father-in-law is casually standing with one foot up on the bench of a picnic table and the other on the ground, leaning with his elbow resting on his elevated knee. Next to him, struggling with all his might to put his foot up on the bench and not fall over is his little son, wanting so much to be like his daddy. The photographer, probably my husband's mother, captured the innocence and sincerity of a child trying to mimic his parent.

Children will try to imitate the adults who have significance in their lives. Little boys may want to help dad in his tool shed and, if encouraged, usually enjoy helping mom in the kitchen. Some little girls play "princess," while others love to help daddy change the car's tire. As they grow older, the children begin to imitate their more dominating peers. A child's worldview is impacted by those who have power over them. It is my understanding that children develop their concept of God from their parents, or from those who are responsible for their nurturing, and that incest impacts a little girl's perceptions so that when she is grown, the way she sees God is distorted.[16]

Research suggests that father-daughter incest has most often been associated with a traditional *patriarchal[17] family structure.[18] Women have become conditioned to think of God as an exploitive male, one to whom they run for help, only to have their feelings and

15. Baker, "How Does the Experience of Incest Distort a Woman's Images of God?"

16. Ibid.

17. See Heath, "The Levite's Concubine: Domestic Violence and the People of God," 12.

18. Alexander and Lupfer, "Family Characteristics and Long-Term Consequences Associated with Sexual Abuse," 234–35.

experiences ultimately discounted and rejected. For centuries, women have been considered "property" of male family members, to be used and abused, sold and discarded.[19] They had no voice that could be heard.

The earliest accounts of patriarchy are found in the pages of the Old Testament. A woman's sexuality was not her own but the exclusive property of whatever man was the head of her household.[20] Fathers expected compensation if their daughters were sexually compromised (Deut 22:28–29), and brothers sought to revenge their sisters' violation (Genesis 34; 2 Samuel 13). In the absence of close male relatives, male cousins could broker the marriages of their female cousins (Esther 2). Nowhere do we read that any of the women in these incidences had a voice in the arrangements.

The early recordings of the rights of children under the patriarchal system are also found in the Old Testament. Honoring parents in Hebrew culture was a divine command (Exod 20:12), and a disrespectful or disobedient child could be stoned to death (Deut 21:18–21). Fathers could give away their daughters for other men's sexual exploitation (Gen 19:8; Judg 19:24). The biblical precedent setting parents' power and rights over their children was so widely recognized that only within the last fifty years, and in just a few countries, has the notion of the rights of children begun to emerge.[21] *History has shown that men have repeatedly abused their power on the women (and children) who were dependent on them.*[22] Statistically, as men typically have greater physical and social power, they are most often the perpetrators of abuse.[23]

Power *Colluding with Patriarchy

Sexual abuse, in whatever form it takes, cuts to the heart of the child. It forever changes her (or his) view of self and others. The child's trust is eroded at its very foundation, and this will affect every relationship she will have for the rest of her life. Imagine living in a home where patriarchy sets all the rules and makes all the decisions. The males in the household have a different set of rules and standards by which they live, and all the female members are to be submissive and obedient. Many of my clients were instructed to serve their fathers and brothers meals before they were allowed to eat, and they were responsible for every aspect of care for the home, including cleaning their brothers' rooms and doing their laundry. They had little, if any, privacy, and whoever, whenever, could enter their bedrooms or bathroom and observe them changing their clothes, using the toilet, or having a bath or shower. "Patriarchy provides a social structure of ownership of women by men, which makes it possible for men to do whatever they want with their women."[24]

Throw into this scenario the fact that this is a "Christian" family, for whom church life is central to its functioning. The father may be highly respected in their faith commu-

19. Eisenstein, *Contemporary Feminist Thought*, 27–28.
20. Weems, *Battered Love*, 4.
21. Ibid., 20.
22. Tracy, *Mending the Soul*, 26.
23. Ibid.
24. Clarke, *Pastoral Care of Battered Women*, 24.

nity, perhaps even being a visible leader or the pastor. Their view of God will be modeled to them by their father's dominance and their mother's submission.

SPIRITUAL INCEST: A FURTHER DEVASTATION

Mark Yantzi believes that parents are the child's first teachers and the first models of God. He has worked for years to bring about restoration between offenders and their victims, saying:

> *Abuse is spiritually devastating.* Survivors find it difficult to believe in a God who protects and sustains what is just and good when an adult entrusted with their care betrayed them. *If an individual has a father who is abusive, the image of God as father can be distressing.* What others experience as a symbol of support and nurture becomes a millstone and a hindrance to spirituality for the abused.[25]

The act of incest crosses more than physical and emotional boundaries. *Spiritual incest occurs when religious abusers distort doctrine and twist scripture in order to justify or rationalize their violence.[26] A father who has sexually abused his daughter may often try to defend his incestuous behavior with Scripture, saying that he turned to his daughter because his wife was not being a "helpmate" and no longer met his needs. As the saying goes, "Spare the rod and spoil and child" (cf. Prov 13:24) is a verse that has been used for centuries to brutalize children, as their fathers tell them, "I am only doing this because I love you." "Women should be silent . . ." (Mark 15:34) is taken out of context and used to shut the mouths of females from crying out and seeking help.

If, however, a little girl is raised in a home where there is respect and mutual submission between her parents, where both her mother and father praise and encourage her appropriately, she can grow up believing that God holds men and women in the same regard and with delight. If she grows up knowing that she can run to her daddy when she is hurt and trusts that he will comfort and protect her, she can learn to believe that God is her defender and consolation in her time of pain. If her mother and father gently discipline her and, by their behavior, show her that love is unconditional, when she is grown she believes that God longs to be in a loving relationship with her, no matter what her choices in life, and that he will always welcome her repentance.

However, if the reverse is true and the child grows up in fear of her father's anger and receives inappropriate discipline and conditional love which are often justified by "twisted" Scripture, she will most likely be disillusioned, believing that God is cold, distant, and unloving. She will wonder what she had done to deserve such brutality and pain. From experience, I have learned that *most sexual abuse survivors believe that they must have done something to cause the abuse.* Women who have experienced fundamental betrayal by one or both of their parents (or parental figures) usually have enormous difficulty putting their faith and trust in God.[27]

---

25. Yantzi, *Sexual Offending and Restoration*, 34–35; emphasis added.

26. Horton, "Practical Guidelines for Professionals Working with Religious Spousal Abuse Survivors," 94.

27. Yantzi, *Sexual Offending and Restoration*, 35.

Misrepresentations from Theology

Christian leaders have, in the majority, taught that suffering is a gift from God. They have preached that suffering is meant for correction,[28] a form of spiritual "pruning,"[29] or a consequence of sin.[30] Just as Job's friends told him to examine himself, since there must be some unconfessed sin in his life (Job 11:13–14), so does this "Scripture twisting" continue to this present day. My own mother was told by a "brother in the faith" that the cancer that would eventually take her life was sent to her by God as a punishment for some sin, and if she repented of the sin, she would be healed.

Suffering in the form of self-sacrifice has also been part of the moral teaching to women. Anna Howard Shaw, a Methodist minister turned *suffragist orator, was quoted as saying, "The greatest defect in the religious teaching to and accepted by women is the dogma that self-abnegation, self-effacement, and excessive humility were ideal feminine virtues."[31]

Patriarchy has so distorted the biblical meanings of submission and obedience that a battered wife or a sexually abused daughter often hears from her pastor, husband, or father that silence is a feminine virtue. These women and children, just like slaves, are victims of captivity and oppression; all have been taught to "stay in your place."[32] Rosemary Radford Ruether summarizes the twentieth-century theologian Karl Barth as saying:

> The covenant of creation dictates a certain order, a relation of priority and posteriority, of A and B. Just as God rules over creation in the covenant of creation, so man rules over the woman. He must be A; he must be first. She is B; she must be second. He must stay in his place. She must stay in hers. She must accept this order as the right nature of things through which she is saved, even if she is abused and wronged by the man.[33]

GOD: A COMPANION IN OUR PAIN

So where is God when a little girl is being molested or her mother beaten? Where is God for the oncology patient or the tsunami survivor? Unlike the patriarchal God/father/judge who uses pain and tragedy to "punish" us for some unknown sin we must have committed, "God suffers when we suffer."[34] Because of his own personal experience of suffering, God asks us to trust him when we are suffering (1 Pet 2:21). God never promised that we would not suffer, but he has promised that he will be with us in the midst of our

---

28. Elliot, *A Path Through Suffering*, 80.

29. Ibid., 36.

30. Sobrino, *The Principle of Mercy*, 28.

31. Hilkert Andolsen, "Agape in Feminist Ethics," 152.

32. Tennis, "Suffering," 204–205.

33. Radford Ruether, *Woman-Church*, 139, summarizing Barth, *Church Dogmatics* III/4, 158–172.

34. Wolterstorff, *Lament for a Son*, 90, "The tears of God are the meaning of history" (Ibid); Ngien, "The God Who Suffers," 38–42.

suffering (Ps 23:4).[35] In the words of Alfred North Whitehead, "God is the fellow sufferer who understands."[36] God truly is a companion in our pain.[37]

Victims of violence need a theology that will teach them that Jesus understands their suffering. He has walked their road of experience, just wearing different "shoes." In Jesus, we see the suffering of God. In order to save the world from the consequences of sin, brought on by humanity's wrong choices and blatant disobedience, God "allowed" his Son to be used as a sacrifice. God did not nail his Son to the cross; the evil choices of men and women hung him there. When his Son was suffering, God could not bear it, causing the sun to eclipse and cover the earth with darkness for several hours. "It was as if the whole creation expressed and experienced the grief of God. God suffered when his Son was crucified."[38] Through Jesus, we see that God is present, even in the middle of pain and violence.

Jesus identified himself with the suffering of others on all levels of life—the blind and the mentally ill, the prostitute, the beggar, the grieving parent, the socially outcast, and the sexual abuse survivor. He knew what it was like to be a victim. He willingly chose to be obedient to God, the Father, and allowed himself to be flogged with a lead-tipped whip, beaten with a stick, spit upon, publicly humiliated, stripped naked, and brutally nailed to a cross (Matt 27:26–31). He knew what it was like to be betrayed by someone he trusted (Matt 26:47–50) and abandoned at his time of need by those he had called "friends" (Matt 26:31). He also knew what it felt like to believe that God had abandoned him in his suffering, when he cried out, *"Eloi, Eloi, lema sabachthani"*—"My God, my God, why have you forsaken me?" (Mark 15:34).

CONCLUSION

Working with survivors of sexual abuse is a privilege, but it comes with a personal price tag. Be prepared to have your heart broken as you listen to unbelievable horror stories. You will hear how her God-image has been deeply crushed by those who were supposed to protect her, and you will never again naively see the church and her pastors as a place of sanctuary for all. In order to be a healthy caregiver, you will need to work through your own emotions as you start to experience some of the same feelings as those of your friends or clients.

The first step in helping an abuse survivor learn how her view of God has been distorted is to understand where her perspective comes from. Ask her to describe how she sees God. Give her permission to be honest, even if this means the "good Christian girl" shares with you that she doesn't believe in God at all. Educate her about how her caregivers (or lack of caregivers) modeled God by their behaviors. If it wasn't demonstrated in her home, where did she see love modeled? For some, it may have been a grade school teacher who affirmed her or the crossing guard who greeted her by name every morning.

---

35. From an address delivered by Dr. Marvin McMickle at Ashland Theological Seminary.

36. Nelson, "Job," 146.

37. Tennis, "Suffering," 206, as quoted in Nelson.

38. Hancock, "The Impatience of Job," 104.

Help her expand the biblical photo gallery of descriptions for God. Have her make a list of other God-images in Scripture, and then have her describe those in her own words (i.e., God as *shepherd*—one who cares for his sheep, defends, protects, feeds, oversees, and so on; and God as *healer*—one who nurtures the sick, who cleans and bandages the wounded). Teach her about the feminine characteristics of God, especially if she was abused by males. Patriarchy has possibly literally "beaten" into her the understanding that God is male and that the only creature made in his image was also male.[39] God said, "Let us make people in our image" (Gen 1:26). "Us" means the Trinity of the *Godhead: Father, Son and Holy Spirit. If women are literally "made in the *image of God," that must mean that God must have female—and not necessarily feminine—characteristics. The distinction between "female" and "feminine" is important, because the first refers to gender while the second refers to culturally defined qualities usually associated with women. The traditionally feminine characteristics given to God are comprised of the tender, nurturing, healing aspects, while the activities in which God administers justice, conquers sin, and establishes peace are called masculine.[40]

Survivors of sexual abuse need to be taught that *all* of their feelings are normal, even anger. We are allowed to be glad and sad, but often preached at that anger is wrong. Scripture gives permission for hurting people to be angry. "Be angry and yet do not sin" (Eph 4:26 NASB). Jesus was so angry when he saw that the temple, the place where God was worshiped, was being violated, that he made a whip and drove out the merchants and knocked over the tables (Matt 21:12). Scripture also calls our bodies a "temple." "Do you not know that your bodies are temples of the Holy Spirit, who is in you, whom you have received from God?" (1 Cor 6:19). If Jesus was angry at a building of brick and stone being misused, how much more angry must he be *for us* when are bodies are being violated.

A pastoral response to a victim of abuse can either condemn her to a life of shame and despair, by sending her back to the abuses from which she has come for help, or it can liberate her. "God seems to choose those who have been made to feel like outcasts and then gives them a new sense of self-worth. God vindicates them in the eyes of their former oppressors."[41]

> "The Spirit of the Lord is upon me,
>   for he has appointed me to bring Good News to the poor.
>   He has sent me to proclaim that captives will be released,
>   that the blind will see,
>   that the oppressed will be set free,
>   and that the time of the LORD's favor has come."
> (Luke 4:18–20)

Like Jesus, we need to stand against the patriarchal leadership of *our* day and model a new way of relating.[42] We are to be the hands and feet of Jesus to the suffering who come to

39. Ezell, "Power, Patriarchy, and Abusive Marriages," 18.

40. McFague, "God as Mother," 140.

41. Gonzalez and Gonzalez, *Liberation Preaching*, 17, as quoted in Thistlethwaite, "Every Two Minutes," 100.

42. Ezell, "Power, Patriarchy, and Abusive Marriages," 19.

our doors. Perhaps we may be the only "Jesus" they ever see. May we look in the mirror and see his reflection.

QUESTIONS FOR DISCUSSION

1. What positive and negative messages did you hear from your parents and/or other caregivers (e.g., "You are a good kid" or "You make me sick") that may have influenced the way you believe God feels about you? From music to literature, how would you describe your view of God? As a therapist or pastor, are you conscious of the metaphors you use for God? How has this chapter helped you think from the survivor's perspective?

2. How were you encouraged to express your feelings as a child? How was love expressed? How have you brought those messages into your present relationships? Consider other sexual abuse survivors you may know: describe their views of God. If you are a survivor, list several things that both your friends and church leadership could do to help you. How has your view of God changed during your lifetime? Read through some of the written prayers in Appendix B, looking for ideas and words that express how you feel.

3. Watch the video "Woman, Thou Art Loosed," produced by Bishop T. D. Jakes. Make note of the parenting messages given to the child, her mother, and her aunt. Discuss how the child's view of God as "father" was impacted by the way men treated her throughout her life. What words did the pastor use that might have been helpful? What other things *could* he have said that might have been of comfort to the young woman in prison?

4. As a therapist or church leader, how would you counsel a woman who was sexually abused as a child and presently lives in a rather "role-oriented" home, though it's not an abusive home at all. Explain what a "suffering God" means for those who've been abused. How do you think male and female survivors can help each other, in light of their painful stories? What do they have in common that can actually bring healing to each other? What *stereotypes do you think need to be addressed in mental health, the church, and society at large, if help for childhood abuse is going to move to the next level?

FOR FURTHER READING

Bilich, Marion, Susan Bonfiglio, and Steven Carlson. *Shared Grace: Therapists and Clergy Working Together*. New York, NY: Haworth Press, 2000.

Kane, Donna, Ph.D. Dissertation. *Women Survivors of Father-Figure Incest: Implications on their View of God*. Maryland: Loyola College, 1990.

Langberg, Diane. *On the Threshold of Hope: Opening the Door to Healing for Survivors of Sexual Abuse*. Wheaton, IL: Tyndale House Publishers, 1999.

Michael, Chester P. *An Introduction to Spiritual Direction*. Mahwah, NJ: Paulist Press, 2004.

Murray-Swank, N. A. Ph.D. Dissertation. *Solace for the Soul: An Evaluation of a Psycho-Spiritual Intervention for Female Survivors of Sexual Abuse.* Bowling Green: Bowling Green University, 2003.

Nason-Clark, Nancy and Catherine Clark Kroeger. *Refuge from Abuse: Healing and Hope for Abused Christian Women.* Downers Grove, IL: Inter-Varsity Press, 2004.

Phelan, James E., Jr. "Women and the Aims of Jesus," *Priscilla Papers* 18 (2004): 7–11.

Ulanov, Ann Belford. *Picturing God.* Einsiedeln: Daimon Verlag, 2002.

22

The Spouses of Adult Survivors

How to Respond Christianly

CLARK BARSHINGER, PhD[1]

ONE OF THE MOST bewildering parts of loving an abuse *survivor is the unexpected *reversal* of your early love. After a promising beginning, the survivor begins to battle with internal confusion, fear, and unfinished business. In *The Mystery of Marriage*, Mike Mason claims that *good love inevitably brings to the surface the deep inner hurts and issues that have been hidden and are in need of repair.*[2] He argues that God leads us into a trusting love that can have the power to challenge and heal our most rejected and hidden inner parts. This is probably no more powerfully true than in the case of marriage with an abuse survivor.

Safe and supportive love creates the conditions under which a hurting survivor of abuse can allow their pain, fears, and anger to slip out through the cracks in their armor, even to torrent out like rivers of sorrow. Brenda Bacon and Laura Lein, in a study of male partners of female *sexual abuse (SA) survivors, record the following statements of male spouses: "She vents on me because she knows she can"; "I'm there and she needs to take it out on somebody"; and "She directs her anger at me because I'm safe."[3] Getting along together is not a simple matter for either party—the abused or their partners. In this chapter we will review some of the research on the problems that spouses of abuse survivors often encounter, explore the typical problems and errors that spouses make in such marriages, and recommend strategies for healing and enriching these marriages.

RESEARCH OF RELATIONSHIPS AFFECTED
BY A PARTNER'S PAST ABUSE

Spouses living with someone's prior *trauma and abuse find themselves struggling with unpredictability in their relationships. "The men could never predict what would ignite anger or when the relationship might deteriorate," say Bacon and Lein.[4] Spouses become

---

1. I would like to thank Michelle Lenz (MMHC) for her assistance in the research of this chapter.
2. Mason, *The Mystery of Marriage*, 198.
3. Bacon and Lein, "Living with a Female Sexual Abuse Survivor," 7.
4. Ibid., 10.

cautious, guarded, and unsure of themselves because they learn that anything can set off an unhappy moment between them and their survivor-partner. In our book, *Haunted Marriage*,[5] we suggest that trying to deal with conflict with an abused spouse is a bit like a scene in the Bruce Lee movie "Enter the Dragon." In a famous scene, Bruce Lee is trying to fight a bad guy in a hall with pillars covered with mirrors. Every time he tries to hit the bad guy, it turns out to be only a reflection of him in a mirror. To solve the problem, Lee has to break all the mirrors first, so he can see which are mere reflections and which is actually the bad guy. *Conflict in a marriage with a survivor is similar in that the apparent problem may only be a reflection of far deeper issues.* To grow in love and safety, couples may need to sort out what they are actually fighting about.

The abuse survivor is usually female, but many men are also abused as children. Therefore, it is often true that marriages struggling with the impact of past abuse and trauma have the male as the survivor and the female as the partner trying to make the best of a difficult situation.

Carolynn P. Maltas reviewed studies on partners of childhood abuse. She states:

> Partners of survivors of *childhood sexual abuse (CSA) may develop a "trauma contagion" marked by high levels of stress, doubts about key personal values and assumptions about the world, and *a tendency to be drawn into unconscious reenactments with the survivor of the abusive relationship.*[6]

She cites Charles R. Figley, ". . . traumatic residue eventually becomes enmeshed in the victim's interpersonal network."[7] Others suggest these marriages get trapped by *repetition compulsion*, in which the expectations of the survivor force a repetition of the abuse dynamics upon the relationship with the partner. This compulsion to repeat the trauma patterns of the past is mostly out of the conscious awareness of either partner in the marriage, especially early in the relationship. *The partner is repeatedly accused of being an abuser in the relationship and may slowly become more angry and aggressive due to frustration with the unfair attacks.*[8]

Often the partner may be seen at the beginning of their love as the wonderful, safe, and kind person the survivor has always been looking for. However, their everyday shortcomings may quickly lead to harsh criticism and emotional attacks for their betrayal. Jody Messler Davies and Mary Gail Frawley suggest that, although the survivor's therapist might be idealized, the survivor's partner is not likely to be so lucky.[9] Carolyn Maltas notes, ". . . to some degree all survivors tend to confuse the partner with the offender . . . no matter how different from the offender or how loving and kind."[10] We note some *sequelae in the survivors struggle.

5. Barshinger et al., *Haunted Marriage*, 56–68.

6. Maltas, "Trauma Contagion in Partners of Survivors of Childhood Sexual Abuse," 5; emphasis added.

7. Figley, *Helping Traumatized Families*, 91.

8. Maltas, "Trauma Contagion," 7; citing van der Kolk, "The Compulsion to Repeat the Trauma," 389–411.

9. Ibid., 8; citing Messler Davies and Frawley, *Treating the Adult Survivor of Childhood Sexual Abuse*.

10. Ibid., 9; citing Maltz, *The Sexual Healing Journey*.

A Portrait of Struggle

Survivors struggle with: (1) uncontrollable, *intrusive memories, (2) "emotional anesthesia" (they can be distant and *detached with little feeling or desire to socialize), and (3) anxiousness (". . . irritability, impaired concentration, sleep disturbance, easily startled . . . *hypervigilance . . . too much adrenalin . . .)."[11] *Hypervigilance refers to the tendency to scan others and life situations for danger, being quick to feel threatened or victimized, and jumping to conclusions.* This is a common characteristic of those who have experienced traumatic events. It often carries the title of *post-traumatic stress disorder (PTSD). Frank M. Ochberg explains that survivors suffer complications such as alcohol and drug abuse, *depression, chronic pain, bereavement, and the tendency to cope and adapt in ways that make them vulnerable to more mistreatment or abuse. He says these survivors have difficulty knowing *whom, when,* and *how* to trust. Partners of abuse survivors can have a "ministry of presence," in which they learn to just be there with the survivor, without necessarily saying anything or pushing any solutions.[12] A male spouse of an abuse survivor should resist a common masculine need to "fix things" or insist on some plan of action. Instead, the spouse should simply listen, *empathize, and reflect what his partner is feeling. Being present with a hurting partner is much more healing than pushing for some quick resolution or spiritualizing the situation.

Whiffen, Judd, and Aube conducted a study in which they found that intimate relationships *moderate the depression suffered by abuse survivors. Abuse survivors tend to fail at forming relationships in which they can trust to give love and trust to be loved. They do not see themselves as lovable or others as safe. Therefore their relationships tend to be unsatisfying. However, this study showed that *abuse survivors who perceive their relationships as reliable, trustworthy, and intimate suffer less depression from their childhood abuse.*[13]

Finally, Brenda Bacon and Laura Lein found that these men had difficult experiences trying to love their partners' unpredictable moods and behaviors, but that they were committed to their relationships and continued to care deeply about their partners and the shared history between them.[14]

DERIVATIVES OF TRAUMA

The unexpected behavior we speak of needs to be better understood by all parties, both the survivor and the partner who loves them. So we note six areas of the survivor's life where deep struggle can manifest itself.

11. Ochberg, "Gift from Within," 3.

12. Ibid., 4.

13. Whiffen et al., "Intimate Relationships Moderate the Association Between Childhood Sexual Abuse and Depression," 942–947.

14. Bacon and Lein, "Living with a Female Sexual Abuse Survivor," 11.

Lost Trust

The abuse survivor often does not know whom to trust. She was unable to defend herself in the past and now she is very vigilant to see incoming abuse and fight it off. The power to say no is experienced as freedom from past pain. However, the abuse survivor's sense of external reality in the marriage is often twisted by her inner emotional memories. Some abuse survivors are so broken by past trauma that they cannot muster the energy to trust—even someone they *rationally* know loves them and is safe. The survivor may not be able to fully relax their guard with a spouse or enter into sexual intimacy because it simply makes them feel too vulnerable.

Transference

In *transference the abuse survivor often cannot emotionally distinguish between the original abuser and their partner, *especially in angry or intimate moments*. It is as if the survivor develops a *phobia in which earlier trauma feelings are aroused and activated by events in the relationship that have some parallel to the original abuse, no matter how vague that similarity might be.

One way to gain leverage over this unconscious transference is to have the survivor talk to his or her partner about their trauma experience(s). By self-disclosing, the couple is drawn closer, the survivor can experience loving empathy, the spouse can better understand the survivor's difficult behaviors, and the spouse can gain further knowledge of what responses of their own might *trigger the survivor's transference.

Anger

The abuse survivor is usually deeply angry over the helplessness they felt and the unfair and cruel ways they were treated in the past. *That anger has usually been suppressed because it was unsafe to express, unspiritual to show, or they felt too shamed, guilty, or compromised to feel free to be honest about their feelings.* The anger sometimes comes out in irrational behavior against the spouse or reckless behavior outside the relationship (e.g., affairs, compulsive spending, stealing, alcohol or drug abuse, etc.). Sometimes the survivor herself reenacts the angry, aggressive, and ugly behavior of her abuser or parents without any awareness of the parallel. Often survivors consciously declare that they intend to be completely different from their parents or abuser yet will repeat many of the same abusive behaviors during times of distress. This is *intergenerational transmission and explains how many toxic relational patterns are passed on from one generation to the next. *Hypnotically, we often learn our *stress responses from our parents or abusers when we are scared of them as little children. Not surprisingly, the abuse survivor tends to be generally tense and guarded, leading to low stress tolerance. *This often results in the survivor being prickly, irritable, easily annoyed, and confrontational.*

Emotional Insulation

The abuse survivor has often learned to adapt in life by not feeling emotions as clearly as other children. By blunting their awareness, they can feel less anxiety and pain in their lives. This *numbing behavior may protect the survivor from pain, but at the cost of less "contactfulness" with the environment around them. Sadly, their inner-circle suffers the most. *With their partner, and others in their sphere of relationships, they are less available, less comfortable with being close, and generally less likely to enjoy social occasions and gatherings.* It is as if they are very wary of the dangers of hurtful experiences when with others, even though they might not be aware of specific thoughts. Over the years they have simply adjusted to life by being more "encased" in their guardedness. Understandably, this style of being in relationship is hurtful to a marriage, with the partner experiencing less intimacy and closeness than the partner would expect and hope for in marriage. Conversely, the survivor might feel the relationship is working, with a balance of companionship and self-protective insulation, but the partner and loved ones around them will no doubt sense the guardedness and distance.

Distorted Sexuality

Given the sense of vulnerability and trauma the abuse survivor feels in daily life, it is not surprising that he or she will be ambivalent and at least vaguely uncomfortable about sexuality. In situations where there was serious sexual or emotional/physical abuse (and they do occur together), the survivor may even struggle with *flashbacks, *panic attacks, or terror during the intimacy of sexuality with their partner. For most survivors there is a hurdle to cross between their natural, God-given sexual desires and their need for safety, control, and distance from being hurt and rejected. That said, for some survivors, their response to sex is just the opposite. They react addictively to sex, with their partner and sometimes with others. They are doing this not so much for intimacy or love making, but to seek the relief that sexual arousal and orgasm provides. The partner can sense feeling almost "used" sexually, and that sex and intimacy are split.

Feeling unlikely to receive love and safety, yielding oneself to sexuality with another person can be unnerving, to say the least. *The risk of rejection, criticism, or feeling inadequate can be overwhelming.* Even though the survivor may well love his or her partner, the partner may have trouble experiencing that love in the marital bed. The partner can feel unloved, even angry, by the unreasonable lack of frequency and fulfillment in their sexual relationship. This is understandably difficult to talk about when the partner does not know what is going on for the survivor *and the survivor can see no positive outcomes for talking plainly and openly about the problem.* One has to remember that the survivor usually comes from a home environment in which any honest and sincere statements of their objection, anger, pain, or confusion were rejected. Similarly, even identifying and expressing real needs may not be a skill the survivor ever learned at home.

So the survivor learned early in life to keep her mouth shut and to distract others from what could be an ugly experience for her. A standoff between the survivor and her partner can occur when the partner does not know why the survivor is avoiding him. *The mystery of shared sexual pleasure and closeness is one aspect of God's plan for healing the shattered lives and insulated hearts of abuse survivors.* The love, pleasure, trusting security, and bond ("becoming one flesh" biblically) can actually help heal the hurting, secret, and flawed parts deep within the abused, which can come to the surface over time and be worked out safely, leading to healing.

Trauma and damage early in life raises the bar so high for this biblical ideal of natural perfection in vulnerability, that, sadly, many couples never get to the sweetness of love that God intended. In a theological sense the struggling spiritual couple is co-creating with God in bringing things back into order. They are part of creation groaning for the day of redemption (Rom 8:22). Is my wife "my neighbor?" Am I to be the "good Samaritan" to her? Is our flawed marriage part of the "fields white unto harvest" (John 4:35)?

Trauma World View

The abuse survivor has been *socialized into a dangerous world. This person is not only on guard and armed for battle or, alternately, driven to helpless submission. He or she also has to fight pre-existing ways they see their world that limit their ability to receive the love they so deeply desire. It is as if the survivor ends up hypnotized, with a "governor" limiting her flexibility to see the options available to her. In sports language, the survivor has poor "field vision" and so cannot see where to throw the ball or how to avoid a tackle. Always getting "a stone instead of bread" (Matt 7:9) from their caregivers in childhood, survivors do not expect anything different as adults. *They experience "victim language" in their head and select words that reinforce their experience as mistreated and victimized.* In this context, it is hard for the partner to be patient with the survivor when the survivor's verbal ways of describing what is going on between them seems so unfair and skewed from reality.

The survivor overreacts, uses *power-over* language and "you statements" such as: "you always betray me"; "you never think about me"; "you can't possibly love me if you think that"; "if you love your friends so much, why don't you go live with *them!*" Struggling to distinguish difficulty from attack, this person generally sees things desperately when upset and uses *reductionistic, black or white, and manipulative thinking. And the result: this alienates the very people who actually love them and who are potential sources for comfort and support. If anger and rejection from others comes as a result of this sort of defense, the survivor will likely experience the rejection as further proof that they will not get a square deal in life. Meanwhile their partner becomes a *secondary abuse survivor*, suffering indirectly from the survivor's original abuse.

Along with severe *defenses, the survivor may compensate for their undersupply of love by turning to transient, compulsive, and addictive pleasures. *Trauma survivors are at serious risk of abusing the pleasures of their environment (e.g., alcohol, drugs, sex, food, spending, hoarding, religiosity, exercise, work, and escapist novels, movies, and TV).* In worse scenarios, the survivor may find an illusion of control through self-inflicted pain (e.g., "cutting"), starvation, or suicide.

In all this it is very hard for the spouse who loves the survivor to understand the logic of what is going on. The spouse would understandably become exasperated and angry, or discouraged and depressed. Creating a steady, stable-state in the relationship that allows these deeper realities to come to light, be addressed, and engage the journey of healing is no easy matter. It requires a solid love-effort on both parts. New memories can be made as the survivor and his or her partner work together on this journey of love and healing.

HEALING BY LOVING

We now turn to the struggles of the spouses to cope with this largely unexpected, uninvited, and unwelcomed life task—they have their own pain to face. *No one signs up for this course in life, but the rewards for successfully showing up for the challenge can reap dividends of growth, maturity, and the ability to give and feel love that were also not planned or expected in life.* The apostles Paul and James counsel that suffering trials and tribulations bring patience, strength, and depth of character and joy. The biblical message is that resolution and peaceful acceptance to life's problems come with obedience, endurance, and a transforming love for God that allows us to accomplish tasks we would not accept "in the flesh."

What Not to Do

Let's start with the easy part: what not to do. It is always easier to fix a problem by eliminating the first over-reactions that are usually ill advised. The survivor was slowly encased in these poor strategies out of their desperation to survive psychologically as a child. The partner, therefore, should be careful to avoid angry, controlling reactions that will not help, and worse, could re-traumatize the survivor.

NOT . . . AGGRESSION

When confronted with overwhelming intensity, anger, and unfair accusations, who won't become angry? The partner of a survivor will be stretched in their ability to remain calm and patient during confrontations. When the abuse survivor's partner is male, the common mistakes of male conflict management prevail. Males typically seek *solutions* and *closure*. To achieve this they often employ an aggressive style, becoming bombastic, challenging, and intimidating. The male *machismo strategy has only one chance of success: short-term. In the long run, overwhelming force only *re-victimizes the survivor, forcing her further underground and in need of more *pathological strategies (e.g., *self-destructive behavior, substance abuse, blowing the budget) to work out her feelings.

Conversely, the survivor may also rise to the challenge of the perceived abuse: "I let my parents get away with bullying me but there is *no* way I am going to let you do it to me!" What results may well be ugly, even violent, fights. *In fact, it can be very healing to avoid reacting to the survivor with counter anger, the way others have in her past.* If she is attacking and angry, let her know it is understandable to you that she is so angry, and that the anger *will not push you away*, because you *want* to hear and understand what she is angry about.

The advice of the old railroad crossing signs is valuable here: "stop, look, and listen." Let the first rush of anger pass, and really look at your spouse's countenance and listen for the positive intention beneath her arguments. A good question to ask yourself when you feel unfairly attacked by your survivor spouse is: "What might be the *positive intention she is trying to reach?" For example, if you surmise that the survivor is desperately trying to defend herself, reassure her that you want to be fair and not to hurt her. Over the years of conducting couples' counseling, I can tell you that one of the most effective responses to an angry, upset spouse is to simply and sincerely restate that you love her very much and do not want to hurt her in any way. Psychologists also advocate *active listening, in which you concentrate on understanding your spouse's positive intention by repeating it back to her or him to clarify if you have it right. This reassures that your primary intention is to listen well and respond well.

Not . . . Preaching and Shaming

A variation on aggression is the abuse of the Christian doctrine of "headship" in marriage. Unfortunately, some men bully and intimidate by preaching Bible verses or offering the example of "local saints" to make the survivor see the light of their sinful, un-submissive attitude. *Shaming is always harmful leadership and does not reflect the love of Christ for the church—or the love of Christ for your spouse. *Dominating through use of guilt or shame avoids the pain of walking the second mile with your partner.* It selfishly diverts attention away from the pain and certainly will not get you the results you seek. There are, of course, times and ways to be "prophetic," but in general, relationships with abuse survivors require the sincere Christian to be humble and sincere. Like verbal aggression, spiritual arrogance will only work briefly, if at all.

Not . . . Conflict Avoidance

Through *conflict avoidance, many men are actually the opposite of aggressive and domineering. They are uncomfortable with confrontation and work to avoid it. They are passive and withdrawn when their spouses are very angry. The more a man withdraws or goes silent, the more upset and angry a woman may get. *Some men shut down because they are scared of angry feelings, but a cycle of poor communication results if partners withdraw when a survivor is angry.*

In truth, both spouses may be reacting to poor childhood training. If childhood abuse was aggressive verbal and physical abuse, the survivor will have a very difficult time looking anger in the eye and staying strong in responding and defending themselves. If, for example, the female in a relationship was a sexual abuse survivor and is very angry and confrontational, and the male is a verbal abuse survivor, the female survivor may find her partner unable to help her contain and work through her anger. A male partner needs to understand and work through his core fear and crippling terror in the face of angry confrontation. *An abuse survivor ideally needs a partner that can take his or her anger, remain calm and objective, and be a worthy opponent, in the sense of not crumbling or overreacting to anger.* It is very reassuring to be with someone who can handle your avalanche of angry feelings and work through them with you until they subside. Such experiences reduce your own fear of your anger and your shame over your own anger. In this light, the old maxim "nice guys finish last" may well be true.

NOT . . . STONEWALLING

John M. Gottman, a famous researcher of marital relationships and marital fighting styles, introduces what he calls "the four horses of the apocalypse" in poor marital conflict resolution.[15] For women the worse offenses, two of the four horses, are criticism and contempt. One of the remaining horses is common of men: *stonewalling. Stonewalling is a type of *passive-aggressive control. *The man withdraws in a punishing silence or even physical absence.* It is as if he is saying to his partner, "Your way of fighting and treating me poorly is so outrageous that I will withdraw from you into my cave where I will nurse my wounds for my unlucky choice of you as a partner." While these words may not be stated, his withdrawal drips of judgment and punishing rejection. This is a strategy of self-pity and usually works intermittently at best. More often the partner either withdraws into an angry silence too, or perhaps worse, she withdraws deeper into her isolated melancholy, learning to live alone or look elsewhere for her comfort and companionship.

Since men tend to be taught to manage conflict by either withdrawal or combat, the rigorous demands of fair fighting with an abuse survivor can be one means God uses to upgrade their humanity. God can increase their capacity to tolerate ambiguity and to have the courage and core strength to work through the frightening specter of abuse-surviving anger.

NOT . . . GIVING UP

Ultimately, whether by exhaustion, discouragement, anger, or cowardice, the partner of the survivor may feel like giving up. There are times when even a Christian may feel they need to give up on a relationship if it is too destructive to their well being or that of their children. Those circumstances are discussed in most self-help books. Here we wish to deal with the emotional feelings of giving up when, in fact, the partner does not intend to actually leave. *The ordeal of the long journey can be very discouraging. No one can judge the failures of either a survivor or their partner in the struggle to survive, endure, and grow.* Yet, the external "game" of punishing your partner by giving up on her or him is just another version of stonewalling. Even if the partner of the abuse survivor is not conscious of trying to create change through guilt, the living death of being in a marriage in which one has withdrawn in anger and whose heart has turned cold is not healthy for either person.

Healing Disciplines for Mutual Recovery

What if you and your abuse-survivor spouse had "perfect parents?" What do healthy parents give? Most books say it is love and discipline. Good families provide love and structure, along with safety and opportunity. Eugene Peterson, in *A Long Obedience in the Same Direction*, argues that most of us have developed a limited attention span to the

---

15. Gottman and Silva, *The Seven Principles for Making Marriage Work*, 33.

"sound bites" of television.[16] If we can't get closure and resolution in thirty seconds, or at least thirty minutes, most of us tend to move on, he suggests. Therefore, the biblical model of lifelong commitments and working on maturity over decades is not common or popular in our culture. Yet, this is the very thing that relationships suffering from the wounds of past trauma and abuse need. Who promised that life would be fair? Who is safe from sudden loss and trauma? Who gets only easy love and marriage? *Most of us have to learn to grow character and faithful love in the trenches of life's brokenness.* Therefore, the healthiest goal in facing past abuse in a relationship is to build commitments for new structures, disciplines, traditions, and love that can replace the lost sense of family from childhood abuse. A Christian model of sacrificial love, without losing *self-care and boundaries, is a heroic vision. What follows are some disciplines for rebuilding and maturing your love.

Discipline of Sharing

Be committed to sharing the trauma as it emerges. Listen, talk, and pray. Create new memories by grieving old memories, *together*. Do not be too busy or scared to engage the partner's need to share and process memories, therapy, and feelings. Frank M. Ochberg calls this a ministry of presence.[17] It is the gift of being really present with the survivor: attentive, caring, tolerant, patient and loving.

Discipline of Protecting the Core Love

The initial attraction traits that drew you together must still be there. *These things you loved about each other must not be lost in the drama of the co-victimization.* In our book, *Haunted Marriage*, we suggest a box be gift-wrapped to represent this core love that emerged between you.[18] It can be taken out during times of key, deep talks to remind you to be committed to protecting your core love as a fragile thing in need of careful treatment. It can also be passed back and forth when each is talking in a tense argument, to be sure that whoever is holding the gift can talk uninterrupted.

There is a wonderful story in 2 Chronicles 34–36, in which Josiah orders the Jerusalem temple to be cleaned and repaired after years of neglect. While clearing out a storage room in the temple, the workers came upon an ancient copy of the Torah.[19] When the king realized what it was and took the time to read it, he tore his clothes, declared a national mourning, and ordered the entire document be read to all the people in one reading, for he realized this was a precious core of God's Word that had been lost and needed to be restored. You should be as vitally committed to God's presence in your core love as this king was.

Discipline of Speaking the Truth in Love

When a spouse has been abused and is angry, it is hard to risk being truthful. Speaking the truth in love (Eph 4:15) is a hard calling, but it is a way to give your partner a bearing in

16. Peterson, *A Long Obedience in the Same Direction*, 7.

17. Ochberg, "Gift from Within," 4.

18. Barshinger et al., *Haunted Marriage*, 80.

19. "Torah" refers to the first part of the Hebrew canon, the Pentateuch (i.e., Genesis–Deuteronomy).

the storm of troubles. When done with loving intention, the courage to be simply honest can forge a path through all the unconsciousness and confusion, though it is hard, costly in time, and can be very unpleasant.

Discipline of Getting Help

There is a tendency to avoid getting help for these problems in a relationship. Getting help can be embarrassing and also financially costly. Men fear looking weak or troubled, especially if the doctor they are seeing is a psychologist. There is also the *taboo against taking any medication for depression or anxiety. Christians often fear that it is wrong to take a pill to get the help they should be relying on the Holy Spirit to do.[20] The discipline to get the help you need is another way to work your way through these difficulties. Individual *psychotherapy, couples counseling, *group therapy for abuse and trauma survivors, and *support groups for spouses of survivors are all very helpful ways to find healing. Short-term medication for depression and anxiety can be beneficial for the survivor and also for the spouse.

Discipline of Christian Community

A healthy Christian community expands the emotional resources and reassurances for "re-parenting" into a healthy family. *If we can be adopted into the spiritual family of God by our faith, we can also be "adopted" into a healthy family in our local church community.* Abuse survivors did not have healthy family experiences. They never learned the joys and security in being in a family they could trust and count on. They never felt truly valued and appreciated. If they practice the discipline of attendance and participation in the life of the local church family, the Holy Spirit can graft them into the spiritual family of God's church. They can be adopted, truly. One is never too old to be adopted by God's family!

Paul says we are all part of one body, the worldwide, mystical family of God throughout generations (1 Cor 12:12–31). How cool is that? Galatians 6:2 tells us to bear one another's burdens and so fulfill all the law of Christ. We are to love one another (1 John 4:7). We are not to neglect the gathering together with our local church family (Heb 10:25). Church life is a discipline that holds promise for healing in our personal relationships when practiced faithfully over the years. It can replace the brokenness, abuse, and disappointment of our first go round with family.

Discipline of Practicing the *Spiritual Disciplines

Throughout church history Christians have been healing their inner wounds by faithfully practicing the ancient and biblical disciplines of prayer, fasting, meditation/reflection, study of Scripture, and service to others (charity).[21] The battle to keep your marriage from being pulled apart can be helped by developing a spiritually intimate marriage. As each of you comes before God in earnestness to make your heart right, spirituality can be a bridge that gives you safe access to each other. Pride, ego, and selfishness can be overcome by the practice of personal spirituality aimed at ministry for your spouse and your own needs.

20. Barshinger et al., "The Gospel According to Prozac," 35.

21. Foster, *Celebration of Discipline*, 16–76, 126–140.

DISCIPLINE OF SIMPLE HEALTHY LIVING

Healthy families have healthy structures, habits, boundaries, and activities. To re-parent the abuse survivor, put into place the healthy choices of healthy families around you. Eat healthy foods; exercise regularly each week together; get adequate rest; reduce poor health habits; share humor; pursue inspirational activity, readings, and movies; build interpersonal community by seeking out healthy friendships as a couple; pursue stable financial planning and advice; and live by "whatsoever is pure . . . lovely . . . and of good repute" (Phil 4:8 NASB).

CONCLUSION

The journey is long, but the ways of God are steady, true, and strong. Committed love and discipline, with patience and self-control, make recovery and healing within your reach, personally and as a couple.

QUESTIONS FOR DISCUSSION

1. Who do you know who loves in ways that you admire? What are the characteristics of their love style? As a pastor, how would you intervene with a couple if one of them is an abuse survivor and does not recognize that they are overreacting to marital stress and frustration? How hard would you confront? How much theory would you bring up? How would you balance gentleness and safety with the need to point out errors and problems? What kind of training in seminary could have helped prepare you to address sexual abuse within the marriage context?

2. How well do you love others in your life who are difficult to love? What parallels do you see between counseling abuse-survivor relationships and other conflicted-relationship counseling principles? What biblical references and principles have you found helpful in working with abuse-survivor scenarios? What did you find most helpful from this chapter? How might "family ministries" leaders better incorporate these insights into their work? Discuss a scenario of an abuse-survivor you know of. How would you define their conflict profile? Whether as a pastor or therapist, what might you emphasize differently now or look for in future cases of abuse-survivors in marriage?

3. As a married couple, how well do you know your own partner? Do you both ever talk about the pains from either party's past? As a pastor or counselor, what problematic behaviors in marriage counseling would lead you to consider the possibility that there could be childhood sexual abuse with one or both of the individuals? Do you have some books in your church library that such individuals could use? What kind of trained professional help are you aware of in your church? At what point would you determine that a couple needs to be referred to a therapist? Does your church or "family pastor" ever teach on these issues? Do they match the recent needs of the church and/or community?

4. On a more reflective level, what did I learn about how to be a safe place for my partner and listen to what might be underlying her hurt instead of reacting to her out of frustration or selfishness? The author referred to the *ministry of presence* that survivors need. If you are a survivor, what would that look like for you? If you are the partner of a survivor, how can you develop a greater *ministry of presence*?

5. As a counselor or therapist, how have you witnessed "conflict avoidance" in your clients? Explain why it is counter-productive. What have you found to be the most helpful ways for couples to address this? How did the author define "repetition compulsion?" What are some other possible reasons for this repetition? Of these views, which one(s) would you say have been most evident in your practice? How would you explain "repetition compulsion" to a Christian elder that may be inclined to simply categorize "sexual fasting" or a sexual addiction as *sin* and require that man or woman to "repent and move on?"

6. As a married couple, how well do I know my own emotional triggers and the emotional triggers of my partner? Consider the author's discussion of the various kinds of abuse (e.g., sexual, physical, emotional) that may be part of your backgrounds. Discuss the implications for this for your communication patterns. As a counselor or pastor, how have you seen this phenomenon of "broken backgrounds" antagonizing both spouses?

7. As a spouse, who do I have to support me and my partner through this? What verses and promises of God can I lean into? How can I expand my capacity to be more empathetic to my partner? Is there a support group for survivor abuse that you can start or help lead? As a pastor, how could you apply these principles in dealing with an abuse-survivor spouse to your sermons or teachings on dealing with conflict in marriage and in relationships?

FOR FURTHER READING

Allender, Dan. B. *The Wounded Heart: Hope for Adult Victims of Childhood Sexual Abuse.* rev. ed. Colorado Springs, CO: NavPress, 1995.

Balswick, Jack O. and Judith K. *The Family: A Christian Perspective on the Contemporary Home.* Third ed. Grand Rapids, MI: Baker, 2007.

Barshinger, Clark E., Lojan E. LaRowe, and Andres T. Tapia. *Haunted Marriage: Overcoming the Ghosts of Your Spouse's Childhood Sexual Abuse.* Downers Grove, IL: InterVarsity Press, 1995.

Davis, Laura. *Allies in Healing: When the Person You Love Was Sexually Abused as a Child.* New York, NY: HarperCollins, 1991.

Ells, Alfred. *Restoring Innocence: Healing the Memories and Hurts that Hinder Sexual Intimacy.* Nashville, TN: Thomas Nelson Publishers, 1990.

Hansen, Paul. *Survivors and Partners.* Longmont, CO: Heron Hill Publishing, 1991.

Oz, Sheri. "When the Wife Was Sexually Abused as a Child: Marital Relations Before and During Her Therapy for Abuse." *Sexual & Relationship Therapy* 16 (2001): 287–298.

23

Childhood Sexual Abuse Survivors as Parents

Navigating a Difficult Path

Patrice F. Penney, MSW, LCSW

*C*HILDHOOD SEXUAL ABUSE (CSA) casts a long and devastating shadow over the subsequent life cycle development of *survivors. The damaging effects of CSA reach deeply into adulthood; it is well known that survivors struggle with a range of mental health problems as adults. More recent psychological research has begun to document the effects of abuse on adult interpersonal relationships as well, particularly survivors' marital relationships. However, while there is an impressive body of knowledge now regarding how a history of CSA impacts later adult functioning, *it has been less clear how the history of abuse also impacts the survivor's functioning as a parent.* Until recently, this was a neglected area of psychological and developmental research, with little known about the impact of surviving CSA on later parenting.

Recent research highlights the complexity of the relationship between CSA and various areas of adult functioning, including relational functioning in marriage and parenting. Childhood sexual abuse occurs in the context of various relational, psychological, social, and cultural factors that influence the course of the survivor's development. These factors, such as poverty, are interwoven with others, such as intervening relationships and events that may buffer the effects of the *trauma (e.g., a positive mentor relationship) and further traumas (e.g., *rape or *domestic violence), resulting in multiple outcomes for adult survivors.[1] Nevertheless, current research and treatment of adult survivors of *sexual abuse (SA), point to connections between the experience of CSA and the difficulties of parenting one's own children as an adult. This chapter considers those vulnerabilities brought to the adult parenting role, examining the problems and challenges that CSA survivors often experience as parents as well as the strengths and resiliencies in the parenting role that are possible outcomes.

---

1. Briere and Jordan, "Childhood Maltreatment, Intervening Variables, and Adult Psychological Difficulties in Women," 376, 382–383.

OVERVIEW OF THE EFFECTS OF CSA

First, it may be helpful to review some of the relevant psychological and developmental research that investigates the relationship between CSA and its impact on the adult survivor, because how the survivor is affected and how he or she functions and relates as an adult in turn affects his or her capacities as a parent. How does the experience of CSA affect the adult survivor psychologically and relationally? And what contributes to the *resilience and relational capacities of the survivor? Because this research draws from a number of different psychological, developmental, and relational perspectives, I will briefly describe these perspectives and how they contribute to our understanding of the effects of surviving CSA. Then I will look at some recent research that has studied CSA survivors as parents, and the implications of this research for survivors' healing and healthy parenting in their families. Finally, I will address how the church can take a more active role in providing acceptance, support, and healing for victims of CSA and their families, becoming a more articulate *advocate for survivors in many contexts.

ADULT SURVIVOR'S MENTAL HEALTH

We know that the effects of CSA do not end when the abuse ends; rather, the experience of CSA is known to create long-term problems that have the ability to significantly disrupt survivor's lives.[2] Childhood sexual abuse has well documented damaging effects on the adult survivor's mental health. While more in-depth discussions of these effects can be found in other chapters of this book, they are summarized here in order to clarify the link between adult survivor mental health issues and their potential impact on parenting. In mental health terms, which focus on *symptom clusters in current functioning, the CSA survivor may struggle with anxiety (including *panic), anger, and *depression, the most common mental health difficulty being depression.[3] While most of the studies looked at women survivors, a study which interviewed twenty-five male survivors of CSA found that 92 percent had experienced depression, and 72 percent had seriously contemplated and/or attempted suicide.[4] *Women are more likely to seek help with mental health issues; only four of the men in the same study had any involvement with the mental health profession, but almost half had a criminal record.*[5]

Survivors may also struggle with *cognitive distortions and "negative working models," which are core beliefs about themselves and the world around which thinking is organized. They may hold maladaptive core beliefs around low self-esteem (e.g., "I'm worthless"), *self-blame, hopelessness, expectations of rejection or abandonment, and preoccupation with danger, as well as disturbance in forming a cohesive identity in adolescence and young adulthood. Related difficulties include *emotional disregulation,

---

2. Alexander, "The Impact of Child Sexual Abuse on Parenting," 267.

3. Briere and Jordan, "Childhood Maltreatment," 376.

4. Etherington, "Adult Male Survivors of Childhood Sexual Abuse," 7.

5. Ibid.

which involves difficulties in the capacity to identify, manage, and appropriately express emotions, and chronic interpersonal difficulties.[6]

PTSD in Adult Survivors

Some researchers have focused on the link between CSA and the development of *post-traumatic stress disorder (PTSD), which without treatment, may be a significant disorder throughout the lifecycle. Post-traumatic stress disorder includes three areas of symptoms and responses to the trauma: (1) *intrusive experiences of reliving the trauma, (2) attempts to avoid people and places that are associated with the abuse, as well as emotional *numbing, (3) and *hyperarousal, including heightened *startle responses, sleep disturbance, and irritability.[7] *The trauma responses that functioned in childhood as survival mechanisms—such as vigilance around danger, which becomes hyperarousal—may in adulthood become part of a pattern of *coping that is generalized to a wide range of life situations,* with negative impact on the survivor's functioning, interpersonal relationships, and overall well-being. The *avoidant pattern of coping, in particular, is associated with increased psychological distress and negative outcomes for adult survivors,[8] because *the avoidance of painful feelings and experiences is not possible without shutting down a wide range of feelings and experiences that are important to healing and stable emotional and interpersonal functioning.* Bessel van der Kolk and Judith Herman have noted that *complex PTSD, which they argue is a better *diagnostic label for the pervasive and complex symptoms of post-traumatic stress, *can become part of the person's *personality structure,* with chronic and pervasive difficulty in the areas of *emotional regulation and arousal, distortions in perceptions of self and others, and belief systems.[9]

CSA Survivors and Attachment: Current Understanding

Because childhood sexual abuse is a relational trauma, it is extremely important to understand its effects in relational terms, using constructs that are valuable for this understanding, particularly for parent-child relationships. The theoretical framework of *attachment developed by John Bowlby,[10] and more recently applied to survivors of CSA by Pamela Alexander,[11] is crucial for understanding the parent-child relationship and how it is foundational to relational development into adulthood, marriage, and parenting. Attachment is basically an emotional bond to another person. Bowlby described attachment as a "lasting psychological connectedness between human beings."[12] *The central theme of *attachment*

6. Briere and Jordan, "Childhood Maltreatment," 376–77.

7. American Psychiatric Association, *Diagnostic and Statistical Manual of Mental Disorders,* 467–468.

8. Wright et al., "Multidimensional Assessment of Resilience in Mothers who are Child Sexual Abuse Survivors," 1187.

9. For further discussion, see Herman, *Trauma and Recovery*; and van der Kolk et al., *Traumatic Stress.*

10. Bowlby, *Attachment and Loss.*

11. Alexander, "Understanding the Effects of Child Sexual Abuse History on Current Couple Relationships."

12. Bowlby, *Attachment and Loss,* 1:194.

theory is that parents who are emotionally available and responsive to their infant's needs es-
tablish a sense of security. The infant knows that the caregiver is dependable, which creates
a secure base for the child to then explore their world. When fearful, the child returns to
the caregiver for safety and stays in close proximity when distressed. Through this secure
relationship, the child learns to trust.

Alexander makes the point that "a child cannot not be attached."[13] This means that for
the sexually abused child, she must maintain a way of being attached to her parent, even
when that parent is also abusing her. Thus the child, when frightened (e.g., during abuse),
seeks comfort "from the very parent who is causing the fear in the first place."[14] For the
sexually abused child, this often results in a *disorganized attachment, which is characterized by controlling (rather than trusting) behavior, anger, caregiving of a parent, as well as
a sense of shame and "badness." In adults, this disorganized attachment translates into a
fearful or unresolved attachment[15] that then impacts the attachment security of the children of that survivor. The presence of another *attachment figure (e.g., a grandmother)
can be a significant emotional buffer for the experience of trauma in childhood. Likewise,
in adulthood, a supportive partner or spouse can *moderate the effects of the CSA on the
survivor. It is important to understand that *childhood and adult attachment patterns have
both obvious and subtle implications for the parenting competence of the survivor, with his
or her spouse*, which will be discussed later. Adequately understanding attachment also argues for utilizing more of a *family systems theoretical approach to understanding CSA,
since both the interactional patterns the survivor experienced and saw modeled in their
family of origin, and the patterns he or she brings to their own parenting, are interrelated,
since these patterns are part of a *web of relationships* and experiences.

CSA SURVIVORS AS PARENTS: CHARACTERISTICS

Some core questions must be addressed for CSA survivors who parent. For example: What
tends to characterize the relationships between parent and children? What makes parenting more likely difficult or problematic? What moderates the effects of being a survivor of
CSA? While there is emerging research on CSA survivors as parents, much more attention
has been paid to the mental health consequences in adulthood for CSA survivors, with
little focus on the survivors' relationships. Many aspects of the survivor-as-parent remain
to be studied in order to adequately understand CSA's effects on this crucial caregiving
role. Nevertheless, the research to date does demonstrate various ways in which the CSA
has impacted the parenting of the survivors. Research has focused almost exclusively on
female survivors as mothers, leaving a significant gap in terms of understanding the experience of male survivors of CSA as parents. I will attempt to address this gap by including
findings from the few studies of men that are available.

Jennie Noll, Penelope Trickett, William Harris, and Frank Putnam found that mothers
with CSA histories were more likely to be teenage mothers, high-school drop-outs, obese,

13. Alexander, "Understanding the Effects," 343.

14. Ibid., 347.

15. Ibid., 351.

have substance abuse problems, and have experienced domestic violence, and their children were more likely to be pre-term births[16] and more likely to be involved in *protective services.[17] Research in the area of intimate partner relationships suggests that CSA survivors' relationships' are characterized by "lower relationship satisfaction, more overall discord, an increased risk of domestic violence, and a greater likelihood of separation or divorce."[18] These characteristics have obvious implications for the health of the family as the marital couple's relationship provides the foundation for family life and development.

At present, there are so few studies of male survivors as parents, that it is difficult to know to what extent male CSA survivors become parents or much about their parenting and family relationships. While clearly some male CSA survivors are parents, *in one study of twenty-five men who were CSA survivors, eighteen—almost three-quarters—were childless.*[19] In one study of male and female survivors of CSA (one of the few with both genders), a significant proportion of the participants were living adult lives "marked by addictions, imprisonment, prostitution, poor health, family instability, and experiences with interpersonal violence, both as *perpetrators and as victims."[20] In another study of incarcerated males, three-fifths of them had a history of CSA, confirming the belief held by many professionals in the criminal justice field that a significant number of incarcerated males are also CSA survivors. This, of course, does not preclude their being parents but would by definition mean that they are absent parents for some periods of time.

Family dynamics in which sexual abuse has occurred include less cohesiveness, less flexibility or adaptability, and more conflict and use of *authoritarian parenting.[21] In the families of the survivors as parents, female survivors report having difficulty speaking up on behalf of the children (particularly when they are being mistreated), not trusting, or trusting too much where it is not warranted.[22]

CSA's Connection to Adult Trauma and Domestic Violence

Victoria Banyard, Linda Williams, and Jane Siegel focused their research on the characteristics of intimate adult relationships of CSA survivors. Their research showed that *CSA is often not isolated but part of a larger context of trauma across the lifecycle.*[23] Thus the study of effects of CSA on adult functioning must take into account the possibility

16. Noll et al., "The Cumulative Burden Borne by Offspring Whose Mothers Were Sexually Abused as Children," 424.

17. In the US and much of Europe, protective services are government agencies that become involved with families when child physical or sexual abuse, or neglect, is indicated. In the two-thirds world, while there are some children's departments, often the child protective role is assigned to police, or is addressed by community leaders.

18. DiLillo and Damashek, "Parenting Characteristics of Women Reporting a History of Childhood Sexual Abuse," 319.

19. Etherington, "Adult Male Survivors," 5.

20. Martsolf and Draucker, "The Legacy of Childhood Sexual Abuse and Family Adversity," 337.

21. Polusny and Follette, "Long-Term Correlates of Child Sexual Abuse," 143–166.

22. Ibid.

23. Banyard et al., "The Long-Term Mental Health Consequences of Child Sexual Abuse," 699–700.

that the adult survivor may have been *re-victimized in adulthood. This re-victimization may include adult sexual assault and rape, as well as *intimate partner violence. As noted earlier, survivors are more likely to be in adult relationships characterized by domestic violence; typically that is man-to-woman violence. In the violent relationships of CSA survivors, there are also higher rates of woman-to-man aggression. In both instances, family members, particularly children, are at increased risk for violence and its effects,[24] including depression and anxiety, substance abuse, PTSD, *cognitive difficulties, *learned helplessness, and social problems.[25]

DEPRESSION

For survivors of CSA, the mental health toll can be enormous: depression and anxiety are the most common mental health problems. What effects do these mental health problems have on CSA survivors' parenting? Depression in mothers has been linked to less emotional availability and responsiveness to their children, negative emotion and negative perspectives toward their children, a critical and rejecting stance, lower levels of parenting competence, and a more "difficult temperament" in their children.[26] In regard to the temperament link, Ariel Lang, Maria Gartstein, Carie Rodgers, and Meredith Lebeck urge a more flexible definition of child temperament, not as *biologically* based and relatively fixed, but as the biological *makeup* of the individual that is influenced by *heredity, maturation, and experience*.[27] In other words, *a child's difficult temperament can be influenced by characteristics of parenting*. To parent a child who is more difficult temperamentally, more parental patience and flexibility are required; these are parenting characteristics that are challenging for any parent and very difficult for parents who are depressed, anxious, and possibly more focused on meeting their own needs—*key needs that were never met for them and may now be extremely difficult for them to attend to in the next generation*.

Overall, children may be significantly affected by the lack of maternal warmth and availability, and by increased negativity, a connection that I will develop more at length in the discussion of attachment effects. To what extent the lack of maternal nurturing is buffered by a supportive and engaged husband and father is also an important area for further study. And while studies of male CSA survivors as parents are only sparsely available, we do know that male survivors also struggle with depression, anxiety, and low self-esteem, and we would anticipate that these difficulties would have effects on their roles as fathers.

24. DiLillo et al., "A Closer Look at the Nature of Intimate Partner Violence Reported by Women with a History of Child Sexual Abuse," 125.

25. For a review of effects on women, see Levendosky and Graham-Bermann, "Parenting in Battered Women," 171–192; and for a review of effects in children, see Margolin and Gordis, "The Effects of Family and Community Violence on Children," 445–479.

26. For a discussion of depression in mothers, see Lang et al., "Impact of Maternal Child Abuse on Parenting an Infant Temperament," 101–102.

27. Ibid., 102.

PTSD in Adult Survivors

Post-traumatic stress disorder also contributes to significantly poorer parenting outcomes in CSA survivors. The PTSD symptoms such as *intrusive memories, *hypervigilance, or avoidance of feelings (i.e., a restricted range of emotions) can significantly interfere with consistent, responsive parenting.[28] Survivors of CSA are especially prone to *avoidance because the emotional states which they commonly experience are negative and over-whelming: depression, anxiety, guilt, shame, rage, and despair. *Because these emotions are so difficult to re-experience, survivors try to avoid these feelings, and as a consequence, also shut down the possibility of positive emotions. Thus parents who are survivors may shut down their own, as well as their children's emotional expression, and they consistently miss opportunities to connect with their children warmly and positively, helping their children developmentally to regulate their emotional experience.*[29]

Disorganized Attachment in Children

Restricting or avoiding emotion is a hallmark of PTSD; it is also a very significant deficit in the attachment relationship, as a secure attachment is one in which the parent is emotionally attuned to the child, and through that sensitivity, acceptance, and *modulation, promotes emotional regulation in the child. In their study, Karlen Lyons-Ruth and Deborah Block found that female CSA survivors, in their parenting role with infants, *are more likely to withdraw from their infants, to behave in emotionally restricted ways, and to establish disorganized attachments with their children.*[30] An important parental capacity is providing emotional regulation for the young child, which includes experiencing a wide emotional range as a parent, noticing emotions and *empathizing with their children, and modeling and helping children learn to regulate—both manage and *self-soothe—their emotions in a healthy manner. The authors discuss the "impossible demand" placed on many traumatized mothers to "flexibly access their own feelings of vulnerability and distress in order to fashion an adequate response to similar infant affective communications."[31] In other words, *the child's emotional responses may feel very threatening to the mother because they intrude on her defense against re-experiencing emotions such as vulnerability or distress.*

In an interesting study, Koren-Karie, Oppenheim, and Getzler-Yosef focused on the *affective dialogues between mothers and their six-year-old children, in light of the mothers' experiences of sexual abuse during childhood. Such dialogues between mother, or other caregiver, and child, are part of the "dance" of *attunement in attachment, in which the mother helps the child to organize his or her emotional experiences in a meaningful way, helping the child to feel understood and secure.[32] This study reveals that mothers

28. Ibid., 101.

29. Lyons-Ruth and Block, "The Disturbed Caregiving System: Relations among Childhood Trauma, Maternal Caregiving, and Infant Affect and Attachment," 273.

30. Ibid., 270–271.

31. Ibid., 272.

32. For a discussion of relevant studies, see Koren-Karie et al., "Mothers Who Were Severely Abused During Childhood and their Children Talk About Emotions," 302.

who have experienced traumas have found that talking about their negative emotions pushed them beyond their emotional capacities. The mothers showed difficulties matching their conversations to their children's emotional expression. Instead, these mothers showed confusing, non-accepting, or overwhelming behavior during their conversations with their children.[33]

The authors also looked at the concept of maternal (parental) insightfulness, as "the capacity to view the child as a separate person with needs, wishes, and emotions of his or her own, particularly when these are different or even contradictory to the mother's."[34] In the conversations of CSA mothers with their children, the authors found a lack of insightfulness, and a tendency to confuse the child's needs and feelings with her own. *This difficulty can be attributed to the CSA survivor's challenge to cope with and heal from the multiple effects of abuse, which have interfered with a cohesive sense of self, good interpersonal boundaries, and with integrated physical, mental, and emotional states.*

Survivors' Children: Risk of Sexual Abuse

Duncan notes that women who have survived CSA have impaired capacity to trust others, including confusion about whom and when to trust.[35] Trust is the foundation of intimate relationships; *for survivors it is difficult to trust others, and survivors sometimes trust the wrong people or fail to trust the right people.* One documented effect of this confusion for parenting is that the children of CSA survivors are more often abused as well. While this may seem contrary to the common sense expectation that a survivor would not be party to an abusive relationship in their adulthood, it is important to recognize that survivors often have distorted belief systems resulting from their own experience of abuse, including the belief that abuse is to be expected, or that "love is always abusive."[36] This belief may contribute to a survivor's failure to protect a child from sexual abuse. Female survivors may be in relationships with male partners who are violent or sexually abusive, or they may continue relationships with their own perpetrators, particularly when the perpetrators are within the immediate or extended family of origin, thus putting their children at risk for victimization.[37] Women may also perpetrate child sexual abuse, although less is understood about this pattern.

Survivors' Children: Risk of Physical Abuse

The connection between CSA and physically abusive parenting on the part of the survivor may seem even more surprising. The link between the two is complicated by the fact that *many victims of CSA also suffered physical abuse, and these multiple abuses create a stronger connection to physically abusive parenting responses.* In fact, Victoria Banyard has confirmed that a maternal CSA history did predict the use of physical violence and

33. Ibid.
34. Ibid., 304.
35. Duncan, "The Impact of Child Sexual Abuse on Parenting," 269.
36. Ibid.
37. See discussion in DiLillo and Damashek, "Parenting Characteristics," 320–321.

harsh parenting as a response to children.[38] This sober finding makes sense when we are reminded of the difficulties with anger and emotional regulation with which survivors of CSA often struggle. Survivors also have problems in the area of distorted cognition and may tend to view their children more negatively or attribute intent to their children's behaviors that are simply impulsive childhood acts or mistakes.

Parenting Skill Deficits

One of the reported characteristics survivors as parents feel is *incompetence*. In one research study, Tamar Cohen looked at parenting skills in survivors of CSA. This investigation addressed the basic functioning of the mothers as parents in seven different domains: *role support, *role image, objectivity, expectations for the child, rapport, communication, and limit-setting.[39] Not surprisingly, Cohen found that mothers with a history of CSA generally functioned on a lower level than mothers who had not experienced this abuse. There were particularly large differences in the areas of role support and communication. The difficulty with role support implies that many of the mothers are not in supportive marital or couple relationships. Communication difficulty also echoes the findings of Koren-Karie et al that show *survivors of CSA are less able to communicate openly about a wide range of feelings because they are avoiding intensely negative feelings.*[40] Victoria Banyard also notes that CSA is a risk factor for further negative parenting, including low self-esteem as a parent and difficulty coping with child discipline.[41]

Role Reversal

From family systems and attachment perspectives, Pamela Alexander studied a specific parent-child pattern which she found to be more common in survivors of CSA—that of *role reversal.[42] Role reversal, also referred to as *parentification in the family systems literature, refers to the pattern of a parent depending on a child for emotional support and companionship, usually accompanied by a qualitatively poor or absent adult relationship (spouse or partner) for that parent. This is a reversal of the healthy pattern of a child depending on the parent for emotional support in a securely attached parent-child relationship. Of concern is that this dynamic of role reversal would become a burden for the child, may interfere with normal child development, and has also been associated with a disorganized attachment in children.[43] In attachment language, *the mother with a history of childhood sexual trauma may turn to her child for comfort when her own attachment anxieties are *triggered, including by the child.* Not only is this a common pattern in parents who are survivors, but also a pattern that survivors frequently experienced in

38. Banyard, "The Impact of Childhood Sexual Abuse and Family Functioning on Four Dimensions of Women's Later Parenting," 1102–1103.

39. Cohen, "Motherhood among Incest Survivors," 1425.

40. Koren-Karie et al., "Mothers Who Were Severely Abused," 302.

41. Banyard, "The Impact of Childhood Sexual Abuse," 1104.

42. Alexander et al., "Childhood Sexual Abuse History and Role Reversal in Parenting," 830.

43. Ibid.

their families of origin, pointing to the power of family *generational patterns as well. The presence of a supportive spouse and *co-parent can mitigate the experience of parenting stress for the survivor as well as the tendency toward role reversal in the children.

Clinical Vignette: Parenting Dynamics of a CSA Survivor

An example from clinical practice will help shed light on the challenges of parenting for a sexual abuse survivor who reflects a number of the issues we've discussed. Naomi's[44] *presentation highlights the effects of child sexual abuse on parenting from the perspectives of mental health symptoms; PTSD, including the avoidant coping style with restriction of a range of emotions; and attachment issues. This case illustrates parenting that is both too permissive and too authoritarian, the generational pattern of role reversal, and the presence of a "supportive" but a largely *absent father. The emotional consequences for the child are also apparent:

> Naomi is a thirty-seven-year-old married mother of two sons: Jeremy, eight, and Joshua, five. She is also a survivor of CSA, which began for her at the age of nine, perpetrated by a male family friend of her father. Her own father left the family when Naomi was eleven, and the abuse ended at that point. Naomi had the burden of caring for her family—cooking and providing childcare for her younger siblings—once her parents separated. *She describes her mother as worried, critical, and dependent on her from that time on.*

As an adult, Naomi has struggled with depression and anxiety, low self-esteem, avoidance of strong feelings and intimacy, *and a chronic sense of threat.* Her core belief is: "The world is not safe." She reports feeling as though, "I exist, and the world outside exists, but I don't connect." She also reports a lot of sadness in her life and the sense that, "I have learned how to avoid letting anything touch me."

Naomi is married to James, whom she describes as "the best thing that ever happened to me." She says he is good to her and would never hurt her, but he is uninvolved with her as a co-parent or directly with the children. She states that he is easily stressed by relationships and so avoids much social interaction. Consequently, Naomi parents both of her boys "solo" and feels isolated and alone much of the time.

Naomi describes a very close emotional bond with her eldest son, Jeremy, and not as much with her younger son, Joshua. Jeremy has difficulties with age-appropriate self-control, anger, bed-wetting, and some *school refusal. Naomi worries about Jeremy constantly. *She reports that she cannot "bear for him to be unhappy"; she also cannot bear to hear his negative feelings, so shuts them down, at which point he becomes very angry.* She also protects Jeremy "like a lion," and tries to control events so that nothing bad happens to him. He responds with counter-control and attempts to control her. Mother and son are engaged in frequent battles, in which both of them become enraged with each other, with much emotional intensity. *Naomi also acknowledges having difficulty allowing him to be with his father, because if anything happened to him in his father's care, she would blame herself.*

---

44. Client names and details have been changed to protect confidentiality.

Naomi views her son Jeremy as fundamentally like her—an extension of herself. She feels very close to him. She expresses *boundary confusion about his thoughts and feelings and her own, and she becomes distressed because her own feelings are stirred by his expression of feelings and become intolerable for her to manage. Paradoxically he tries to soothe her and take care of her distress, and yet he also tries to control her, resulting in each of them becoming very angry. Naomi is very fearful that she will lose her close relationship with him, and his care of her, if the conflict continues as he grows older. *She is also fearful that she will abuse him physically in her rage, and she is aware her relationship with him is already often emotionally abusive.*

In this vignette, several themes of CSA survivors as parents that have been discussed are illustrated: (1) Naomi struggles with her own mental health issues as a result of CSA, including depression, anxiety, and post-trauma related cognitive distortions; (2) she married someone who was "safe" but emotionally an absent father; (3) her relationship with her eldest son, Jeremy, is characterized by role reversal (which is also a generational pattern since she took care of her mother), emotional abuse, and an impaired capacity to tolerate her son's feelings, particularly his negative feelings, or help him manage them; (4) Jeremy struggles with an insecure attachment and behavior problems that stem from that, such as emotional disregulation, and control.

MALE SURVIVORS OF CHILDHOOD SEXUAL ABUSE

In the research literature, it is difficult to find studies regarding male survivors of CSA, especially studies that address relational issues, such as parenting. This dearth of literature has its own effects in perpetuating the silence on an important issue and, in turn, preventing health and mental health professionals from recognizing and treating male CSA survivors appropriately. *The lack of focus on men as survivors may be in part due to a larger cultural context that shames men for experiences and feelings that show possible weakness, emotional need, or need for professional support.*[45] I have noted previously that men with a history of CSA are over-represented in criminal justice and under-represented in mental health, which is a tragedy worth acknowledging and addressing. The few studies that are available find that male survivors of CSA experience difficulty with intimacy in relationships, emotional discomfort, and restricted expression of feelings, alienation, and anger.[46] They also struggle with depression and may externalize their overwhelming feelings in behaviors that are isolating or aggressive. *Clearly the men in this study are struggling with issues similar to their female counterparts: learning to tolerate emotional distress; trying to trust again after the experience of abuse, which shattered trust; wanting to belong and to feel secure and safe.* Unlike women who are CSA survivors, men must also address their own socialization in cultural and religious spheres of *shaming; social environments that do not leave sufficient room for men to have emotional needs. And since so little is known about male CSA survivors as parents, research obviously needs to take the next step and address this issue, both how CSA affects men's parenting relationships and outcomes in their families.

45. Pollack, *Real Boys*, 23–24.

46. Kia-Keating et al., "Relational Challenges and Recovery Processes in Male Survivors of Childhood Sexual Abuse," 666.

POSSIBILITIES FOR MODERATING THE EFFECTS
AND STRENGTHENING RESILIENCE

Many studies have addressed resilience, the capacity for individuals to emerge from the experience of adversity stronger and more able to cope. Several of the studies of CSA survivors have also focused on resilience, in terms of positive coping styles and making meaning of the adversity in their lives.[47] Positive *coping skills that are productive for survivors included problem solving, seeking support, setting boundaries in relationships, having realistic expectations for oneself, and a focus on *self-care. The study by Wright, Fopma-Loy, and Fischer highlighted a range of factors, including a supportive marriage, that promotes resilience in the areas of functioning in the role of parents, overall well-being, and general quality of life.[48]

Froma Walsh addresses resilience in a relational and family context, which I appreciate, as she highlights the importance of *relational aspects of resilience*—in other words, the ways in which relationships can promote coping and strengthen functioning.[49] Looking at resilience in a relational context highlights the importance of connection to others for the health and functioning of the survivor. Walsh addresses three characteristics of resilient families: (1) open communication, with a tolerance of negative emotion, (2) flexible connectedness, (3) and the capacity to make meaning of adversity. These characteristics should become part of the focus of treatment in families affected by CSA, helping these families make meaning out of the adversity. These factors have tremendous implications for Christians responding to CSA with the hope of the Gospel.

For many survivors, the foremost factor in mitigating the effects of CSA in their parenting is a strong and supportive marital relationship. Many family theorists have underscored the significance of a supportive marital relationship as the foundation of strong families with healthy relationships. Pamela Alexander, among others, notes that partner relationship satisfaction interacts with the abuse history in predicting the health of the parent-child relationship.[50] Particularly for sexual abuse survivors, a supportive spouse or partner can provide a more secure adult attachment, providing a relationship in which the survivor's emotional needs are more reliably met, and in which there is support for a wider range of feelings. At the same time, *spouses of CSA survivors often struggle with the emotional upheaval of living with a survivor and may experience *secondary traumatization through the traumatic stress responses of their spouses.* These spouses can also experience depression and anxiety as they live with levels of unpredictability in the marital and family relationships.[51] Nevertheless, when the marital relationship is more secure, survivors evidence fewer depressive symptoms, feel more competent, and are more able to adequately function in their parental role.[52] Not only is the female survivor more able

47. Ibid., 680.

48. Wright et al., "Multidimensional Assessment of Resilience in Mothers," 1185–1188.

49. See discussion in Walsh, *Strengthening Family Resilience*.

50. Alexander, "Understanding the Effects," 355.

51. Ibid., 351.

52. Wright et al., "Multidimensional Assessment of Resilience in Mothers," 1188.

to respond appropriately to her child's needs and feelings, but the child is less likely to be drawn into meeting the parent's emotional needs.

IMPLICATIONS FOR SURVIVORS AS PARENTS
AND THE CHRISTIAN COMMUNITY

What Do Survivors Need in Order to be Strong Parents?

Despite the real possibilities of resilience for survivors of CSA, of concern for all of the researchers and writers cited in this chapter is the continued vulnerability of CSA survivors in many areas of their functioning as parents. While this is not intended to minimize resilience, *this core concern underscores the need for therapeutic treatment, social services, an understanding faith community, and a safe, reliable, and caring social network for survivors struggling with the traumatic effects of CSA.* Karen Duncan reminds us that women are the major consumers of healthcare for themselves as mothers and their children, and it is within the access to healthcare and community services that CSA survivors can be helped: through screening for the trauma, providing information to survivors, discussing healing and recovery, and providing counseling and other treatments. Duncan writes:

> When we consider the number of women who have experienced this trauma in childhood along with the significant number of problems associated with it and the continuing risk to women for *re-victimization once this trauma has occurred, there is no plausible reason for screening, education, treatment, and recovery not to be a part of the mainstream of healthcare for women and children.[53]

I would only add that men should become a part of this focus on screening and providing supportive resources.

As with Naomi, some survivors of CSA who are parents will need ongoing counseling or psychotherapy to support their own healing and to strengthen and support their marital and parental roles. In Naomi's therapy, we worked on her setting appropriate limits with her son, learning to view him as separate from her, and developing good interpersonal boundaries. She developed a stronger capacity to accept and support her son's emotional expression, while regulating her own anxiety, sadness, and fear with less reliance on Jeremy to take care of her feelings (see *self-regulation). Of enormous help in that process was the support of James, her husband, who reluctantly attended therapy, *only to recognize more clearly his wife's struggles to parent and to commit to involve himself more significantly in the life of the family as a co-parent with her.* This case vignette illustrates the need for relational healing and *intervention, focused not only on the survivor, but on the marital and co-parenting relationships and the complexity of family relationships impacted by the CSA. This is a point that some therapies, therapists, and church ministers who work with survivors have missed, namely, *that survivor healing and growth must take place in the context of family relationships in which the survivor is involved so that they can*

---

53. Duncan, "The Impact of Child Sexual Abuse on Parenting," 270.

adequately address the health of those relationships and interrupt the intergenerational patterns around the trauma and its effects that occur in a web of relationships.[54]

The Christian Response

From a Gospel perspective, Christians should be vitally concerned about the impact of CSA. Childhood sexual abuse profoundly damages children and adults at a core level of trust, attacking their sense of self and identity, and it has enduring effects which may perpetuate psychological and relational damage in *generational patterns. Family relationships are foundational to how people grow and develop, and how we experience love, authority, *forgiveness, and grace. The Christian community and its family pastors should be deeply concerned about supporting health in families and nurturing children who can grow and develop free of the legacy of CSA, or who can heal once they've been damaged by its effects. N. T. Wright reminds us that if Christians are obedient to the Gospel, if we are following Jesus, then we are "to build for the kingdom"; every act of love, healing, care, nurture, or comfort will become part of God's new creation,[55] the work that he is accomplishing. When those acts focus on supporting and nurturing families who have been damaged by CSA, then the church is actively involved in the process of healing from a generational trauma and halting the impact of the abuse on the next generation of children.

Thus the larger context for survivors and their families in local church communities needs to be one of acknowledgement and support for the difficulties faced by CSA survivors as this can be a stunningly arduous path they navigate as parents. Survivors need information, encouragement, acceptance, and skill-building in order to be the parents they want to be. Christian communities must be better educated about the struggles of survivors as parents and more willing to create an accepting and supportive environment in which these parents can heal. In many ways and in different contexts, the local church can support parents: (1) through marriage ministries and aggressive pre-marital counseling, (2) through ministries to women preparing to be mothers, including unwed mothers, (3) and through ministries to mothers of infants and mothers of older children, including divorced and single-parent mothers. Also needed are parenting skills and mentoring programs for parents and other supportive programs for mothers and children. Most of the programs suggested here function in group settings, where parents meet together. *In those settings in the church, intentional focus should be placed on the experience of women as survivors, so that these women do not have to break the silence or share "the secret" without any public acknowledgement or understanding of the trauma of abuse.* One of the strongest factors for healing in a group is the sense of "I am not alone!" (see *support group). In such group settings, survivors are able to obtain the social support that they need in order to cope more positively with their challenges of parenting.

---

54. Alexander, "Understanding the Effects of Child Sexual Abuse," 342–343, 356–359. Alexander cautions clinicians that treating survivors without addressing family relationships can have *iatrogenic effects (356).

55. Wright, *Surprised by Hope*, 208.

The church should also be more intentional in addressing the effects of CSA so that children are buffered from the generational damage of their parent's CSA and have the opportunity to grow and thrive in healthy ways. Christian education programs that minister the love of Jesus to hurting children can also provide hope to children affected by CSA in their families. Programs for children that provide safety, relationships, and mentoring can "stand in the gap" for children at risk in their families. For almost twenty years I worked with an outreach program outside of Chicago[56] that created supports for parents and their children, including after-school and summer programs, tutoring, and mentoring for children. *The strength of these programs lay in the belief that directly intervening with "at risk" families and children meant that the intergenerational impact of abuse, among other stressors, could be mitigated and even halted by supportive relationships and programs in the community.* But understanding and outreach actually encompasses a spectrum of complex needs.

CSA and Intervention: Complexities of Cross-Cultural Contexts

Child sexual abuse is a serious problem in the North American culture, but it is also a compelling problem in other cultures across the Western and two-thirds world. As Christians, we must be broken-hearted about CSA and its devastating impact across generations of families, and we must understand that CSA is part of a web of abuse and injustice perpetrated in diverse cultural contexts across the world. As Gary Haugen writes in *Good News About Injustice*, God gives us a mandate to seek justice because He is a God of justice and compassion, and he empowers us to seek justice and healing where we see it is needed.[57]

I would argue that if we are to seek justice and be involved in compassionate ministry in these diverse cultural contexts, then we must be concerned with those patterns, cultural traditions, and institutions that sanction violence against women and children—both physical and sexual violence. While addressing SA is complex enough; we cannot simply universalize Western clinical models, tenants of individualism, or *hermeneutical approaches to Scripture and then expect the same results in vastly different cultural contexts. Abuse advocacy must learn to adapt to the complex social dynamics in the countries of Asia, Africa, and the Middle East, for example. In such countries, family solidarity, honor, authority, and gender are not defined according to European traditions. Regardless, this dialogue must move into the two-thirds world.

There is a great need for a more articulate and compelling public Christian voice that acknowledges the devastating global social issues of our time. These issues impact men, women, and children and interact with CSA in terms of cause and effect. Such issues include: *human trafficking of women and children; the international sex trade, that forces children and women into prostitution; family and cultural practices that support child abuse, rape and prostitution; pornography; the rape and subjugation of women and

---

56. With *Outreach Community Center* of *Outreach Community Ministries*, Carol Stream, Illinois, from 1986–2003.

57. Haugen, *Good News about Injustice*, 69–70.

children in wars and regional conflicts throughout the world. How does a child who was sold into slavery and prostitution go on to parent her own children? How does a woman who was raped as a child and suffered in silence now parent? How does a boy child soldier, who was subjugated through physical and sexual violence, grow up to be a loving father? These are complex issues we must grapple with, even as our hearts are moved, so that we take up the mandate of seeking justice and developing compassionate responses in various contexts of our world.

It is beyond the scope of this chapter to discuss cross-cultural responses to CSA, except to acknowledge that *these contexts require that Christians take a learner's perspective and also have a heart of compassion and humility.* There are significant cultural issues with which we must grapple. For instance, in some traditional cultures, it is *taboo to for children to know about or even discuss sexuality, so if a child is sexually abused, he or she will keep silent for fear of a punitive response, even becoming ostracized from the family. In Kenya, in a discussion with several rural pastors, I learned that they thought CSA victims or adult rape victims should leave their communities without naming the abuse so as not to bring shame on themselves or their families.[58] These cultural practices powerfully interact with CSA and its effects and have been protective of the culture, yet they may make it very challenging to bring CSA and its effects to light, hold perpetrators accountable, or access healing and support in the community and in the church.

CONCLUSION

Childhood sexual abuse does enormous damage across the lifecycle of the survivor, and as I have discussed in this chapter, has a significant impact on the role of adult survivors' parenting—raising the next generation of children, and the next. My hope is that I have shown evidence of a strong link between the childhood experience of sexual abuse, the consequences for the adult in terms of mental health, PTSD, attachment, and personhood, and the parenting capacities of the survivor caring for his or her own children. Clearly, while much more research needs to be undertaken around male and female survivors' experiences of parenting, a compelling connection is already emerging that means: (1) survivors need not only the opportunity to heal personally but also to be supported to address their parenting of their children of creation in a family context, (2) spouses of survivors also need understanding and support to stay engaged, (3) and children, the most vulnerable, need support and protection. Christians face the challenge of making the church a place of acknowledgement, hope, support, and comfort for survivors and their families, both in the North American context, and in other contexts of injustice throughout our world.

58. From the author. Discussion in a graduate course on trauma at *Africa International University,* Nairobi, Kenya.

QUESTIONS FOR DISCUSSION

1. Based on this discussion, what are some key reasons for disorganized attachment as an adult? How do adult attachment issues affect co-parenting responsibilities? How might pre-marital counseling incorporate some of these insights for couples about to be married? Discuss the various ways that socialization patterns in society and the church have discouraged male CSA survivors from seeking professional help. If possible, ask a male survivor to discuss various elements in his "disclosure"; have these elements of his story professionally critiqued by a therapist. List some practical steps counselors and pastors can do *together* to bring change.

2. A mother is a CSA survivor, abused by her own mother in her teen years; explain how both attachment issues and avoidant coping could present in her life as: (1) a mother to her teenagers, and (2) as an intimate partner with her husband. Reverse this abuse scenario: explain how a boy abused by a male figure might struggle later with his responsibilities as a father and husband. How are these kinds of scenarios addressed—adequately or inadequately—in the training contexts of therapists, seminaries, and local church family ministries?

3. Tragically, CSA survivors often abuse their own children. Based on this chapter, why would a deeply wounded adult (male or female) perpetuate their own trauma? List several elements that non-abused "outsiders" might *wrongly* conclude from inter-generational sexual abuse. Think of an abuse case you know of in which intergenerational abuse has occurred—what does healing look like for that CSA adult parent? How might they have been better helped if caretakers were better informed? How does one rehabilitate an adult survivor's view of marriage, sexual intimacy, parenting, and having children?

4. Explain how role reversal works. Why can it affect both the child and the other spouse in the same home? Whether you are a counselor, professor of ethics, social worker, or minister, what kind of training have you received to address CSA survivors as parents? How might "family pastors" in churches better detect, instruct, and counsel families caught in these unhealthy relationships? List several specific items you feel that seminary training should address for men and women who will face sexual abuse issues in ministry. List two biblical passages (an Old Testament and New Testament text) that illustrate the issues raised in this chapter, then discuss ways these could be sensitively preached.

5. Regarding male CSA survivors as parents, what might account for the lack of research and literature on this group? List some myths or *stereotypes that exist for male survivors? Discuss a recent scenario of a male survivor you are aware of and how this chapter helps answer key problems. Given that so many perpetrators are men, what's at risk for not adequately understanding and addressing cultural socialization and particular struggles of male CSA survivors? What kinds of programs exist for male survivors in your church, therapy office, or community?

6. Interview a missionary who works with sexual abuse, trauma, and family counseling in a two-thirds world country. What is the unique presentation of CSA in that culture? Consider letting a missionary speak at your school, church, or missions program. What are the particular cultural issues they are facing working with CSA survivors in a cross-cultural context? How should missionaries be trained to work with CSA survivors in such countries? What can "Western" therapy practices learn from cross-cultural experiences?

FOR FURTHER READING

Barshinger, Clark E., Lojan E. Larowe, and Andrés Tapia. *Haunted Marriage: Overcoming the Ghosts of Your Spouse's Childhood Abuse.* Downers Grove, IL: InterVarsity, 1995.

Duncan, Karen. *Healing from the Trauma of Childhood Sexual Abuse: The Journey of Women.* Westport, CT: Praeger, 2005.

Graber, Ken. *Ghosts in the Bedroom: A Guide for Partners of Incest Survivors.* Deerfield Beach, FL: Health Communications, 1991.

Hughes, Daniel. *Attachment-Focused Parenting: Effective Strategies to Care for Children.* New York, NY: W.W. Norton and Co., 2009.

Hunt, Laura. "Missions in the Context of Recovery from Childhood Sexual Abuse." *Missiology* 38 (2010): 321–333.

Kia-Keating, Maryam, Lynn Sorsoli, and Frances Grossman. "Relational Challenges and Recovery Processes in Male Survivors of Childhood Sexual Abuse." *Journal of Interpersonal Violence* 25 (2010): 666–683.

Mazor, Aviva. "Relational Couple Therapy with Post-Traumatic Survivors: Links Between Post-Traumatic Self and Contemporary Intimate Relationships." *Contemporary Family Therapy* 26 (2004): 3–21.

Murphey, Cecil. *When a Man You Love Was Abused: A Woman's Guide to Helping Him Overcome Childhood Sexual Molestation.* Grand Rapids, MI: Kregel, 2010.

Siegel, Daniel, and Mary Hartzell. *Parenting from the Inside Out.* New York, NY: Penguin, 2003.

Wallin, David. *Attachment in Psychotherapy.* New York, NY: Guilford Press, 2007.

Appendix A

Stories of Survivors

DIANE'S STORY

"God is good."
Is he, really?
If he is, then how could he allow this evil to happen to me?

I circle through this sequence on a regular basis. In fact, I am currently writing a research paper on the goodness of God and the presence of evil, and I will use it as a springboard for my thesis at the Institute for Spiritual Formation (ISF), Talbot School of Theology. God brought me there to heal my soul and has done so through the loving and insightful community of faculty, staff, and students at ISF. It has been an exhausting and invigorating journey because I entered with a tremendous weight of sorrow. The load is getting lighter.

I am a forty-seven-year-old woman who is a survivor of childhood sexual trauma. My father abused me until I was four years old. He threatened to kill my mother or younger brother if I told. He was hostile and psychotic, addicted to everything. Yet my mother continued to keep us in that environment. They eventually divorced when I was six, but not because of what he did to me. He terrorized our family until his death in 2009.

After her divorce, my mother had affairs—the first one involved a priest; the other, a married man. The priest was sexually inappropriate with me; my mother's paramour molested me when I was eighteen. I said nothing to her when it happened and pushed it out of my memory. I married eight years later, and as my husband relentlessly tickled me one evening, the memory of that most recent molestation was triggered.

I sought my second round of therapy. I was told to reveal to my mother what occurred, and I did. This resulted in my mother and brother turning on me. Ten years or so later, my mother married the very man who molested me.

I said nothing about my father for decades—I kept it all inside. My brother and I were well trained to never upset our mother. The selfish manner in which my mother raised me affects me to this day. I lived a perfectionistic and performance-oriented childhood, ignoring my own needs in order to keep her happy. Growing up was also filled with constant health issues, nightmares about being chased and raped, and a desire to have normal relationships with boys—and eventually, men. I was afraid of being hurt, yet more fearful of not having someone.

Struggling with all of this in addition to the abuse led me to a breakdown when I was thirty. While in the hospital, the psychiatrists and therapists urged me to tell my mother what my father had done. I was panic-stricken. I did not want further rejection and invalidation from my mother and brother. But, I knew I had to say something. I was trapped again, and suicidal—a lifelong issue. I was actually willing to take this secret to the grave by ending my life in order to avoid harming my mother.

After several agonizing days in the hospital, I told my mother and brother about the abuse. They, of course, did not believe me. Not only this, but shortly afterward my mother, brother, and now stepfather concluded I was insane regarding both my father's incest and my stepfather's molestation. They believe I made up both events merely out of malice for my mother. Instead of seeing me as the victim, instead of using this as a vehicle for apologies and reconciliation with me, they saw me as the culprit. Unbelievable! This has damaged and grieved me almost as much as the abuses did.

I have felt alone and unprotected most of my life. I knew God was there, but his promises were not for me. Why was I given this incredibly unfair and unwanted burden? I kept serving him out of fear and a sense of duty. It was performance-oriented: "If only I do or think x, y, z—he'll accept me and take away this horror-filled life of mine. If he loves me, he'll open their eyes, they will believe me, and all will be resolved."

Never happened. Never will.

I have been his disciple for more than thirty-five years. Mine has been a life of ministry to and sacrifice for others, but I have always felt inadequate or insufficient. Although I sought and served God with all of my strength, I still felt a wall and a distance between us. What my head knew as theological truth could not filter down to my heart. I was furious with God. I was also terrified of him, but longed to be close to and secure in him. In my first semester at ISF, I sat with one of my professors who knew a bit of my background. I wept as I told her how much I wanted a deeper relationship with God but hadn't figured out how to do so. So much has happened, and I have great difficulty trusting God. Her reply startled me: "How could you *not* have trust issues with him?" No judgment or chastisement in her tone. It was validating. It was freeing. I knew at that moment I didn't have to pretend anymore. It was OK that I wasn't firing on all cylinders. This was the beginning of the deep healing I have now experienced for the past four years.

It takes a great deal of tenderness and patience to walk alongside me in my journey, but I have learned to surround myself with people who are safe and are able to minister to me. My second husband is truly understanding, as is the ISF community and other good friends. God has used them greatly as I heal from the flashbacks, nightmares, PTSD, OCD, depression, fear, anger, and anxiety. I also feel like "used goods" at times, and as mentioned, have difficulty trusting God, others, and myself. Feelings of worthlessness and uselessness surface quite often.

Additionally, a host of physical maladies have accompanied me throughout my life, including lung, intestinal, chronic pain, and chronic fatigue issues. I have bouts of insomnia when the flashbacks and nightmares are in full swing, and then there are times I cannot get out of bed because I am so drained. On those days, my ten-year-old will snuggle up and we read together or watch TV. She is joyful and delightful, my greatest gift from

God. I see in her how I could have been, were it not for my twisted family of origin. And I worry that although I persist in my healing, I will damage her somehow. The neurotic cycle never ends.

If this were not overwhelming enough, the abuse also left me vulnerable to one phenomenon I knew was true, but did not know why. Within two semesters, three professors (two of whom were my spiritual warfare instructors) explained how sexual abuse (or sexual sin) and anger are the main entry points for demonic activity. Triple whammy for me because my first husband was unfaithful with prostitutes. I have had sightings and experiences throughout my life, and I now know what to do. I have had warfare prayer numerous times, and it was powerful. I have had inner-healing prayer, soaking prayer, and my colleagues and professors have prayed over me. I cannot emphasize enough the importance of prayer with trained intercessory warriors. Our classes at ISF not only teach about prayer but also teach us how to pray. We are taught prayers by the church fathers and mothers, and others throughout church history. We are also trained how to sit with God and be silent, very difficult for one like me who is afraid of being alone—flashbacks, and so on constantly going through my mind. But I have learned. And I have grown closer to my God.

God continues to redeem my past. Although I cannot "rejoice" in the atrocities I have experienced, I am grateful God has preserved me. And I finally realized that if those things had not happened, I very possibly could have become like my family of origin. God plucked me out of that ghastly cycle, and I turned toward him instead of away from him—by his grace. I do not seek their approval any longer; I do not care if they believe me. I cut off all contact two years ago and am healing at a much better pace than I had before.

It is the goodness of God that heals me. That took years to work through. I have moments of doubt, but I can see his guidance as I look back, guidance that led me through the deepest of valleys into places where I actually experience streams of living water. I may never know why it had to be sexual abuse of all things to draw me closer to Him, but I praise Him. Although he did not protect me from the abuse, he has kept my soul safe. I belong to him. Perhaps he kept worse evils from occurring—my life was spared as a child. My life has been spared several times recently—I have had three or four near-death experiences in the past five years. I have had serious medical issues, and I recently survived a head-on collision. I felt a tremendous sense of his mercy, especially in the accident. Like Job, I do not understand all the reasons things have happened the way they have, but:

> "I know that my redeemer lives,
>   and that in the end he will stand on the earth.
>   And after my skin has been destroyed,
>   yet in my flesh I will see God;
>   I myself will see him
>   with my own eyes—I, and not another.
>   How my heart yearns within me!" (Job 19:25–27 NIV)

For someone with my background, trained and experienced Christian professionals are vital. We are required to have a spiritual director and therapist in ISF, and although the work can be excruciating, it is worth it. Community—authentic followers of the Lord

Jesus—is a basic necessity. To journey with people who know their identity is in Christ is incredibly healing. We need to surround ourselves with people who are genuine, who are not afraid to look at their own sin, who do not hide from God, others, and themselves. I have witnessed the Spirit's power in my life and the lives of my brothers and sisters as we open to God and present ourselves to him with intentionality and humility.

Although I am well taken care of by my ISF family, I am concerned about the "hurry up" approach of most church ministries. Not many pastors, let alone lay people, are willing or able to invest the time it takes to journey with someone such as myself. Yet this is what the Lord Jesus and Apostle Paul lived and taught us by example. As a family, the body of Christ is to weep with one another, carry one another's burdens, and participate in all of the "one another's" the New Testament describes. This is the investment of a lifetime! This is how we pour out ourselves as living sacrifices, by meeting the needs of others—no matter how difficult.

I have worked on several church staffs over the past thirty years, but only two pastors took a real interest in my spiritual growth and me as a person. Two. The pastor I work for currently is under the impression (as are many, if not most) that "one quick prayer ought to do it." No. Neither is forgiveness a one-time event; it is a process. I pray the Spirit works on this with his people. Forgiveness takes time and tears. The Lord Jesus commands it, yes, but it is also a relational exercise—it cannot be experienced in a vacuum. Forgiveness has to be modeled and practiced in a safe setting, as the church was meant to be.

However vital forgiveness is to the corporate body and the individuals within, it is not my main issue as a survivor. I struggle most often with: (1) the inability to trust God, others, and myself, and (2) feelings of self-worth. Again, these are areas that can only be healed as I see and experience authentic love by authentic disciples of the Lord Jesus. Whether the issue is sexual abuse or something less complicated, God's healing comes when we deeply connect with him and others. Surface affiliations cannot accomplish God's profound purposes when it comes to healing the wounded. It takes time to develop relationships, but it is the way he designed us—we need one another. We need to be bound by the love of the Father, Son, and Holy Spirit in order to lock arms against the enemy and his wicked schemes. We need to learn how to love each other authentically and sacrificially because perfect love casts out fear, and it covers a multitude of sins.

DILLON'S STORY

It was hard to explain to my father that I'd be spending the night at a hotel with the conference speaker who just taught about healing from homosexuality, the preacher proclaiming "Peace! Peace!," and I, in a line of two waiting to talk with him after, had received a cordial invitation to spend a little more time with him. Then, it wasn't too strange. Another friend shared the room with us and we only talked through the night. We sat on a balcony overlooking the parking lot, watching fireworks blast from over the hills. It didn't matter much that I was sixteen—both still laughed and included me in their conversation, and his friend even let me sleep in his bed.

The next day he took me to a theme park nearby, and we ran to each ride and smiled all afternoon. We were now friends—he gave me a nickname and paid for my lunch. His favorite ride was the haunted house; the monsters were funny to him, cute ghosts in the walls. Though they shouted, he did not flinch like the other riders. I thought he was confident, bold, an exceptional man. When he left the next day to resume his speaking tour, I started painting him a picture of the ghost ride, dark blue and green paint on canvas. Maybe he'd never come back here again, but I'd send it to thank my new mentor for how much he'd taught me about freedom and fire.

He was both—aflame and free. His prayers were in many tongues, mystical tongues that only angels knew, a higher way to speak to our God who also speaks to us. His words are available for anyone, and my mentor always hears them. "The sheep know my voice," he would quote. "We just need to listen." Then we'd rock on our knees praying in tongues. What a godly man—he knew such bright truths about the Scriptures that I didn't grow up with but quickly adopted.

At his next conference stop, we talked in the evenings on web cameras, the first time for about an hour, then for nearly two hours a few times each week throughout his whole tour. I'd told him in the hotel about my history of sexual pain, of all the pictures of men I'd seen on the Internet, and how ill I felt for enjoying them. He promised healing and offered his stories that were so similar, so exactly parallel with mine that I couldn't help but listen, amazed. Am I not alone in the world? I'd felt like it—a secret life and feminine habits had alienated me from my peers, and though other mentors had started to listen, few could help me like this one.

He introduced me to his friends on the camera, and none of them seemed distracted by my age or my past. The Preacher was very sociable with them, proven by hugs and uplifting voice. They would wrestle on the camera, and I watched, laughing. He always wrestled with friends; it was part of his healing. Alienation from the same gender was causative of same-sex attraction. His book carried this message (and he'd given me an autographed copy). So replacing negative touch with healthy touch should be a good thing, a safe thing. Some of his friends shared queen beds, took showers without curtains, then stood undressed after the shower without any feeling of shame. They aimed to normalize things once mysterious.

The Preacher finished his tour and ended up visiting a suburb near mine. My parents knew I was fond of him, and considering his résumé and what they knew of my past, they figured him God-sent. Dad would be in Kenya for the month teaching at a Bible conference, and Mom would join him after a week to teach the women. Instead of me staying with a friend and assigning our grandparents to check in on the home, I might be able to stay at our house with the Preacher. His host got called out of town, and my mentor needed to find a new place to stay—it all seemed so ordained by God the Healer!

Mom dropped off Dad at the airport. The Preacher arrived at our home just before her, and we talked happily on the couch next to each other, his arm around me, normalizing touch for the boy who hadn't had much from his Dad. Mom saw us on the couch with his hand resting on the inner curve of my thigh.

She put her groceries away in the pantry and tried to ignore it, and then we moved to the kitchen table and pushed two chairs together to share. We talked and talked, always on the same side of the table, looking at each other sideways with our arms clamped around the other.

Mom didn't trust my healing. "Dillon, why don't you go move your guitar and some clothes into your brother's room so your friend can move into yours?" I slept in the biggest room in the house, decked with a bunk bed and futon and whole drum set with plenty of floor space left over. We often had Africans here for church conferences or just to visit, and it seemed absurd for me to move into my brother's one-bed, one-desk room with hardly the space to do pushups, or to wrestle, which I figured we would do.

I resented her separation, but that night once Mom was asleep I snuck into the Preacher's dark room where he lay awake on the top bunk by himself. To sleep alone was abnormal, or at least undesirable. So many of his ex-gay friends exchange physical touch in hugs, holding hands. One won't ever sleep in a bed by himself. My mentor should not be alone. And he invited me into the bed without words, and I lay sideways beside him, his arms around me for a long duration of peace. He joked that my listening to his heartbeat was like John on the bosom of Christ. It felt like Christ, felt like heaven. And it was totally normal, he taught—the best way to heal. "But you should get out of the bed in case your mom comes," he said, so I snuck away.

I could number the times I'd hugged my Dad since fourth grade, and most were at airports and school graduations. He'd always told me to keep far from the male body—once before leaving to a sleepover birthday party, the only advice he gave was, "Dillon, I don't want you to take off your clothes at that house." Both of his brothers were altar boys fondled in one of the first scandals of a priest uncovered, and though my Dad stayed on his side of the confessional booth, his birth father abused him when drunk, if not sexually then in every other way that guns and fists and neglect could afford. But Dad didn't make sense; he was pathetic. My new mentor and was aflame, alive!—Dad only pushed boundaries and self-restraint.

The next morning I went back to his room and we had a match of wrestling before breakfast. He was much stronger and threw me down without trying, and though I couldn't win, I didn't want to ruin our normal activity by cutting it short. When I'd get on bottom, I could feel his crotch through my clothing, often pressing against mine while I lay on my back. He eventually made a rule that we couldn't pin the other like that anymore—I was always on bottom—because it was too risky a pose. He told me this in a car lit by the sunroof, the sun shining on his hand holding mine over the gearshift. "People will assume you're not safe when you tell them you're an ex-gay, so you really can't let those kinds of stories get out. If it were twisted, it could be enough to ruin a ministry." So since that was abnormal, we changed our positions but wrestled no less frequently.

On the third day, my sister and I already at school, Mom called the Preacher downstairs to talk. "It says in your book," she holds up the page, stained pink with highlighter marks from me, like most of the lines on all of the pages. "It says that men struggling with same-gender attraction shouldn't be seeking healing touch from their counselors, or from each other." She shook the page. "You're both of those."

"Well," a fire bloomed in his eyes. "This is a little bit different."

He whispered a prayer. "The sheep know the voice of their Shepherd."

Mother was stunned. "What do you mean?"

"God told me to do it." A pause. "It's different with your son Dillon."

He'd had visions and voices, none of them discouraging his touch with the boy. And when he did feel guilt, he named it for what it was: a demonic attack by the accuser, that's all. After a dangerous wrestling match, we'd rock on our knees and pray against Satan for causing false guilt when we were only trying to be healed. Then we'd hold hands and move on. Our prayers against Satan far outnumbered those offered to God. This is what healthy spirituality looked like, he said.

But Mom was a little bit ignorant. And because Dad was in Africa, she'd have to deal with this on her own. The women in her small group would condemn her as crazy if she let it persist. She'd met with my youth pastor—he felt the same way, judging only by the latching behavior we displayed in the Sunday pews. Their opinions were built from what they saw in passing, and though they'd met him but once, none of them trusted my mentor.

Mom had walked in on our wrestling, seen our enchantment, heard me take on his accent and mannerisms like replacing the *l* and *y* sounds of "I love you" to *w*'s. But maybe she'd just imagined it. Maybe it wasn't so bad. She'd talked with me about her fears, but I assured her it was all just how it should be, and better! God was redeeming my life and pain through the chest of my mentor. Who cared if it wasn't ordinary? "God's ways are countercultural," the Preacher had said.

To honor the weaker sister, we vowed to wrestle only when she wasn't home, but our pins became more distinct as every part of our bodies managed to touch in slow motion, and every minute in bed—there were dozens, just lying—became noticeably a little abnormal and long. We watched each other undress before showers, trying to normalize the body as well. But I knew the contours of his belly and groin without looking, and he, all of mine.

By the fifth day, Mom had met with each of us twice, adamant to stifle the heat before she left to the airport. Against all trust and convenience, she threw him out and made me stay with a friend, leaving me in a rage of pain. How badly she'd hurt me!—to think that my Mom had no trust, and to know she had gossiped to friends with an aim to ruin my wonderful healing.

Hardly a week passed and I saw the Preacher again. Without asking my new guardians, I drove over an hour to sleep in his house, in his same bed and close to his breathing chest. He woke up early to leave for the airport, but knelt first by the bed for a ritual of passing. A crucifix necklace hid under his collar.

"You'll be in my place next, little brother." He removed the jewelry then tied it around my neck and kissed me on the forehead. "Lock everything up when you leave."

Three hours later, I woke in a smiling bliss then straightened the sheets on my way out. Every window I closed, and I turned out all the lights. But on the way out the garage, I felt in my pocket for car keys and turned around just as the door slammed shut behind me. They were locked inside. I took out my phone—it died when I opened it.

I went to the neighbor's home, but the man at the door only spoke Spanish, and the next neighbor, and every house on the Latino block. Anxiety swelled, and when I'd finally found someone I could talk to, I was shaking in tears at her front door. The horror of it, locked out of my car at a house far away, but even worse than the trouble came a flooding of shame. I imagined my other mentors bowing their heads in disapproval, a chorus of correction that I'd shut my ears to. Did I shut my ears—did I?—or had they been plugged? It felt miry and dark, like I was pushed into oil but had stayed there swimming.

Four years later, a sophomore in college, I received hugs with unease and a painted smile. I didn't know where it came from, or why I'd lost all eagerness to tell of God's redemption in my earlier trials. The story used to be very encouraging—deliverance from same-gender attraction! I'd wanted to make it my ministry, but now I was guarded without knowing why. My relational energy and ability to risk was stifled around younger people, often nervous that maybe their parents might be watching, afraid of their disapproval and cautious to do anything odd.

Then one day in a friend's room, I was lying alone and he jumped playfully on top of me, indenting my body with his. My senses exploded. His belly—beneath it—each curve was electric, stabbing. I lay still as a grave, then left his room limply. I carried my backpack to the elevator, and there saw a sign by the door. "Sexual Abuse: Naming, Healing, Comforting," an announcement for a chapel at the end of the month. "Survivors may submit their stories to be read anonymously at the chapel. They will be destroyed after the service." One of my professors was hosting it. "Good for him," I thought, then looked back down the hall. I thought of the bed then looked at the poster. I hadn't once tried to remember the episode with the Preacher. The shame was too much—when Mom and Dad came back from Africa, I didn't even mention him. I'd thrown out his book, erased his phone number, blocked him on emails, and apparently, locked him out of my mind. I went back to my room and wrote in my journal from sunrise to noon, horrible words on the page that I'd never even pronounced in my imagination.

A man's voice backstage read my story at the chapel, along with dozens of others. I bit my lip and clenched, and I spent many long days after trying to remember more than a few sentences of what really happened. At first I blamed myself, having no categories for responsibility or perversion, no way to see through his cheap preaching—which he really believed. I thought he had good intentions and assumed I was the initiator. He'd preached about healing, then damaged. He'd promised life, and I died. The one who had vowed to help destroyed me, and all in the name of Christ. "The sheep know the voice of the Shepherd."

His necklace still hangs on my desk lamp, a present caution of life without boundaries and a reminder to pray for my enemies. At the end of just-begun counseling, I plan to bury it, along with a poem and an unsent letter to him. My friends will stand with me, then try to hug me, and I'll try my best to receive it as normal. But they'll take off their shoes on holy soil where crosses are buried. Yes, instead of my body and senses, I'll bury a cross in hopes that this flesh might resurrect little by little, slowly and tiring, endless and long.

MIRANDA'S STORY

I grew up in a Christian home where Jesus was mentioned frequently. My grandparents taught me at a very young age the importance of prayer and God's Word. When I was six years old, I heard my Sunday school teacher talk about Jesus as if she knew him, and I wanted to know Jesus that way. So I prayed with childlike faith to receive Christ into my heart and that he would forgive me of my sins. As I continued to grow up, I truly loved God and wanted to please him and desired to know him more.

I lived protected and sheltered from the world for the most part, and I loved and trusted others easily. At that time in my life, I didn't understand the strong presence of sin that is in this world, or that Satan, the adversary of our souls, is alive and well—seeking whom he can devour and coming "only to steal, kill and destroy."

When I was twelve years old, something happened to me that changed my life, changed my perspective of God, of myself, and of love. A friend, who was like an older brother to me, began to sexually abuse me. As I look through the lens of time, I can see now that I changed from a girl who was full of joy, loved life, trusted others, and felt free and became a girl who was afraid, suspicious of others, and felt like she needed to hide. It was as if I stopped growing emotionally for a period of time. I became shy, fearful, and ashamed. It was like a prison of fear came over me, but I lived my life not fully realizing what had happened and how it affected me and the future relationships I would have, especially with men.

For a long time, even after the abuse and sexual molestation stopped, I blamed myself for the abuse, thinking it was my fault, that I maybe I said or did something to provoke him. Later I realized that I was a victim during those times, and that it wasn't my fault. The guy who sexually abused me was in his midtwenties and engaged to be married. I struggled with wanting to tell someone but also wondered who would believe me; he came from an immigrant family and was the head of the household. He held the authority in that home.

I eventually told my best friend Erin what had happened, and she didn't believe me and said, "How dare you accuse my brother of such a thing!" It wasn't until we were both out of college that she and I met for coffee and she actually asked me to forgive her for not believing me. She told me that she found out that their uncle had molested Adam when he was a little boy, and that his molesting me was only a part of his troubles.

A couple years after the sexual abuse ended, I was in my sophomore year of high school and I dated a guy who I thought would protect me. He was co-captain of the football team, looked strong and built, and seemed like a nice guy. I was hungry for love, looking for someone to undo the wrong that was done to me at twelve years old, someone who would make me feel wanted and loved, not dirty and used. I would let him kiss me, or be intimate with me—never all the way—but more than I truly wanted to. I was looking for love, and since I thought my body was the only part of me that would interest guys, it became a way for me to try to feel loved. But instead of feeling loved, I was left feeling more empty, hurt, and broken.

When I began dating another guy in college, I was still struggling to recover my value and worth as a person. I believed I was still a virgin because I hadn't "gone all the way." I told him that I was saving sex for marriage, which he said he respected, but over time he began to pressure me and boundaries were crossed. I believed that he loved his ex-girlfriend more than me because she'd had sex with him.

Over time, I was tempted more and more, not physically, but more in my heart and emotions. Thoughts entered my mind, thoughts of competition and temptation saying things like, "How will you ever know he loves you more than his ex-girlfriend unless you have sex with him?" and, "She will always have one up on you if you don't sleep with him."

I eventually gave in to the temptations and the deceptions of my own heart and had sex with him. I was eighteen when I gave my virginity to him. It wasn't fireworks and all that—it was actually one of the darkest days of my life. For the first time, I felt truly separated from God. I felt like a dark cloud came over me, and immediately afterward tormenting thoughts entered my mind, like "How can you call yourself a Christian, now, after what you have done?" "How will God ever love you now?" I remember crying because I was ashamed of what we had done. I thought he would understand how I felt. After all, he had told me he loved me. For over a year he had bought me gifts and was there for me, but soon after we had sex he became angry and said he couldn't believe I was making such big deal out of it.

I didn't feel loved by having sex with him—I felt like he took something from me. When I asked him what he would do if I got pregnant, he said he would come over and visit the kid once in a while because he had goals and dreams that he wanted to pursue in his life. At that moment, I realized that his plans really didn't include me.

Fortunately, I wasn't pregnant—but the next time he came over he brought a condom. I looked at him with disgust because he was only thinking about himself. I grabbed the condom out of his hand and threw it across the room telling him to get out of my house. Still, I stayed with him until a few months later when I found out from his sister that he had been dating someone else. That hurt—a lot. I began to realize how much of my life revolved around him, and I became very depressed. Thoughts of suicide even entered my mind, and the guilt and shame of what I had done overwhelmed me. I didn't like who I was becoming or how I felt inside. The love I had for God and my desire to live for him was buried now, even though I longed to be free again.

I remember falling to my knees in my college apartment asking God to take me back, saying that I would do anything, just like the prodigal returning home to his father saying he would be one of his servants. But it was at that moment that I knew and felt the love of God, his everlasting love for me, and that he was drawing me to him and had been pursuing me all along. It was at that moment that I truly knew what it meant for Jesus to be my Savior, not just in my head, but a real and personal Savior for me.

I couldn't do anything to earn salvation, to earn God's forgiveness and grace, nor could I do anything to heal or free myself from the pain and shame that I carried from what happened to me at age twelve. Christ took my pain, my shame, my guilt, and my sin upon his cross when he died. He paid the price for me so that I could be free, so that I could have life—abundant life. He broke the power of sin, destroyed the works of Satan, and purchased me with his blood. Jesus was the one I was really searching for—the power of his cross.

It was a story I believed in as a little girl, yet I didn't really know or understand the power of the cross for myself or what it meant for his kingdom to reign and rule in my heart. Jesus is the one who fixed me, who restored me and redeemed me. I surrendered all and repented truly that day, and I made a commitment to allow Christ to change my life; to make a new start and to serve God with my life; to embrace his will and calling for me, whatever he had destined for me, and to live my life to bring glory to his name—to love him with all my "heart, soul, mind, and strength." I had been trying to drink from broken cisterns, looking to guys to bring the healing that only Christ could and wanted to. I had made idols in the midst of the suffering. Now, I am learning more and more to drink of Jesus' living water and to go deeper in intimacy with him. It's truly been a beautiful journey.

God has brought amazing healing to my heart and has set my captive soul free in so many ways. I understand more and more that Jesus is the one who loves me perfectly, and that the presence of the Holy Spirit is and always will be my comfort and strength. God has restored joy that was lost and has made me alive again. He gave me the grace to forgive Adam, and I knew that my heart was changed when I surprisingly saw him again over ten years after the abuse and noticed that there was no hate in my heart, only compassion.

I've had to grieve parts of my childhood that I lost and to allow God to restore the little girl in me. I have found such moments of deep intimacy with Christ even through the suffering. My image of God as a loving heavenly Father is one that continues to be restored and strengthened. He is teaching me how to rest in his love and to enjoy being his daughter, his beloved.

God has brought healing through godly and healthy relationships I've had, readings I've done, and the community of believers I've been a part of and been able to serve with the gifts he has given me, along with inner-healing prayer and times of counseling and therapy. Some of the readings have been theologically grounded and have been centered in the character and nature of God, spiritual formation, identity in Christ, spiritual warfare, healing of damaged emotions, freedom prayer, setting healthy boundaries, and other areas of psychology. The counseling and therapy I have had hasn't been extensive but has been important. It wasn't until I was around twenty-nine years old that I began to recognize how my "issues" in relationships (e.g., settling for mediocre relationships, looking for love in all the wrong places, and trying to "fix" guys I may date) was related to my being abused as a little girl. The oppression, hypervigilance, fear, and overall preoccupation with trying to make sure I was safe was controlling me in many ways. I also noticed that some of the guys I dated were addicted to pornography, and this unsettled me. I have a heart for men who want to be free from that, but I do not necessarily want to be involved in a romantic relationship with someone who is addicted to pornography or even casually glances at it. I have had a difficult time distinguishing between love and lust at times, and between which guys are safe for me and which guys are not good for me. Oftentimes I have learned to trust the promptings of the Holy Spirit in me, and I have appreciated that my hatred for what is evil has been a blessing that has come out of being abused.

One of my counselors used cognitive-behavioral and narrative therapy with me. He shared how he saw me as one that God had really protected, keeping his Spirit very active and alive in me. He also shared that many women who have been abused end up being very promiscuous, deeply depressed, and sometimes unable to form any kind of healthy relationship with a man. My counselor noticed that God has really preserved me and continues to protect me. He helped me to see myself more as God sees me and to not define myself as a sexually abused woman, but rather as a woman who experienced sexual abuse. He helped me to work through some of my "victim" thinking and pointed to areas he saw in me that were full of life and full of hope; he helped the "little girl" in me gain back her voice. I liked that he was also sensitive to the Holy Spirit and that we could talk about faith openly. He gave me the opportunity to process through the grief, loss, and anger related to the sexual abuse. He also used the open-chair technique and asked me to imagine what I would say to Adam about how I felt about his abusing me as a little girl if he were sitting there in front of me. We were also able to talk about the theology of suffering, which I found to be extremely helpful as well.

Other times of counseling and therapy that I have found to be the most effective have been ones that include inner-healing prayer, forms of Theophostic- or Emmanuel-Healing Prayer. I was able to do some of my work while interning at a counseling ministry in Illinois. I also participated in an eight-week support group at a local church, which used Dan Allender's book *The Wounded Heart: Hope for Adult Victims of Childhood Sexual Abuse*. I found the support group to be helpful in understanding my struggles more clearly and in meeting other women who had experienced similar trauma. I enjoyed the times we could use with writing, art, and music as part of our group; I found these to be especially therapeutic for me. Looking back on the group, I would have wanted there to be more times of prayer, re-framing, and opportunities to experience God's healing presence as well.

I still want to continue to have God heal areas of my heart related to this trauma and other things I have suffered, so that I can be freer to love, to receive his love, and to live the life he has called me to live. Through the work I have done so far, God has shown me that he is after my healing and wants to draw me into deeper intimacy with him even through suffering, and that he will use different tools to restore my soul.

Through the working of the Holy Spirit in me, I have been able to give Jesus the burden of caring for me. For so long I battled with trying to "protect myself," making sure the little girl in me was safe. Through times of healing prayer, God has brought deep healing to my soul and spirit and has freed me from the sexual perversions and oppression that I was exposed to as a little girl through those acts of abuse. There are times that I still struggle with wondering who to trust, especially when it comes to men. I am thankful that God has made me sensitive to his Holy Spirit. God has taught me to trust him and the discernment he has given me, to not be afraid, and to live fully knowing that he is for me and is carrying me. I am so thankful for all the gifts and opportunities he has given me to share his love and healing with others.

He is still working in me, and I know that he will complete what he has started in me. Through prayer, seeking him, time in his Word, circumstances, and his speaking through others, my calling to minister to women and youth has become clearer over the years. I want my life to make Jesus famous so that others may know of his love, his healing and restoration, his saving grace, and his power to transform lives for his glory.

> *I have loved you with an everlasting love;*
> *I have drawn you with unfailing kindness.*
> —Jer 31:3

SEAN'S STORY

In 1970 my father had just returned home from the Vietnam War. He took a job at a waste-water treatment plant outside of Austin, Texas, where he met my mother. Early that year, I was conceived out of wedlock. At the urging of my maternal grandparents, my mother wed Teddy Wesley.

Their insistence on the marriage was essentially driven by a desire for their family to save face in the church and community. The marriage was doomed from the start. My father, having grown up in an abusive family, would perpetrate the same against my mother. In addition to being emotionally abusive, he was also physically abusive to the point of pistol-whipping my mother and threatening her life. My mother left him before my third birthday and never looked back.

Mom secured work as a hotel restaurant waitress and found an apartment that would fit her limited budget. It wasn't long before she caught the eye of one of the cooks. And it wasn't long before she caught the fury of her family. Now it wasn't that her newfound beau was a bad guy; it was that he was a black guy. To say that interracial relationships touched a very raw social nerve in the 70s would be an understatement. In my mother's case, not only did it touch a nerve—it tore up a family. Declining her parents' $2,000 cash offer to say "I don't," she walked the aisle on November 14, 1976, and said, "I do."

Whatever the poverty threshold was back then, I'm sure we were well below it. I often joke that we were so poor that when my mother got a sweet tooth she had to lick an envelope. With finances being what they were and having both parents at work, I became a latchkey kid. So, after school and all throughout the summer months, I was left totally unsupervised. If there was trouble to be found, I could be counted on to find it, if it didn't find me first.

Being that money was hard to come by, my stepfather would (in addition to working two jobs) salvage aluminum cans, copper wire, computer paper, glass, etc.—anything that could be redeemed. Unfortunately, he also salvaged discarded pornographic magazines—magazines that I had no trouble finding in all of my unsupervised spare time around the house. These images, coupled with the natural explorative curiosities that accompany the early years, combined to ignite in me an addictive fascination with all things sexual. Pandora's Box had been opened.

Although my mother was estranged from her family, they were not estranged from me. At this point my grandfather was working as a bank president. He lived in (what seemed to me) a mansion. It was a two-story, four-bedroom, rock house situated on a quiet cul-de-sac in an upscale neighborhood, a far cry from the world I knew. To this day my best childhood memories can be traced back to spending several weeks with them each summer. It was somewhat surreal. Vacations to exciting theme parks, overnight camping and fishing excursions, going swimming at their country club, attending church camp, running errands with my grandmother, enjoying fried everything and devouring her famous "blondies" (the best chocolate chip brownies in the world).

Normally visits to "MaMa and PaPa's" house included one or two of my cousins, the oldest being seven years my elder. Of all seven cousins, not only was he the oldest, he was the coolest. As a tall, well-built, good-looking guy, he was a head-turner for the ladies. I still remember him showing me pictures of his drop-dead gorgeous girlfriends. He wore cool clothes, listened to great music, and drove the very popular two-tone brown-and-tan Trans-Am with T-tops (complete with the firebird decal on the hood). This was the guy that every kid wanted to be like. So you can imagine my excitement when I learned the cousin I had come to idolize was going to be with me at our grandparents' house at the same time. Sadly, the excitement soon turned to confusion, embarrassment, guilt, and shame.

Though the details of the initial proposition escape me, the anguish of sexual molestation never will. Even as a young boy I knew immediately that my "hero" had crossed a very sacred line. The frantic beating in my chest was matched only by the severe anxiety that shot through my mind every time he violated me. Although I instinctively knew that what he was doing to me was wrong, I did not have the courage to confront my abuser at the time. To this day I still lament my silence because I am convinced that it was mistakenly construed as compliance—compliance that contributed to the furtherance of the abuse.

My heart raced with paralyzing fear and crippling guilt at every encounter. In rapid succession, my conscience supplied a steady stream of warning flares. My mind was flooded with soul-penetrating questions. What is going on? Is this really happening to me? What if someone finds out? Does this mean something's wrong with me? If it's so bad, why is this "great guy" doing it? I had now entered into the world of being a sexualized boy.

Unfortunately, the abuse served to heighten my interest in all things sexual. In the early 80s my mother and her brother (the perpetrator's father) began rebuilding the relationship fractures that were brought on by her marriage to my black stepdad. What this meant was that I would be seeing more of my uncle as well as my cousin. Being invited to spend the night in their home meant that I could hang out with my favorite cousin Devin, who was just a year younger than me. But it also meant I'd be in close quarters with his oldest brother who had been taking advantage of me. Though I never refused his advances, there was one occasion that stands out in my mind. Late one night he slipped into my room and persistently attempted to rouse me my from my sleep, being careful not to wake my younger cousin (his youngest brother) who was sleeping in the same bed with me. To this day I still find a measure of personal pride in knowing that I was able to manage at least one successful stand against his twisted advances.

During this time I was exposed, not only to more pornographic magazines, but also to pornographic movies. Sexual exploration and deviation had taken firm root in my heart. Illicit fantasizing consumed my thought life. By the time I was in eighth grade, I was sexually active.

Growing up, no one ever knew what happened. As far as I was concerned, these secrets would go with me to my grave. Years later, when I confided in my mother about my ordeal, all she could say was, "I'm so sorry." Then I learned that she, too, had been sexually violated by a family member growing up.

As a teenager, I was troubled by the fact that I had been violated. I felt dirty and ashamed inside. But what bothered me the most is that when my high school girlfriend went away to college, I became so desperate for sexual satisfaction that I actually sought out my perpetrator. Now I was beginning to wonder if I had become a homosexual.

At this juncture I was psychologically tormented because now I had violated my own sense of right and wrong. All the warnings of my conscience went completely ignored. Somehow I managed to surrender what little was left of my integrity, what I knew deep down to be true, just so that I could once again gratify the insatiable sexual cravings that had come to define my life. That intrinsic moral code that had been indelibly written on my heart was being completely suppressed by my own deceitful desires. This is not to say that there was ever a time that I felt good about this type of experimentation. Through it all, I constantly sought to rationalize my devious decisions to indulge these dark desires. After all, he still had many beautiful girlfriends. In fact, he even promised to arrange an encounter with one of them for me. He still drove a hip car (a 280ZX with T-tops), wore the coolest clothes, and listened to the best music.

So here I was. nineteen years old. The product of a broken home. No sense of direction, purpose, worth, or identity. A slave to all kinds of sordid sexual impulses; on the verge of becoming hopelessly enmeshed in a lifestyle I knew was terribly wrong. On the precipice of destruction, I stood with my entire life ahead of me. Were there any real options for escaping what I knew was not right and true? Or was I broken beyond repair with no alternatives for escaping these life-defining, life-dominating, and life-depleting tyrannical desires? This is not the person I wanted to become. I was ashamed, embarrassed, confused, and conflicted because I had now gone from being an unwilling victim in years past to a willing participant in time present. My conscience had been ignored. My sense of right and wrong had been inverted. My integrity had been shattered. No longer was I simply the boy who had been betrayed—now I was the young man who had betrayed himself.

The summer of 1990 would prove to be a pivotal turning point in my life. A complete stranger placed in my hands a copy of the Gospel of John, the fourth gospel in the New Testament on the life and teachings of Jesus Christ. Please understand that I was not a good student in school, nor was reading something I enjoyed. But as I began to absorb the contents of this little booklet, a penetrating light began to pierce the great darkness that had come to characterize my life. For the first time in my life I saw my sin for what it was against the backdrop of the blazing holiness of Almighty God. My initial instinct was to close the booklet, put it down, and walk away. Seeing yourself as you really are is a terribly troubling reality. Yet I was strangely and irresistibly drawn to this holy God who somehow seemed to be strangely and irresistibly drawn to me.

In these pages of Holy Writ, this troubled man found forgiveness, redemption, healing, and freedom through the One who came looking for people just like me—he, the

Lord Jesus Christ. He took my sin. I received his righteousness. He washed me clean by offering to God the only sacrifice that could remove the sin that had made me unacceptable in God's sight. That offering was his sinless body and blood. Christ entered my life on August 10, 1990, and I have never been the same. Because of his loving kindness to me, I am now totally forgiven, completely accepted, fully pleasing, and wonderfully loved. Through this forgiveness I have been enabled to forgive my abuser, live in new freedom, enjoy a deeply satisfying relationship with my wife, and experience healthy relationships with my family and friends—pointing to the One who made it possible all the way.

This is my first time to put my story in writing. Retracing my steps proved to be more psychologically grueling and emotionally taxing than I had anticipated. Be that as it may, my prayer is that you, the reader, would find the cleansing, liberating, life-giving, hope-restoring, joy-producing power of God's forgiveness to be entirely sufficient and supremely satisfying in your journey home. May it be that my pain and my sin and my redemption serves you well as you seek to serve God, in spite of the abuse you may have known.

Had you known me for the first nineteen years of my life, you would have found (just like me) ridiculous amusement at the thought of me ever becoming a pastor. Yet in God's inscrutable providence, I am just that—a pastor. In addition to being a pastor, I am a happily married husband of fifteen years, the proud father of two adopted sons.

> He will wipe every tear from their eyes. There will be no more death' or mourning or crying or pain, for the old order of things has passed away.
>
> —Rev 21:4 NIV

Soli Deo Gloria

WHITNEY'S STORY

Half my childhood was spent in an upper-class suburb of Los Angeles, a carefree, mansion-dwelling kid. The neighborhood kids spent afternoons playing at one another's homes. Our parents attended one another's cocktail parties. It was a close-knit community.

My best friend was from a family of color, and her parents were looked up to as proof that the civil rights movement had succeeded. It was her father who exposed me to pornography. I knew it was wrong, but I also knew no one would believe me if I told them—even my own parents. His pedestal of community respect kept me silent. I had sexual knowledge beyond my years and carried a secret that could harm our community identity; it made me feel ashamed and very alone.

Our life there ended when my father was falsely accused of being a drug dealer. He moved us from the mansion to a tiny ski-cabin in a small mountain town. It was his dream, but Mom was a city girl, and it became a nightmare for her. In close proximity, I realized they drank to drunkenness every night, and that the shouting the mansion had muffled was loud and clear in that cabin. Somehow, I thought it was my fault. We went from rich to poor, and Mom went to work as a nurse for a family planning clinic. Everything had changed.

As I went through puberty, Dad often made lewd comments about my developing body. As his relationship with mom worsened, he made me his confidante, sharing things that I now know were inappropriate. I was repelled by his attention but hungry for his approval, and I felt a responsibility to help their marriage. She was jealous of my closeness with Dad; I felt like I was betraying her. Mom talked to me a lot about sex, and so did Dad, as if it was a recreational sport. When I was fourteen, to my shock, Mom gave me birth control and told me that if I ever needed an abortion, "Just go to the next county."

At sixteen, I began to consider my virginity a burden, and a twenty-seven-year old man took care of that. I was starved for affection but discovered I was just a toy to him. He introduced me to drugs and broke my heart when he replaced me with another underage girl. I found others and continued into a downward cycle of using and being used, looking for someone to love me. My parents were happy I could have the sexual freedom they had wanted, never mentioning that what these men were doing was illegal—or what it was costing my soul.

I cried out to God for help, although I knew nothing about him other than sensing his presence in the wind of my sailboat. On my own, I had attended a mainline church for a while, but the priest was more interested in learning about the Wicca I had been studying than in teaching me about Christ. But my Nana had given me a Bible, and every night when the yelling carried on and it seemed like the evil in my room would swallow me, Psalm 18 was my comfort.

College gave me hope for a new beginning, but I lost scholarships with wild living and dropped out. I began to study Wicca again for the control it promised, and just as I got closer to darkness, a neighbor shared with me about forgiveness in Jesus Christ. It took a power encounter, facing evil in the name of a Jesus I didn't even know yet, to get my attention. I became God's child and found the love and acceptance I had longed for. I was a completely new person, full of joy in the gift he had given. I shared what Jesus had done with abandon. My church leadership began to wonder if God was calling me to serve him.

Two years later, the call was clear, and I left to serve in Europe among refugees. My testimony did not include sexual abuse—had I not had a "wonderful childhood?" Several of my co-workers were taking a course called "Survivors of Abuse: Leadership Training Seminars," exploring the ramifications of their childhood abuse. I didn't "get it" then, and I wondered why they just couldn't get over it and move forward in victory. I met a wonderful man on the field, and his love, loyalty, and faith in marriage was a source of the Lord's healing.

We moved to the Middle East to work with refugees. Living in a third-world neighborhood, I was shocked by the staring and attempted groping of the men. As I learned the language, I discovered that the men (and their wives) assumed I was a promiscuous, which covered me with a shame I couldn't shake. I started acting like the other women, looking at the ground outside, wearing very long sleeves and skirts, even covering my hair. Even this didn't stop the staring, and with each stare another layer of shame settled over me—I had been what they thought I was; they could not see how Christ had changed me; I deserved it. Sharing my testimony proved a shaming experience in the Arab church;

sexual sins are not covered by Christ's blood. One Christian friend told me I could never tell my story publicly since it would damage my husband's reputation—another layer of shame in place.

Our field director was concerned that it seemed I had lost my identity and he recommended counseling. A wise woman listened and spoke God's words of healing. Living in a shame-based culture had revealed areas of my own hidden shame. She explained how premature sexualization can affect a girl, how my father's actions were a form of emotional incest, and how I didn't have to ask God for forgiveness for being abused. It was an "aha" moment, and random pieces of my life began to fit together for the first time. Soon thereafter, I went to a week-long conference for survivors of sexual abuse, the same course my co-workers had taken.

I came home changed. I shared what I learned with a national group of pastors' wives who told me they were seeing women with SA issues in premarital counseling. In this region, if a woman is not a virgin, for whatever reason, she will never get married. It was such a taboo topic that it was the first time most of them had ever vocalized the words. Within a month, I was teaching them the material I had just learned. Their husbands were skeptical, so we planned a seminar with a local member of the family protection unit who talked about the prevalence of SA in the country—seventy pastors, their wives, and church leaders attended!

God challenged me that if women were going to trust me with their secrets of shame, I had to be willing to risk my reputation and reveal mine. I began to share his faithfulness in bringing me to healing, and the response was amazing. In the eight years since then, over one hundred women and fifteen men have been in grace groups and have taken the twelve-week course in abuse recovery. My abuse became my ministry. Walking with other women on the road to recovery has become one of my chief joys in life.

I can say with absolute surety that Jesus Christ has fulfilled the words of the prophet Isaiah in healing the brokenhearted, setting prisoners free, comforting those who mourn and exchanging their ashes for beauty, the oil of joy for mourning, and the spirit of heaviness for a garment of praise. He did that for me. He has done that for Arab believers. And he can do it for you too.

Appendix B

Some Written Prayers for Survivors

Be My God of Control

Be my control, for I have none,
    And some of the most influential people in my life have
        Betrayed their trust to You
        And my trust in them.
With a perversion of power, they've distorted my view of spiritual models.

Be my control, for I see none.
    Help me see a new father in my museum of painful portraits.
    Many in my company of experience have left You;
        Their confusion exceeds their faith,
        Nor has mine been left intact.
With a perversion of love, they've distorted my sense of the lovely.

Be my control, for I find none.
    Write a new script for my play; the old drama is overwhelming me,
        And too many characters have become grotesque.
    I do not want a new universe around me,
        Only a deepening vision to live in the present one.
    Nor do I seek a fiefdom to guard my own freedom,
        But a commanding zone of security within Your best.
As you commanded chaos, so confine mine to the depths of a new dependence.

Secure some room *beside* your throne for the "betrayed."
    For while the martyrs *beneath* seek vindication,
        We huddle for security to praise.
    Our childhood trust has been martyred,
        So comfort us in the shadow of Your strength.
    For us, Your strong arm is our needed love,
        Your protection is our richest praise,
        Your defense, our greatest delight.
Then hide us in *The Chorus of the Flawless*, where
    Memories no longer haunt,
    Accusations no longer sting,
    And minds no longer paralyze,
        So *The Scared* will be welcomed in *The Parade of the Jubilant*.

This ongoing prayer we offer in the securing name of Jesus Christ, who
    Was betrayed by brothers,
    Abandoned by family, and Father,
    Deprived of advocates,
    Wounded for our sin,
        Carrying some earthly scars for the frightened.

AMEN

Be Our Earthly Father, Too

So great is our distortion,
    we are hardly able to pray "Our Father,"
    or view You as "Heavenly Father."

Our earthly model has soured our sense of heavenly trust.
These have been years of tears.
    For the imagery of his: face,
                           arms,
                           hands,
                           speech,
have bent our earliest picture of Your fatherliness.

Superimpose Your calm countenance over the flinted face.
Extend Your secure embrace that overwhelms the brutish grasp.
Open Your creative touch that heals illicit senses.
Sing Your soothing rhymes that comfort daggered speech.

Please tell us Your fathering does not: intimidate the insecure,
                                         break the boundaries,
                                       seduce the sensitive,
                                       coerce the compliant,
                                       undress the unsuspecting,
                                       discard the disillusioned,
                                       rationalize the restricted,
                                       punish the powerless,
                                       castigate the confused,
                                       slander the survivor,
    and . . .

While we believe such things are not true of Your fathering,
    do You see why these associations have become anything but
        patterns of purity,
        models of maturity,
        sources of security?

We now live in a haunted house
    with many cracks and creaks.
We now realize that You are actually offended *for* us—you are angry too!
    Your trust to others has been abused!
    You have been defamed and misrepresented!

Until You welcome us to Your House of Healing
    on Secure Street—where there is no scary nighttime—may we call You our
    Shepherd, instead. What we know of shepherds is caring imagery.

We pray in the name of Jesus Christ—our Great Shepherd,
    who went to prepare for us in Heaven
    what neither He nor we ever had on earth.

AMEN

Broken Into Healing

(Helping the Abused at Communion)

We ask for your strength,
    To celebrate and perform this "exchange"—of another broken body.

Paradoxically, we also request:

    To be broken toward You,
    Be broken with You,
    Broken for You,
    And in You.

    ~*Toward* You in Your community-commitment
        of those who would abandon,
            or we, too, may flee in harmful directions.
    ~*With* You in Your servant-selflessness
        of those who would contend,
            or we, too, may resort to the fleeting refuge of rights.
    ~*For* You in Your daring-devotion
        of those who would deny,
            or we, too, may opt for acceptance over justice.
    ~*In* You in Your royal-release
        for those too prideful to bend the knee,
            or we, too, may stumble over Your gift.

But we, your broken beggars, have come to relish your
    Cruciform body and blood,
    For we survive as living pieces of your storied sacrifice.

    In You alone, we are broken into healing.

Our *Rapha* Rescuer and Broken Lamb,
    we recognize Your violence—renew us also in Your scarred victory.

In You alone, we are broken into healing.

We do this, contemplate this, share this, grieve this, and yet cherish this,
   . . . *in remembrance*, reverence, awe, hope, and healing,
   . . . *of You*, toward You, with You, for You, and in You.

In You alone, we are breaking into healing.

As we recall Your wounding, celebrate with us our healing,
   till the broken remember this paradox no more!

AMEN

Christ is Risen!
Other Tombs May Open

(Helping the Abused on Easter)

Christ is risen—for the hope of all.

    All who need a Savior . . .
    Many who live in crippling deformity,
    Many who fight the darkness of depression,
    Many who are drained of life in the death of another.

      But: too many still hear the violator's voice,
              too many still sense the abuser's arrogance,
              too many still freeze from the:
                    innocent stare
                    innocent touch
                    innocent words of the reckless-redeemed.

Hear, O Risen King, the voices of the violated ~
    Raise high their feeble anthem!
See, O Risen Lord, the angst of the abused ~
    Raise high their allusive assurance!
Carry, O Risen Shepherd, the frozen of your flock ~
    Raise high their frail limbs!

    From our crippling to your resurrecting leap,
        Grant a renewed life toward wholeness.
    From our darkening to your resurrection light,
        Grant a renewed life toward liberty.
    From our mourning to your resurrection might,
        Grant a renewed life capable of jubilation.

Swell the ranks of your resurrection-witnesses,
    With the violated ~
        Easter them from their share in your scorn.
    With the abused ~
        Easter them from their share in your trauma.
    With the frozen ~
        Easter them from their share in your grave.

As the broken among your Bride,
    We plead in the name of Jesus Christ,
        Our compassionate Shepherd,
            who was tempted as all and violated as many,
    Having exchanged the cruelty and violence,
        For glory and empathy.

AMEN

Appendix B

Lord of Metaphor

What meaning is right   When none is left,
                         When now is spoiled,
                         When the child is deflowered?

What has become of metaphor?
      Who remains to   prize the phrase,
                           value the figure,
                           nurture the nuance?
What has become of metaphor—slowly it died.

When the earthly father strips the flower,
      The earthly child loses their way on earth:
            Without their hero,
            Without their magician,
            Without their metaphor.
                  How do they trust a heavenly Father
                  When the earthly father has so little honor?

When the earthly mother ignores the drooping flower,
      The earthen child makes their bed on the dampened earth:
            Bereft of model,
            Bereft of nurturer,
            Bereft of metaphor.
                  Shall they find enough warmth under a blanket of stars
                  When the earthly mother has lost her myth?

Heavenly Fa . . . Moth . . . Weeper—Child of this scarred earth,
      These metaphors were Your ambassadors,
            But how destructive their distinction,
                  How traumatic their terror . . .

Reader of mangled metaphors, Collector of the fragile frightened,
Creator of the whole meaning, the whole person,
      Grant us   New metaphors,
                     In new embraces,
                     With new meanings.

We pray in the name of   The Sacrificed Shepherd,
                           The Fallen King,
                           The Crushed Rock,
Our Metaphor Crucified—who wept first,
    Jesus Christ.

AMEN

On This Day of Mothers and Fathers

(To Help the Abused on Mother's and Father's Day)

On this day . . . grief is mixed with smiles,
    healing with loss,
    safety with haunting memories . . . is there a rose left for us?

Too many memories of loud insults and silent wounds,
Too much confusion over what healing really means,
Too much grief unheard, unheeded, unhealed . . . especially on this day!
    For parents who did it right—we are glad.
        for happy sons and daughters, though we cannot identify
            with either honest parents
            or well-adjusted teens.

Give these parents flowers for all the fragrant memories
    that they've planted in their children's hearts.
But what beauty remains
    for the deflowered on Father's Day?
What sweet fragrance lingers
    on hypocritical roses of Mother's Day?

On this day . . . what should we give to mothers and fathers
    who stole so much and admitted so little?

We do have: Promises for our little ones ~
    God help us do right by them!
        Smiles and some laughter for new families ~
            may new rituals bury the old!
        Letters to be read one day, when we're gone ~
            let them grieve with insight!
        Tears for the ground that has felt them before ~
            let new memories grow there!

But flowers!
    Yes, some flowers for mothers and fathers . . .
        not our own, but those who have held us
           and taught us to hold.

On this day, we have warm tears
    for our broken mothers and fathers.
But to special friends who shed the Samaritan's tear . . .
        for them, we have flowers.
A testimony offered in the name of the One
    Who: created,
           wept,
           and was buried in a garden.
Jesus Christ, our sweet Flower of Glory,
    The "Rose of Sharon" is ours, gifted to us,
        flowering most fragrantly in broken hearts.

AMEN

We Bring Our Sacrifice of . . .

We bring our sacrifice of   . . .   innocence lost.
   ~We would offer You more, but we can't.
We bring our sacrifice of   . . .   deep anger.
   ~We would offer You other, but we must grieve unmentioned horrors.
We bring our sacrifice of   . . .   crushed expectations.
   ~We would offer You better, but we must fall back on cruel realities.
We bring our sacrifice of   . . .   social brokenness.
   ~We would offer You healthier, but we've been reduced to awkwardness.

We bring our sacrifice of   . . .   mistrust toward You.
   ~We would offer You the spectacular, but even You didn't step in.

So, if we continue our walk with You, don't:

> Recoil when we do,
> Cry out when we do,
> Look away when we do,
> Limp when we do,
> Hide in "safe corners" when we do.

For from these contorted linens
   we must dress ourselves
And from these confusing effects
   we search for an offering.

We bring our sacrifice of   . . .   dissociation.
   ~We would offer You wholeness, but frightening fractures dog us.
We bring our sacrifice of   . . .   silence.
   ~We would offer You anthems, but our names were lost with our voice.
We bring our sacrifice of   . . .   suspicion.
   ~We would offer You a child's embrace, but fear still seizes that child just as accusations still echo.
We bring our sacrifice of   . . .   illnesses.
   ~We would offer You stature and might, but the toxin has left atrophy and illness.

We bring our sacrifice of   . . .   confusion.
~We would offer You wit and imagination, but sleep comes hard and waking is
for vigilance—if only to stumble on another fixation.

This is our praise, offered to One who must have
lost so much in his incarnation—including the praise of angels—
to take on the embodiment of:
disfigurement, isolation, scorn, rebuke, suspicion . . .

. . . and brokenness of a kind close enough
to understand this kind of praise.

AMEN

Restore Some Beauty

Creator of Life,
    Maker of Perfect Memory,

        restore precious moments to our waning days;
        interject tasks of more eternal meaning;
            we need them desperately.

Like the Laments of old,
    teach us both pain's honesty
        and the vigor of praise.

So, between pain and praise,
    restore some beauty that nurtures.

Too long have painful memories hounded us:
    What we've done,
    What others have done,
    What we're afraid may return.

Overwhelm our burdened minds with:
    Glimpses of beauty ~ images not our own.
    Angelic friends ~ insights gifted to us.
    Hope of healing ~ sheer release
        from the toilsome cares outside Eden.

Then, fed with
    healing, wisdom, and beauty,
chart us a new course of
    caring, mending, and building.
For any healing you bring is really beauty restored.

Dock us in deep waters of brokenness,
    So we may be agents of comfort,
        as we too, have been
            comforted,
            named,
            and restored.

We pray in the name of our Broken Savior,
    Whose Name we love,
        fragrance we feel,
        and beauty we share.

AMEN

To The Brilliantly Misinformed

FROM: The living-scorned
TO: The brilliantly misinformed
RE: "The secret" you won't accept—
           we would have you know the truth!

We were innocent children once, until:
           our playrooms were invaded,
           the lights were turned off,
           and our pictures torn up.

~ We believe: basements make good cages,
           PJs only protect from the cold,
           nighttime is really fright-time,
           and bed sheets can feel like body bags.

We were silenced for speaking out, until:
           our siblings were harmed,
           our children were endangered,
           our panic attacks named what we couldn't.

~ We know: time doesn't heal all wounds,
           loyalty trumps ethics for some,
           systems and persons violate others,
           why many believers no longer believe.

We have learned to survive, but now:
           we will flee to our spouse, not from,
           we will cherish teenage ways, not chide,
           we will thrive amid Christian love, not hide.

~ We resolve: to face the same fears in others,
           to be advocates for the speechless,
           to contemplate the wounding of our Lord,
           to patiently train leaders in Christ's Church.

We found that our stories of rape, betrayal, abuse, exploitation, and violence
    were already known to: Dinah, Joseph, Tamar, Bathsheba, and Jesus.

This MEMO is prayerfully written on behalf of those with unwanted testimonies,
    to the people of God's House:
        "Jew or Greek, slave or free, male or female."
    We are no longer bound, and you are no longer ignorant!

In memory of the Shepherd who would have us all know the truth,
    The Savior who was the Truth,
    The Slain Lamb, who brought such costly Truth to us all.

AMEN

Those Charged with Our Security

Protective Father, please know that those charged with our senses, security, and sexuality have pawned them off.

The property we hardly knew was ours has been:
 Stolen without our permission,
 Used without our consent,
 Traded in the dark for an image touted in the light.

Now the senses needed to own and even understand our sexuality are working overtime.
 Horrified ~ by an unlawful knowledge!
 Repulsed ~ to the extent of dissociation!
 Suspicions ~ of loud authorities, commanding gazes, and even little children that remind us of ourselves!

Unselfish Father, please hear in the sanitized language of our sobs:
 What we cannot vocalize to others ~ though words have accosted us!
 What some refuse to believe ~ though insist on flaunting their reality!
 What the "privileged-normal" claim to understand . . .
 Nevertheless, what churches may stifle, a growing throng knows only too well.
 These are the "shrieking silent" who long for control of their:
  dreams,
  tears,
  anxiety attacks.

Mending Father, give us physical comfort and perceptive words,
 For bodies now frozen and minds still imprisoned.

Watchful Father, charge the guilty accordingly,
 Since we are the worst of orphans, hardly wanted even by ourselves.
 Audit their religious claims for spiritual incest and moral hypocrisy.
 Hand down the verdict of true reality to those who distorted ours.
 We do not seek their violence, for we have: known enough
  seen enough,
  lost enough.

Creative Father, those charged with shaping our imaginations invaded our child-like
   dreams, and we woke up to a scarred sexuality.

To those struggling to believe in a loving Heavenly Father,
   We beg You to call in their moral debt;
   Arrest the arrogant with Your angels of advocacy;
   Help the hopeful-wounded understand:
         what maturity now means,
         what trust can grow,
         what closure can salve.
   Help the sexually scarred to accept permanent loss.

Our *Attending Father*, this we plead in the safe authority of Jesus;
   Himself victimized, and now preparing our Safe House of healing.

AMEN

Though Pain Remains . . .

Though pain remains, life grows on.
  In the fright,
  Into the future
  In between grief consoled
    and plaguing questions.

In the fright ~ life grows on.
  Nurture what is fragile
    and mend what is broken.
      Though undone, we cling in hope.
      May our fright fade in life renewed.

Into the future ~ life grows on.
  Cherish what is determined
    and enrich what persists.
      Through the unknown, we move into healing.
      May our future flower into life respected.

In between the consoling and plaguing ~ life grows on.
  Gentle Gardner, *Plant*   safe places,
                 fragrant graces,
                 hidden spaces,
    where You alone can meet with us ~
      in between: Terror and Trust,
             Brokenness and Boundary,
             Fire and Faith.

  Curator of the broken,
    Water what remains by Your own comfort.
    Graft us into the Chorus of the Renewed.
    May our questions that linger find final release,
      in Your embrace, Lover of the Limping-in-Between.
      How we cherish Your wounds and tears.
      We treasure them as they treasure us.

We pray in the name of the One
    whose most painful moments were in gardens,
      in-between kingdom and cross,
          determination and desertion.
    whose own grief teaches us to grow on ~
      in the resolve of the Nobody of Nazareth,
      Jesus Christ.

          AMEN

We Are Majestically Broken

Collector-of-Fragments, we are broken now.

    Fragmented are simple expectations.
    Fragmented are life-giving hopes.
    Fragmented are ligaments of faith.

    How good are you at:

        Finding,
        Cleaning,
        Mending pieces of lives?

The dismembered, displaced, and disoriented need to know.

Our faith has been reduced to trust . . .
    ~ a trust in goodness far beyond our experience,
    ~ a trust in safety far beyond our fears,
    ~ a trust in healing far beyond our means.

Please mend well what others have shattered.
Please forgive through us where our strength has run out.

But, in Your mending and healing work,
    Leave some cracks for memorial:

        Of where we came from,
        Of how You gathered us,
        Of how You cradle the majestically broken.

We pray this in the compassionate name of Your Majestic Broken One,
 Bruised and broken for the broken and bruised,
 Lover of the limping,
 The Finder-of-Fragments,
  Who still weeps more than we do,
  Jesus Christ.

AMEN

Your Haunting Silence

Our Father, our final protecting One,
    The violence observed by some
    Has been frighteningly experienced by many.
From the outside we say, "Mercy! Enough!"
    But from the inside we cry, "Where were You?!"

How are we to tend the little ones given to us
    With our frail strength and limited wisdom?
    Yet You, with the Creator's might and divine wisdom
    Chose not to step in and arrest our abuser! We cower confused and confounded.
A wail of the masses rises, "My God, My God, why have You forsaken me?!"
    A desperate question or gasping exclamation ~ we dare not say.
From the outside is heard, "Mercy! Enough!"
    But from the inside we mutter, "Where were You?!"

Some in the *Chorus of The Used* have ceased to ask ~
    They are no longer children and they no longer pray.
Some in the *Chorus of the Beaten* were broken before they could plead again ~
    They no longer live; nor were they granted humanity in life.
Some in the *Chorus of the Scarred* survive "nameless" ~
    They cling to life or do not know they still live.
Some in the *Chorus of the Traumatized* have found a healing path, a quiet path ~
    Yet one fraught with questions that exceed their strength.
From the outside one hears, "Mercy! Enough!"
    But from the inside the failing cry, "Where were You?!"

For us that remain in faith, show us:
    That the gospel can sustain as well as save,
    That our children can have our wisdom without our pain,
    That heaven will be patient with the abused,
    That Your heart is also broken,
    That Your silence is not Your absence.
As an *insider* speaking for the speechless,
    Please reward us for the unnatural candor we need to survive,
    Even if You cannot heal us in this life.

We plead in the rescuing name of Jesus Christ,
Who will gift a new name to the forgotten,
a new voice to the silenced,
a new family to the frightened.
Who himself was brutalized for his name,
Your own *insider*, whom You rejected,
Who left His story to fill the silence.

AMEN

Appendix C

Web-based Resources

Adult Survivors of Child Abuse
    www.ascasupport.org

American Association of Christian Counselors:
    www.aacc.net

American Association for Marriage and Family Therapy
    www.aamft.org

American Psychiatric Association
    www.psych.org

American Psychological Association
    www.apa.org

Association for the Treatment of Sexual Abusers
    www.atsa.com

The American Bar Association Commission on Domestic Violence
    www.abanet.org/domviol

Child and Adolescent Bipolar Foundation
    www.bpkids.org
    www.depressedteens.com

Childhelp USA
    www.childhelpusa.org

Child Molestation Research & Prevention Institute
    www.childmolestationprevention.org

Clergy Sexual Abuse Project
    www.baylor.edu/clergysexualmisconduct

Girlthrive
    www.girlthrive.com

Gift from Within

www.giftfromwithin.org

G.R.A.C.E. (Godly Response to Abuse in a Christian Environment)
www.netgrace.org

Help Guide, "Child abuse and neglect"
www.helpguide.org

Hidden HurtDomestic Violence InformationMarital Rape:
ww.hiddenhurt.co.uk/Articles/maritalrape.htm

Incest Resources, Inc.
www.incestresourcesinc.org

Locating a Therapist:
www.therapistlocator.net

Men Who Have Had Abusive Sexual Experiences:
www.1in6.org

Missionary Kids Safety Net:
www.mksafetynet.net

National Association of Social Workers
www.socialworkers.org

National Center for Missing & Exploited Children
www.missingkids.com

National Center for the Victims of Crime
www.ncvc.org

National Clearinghouse on Child Abuse and Neglect Information
www.nccanch.acf.hhs.gov

National Domestic Violence Hotline:1-800-799-SAFE (7233):
www.ndvh.org

National Sexual Violence Resource Center
www.nsvrc.org

National Sexual Violence Resource Center
www.nsvrc.org

Rape, Abuse & Incest National Network
(RAINN):1-800-656-HOPE (4673):

www.rainn.org

The RAVE Project (Religion and Violence e-Learning)
    www.theraveproject.org

State Registries of Sexual Offenders
    www.prevent-abuse-now.com

Stigma
    www.stigmatized.org

Survivors of Incest Anonymous
    www.siawso.org

Surviving to Thriving
    www.survivingtothriving.org

United States Department of Justice, Office on Violence against Women
    www.usdoj.gov/ovw

The Voices and Faces Project
    www.voicesandfaces.org

The Washington Coalition of Sexual Assault Programs
    www.wcsap.org

World Health Organization, Department of Gender, Women, and Health
    www.who.int/gender/en

ORGANIZATIONS BY PHONE NUMBER

800-531-HUG-U—Adult Survivors of Child Abuse

800-448-3000—Boystown National Hotline

800-248-8020—Child Quest International (Missing and Abused Children)

800-4-A-CHILD—Childhelp USA Child Abuse Hotline

800-477-2676—Colorado Outward Bound School (For Survivors of Child Abuse)

800-843-5678—National Center for Missing and Exploited Children

800-222-2000—National Council on Child Abuse and Family Violence Helpline

800-851-3420—National Criminal Justice Referral Service

800-227-5242—National Resource Center on Child Abuse and Neglect

800-KIDS-006—National Resource Center on Child Sexual Abuse

800-421-0353—Parents Anonymous National Office (for overwhelmed parents)

800-627-3675—Red Flag/Green Flag Resources (sexual abuse and domestic violence)

800-786-4328—Voices in Action, Inc. (for incest survivors)

ORGANIZATIONS BY ADDRESS

Adult Survivors of Child Abuse (ASCA) Treatment Centers
10251 E. Artesia Boulevard, Suite 215
Bellflower, CA 90706
(310) 866-5810
(800) 531-HUG U

American Medical Association
Department of Mental Health
515 North State Street
Chicago, IL 60610
(312) 464-5000

American Professional Society on the Abuse of Children
332 South Michigan Avenue
Suite 1600
Chicago, IL, 60604
(312) 554-0166
Responds to inquiries from professionals involved in combating child maltreatment.

Boys and Girls Clubs of America
Government Relations Office
611 Rockville Pike, Suite 230
Rockville, MD 20852
(301) 251-6676
1,200 clubs nationwide serving over 1.6 million boys and girls.
Offers child safety curriculum.

C. Henry Kempe Center for Prevention and Treatment of Child Abuse and Neglect
1205 Oneida Street
Denver, CO 80220
(303) 321-3963
Offers a clinically based resource for training, consultation, program development and evaluation, and research in all types of child maltreatment.

Childhelp USA
6463 Independence Avenue
Woodland Hills, CA 91367
(800) 4-A-CHILD
(800) 422-4453
Provides comprehensive crisis counseling by mental health professionals for adult and child victims of child abuse and neglect, offenders, parents who are fearful of abusing or who want information on how to be effective parents. The Survivors of Childhood

Abuse Program (SCAP) disseminates materials, makes treatment referrals, trains professionals, and conducts research.

Clearinghouse on Child Abuse and Neglect Information
Box 1182
Washington, DC 20013
(703) 385-7565
1-800-394-3366 outside metropolitan Washington, DC

This Clearinghouse, a component of the National Center on Child Abuse and Neglect, is a major resource center for publications and public awareness and child abuse. Their database provides bibliographies, program directories, and public awareness materials. From this database and other resources, the Clearinghouse develops publications on a variety of subjects including sibling abuse, cultural sensitivity, sexual abuse prevention and treatment, and substance abuse.

Incest Resources, Inc.
46 Pleasant Street
Cambridge, MA 02139
(617) 492-1818
(requests by mail only)

Incest Survivors Resource Network International
P.O. Box 7375
Las Cruces, NM 88006-7375
(505) 521-4260

National Center for Missing and Exploited Children
2101 Wilson Boulevard
Suite 550
Arlington, VA 22201
(703) 235-3900
(800) 843-5678

Toll-free number for reporting missing children, sightings of missing children, or reporting cases of child pornography. Provides free written materials for the general public on child victimization as well as technical documents for professionals.

National Center for Prosecution of Child Abuse
1033 N. Fairfax St., Suite 200
Alexandria, VA 22314
(703) 739-0321

A Program of the American Prosecutors Research Institute, promotes the prosecution and conviction of child abusers by offering information and practical assistance to prosecutors involved in child abuse litigation. Publishes manuals on legal issues and provides technical assistance, referral services, and training seminars on child abuse litigation for prosecutors.

National Center for Prosecution of Child Abuse
National Prosecutors Research Institute
   1033 N. Fairfax St., Suite 200
   Alexandria, VA 22314
   (703) 739-0321
   The National Center for Prosecution of Child Abuse aims to improve the investigation and prosecution of child abuse through court reform, profession specialization, and interagency coordination. It provides training, technical assistance, and an information clearinghouse for child abuse prosecutors and others.

National Coalition Against Sexual Assault
   P.O. Box 21378
   Washington, D.C. 20009
   (202) 483-7165
   The National Coalition Against Sexual Assault was founded in 1979 to lead a national movement to promote awareness about sexual violence and advocate for services for survivors. Members include rape crisis centers, counseling services, educational programs, women's shelters and concerned individuals.

National Committee for Prevention of Child Abuse
   332 South Michigan Avenue
   Suite 1600
   Chicago, IL 60604-4357
   (312) 663-3520
   Sixty-eight local chapters (in all 50 states). Provides information and statistics on child abuse and maintains an extensive publications list. The National Research Center provides information for professionals on programs, methods for evaluating programs, and research findings.

National Exchange Club Foundation for Prevention of Child Abuse
   3050 Central Avenue
   Toledo, OH 43606
   (419) 535-3232
   Provides volunteer parent aide services to abusive and neglecting families in 37 cities.

National Organization for Victim Assistance
   1757 Park Road, N.W.
   Washington, D.C. 20010
   (202) 232-6682
   Provides information and referral for child victims as well as crisis counseling.

National Resource Center on Child Sexual Abuse
   106 Lincoln Street
   Huntsville, AL 35801
   (205) 534-6868
   1-800-543-7006

The toll-free number serves requests from the general public on information on child sexual abuse. The National Resource Center publishes the *National Directory of Child Sexual Abuse Treatment Programs* and has developed methods to increase professional awareness on issues including male survivors of sexual abuse, case management, and sexual abuse allegations in child custody litigations.

Parents United/Daughters and Sons United/Adults Molested as Children United
232 East Gish Road
San Jose, CA 95112
(408) 453-7616
One hundred fifty chapters nationwide. Provides guided self-help for sexually abusive parents as well as child and adult victims of sexual abuse.

Survivors of Incest Anonymous, Inc.
P.O. Box 21817
Baltimore, MD 21222
(301) 282-3400
(requests by mail only)

Survivors United Network
3607 Martin Luther King Blvd.
Denver, CO 80205
(303) 355-1133

Voices in Action, Inc.

(Victims of Incest Can Emerge Survivors)
P.O. Box 148309
Chicago, IL 60614
(800) 786-4238
(301) 282-3400

Glossary

The following terms are taken from the preceding chapters of *The Long Journey Home*. These definitions are intended to aid general readership by bringing clarity to some technical terms, providing additional information to key concepts, and helping facilitate trans-disciplinary understanding and dialogue.

Abdicate, Abdication. To relinquish or give up power, rights, or responsibility. In a family, one member can abdicate his or her responsibilities to or for other members in the relationship, which can lead to a dysfunctional dynamic.

Absent Father. One who is a biological parent, but not a parent actively or emotionally involved in raising his children.

Absolution. Setting free from guilt, sin, or penalty; forgiveness of an offense.

Acculturative Stress. Stress related to the adjustment difficulties and challenges involved in the adoption of the behavior patterns and attitudes of another culture within which one must function.

Accusative Case. The noun that marks the direct object, the recipient of the action (e.g., "I hit *the ball*").

Active Listening. A process of listening, often utilized in psychotherapy, where the listener pays close attention to verbal and nonverbal communication, seeks to understand the content and emotional meaning of the message, asks clarifying questions as needed, and reflects the message back to the speaker for clarification and correction. (See also **Empathy**)

Actuarial Assessments/ Factors. A statistically calculated estimation of the probability that a person will engage in a certain behavior or be involved in a certain outcome given the existence of key predictive variables.

Adrenal System. The adrenal glands are chiefly responsible for releasing hormones in reaction to stress, which then leads to certain automatic physiological reactions such as increased heart rate, constriction of blood vessels, and dilation of air passages, the purpose of which is designed to have survival value in preparing the individual for "fight or flight." (See also **Sympathetic Nervous System**)

Adult Bible Fellowship. Adult Bible fellowship is a group of adults who gather together for a Bible or book study in the context of developing relationships. The adults are most often comprised of people in similar stages of life. Time is given for getting to know one another, sharing prayer requests, and for social activities outside of class.

Adversarial Legal System. A system of law where opposing sides formally represent their positions before an impartial person or group of people, usually a judge or jury which then tries to determine the truth of the case based on the evidence presented.

Advocacy. Acting positively and constructively on behalf of one's own cause or on behalf of the cause of another, whose legitimate needs might otherwise be overlooked or ignored.

Affect. The personal experience of emotion that can range from anger to joy or enthusiasm to despair, being a reactive emotional response to a situation that gives information to the individual as to the personal or symbolic meaning of the situation.

Affective Experience. See **Affect.**

Affect Regulation. The self-regulatory ability to appropriately understand and cope with one's emotions, including the ability to increase positive emotions and minimize stress and negative emotional states.

Affective Dialogue. A therapeutic mode of communication that is emotionally focused (as opposed to being more intellectualized) and thus attuned to cognitions and responses that are considered "hot" such that a person's awareness, recollections, and motivation are heightened in the moment thus attaining an increased level of meaning and depth.

Affective Processes. The influence of emotions on mental processing that gives information to the individual regarding the personal or symbolic meaning of a given situation.

Amnesia. The partial or total inability to remember that is usually due to a significant shock or to brain damage. Dissociative amnesia refers to amnesia that is not due to a physiological problem (e.g., brain injury or dementia). (See also **Dissociation**)

Amulet. Latin (*amuletum*). Taking a variety of small portable forms, an amulet functions as a charm (or ornament). Similar to a talisman or phylactery, the amulet is typically inscribed with magic phrases, words (i.e., incantation) or a symbol to aid the wearer or protect against evil, disease, or witchcraft.

Analytic Clinician. Typically refers to a practitioner who utilizes the theories and methods of Carl Jung to help uncover the unconscious meaning and symbolic significance of an individual's behavior.

Anamnesis. The recollection of one's personal history; clinically this refers to one's individual development, relevant family information, and medical history prior to the onset of symptoms of a psychological disorder.

Androcentric Language. A manner of communication that emphasizes the male perspective and that may also diminish the value and validity of women's experiences. (See also **Feminist Hermeneutic, Patriarchy**)

Animal Magnetism. The view that human beings were influenced by magnetic forces or those that operated similarly to magnets. Uses of these properties were attempted as cures for diseases.

Anthropology. The study of human beings that involves describing characteristics of and explaining reasons for observed similarities and differences (physical and cultural) between groups of people.

Antisocial Behavior. Behavior that deviates significantly from the prevailing norms and values of society and that typically violates the rights of others. (See also **Antisocial Personality Disorder**)

Antisocial Cognitions. Perceptions, thoughts, and images associated with values and beliefs that run counter to societal norms and which can then lead to antisocial actions.

Antisocial Personality Disorder. According to the *DSM-IV-TR*, a personality disorder that involves a pattern of chronic and pervasive antisocial thinking and behavior; sometimes referred to as psychopathy or sociopathy. (See also **Antisocial Cognitions, DSM-IV-TR, Psychopathy**)

Assessment. A systematic procedure for gathering relevant information about an individual's social patterns, personality, intellectual, and behavioral functioning. Strategies used in this endeavor may include formal testing as well as clinical interview. (See also **Presenting Symptoms**)

Atonement. Amends or reparation made for wrongdoing; in Christianity, the reconciliation of God and man that is brought about by the redemptive work of Jesus Christ. (See also **Reconciliation, Restitution**)

Attachment Development. Attachment theory describes the important developmental need for infants and children to form close emotional bonds with significant others. Secure, reliable attachment is related to positive psychological and relational growth and development; disruption in the formation of such attachment is thought to be related to discontinuity in the development of a healthy and stable sense of self and others. (See also **Attachment Figure, Attachment Theory, Developmental Theory**)

Attachment Figure. A significant adult or older child with whom the infant or young child develops a close emotional bond; and on whom the child relies for security, organization of experience, and the capacity to trust and develop emotionally. This is typically a parent but may also be another family member or caregiver (who engages the child in an emotionally significant relationship), particularly in two-thirds world contexts.

Attachment Theory. Emphasizes the inborn need to form close emotional bonds with significant others. Attachment characterizes the type and quality of the relationship between infants and caregivers and is believed to affect later social development and emotional stability.

Attunement. The sharing or matching of affect, so that one person feels understood by the other, typically employed to describe a positive experience of parent-child attachment. (See also **Empathy**)

Authoritarian. A restrictive and controlling style of parenting; the father stresses loyalty and strict obedience to rules; often involving punitive forms of punishment to gain compliance.

Automatisms. Involuntary or reflex biological movements in an organ or other body part, such as the beating of the heart or the dilation of the pupil of the eye; also refers to brief, automatic movements that are not under conscious control, such as tremors during a seizure.

Avoidance Effort. A way of coping with perceived danger by fleeing, escaping, or relationally withdrawing.

Avoidant Pattern. A self-protective pattern of response in those diagnosed with post-traumatic stress disorder, which includes avoidance of the stimuli associated with the trauma, emotional numbing, and restricted range of emotion, loss of interest in activities, and detachment from others. Such may operate on a conscious or subconscious level of awareness. (See also **Blunted Affect, Trigger**)

Ban. Generally, a prohibition. In the Bible, God's decree that everything be destroyed or dedicated in an almost sacrificial manner (cf. Lev 27:28–29; Joshua 6–7).

BASK Model of Dissociation. A way of explaining dissociation of experience using the acronym of Behavior, Affect, Sensation and Knowledge.

Behavioral Contracting. An agreement, usually written down, that stipulates the specific steps or responsibilities that an individual will carry out under specified conditions and within a certain time frame toward the goal of managing a problem behavior.

Behavioral Techniques. Therapeutic strategies used to manage problem behaviors and situations, often involving learning, reinforcement, modeling, punishment, replacement behaviors, and conditioning.

Best Practice. Those strategies and procedures that have been recognized and endorsed by the professional community as having empirical support (i.e., are validated through careful research) and having demonstrated effectiveness for the particular issue and population in question.

Biastophilia. A sexual disorder in which unusual fantasies or behaviors based on surprising or attacking a stranger sexually are needed in order to generate sexual excitement. (See also **Paraphilias**)

Biblical Theology. Emphasizing the overarching message of Scripture, biblical theology is study of the Bible from the perspective of the text's own internal themes and progressive history of God in revealing himself to humankind throughout the Old and New Testaments.

Bigamy. The illegal act of marrying one person when already married to someone else.

Biological Antecedents. A biological event, circumstance, or stimulus that precedes or comes before some other event and often elicits, signals, or sets the stage for a particular behavior or response.

Biopsychosocial. The systematic integration of biological, psychological, and social information to understand human functioning. A part of a formal assessment process, commonly completed during the preliminary part of a mental health intake interview.

Bipolar Disorder. As listed in the *DSM-IV-TR*, a psychiatric disorder involving significant problems in mood regulation that includes a history of both manic and depressive symptoms in varying combinations and to various degrees. Previously known as manic depressive disorder. (See also ***DSM-IV-TR***)

Bisexual. Sexual attraction to or sexual behavior with both men and women.

Blame Shifting. A defensive maneuver whereby responsibility for an act is directed away from oneself toward another individual so as to absolve oneself of any responsibility for the problems associated with the act. (See also **Defense Mechanisms**)

Blunted Affect. An individual shows little or no apparent emotion. Often part of a depressive process. (See also **Affect, Depression**)

Body Memories. The idea that memories, often connected to trauma, can be stored outside the brain in locations throughout the body. This phenomenon is offered as an explanation for the existence of physical symptomatology (e.g., bruising, stomach ache) that is thought to be related to some earlier abuse, typically of a sexual nature, that involved that particular area.

Borderline Personality Disorder (BPD). According to the *DSM-IV-TR* a disorder characterized by a pattern of marked instability in mood, interpersonal relationships, and self-perception that is severe and causes great distress and interference with interpersonal and work-related functioning. (See also ***DSM-IV-TR***)

Boundary Confusion. In a family or other structured relationship refers to a loss of clarity around each individual's personal functioning, so that role expectations are not clear. For instance, who is the parent and who is the child, as is the case when the parent subjects himself or herself so that the child is inappropriately put in the position of taking care of the parent's needs in some contexts while being expected (often via unspoken rules) to revert back into the role of the child in other circumstances. (See also **Enmeshment**)

Call to Worship. A message, in song or speech, directed toward the people as an invitation to worship.

Case Analysis. Careful review of the details surrounding a particular type of occurrence or clinical case so as to learn about causal connections that led to a particular outcome.

Catharsis. The release of intense affect (emotion) into present experience that has been connected to a prior traumatic event. Often the traumatic event was threatening or overwhelming to an individual and as a result had been buried or repressed (i.e., pushed out of conscious awareness), being too overwhelming to allow into conscious awareness.

Catharism. Related to a Christian sect that flourished in Western Europe in the twelfth and thirteenth centuries that taught a dualistic belief emphasizing ascetic (i.e., the practice of rigorous self-discipline) renunciation of the world; this sect was condemned by the church as heretical. (See also **Docetism, Dualism, Gnosticism**)

Celtic Blessing Circles. A service of communal group prayer where those who gather form a circle and offer prayers and blessings to facilitate healing for those experiencing loss, grief, and sorrow.

Cerebral Imaging Technology. A set of clinical scanning strategies used to view the structure and function of different parts of the brain, including CAT scan, PET scans, MRI and FMRI scans. Certain scans can indicate which parts of the brain are most active under different types of circumstances.

Chattel. Old Norman for "cattle," from Latin (*capitalis*, "head") and referred to an article of personal movable property, such as livestock. At times, this included another person over whom one had complete control.

Chiastic Structure. Derived from the Greek letter *chi* (X), it is a literary device employing words and poetic lines that are inversely repeated for rhetorical effect. Chiastic structures shape episodes, speeches, or entire stories (e.g., Amos 5:4b–6a). (See also **Rhetorical Analysis**)

Child Bride. An underage girl (in some cases pre-pubertal) who is married to an older man. Such marriages are typically foisted upon a child who lacks the cognitive capacity to understand the ramifications (and thus cannot give true consent), and who is also vulnerable in terms of power dynamics (and thus may find it impossible to resist).

Child/hood Sexual Abuse (CSA). A form of child abuse where an adult or older adolescent uses a child for sexual gratification by pressuring a child to engage in various sexual activities, which may include either contact or non-contact abuse: exposing one's genitals to a child, showing pornography to a child, having physical contact with the child's genitals, viewing of the child's genitalia, or using a child to create child pornography. (See also **Child Protective Agencies, Sexual Abuse**)

Child Protective Agencies. Governmental agencies charged with protecting the safety, health, and welfare of children. Such will investigate allegations of suspected abuse and neglect. (See also **Child/hood Sexual Abuse**)

Civil Commitment. A legal process where a judge decides whether a person who is believed to be mentally ill should be required to go to a psychiatric hospital or to accept other mental health intervention. A civil commitment is not a criminal conviction and does not go on a criminal record.

Close-binding Mother. The view in psychoanalytic theory that homosexuality may develop in a male child as the result of having an overly involved, dominant mother and a rejecting, detached, or absent father, the combination of which thwarts the development of a secure sense of male identity. This dynamic undermines the boy's identification with his father or otherwise makes the mother-son relationship so strong that psychological separation from the mother is impossible. (See also **Attachment Figure, Psychoanalytic Theory**)

Close Reading. A process of reading [Scripture] that accounts for the detail of a text (e.g., plot, setting characterization, point of view, repeated terms, etc.). Conscious literary artistry is emphasized, paying careful attention to individual words, syntax, speakers, and the order in which sentences and ideas unfold as stories develop and are "reused" (e.g., Nathan's parable [2 Sam 12:1–4] that reemploys key terms from David's sin/rape of Bathsheba [2 Sam 11]: "eat," "drink," "bosom"). (See also **Rhetorical**)

Coercive Control. Behaviors used to control the victim for the purposes of the abuser; a pattern of sexual mastery where the abuser (usually male) mixes repeated physical intimidation and abuse, isolation, and control to accomplish his purposes.

Coercive Pornography. A type of pornography that depicts the victim as being forced into an unwanted sex act (related to "bondage").

Cognitive-Behavioral Theory. An active and usually time-limited form of psychotherapy that attends to cognitive (i.e., thinking) and behavioral elements of psychological disorders. Treatment is typically directed to identifying and changing the client's core beliefs, maladaptive thought processes, and problematic behaviors through cognitive restructuring and behavior modification strategies.

Cognitive Deficits. Limitations in performance or capacity of thinking that are substantially lower than expected for a person of a given age and education, and which create some degree of impairment for the person.

Cognitive Development Theory. Theories that set out to explain what accounts for the growth and maturation of thinking processes. Such theories often depict cognitive development as occurring in a series of fairly predictable stages, with different challenges to be resolved at each in order for development to proceed normally.

Cognitive Disorder. Impaired ability in one or more aspects of thinking that are involved in such things as self-control, organization, perception, planning, reasoning, emotional control, judgment, memory, and decision-making.

Cognitive Dissonance. An uncomfortable feeling of psychological tension caused by simultaneously holding contradictory ideas about an issue. The individual is motivated to reduce this tension by modifying beliefs or the meaning of behaviors related to the issue.

Cognitive Distortion. A faulty or inaccurate thinking, believing, imaging, or perceiving.

Cognitive Framework. A particular perspective used for understanding and evaluating information, providing a structure from which to meaningfully organize new information; a set of lenses, so to speak, for viewing the world according to certain rules or theories.

Cognitive Processing Therapy (CPT). This form of therapy is often used in treating post-traumatic stress disorder (PTSD) to assist in the identification and expression of appropriate thoughts and emotions related to the event, thus leading to constructive changes in the beliefs and attitudes toward self, others, and the world of the affected individual. (See also **Post-traumatic Stress Disorder**)

Cognitive Strategies. Coping skills used to manage the process and content of thought, often involving things like self-talk, imagery, and the recognition and alteration of errors or extremes in thinking. (See also **Coping Skills**)

Cohabitation. A living arrangement where individuals live together as though married but without being legally married.

Collude/ Collusion. The unintended effect of contributing to harm. A secret agreement or understanding between individuals, usually for accomplishing fraudulent or treacherous purposes.

Collusive Partner. An individual who agrees (implicitly or explicitly) to act in secret understanding with another toward some commonly accepted goal, that is often self-serving, negative, or underhanded. (See also **Conspiracy of Silence, Denial**)

Community Consultation. The coordinated integration of various community agencies and organizations to help provide for the best level of care and support for targeted individuals and groups. Such usually involves a collaborative relationship among hospitals, mental health and substance abuse treatment agencies, as well as other supportive organizations.

Community Referral. A system of connecting people in need and various assistance services which are geographically contiguous and financially viable.

Complex PTSD. A syndrome resulting from prolonged and repeated trauma, usually when the victim is held in a state of captivity by the perpetrator. Coercive control is often involved due to the inescapability of the situation for the victim. (See also **Post-traumatic Stress Disorder**)

Compulsive Masturbation. The frequent stimulation of the genitals to achieve sexual gratification, usually leading to orgasm. Such is often perceived by the person as an uncontrollable and overruling urge.

Concubinage. An ongoing, marriage-like relationship between a man and woman, wherein the man cannot marry for a specific reason but keeps the woman as a sort of pseudo-wife. The reason may be because of issues like social circumstance or because the man is already married.

Conflict Avoidance. A method of managing the anxiety and trouble of conflict by not directly confronting the issue at hand, usually because such confrontation is seen as too threatening. Such strategies may include changing the subject, putting off a discussion until later, or simply not bringing up the subject of contention, none of which, however, resolve the original issue.

Conjugal Rights. Mutual rights and privileges that have their basis in a marital union, including those involving companionship, aid and support, and sexual relations.

Conspiracy of Silence. Having to do with a condition or matter which is known to exist in a family or other social group but which, by implied or unspoken agreement, is not talked about or acknowledged. Such matters are typically considered to be shameful or taboo (e.g., of a family regarding their abusing member). (See also **Taboo**)

Constriction. Narrowing the range or cutting off aspects of personal experience that is threatening or uncomfortable for an individual. (See also **Avoidant Pattern, Blunted Affect, Numbing**)

Co-parenting. The idea of two parents who are divorced or separated, or other parent figures who are not living together (e.g., stepparents, extended family members, or anyone who shares parenting responsibilities), and are involved in sharing parenting responsibilities.

Coping. See **Avoidant Pattern.**

Coping Skills. Strategies learned so as to be able to better manage the stressful demands of a situation that might otherwise tax or exceed one's existing resources. (See also **Avoidant Pattern**)

Corporeal. Latin: *corpus*. Of, relating to, or characteristic of physicality; the body. (See also **Embodiment**)

Corrective Rape. A criminal practice where men rape lesbian women, purportedly as a means of "curing" the woman of her sexual orientation.

Counter-transference. A therapist's unconscious reactions to a patient that are based on the therapist's own psychological needs and conflicts. (See also **Transference**)

Creation Mandate. The Creation Mandate (Gen 1:28) is God's royal blessing of man and woman. Though a grammatical command, its function is a blessing of ethical stewardship toward all life (Gen 2:15), involving a vitality of relationship, charge, and capability for both sexual propagation ("be fruitful . . .") and governance ("rule over . . ."; cf. Gen 9:1–7; Exod 1:7; Psalm 8).

Creation Theology. The theological portrait of God's creative work seen throughout Scripture. Unique to Scripture is a sovereign artisan, who creates without a consort, and whose work is ideal for all life and entrusted to royal human ambassadors. Creation theology highlights the Creator's relational involvement within his creation through three key modalities: (1) *beginning* (Gen 1:1–2:3; 2:4–25), (2) *continuation* (Psalms 8, 19, 33; Job 38:12–41:34), and (3) *consummation* (Isaiah 40–55; John 1:1–9). The coming of Christ inaugurated a new age and therefore a new creation (2 Cor 5:17; Col 1:17; Rev 20:2–3). (See also **Biblical Theology, Eschatology**)

Criminogenic Factors. Factors or issues in a person's life that are believed to contribute to the development of criminal tendencies or the repetition of such behavior.

Cultural Norms. Societal rules, values, or standards that define what is accepted and appropriate behavior within a given culture.

Cybersex. Cybersex, computer sex, or Internet sex is a virtual or digital sex encounter in which two or more persons connected remotely via computer send each other sexually explicit messages describing a sexual experience. Participants may pretend they are having actual physical sex with each other.

Cyclical Transactional Patterns. Having to do with the continuing process of interaction and influence between a person and the physical or social environment in which he or she functions. This is a mutual process of influence such that it is difficult to truly understand the meaning of behavior when viewing the individual out of context.

Date Rape. Also known as *acquaintance rape*, date rape is an act of aggression or violence that involves forced, nonconsensual sex between two people who already know each other, where the will of one is imposed upon the other. (See also **Corrective Rape, Gang Rape**)

Dative Case. In syntax, marking the indirect object of a verb. Often the recipient of speaking or giving verbs (e.g., "I threw the ball *to my dog*").

Deconstruction. Deconstruction has a basic suspicion of all traditional models of defining and understanding history, literature, subjectivity, and knowledge, and so seeks to expose and challenge conceptual limits and foundations; philosophical movement and theory of literary criticism that questions the ability of language to represent reality, truth, and origin. In its more radical uses, a reader-response approach to texts focuses on the reader's interests to interact with the text and create meaning. (See also **Feminist Hermeneutic, Hermeneutic of Suspicion, Postmodernism**)

Defense Mechanisms. A psychoanalytic term used to describe various unconscious ways in which individuals protect themselves from being overwhelmed with anxiety, typically by denying, deflecting, or distorting reality in some way. The full term is *ego defense mechanism*. (See also **Abdication, Avoidance, Denial**)

Denial. A defense mechanism whereby unpleasant thoughts, feelings, wishes, or events are excluded from conscious awareness, thereby reducing anxiety or emotional conflict by refusing to acknowledge the reality of an event. (See also **Avoidant Pattern, Blunted Affect, Defense Mechanisms**)

Depersonalization. A sense of detachment from self and body. One of the *DSM-IV-TR* dissociative symptom areas. (See also **Dissociative Disorders**)

Depravity. Generally, a reference to human corruption or degradation. In theology, a description of sin as a state affecting the entire person: body, mind emotions, and will (cf. Rom 6:6, 17; 2 Cor 3:14–15; Gal 5:24), who is unable to qualify for God's favor.

Depression. A deviation from a normal mood state that is characterized by sadness, pessimism, a loss of drive, or feelings of despondency. When extreme and unremitting, a formal psychiatric diagnosis of *Dysthymia* or *Major Depression* may be considered. (See also **Dysphoria, Symptom Clusters**)

Derealization. A sense that people or places seem strange or unreal. One of the *DSM-IV-TR* dissociative symptom areas. (See also **Dissociative Disorders**)

Detachment. The feeling of emotional or psychological disengagement that may be a defensive reaction to trauma and abuse that is achieved by psychologically removing oneself from a real or imagined situation. (See also **Dissociation, Dissociative Symptoms**)

Developmental Perspective. Interpreting behavior according to validated and predictable sequences or phases in maturation that are a normal function of chronological age. New challenges opportunities for growth are typical for each stage of development; however, when thwarted, normal development may get sidetracked.

Developmental Theory. Theories that postulate the importance of early experiences in helping to shape personality. Developmental (i.e., a progressive series of changes and adaptations moving the individual toward maturation) needs and tasks are thought to be common to all, with successful resolution of such forming the basis for healthy personality. (See also **Attachment Development, Developmental Perspective**)

Deviant Sexual Behavior. Any sexual behavior that falls out of the norm, including homosexuality, voyeurism, fetishism, masochism, sadism, incest, pedophilia, and transvestitism. (See also **Incest, Pederasty, Sadism, Sexual Deviance, Voyeurism**)

Diagnostic Label. A clinical term signifying a concise description of a meaningfully related cluster of symptoms that is exhibited by an individual with a particular disorder which then helps facilitate a form of shorthand communication between professionals. Typically reflects a formal *DSM-IV-TR* diagnosis. Labels can become problematic if such becomes the central focus of attention to the exclusion of other important (and non-pathological) qualities of the individual in question. (See also *DSM-IV-TR*)

Diagnostic and Statistical Manual of Mental Disorders—4th Edition—Text Revision (DSM-IV-TR) (p. 423).

Dialectic Behavioral Therapy (DBT). A form of therapy that combines various ideas from Behavior Therapy, Cognitive Therapy, and Mindfulness Therapy, and which promotes both acceptance and change. Often used with disorders difficult to treat such as borderline personality disorder (BPD). (See also **Borderline Personality Disorder**)

Differentiate. The psychological state of being different from others and as seeing oneself as a unique individual (e.g., as a child becomes differentiated from parents over time). In some cases, the process of differentiation is thwarted and the child becomes enmeshed with a parent, thus having a sort of combined identity with no real distinct sense of him or herself. (See also **Boundary Confusion, Individuate**)

Disorganized Attachment. An insecure attachment pattern in a child that is unpredictable under stress; marked by rigid control rather than trust, putting the child at risk for psychological problems in childhood and adulthood. (See also **Attachment Development, Attachment Theory**)

Dissociation. A disruption in the usually integrated mental functions of consciousness memory and identity, in order to avoid painful or traumatic associations or perception of the environment, sensation, and motor functioning. (See also **Associative Disorder**)

Dissociative Disorder. There are five *DSM-IV* dissociative disorders: dissociative amnesia, dissociative fugue, depersonalization disorder, dissociative disorder not otherwise specified, and dissociative identity disorder (Compare to ***DSM-IV-TR***)

Dissociative Disorder Not Otherwise Specified (DDNOS). According to the *DSM-IV-TR*, a dissociative disorder that does not meet full diagnostic criteria for one of the other dissociative disorders (e.g., *dissociative identity disorder*) and includes individuals with internally fragmented parts of self-involving consciousness, memory, and identity. Often occurs in individuals who have experienced prolonged and forced persuasion, such as brainwashing and indoctrination while captive. (See also ***DSM-IV-TR*, Dissociative Identity Disorder**)

Dissociative Experiences Scale–II (DES). A brief screening instrument to determine the extent an individual experiences both normal and pathological dissociation. (See also **Pathological**)

Dissociative Identity Disorder (DID). Formerly called multiple personality disorder (MPD). According to the *DSM-IV-TR*, this is a mental disorder in which two or more distinct personalities take over executive functioning of an individual's thoughts, feelings, and behaviors. (See also **Multiple Personality Disorder**)

Dissociative Symptoms. There are five *DSM-IV-TR* dissociative symptom areas: amnesia, depersonalization, derealization, identity confusion, and identity alteration. (See also **Depersonalization, Derealization, Identity Alteration, Identity Confusion**)

Disorders of Extreme Stress Not Otherwise Specified (DESNOS). A diagnostic category utilized by trauma specialists to describe symptoms associated with a history of prolonged, repeated, severe sexual or physical victimization.

Docetism. An early Christian heresy, associated with the Gnostics, that denied the full humanity, suffering, and death of Jesus (i.e., Jesus only "seemed" to be incarnate; cf. 1 John 1:1–4). (See also **Catharism, Gnosticism**)

Dogma. A doctrine or body of theological belief that relates to matters such as morality and faith, and which is set forth in an authoritative manner by an organized group such as the church; an authoritative principle or belief.

Domestic Violence. Any pattern of violence or abuse (e.g., physical, sexual, emotional) that occurs within the context of the home or other intimate relationships. (See also **Sexual Abuse**)

Diagnostic and Statistical Manual of Mental Disorders—4th Edition—Text Revision (*DSM-IV-TR*). The diagnostic system for mental illness published by the American Psychiatric Association and typically used by mental health professionals in North America and other countries in the world. The *DSM* undergoes periodic updating and revision to reflect the current state of understanding in the field of psychiatry. As of this writing, the *DSM-V* is in preparation and is scheduled for release in 2013.

Doxology. Greek, *doxa* ("praise, glory") and *lego* ("to declare"). A liturgical form of direct praise and worship of God, focusing on his unique character and acts to in order to highlight his glory (cf. Psalm 150; Phil 4:20; Rev 1:6). (See also **Liturgy**)

Dualism. The concept that the world is ruled by opposing realities, whether visible and invisible or forces of good and evil; the concept that humans have two basic natures, the physical and the spiritual, body and soul or mind and matter. Most dualistic philosophies celebrate the soul or spirit while denigrating flesh, bodies, and material creation. (See also **Catharism, Docetism, Gnosticism**)

Dynamic Factors. The various motives, emotions, and drives within an individual, the interplay of which can influence behavior and thinking.

Dysfunction. Broad description meaning impaired, problematic, or unhealthy behavior; often in an interpersonal group. (See **Family Dysfunction**)

Dysphoric. A mood state characterized by sadness, discontent, and sometimes restlessness. (See also **Depression**)

Electra Complex. See **Oedipal Complex.**

Embodiment (Theology). The recognition that our sense of self, others, and the sacred is body-mediated; the study of relationships between embodied persons. The idea in cognitive psychology and philosophy that emphasizes the role that the body plays in the shaping of the mind, whereby much of human thinking is viewed as a sort of extension of experiences from the interplay between the body and its immediate surroundings. (See also **Catharism, Docetism, Dualism, Gnosticism**)

Emotional Regulation. The ability to modulate or control one's emotion. (See also **Affect Regulation**)

Emotional Sequelae. The emotional aftereffect or "debris" following the experience of a negative or traumatic event, sometimes occurring relatively soon after the trauma, sometimes occurring more distally. (See also **Sequelae**)

Empathy. The ability to compassionately and deeply understand another person from that person's unique frame of reference and communicate this understanding to the person. (See also **Active Listening, Entitlement**)

Enmeshment/ Enmeshed Relationship. A lack of good emotional and psychological boundaries between individuals in a close relationship or family unit such that members may become overly involved in each other's lives, thus limiting healthy growth of one's sense of self. (See also **Boundary Confusion, Disorganized Attachment**)

Entitlement (of Offender). An attitude held by the *offender* where he or she believes that they deserve or have a right to something, such as a sexual experience of some type, and so feels entitled to that, regardless of the "rightness," domestic boundaries, or acceptability of the particular act.

Erotophonophilia. A paraphilia that involves sexual arousal or gratification that depends on the death of a human being. This type of crime is often manifested either by murder during sexual intercourse and/or by mutilating the sexual organs or areas of the victim's body. It sometimes includes such activities as removing clothing from the body or the posing and propping of the body in different positions, generally sexual ones. (See also **Paraphilia**)

Eschatology. The branch of theology that is concerned with final or end things, such as death, resurrection, the return of Christ, the Last Judgment, heaven and hell, and the ultimate destiny of humankind. Prophetic eschatology is a continuation of the present, whereas apocalyptic eschatology is a decisive break with the present age. (See also **Biblical Theology, Embodiment**)

Etiology. A term denoting the study of the causes and origins of a disorder or abnormality.

Evangelical. A Christian point of view, emphasizing: conversion experience, an active laity sharing the gospel and engaged in good works, the sole authority of the Bible as divinely inspired, and salvation through the work of Christ on the cross (cf. 1 Cor 2:2).

Evidence-based Practice. The use of therapeutic procedures and strategies that have been validated through controlled empirical research for the treatment of specific disorders or groups of people.

Exegesis. Greek, *exegeomai* ("to lead, draw out"). The process of critical analysis and explanation of a text of Scripture. The goal is to analyze biblical passages so that the words and intent of the text are as clear as possible. Rather than speculation, focused attention is given to meaning of words, syntax, genre, literary structure, historical context, and theology. (See also **Biblical Theology, Deconstruction, Feminist Hermeneutic**)

Exhibitionism. In general terms, the tendency to draw attention to oneself in conspicuous ways. As a paraphilia, such often involves exposing one's genitals to unsuspecting strangers for the purpose of gaining sexual excitement, but without any attempt to engage the other person in sexual contact. (See also **Paraphilia, Sexual Deviance**)

Exposure Therapy. A form of behavior therapy that is useful in treating anxiety disorders. This treatment involves scheduled, controlled confrontation with a feared object or situation, until habituation (i.e., getting used to the object or acquiring a different perspective on the object) occurs and the person becomes less and less anxious over the duration of the treatment. (See also **Trauma Breaks, Trigger**)

Eye Movement Desensitization and Reprocessing (EMDR). A method of treatment used to reduce the emotional impact that is related to a traumatic event. For example, one may be trained to think about the traumatic event while simultaneously visually concentrating on the rapid lateral movements of the therapist's finger. (See also **Trauma**)

Fall, the. In theology, the act of rebellion when Adam and Eve succumbed to the serpent's temptation (Genesis 3) to reject the clear directive of God and assert their own will in doing that which God had forbidden (Gen 2:16–17), resulting in the loss of the original relationship with God and the introduction of sin and judgment into the world and to all humankind (Rom 5:12–19, 20–21). (See also **Retribution, Theodicy, Vengeance**)

Family Dysfunction. Family dysfunction is any interactive process in the family that limits the effective and healthy development of family members. Such processes may include things like poor communication patterns, enmeshed relationships, poor boundaries between members, unclear roles, spiritual chaos, and poor problem-solving. (See also **Boundary Confusion, Enmeshed Relationship**)

Family Structure. The composition of the family and the organization and patterning of relationships among individual family members that can affect how well a family operates. A key point of study in the form of Family Systems Theory, also known as Structural Family Therapy. (See also **Family Systems Theory**)

Family Systems Theory. A broad conceptual model that underlies various approaches to family therapy. The family is viewed as a functional unit, as a whole, and as more than a just a collection of individuals. As such, therapy and theory focus on the entire family and the interrelationships between its members. Any change in one aspect of the family unit impacts everyone. The family then adapts to the change or else seeks to restore itself to its prior level of functioning. The personal problems of any individual are thought to be symptomatic of problems in broader family functioning.

Fatalism. A philosophical worldview believing that events are fixed in advance so that human beings are powerless to change them (e.g., being fatalistic about war).

Father. See **Authoritarian.**

Feedback Mechanisms. In systems theory, a sort of self assessment process by which the family regulates itself by determining whether the current operation of the system is useful or acceptable and, if not, attempts to make the needed changes. (See also **Systems Theory**)

Female Circumcision. Formally referred to as a *clitoridectomy*, this involves the removal of all or part of the clitoris, usually performed on young girls, and being practiced among certain cultures for different reasons including the curbing of sexual desire, prevention of premarital sex, or some form of initiation. (See also **Infibulation**)

Feminist (Hermeneutic). Reading Scripture from a feminist perspective includes: prioritizing the woman's experience as a worldview; emphasizing equality and mutuality, autonomy and rationality; rejecting any inequality in gender. Focusing on liberation, the hermeneutical goal is to expose and critique a variety of areas where patriarchal structures are self-perpetuating and self-legitimating and thereby to transform society, particularly in terms of social relations. (See also **Androcentric Language, Deconstruction, Hermeneutic of Suspicion, Patriarchy, Postmodernism, Womanist**)

Fertility Cult. In general, fertility cults have believed there is a causal connection between the fertility and blessing of the cropland, herds, and other such forms of prosperity to the sexual relations enacted by the "divine couple," priests and priestesses, or by cult prostitutes. Such activity is viewed as an act of worship intended to emulate the gods' creative abilities, or seen as an act of imitative magic by which the gods are then compelled to preserve the earth's fertility.

Flashbacks. The vivid and emotional reliving of a traumatic event by the victim after the original trauma has occurred. (See also **Post-traumatic Stress Disorder, Triggers**)

"Fight or Flight" Reaction. An emotional and visceral response to an emergency situation that is activated by the release of adrenalin and is designed to prepare the individual for attacking or fleeing from the source of threat or danger.

Forensic Psychology. The application of knowledge from psychology to situations involving the legal system, including assessment, diagnosis, and treatment of offenders.

Forgiveness. Forgiveness extends grace to the offender for a relationship that has been ruptured due to the violation or sin of one party against the other. Forgiveness does not cancel any legal verdict, nor does it dismiss, minimize, ignore, or forget the pain. In forgiveness, the offended party relinquishes the right to vengeance, thus often called *the act* of forgiveness. (See also **Forgiveness Intervention, Performative Statement, Reconciliation, Reparative Therapy, Restitution, Vengeance**)

Forgiveness Intervention. A therapeutic approach to assisting victims who have suffered some form of unjust or unfair treatment from others, such as sexual abuse, family murder, or incest, to be able to deal with the negative aftereffects (e.g., subsequent anger, depression, anxiety, etc.) of the offense so as to find release and be able to move on to a more healthy and productive life. (See also **Forgiveness, Restitution, Reparative Therapy**)

Fornication. Hebrew, *zana*; Greek, *porneia*. Generally, illicit sexual intercourse, a violation of the seventh commandment (Exod 20:14) that was meant to protect the integrity of the family. Fornication can be linked to adultery (Matt 5:32) or distinguished (Mark 7:21; cf. Acts 15:20, 29).

Frigid. Impaired sexual desire or inability to achieve full sexual gratification in women.

Frotteurism. A paraphilia practice involving a person intentionally and regularly seeking sexual gratification by rubbing against other people, usually in a public place. Also *frottage*. (See also **Paraphilia, Sexual Deviance**)

Frozen Visual Memories. When an individual experiences a traumatic event, their memory can be affected in many ways. One way is to store the traumatic memory is to create a very vivid "snapshot" in the brain. When the person remembers the traumatic event they then call up this vivid snapshot and may also re-experience the associated thoughts, emotions, and physical sensations. Therapy to resolve frozen visual memories includes having the individual reprocess the trauma and *un-couple* the strong thoughts, emotions, and physical sensations so the person can experience some relief. (See also **Triggers**)

Gang Rape. When a person is raped in a group situation, successively by several attackers. (See also **Corrective Rape, Marital Rape**)

Gay. Homosexual; having a sexual attraction to persons of the same sex.

Gay Bashing. Hatred and fear of gay men and lesbians that leads to prejudice, anger, and violence directed toward them.

Gay Identity. The sense of self-definition as a person that reflects an embracing of the physical and psychological characteristics shared by gay individuals.

Generational Patterns. Repeated patterns of behavior and ways of being that characterize the certain regularities in family functioning across multiple generations. Such may be positive and constructive or negative and destructive in terms of the impact on individual and family behavior. (See also **Intrafamilial**)

Genotype. The genetic makeup or constitution of an individual.

Gestalt Techniques. Experiential clinical strategies used in Gestalt therapy which emphasize the client's total functioning in the present, as opposed to spending time investigating an individual's personal history and development. Techniques are designed to bring out spontaneous feelings and self-awareness that might remain otherwise hidden or stifled so as to promote growth and self-direction.

Glossolalia. The New Testament gift known as "speaking in tongues," and first occurred on the day of Pentecost (Acts 2:1–13); a prayerful language that one has never formally learned but is given as a gift by the Holy Spirit (1 Cor 12:10, 28) and is typically used in the praise of God.

Gnosticism. Flourishing between the first century BC and the fourth century AD, a religious orientation advocating *gnosis* (i.e., secret knowledge, specialized or esoteric belief) as the way to release or free a person's spiritual element; considered heresy by Christian churches; usually emphasizing the corruption of anything that is physical. (See also **Dualism**)

Godhead. The Trinity; in theology, the divine nature and being of God.

Grooming Techniques. Specific strategies or actions used to manipulate individuals (usually children or impaired adults) in order to commit sex crimes against them. Grooming is typically used to gain access to victims, build trust with the intended victim or the victim's caretakers, minimize physical resistance, reframe abusive behavior as "special" or "loving," and get the victim to believe that he or she is at least partially responsible for the sexual behavior.

Group Therapy. Treatment technique used for certain psychological problems where several participants interact with each other with the guidance of a therapist who acts as a facilitator and interpreter of the process.

Hendiadys. A figure of speech using two parts (noun or verb), connected by a conjunction, to express a single idea (e.g., "pain and trembling" = "labor pains" [Gen 3:16a]; "full of grace and truth" = "God's gracious truth" [John 1:17]).

Hermeneutic. The interpretative approach one uses in reading and studying texts; the study of the locus of meaning and the principles of interpreting texts. (See also **Exegesis, Hermeneutic of Suspicion**)

Hermeneutic of Suspicion. An interpretative approach based on the assumption that biblical texts were written in androcentric language and reflect patriarchal structures. Feminist critics read with "suspicion" or more aggressively with "resistance" in order to uncover suppressed traditions (e.g., maternal God-language, women apostles, New Testament models of male leadership, and the use of gender-exclusive language or "linguistic sexism"). (See also **Androcentric Language, Deconstruction, Feminist Hermeneutic, Patriarchy, Postmodernism**)

Heterogeneous. That which consists of mixed elements or parts; not similar; completely different; incongruous.

Hierarchy. A group of persons, levels of values, responsibilities, or roles arranged in order of rank, class, or authority. A key assumption in feminist studies is that such roles and values are established by men to reflect and legitimate male power. However, contemporary scholars increasingly prefer more nuanced terms such as "heterarchy" that cuts across formal hierarchical structures of society, acknowledging "guilds" and "professional" associations of women. (See also **Androcentric Language, Feminist Hermeneutic, Patriarchy, Power Structures**)

Holy Innocents Day. A day (December 28) observed by worship in commemoration of the children slain by Herod at Bethlehem (Matt 2:16). It is a time for children to be especially blessed in church.

Honor Killing. The murder of a member of a cultural group or family by other members of that group that is motivated by the belief that the victim has brought dishonor to the group.

"Hook Up." A casual, brief encounter or connection that may involve sexual activity with no particular commitment to an ongoing relationship.

Homeostasis. The ability or tendency of an organism to maintain a state of internal equilibrium or consistency by adjusting its physiological processes to account for changes in its surroundings. (See also **Family Systems Theory**)

Homoerotic Attraction. A sexual/erotic desire for people of one's own gender.

Homosexuality. Sexual attraction or activity between members of the same sex. (See also **Gay, Lesbian, Same-sex Attraction**)

Homosexual Gang Rape. When a person is raped successively by several attackers who are of the same gender as the victim. (See also **Corrective Rape, Date Rape, Gang Rape**)

Household Code. In biblical studies, a "household code" refers to a set of rules that outline the relationships within the household: master/ slave, husband/ wife, and father/ children (e.g., Col 3:18–4:1; Eph 5:22–6:9; 1 Pet 2:13–3:7).

Human Trafficking. The activity of recruiting, transporting, buying, or kidnapping individuals, adults, or children to serve an exploitative purpose, such as sexual slavery or forced labor. (See also **Sex Trafficking**)

Hyperarousal. A state of increased psychological and physiological tension marked by such effects as reduced pain tolerance, anxiety, exaggeration of startle responses, insomnia, fatigue, and accentuation of personality traits.

Hypermasculine. The exaggerated expression or valuing of stereotypic male characteristics such as strength, virility, aggression, and the like. (See also **Machismo**)

Hypervigilance. A condition, usually fueled by anxiety, of maintaining an abnormally acute awareness of one's environmental surroundings; may include a heightened startle response. (See also **Startle Response**)

Hypnosis. The act of inducing an altered state of consciousness in an individual that is wakeful, focused, and highly suggestible.

Hysteria. Formerly used diagnostic term to describe a mental illness where physical symptoms have psychological rather than biological causes.

Iatrogenic. Greek, *iatros* ("physician"). A client effect or condition inadvertently induced by a doctor, clinician, or diagnostic procedure.

Identity Alteration. Objective behavior indicating the assumption of different identities much more distinct than different roles. One of the *DSM-IV-TR* dissociative symptom areas. (See also **DSM-IV-TR**)

Identity Confusion. Subjective feelings of uncertainty or conflict with regard to sense of self or identity. One of the *DSM-IV-TR* dissociative symptom areas. (See also **Dissociative Symptoms, *DSM-IV-TR***)

Ideomotor Signaling. Use of finger signals to access aspects of self outside of conscious awareness.

Imago Dei. Latin, "image of God." Image of God is a phrase used in theology to describe the uniqueness of humankind among God's creatures (Gen 1:26–27). Theologians differ on what the "image of God" actually refers to, but there seems to be some combination of internal and external aspects, though reason, will, and relationality have traditionally received greater emphasis. Whether or not the image of God was actually damaged in the Fall is also debated (cf. Gen 9:6; Jam 3:9). (See also **Fall, the**)

Impulsive Action. Behavior that is under-regulated; acting without giving much forethought to one's actions or to the possible consequences or implications of those actions.

Impulse Control. The ability to exert appropriate self-regulation or redirection of one's response in the presence of the strong urge or desire to behave in a certain way. (See also **Self-regulation**)

Incarnation. The theological doctrine that Jesus Christ, the Eternal Word (John 1:1–2) and second person of the Trinity, took on human embodied form, without any loss of his divine nature (Phil 2:6–11; cf. Rom 5:9–10; Col 1:15–20; Heb 1:1–3; 10:9–14). (See also **Godhead, Trinity, Embodiment**)

Incest. Sexual relations between persons to whom marriage is prohibited by custom, no matter how distant the relationship, or law because of their close kinship, such as within a family. Though it varies by country, age eighteen may be the legal limit. (See also **Child/hood Sexual Abuse, Intrafamilial Sexual Abuse, Sexual Abuse, Spiritual Incest**)

Individuation. The gradual process of the development of a unified and integrated sense of oneself as being a unique and autonomous individual.

Infanticide. The act of killing an infant.

Infibulations. A surgical procedure involving the sewing together of a female's labia majora so as to partially seal the opening of the vagina; typically performed on girls entering puberty to help ensure chastity. Where practiced, such is seen as a visible indication of virginity. (See also **Female Circumcision**)

Informed Consent. A legal and ethical principle to ensure that an individual knows all of the risks and costs involved in a procedure such as clinical treatment. Elements of informed consent include informing the individual of the nature of the treatment, possible alternative treatments, and the potential risks and benefits of the treatment. Key is the idea that the individual in question has the capacity to make truly informed consent (e.g., minors, cognitively impaired individuals may be considered as unable to give true informed consent).

Intergenerational Transmission. When particular social and behavioral patterns are carried on between successive generations of families. The complexity of socio-religious traditions protect and facilitate the transmission of both constructive and destructive social patterns from one family to the next. Any criminal act of an individual has a preceding social backdrop that can inform and even justify some activities. (See also **Generational Patterns, Spiritual Incest, Family Structure**)

Internalization. To make an idea, attitude, norm, belief, etc., a part of one's own patterns of thinking and being.

Intervention. Therapeutic techniques or strategies used by a therapist to treat the specific emotional and behavioral problems presented by the client.

Intrainterview Amnesia. A phenomenon that may occur during clinical interviews with severely traumatized patients who may be suffering from multiple personality disorder (MPD). One marker of MPD is intrainterview amnesia whereby a patient demonstrates in session an alter personality, first admitting to and then denying symptoms, being unable to later recall what had happened earlier in the session. (See also **Dissociative Identity Disorder, Multiple Personality Disorder**)

Intimate Partner Sexual Assault. Intimate partner sexual assault is a forced sexual encounter that is committed by a current or past spouse or boyfriend. Forced intercourse within a marriage is often called "marital rape." (See also **Rape, Wife/ Marital Rape**)

Intrafamilial. That which occurs *within* a family and in contrast to "interfamilial," that which occurs *between* families. (See also **Family Structure, Generational Patterns**)

Intrafamilial Sexual Abuse. Sexual abuse that occurs within a family. (See also **Child/ hood Sexual Abuse, Incest, Sexual Abuse, Taboo**)

Intrusive Thoughts/ Memories. Unwanted thoughts or images that intrude upon the flow of ongoing, task-related thinking despite personal efforts to avoid those thoughts.

"In Vivo" Exposure Therapy. A form of behavior therapy in which a client is exposed to anxiety-generating situations in actual, real-world conditions so as to be able to experience and then master their anxiety while in the presence of those provocative stimuli. (See also **Exposure Therapy**)

Jesuits. The Society of Jesus is the largest male Catholic religious order.

Judicial. Having to do with the court system.

Kingdom of God. God's sovereign rule over the people of God and the entire created order. Building on imagery of kingship in the Old Testament, the kingdom of God/heaven is a significant concept for understanding the teaching and ministry of Jesus in the Gospels (Matt 6:33; Luke 6:20). In the New Testament, the kingdom is present in the person and teaching of Jesus (Luke 10:9; 17:21), while still awaiting its future consummation (Luke 13:29; 22:18).

Koinonia. Greek; Christian *fellowship* or communion with God. Emphasizes close mutual involvement and relationship with others, implying wholesome intimacy, trust, sharing, and harmony (cf. Acts 2:42; Phil 2:1; Heb 13:16; 1 John 1:6).

Kyrie. Latin; a short liturgical prayer or petition including the phrase *kyrie* or "Lord, have mercy." (See also **Liturgy**)

Lament. A lament can be a biblical psalm of "complaint," a poem, or piece of music from either an individual or community expressing grief, suffering, oppression, or mourning. Biblical laments contain: (a) a call to God, (b) description of need, (c) request for help, (d) reasons God should intervene, (e) statement of trust, (f) and concluding praise. Laments are significant for their candor, honesty, even "raw" expression to God (e.g., Psalm 13).

Learned Helplessness. The condition in which someone has learned that his or her behavior has no effect on the environment, and as a result behaves helplessly, such as a child who is physically or sexually abused or an adult in a domestically violent relationship. Found to be strongly related to the development of depression. (Contrast with **Resilience**) (See also **Child/hood Sexual Abuse, Depression, Enmeshment**)

Lectio Divina. Latin for "divine reading," spiritual reading, or "holy reading," and represents a traditional Christian practice of prayer and scriptural reading intended to promote communion with God and to increase in knowledge of God's Word. (See also **Spiritual Disciplines, Spiritual Formation**)

Lesbian. A woman whose sexual orientation is to other women. (See also **Gay, Gay Identity, Homoerotic Attraction, Same-sex Attraction**)

Lex Orandi, Lex Credendi, Lex Agendi. Latin; the rule of prayer (or, more generally, worship) is the rule of belief and the rule of action; refers to the relationship between worship and belief.

Lex Talionis. Latin; "law of retribution." Often referencing the Old Testament "fix ratio" of legal principle (not interpersonal) of justice that is not based on class or money, but the *kind* of crime; thus, "eye for eye" (Gen 9:6; Exod 21:12; Lev 24:17, 21). The penalty was rooted in the nature of the crime, and thus controlled rogue vengeance, applying punishment equally to all. The New Testament stresses benevolence over retaliation (cf. Matt 5:38; Rom 12:17; 1 Thess 5:15; 1 Pet 3:9). (See also **Forgiveness, Restitution, Retribution, Vengeance**)

Limbic System. A group of brain nuclei that are involved in the kind of cognitive processing that is related to emotion and learning.

Limits of Confidentiality. Confidentiality is a key principle of professional ethics for mental health providers, requiring them to limit the disclosure of a client's identity as well as the details of his or her treatment, including the content of what is talked about. However, there are legal limits to confidentiality, including information related to sexual abuse, danger to self, and danger to others. In such cases the therapist is required for the purposes of safety and welfare to report such activity to the relevant parties or authorities.

Litany. A formal and repetitive prayer consisting of a series of petitions recited by a leader, followed in alternating fashion by prescribed responses from the congregation. (See also **Ritual**)

Liturgy. A predetermined or prescribed set of rituals that are performed, usually in a church. (See also **Lament**)

Longitudinal Study. The systematic, experimental investigation of certain variables of interest over time, sometimes several years, for the purpose of better understanding how certain phenomena change or develop.

Machismo. Spanish; prominent or exaggerated masculinity; attributes like virility, courage, strength and even entitlement are valued. (See also **Hypermasculine**)

Magnificat. Latin; known as *Mary's Song* of praise to the Lord: "My soul magnifies the Lord" (Luke 1:46). Modeled after Hannah's song (1 Sam 2:1–10), the Magnificat is frequently sung (or spoken) liturgically in Christian church services. (See also **Liturgy**)

Mandated Reporting. Related to the limits of confidentiality, mental health workers and other identified individuals are legally required as mandated reporters to breach a client's confidentiality under circumstances to help ensure the safety of individuals, as in the case of suspected child abuse, elder abuse, suicidal or homicidal plans as reported by the client to the therapist. (See also **Limits of Confidentiality**)

Mikvah. Hebrew; a ritual bath used for immersion in Judaism.

Millennium. The one thousand year reign of Jesus Christ on earth that is in fulfillment of many Old Testament prophesies that speak of an indeterminate length of time (Isah 65:17–25; Zech 9:9–10). New Testament references include 1 Cor 15:23–28 and Rev 20:4–6. Like patristic evidence, modern Christians are divided over whether the language is literal or figurative (i.e., millennialism vs. amillennialism).

Mindfulness. Having full awareness of one's internal states and surroundings. This idea has been applied to various types of psychotherapy to help individuals manage destructive or automatic habits and behaviors by learning to become better observers of their own thoughts and emotions. (See also **Self-care, Self-regulation, Self-soothe**)

Minor. A person who is not legally an adult; being "under age" and therefore unable to give trueinformed consent.

Modeling Experience. According to social learning theory, this signifies a type of vicarious learning that occurs through the experience of watching a model perform certain behavior. The impact of the experience on learning is related in part to whether the model is viewed as desirable, is someone the learner can relate to, and whether the model ultimately benefits from or is punished as a result of performing the behavior in question.

Moderate. When the presence of one variable (e.g., a behavior, trait, or situation, etc.) alters the relationship between other variables. For example, social support is said to *moderate* against the potential negative impact of chronic stress in terms of whether the individual develops stress-related physical (e.g., ulcer) or psychological (e.g., depression/anxiety) complications.

Modulating Emotion. To adjust, regulate, adapt, or otherwise temper an emotional response.

Molestation. The crime of committing sexual acts with minors, including such activities as touching private areas, exposure of genitalia, taking of pornographic pictures, rape, inducing sexual acts with the molester or with other children, and variations of these acts. Molestation also applies to incest by a relative with a minor family member, and any unwanted sexual acts with adults falling short of rape. (See also **Sexual Abuse**)

Mores. See **Cultural Norms.**

Multiple Personality Disorder. Known currently as dissociative identity disorder according to the *DSM-IV-TR*, this represents the presence of two or more distinct identities or personality states within an individual that each recurrently takes control of the individual's behavior. Such is often associated with severe and prolonged physical and sexual abuse, especially if occurring during childhood. (See also **Dissociative Identity Disorder**, *DSM-IV-TR*, **Trauma**)

Narrative Therapy. A form of psychotherapy that helps clients to reinterpret and rewrite, so to speak, their life events into true but more life-enhancing and growth-promoting narratives or stories. (See also **Anamnesis**)

"Nature and/vs. Nurture." Having to do with the discussion regarding the degree to which heredity (inborn factors) and environment (situational factors) interact to contribute to influence the development of individuals and their behavior.

Neurological. Having to do with or based in the operation of the nervous system.

New Covenant. In theology, the new relationship and agreement between God and humankind that is mediated by Jesus Christ, either through the effects of Christ's death (Heb 8:8–13; 10:16–17) or the expected renewal of the original covenant (Jer 31:31–34). (See also **Incarnation**)

Nightmares. A frightening or disturbing dream that involves strong feelings of fear, sadness, despair, and the like. The visual imagery in nightmares is usually quite vivid and can involve physiological reactions of terror. (See also **Affect Experience**)

Noetic. Greek, *noētikos, noein* ("intellectual," "to think"); focusing on that which is intellectual; associated with or requiring the use of the mind or process of knowing.

Normalization. To reframe or make normal so as to allow an individual to process or move past an event that seemed out of the norm for them; to make publically "normal" or recognized by reducing to a standard and thereby transforming social variables to a needed end (e.g., "Sexual abuse needs to be *normalized* in the church in order to adequately address it").

Normalizing Symptoms. The process of establishing the plausibility of symptoms as a natural and understandable ramification of having experienced a particular event such as trauma.

Numbing/Numbness. When abuse is present, the resulting emotions are typically distressing (fear, doubt, rage, shame, humiliation) and are often associated with pain. In an unconscious attempt to avoid painful emotions a survivor may experience a deadening of emotions, possibly as the result of the defense mechanism of *repression*. For a survivor, the state of a lack of any emotions may become their new definition of "happiness." (See also **Constriction, Defense Mechanism, Post-traumatic Stress Disorder**)

Objectification. To present or regard something or someone as an object or a thing; to separate out any personal or humanizing quality so as to limit or eliminate any associated feelings that may cause discomfort.

Oedipal Complex. From psychoanalytic theory, the Oedipal complex is a complicated concept and has to do with the erotic feelings a son is theorized to have toward his mother, which are accompanied by a sense of hostility and competition directed toward the father over the mother's affection. The boy fears retaliation by the father and so resolves this dilemma by identifying with his father. According to the theory, this is a predictable phase of development that young boys go through, which needs to be resolved successfully for healthy development and identity formation to occur. The female version of the Oedipal complex is termed the Electra complex, with somewhat different dynamics involved but which also must be successfully resolved in the young girl in order for healthy development and female identification to occur. (See also **Psychoanalytic Theory**)

Offense Cycle. For one who commits sexual offenses, the pattern or sequence of specific thoughts, feelings, and behaviors, combined with identifiable setting events, that lead to and are thereby "resolved" (i.e., the tension is reduced for the perpetrator) by the offending act.

Order of Protection. A legal document, signed by a judge, that is filed against a specific individual that forces that individual to keep at a defined distance from another named person and is intended to prevent abusive or other harmful and intimidating behavior toward the named person. Also called a restraining order.

Orgy. A gathering of individuals wherein a number of people engage in sexual activity with each other that is often unrestrained and without limits. (See also **Sexual Deviance**)

Oxymoron. Greek; statement or a concept that is made up of contradictory or incompatible elements (e.g., cruel kindness).

Panic Attack. A sudden onset of intense feelings of apprehension and fearfulness, not necessarily triggered by actual danger, along with other physical symptoms such as palpitations, shortness of breath, chest pain or tightness, choking, sweating, and dizziness, during which time the individual may fear that he or she is losing one's sanity or dying.

Paraphilia. A category of sexual disorders listed in the *DSM-IV-TR* characterized by various unusual or bizarre fantasies and/or behaviors that are needed in order to generate sexual excitement in the individual. (See also ***DSM-IV-TR***)

Parentification. Also called parentified child. A temporary or continuous reversal of roles between parent and child, leading to a distortion of the normal relationship wherein the adult places the child in the position of parent such that the child then must assume developmentally inappropriate responsibilities. (See also **Role Reversal**)

Partner Violence. A form of physical abuse that occurs between two people who are in a close relationship. (See also **Domestic Violence/ Abuse, Wife/ Marital Rape**)

Paschal. Greek; *pascha*, derived from the Hebrew *pesach*; an archaic name for the Passover or Easter.

Pastoral Care. Counseling or comfort that is given by ministers, priests, rabbis, trained spiritual leaders, etc., to those in need of help with their emotional, spiritual or relational problems or stressful situations.

Passing the Peace. In church liturgy and worship, often in preparation for receiving communion, the gathered community greets each other with the words: "Peace be with you."

Passive-Aggressive. Behavior that gives the appearance of being incidental, accidental, or neutral but that indirectly and more safely conveys a degree of aggression or anger toward another person (e.g., not following through on a task or being strategically forgetful, etc.), without running the risk of open confrontation.

Patriarchy. A social system in which the father is the head of the family and where men have authority over women and children. A term current in critical theory for male domination of women. Feminist critics claim that patriarchal structures in any culture both legitimate and perpetuate a marginalizing of women, via economics, religion, politics, and sex. Recent scholarship also acknowledges that the term "patriarchy" is not only anachronistic, but an overgeneralization based on Western concepts of social organization. Because male slaves were beneath some wives, patricentric is used by some. (See also **Androcentric Language, Deconstruction, Feminist Hermeneutic, Hermeneutic of Suspicion, Hierarchy, Reductionism**)

Pathological. Behavior that is extreme, excessive, markedly abnormal; symptomatic of a disturbed condition.

Pederasty. A sexual relationship between an older male and an adolescent boy that is romanticized as spiritual, pure, and virtuous. The age of the victim is typically older than pedophilia, which is usually focused on pre-puberty, and yet too young for consensual adult homosexuality. While idealized in early Greek and Roman culture, pederasty is considered child abuse in most countries today.

Pedophile. One who has a sexual interest in children; engages in sexual acts or fantasies with pre-pubertal children as the preferred method of gaining sexual excitement. (See also **Child/hood Sexual Abuse [CSA]**)

Performative Statement. Also called utterance. In speech act theory, a performative *statement* is an action in and of itself (e.g., oaths; "I forgive you"; "I establish my covenant with you," Gen 6:18, [illocutionary acts]) or *ceremonial* events of "performance" (e.g., marriage; "I now declare you husband and wife," [perlocutionary acts]).

Perpetrator. Someone who is responsible for or who commits an offense or crime. (See also **Molestation**)

Personality Disorder. A chronic and pervasive pattern of viewing, relating to, and thinking about the self and the world that is dysfunctional and interferes in various ways with the overall functioning of the individual. The *DSM-IV-TR* lists ten different personality disorders. (See also **Personality Structure, Borderline Personality Disorder (BPD), Dissociative Identity Disorder (DID),** *DSM-IV-TR*)

Personality Structure. Refers to the way the personality is organized according to the interrelationship and relative influence among assorted variables or traits. Descriptions of personality structure vary somewhat according to the differing theoretical schools of thought. (See also **Personality Disorder**)

Phenomenology. A point of view in philosophy which, when applied to psychotherapy, emphasizes a focus on the here-and-now, personal meaning, and the process of self-discovery. Characteristic of existential and humanistic approaches to therapy. (See also **Gestalt Techniques**)

Phenotype. The observable characteristics of an individual based on the interaction of the genotype and environment.

Phobia. A persistent, irrational, and intense fear of a specific object or situation that leads to an avoidant behavior. (See also **Avoidance Coping, Avoidance Effort**)

Play Therapy. A psychotherapeutic modality of treatment, typically used with younger children, that is typically nondirective and makes use of toys and other developmentally appropriate play activity in order to help the child express and work through personal issues. Play becomes the symbolic language through which the child communicates to the therapist.

Polygamy. The marriage of either sex to more than one spouse at the same time.

Positive Intention. As used in neuro-linguistic programming (a form of psychotherapy), this is the therapeutic sentiment that "behind every behavior is a positive intention," which, if identified, provides a path to getting behind problematic behaviors so they can be modified without losing the learning-benefits that their presence potentially provide.

Post-traumatic Avoidance Symptoms. One of the diagnostic criteria for post-traumatic stress disorder involving avoidance of situations, thoughts, or feelings that are associated with a previous traumatic experience. (See also **Avoidance Coping, Avoidance Effort, Post-traumatic Stress Disorder, Trauma**)

Post-traumatic Growth. Positive psychological change one experiences as a result of having struggled with and worked through highly challenging life circumstances such as personal trauma. (See also **Trauma**)

Post-traumatic Re-experiencing Symptoms. One of the diagnostic criteria for post-traumatic stress disorder involving re-experiencing of a traumatic event (e.g., in the form of flashbacks, nightmares, overwhelming affect, etc.). (See also **Flashbacks, Nightmares, Post-traumatic Avoidance Symptoms, Post-traumatic Stress Disorder, Trigger**)

Post-traumatic Stress Disorder (PTSD). A *DSM-IV-TR* diagnosis for individuals who have been exposed to a traumatic event and develop symptoms associated with the trauma including re-experiencing the event through nightmares or flashbacks, avoidance of experiences associated with the trauma, and hyperarousal. (See also **Cognitive Processing Therapy (CPT)**, *DSM-IV-TR*, **Hyperarousal, Post-traumatic Avoidance Symptoms, Trauma, Trigger**)

Postmodern(ism). Designating a variety of intellectual and cultural developments, postmodern(ism) is a *mood* more than an era. Postmodernism exists alongside pre-modern and modern communities, highlighting its *pluralism*. Its several characteristics could include: opposition to modernity's bent for the abstract and individualistic in favor of relational and communal, opposition to any narrative that would legitimize all knowledge, embrace of multiple value systems, emphasis on rhetoric over truth, concern for perception more than reality, rejection of the universal for the local, and commitment to social construction over "givens." (See also **Androcentric Language, Deconstruction, Feminist, Hermeneutic of Suspicion**)

Predator. An individual who systematically preys upon and victimizes others for personal gain. (See **Sexually Violent Offender**)

Power Structures. A power struggle involves two people or groups, each of whom is equally committed to winning. This often occurs within close relationships where competing agendas that have not been resolved through compromise are present, where something important is at stake, and where the outcome involves winners and losers. This cycle can be imbedded in culture, ongoing, and quite political. (See also **Feminist, Postmodernism**)

Presenting Symptoms. Symptoms that are manifested by a client at the point of a clinical assessment which help form the basis for making a diagnosis and constructing an initial treatment plan. (See also **Assessment**)

Prevalence. The degree or frequency of occurrence of a phenomenon within a defined population at a given time. Sometimes used synonymously with prevalence rate. (See also **Prevalence Rates**)

Prevalence Rates. The ratio of the number of existing cases of a condition or disease compared to the total number of people within a population at a given time.

Pre-narrative. Having little or no coherent narrative structure linking the presentation of segments.

Pro-offending. Attitudes that condone or minimize the impact of criminal behavior. Common pro-offending beliefs among sex offenders include a sense of personal entitlement; laws apply to others; belief that women want, deserve, or harbor fantasies of being raped; if a woman flirts with you she has consented to sex; children are not harmed by sex with adults, etc. (See also **Entitlement**)

Proportionality. Having to do with statistics, this involves a relationship between two variables (e.g., variables *a* and *b*) that are directly proportion such that when one changes, the other will change as well (positively or negatively) according to a constant ratio that exists between them (e.g., when *a* increases or decreases by *x* amount, *b* will fluctuate systematically in proportion to the movement in *a*).

Protective Services. The governmental agency that responds to reports of abuse (e.g., physical, sexual, emotional) or neglect of vulnerable populations (e.g., children, elders, developmentally disabled). Any citizen may report suspected abuse to the protective service agency; however, certain individuals/professions are mandated reporters, meaning that those persons are required by law to report suspected abuse or neglect to this agency. Mandated reporters are defined by individual state laws and can include mental health workers, teachers, medical professionals, and clergy (consult your state's laws for specific information in this regard). (See also **Child Protective Agencies**)

Psychic. Broadly speaking, phenomena having to do with the workings of the mind; that which is mental and outside the range of physical science.

PsychINFO Search. PsycINFO is an abstract database that provides systematic coverage of the psychological literature from the 1800s to the present, a service provided by the American Psychological Association.

Psychoanalysis. A depth approach to psychotherapy that was developed by Sigmund Freud. This approach emphasizes the importance of the influence of unconscious psychological processes on emotion, thought, and behavior. The psychoanalytic solution to problems includes making the unconscious conscious through a process of interpretation of the symbolic meanings of an individual's thoughts and behavior. Insights thus gained help to form the basis for "working through" one's psychological conflicts. (See also **Psychoanalytic Theory**)

Psychoanalytic Theory. A theory of development, psychopathology, and treatment, developed originally by Sigmund Freud, which strives to comprehensively and deeply understand the unconscious motivations and behaviors of people. Strongly drive oriented and deterministic in its view of human behavioral dynamics. (See also **Psychoanalysis**)

Psychological Sequelae. The cognitive and emotional consequences or ramifications of an event in a person's life. (See also **Sequelae**)

Psychopathy. The term signifying a personality trait characterized by marked egocentricity, impulsivity, and lack of emotions like guilt and remorse, being particularly prevalent among repeat offenders diagnosed with antisocial personality disorder. (See also **Entitlement, Pro-offending**)

Psychopathology. The scientific study of mental disorders that includes understanding causes, course, diagnosis, and treatment.

Psychosis. A serious mental state marked by significant problems in higher brain functioning that is manifested by delusions, hallucinations, and significant cognitive disorganization. (See also **Cognitive Deficits, Cognitive Disorder, Cognitive Distortion**)

Psychosexual Disorder. Listed in a previous version of the Diagnostic and Statistical Manual of Mental Disorders (*DSM-III*), a group of disorders of sexuality that result from psychological factors, not organic or biological factors.

Psychotherapy. Any psychological service (there are different forms of psychotherapy) provided by a trained professional that is used to treat emotional, relational, and behavioral dysfunction.

Psychotropic Medication. Medications used to treat psychological disorders, typically prescribed by a psychiatrist, and varying according to the particular disorder being treated.

Queer. A slang term for a homosexual person. (See also **Gay**)

Rape. A criminal offense defined in most states as forcible sexual relations with a person against that person's will. (See also **Corrective Rape, Date Rape, Gang Rape, Wife/Marital Rape, Stranger Rape**)

Recidivism. Signifying the relapse or chronic repetition of a behavior; especially criminal behavior.

Reconciliation. Central to Christian doctrine, God reconciling the world to himself through Christ's death (2 Cor 5:19). The process of restoring or renewing a broken relationship; moving from hostility to peace. Reconciliation (i.e., between parties) may be the biblical goal of forgiveness though it is not the same as forgiveness (i.e., from one party). Unlike forgiveness, reconciliation requires positive movement from both parties in order to heal the relationship. (See also **Forgiveness, Performative Statement, Restitution**)

Reductionism. Reducing complex data to simple terms. As an ideological or tactless use of critical thought, however, reductionism is an oversimplification, occurring in a "nothing but . . ." kind of thinking or argument (e.g., "If only the homeless would just get a job," or "Just forgive and move on!"). (See also **Patriarchy, Stereotype**)

Referring Agencies. Those individuals or organizations that refer a person to receive professional services.

Reintegration (of the Self). The process of restoring or reorganizing mental processes to health after such have been disorganized or distorted by a psychological disorder, especially when psychosis is involved. (See also Cognitive Distortion, Psychosis)

Relational Ecosystem. Based on creation theology, the relational ecosystem refers to the interrelationship all created life: God with humankind, humankind with animals, humankind with the earth, and man with woman (Genesis 1–2; Psalms 8, 104, 148). These are *core bindings* that help define personhood, function, ethics, and human stewardship in the Creation Mandate (Gen 1:28). Sin's consequences tear apart the Relational Ecosystem (cf. Rom 8:19–22). (See also **Creation Mandate, Creation Theology, Image of God**)

Remission. A temporary and/or incomplete subsiding of a disease or condition; the act or process of diminishing or canceling.

Reparative Therapy. A form of therapy that is given to people who have experienced sexual assault, including childhood sexual abuse and adult rape, wherein the emotional trauma, and self-blame are worked through. (See also **Self-care**)

Repression. Based in Freudian theory, a defense mechanism involving unconscious hiding of anxiety-producing thoughts, feelings, desires, and events. (See also **Defense Mechanisms**)

Repressed Family. Family members regard all sexual thoughts, feelings, and behavior as dirty, shameful, and sinful, often twisting religious teachings to promote the evils of sex and fear of punishment. All sexual discussions are considered to be taboo, making the subject unexplained and secretive. (See also **Boundary Confusion, Family Dysfunction, Taboo**)

Repressed Memories. Memories that are blocked from conscious awareness due to their extremely distressing quality, such as memory of a personal traumatic event that might otherwise overwhelm the individual's capacity to function were they allowed entrance into the normal stream of thought. This is not the aberrant theory of "recovered memories." (See also **Dissociative Symptoms, Repression, Trauma**)

Resilience. The ability to adapt positively to challenging or unusually difficult life circumstances so as to thrive and continue to grow despite those difficulties. Resilience has been found to relate positively to psychological health.

Restitution. Restitution can be as basic as a sum of money paid in compensation for loss or injury. But more complex personal and relational damage can also require a form of "restoring" or repairing of something to its normal, needful, or required state. Whether material or symbolical, rituals of restitution can be very significant for a victim's healing and relational restoration. (See also **Rituals**)

Retribution. Retribution is "giving what is due"; what is justly deserved, such as a penalty for a misdeed or correction for a wrong doing. "Complete justice" or "fairness" is not part of this life (Jer 12:1; Job 33). Within Christian theology, retribution is an application of God's holiness that purifies the world for his kingdom of peace. God's *reasons* for retribution center on disobedience and injustice, while His *purposes* are essentially restorative and developmental. Thus retribution gives hope to fallen humanity for sin acknowledged and unacknowledged, anticipating the triumph of righteousness (Ps 58:11). Retribution grants rationality and stability to humanity, promotes closure in crisis, and fosters hope—a forerunner of the ultimate judgment before the King's throne (Matt 25:31–46; Rev 21:1–8; 22:1–5). (See also **Kingdom of God, Theodicy, Vengeance**)

Revictimization. The experience of a survivor being further victimized or traumatized after the original traumatic episode by how those events are handled by others. In sexual abuse, common forms include: tactless questions, family ostracizing, spiritual leaders pressuring the survivor for forgiveness, insensitive interviews or interactions with media, harsh medical professionals, etc. Revictimization also comes from legal professionals, pastors/ministers, siblings, family relatives, the court system, skewed reporting and books, and therapists. (See also **Secondary Trauma**)

Rhetorical (Analysis). The study of how language is used to persuade; the analysis of rhetorical structures, terms, and themes used in a text, particularly the strategies of construction (e.g., how "brother" is used to highlight both responsibility and violence in the Cain and Abel story of Gen 4:1–12). (See also **Close Reading, Deconstruction**)

Risk Assessment. The formalized process of determining ahead of time the potential or likelihood that some negative event may occur.

Rituals. Prescribed or acquired patterns of behavior that are carried out according to a schedule with idiosyncratic meaning and purpose. Such may be symbolic and ceremonial so as to enhance the significance of an experience, or compulsive and irresistible so as to manage distress or anxiety. (See also **Ritualistic Abuse**)

Ritualistic Abuse. Organized, repetitive, and sadistic abuse (physical, sexual, or emotional), often committed against children. Rituals and symbols from religion, the occult, secret societies and the like are often employed. Victims may be forced into silence about the abuse by threat of retaliation. (See also **Sexual Deviance, Sadistic Sexual Abuse, Sexual Abuse**)

Role Competence. The ability of an individual to carry out a set of duties or expected behaviors that are accepted by or ascribed to an individual.

Role Distortion/ Confusion. A state of personal uncertainty about a given social role. This may include demonstrating gender role behavior that is associated with the opposite sex.

Role Image. The image a person has within a role, such as parenting, which can be positive, negative, or mixed (e.g., a confident parent vs. an anxious parent).

Role Play. A technique sometimes used in psychotherapy where individuals, coached by the therapist, dramatically act out various prescribed roles pertaining to certain problematic situations in which they may have to function in real life, thereby allowing the individual to prepare to handle such situations optimally.

Role-reversal. Occurs in families when a child regularly provides for the emotional needs of a parent, thus missing the nurturance the child needs to reliably receive. Role reversal is implicated in negative long-term effects in the child, including anxious attachment and depression. (See also **Boundary Confusion, Enmeshed Relationship, Parentified Child**)

Role Support. The degree of supportive and cooperative interaction between two or more family members that enables each to continue in his or her role; such as parents who share responsibilities in co-parenting. (See also **Co-parenting**)

Rumination (of Stalker). Stalkers mentally rehearse scenes in their minds of imagined relationships, encounters, and fantasies with their victim. These mental fantasies serve as rewards and reinforce their distorted views of their role in the victim's life in the face of contrary evidence and messages from the victim. (See also **Entitlement of Offender**)

Rumination (of Victim). Victims often play out traumatic or abusive scenes in their minds as they attempt to imagine what they could have done differently, if they said or did something that justified what happened, or what they would do differently in the future. Victims are often beset by intrusive thoughts, images, sounds, sensations, and smells of the abuse, which can be very disturbing and can perpetuate the perception of being unsafe, vulnerable, and powerless. (See also **Intrusive Thoughts**)

Sacred Space. The dignity, health and integrity of the self, often in a potentially dangerous social environment. In the Scripture, and particularly the Old Testament, "sacred space" revolved particularly around the tabernacle/temple and the holy of holies. Thus, sacred space created a "sacred compass" that guarded and calibrated peoples' access to the presence of the holy God. In the New Testament, Christ as sacred person eclipsed sacred space: "Remain in me . . ." (John 15:4); and elsewhere, "For God was pleased to have all his fullness dwell in him, and through him to reconcile to himself all things, whether things on earth or things in heaven . . ." (Col 1:19).

Sadism. Obtaining gratification through inflicting pain or humiliation on a sexual partner. (See also **Entitlement of Offender, Sadistic Sexual Abuse, Sexual Deviance**)

Sadistic Sexual Abuse. Sexual abuse in which the offender tries to incite reactions of dread, horror, or pain in the victim as a means of increasing the offender's own sexual arousal during the abuse. (See also **Ritualistic Abuse, Sexual Abuse, Sexual Deviance**)

Safety Plan. A *safety plan* delineates various practical and specific ways a family can proactively help protect children from child sexual abuse by creating a safer environment, open communication, and a more supportive network. It is also a systematic and proactive plan that is designed to help ensure the safety and welfare of vulnerable individuals from specific dangers. Various professional organizations exist to help as a "safety net."

Same-sex Attraction. A person's feelings of sexual attraction to members of the same gender identity. (See also **Gay, Lesbian, Sexual Identity, Sexual Orientation**)

Schemas. A fundamental outlook or basic belief held by an individual regarding the self, others, and the world that is resistant to change and which influences attitudes, perceptions, and behavior. Some schemas are healthy and adaptive while others are dysfunctional and can lead to problems in living.

School Refusal. A persistent resistance to go to school that is often fueled by anxiety and separation issues; most typically exhibited among younger children.

Secondary Abuse Survivor. Family members or others who care about the abuse victim and who are negatively and vicariously impacted by the reality and effects of the abuse against their loved one. (See also **Secondary Trauma, Transference**)

Secondary Trauma. Also called vicarious trauma, secondary trauma occurs as a result of contact or work with those who have been the direct or primary victims of a traumatic event. Sometimes referred to as an occupational hazard of those who work with traumatized individuals, such as mental health workers or hospital emergency room staff. Symptoms can include anxiety, anger, poor concentration, sleep problems, withdrawal, replaying an experience that has been reported to the helper, etc. (See also **Secondary Abuse Survivor**)

Seduction Theory. An early Freudian theory suggesting that the development of certain psychological or somatic symptoms in adulthood, for which there is no apparent biological foundation, was possibly due to the trauma of early childhood sexual molestation experiences that were repressed (i.e., the individual adult is not aware that such abuse had occurred) and thereafter manifested as a somatic symptom.

Self-blaming. To hold oneself accountable for crimes and actions (e.g., abuse) committed against oneself. For instance, a victim may think that she should have done something differently, which would have then forestalled the abuse done to her. Or, the victim may believe that there is just something wrong with her which makes her prone to abuse. (See also **Self-loathing**)

Self-care. Activities required for personal care, such as eating, dressing, or grooming, and tending to one's own emotional needs that can be managed by the individual without assistance.

Self-destructive Behavior. Self-directed, harmful, and sometimes repetitive behaviors that are physically, emotionally, or relationally damaging (e.g., "cutting").

Self-immolation. A deliberate and willing sacrifice of oneself by fire.

Self-loathing/hatred. Sometimes referred to as autophobia, this idea refers to an extreme dislike of oneself, or being angry at oneself. (See also **Self-blaming**)

Self-regulation. The ability to exert conscious and deliberate control over one's own actions, thoughts, and feelings though self-monitoring, self-evaluation, self-reinforcement so as to facilitate the occurrence of desired or necessary behavior.

Self-report. A report about one's own experience, circumstance, or behavior that is made to some other individual or agency, in contrast to the report being on behalf of the individual by another person. In some cases involving intimate, embarrassing or socially unacceptable situations, or when there is coercion by a perpetrator with the threat of reprisal, the tendency to self-report may be diminished due to concerns about embarrassment, ostracism or safety.

Self-soothe. A form of self management involving the regulation of one's emotions; being able to adaptively manage difficult emotions by the application of certain stress reducing and comforting activities. (See also **Coping Skills**)

Sequelae. The direct and indirect negative after-effects (e.g., depression, anxiety) that result from having gone through a harsh or difficult experience such as abuse. (See also **Depression, Emotional Sequelae**)

Serial Offenders. An offender whose motivation for the action in question is often based on psychological gratification. The offenses may have been attempted or completed in a similar fashion and the victims may have had something in common.

Serotonin. A neurotransmitter in the brain and other parts of the central nervous system that is involved in various biological-regulatory processes involving mood, sleep, and appetite, and is implicated in various psychological conditions such as depression, anxiety, and aggression.

Sex Offender. A person committing a sex offense, which is a sex act that is prohibited by law. (See also **Perpetrator**)

Sex Trafficking. Sex trafficking is a modern-day form of slavery in which a commercial sex act (i.e., sexual act done to earn the trafficker money) is induced by the trafficker through the use of force, fraud, or coercion, or in which the person induced to perform such an act is a minor (e.g., under eighteen years). (See also **Chattel, Human Trafficking**)

Sexting. The act of sending sexually explicit messages or photos electronically, primarily between mobile phones. (See also **Telephone Scatalogia**)

Sexual Abuse (SA). Sexual abuse (SA) generally, and particularly childhood sexual abuse (CSA), is any behavior that exploits a child/person for the sexual gratification of another. The types of sexual exploitation may include: physical force, intimidation, bribery, and abuse of power, such as using one's greater authority, status or knowledge, position, and age. A distinction can be made between (a) *contact* and (b) *non-contact* SA. The former can include excessive rubbing, fondling, or forced vaginal, oral, or anal intercourse. The latter can include exhibitionism, voyeurism, exposure to pornography, obscene sexual phone calls, and intrusive behavior such as not allowing a child to undress or use the bathroom in privacy. While definitions vary, SA can be defined within a rubric of four key elements: (a) traumatic sexualization, (b) relational betrayal, (c) personal powerlessness, (d) and socio-religious stigmatization. Sexual abuse can be a spectrum of experiences and behaviors. (See also **Child/hood Sexual Abuse (CSA), Coercive Pornography, Exhibitionism, Incest, Intrafamilial Sexual Abuse, Sexualization, Telephone Scatalogia, Voyeurism**)

Sexual Addiction. A problematic sexual behavior that has become out of control; has significant negative consequences, and which the individual is unable to organize, despite wanting to do so.

Sexual Deviance. Sexual behavior that is significantly different from the norm. (See also **Sexual Ethics**)

Sexual Diffusion. Diffusion refers to the spread of something, such as a story, information, or an infection, through a population. There is growing concern regarding the sexual diffusion of HIV from core groups such as injecting drug users (IDUs) and men who have sex with men (MSM) to more general population groups (i.e., non-injectors and heterosexuals). In regard to sexual offenders, sexual diffusion is a concept that has to do with a theory about why perpetrators might engage in such activity and how to help abate that drive or desire.

Sexual Dysfunction. In the *DSM-IV-TR*, a category of sexual disorders having to do with problems in some aspect of the sex-response cycle (e.g., erectile dysfunction, female orgasmic disorder, etc.). (See also ***DSM-IV-TR***)

Sexual Ethics. Standards or rules of conduct regarding matters related to sexual behavior. Such would include moral beliefs about the appropriateness or rightness of various types of sexual behavior.

Sexual Harassment. Conduct (communication or behavior) toward another of a sexual nature that is unwelcome and offensive, especially in the workplace.

Sexual Identity. A person's internal sense of identification with either a heterosexual, homosexual, or bisexual preference, thus having to do with one's sexual orientation. (See also **Sexual Orientation**)

Sexual Minority. A group whose sexual identity, orientation, or practices differ from the majority of the surrounding society. (See also **Sexual Orientation**)

Sexual Orientation. A person's enduring sexual attraction to individuals of a particular gender (or both genders). (See also **Gay**, **Lesbian**, **Sexual Identity**)

Sexual Risk-taking Behavior. High risk or potentially dangerous sexual activity (e.g., unprotected sex, sex with multiple partners, sex with strangers, etc.), where the potential negative ramifications are not carefully considered.

Sexualization. Refers to the process whereby a person, group, or thing comes to be seen as sexual in nature or for a person to become aware of sexuality. Can also refer to the making of an interpersonal relationship into a sexual relationship. (See also **Sexualized Behavior**, **Sexualized Childhood**, **Sexualized Family**, **Sexualized Thoughts**)

Sexualized Behavior. Behavior, especially in young children, that exhibits developmentally inappropriate knowledge and actions that are sexual in nature. Such actions may be exhibited in play with toys such as dolls, or in interactions with peers or other adults, such as engaging in sensual kissing or inappropriate touching. Such behavior is usually learned as the result of exposure to pornographic media, modeling, or sexual abuse. (See also **Sexualization**)

Sexualized Childhood. When children early in development are exposed to, influenced by, and encouraged to prematurely adopt adult-like modes of dress and social activity that is indicative of sexual maturity, awareness, and interest. Such children are typically not developmentally ready to deal with the ramifications of this sort of influence and may lose out on certain basic elements that are important to healthy child development. (See also **Sexualized**, **Sexualized Family**)

Sexualized Family. A family characterized by a heightened sense of sexual arousal from their environment, an inordinate preoccupation with sex, poor family sexual boundaries, and eroticization of family relationships. (See also **Sexualized Behavior**, **Sexualized Childhood**)

Sexualized Thoughts. Thoughts that are influenced by or characterized by sexual content or images. Such thoughts may be chronic and intrusive and as such may be a source of significant distress for the individual. May be seen as a marker of possible sexual abuse when present in children. (See also **Sexualized Behavior**)

Sexually Violent Offender. Broadly speaking, sexual predators are people who commit sexual crimes on others. Predators are typically repeat offenders who find pleasure in "the hunt." Predators often attack a particular type of victim, such as children or people with certain physical or social characteristics. Violent offenders are those whose mode of apprehension is characterized by some form of violence. In either case, the method of offence usually elicits intense sexual excitement for the perpetrator. (See also **Predator**, **Sexual Deviance**)

Shalom. Hebrew. A word basically meaning "peace" or "welcome" when used as a greeting. Used as a benediction or blessing, the idea is "completeness"; also with notions of recompense and uninjured (cf. Gen 33:18; Jer 18:20). With internal and external significance, "granting someone *shalom*," for example, is incorporating them into your fellowship—giving them identity, safety, well-being, and fellowship.

Shaming Mechanisms. Social processes of expressing disapproval, which have the intention or effect of controlling behavior by invoking humiliation and self-condemnation in the person being shamed.

Socialization. The process (includes formal and informal learning) whereby a child learns to get along with other people and to behave in socially prescribed ways and so fit in with the rest of society.

Sodomy. Anal intercourse between people or sexual intercourse between a person and an animal. (See also **Gang Rape, Sexual Deviance**)

Somatic Symptoms. Physical symptoms associated with certain psychological disorders or medical conditions.

Somatization. The physical expression of symptoms of a psychological disorder.

Somatoform Dissociation. Failure to integrate somatic experiences such as pain or pleasure.

Spiritual Formation/ Disciplines. The growth and development of the whole person by an intentional focus on one's spiritual and interior life and the spiritual practices/disciplines such as prayer, the study of Scripture, fasting, simplicity, solitude, confession. Spiritual formation is a relational ministry between Christians, supporting the ongoing transforming work of the Holy Spirit so that believers become more conformed to the image of Christ.

Spiritual Incest. Spiritual incest describes the power-plays and narcissism standard in physical incest; only it is applied to *religious control* (similar to the profile of religious cults and their leaders). Spiritual incest is characterized by: religious syncretism, rigid hierarchies, religious chaos in the home or social group, doctrinal brainwashing, spiritual ideas/terms used as "mantras" (e.g., "I can trust you, but not your flesh"), and instilling an "in-group vs. out-group" spiritual elitism. Shaming techniques are used against dissent (e.g., "God is going to punish you for . . . !"). Survivors can feel a profound sense of spiritual betrayal, spoiling of religious heritage, lack of intellectual agency, and personal "ruin" when they try to process their experience. (See also **Authoritarian, Dualism, Hierarchy, Reductionism, Shaming Mechanisms**)

Spousal Rape. Any unwanted sexual act by a spouse or ex-spouse that is done without consent, and done with the use or threat of force and intimidation. (See also **Gang Rape, Rape, Wife/Marital Rape**)

Stalking. A pattern of following, tracking, or observing a person that is obsessive and may be harassing.

Startle Response. The response of mind and body to a sudden unexpected stimulus that includes activation of the sympathetic nervous system. (See also **Hypervigilance, Sympathetic Nervous System**)

Stations of the Cross. A devotion consisting of prayers and meditations on fourteen events commemorating the events of the Passion of Jesus.

Status Quo. The normal or existing state of affairs; the way things currently are.

Statutory. Pertaining to a law that is legally punishable by the state.

Statutory Rape. Sexual relations with a person who has not reached the statutory (i.e., legal) age of consent. (See also **Date Rape, Rape**)

Stereotype. A conventional and oversimplified notion or categorization of a person or group of people (e.g., according to race, aptitude, gender, socioeconomic status, religious belief, etc.) that often influences subsequent opinions about and behavior toward that person or group in ways that are often unfair, hypocritical, or short-sighted (e.g., "That's the view of the religious right/ liberal left"; "You know men!"). (See also **Reductionism**)

Stonewalling. A tactic of obstruction; a stubborn denial or refusal to acknowledge that a condition or state of affairs exists despite overwhelming evidence. (See also **Avoidant Pattern**)

Stranger Rape. A rape where the victim does not know the rapist. (See also **Rape**)

Stress Inoculation Training (SIT). A form of Cognitive Behavior Therapy where clients are taught specific strategies to recognize and manage stress and anxiety. (See also **Cognitive Behavior Therapy**)

Stress Responses. Psychological and physical reactions following exposure to acute or chronic stress.

Structured Clinical Interview for DSM-IV Dissociative Disorders (SCID-D). Semi-structured DSM-IV formatted diagnostic interview for assessment of dissociative symptoms and dissociative disorders.

Subsystems. Smaller systems or components within the structure of a larger system such as a family that exist to carry out various tasks that help promote the survival of the system. (See also **Systems Theory**)

Suffragist. Historically, one who advocates for a woman's right to vote.

Suicidal Ideation. Thoughts about or preoccupation with suicide; sometimes a symptom of depression. Suicide ideation does not necessarily progress to a suicide attempt.

Support Group. Somewhat like a self-help group, members who have a similar problem meet to provide each other with help and support in dealing with those issues. Leaders of such groups are usually trained professionals who act as facilitators and so do not share the problem around which the group was established (in contrast to a typical self-help group format).

Survivor. One who was the victim of sexual abuse or assault and who has attempted to deal productively and realistically with the reality of their victimization. As a declaration of healing, empowerment, and personal agency, the term "survivor" (also "thriver") is preferred by many over "victim."

Sympathetic Nervous System. The part of the autonomic nervous system that under stress raises blood pressure and heart rate, constricts blood vessels, and dilates the pupils as preparation for fight or flight. (See also **Adrenal System, Startle Response**)

Symptom Clusters. A grouping or constellation of symptoms that together relate to a given diagnosis, such as persistent sad mood, loss of pleasure in usual activities, feelings of guilt and worthlessness, and fatigue that cluster for depression.

Symptomatic Behavior. The signs, markers, or indications of a disease or disorder.

Symptomatic Distress. The subjective level of distress that an individual experiences from the symptoms of their disorder.

Systemic Disruption. An event or events whose impact has the potential to threaten the stability of the family system. (See also **Systems Theory**)

Systems Perspective. Viewing individual problems as reflecting system dysfunction rather than individual pathology, where problems experienced by any one family member (e.g., depression in a child) are interpreted as being symptomatic of systemic (i.e., whole family) dysfunction. Thus, it is believed that change efforts that are most durable need to be directed toward the entire family unit, not just the individual symptom-bearer. Some clinicians who have this perspective will not meet with an individual family member for treatment. (See also **Systems Theory**)

Systems Theory. A system is comprised of many parts, which relate to each other in a consistent fashion. Since these relationship patterns form the structure and regulate the system, the individual components of the system can only be understood within the context of the whole "family organism." (See also **Systems Perspective**)

Taboo. Signifying that which is forbidden. A ban on an unacceptable action that carries with it significant social ramifications if violated.

Taize Service. A worship service (drawing on practices of the Taize community) incorporating ancient Christian traditions of prayer and healing with simple chant, prayers, Scripture, meditative silence and song.

Telephone Scatalogia. To derive sexual arousal and/or gratification from making obscene, provocative telephone calls, usually at random.

Theodicy. The branch of theology that contemplates and defends God's actions in the face of the existence of evil. Posed from the perspective of God's goodness and love: "How can an all-powerful, sovereign, and loving God allow dehumanizing evil and suffering?" or posed from the human perspective regarding God's justice: "Why do bad things happen to good people?" or "Why do innocent people suffer?" (See also **Retribution**)

Therapeutic Modalities. Signifies the differing approaches and theories to understanding and treating psychological disorders, such as: behavioral, existential, cognitive-behavioral, psychoanalytic, narrative, Gestalt, family systems, etc.

Transitive Verb. A verb that needs a direct object to complete its meaning. For example, *bring, enjoy,* and *prefer* are transitive verbs. In each case, a direct object of the transitive verb is needed in order to be meaningful (i.e., "bring apples," "enjoy life," and "prefer cash").

Transference. A core psychoanalytic concept having to do with the displacement or projection of unconscious feelings and desires by a client onto their therapist; wishes and desires that were originally felt toward important individuals in a client's earlier life, such as parents, are directed onto the therapist. This is seen as an expected and necessary part of treatment in order for the client's problematic unconscious material to be brought to the surface, re-experienced, and worked through (i.e., resolved) in treatment. (See also **Counter Transference**)

Trauma. An event in which a person views or personally experiences a threat to his or her own life and safety, or to that of others, which results in intense fear, terror, or a sense of helplessness. Such can cause a change in the way a person views the world and in some cases may lead to a psychological disorder such as post-traumatic stress disorder. (See also **Post-traumatic Stress Disorder, Revictimization, Secondary Trauma**)

Trauma Breaks. Specific interventions, either helper-directed or self-directed, used when a client experiences hyperarousal and/or flashbacks, in order to decrease physical symptoms, increase a sense of safety, and allow some control over traumatic memories. (See also **Flashbacks, Hyperarousal, Intrusive Memories**)

Trauma-focused Cognitive Behavioral Therapy (TF-CBT). Trauma-focused cognitive behavioral therapy (TF-CBT) is an evidence-based treatment approach shown to help children, adolescents, and their caretakers overcome trauma-related difficulties. (See also **Cognitive Behavioral Theory**)

Trigger. A stimulus or situation that elicits a certain reaction, such as when the occurrence of a present event causes an individual to recall something unpleasant for earlier in their life, or causes a specific behavioral reaction. (See also **Flashbacks, Hyperarousal**)

Trinity. Distinctive Christian teaching that the Creator God revealed in history is the God of Israel and that the God and Father of Jesus Christ is tri-personal; that is: God the Father, God the Son, and God the Holy Spirit, a tri-unity. Indirectly found in the Old Testament (Gen 1:2, 26; Exod 23:23; Ps 33:6; Prov 8:12), the Trinity is explicit in the New Testament (Matt 3:16; 28:19; 2 Cor 13:13).

Type-scene. A type-scene is a literary device in which the repetition of conventions of speech and behavior occur in analogous situations (e.g., birth, initiatory trial, betrothals, annunciations, rivalries between the barren and fertile wives, trials in the wilderness, revival of the dead child, and the deathbed). In a story, a type-scene produces expectations in a reader (e.g., "Once upon a time"), which can then be reworked for emphasis by the narrator.

Utterance. See **Performative Statement.**

Vengeance. Punishment used as just retribution for prior harm against persons. Scripture considers vengeance to be an attribute of God (Nah 1:2; Rom 12:19). The Old Testament puts bounds on human vengeance (Deut 19:1–13) while discouraging it is a key element of Jesus' teaching (Matt 5:38–48). (See also **Retribution, Theodicy**)

Victim Panels. Organized groups of survivors who speak out about the effects of being the direct or indirect victim of abuse with the hope of educating others, including offenders, about the real life impact of abuse on people.

Voyeurism. A paraphilia where the preferred type of sexual interest and arousal is that of viewing unsuspecting people who are nude or are undressing. The voyeur does not seek sexual activity with the person observed; however, the individual may experience an orgasm, usually by masturbating, while watching the victim. (See also **Paraphilia**)

Wife/Marital Rape. Unwanted sexual activity that is forced upon a spouse within the context of marriage, sometimes involving coercion, aggression, or violence. (See also **Corrective Rape, Intimate Partner Sexual Assault, Rape, Spousal Rape**)

Womanist (Hermeneutic). A hermeneutic among black feminists who feel excluded from both black male liberation theology and white middle/upper class feminists defined more by station and power. What is prioritized is the experience of poor and marginalized black women. The hermeneutic is characterized by community, faith, liturgy, teaching, and "this-life" experience, not eschatology. (See also **Deconstruction, Feminist, Patriarchy**)

Bibliography

Abel, Gene, and Nora Harlow. *The Stop Child Molestation Book: What Ordinary People Can Do in Their Everyday Lives To Save Three Million Children*. Philadelphia, PA: Xlibris Corporation, 2001.

Ackermann, Denise. *After the Locusts: Letters from a Landscape of Faith*. Grand Rapids, MI: Eerdmans, 2003.

Adams-Curtis, Leah E., and Gordon B. Forbes. "College Women's Experiences of Sexual Coercion: A Review of Cultural, Perpetrator, Victim, and Situational Variables." *Trauma, Violence, & Abuse* 5 (2004) 91–122.

Ainscough, Carolyn, and Kay Toon. *Breaking Free: Help for Survivors of Child Sexual Abuse*. London: SPCK, 1993.

Alanko, K., et al. "Psychiatric Symptoms and Same-Sex Sexual Attraction and Behavior in Light of Childhood Gender Atypical Behavior and Parental Relationships." *Journal of Sex Research* 2 (2009) 1–11.

Alexander, Pamela C., and S. L. Lupfer. "Family Characteristics and Long-term Consequences Associated with Sexual Abuse." *Archives of Sexual Behavior* 16 (1987) 235–245.

———, et al. "Childhood Sexual Abuse History and Role Reversal in Parenting," *Child Abuse and Neglect* 24 (2000) 829–838.

———. "The Impact of Child Sexual Abuse on Parenting: A Female Perspective." In *VISTAS: Compelling Perspectives on Counseling*, edited by G. R. Walz and R. K. Yep. Alexandria, VA: American Counseling Association, 2005.

———. "Understanding the Effects of Child Sexual Abuse History on Current Couple Relationships: An Attachment Perspective." In *Attachment Processes in Couple and Family Therapy*, edited by Susan M. Johnson and Valerie E. Whiffen, 342–365. New York, NY: Guilford Press, 2005.

Allen, Beverly. *Rape Warfare: The Hidden Genocide in Bosnia-Herzegovina and Croatia*. Minneapolis, MN: University of Minnesota Press, 1996.

Allender, Dan. *The Wounded Heart: Hope for Adult Victims of Childhood Sexual Abuse*. rev. ed. Colorado Springs, CO: NavPress, 2008.

Almosaed, Nora. "Violence against Women: A Cross-Cultural Perspective." *Journal of Muslim Minority Affairs* 24 (2004) 67–88.

Alpert, Judith L., et al. "Symptomatic Clients and Memoires of Childhood Abuse: What the Trauma and Child Sexual Abuse Literature Tells Us." *Psychology, Public Policy and Law* 4 (1998) 941–955.

———. "Final Conclusions of the American Psychological Association Working Group on Investigation of Memories of Childhood Abuse." *Psychology, Public Policy, and Law* 4 (1998) 933–940.

Alter, Robert. *The Art of Biblical Narrative*. New York, NY: Basic Books, 1981.

———. *The Art of Biblical Poetry*. New York, NY: Basic Books, 1985.

———. *The Five Books of Moses: A Translation with Commentary*. New York, NY: W. W. Norton & Company, 2004.

American Psychiatric Association. Diagnostic and Statistical Manual of Mental Disorders: DSM-IV-TR. 4th ed. Washington, DC: American Psychiatric Publishing, 2000.

Anderson, Herbert, and Edward Foley. *Mighty Stories, Dangerous Rituals*. San Francisco, CA: Jossey-Bass, 1998.

Anderson, Ray S. *On Being Human: Essays in Theological Anthropology*. Grand Rapids: Eerdmans, 1982.

———. *Self Care: A Theology of Personal Empowerment & Spiritual Healing*. Pasadena, CA: Fuller Seminary, 2000.

Anderson, Shayne, and Richard Miller. "The Effectiveness of Therapy with Couples Reporting a History of Child Sexual Abuse: An Exploratory Study." *Contemporary Family Therapy: An International Journal* 28 (2006) 353–366.

Bibliography

Andersen, Torbjorn Herlof. "Men Dealing with Memories of Childhood Sexual Abuse: Conditions and Possibilities of 'Positive Deviance.'" *Journal of Social Work Practice* 22 (2008) 51–65.

Angelou, Maya. *I Know Why the Caged Bird Sings*. New York, NY: Bantman Books, 1969.

Annis, Ann W., and Roger R. Rice. "A Survey of Abuse Prevalence in the Christian Reformed Church." *Journal of Religion and Abuse* 3 (2001) 7–40.

Anonymous M.D. *Unprotected: A Campus Psychiatrist Reveals How Political Correctness in Her Profession Endangers Every Student*. New York, NY: Sentinel, 2006.

Aquinas, St. Thomas. *Summa Theologica* III. New York, NY: Benzinger, 1947.

Arata, C.M. "Coping with Rape: The Roles of Prior Sexual Abuse and Attribution of Blame." *Journal of Interpersonal Violence* 14 (1999) 62–78.

Arnold, Bill T., and Bryan E. Beyer, eds. "Enuma Elish." In *Readings from the Ancient Near East: Primary Sources for Old Testament Study*. Encountering Biblical Studies. Grand Rapids, MI: Baker, 2002.

———, and John H. Choi. *A Guide to Biblical Hebrew Syntax*. Cambridge: Cambridge University Press, 2003.

———. *Genesis*. New Cambridge Bible Commentary. Cambridge: Cambridge University Press, 2009.

Arreola, Sonya Grant, et al. "Higher Prevalence of Childhood Sexual Abuse among Latino Men Who Have Sex with Men than Non-Latino Men Who Have Sex with Men: Data from the Urban Men's Health Study." *Child Abuse & Neglect* 29 (2005) 285–290.

———, et al. "Childhood Sexual Experiences and Adult Health Sequelae among Gay and Bisexual Men: Defining Childhood Sexual Abuse." *Journal of Sex Research* 45 (2008) 246–252.

———, et al. "Childhood Sexual Abuse and the Sociocultural Context of Sexual Risk among Adult Latino Gay and Bisexual Men." *American Journal of Public Health* 99 (2009) 432–438.

Armstrong, Judith G., et al. "Development and Validation of a Measure of Adolescent Dissociation: The Adolescent Dissociative Experiences Scale." *Journal of Nervous & Mental Disease* 8 (1997) 491–497.

Armsworth, Mary, and Karin Stronck. "Intergenerational Effects of Incest on Parenting: Skills, Abilities and Attitudes." *Journal of Counseling and Development* 77 (1999) 303–315.

Aronson Fontes, Lisa. "Sin Verguenza: Addressing Shame with Latino Victims of Child Sexual Abuse and Their Families." *Journal of Child Sexual Abuse* 16 (2007) 61–81.

Austin, S. B., et al. "Disparities in Child Abuse Victimization in Lesbian, Bisexual, and Heterosexual Women in the Nurses' Health Study II." *Journal of Women's Health* 17 (2008) 597–606.

———, et al. "Sexual Violence Victimization History and Sexual Risk Indicators in a Community-Based Urban Cohort of 'Mostly Heterosexual' and Heterosexual Young Women." *American Journal of Public Health* 98 (2008) 1015–1020.

Bach, Alice. "Rereading the Body Politic: Women and Violence in Judges 21." In *Judges: A Feminist Companion to the Bible*, edited by Athalya Brenner, 143–159. FCB 2/4. Sheffield: Sheffield Academic Press, 1999.

Bacon, Brenda L., and Laura Lein. "Living with a Female Sexual Abuse Survivor: Male Partner's Perspectives." *Journal of Child Sexual Abuse* 5 (1996) 1–16.

Bailey, D. P. "Jesus As the Mercy Seat: The Semantics and Theology of Paul's Use of *Hilasterion* in Romans 3:25." PhD diss., University of Cambridge, 1999.

Bailey, Randall C. *David in Love and War: The Pursuit of Power in 2 Samuel 10–12*. Sheffield: JSOT Press, 1990.

Baker, A., and S. Duncan. "Child Sexual Abuse: A Study of Prevalence in Great Britain." *Child Abuse and Neglect* 9 (1985) 457–467.

Baker, Morven R. "How Does the Experience of Incest Distort a Woman's Images of God?" DMin Final Project Document. Ashland Theological Seminary, 2005.

Bal, Mieke. *Lethal Love: Feminist Literary Readings of Biblical Love Stories*. Bloomington, IN: Indiana University Press, 1987.

Ballard, D. T., et al. "A Contemporary Profile of the Incest Perpetrator: Background Characteristics, Abuse History, and Use of Social Skills." In *The Incest Perpetrator: A Family Member No-One Wants to Treat*, edited by A. L. Horton, et al., 43–64. Newbury Park, CA: Sage, 1990.

Balsam, Kimberly F., et al. "Victimization Over the Life Span: A Comparison of Lesbian, Gay, Bisexual, and Heterosexual Siblings." *Journal of Consulting and Clinical Psychology* 73 (2005) 477–487.

Bancroft, J., and Z. Vukadinovic. "Sexual Addiction, Sexual Compulsivity, Sexual Impulsivity, Or What? Toward A Theoretical Model." *Journal of Sex Research* 41 (2004) 224–234.

Banyard, Victoria. "The Impact of Childhood Sexual Abuse and Family Functioning on Four Dimensions of Women's Later Parenting." *Child Abuse and Neglect* 21 (1997) 1095–1107.

———, et al. "The Long-Term Mental Health Consequences of Child Sexual Abuse: An Exploratory Study of the Impact of Multiple Traumas in a Sample of Women." *Journal of Traumatic Stress* 14 (2001) 697–715.

Bar-Efrat, Shimeon. *Narrative Art in the Bible*. Journal of the Society of the Old Testament Suppplement 70. Sheffield: JSOT Press, 1989.

Barasch, Marc Ian. *The Healing Path: A Soup Approach to Illness*. New York, NY: Putnam, 1993.

Barcus, Robert A. "Partners of Survivors of Abuse: A Men's Therapy Group." *Psychotherapy* 34 (1997) 316–323.

———, et al. "Victim-Perpetrator Reconciliation." *Violence Against Women* 3 (1997) 515–532.

Bard, Leonard., et al. "A Descriptive Study of Rapists and Child Molesters: Developmental, Clinical, and Criminal Characteristics." *Behavioral Sciences and the Law* 5 (1987) 203–220.

Barker-Collo, S. L. "Adult Reports of Child and Adult Attributions of Blame for Childhood Sexual Abuse: Predicting Adult Adjustment and Suicidal Behaviors in Females." *Child Abuse & Neglect* 25 (2001) 1329–1431.

Barnes Lampman, Lisa, ed. *God and the Victim: Theological Reflections on Evil, Victimization, Justice, and Forgiveness*. Grand Rapids, MI: Eerdmans, 1999.

Barshinger, Clark E., Lojan E. LaRowe, and Andrés Tapia. *Haunted Marriage: Overcoming the Ghosts of Your Spouse's Childhood Abuse*. Downers Grove, IL: InterVarsity, 1995.

———, et al. "The Gospel According to Prozac: Can a Pill Do What the Holy Spirit Could Not?" *Christianity Today* (August 1995) 34-37.

Barth, Karl. *Church Dogmatics*. III/1. Edinburgh: T. & T. Clark, 1966.

Barth, Markus. *Ephesians*. AB 34A. New York, NY: Doubleday, 1974.

Bartoi, M. G., & B. N. Kinder. "Effects of Child and Adult Sexual Abuse on Adult Sexuality." *Journal of Sex and Marital Therapy* 24 (1998) 75–90.

Basile, K. C. "Prevalence of Wife Rape and Other Intimate Partner Sexual Coercion in a Nationally Representative Sample of Women." *Violence and Victims* 17 (2002) 511–524.

Baskin, Thomas W., and Robert D. Enright. "Intervention Studies on Forgiveness: A Meta-Analysis." *Journal of Counseling and Development* 82 (2004) 79–90.

Bass, Ellen, and Laura Davis. *The Courage To Heal: A Guide for Women Survivors of Child Sexual Abuse*. New York, NY: Harper & Row, 1998.

Baumli, Francis. "On Men, Guilt and Shame," in *Men Healing Shame: An Anthology*, edited by Roy U. Schenk and John Everingham, 155–166. New York, NY: Springer, 1995.

Beale, Greg K. *The Book of Revelation*. New International Greek Testament Commentary. Grand Rapids, MI: Eerdmans, 1999.

———. *We Become What We Worship: A Biblical Theology of Idolatry*. Downers Grove, IL: InterVarsity, 2008.

Bear, Euan with Peter T. Dimock. *Adults Molested As Children: A Survivor's Manual for Women and Men*. Orwell, VT: Safer Society Press, 1988.

Bechtel, Lyn M. "What if Dinah Is Not Raped? (Genesis 34)." *Journal for the Study of the Old Testament* 62 (1994) 19–36.

Beckenbach, John. *Sexual Abuse and Forgiveness*. Unpublished Doctoral Diss. Dekalb, IL: Northern Illinois University, 2002.

Becvar, Dorothy Stroh, and Raphael J. Becvar. *Family Therapy: A Systemic Integration*. 5th ed. Boston, MA: Ally and Bacon, 2003.

Benner, David G. *Strategic Pastoral Counseling*. Grand Rapids: Baker, 1992.

Bennett, Ralph W., and Daryl F. Gates. "The Relationship Between Pornography and Extrafamilial Child Sexual Abuse." *The Police Chief* 58 (1991) 14–20.

Bennice, Jennifer A., and Patricia A. Resick. "Marital Rape: History, Research, and Practice." *Trauma, Violence, and Abuse* 4 (2003) 228–246.

Benkert, Marianne, and Thomas P. Doyle. "Clericalism, Religious Duress and Its Psychological Impact on Victims of Clergy Sexual Abuse." *Pastoral Psychology* 58 (2009) 223–238.

Bergen, Jeremy M. *Ecclesial Repentance: The Churches Confront Their Sinful Pasts*. Edinburgh: T&T Clark, 2011.

Bibliography

Bergen, Raquel Kennedy. *Wife Rape: Understanding the Response of Survivors and Service* Providers. Newbury Park, CA: Sage Publications, 1996.

———. "Studying Wife Rape." *Violence against Women* 10 (2004) 1407–1416.

Bergen, Robert D. *1, 2 Samuel*, vol. 7, New American Commentary. Nashville, TN: Broadman and Holman, 1996.

Berger, Leslie Beth. *Incest, Work and Women: Understanding the Consequences of Incest of Women's Careers, Work and Dreams*. Springfield, IL: Charles C. Thomas, 1998.

Bernstein, Jerome S. "The Decline of Rites of Passage in Our Culture: The Impact on Masculine Individuation." In *Betwixt and Between: Patterns of Masculine and Feminine Initiation*, edited by Louise Carus Mahdi, et al. La Salle, IL: Open Court, 1987.

Besharov, Douglas J. *Recognizing Child Abuse: A Guide for the Concerned*. New York, NY: Free Press, 1990.

Beste, Jennifer. *God and the Victim: Traumatic Intrusions on Grace and Freedom*. Oxford: Oxford University Press, 2007.

———. "Mediating God's Grace Within the Context of Trauma: Implications for a Christian Response to Clergy Sexual Abuse." *Review & Expositor* 105 (2008) 245–260.

Beth, Sterling. *The Thorn of Sexual Abuse*. Grand Rapids, MI: Fleming H. Revell, 1994.

Biddle, Mark E. *Missing the Mark: Sin and Its Consequences in Biblical Theology*. Nashville, TN: Abingdon, 2005.

———. "Genesis 3: Sin, Shame and Self-Esteem." *Review & Expositor* 103 (2006) 359–370.

Bieber, Irving, et al. *Homosexuality: A Psychoanalytic Study of Male Homosexuals*. New York, NY: Basic Books, 1962.

Bilich, Marion, et al. *Shared Grace: Therapists and Clergy Working Together*. New York, NY: Haworth Press, 2000.

Billington, Clyde E. "Ancient Exorcists, Demons, and the Name of Jesus: Part One." *Artifax* 25 (2010) 15–21.

Billman, Kathleen, and Daniel Migliore. *Rachel's Cry: Prayer of Lament and Rebirth of Hope*. Cleveland, OH: United Church, 1999.

Birch, Bruce C., et al. *A Theological Introduction to the Old Testament*. Nashville, TN: Abingdon, 1999.

Bisson, Jonathan, M. Andrew. "Psychological Treatment of Post-traumatic Stress Disorder (PTSD)." *Cochrane Database of Systematic Reviews* 3 (2007): Art. No.: CD003388. DOI: 10.1002/14651858.CD003388.pub3.

Blasingame, Gerry. *Developmentally Disabled Persons with Sexual Problems*. Oklahoma, OK: Wood "N" Barnes, 2001.

Blume, E. Sue. *Secret Survivors: Uncovering Incest and its Aftereffects in Women*. New York, NY: John Wiley and Sons, 1990.

Bly, Robert. "Seven Sources on Men's Shame." In *Men Healing Shame: An Anthology*, edited by Roy U. Schenk and John Everingham, 50–72. New York, NY: Springer, 1995.

Blyth, Caroline. "Terrible Silence, Eternal Silence: A Consideration of Dinah's Voicelessness in the Text and Interpretive Traditions of Genesis 34." PhD diss., Edinburgh: University of Edinburgh, 2008.

Boakye, Kofi E. "Culture and Nondisclosure of Child Sexual Abuse in Ghana: A Theoretical and Empirical Exploration." *Law & Social Inquiry* 34 (2009) 951–979.

Boda, Mark J. *A Severe Mercy: Sin and Its Remedy in the Old Testament*. Siphrut 1, Literature and Theology of the Hebrew Scriptures. Winona Lake, IN: Eisenbrauns, 2009.

Bohonos, Sybil. *Why Me, Lord?* Edmonton, Alberta: Heart Communications, 1992.

Bolen, R. M., and M. Scannapieco. "Prevalence of Child Sexual Abuse: A Corrective Meta-analysis." *Social Service Review* 73 (1999) 281–313.

Bolen, Rebecca. "Child Sexual Abuse and Attachment Theory: Are We Rushing Headlong into Another Controversy?" *Journal of Child Sexual Abuse* 11 (2002) 95–124.

———. "Child Sexual Abuse: Prevention or Promotion." *Social Work* 48 (2003) 174–185.

Bolton, Frank G., et al. *Males at Risk*. Newbury Park, CA: Sage Publications, 1989.

Bonhoeffer, Dietrich. *The Cost of Discipleship*, trans. Reginald Horace Fuller. New York, NY: Macmillan, 1963.

———. *Life Together*. trans. John W. Doberstein. New York, NY: Harper & Row, 1976.

Bornkamm, Günther. *Paul*, trans. D. M. G. Stalker. New York, NY: Harper & Row, 1817.

Boszormenyi-Nagy, Ivan, and Geraldine M. Spark. *Invisible Loyalties*. New York, NY: Brunner/Mazel, 1984.

Bourke, Michael. "Response from the Researcher." *Monitor on Psychology* 41 (2010) 8, 65.

Bowlby, John. *Separation: Anxiety and Anger.* New York, NY: Basic Books, 1973.

———. *The Making and Breaking of Affectional Bonds.* London: Tavistock, 1979.

———. *Attachment and Loss,* vol. 1. New York, NY: Basic Books, 1982.

———. *A Secure Base: Parent-child Attachment and Healthy Human Development.* London: Routledge, 1988.

Boyarin, Daniel. *A Radical Jew: Paul and the Politics of Identity.* Berkeley, CA: University of California Press, 1994.

Bradshaw, John. *Healing the Shame that Binds You.* Deerfield Beach, FL: Health Communications, 1988.

———. *The Family.* Deerfield Beach: FL: Health Communications, 1988.

———. *Homecoming.* New York, NY: Bantam Books, 1990.

Brannon, Yolanda Nicole, et al. "Attitudes About Community Notification: A Comparison of Sexual Offenders and the Non-offending Public." *Sexual Abuse* 19 (2007) 369–79.

Branscombe, N. R., et al. "Counterfactual Thinking, Blame Assignment, and Well Being in Rape Victims." *Basic and Applied Social Psychology* 25 (2003) 265–273.

Braun, Bennett G. "The BASK Model of Dissociation: Clinical Applications." *Dissociation* 1 (1988) 16–23.

———. "Dissociative Disorders as a Sequelae to Incest." In *Incest-Related Syndromes of Adult Psychopathology,* edited by R. Kluft, 227–245. Washington, DC: American Psychiatric Press, 1990.

Brennan, Sharon. "Sibling Incest Within Violent Families: Children under 12 Seeking Nurture." *Health Sociology Review* 15 (2006) 287–92.

Briere, John. *Child Abuse Trauma: Theory and Treatment of the Lasting Effects.* Newbury Park, CA: Sage, 1992.

———. "Treating Adults Severely Abused as Children: The Self Trauma Model." In *Child Abuse: New Directions and Treatment Across the Lifespan,* edited by D. A. Wolfe, R. J. McMahan and R. D. Peters, 177–204. Thousand Oaks, CA: Sage Publishers, 1997.

———, et al. "Childhood Maltreatment, Intervening Variables, and Adult Psychological Difficulties in Women: An Overview." *Trauma, Violence, and Abuse* 10 (2009) 375– 388.

Briggs, Freda, and Russell M. F. Hawkins. "A Comparison of the Childhood Experiences of Convicted Male Child Molesters and Men Who Were Sexually Abused in Childhood and Claimed to Be Nonoffenders." *Child Abuse and Neglect* 20 (1996) 221–233.

Briggs, L., and P. R. Joyce. "What Determines Post-Traumatic Stress Disorder Symptomatology for Survivors of Childhood Sexual Abuse?" *Child Abuse & Neglect* 21 (1997) 575–582.

Brillon, P., et al. "Influence of Cognitive Factors on Sexual Assault Recovery: Descriptive Review and Methodological Concerns." *Scandinavian Journal of Behaviour Therapy* 28 (1999) 119–137.

Brison, Susan J. *Aftermath: Violence and the Remaking of a Self.* Princeton, NJ: Princeton University Press, 2002.

Broht, K. *When Your Child has Been Molested: A Parent's Guide to Healing & Recovery.* San Francisco, CA: Jossey-Bass, 2004.

Bromley, M. B. *Hush: Moving from Silence to Healing after Childhood Sexual Abuse.* Chicago: Moody, 2007.

———. *Breathe: Finding Freedom to Thrive in Relationships after Childhood Sexual Abuse.* Chicago: Moody, 2009.

Bromberg, D. S. and B. T. Johnson. "Sexual Interest in Children, Child Sexual Abuse, and Psychological Sequelae for Children." *Psychology in the Schools* 28 (2001) 343–355.

Brooks Thistlethwaite, Susan. "Every Two Minutes: Battered Women and Feminist Interpretation." In *Feminist Interpretation of the Bible,* edited by Letty Russell, 377–386. Louisville, KY: Westminster John Knox Press, 1985.

Browne, A., and D. Finkelhor. "Impact of Child Sexual Abuse: A Review of the Literature." *Psychological Bulletin* 99 (1986) 66–77.

Brown, Sally A. and Patrick D. Miller. *Lament: Reclaiming Practices in Pulpit, Pew, and Public Square.* Louisville, KY: Westminster John Knox, 2005.

Brown, William P. *The Ethos of the Cosmos: The Genesis of Moral Imagination in the Bible.* Grand Rapids, MI: Eerdmans, 1999.

———. "Creation." In *Eerdmans Dictionary of the Bible,* edited by David Freedman, 293–294. Grand Rapids: Eerdmans, 2000.

Browning, Robert L., and Roy A. Reed, ed. *Forgiveness, Reconciliation, and Moral Courage: Motives and Designs for Ministry in a Troubled World*. Grand Rapids, MI: Eerdmans, 2004.

Brownmiller, Susan. *Against Our Will*. New York, NY: Simon and Schuster, 1975.

Brueggemann, Walter. "The Formfulness of Grief." *Interpretation* 31 (1977) 263–275.

———. *Genesis: Interpretation: A Bible Commentary for Teaching and Preaching*. Atlanta, GA: John Knox, 1982.

———. *The Message of the Psalms: A Theological Commentary*. Minneapolis, MN: Augsburg, 1984.

———. "The Costly Loss of Lament." *Journal for the Study of the Old Testament* 36 (1986) 57–71.

———. *The Psalms and the Life of Faith*. Minneapolis, MN: Fortress, 1995.

———. "Sexuality." In *Reverberations of Faith: A Theological Handbook of Old Testament Themes*, 190–195. Louisville, KY: Westminster John Knox, 2002.

———. "Listening." In *Reverberations of Faith: A Theological Handbook of Old Testament Themes*, 123–125. Louisville, KY: Westminster John Knox, 2002.

———. *An Unsettling God: the Heart of the Hebrew Bible*. Minneapolis, MN: Fortress, 2009.

Breuer and Freud. "Studies on Hysteria." In *Standard Edition*. trans. J. Strachey, vol. 2, 35. London: Hogarth Press, 1955.

Bromley, Nicole Braddock. *Breathe: Finding Freedom to Thrive in Relationships after Childhood Sexual Abuse*. Chicago: Moody, 2009.

Bryant, S., and L. Range. "Suicidality in College Women Who Were Sexually and Physically Abused and Physically Punished by Parents." *Violence and Victims* 10 (1995) 195–201.

Buchwald, Emilie, et al. *Transforming a Rape Culture*. Rev. ed. Minneapolis, MN: Milkweed Editions, 2005.

Budrionis, Rita, and Arthur E. Jongsma, Jr. *The Sexual Abuse Victim and Sexual Offender Treatment Planner*. Hoboken, NJ: John Wiley and Sons, 2003.

Bultmann, Rudolph. *Theology of the New Testament*, trans. Kendrick Grobel. 2 Vols. New York, NY: Charles Scribner's Sons, 1951–1955.

Burnett, Joel S. *Where is God? Divine Absence in the Hebrew Bible*. Minneapolis, MN: Fortress, 2010.

Butler, Sandra. *Conspiracy of Silence: The Trauma of Incest*. San Francisco, CA: Volcano Press, 1985.

Buttenheim, M., and A. Levendosky. "Couples Treatment for Incest Survivors." *Psychotherapy* 31 (1994) 407–414.

Burgess, Ann Wolbert, et al. "Educator Sexual Abuse: Two Case Reports." *Journal of Child Sexual Abuse* 19 (2010) 387–402.

Burgess, Wes. *The Bipolar Handbook: Real-Life Questions with Up-to-Date Answers*. New York, NY: Avery/Penguin Group, 2006.

Burkett, Edan. "Victory for Clergy Sexual Abuse Victims: The Ninth Circuit Strips the Holy See of Foreign Sovereign Immunity in Doe v. Holy See." *Brigham Young University Law Review* 1 (2010) 35–50.

Byars, Ronald. *The Future of Protestant Worship*. Louisville, KY: Westminster John Knox, 2002.

Calvin, John. *Institutes of the Christian Religion*. vol. 1, trans. F. L. Battles, edited by J. T. McNeill. Philadelphia, PA: Westminster. 1960.

———. *Institutes of the Christian Religion*. vol. 4, trans. F. L. Battles, edited by J. T. McNeill. Philadelphia, PA: Westminster, 1960.

Cameron, Catherine. *Resolving Childhood Trauma: A Long-Term Study of Abuse Survivors*. Thousand Oaks, CA: Sage, 2000.

Cameron, P., et al. "Child Molestation and Homosexuality." *Psychological Reports* 58 (1986) 327–337.

Camilleri, Joseph A., and Vernon L. Quinsey. "Pedophilia: Assessment and Treatment." In *Sexual Deviance: Theory, Assessment, and Treatment*, edited by D. Richard Laws and William T. O'Donohue, 183–212. New York, NY: The Guilford Press, 2008.

Campbell, Rebecca, et al. "The Co-Occurrence of Childhood Sexual Abuse, Adult Sexual Assault, Intimate Partner Violence, and Sexual Harassment: A Mediational Model of Posttraumatic Stress Disorder and Physical Health Outcomes." *Journal of Consulting and Clinical Psychology* 76 (2008) 194–207.

Canavan, Margaret M., et al. "The Female Experience of Sibling Incest." *Journal of Marital and Family Therapy* 18 (1992) 129–142.

Cantón-Cortés, David, and José Cantón. "Coping with Child Sexual Abuse among College Students and Post-Traumatic Stress Disorder: The Role of Continuity of Abuse and Relationship with the Perpetrator." *Child Abuse & Neglect* 34 (2010) 496–506.

Capacchione, L. *The Power of Your Other Hand*. North Hollywood, CA: New Castle Publishing, 1988.

Carballo-Dieguez, A., and C. Dolezal. "Association between History of Childhood Sexual Abuse and Adult HIV-Risk Sexual Behavior in Puerto Rican Men Who Have Sex with Men." *Child Abuse & Neglect* 19 (1995) 595–605.

Carlson, Eve B. "Studying the Interaction between Physical and Psychological States with the Dissociative Experiences Scale." In *Dissociation: Culture, Mind and Body*, edited by David Spiegel, 41–58. Washington, DC: American Psychiatric Press, 1994.

———, et al. "Sibling Incest: Reports on Forty-One Survivors." *Journal of Child Sexual Abuse* 15 (2006) 19–34.

Carlson, Elizabeth, et al. "Dissociation and the Development of the Self." In *Dissociation and the Dissociative Disorders: DSM-V and Beyond*, edited by Paul F. Dell and John A. O'Neil, 39–52. New York, NY: Routledge, 2009.

Carlson, Lee W. *Child Sexual Abuse: A Handbook for Clergy and Church Members*. Valley Forge, PA: Judson Press, 1988.

Carnes, Patrick. *Out of the Shadows*. Minneapolis, MN: CompCare Publishers, 1983.

Carosella, Cynthia. *Who's Afraid of the Dark? A Forum of Truth, Support, and Assurance for Those Affected by Rape*. New York, NY: HarperCollins, 1995.

Carr, David M. *The Erotic Word: Sexuality, Spirituality, and the Bible*. Oxford: Oxford University Press, 2003.

———. "Genesis." In *The New Oxford Annotated Bible: New Revised Standard Version with Apocrypha*, edited by D. M. Coogan, M. Z. Brettler and C. A. Newsom, 9-81. An Ecumenical Study Bible, Third Edition. Oxford: Oxford University Press, 2007.

Carson, D. A. *The Gospel According to John*. Downers Grove, IL: Inter Varsity, 1991.

———. *How Long O Lord? Reflections on Suffering and Evil*. 2nd Edn. Grand Rapids: Baker, 2006.

Casey, Keree. "Surviving Abuse: Shame, Anger, Forgiveness." *Pastoral Psychology* 46 (1998) 223–231.

Casey, Erin A., and Paula S. Nurius. "Trends in the Prevalence and Characteristics of Sexual Violence: A Cohort Analysis." *Violence and Victims* 21 (2006) 629–644.

Cashman, Hilary. *Christianity and Child Sexual Abuse*. Society for Promoting Christian Knowledge. London: SPCK, 1993.

Caspi, Mishael. "The Story of the Rape of Dinah: The Narrator and the Reader." *Hebrew Studies* 26 (1985) 25–45.

Castillo, Richard J. "Dissociation." In *Culture and Psychopathology: A Guide to Clinical Assessment*, edited by Wen-Shing Tseng and Jon Steltzer, 101–123. New York, NY: Brunner/Mazel, 1997.

Cecil, H. and S. C. Matson. "Differences in Psychological Health and Family Dysfunction by Sexual Victimization Type in a Clinical Sample of African American Adolescent Women." *Journal of Sex Research* 42 (2005) 203–214.

Celano, M. P. "A Developmental Model of Victims' Internal Attributions of Responsibility for Sexual Abuse." *Journal of Interpersonal Violence* 7 (1992) 57–69.

———, et al. "Attribution Retraining with Sexually Abused Children: Review of Techniques." *Child Maltreatment* 7 (2002) 65–76.

Cermak, Pamela, and Christian E. Molidor. "Male Victims of Child Sexual Abuse." *Child and Adolescent Social Work Journal* 13 (1996) 385–401.

Chan, Simon. *Liturgical Theology: The Church as Worshiping Community*. Downers Grove, IL; InterVarsity, 2006.

Chapman, Alexander L., and Kim L. Gratz. *The Borderline Personality Disorder Survival Guide: Everything You Need to Know About Living with BPD*. Oakland, CA: New Harbinger Publications, 2007.

Chopp, Rebecca S. *The Power to Speak: Feminism, Language, God*. New York, NY: Crossroad, 1991.

Chouliara, Zoë, et al. "Vicarious Traumatization in Practitioners Who Work with Adult Survivors of Sexual Violence and Child Sexual Abuse: Literature Review and Directions for Future Research." *Counseling & Psychotherapy Research* 9 (2009) 47–56.

Christenson, Randall M. "Parallels Between Depression and Lament." *Journal of Pastoral Care & Counseling* 61 (2007) 299–308.

Chu, J., L. M. Frey, B. L. Ganzel, and J. A. Matthews. "Memories of Childhood Abuse: Dissociation, Amnesia and Corroboration." *American Journal of Psychiatry* 156 (1999) 749–755.

——, D. Dill. "Dissociative Symptoms in Relation to Child Physical and Sexual Abuse." *American Journal of Psychiatry* 147 (1990) 887–892.

——. "Psychological Defense Styles and Childhood Sexual Abuse." *American Journal of Psychiatry* 157 (2000) 1707.

——, et al. "Trauma and Dissociation: 20 years of Study and Lessons Learned along the Way," *Journal of Trauma & Dissociation* 1 (2000) 5–20.

Chung, Sung Wook. "Toward the Reformed and Covenantal Theology of Premillennialism." In *A Case for Historic Premillennialism: An Alternative to 'Left Behind' Eschatology*, edited by C. L. Blomberg and S. W. Chung, 133-146. Grand Rapids: Baker, 2009.

Cicchetti, D. "The Impact of Child Maltreatment and Psychopathology on Neuroendocrine Functioning." *Development and Psychopathology* 13 (2001) 783–804.

Clark, Donald. "Sexual Abuse in the Church: The Law Steps In." *The Christian Century* 110 (1993) 396–398.

Clark, Elizabeth A. "The Celibate Bridegroom and His Virginal Brides: Metaphor and the Marriage of Jesus in Early Christian Ascetic Exegesis." *Church History* 77 (2008) 1–25.

Clark, R. and J. Clark. *The Encyclopedia of Abuse.* New York, NY: Facts on File, Inc., 1989.

Clark Kroeger, Catherine. "Let's Look Again at the Biblical Concept of Submission." In *Sexuality and the Sacred: Sources for Theological Reflection*, edited by James B. Nelson and Sandra P. Longfellow, 135–140. Louisville, KY: Westminster John Knox Press, 1994.

——, and James Beck. *Women, Abuse and the Bible.* Grand Rapids: Baker Books, 1996.

——, and Nancy Nason-Clark. *No Place for Abuse: Biblical and Practical Resources to Counteract Domestic Violence.* 2nd ed. Downers Grove, IL: InterVarsity Press, 2010.

Clarke, Rita-Lou. *Pastoral Care of Battered Women.* Philadelphia, PA: Westminster Press, 1986.

Classen, Catherine. et al. "Sexual Revictimization: A Review of the Empirical Literature." *Trauma, Violence & Abuse* 6 (2005) 103–129.

Clinton, Timothy E., and Mark R. Laaser. *The Quick-reference Guide to Sexuality & Relationship Counseling.* Grand Rapids, MI: Baker, 2010.

Cloke, K. "Revenge, Forgiveness, and the Magic of Mediation" *Mediation Quarterly* 11 (1993) 67–78.

Coe, John H., and Todd W. Hall. *Psychology in the Spirit: Contours of a Transformational Psychology.* Downers Grove, IL: InterVarsity, 2010.

Coetzee, J. H. "'Outcry' of the Dissected Woman in Judges 19–21: Embodiment of a Society." *Old Testament Essays* 15 (2002) 52–63.

Coffey, P., et al. "Mediators of the Long-term Impact of Child Sexual Abuse: Perceived Stigma, Betrayal, Powerless, and Self-blame." *Child Abuse & Neglect* 20 (1996) 447–455.

Coffey, Rebecca. *Unspeakable Truths and Happy Endings: Human Cruelty and the New Trauma Therapy.* Lutherville, MD: Sidran Press, 1998.

Cohen, Judith A., and A. P. Mannarino. "Addressing Attributions in Treating Abused Children." *Child Maltreatment* 7 (2002) 82–86.

——, et al. "Trauma-focused Cognitive-Behavioral Therapy for Sexually Abused Children." *Psychiatric Times* 21 (2004) 1–2.

——, et al. "A Multi-site, Randomized Controlled Trial for Children with Sexual Abuse-related PTSD Symptoms." *Journal of the American Academy of Child and Adolescent Psychiatry* 43 (2004) 393–402.

Cohen, Tamar. "Motherhood among Incest Survivors." *Child Abuse and Neglect* 19 (2000) 1423–1429.

Cole, Jan, and Kay Jones. "'Universal Precautions': Perinatal Touch and Examination after Childhood Sexual Abuse." *Birth: Issues in Perinatal Care* 36 (2009) 230–236.

Cole, Pamela M., et al. "Parenting Difficulties: Adult Survivors of Father-Daughter Incest." *Child Abuse and Neglect* 16 (1992) 39–49.

Coleman, Monica. *The Dinah Project: A Handbook for Congregational Response to Sexual Violence.* Cleveland, OH: Pilgrim, 2004.

Collins, C. John. *Genesis 1–4: A Linguistic, Literary, and Theological Commentary.* Phillipsburg, NJ: P&R Publishing, 2006.

Collins, Raymond F. *Sexual Ethics and the New Testament: Behavior and Belief.* New York, NY: Crossroad, 2000.

Collins, Wanda Lott. "Silent Sufferers: Female Clergy Sexual Abuse." *Family and Community Ministries* 23 (2009) 10–17.

Connolly, Marie, and Richard Woollons. "Childhood Sexual Experience and Adult Offending: An Exploratory Comparison of Three Groups." *Child Abuse Review* 17 (2008) 119–132.

Conroy, Mary Alice. "Evaluation of Sexual Predators." In *Handbook of Psychology, Volume 11 Forensic Psychology*, edited by Alan M. Goldstein and Irving B. Weiner, 463–484. New York, NY: Wiley, 2003.

Cook, Sarah L., and Mary P. Koss. "More Data Have Accumulated Supporting Date and Acquaintance Rape as Significant Problems for Women." In *Current Controversies on Family Violence*, edited by Donileen R. Loseke et al, 97–116. Thousand Oaks, CA: Sage, 2005.

Cooper-White, Pamela. *The Cry of Tamar: Violence against Women and the Church's Response*. Minneapolis, MN: Fortress, 1995.

Copeland, M. Shawn. *Enfleshing Freedom: Body, Race, and Being*. Minneapolis, MN: Fortress, 2010.

Copelon, Rhonda. "Gendered War Crimes: Reconceptualizing Rape in Time of War." In *Women's Rights, Human Rights: International Feminist Perspectives*, edited by Julie Peters and Andrea Wolper, 197–214. New York, NY: Routledge, 1995.

Corcoran, Kevin J. *Rethinking Human Nature: A Christian Materialist Alternative to the Soul*. Grand Rapids, MI: Baker, 2006.

Corey, Gerald. *Theory and Practice of Counseling and Psychotherapy*, 8th ed. Fullerton, CA: Thomson, 2009.

Corliss, Heather L., et al. "Reports of Parental Maltreatment During Childhood in a United States Population-based Survey of Homosexual, Bisexual, and Heterosexual Adults." *Child Abuse & Neglect* 26 (2002) 1165–1178.

Cormier, Bruno, et al. "Psychodynamics of Father-daughter Incest." *Canadian Psychiatric Association Journal* 7 (1962) 203–217.

Countryman, Louis William. *Dirt, Greed, and Sex: Sexual Ethics in the New Testament and Their Implications for Today*. Philadelphia, PA: Fortress, 1988.

Courtois, Christine A. *Healing the Incest Wound: Adult Survivors in Therapy*. New York, NY: W.W. Norton, 1988.

———. *Theory, Sequencing and Strategy in Treating Adult Survivors*. "Treating Victims of Child Sexual Abuse" 51 (1991) 47–60.

———. *Healing the Incest Wound: Adult Survivors of Child Sexual Abuse*. Milwaukee, WI: Families International, 1993.

———. "Assessment and Diagnosis." In *Treating Women Molested in Childhood*, edited by Catherine Classen, 1–35. San Francisco, CA: Jossey-Bass Publishers, 1995.

———. "Complex Trauma, Complex Reactions: Assessment and Treatment." *Psychological Trauma: Theory, Research, Practice, and Policy* 1 (2008) 86–100.

———, and Julian D. Ford. *Treating Traumatic Complex Stress Disorders: An Evidence-based Guide*. New York, NY: The Guilford Press, 2009.

Cowdell, Scott. "An Abusive Church Culture? Clergy Sexual Abuse and Systematic Dysfunction in Ecclesial Faith and Life." *St Mark's Review* 205 (2008) 31–49.

Cox Miller, Patricia. *The Corporeal Imagination: Signifying the Holy in Late Ancient Christianity*. Philadelphia, PA: University of Pennsylvania Press, 2009.

Cozzens, Donald. *Sacred Silence: Denial and the Crisis in the Church*. Collegeville, MN: Liturgical Press, 2004.

Cramer, Elizabeth, et al. "Violent Pornography and Abuse of Women: Theory to Practice." *Violence and Victims* 13 (1990) 319–332.

Craven, S., et al. "Sexual Grooming of Children: Review of Literature and Theoretical Considerations." *Journal of Sexual Aggression* 12 (2006) 287–299.

Crenshaw, James. *Samson: A Secret Betrayed, a Vow Ignored*. Atlanta, GA: John Knox, 1978.

Crewdson, John. *By Silence Betrayed: Sexual Abuse of Children in America*. Boston, MA: Little, Brown, 1988.

Criassati, Jackie. "Sexual Violence against Women: A Psychological Approach to the Assessment and Management of Rapists in the Community." *Probation Journal: The Journal of Community and Criminal Justice* 52 (2005) 401–422.

Crisci, G., et al. *Paper Dolls and Paper Airplanes: Therapeutic Exercises for Sexually Traumatized Children*. Indianapolis, IN: Kidsrights, 1998.

Crisp, Beth R. "Spiritual Direction and Survivors of Sexual Abuse." *The Way* 43 (2004) 7–17.

———. "Spirituality and Sexual Abuse: Issues and Dilemmas for Survivors." *Theology & Sexuality* 13 (2007) 301–314.

———. "Beyond Crucifixion: Remaining Christian after Sexual Abuse." *Theology & Sexuality* 15 (2009) 65–76.

———. "Silence and Silenced: Implications for the Spirituality of Survivors of Sexual Abuse." *Feminist Theology* 18 (2010) 277–293.

Crompton, Vicki, and Ellen Z. Kessner. *Saving Beauty from the Beast: How To Protect Your Daughter from an Unhealthy Relationship.* Boston, MA: Little, Brown and Company, 2003.

Crosby, Michael H. *The Dysfunctional Church: Addiction and Codependency in the Family of Catholicism.* Notre Dame, IN; Ave Maria Press, 1991.

Cross, Theodore P., et al. "Criminal Justice Outcomes of Prosecution of Child Sexual Abuse: A Case Flow Analysis." *Child Abuse and Neglect* 19 (1995) 1431–1442.

Crowder, A. *Opening the Door: A Treatment Model for Therapy of Male Survivors of Sexual Abuse.* New York, NY: Bruner/ Mazel, 1995.

Cummings, Louise. *Eyes Wide Open: Spiritual Resources for Healing From Childhood Sexual Assault.* Winfield, BC: Wood Lake Books, 1994.

Cunningham, R. M., et al. "The Association of Physical and Sexual Abuse with HIV Risk Behaviors in Adolescence and Young Adulthood: Implications for Public Health." *Child Abuse & Neglect* 18 (1994) 233–245.

Dallas, Joe and Nance Heche, eds. *The Complete Christian Guide to Understanding Homosexuality: A Biblical and Compassionate Response to Same-Sex Attraction.* Eugene, OR: Harvest House, 2010.

D'Angelo, Mary Rose. "Feminist Ethics and the Sexual Abuse of Children: Reading Christian Origins." In *A Just & True Love: Essays in Honor of Margaret A. Farley,* edited by Maura A. Ryan, Brian F. Linnane, 234–272. Notre Dame, IN: University of Notre Dame Press, 2007.

Danieli, Yael. *International Handbook of Multigenerational Legacies of Trauma.* New York, NY: Springer, 1998.

Davenport, D. S. "The Function of Anger and Forgiveness: Guidelines for Psychotherapy with Victims." *Psychotherapy* 28 (1991) 130–143.

Davidson, Julia. "Victims Speak: Comparing Child Sexual Abusers' and Child Victims' Accounts, Perceptions, and Interpretations of Sexual Abuse." *Victims and Offenders* 1 (2006) 159–174.

Davidson, Richard M. "Did King David Rape Bathsheba? A Case Study in Narrative Theology." *Journal of the Adventist Theological Society* 17 (2006) 81–95.

———. *Flame of Yahweh: Sexuality in the Old Testament.* Peabody, MA: Hendrickson, 2007.

Davis, Joseph E. *Accounts of Innocence: Sexual Abuse, Trauma, and the Self.* Chicago, IL: University of Chicago Press, 2006.

Davis, Laura. *The Courage to Heal Workbook: For Women and Men Survivors of Child Sexual Abuse.* New York, NY: Harper & Row, 1990.

———. *Allies in Healing: When the Person You Love Was Sexually Abused as a Child.* New York, NY: Harper Perennial, 1991.

de Gruchy, John W. *Reconciliation: Restoring Justice.* London: SCM Press, 2002.

Deacy, Susan and Karen F. Pierce, eds. *Rape in Antiquity: Sexual Violence in the Greek and Roman Worlds.* London: Duckworth, 1997.

DeMaio, Christine M., et al. "The Use of Clarification Sessions in the Treatment of Incest Victims and Their Families: An Exploratory Study." *Sexual Abuse* 18 (2006) 27–39.

DeMause, Lloyd. *The History of Childhood.* New York, NY: the Psychohistory Press, 1974.

———. "The History of Child Assault." *The Journal of Psychohistory* 18 (1990) 1–29.

Deming, Will. "Mark 9:42–10:12, Matthew 5:27–32, and *B. Nid.* 13b: A First Century Discussion of Male Sexuality." *New Testament Studies* 36 (1990) 130–141.

DeMott, Benjamin. "The Pro-Incest Lobby." *Psychology Today* 13 (March, 1980) 11–16.

Dennis, Trevor. *Sarah Laughed: Women's Voices in the Old Testament.* Nashville: Abingdon, 1994.

DePrince, Anne P., and Jennifer J. Freyd. "Trauma-induced Dissociation." In *Handbook of PTSD: Science and Practice,* edited by Matthew J. Friedman, Terence M. Keane, and Patricia A. Resick, 135–150. New York, NY: Guilford Press, 2007.

De Younge, M. *The Sexual Victimization of Children.* Jefferson, NC: McFarland, 1982.

Dhaliwal, G. K., et al. "Adult Male Survivors of Childhood Sexual Abuse: Prevalence, Sexual Abuse Characteristics, and Long-term Effects." *Clinical Psychology Review* 16 (1996) 619–639.

Dhawan, Sonia, and W. L. Marshall. "Sexual Abuse Histories of Sexual Offenders." *Sexual Abuse: A Journal of Research and Treatment* 8 (1996) 7–15.

Diamond, L. "Female Bisexuality from Adolescence to Adulthood: Results from a 10-Year Longitudinal Study." *Developmental Psychology* 44 (2008) 5–14.

———. *Sexual Fluidity: Understanding Women's Love and Desire*. Cambridge, MA: Harvard University Press, 2008.

DiBlasio, F. A. "Practitioners, Religion and the Use of Forgiveness in the Clinical Setting." *Journal of Psychology and Christianity* 10 (1992) 181–187.

Dienemann, Jacqueline, et al. "Intimate Partner Abuse Among Women Diagnosed with Depression." *Issues in Mental Health Nursing* 21 (2000) 499–513.

DiLillo, David, et al. "A Closer Look at the Nature of Intimate Partner Violence Reported by Women with a History of Child Sexual Abuse." *Journal of Interpersonal Violence* 16 (2001) 116–132.

———, et al. "Parenting Characteristics of Women Reporting a History of Childhood Sexual Abuse." *Child Maltreatment* 8 (2003) 319–333.

———, et al. "Child Maltreatment History Among Newlywed Couples: A Longitudinal Study of Marital Outcomes and Mediating Pathways." *Journal of Consulting and Clinical Psychology* 77 (2009) 680–692.

Dimock, P. T. "Adult Males Sexually Abused as Children: Characteristics and Implications for Treatment." *Journal of Interpersonal Violence* 3 (1988) 203–221.

Di Vito, Robert A. "Old Testament Anthropology and the Construction of Personal Identity." *Catholic Biblical Quarterly* 61 (1999) 217–238.

———. "Anthropology, OT Theological." *New Interpreter's Dictionary of the Bible*, edited by Katharine Doob Sakenfeld, 171–174. Nashville, TN: Abingdon, 2006.

Doak, Melissa J. *Violent Relationships: Battering and Abuse Among Adults*. Farmington Hills, MI: Thomson/Gale, 2005.

Dobash, R. Emerson and Russell Dobash. *Violence against Wives: A Case against the Patriarchy*. New York, NY: Free Press, 1979.

Dobbs-Allsopp, F. W., and Tod Linafelt. "The Rape of Zion in Thr 1,10." *Zeitschrift für die Alttestamentliche Wissenschaft* 113 (2001) 77–81.

Doka, Kenneth. "Disenfranchised Grief." In *The Path Ahead: Readings in Death and Dying*, edited by Lynne DeSpelder and A Strickland, 271–275. Mountain View, CA: Mayfield, 1989.

Dolan, Yvonne. *Resolving Sexual Abuse: Solution-Focused Therapy and Ericksonian Hypnosis for Adult Survivors*. New York, NY: W. W. Norton & Company, 1991.

Donnelly, Susie, and Tom Inglis. "The Media and the Catholic Church in Ireland: Reporting Clerical Child Sex Abuse." *Journal of Contemporary Religion* 25 (2010) 1–19.

Donnerstein, Edward, et al. Victim Reactions in Erotic Films as a Factor in Violence against Women. *Journal of Personality and Social Psychology* 41 (1981) 710–724.

Doren, Dennis M. "Recidivism Risk Assessments: Making Sense of Controversies." In *Sex Offender Treatment: Controversial Issues*, edited by William L. Marshall, et al., 3–15. New York, NY: Wiley, 2006.

Doris, J. (Ed.). *The Suggestibility of Children's Recollections: Implications for Eyewitness Testimony*. Washington, DC: American Psychological Association Press, 1991.

Douglas, Anne. "Reported Anxieties Concerning Intimate Parenting in Women Sexually Abused as Children." *Child Abuse and Neglect* 24 (2000) 425–434.

Doyle, Thomas P. "Clericalism: Enabler of Clergy Sexual Abuse." *Pastoral Psychology* 54 (2006) 189–213.

———. "The Spiritual Trauma Experienced by Victims of Sexual Abuse by Clerical Clergy." *Pastoral Psychology* 58 (2009) 239–260.

Drapeau, Martin, et al. "What Sex Abusers Say About Their Treatment: Results from a Qualitative Study on Pedophiles in Treatment at a Canadian Penitentiary Clinic." *Journal of Child Sexual Abuse* 14 (2005) 91–115.

Draper, B., et al. "Long-term Effects of Childhood Abuse on the Quality of Life and Health of Older People: Results from the Depression and Early Prevention of Suicide in General Practice Project." *Journal of the American Geriatrics Society* 56 (2008) 262–271.

Driver, Tom. *The Magic of Ritual: Our Need For Liberating Rites that Transform Our Lives and Our Communities.* San Francisco, CA: Harper, 1991.

Duck, Ruth, and Patricia Wilson-Kastner. *Praising God: The Trinity in Christian Worship.* Louisville, KY: Westminster John Knox, 1999.

———. "Hospitality to Victims: A Challenge for Christian Worship." In *The Other Side of Sin: Woundedness from the Perspective of the Sinned-Against,* edited by Andrew Park and Susan Nelson, 165–180. Albany, NY: State University of New York, 2001.

Duffy, Shannon. *3rd Circuit Bars Prosecution Threat for Teen "Sexting." The Legal Intelligencer,* March 18, 2010.

Duncan, Karen. "The Impact of Child Sexual Abuse on Parenting." In *VISTAS: Compelling Perspectives on Counseling,* edited by G. R. Walz and R. K. Yep. Alexandria, VA: American Counseling Association, 2005.

Dunnill, John. "Out of the Dark: Child Sexual Abuse and the Web of Sin." *St Mark's Review* 205 (2008) 69–86.

Durham, M. Gigi. *The Lolita Effect: The Media Sexualization of Young Girls and What We Can Do About It.* New York, NY: The Overlook Press, 2008.

Dworkin, Andrea. *Letters from a War Zone.* London: Secker & Warburg, 1988.

East, Norwood W., and William Henry de Bargue Norwood. *Report on the Psychological Treatment of Crime.* London, Great Britain: H.M. Stationery Off, 1939.

Eisenstein, Hester. *Contemporary Feminist Thought.* Boston, MA: G. K. Hall, 1983.

El-Bassel, N., et al. "The Relationship between Drug Abuse and Sexual Performance among Women on Methadone: Heightening the Risk of Sexual Intimate Violence and HIV." *Addictive Behaviors* 28 (2003) 1385–1403.

Ellens, J. Herald. "Sin or Sickness: The Problem of Human Dysfunction." In *Seeking Understanding: The Stob Lectures, 1986-1998,* edited by M. Van Denend. Grand Rapids, MI: Eerdmans, 2001.

Ellens, J. Harold. *Sex in the Bible: A New Consideration.* Psychology, Religion, and Spirituality. Westport, CT: Praeger, 2006.

Elliot, Elisabeth. *A Path Through Suffering: Discovering the Relationship Between God's Mercy and Our Pain.* Ann Arbor, MI: Vine Books/ Servant Publications, 1990.

Elliott, Robert, Kenneth L. Davis, and Emil Slatick. "Process Experiential Therapy for Post-traumatic Stress Difficulties." In *Handbook of Experiential Psychotherapy,* edited by L. Greenberg, G. Lietaer, and J. Watson, 249–271. New York, NY: Guilford Press, 1998.

Ellis, J. Edward. *Paul and Ancient Views of Sexual Desire: Paul's Sexual Ethics in 1 Thessalonians 4, 1 Corinthians 7, and Romans 1.* London: Continuum, 2007.

Emerson Dobash, R., and Russell Dobash. *Violence Against Wives: A Case Against the Patriarchy.* New York, NY: Free Press, 1979.

Emerson, Judy. *In the Voice of a Child.* Nashville, TN: Thomas Nelson, 1994.

Engel, Beverly. *The Right to Innocence.* Los Angeles, CA: Jeremy P. Tarcher, 1989.

———. *Partners in Recovery.* New York, NY: Ballantine Books, 1991.

———. *Families in Recovery: Working Together to Heal the Damage of Child Sexual Abuse.* Los Angeles, CA: Lowell House, 1995.

Engel, Mary Potter. "Evil, Sin and Violation of the Vulnerable." In *Lift Every Voice: Constructing Christian Theology from the Underside,* ed. Mary Potter Engel, 152–164. Maryknoll, NY: Orbis Books, 1998.

Engle, Michael J., et al. "The Attitudes of Members of the Association for the Treatment of Sexual Abusers toward Treatment, Release, and Recidivism of Violent Sex Offenders: An Exploratory Study." *Journal of Offender Rehabilitation* 44 (2007) 17–24.

Enright, Robert D., and the Human Development Study Group. "Counseling Within the Forgiveness Triad: On Forgiving, Receiving Forgiveness, and Self-forgiveness." *Counseling and Values* 40 (1996) 107–126.

———, and Joanna Clark, *Exploring Forgiveness.* Madison, WI: University of Wisconsin Press, 1998.

———. *Forgiveness is a Choice: A Step by Step Process for Resolving Anger and Restoring Hope.* Washington, DC: American Psychological Association, 2001.

Epperly, Bruce. *Healing Worship: Purpose and Practice.* Cleveland, OH: Pilgrim, 2006.

Erikson, Eric H. *Childhood and Society.* 2d ed. New York, NY: Norton, 1963.

Esterson, A. "Seduction Theory." In *The Freud Encyclopedia: Theory, Therapy, and Culture*, 515–519. New York, NY: Routledge, 2002.

Etherington, Kim. "Adult Male Survivors of Childhood Sexual Abuse." *Counseling Psychology Quarterly* 8 (1995) 233–241.

Evans, Abigail. *Healing Liturgies for the Seasons of Life*. Louisville, KY: Westminster John Knox, 2004.

Evans, Ray B. "Childhood Parental Relationships of Homosexual Men." *Journal of Consulting and Clinical Psychology* 33 (1969) 129–135.

Everingham, John. "Inadvertent Shaming: Family Rules and Shaming Habits." In *Men Healing Shame: An Anthology*, edited by Roy U. Schenk and John Everingham, 228–253. New York, NY: Springer, 1995.

Everly, George S., Jr. "Psychotraumatology." In *Pyschotraumatology: Key Papers and Core Concepts in Post-traumatic Stress*, edited by George S. Everly, Jr., and Jeffrey M. Lating, 3–8. New York, NY: Plenum Press, 1995.

Exline, Julie J. "Religious Framing by Individuals With PTSD When Writing About Traumatic Experiences." *International Journal for the Psychology of Religion* 15 (2005) 17–33.

Ezell, Cynthia. "Power, Patriarchy, and Abusive Marriages." In *Healing the Hurting: Giving Hope and Help to Abused Women*, edited by Catherine Clark Kroeger and James R. Beck, 15–39. Grand Rapids, MI: Baker, 1998.

Fackenheim, Emil. *God's Presence in History*. New York, NY: Harper & Row, 1970.

Faiez, Rahim. "Are Afghans Revising Laws That Will Legalize Marital Rape?" July 9, 2009.

Faller, K. "Women Who Sexually Abuse Children." *Violence and Victims* 2 (1987) 263–276.

Farley, Wendy. *Tragic Vision and Divine Compassion*. Louisville, KY: Westminster, 1990.

Fast, Julie A., and John Preston. *Loving Someone with Bipolar Disorder: Understanding and Helping Your Partner*. Oakland, CA: New Harbinger Publications, 2004.

Fee, Gordon. "Hermeneutics and the Gender Debate." In *Discovering Biblical Equality: Complementarity without Hierarchy*, edited by Ronald W. Pierce and Rebecca Merrill Groothuis, 364–381. Downers Grove, IL: InterVarsity, 2004.

Feerick, M. M., and K. L. Snow. "The Relationship between Childhood Sexual Abuse, Social Anxiety, and Symptoms of Posttraumatic Stress Disorder in Women." *Journal of Family Violence* 20 (2005) 409–419.

Feinauer, Leslie, H. Gill Hilton, and Eddy Howard Callahan. "hardiness as a Moderator of Shame Associated with Childhood Sexual Abuse." *American Journal of Family Therapy* 31 (2003) 65–78.

Feiring, C. et al. "Trying to Understand Why Horrible Things Happen: Attribution, Shame, and Symptom Development Following Sexual Abuse." *Child Maltreatment* 7 (2002) 26–41.

Feldmeth, Joanne, and Midge Finley. *We Weep for Ourselves and Our Children: A Christian Guide for Survivors of Childhood Sexual Abuse*. San Francisco, CA: HarperSanFrancisco, 1990.

Felker Jones, Beth. *Marks of His Wounds: Gender Politics and Bodily Resurrection*. New York, NY: Oxford University Press, 2007.

Ferguson, David M., and Paul E. Mullen. *Childhood Sexual Abuse: An Evidence-Based Perspective*. Thousand Oaks, CA: Sage, 1999.

Ferrara, F. Felicia. *Child Sexual Abuse: Developmental Effect Across the Lifespan*. Pacific Grove, CA: Brooks/Cole, 2002.

Ferro, Christine, et al. "Current Perceptions of Marital Rape: Some Good and Not-So-Good News." *Journal of Interpersonal Violence* 23 (2008) 764–779.

Fetchenhauer, D., et al. "Belief in a Just World, Causal Attributions, and Adjustment to Sexual Violence." *Social Justice Research* 18 (2005) 25–42.

Feueresien, Dr. Patti, with Caroline Pincus. *Invisible Girls: The Truth about Sexual Abuse*. Emeryville, CA: Seal Press, 2005.

Fields, Weston W. *Sodom and Gomorrah: History and Motif in Biblical Narrative*. JSOTSup 231. Sheffield: Sheffield Academic Press, 1997.

Figley, Charles R. *Helping Traumatized Families*. San Francisco, CA: Jossey-Bass, 1989.

Fincham, F. D. "Child Abuse: An Attribution Perspective [Commentaries on the Focus Section]." *Child Maltreatment* 7 (2002) 77–81.

Fine, C. G. "The Cognitive Sequelae of Incest." In *Incest-Related Syndromes of Adult Psychopathology*, edited by R. Kluft, 161–182. Washington, D.C.: American Psychiatric Press, 1990.

Finkelhor, David, et al (eds.). *The Dark Side of Families: Current Family Violence Research*. Newbury Park, CA: Sage Publications, 1983.

———. *Child Sexual Abuse: New Theory & Research*. New York, NY: Free Press, 1984.

———, and Angela Browne. "The Traumatic Impact of Child Sexual Abuse: A Conceptualization." *American Journal of Orthopsychiatry* 55 (1985) 530–541.

———. *A Sourcebook on Child Sexual Abuse*. Newbury Park, CA: Sage Publications, 1986.

———. *Nursery Crimes: Sexual Abuse in Day Care*, edited by David Finkelhor, et al. Newbury Park, CA: Sage, 1988.

———, et al. "Sexual Abuse in a National Survey of Adult Men and Women: Prevalence, Characteristics, and Risk Factors." *Child Abuse and Neglect* 14 (1990) 19–28.

———. "Early and Prolonged Effects of Child Sexual Abuse: An Update." *Professional Psychology Research and Practice* 21 (1990) 325–330.

———. "The International Epidemiology of Child Sexual Abuse." *Child Abuse and Neglect* 18 (1994) 409–417.

———. "Current Information on the Scope and Nature of Child Sexual Abuse." *The Future of Children* 4 (1994) 31–53.

———, and L. Berliner. "Research on the Treatment of Sexually Abused Children: A Review and Recommendations." *Journal of the American Academy of Child and Adolescent Psychiatry* 34 (1995) 1408–1423.

———, et al. "The Victimization of Children and Youth: A Comprehensive National Survey." *Child Maltreatment* 10 (2005) 5–25.

Finney, Lynne, JD, MSW. *Reach for the Rainbow: Advanced Healing for Survivors of Sexual Abuse*. New York, NY: Perigee Books, 1992.

Firmin, M. W., and M. Tedford. "An Assessment of Pastoral Counseling Courses in Seminaries Serving Evangelical Baptist Students." *Review of Religious Research* 48 (2007) 420–427.

Fisher, B. et al. *The Sexual Victimization of College Women*. Washington, DC: US Department of Justice, 2001.

Fisher-Townsend, Barbara, Nancy Nason-Clark, Lanette Ruff and Nancy Murphy. "I am Not Violent: Men's Experience in Group." In *Beyond Abuse in the Christian Home: Raising Voices for Change*, edited by Catherine Clark Kroeger, Nancy Nason-Clark, and Barbara Fisher-Townsend, 78–99. Eugene, OR: Wipf and Stock, 2008.

Fitzgibbons, P. R. "The Cognitive and Emotive Uses of Forgiveness in the Treatment of Anger." *Psychotherapy* 2 (1986) 629–633.

Flaherty, Sandra. *Woman, Why Do You Weep? Spirituality for Survivors of Childhood Sexual Abuse*. Mahwah, NJ: Paulist, 1992.

Flynn, Kathryn. *The Sexual Abuse of Women by Members of the Clergy*. Jefferson, NC: McFarland & Company, 2003.

Foa, Edna B., et al. "Treatment of Posttraumatic Stress Disorder in Rape Victims: A Comparison between Cognitive Behavioral Procedures and Counseling." *Journal of Consulting and Clinical Psychology* 59 (1991) 715–723.

———, et al. *Effective Treatments for PTSD: Practice Guidelines from the International Society for Traumatic Stress Studies*. 2nd ed. New York, NY: The Guilford Press, 2008.

Foote, Catherine. *Survivor Prayers: Talking with God about Childhood Sexual Abuse*. Louisville, NY: Westminster/John Knox, 1994.

Ford, Julian D. "Neurobiological and Developmental Research: Clinical Implications." In *Treating Complex Traumatic Stress Disorders: An Evidenced-Based Guide*, edited by Christine A. Courtois and Julian D. Ford, 31–58. New York, NY: Guilford Press, 2009.

Fortney, T., and J. N. Baker. "A Look in the Mirror: Sexual Abuse Professionals' Perceptions about Sex Offenders." *Victims and Offenders* 4 (2009) 42–57.

Fortune, Marie. *Keeping the Faith: Questions and Answers for the Abused Woman*. San Francisco, CA: Harper & Row, 1987.

———. *Violence in the Family: A Workshop Curriculum for Clergy and Other Helpers*. Cleveland, OH: Pilgrim, 1991.

———. "Forgiveness: The Last Step." In *Violence Against Women and Children: A Christian Theological Sourcebook,* edited by Carol Adams and Marie Fortune, 201–206. New York, NY: Continuum, 1995.

Forward, Susan, and Craig Buck. *Toxic Parents.* New York, NY: Bantam, 1989.

Fossum, Merle A., and Marilyn J. Mason. *Facing Shame: Families in Recovery.* New York, NY: W. W. Norton & Company, Inc., 1986.

———. *Catching Fire: Men Coming Alive in Recovery.* San Francisco, NY: Harper, 1989.

Foster, Richard A. *Celebration of Discipline: The Path to Spiritual Growth.* New York, NY: HarperCollins, 1988.

———. "Spiritual Formation Agenda: Three Priorities for the Next 30 Years." http://www.christianitytoday.com/ct/2009/january/26.29.html.

Fourez, Gerard. *Sacraments and Passages.* Notre Dame, IN: Ave Maria, 1983.

Fox, Matthew. *Sins of the Spirit, Blessings of the Flesh: Lessons for Transforming Evil in Soul and Society.* New York, NY: Harmony Books, 1999.

Frank, Jan. *Door of Hope.* Nashville, TN: Thomas Nelson, 1995.

Fraser, Sylvia. *My Father's House: A Memoir of Incest and of Healing.* New York, NY: Harper & Row, 1989.

Fraser, Meredith. "A Feminist Theoethical Analysis of White Pentecostal Australian Women and Marital Abuse." *Journal of Feminist Studies in Religion* 19 (2003) 145–167.

Frazier, P. A. "Victim Attributions and Post-Rape Trauma." *Journal of Personality and Social Psychology* 59 (1990) 298–304.

———, et al. "Coping Strategies as Mediators of the Relations among Perceived Control and Distress in Sexual Assault Survivors." *Journal of Counseling Psychology* 52 (2005) 267–78.

Fredrickson, David. "Passionless Sex in 1 Thessalonians 4:4–5." *Word and World* 23 (2003) 23–30.

Freedman, S. R., and Robert D. Enright. "Forgiveness as an Intervention Goal with Incest Survivors." *Journal of Consulting and Clinical Psychology* 64 (1996) 983–992.

Fretheim, Terence E. "The Book of Genesis: Introduction, Commentary, and Reflections." In *The New Interpreter's Bible: A Commentary in Twelve Volumes,* 321–674. Nashville, TN: Abingdon, 1994.

———. "Law in the Service of Life: A Dynamic Understanding of Law in Deuteronomy." In *A God So Near: Essays on Old Testament Theology in Honor of Patrick D. Miller,* edited by Brent A. Strawn and Nancy R. Bowen, 183–200. Winona Lake, IN: Eisenbrauns, 2003.

———. *God and World in the Old Testament: A Relational Theology of Creation.* Nashville, TN: Abingdon, 2005.

———. "God, OT View of." In *The New Interpreter's Dictionary of the Bible.* vol. 2., edited by Katherine Doob Sakenfeld, 603–618. Nashville, TN: Abingdon Press, 2006.

Freud, Anna. "A Psychoanalyst's View of Sexual Abuse by Parents." In *Sexually Abused Children and Their Families,* edited by P. B. Mrazek and C. H. Kempe, 33–34. New York, NY: Pergamom Press, 1981.

Freud, Sigmund. "The Aetiology of Hysteria." In *Standard Edition,* trans. J. Strachey, vol. 3. London: Hogarth Press, 1962.

Freund, Kurt, et al. "The Courtship Disorders," *Archives of Sexual Behavior* 12 (1983) 369–379.

Freyd, Jennifer, et al. "The State of Betrayal Trauma Theory." *Memory* 4 (2007) 295–311.

Frymer-Kensky, Tikva. *Reading the Women of the Bible.* New York, NY: Schocken, 2002.

———. MAL A §23; *The Context of Scripture,* edited by W. W. Hallo, 2:355–356. Leiden: E. J. Brill, 1997–2002.

Fuchs, Esther. *Sexual Politics in the Biblical Narrative: Reading the Hebrew Bible as a Woman.* Journal for the Study of the Old Testament: Supplement Series, 310. Sheffield: Sheffield Academic Press, 2000.

Furniss, Tilman. *The Multi-Professional Handbook of Child Sexual Abuse: Integrated Management, Therapy and Legal Intervention.* London: Routledge, 1991.

Fürst, Dieter. "Confess." In *The New International Dictionary of New Testament Theology.* vol. 1, edited by Colin Brown, 344–347. Grand Rapids, MI: Zondervan, 1979.

Gagnon, John. "Basic Male Shame." In *Men Healing Shame: An Anthology,* edited by Roy U. Schenk and John Everingham, 167–183. New York, NY: Springer, 1995.

Gagnon, Robert A. J. *The Bible and Homosexual Practice.* Nashville, TN: Abingdon, 2001.

———. "Sexuality." In *Dictionary for Theological Interpretation of the Bible,* edited by Kevin J. Vanhoozer, 739–748. Grand Rapids, MI: Baker, 2005.

———. "Article Review of Stacy Johnson, *A Time to Embrace.*" *Scottish Journal of Theology* 62 (2009) 61–80.

Bibliography

Gane, Roy. *God's Faulty Heroes*. Hagerstown, MD: Review and Herald, 1996.

Gannon, Theresa A., et al. "Cognitive Distortions in Child Molesters: Theoretical and Research Developments Over the Past Two Decades." *Aggression and Violent Behavior* 12 (2007) 402–416.

———, et al. "Rape: Psychopathology and Theory." In *Sexual Deviance: Theory, Assessment, and Treatment*, edited by D. Richard Laws and William T. O'Donohue, 336–355. New York, NY: The Guilford Press, 2008.

———, et al. "Does the Polygraph Lead to Better Risk Prediction for Sexual Offenders?" *Aggression and Violent Behavior* 13 (2008) 29–44.

Garbarino, J., and F. Scott. *What Children Tell Us: Eliciting, Interpreting, and Evaluating Information from Children*. San Francisco, CA: Jossey-Bass, 1989.

Garland, Diana R. "When Wolves Wear Shepherds' Clothing: Helping Women Survive Clergy Sexual Abuse." *Journal of Religion & Abuse* 8 (2006) 37–70.

———, et al. "The Abused/Abuser Hypothesis of Child Sexual Abuse: A Critical Review of Theory and Research." In *Pedophilia: Biosocial Dimensions*, edited by J. Feierman, 488–509. New York, NY: Springer-Verlag, 1990.

Garrett, Greg. *Stories from the Edge: A Theology of Grief*. Louisville, KY: Westminster John Knox Press, 2008.

Garsiel, Moshe. "The Story of David and Bathsheba: A Different Approach." *Catholic Biblical Quarterly* 55 (1993) 244–262.

Gartner, R. D. *Betrayed as Boys: Psychodynamic Treatment of Sexually Abused Men*. New York, NY: Guilford Press, 1999.

Gavrielides, Theo, and Dale Coker. "Restoring Faith: Resolving the Roman Catholic Church's Sexual Scandals through Restorative Justice (Working Paper I)." *Contemporary Justice Review* 8 (2005) 345–365.

Gelinas, D. J. "Family Therapy: Characteristic Family Constellation and Basic Therapeutic Stance." In *Vulnerable Populations: Evaluation and Treatment of Sexually Abused Children and Adult Survivors*, vol. 1, edited by S. Sgroi, 25–49, 51–76. Lexington, MA: Lexington Books, 1988.

Gettleman, Jeffrey. "Rape Epidemic Raises Trauma of Congo War." *New York Times*, October 7, 2007.

Gibbs, N. "Can These Parents Be Saved?" *Time*, November 30 (2009) 54–57.

Giles, John. "Forgiving the Unforgivable: Overcoming Abusive Parents." In *Men Healing Shame: An Anthology*. Springer Series Focus on Men, edited by Roy U. Schenk and John Everingham, 215–227. New York, NY: Springer, 1995.

Gill, Eliana. *Outgrowing the Pain: A Book For and About Adults Abused as Children*. New York, NY: Dell, 1983.

———. *Treatment of Adult Survivors of Childhood Abuse*. Walnut Creek, CA: Launch Press, 1988.

———. *The Healing Power of Play: Working with Abused Children*. New York, NY: The Guilford Press, 1991.

———, and Toni Cavanagh Johnson. *Sexualized Children: Assessment and Treatment of Sexualized Children and Children Who Molest*. Rockville, MD: Launch Press, 1993.

Gill, M., and L. M. Tutty. "Male Survivors of Childhood Sexual Abuse: A Qualitative Study and Issues for Clinical Consideration." *Journal of Child Sexual Abuse* 7 (1999) 19–33.

Gilmartin, Pat. *Rape, Incest, and Child Sexual Abuse*. New York, NY: Garland Publishing, 1994.

Gingrich, Heather D. "Trauma and Dissociation in the Philippines." *Journal of Trauma Practice* 4 (2005) 245–269.

———. *Trauma and Dissociation in a Cross-Cultural Perspective: Not Just a North American Phenomenon*, edited by George Rhoades Jr. and Vedat Sar, 245–269. New York, NY: Haworth Press 2005.

———. "Assessing Dissociative Symptoms and Dissociative Disorders in College Students in the Philippines." *Journal of Maltreatment, Aggression, & Trauma* 18 (2009) 403–418.

Gobin, R. L., and J. F. Freyd. "Betrayal and Revictimization: Preliminary Findings." *Psychological Trauma: Theory, Research, Practice and Policy* 1 (2009) 242–257.

Goldingay, John. *Old Testament Theology: Israel's Gospel*, vol. 1. Downers Grove, IL: InterVarsity, 2003.

Gonzalez, Justo, and Catherine Gonzalez. *Liberation Preaching: The Pulpit and the Oppressed*. Nashville, TN: Abingdon, 1980.

Goodhart, Michael. "Sins of the Fathers: War Rape, Wrongful Procreation, and Children's Human Rights." *Journal of Human Rights* 6 (2007) 307–324.

Goodwin, J. M. "Applying to Adult Incest Victims What We Have Learned from Victimized Children." In *Incest-Related Syndromes of Adult Psychopathology*, edited by R. Kluft, 57–74. Washington, DC: American Psychiatric Press, 1990.

Gordon, M. "Males and Females as Victims of Childhood Sexual Abuse: An Examination of the Gender Effect." *Journal of Family Violence* 5 (1990) 321–332.

Gore-Felton, C. et al. "Psychologists' Beliefs and Clinical Characteristics: Judging the Veracity of Childhood Sexual Abuse Memories." *Professional Psychology Research and Practice* 31 (2000) 372–377.

Gostecnik, Christian. "Sexuality and the Longing for Salvation." *J Relig Health* 46 (2007) 580–590.

Gottman, John M., and N. Silva. *The Seven Principles for Making Marriage Work*. New York, NY: Norton, 1994.

Gottschall, Marilyn. "Embodiment." In *New and Enlarged Handbook of Christian Theology*, edited by Donald W. Musser and Joseph L. Price, 155–157. Nashville, TN: Abingdon, 2003.

Gould, James B. "Spiritual Healing of Disrupted Childhood." *The Journal of Pastoral Care and Counseling* 60 (2006) 263–271.

Graber, K. *Ghosts in the Bedroom: A Guide for Partners of Incest Survivors*. Deerfield Beach, FL: Health Communications, 1991.

Grant, Beth and Cindy Lopez Hudlin (eds). *Hands That Heal International Curriculum for Training Caregivers of Trafficking Survivors—Community-Based Editions—Part I; Part II*. Springfield, MO: Project Rescue International and FAAST, 2007.

Grant, Michael. *Saint Paul*. New York, NY: Scribner's Sons, 1976.

Green, Anthony and Douglas Baird. "Prostitution and Ritual Sex." In *Dictionary of the Ancient Near East*, edited by Piotr Bienkowski and Alan Millard, 235–236. Philadelphia, PA: University of Pennsylvania Press, 2000.

Green, Arthur H. "Children Traumatized by Physical Abuse." In *Post-Traumatic Stress Disorder in Children*, edited by Spencer Eth and Robert S. Pynoos, 134–154. Washington, DC: American Psychiatric Press, 1985.

Green, Joel B. *Body, Soul, and Human Life: The Nature of Humanity in the Bible*. Studies in Theological Interpretation. Grand Rapids, MI: Baker Academic, 2008.

Greenberg, Moshe. *Ezekiel 1–20: A New Translation with Introduction and Commentary*. Anchor Bible 22. Garden City, NY: Doubleday, 1983.

Grenz, Stanley J. *The Social God and the Relational Self: A Trinitarian Theology of the Imago Dei*. Louisville, KY: Westminster John Knox Press, 2001.

———. "The Social Imago: The Image of God and the Postmodern (Loss of) Self." In *The Papers of the Henry Luce III Fellows in Theology*, edited by C. I. Wilkins, 49–78. Pittsburgh, PA: Association of Theological Seminaries, 2003.

Grobb, Gerald. *The Mad Among Us: A History of the Care of America's Mentally Ill*. Cambridge, MA: Harvard University Press, 1994.

Groth, A. N. "The Incest Offender." In *Handbook of Clinical Intervention in Child Sexual Abuse*, edited by S. Sgroi, 215–218. Lexington, MA: Lexington Books, 1982.

———. et al. "The Child Molester: Clinical Observations." In *Social Work and Child Sexual Abuse*, edited by J. Conte and D. Shore. New York, NY: Haworth, 1982.

Grossman, Susan F., et al. "Service Patterns of Adult Survivors of Childhood Versus Adult Sexual Assault/Abuse." *Journal of Child Sexual Abuse* 18 (2009) 655–672.

Gruber, Mayer I. "A Re-examination of the Charges against Shechem Son of Hamor." *Beit Mikra* 157 (1999) 119–127.

Grubman-Black, S. D. *Broken Boys and Mending Men: Recovery from Childhood Sexual Abuse*. Blue Ridge Summit, PA: TAB Books, 1990.

Gudorf, Christine E. *Victimization: Examining Christian Complicity*. Philadelphia, PA: Trinity Press International, 1992.

Guenther, Margaret. *Holy Listening: The Art of Spiritual Direction*. Cambridge, MA: Cowley Publications, 1992.

Guroian, Vigen. *Life's Living Toward Dying*. Grand Rapids: Eerdmans, 1996.

Gustav, Erik Alexius Berggren. *The Psychology of Confession*. Leiden: E.J. Brill, 1975.

Haid, Gert Martin, et al. "Pornography and Attitudes Supporting Violence against Women: Revisiting the Relationship in Non-Experimental Studies." *Aggressive Behavior* 36 (2010) 14–20.

Halbwachs, Maurice. "The Social Frameworks of Memory." In *On Collective Memory*, edited and trans. by Lewis A. Coser. Chicago: University of Chicago Press, 1992.

Hall, M. Elizabeth, Eric Johnson. "Theodicy and Therapy: Philosophical/Theological Contributions to the Problem of Suffering." *Journal of Psychology and Christianity* 20 (2001) 5–17.

Hall, Terese. "Spiritual Effects of Childhood Sexual Abuse in Adult Christian Women." *Journal of Psychology and Theology* 23 (1995) 129–134.

Halling, S. "Shame and Forgiveness." *The Humanistic Psychologist* 22 (1994) 74–87.

Hamilton, Victor P. *The Book of Genesis: Chapters 1–17*. New International Commentary on the Old Testament. Grand Rapids, MI: Eerdmans, 1990.

Hampl, Patricia. *I Could Tell You Stories: Sojourns in the Land of Memory*. New York, NY: W. W. Norton & Company, 1999.

Hansen, Tracy. *Seven for a Secret: Healing the Wounds of Sexual Abuse in Childhood*. London: Triangle/SPCK, 1991.

Hanson, R. Karl, and S. Slater. "Sexual Victimization in the History of Child Sexual Abusers: A Review." *Annals of Sex Research* 1 (1988) 485–499.

———, and Monique T. Bussiere. "Predicting Relapse: A Meta-analysis of Sexual Offender Recidivism Studies." *Journal of Consulting and Clinical Psychology* 66 (1998) 348–362.

———. Stability and Change: Dynamic Risk Factors for Sexual Offenders." In *Sexual Offender Treatment*, edited by William L. Marshall et al., 17–31. New York, NY: Wiley, 2006.

———, and Kelly E. Morton-Bourgon. "The Accuracy of Recidivism Risk Assessments for Sexual Offenders: A Meta-Analysis of 118 Prediction Studies." *Psychological Assessment* 21 (2009) 1–21.

Hanson. et al., "The Principles of Effective Correctional Treatment Also Apply to Sexual Offenders: A Meta-Analysis." *Criminal Justice And Behavior* 36 (2009) 865–891.

Hardy, Marjorie S. "Physical Aggression and Sexual Behavior among Siblings: A Retrospective Study." *Journal of Family Violence* 16 (2001) 255–68.

Hargrave, Terry D. *Families and Forgiveness: Healing Wounds in the Intergenerational Family*. New York, NY: Brunner/Mazel, 1994.

Harrington, Daniel J., and James F. Keenan. *Jesus and Virtue Ethics: Building Bridges between New Testament Studies and Moral Theology*. New York, NY: Roman & Littlefield, 2002.

Harris, Andrew, et al. *Static-99 Coding Rules Revised 2003*. Ottawa: Public Safety Canada, 2003.

Harris, Chris. *Creating Relevant Rituals: Celebrations for Religious Education*. Newtown, Australia: E. J. Dwyer, 1992.

Harris, J. Irene et al. "Christian Religious Functioning and Trauma Outcomes." *Journal of Clinical Psychology* 64 (2008) 17–29.

Harris, Stephen. *The New Testament: A Student's Introduction*, 6th ed. Boston: McGraw Hill, 2009.

Hart, Archibald D. et al. *Secrets of Eve: Understanding the Mystery of Female Sexuality*. Nashville, TN: Word, 1998.

Harter, Susan. "The Effects of Child Abuse on the Self-System." In *Multiple Victimization of Children: Conceptual, Developmental, Research, and Treatment Issues*, edited by B. B. Robbie Rossman and Mindy S. Rosenberg, 147–170. New York, NY: Haworth Maltreatment and Trauma Press, 1998.

Hartman, Carol R., and Ann W. Burgess. "Sexual Abuse of Children." In *Child Maltreatment: Theory and Research on the Causes and Consequences of Child Abuse and Neglect*, edited by Dante Cicchetti and Vicki Carlson, 98–128. Cambridge: Cambridge University Press, 1989.

Hatzfeld, J. *Machete Season: The Killers in Rwanda Speak*. New York, NY: Farrar, Straus & Giroux, 2006.

Haugen, Gary A. *Good News about Injustice: A Witness of Courage in a Hurting World*. Downers Grove, IL: IVP Books, 2009.

Hawkins, J. "Rowers on the River Styx: An Interview with Dr. Judith Herman." *Harvard Magazine* 91 (1991) 43–52.

Haydon, Abigail A., et al. "Childhood Abuse and Neglect and the Risk of STDs In Early Adulthood." *Perspectives on Sexual & Reproductive Health* 43 (2011) 16–22.

Hays, Richard B. *The Moral Vision of the New Testament: A Contemporary Introduction to New Testament Ethics*. San Francisco, CA: HarperSanFrancisco, 1996.

———. "The Letter to the Galatians: Introduction, Commentary, and Reflections." In *2 Corinthians, Galatians, Ephesians, Philippians, Colossians, 1 & 2 Thessalonians, 1 & 2 Timothy, Titus, Philemon. NIB* 11. Nashville, TN: Abingdon, 1997.

Hazlewood, Robert R., and Ann Wolbert Burgess. *Practical Aspects of Rape Investigation: A Multidisciplinary Approach, Practical Aspects of Criminal & Forensic Investigations.* New York, NY: Elselvier, 2008.

Hazzard, A., et al. "Factors Affecting Group Therapy Outcome for Adult Sexual Abuse Survivors." *International Journal of Group Psychotherapy* 43 (1993) 453–468.

Heath, Elaine. "The Levite's Concubine: Domestic Violence and the People of God." In *Priscilla Papers* 13 (1999) 10.

Hébert, Martine, et al. "Prevalence of Childhood Sexual Abuse and Timing of Disclosure in a Representative Sample of Adults from Quebec." *Canadian Journal of Psychiatry* 54 (2009) 631–636.

Hedges-Goettl, Len. *Sexual Abuse: Pastoral Responses.* ed. Daniel G. Bagby. Nashville, TN: Abingdon, 2004.

Heggen, Carolyn Holderread. *Sexual Abuse in Christian Homes and Churches.* Scottdale, PA: Herald Press, 1993.

Heim, C., et al. "Pituitary-Adrenal and Autonomic Responses to Stress in Women After Sexual and Physical Abuse in Childhood." *Journal of the American Medical Association* 284 (2000) 592–597.

Heimbach, Daniel R. *True Sexual Morality: Recovering Biblical Standards for a Culture in Crisis.* Wheaton, IL: Crossway Books, 2004.

Heiser, Michael S. "Divine Council." In *Dictionary of the Old Testament: Wisdom, Poetry and Writings*, edited by Tremper Longman III, Peter Enns, 112–116. Downers Grove, IL: InterVarsity, 2008.

Heitritter, L., and J. Vought. *Helping Victims of Sexual Abuse: A Sensitive Biblical Guide for Counselors, Victims, & Families.* Bloomington, MN: Bethany House, 2006.

Helm, Herbert W., et al. "The Implications of Conjunctive and Disjunctive Forgiveness for Sexual Abuse." *Pastoral Psychology* 54 (2005) 23–34.

Hendel, Ronald, Chana Kronfeld, and Ilana Pardes. "Gender and Sexuality." In *Reading Genesis: Ten Methods*, edited by Ronald Hendel, 71–91. Cambridge: Cambridge University Press, 2010.

Henderson, J. Frank. *Liturgies of Lament.* Chicago, IL: Liturgy Training, 1994.

Hengel, Martin. *Crucifixion in the Ancient World and the Folly of the Message of the Cross.* Philadelphia, PA: Fortress, 1977.

Herman, Judith L. "Discussion." In *Incest-Related Syndromes of Adult Psychopathology*, edited by R. Kluft, 289–293. Washington, D.C.: American Psychiatric Press, 1990.

———. "Complex PTSD: A Syndrome in Survivors of Prolonged and Repeated Trauma." In *Psychotraumatology: Key Papers and Core Concepts in Post-traumatic Stress*, edited by George S. Everly, Jr., and Jeffery M. Lating, 87–102. New York, NY: Plenum Press, 1995.

———. *Trauma and Recovery: The Aftermath of Violence—From Domestic Abuse to Political Terror.* New York, NY: Basic Books, 1997.

———. *Father-Daughter Incest.* Rev. ed. Cambridge, MA: Harvard University Press, 2000.

Herman, Steve. "The Role of Corroborative Evidence in Child Sexual Abuse Evaluations." *Journal of Investigative Psychology & Offender Profiling* 7 (2010) 189–212.

Hermisson, Hans-Jürgen. "Observations on the Creation Theology in Wisdom." In *Creation in the Old Testament*, edited by Bernhard W. Anderson, 118–134. Issues in Religion and Theology 6. Philadelphia, PA: Fortress, 1984.

Herring, Stephen L. "A 'Transubstantiated' Humanity: The Relationship between the Divine Image and the Presence of God in Genesis 1:26f." *Vetus Testamentum* 58 (2008) 480–494.

Hess, Kathryn D., and Paul Brinson. "Mediating Domestic Law Issues." In *The Handbook of Forensic Psychology*, 2d ed, edited by Allen K. Hess and Irving B. Weiner, 63–103. New York, NY: Wiley, 1999.

Herman, Judith. *Trauma and Recovery.* New York, NY: Basic, 1992.

Heschel, Abraham J. "The Mystical Element in Judaism." In *Understanding Rabbinic Judaism: From Talmudic to Modern Times*, edited by Jacob Neusner, 279–300. New York, NY: Ktav, 1974.

Hess, Richard. "Adam." In *Dictionary of the Old Testament: Pentateuch*, edited by T. Desmond Alexander and David W. Baker, 18–21. Downers Grove, IL: InterVarsity, 2003.

Hicks, Peter. *The Message of Evil and Suffering*, edited by Derek Tidball. The Bible Speaks Today. Downers Grove, IL: IVP, 2006.

Hiebert, Theodore. "Creation." In *The New Interpreter's Dictionary of the Bible, A-C*, 780–788. Nashville, TN: Abingdon, 2006.

Hilkert Andolsen, Barbara. "Agape in Feminist Ethics." *The Journal of Religious Ethics* 9 (1981) 69–83.

Hill, Catherine and Elena Silva. *Drawing the Line: Sexual Harassment on Campus*. Washington, DC: American Association of University Women Educational Foundation, 2005.

Hindman, J., and J. Peters. "Polygraph Testing Leads to Better Understanding Adult and Juvenile Sex Offenders." *Federal Probation* 65 (2001) 8–15.

Hobbs, Christopher J., et al. *Child Abuse and Neglect: A Clinician's Handbook*. Edinburg: Churchill Livingstone, 1993.

Hobfoll, S. E., et al. "The Impact of Perceived Child Physical and Sexual Abuse History on Native American Women's Psychological Well-being and AIDS Risk." *Journal of Consulting and Clinical Psychology* 70 (2002) 252–257.

Hodges, Elizabeth A., and Jane E. Myers. "Counseling Adult Women Survivors of Childhood Sexual Abuse: Benefits of a Wellness Approach." *Journal of Mental Health and Counseling* 32 (2010) 139–153.

Hoekema, Anthony A. *Created in God's Image*. Grand Rapids, MI: Eerdmans, 1986.

Holcomb, Lindsey A., et al. *Rid of My Disgrace: Hope and Healing for Victims of Sexual Assault*. Wheaton, IL: Crossway, 2001.

Holderread-Heggen, Carolyn. *Sexual Abuse in Christian Homes and Churches*. Scottdale, PA: Herald Press, 1993.

Hollinger, Dennis P. *The Meaning of Sex: Christian Ethics and the Moral Life*. Grand Rapids, MI: Baker, 2009.

Hollingsworth, Jan. *Unspeakable Acts: The True Story of One Community's Nightmare*. New York, NY: Congdon & Weed, 1988.

Holmes, W. C. "Association between a History of Childhood Sexual Abuse and Subsequent, Adolescent Psychoactive Substance Use Disorder in a Sample of HIV Seropositive Men." *Journal of Adolescent Health* 20 (1997) 414–419.

———, and G. B. Slap. "Sexual Abuse of Boys: Definition, Prevalence, Correlates, Sequelae, and Management." *Journal of the American Medical Association* 280 (1998) 1855–1862.

Hooper, Carol-Ann. *Mothers Surviving Child Sexual Abuse*. New York, NY: Routledge, 1992.

———, and Catharine Humphreys. "What's in a Name—Reflections on the Term 'Non-Abusing Parent.'" *Child Abuse Review* 6 (1997) 298–303.

Horton, Anne L. "Practical Guidelines for Professionals Working with Religious Spousal Abuse Survivors." In *Abuse and Religion: When Praying Isn't Enough*, edited by Anne L. Horton and J. A. Williamson, 94. Lexington, KY: Lexington Books, 1988.

Horton, C. B. and T. K. Cruise. "Sexual Abuse." In *Children's Needs III: Development, Prevention, & Intervention*, edited by G. Bears and K. Minke, 821–833. Bethesda, MD: NASP Publications, 2006.

Hotz, Kendra, and Matthew Matthews. *Shaping the Christian Life: Worship and the Religious Affections*. Louisville, KY: Westminster John Knox, 2006.

House, Paul R. "Biblical Theology and the Wholeness of Scripture: Steps Toward a Program for the Future." In *Biblical Theology: Retrospect and Prospect*, edited by Scott J. Hafemann, 267–279. Downers Grove, IL: InterVarsity, 2002.

Howells, K. "Child Sexual Abuse: Finkelhor's Precondition Model Revisited." *Crime & Law* 1 (1994) 201–214.

Hunt, Laura. "Missions in the Context of Recovery from Childhood Sexual Abuse." *Missiology* 38 (2010) 321–333.

Hunter, Mic. *Abused Boys: The Neglected Victims of Sexual Abuse*. New York, NY: Fawcett Columbine, 1990.

Hunter, Sally V. "Evolving Narratives about Childhood Sexual Abuse: Challenging the Dominance of the Victim and Survivor Paradigm." *Australian & New Zealand Journal of Family Therapy* 31 (2010) 176–190.

Ipsen, Avaren. *Sex Working and the Bible*. London: Equinox, 2009.

Isley, Paul. "Child Sexual Abuse and the Catholic Church: An Historical and Contemporary Review." *Pastoral Psychology* 45 (1997) 277–299.

Jacobs, Janet. "Religious Ritual and Mental Health." In *Religion and Mental Health*, edited by John Schumaker, 291–99. Oxford: Oxford, 1992.

Jacoby, Mario. *Individuation and Narcissism: The Psychology of Self in Jung and Kohut.* London: Routledge, 1990.

Jackson, Joan L., et al. "Young Adult Women Who Report Childhood Intrafamilial Sex Abuse: Subsequent Adjustment." *Archives of Sexual Behavior* 19 (1990) 211–221.

Jackson, Lisa A., and John S. March. "Post-traumatic Stress Disorder." In *Anxiety Disorders in Children and Adolescents*, edited by John S. March, 276–300. Cambridge, MA: Harvard University Press, 1995.

Jansen, Melanie. *From the Darkest Night: Meditations for Abuse Survivors.* Grand Rapids: Faith Alive/CRC, 2001.

Jenkins, Alan. *Invitations To Responsibility: The Therapeutic Engagement of Men Who are Violent and Abusive.* Adelaide, Australia: Dulwich Centre, 1990.

Jenson, Robert. "Cruel to Be Hard: Men and Pornography." *Sexual Assault Report.* January/February 2004.

Jespersen, Ashley F., et al. "Sexual Abuse History among Adult Sex Offenders and Non-Sex Offenders: A Meta-Analysis." *Child Abuse and Neglect* 33 (2009) 179–192.

Jewkes, Rachel et al. *Understanding Men's Health and Use of Violence: The Interface of Rape and HIV in South Africa.* Pretoria, South Africa: Medical Research Council, 2009.

Jinich, S., et al. "Childhood Sexual Abuse and HIV Risk-Taking Behavior among Gay and Bisexual Men." *AIDS Behavior* 2 (1998) 41–51.

Jobes, Karen H. *Esther.* NIV Application Commentary. Grand Rapids, MI: Zondervan, 1999.

John Jay College of Criminal Justice. *The Nature and Scope of the Problem of Sexual Abuse of Minors by Catholic Priests and Deacons in the United States.* Washington, DC: United States Conference of Catholic Bishops, 2004.

Johnson, David, and Jeff VanVonderen. *The Subtle Power of Spiritual Abuse.* Minneapolis, MN: Bethany, 1991.

Johnson, Dawn M., et al. "Factors Predicting PTSD, Depression, and Dissociative Severity in Female Treatment-Seeking Childhood Sexual Abuse Survivors." *Child Abuse & Neglect* 25 (2001) 179–98.

Johnson, Eric L. *Foundations for Soul Care.* Downers Grove, IL: InterVarsity, 2007.

Johnson, Janis Tyler. *Mothers of Incest Survivors: Another Side of the Story.* Bloomington, IN: Indiana University Press, 1992.

Johnson, R. L. & D. K. Shrier. "Sexual Victimization of Boys: Experience at an Adolescent Medicine Clinic." *Journal of Adolescent Health Care* 6 (1985) 372–376.

Johnson, Susan M. *Emotionally Focused Couple Therapy with Trauma Survivors: Strengthening Attachment Bonds.* New York, NY: The Guilford Press, 2002.

Johnson, T. C. *Understanding Children's Sexual Behaviors—What's Natural and Healthy.* South Pasadena, CA: Author, 1998.

Jones, Beth Felker. *Marks of His Wounds: Gender Politics and Bodily Resurrection.* New York, NY: Oxford University Press, 2007.

Jones, L., D. Finkelhor, and K. Kopiec. "Why is Child Sexual Abuse Declining?" *Child Abuse and Neglect* 25 (2001) 1139–58.

Jones, Gregory. *Embodying Forgiveness: A Theological Analysis.* Grand Rapids, MI: Eerdmans, 1995.

Jones, Stanton L., and Mark A. Yarhouse. *Homosexuality: The Use of Scientific Research in the Church's Moral Debate.* Downers Grove, IL: InterVarsity Press, 2000.

———, and Mark A. Yarhouse. *Ex-Gays? A Longitudinal Study of Religiously-Mediated Change in Sexual Orientation.* Downers Grove, IL: InterVarsity Press, 2007.

Justice, B., and R. Justice. *The Abusing Family.* New York, NY: Plenum Press, 1990.

Justice, William, and Warren Lambert. "A Comparative Study of the Language People Use to Describe the Personalities of God and Their Earthly Parents." *Journal of Pastoral Care* 40 (1986) 166–172.

Kalichman, Seth C., et al. "Trauma Symptoms, Sexual Behaviors, and Substance Abuse: Correlates of Childhood Sexual Abuse and HIV Risks among Men Who Have Sex with Men." *Journal of Child Sexual Abuse* 13 (2004) 1–15.

Kallstrom-Fuqua, A. C., et al. "Childhood and Adolescent Sexual Abuse of Community Women: Mediated Effects on Psychological Distress and Social Relationships." *Journal of Consulting and Clinical Psychology* 72 (2004) 980–992.

Kamitsuka, Margaret D. (Ed.). *The Embrace of Eros, Bodies, Desires, and Sexuality in Christianity.* Minneapolis, MN: Fortress, 2010.

Bibliography

Kane, Donna. "Women Survivors of Father-Figure Incest: Implications on their View of God." PhD diss., Maryland: Loyola College, 1990.

———. "Perception of God by Survivors of Childhood Sexual Abuse: An Exploratory Study in an Underresearched Area." *Journal of Psychology and Theology* 21 (1992) 228–237.

Kane, Michael N. "A Qualitative Survey of the Attitudes of Catholic Priests toward Bishops and Ministry Following the Sexual Abuse Revelations of 2002." *Pastoral Psychology* 57 (2008) 183–198.

Kapp, C. "Rape on Trial in South Africa." *The Lancet* 367 (2006) 718–719.

Käsemann, Ernst. *New Testament Questions of Today.* trans. W. J. Montague. London: SCM Press, 1969.

Kaufman, Gershen. *Shame: The Power of Caring.* 3rd ed. rev. & expanded. Rochester, VT: Schenkman, 1992.

———. "Men's Shame." In *Men Healing Shame: An Anthology,* edited by Roy U. Schenk and John Everingham, 31–49. New York, NY: Springer, 1995.

———, and Robert Bly. "Healing Internalized Shame." In *Mean Healing Shame,* edited by Roy U. Schenk and John Everingham. New York, NY: Springer, 1995.

Katz, Sedelle and Mary Ann Mazur. *Understanding the Rape Victim: A Synthesis of Research Findings.* New York, NY: John Wiley & Sons, 1979.

Kearney, R. Timothy. *Caring for Sexually Abused Children: A Handbook for Families and Churches.* Downers Grove, IL: InterVarsity, 2001.

Keefe, Alice A. "Rapes of Women/Wars of Men." *Semeia* 61 (1993) 90

Keenan, James F. "Contemporary Contributions to Sexual Ethics." *Theological Studies* 71 (2010) 148–167.

Keene, Frederick W. "Structures of Forgiveness in the New Testament." In *Violence Against Women and Children: A Christian Theological Sourcebook,* edited by Carol J. Adams and Marie M. Fortune, 121–134. New York, NY: Continuum, 1995.

Keene, Jane. *A Winter's Song: A Liturgy for Women Seeking Healing from Sexual Abuse in Childhood.* New York, NY: Pilgrim, 1991.

Keener, Craig S. "Some Biblical Reflections on Justice, Rape, and an Insensitive Society." In *Women, Abuse, and the Bible: How the Scripture Can Be Used To Hurt or To Heal,* edited by Catherine Clark Kroeger and James R. Beck, 117–130. Grand Rapids: Baker, 1996.

Kelly, Annie. "Raped and Killed for Being a Lesbian: South Africa Ignores 'Corrective' Attacks." *The Guardian.* March 12, 2009.

Kelly, Diann Cameron, and Elizabeth Palley. "Severe Sexual Maltreatment & Social Inclusion: A Case Study on Insecure Attachment." *Journal of Pastoral Counseling* 43 (2008) 79–92.

Kelly, Liz. *Surviving Sexual Abuse.* Minneapolis, MN: University of Minnesota, 1988.

Kelly, R. J., et al. "Effects of Mother-son Incest and Positive Perceptions of Sexual Abuse Experiences on the Psychosocial Adjustment of Clinic-referred Men." *Child Abuse and Neglect* 26 (2002) 425–442.

Kendall, K. A., et al. "Impact of Sexual Abuse on Children: A Review and Synthesis of Recent Empirical Studies." *Psychological Bulletin* 11 (1993) 164–180.

Kendall-Tackett, K., et al. "Impact of Sexual Abuse on Children: A Review and Synthesis of Recent Empirical Studies." *Psychological Bulletin* 113 (1993) 164–180.

Kennedy, Philip. *Deus Humanissimus: The Knowability of God in the Theology of Edward Schillenbeecks.* Fribourg: Fribourg University Press, 1993.

Keshgegian, Flora. *Redeeming Memories.* Nashville, TN: Abingdon Press, 2000.

Kessler, John. "Sexuality and Politics: The Motif of the Displaced Husband in the Books of Samuel." *Catholic Biblical Quarterly* 62 (2000) 409–423.

Kessler, M. R. H., et al. "Group Treatments for Women Sexually Abused as Children: A Review of the Literature and Recommendations for Future Outcome Research." *Child Abuse and Neglect* 27 (2003) 1045–1061.

Kia-Keating, Maryam, Lynn Sorsoli, and Frances Grossman. "Relational Challenges and Recovery Processes in Male Survivors of Childhood Sexual Abuse." *Journal of Interpersonal Violence* 25 (2010) 666–683.

Kilner, John F. "Humanity in God's Image: Is the Image Really Damaged?" *Journal of the Evangelical Theological Society* 53 (2010) 601–617.

Kim, Kihyun, et al. "Childhood Experiences of Sexual Abuse and Later Parenting Practices among Non-Offending Mothers of Sexually Abused and Comparison Girls." *Child Abuse & Neglect* 34 (2010) 610–622.

King, N. J., et al. "Sexually Abused Children Suffering for Post-Traumatic Stress Disorder: Assessment and Treatment Strategies." *Cognitive Behavior Therapy* 32 (2003) 2–12.

Kingston, D. A., et al. "The Importance of Individual Differences in Pornography Use: Theoretical Perspectives and Implications for Treating Sexual Offenders." *Journal of Sex Research* 46 (2009) 216–232.

Kingston, S., and C. Raghavan. "The Relationship of Sexual Abuse, Early Initiation of Substance Use, and Adolescent Trauma to PTSD." *Journal of Traumatic Stress* 22 (2009) 65–68.

Kinnear, Karen L. *Childhood Sexual Abuse: A Reference Handbook.* Santa Barbara, CA: ABC-CLIO, 1995.

Kirk-Duggan, Cheryl A. "Slingshots, Ships, and Personal Psychosis: Murder, Sexual Intrigue, and Power in the Lives of David and Othello." In *Pregnant Passion: Gender, Sex, and Violence in the Bible*, 37–70. Semeia Studies 44. Atlanta, GA: Society of Biblical Literature, 2003.

Kiselica, Mark S., and Mandy Morrill-Richards. "Sibling Maltreatment: The Forgotten Abuse." *Journal of Counseling and Development* 85 (2007) 148–160.

Kleber, Rolf, et al, eds. *Beyond Trauma: Cultural and Societal Dynamics.* New York, NY: Plenum Press, 1995.

Klein, Lillian R. "Bathsheba Revealed." In *Samuel and Kings: A Feminist Companion to the Bible*, edited by Athalya Brenner, 47–64. FCB 2/7. Sheffield: Sheffield Academic Press, 2000.

Klein, Richard. *'If It Feels Good, Don't Do It.'* A Review of David Shaw's *The Pleasure Police: How Bluenose Busybodies and Lily-Livered Alarmists are Taking All the Fun Out of Life.* New York, NY: Doubleday, 1996.

Klingbeil, Gerald A. "Between 'I' and 'We': The Anthropology of the Hebrew Bible and Its Importance for a 21st-Century Ecclesiology." *Bulletin for Biblical Research* 19 (2009) 319–33.

Klug, Ron. *How to Keep a Spiritual Journal.* Minneapolis, MN: Augsburg Books, 1993.

Koenig, Linda J., et al (eds.). "From Child Sexual Abuse to Adult Sexual Risk: Trauma, Revictimization, and Intervention." Washington, DC: American Psychological Association Press, 2003.

———, (ed). *From Child Sexual Abuse to Adult Sexual Risk: Trauma, Revictimization, and Intervention.* Washington, DC: American Psychological Association, 2004.

Kolko, D. J., et al. "Children's Perceptions of Their Abusive Experience: Measurement and Preliminary Findings." *Child Maltreatment* 7 (2002) 42–55.

Koren-Karie, Nina, David Oppenheim, and Rachel Getzler-Josef. "Mothers Who Were Severely Abused During Childhood and their Children Talk About Emotions: Co-Construction of Narratives in Light of Maternal Trauma." *Infant Mental Health Journal* 25 (2004) 300–317.

Koskenniemi, Erkki. *The Exposure of Infants among Jews and Christians in Antiquity.* The Social World of Biblical Antiquity, 4. Sheffield: Sheffield Phoenix Press, 2009.

Koss, M. P., et al. "Cognitive Mediation of Rape's Mental, Physical, and Social Health Impact: Test of Four Models in Cross-Sectional Data." *Journal of Counseling and Clinical Psychology* 70 (2002) 926–941.

Krahé, Barbara. "Child Sexual Abuse and Revictimization in Adolescence and Adulthood." In *Post-traumatic Stress Theory*, edited by Jon Harvey and Brian Pauwels, 49–66. Philadelphia, PA: Brunner/Mazel, 2000.

Kramer, J. *Family Interfaces: Transgenerational Patterns.* New York, NY: Brunner/Mazel, 1985.

Kreklewetz, C., and C. Piotrowski. "Incest Survivor Mothers: Protecting the Next Generation." *Child Abuse and Neglect* 22 (1998) 1305–1312.

Kretzschmar, Louise. "Women and Children in Africa: A Theological-Ethical Analysis of a Path Beyond Exploitation." *Perspectives in Religious Studies* 36 (2009) 217–231.

Kristof, Nicholas D. "After Wars, Mass Rapes Persist." *New York Times*, May 21, 2009.

Kuan, K. Jeffrey. "Configurations of Rape: Some Issues for Conversation." *Reviews in Religion and Theology* 17 (2010) 256–260.

Kübler-Ross, Elisabeth. *On Death and Dying.* New York, NY: Macmillan Publishing, 1969.

Kuehnle, Kathryn. "Child Sexual Abuse Evaluations." In *Handbook of Psychology, Volume 11 Forensic Psychology*, edited by Alan M. Goldstein and Irving B. Weiner, 437–439. New York, NY: Wiley, 2003.

Kushner, Harold S. *When Bad Things Happen to Good People.* New York, NY: Avon Books, 1983.

La Fontaine, Jean. *Child Sexual Abuse.* Oxford: Polity Press, 1990.

Lalor, Kevin, and Rosaleen McElvaney. "Child Sexual Abuse, Links to Later Sexual Exploitation/High-Risk Sexual Behavior, and Prevention/Treatment Programs." *Trauma, Violence & Abuse* 11 (2010) 159–177.

Lalumière, Martin L., et al. *The Causes of Rape: Understanding Individual Differences in Male Propensity of Sexual Aggression.* Washington, DC: American Psychological Association, 2005.

Lambert, Michael J., and Benjamin M. Ogles. "The Efficacy and Effectiveness of Psychotherapy." In *Bergin and Garfield's Handbook of Psychotherapy and Behavior Change*, 5th ed., edited by Michael J. Lambert, 139–193. New York, NY: Wiley, 2004.

Lang, Ariel J., et al. "Impact of Maternal Child Abuse on Parenting an Infant Temperament." *Journal of Child and Adolescent Psychiatric Nursing* 23 (2010) 100–110.

Langberg, Diane Mandt. *On the Threshold of Hope: Opening the Door to Healing for Survivors of Sexual Abuse.* Wheaton, IL, Tyndale House: 1999.

———. *Counseling Survivors of Sexual Abuse.* Longwood, FL: Xulon Press, 2003.

Langan, Patrick, and Caroline Wolf Harlow. "Child Rape Victims, 1992." *Crime Data Brief,* US Department of Justice. Office of Justice Programs, Bureau of Justice Statistics, 1994.

Lange, Dirk G. "Trauma Theory and Liturgy: A Disruption of Ritual." *Liturgical Ministry* 17 (2008) 127–132.

———. *Trauma Recalled: Liturgy, Disruption, and Theology.* Philadelphia, PA: Fortress, 2009.

Langevin, R., et al. "Are Incestuous Fathers Pedophilic and Aggressive?" In *Erotic Preference, Gender Identity and Aggression,* edited by R. Langevin. New York, NY: Erlbaum Associates, 1983.

Lasine, S. "Guest and Host in Judges 19: Lot's Hospitality in an Inverted World." *Journal for the Study of the Old Testament* 29 (1984) 37–41.

Lauck, Jennifer. *Blackbird: A Childhood Lost and Found.* New York, NY: Pocket Books, 2001.

Lauer, Teresa M. *The Truth About Rape: Emotional, Spiritual, Physical, and Sexual Recovery from Rape.* Gold River, CA: Raperecovery.com, 2002.

Laumann, E. O., et al. *The Social Organization of Sexuality: Sexual Practices in the United States.* Chicago and London: The University of Chicago Press, 1994.

Lavin, Michael. "Voyeurism: Psychopathology and Theory." In *Sexual Deviance: Theory, Assessment, and Treatment.* 2nd Edition, edited by D. Richard Laws and William T. O'Donohue, 305–319. New York, NY: The Guilford Press, 2008.

Laws, D. Richard. "Central Elements in Relapse Prevention Procedures with Sex Offenders." *Psychology, Crime & Law* 2 (1995) 41–53.

———. "The Public Health Approach." In *Sexual Deviance: Theory, Assessment, and Treatment,* 2nd Edition, edited by D. Richard Laws and William T. O'Donohue, 611–628. New York, NY: The Guilford Press, 2008.

Leahy, T. et al. "Child Sexual Abuse Narratives in Clinically and Nonclinically Distressed Adult Survivors." *Professional Psychology Research and Practice* 34 (2003) 657–665.

Leehan, James. *Defiant Hope: Spirituality for Survivors of Family Abuse.* Louisville, KY: Westminster/John Knox, 1993.

Lees, Susan. *Carnal Knowledge: Rape on Trial.* London: H. Hamilton, 1996.

Lemelin, R. Harvey. "Running to Stand Still: The Story of a Victim, A Survivor, a Wounded Healer—A Narrative of Male Sexual Abuse from the Inside." *Journal of Loss & Trauma* 11 (2006) 337–350.

Lemieux, S. R., and E. S. Byers. "The Sexual Well-being of Women Who Have Experienced Child Sexual Abuse." *Psychology of Women Quarterly* 32 (2008) 126–144.

Lemoncelli, John, and Andrew Carey. "The Psychospiritual Dynamics of Adult Survivors of Abuse." *Counseling and Values* 40 (1996) 175–185.

Lenderking, William R., et al. "Childhood Sexual Abuse Among Homosexual Men: Prevalence Associated with Unsafe Sex." *Journal of General Internal Medicine* 12 (1997) 250–253.

LenkaBula, Puleng. "From the Womb into a Hostile World: Christian Ethics and Sexual Abuse against Children in South Africa." *Journal of Theology for Southern Africa* 114 (2002) 55–68.

Leonard, Leah M, et al. "Sexual Functioning and Sexual Satisfaction among Women Who Report a History of Childhood and/or Adolescent Sexual Abuse." *Journal of Sex & Marital Therapy* 34 (2008) 375–384.

Leserman, Jane. "Sexual Abuse History: Prevalence, Health Effects, Mediators, and Psychological Treatment." *Psychosomatic Medicine* 67 (2005) 906–915.

Leslie, Kristen J. *When Violence Is No Stranger: Pastoral Counseling with Survivors of Acquaintance Rape.* Minneapolis, MN: Fortress, 2003.

Lester, Andrew D. *Anger: Discovering Your Spiritual Ally.* Louisville, KY: Westminster John Knox, 2007.

Leupp, Roderick T. *The Renewal of Trinitarian Theology: Themes, Patterns and Explorations.* Downers Grove, IL: InterVarsity Press, 2008.

Lev-Wiesel, Rachel, Marianne Amir, and Avi Besser. "Posttraumatic Growth among Female Survivors of Childhood Abuse in Relation to the Perpetrator Identity." *Journal of Loss & Trauma* 10 (2005) 7–17.

Levendosky, Alytia, et al. "Parenting in Battered Women: The Effects of Domestic Violence on Women and Their Children." *Journal of Family Violence* 16 (2001) 171–192.

Levenson, Jill S., et al., "Perceptions of Sex Offenders about Treatment: Satisfaction and Engagement in Group Therapy." *Sexual Abuse: A Journal of Research And Treatment* 21 (2009) 35–56.

Levenson, Jon D., and Baruch Halpern. "The Political Import of David's Marriages." *Journal of Biblical Literature* 99 (1980) 507–518.

———. "Genesis: Introduction." In *The Jewish Study Bible: Torah, Nevi'im, Kethuvim*, edited by Adele Berlin and Marc Zvi Brettler, 8–11. New York, NY: Oxford University Press, 2004.

Levin, Diane E., and Jean Kilbourne. *So Sexy So Soon: The New Sexualized Childhood and What Parents Can Do to Protect Their Kids.* New York, NY: Ballantine Books, 2008.

Levitt, Laura, and Sue Ann Wasserman. "*Mikvah* Ceremony for Laura." In *Confronting Rape and Sexual Assault*, edited by Mary E. Odem and Jody Clay-Warner, 25–31. Wilmington, DE: Scholarly Resources, 1998.

Lev-Wiesel, R. "Quality of Life in Adult Survivors of Childhood Sexual Abuse Who Have Undergone Therapy." *Journal of Child Sexual Abuse* 9 (2000) 1–13.

Lew, Mike, et al. *Victims No Longer: The Classic Guide for Men Recovering from Sexual Child Abuse.* Revised and Updated. New York, NY: HarperCollins, 2004.

Lewis, C. S. *The Problem of Pain.* New York, NY: Simon and Schuster, 1978.

Lile, Sherry, et al. "Counting the Cost: Caregiver Issues." In *In Hands That Heal: International Curriculum for Training Caregivers of Trafficking Survivors—Academic Edition*, edited by Beth Grant and Cindy Lopez Hudlin, 290–324. Springfield, MO: Project Rescue International and FAAST, 2007.

Lindholm, K. J., and R. Willey. "Ethnic Differences in Child Abuse and Sexual Abuse." *Hispanic Journal of Behavioral Sciences* 8 (1986) 111–125.

Linehan, Marsha M. *Cognitive Behavioral Treatment of the Borderline Personality Disorder.* New York, NY: The Guilford Press, 1993.

Linley, P. Alex, Stephen Joseph. "Positive Change Following Trauma and Adversity: A Review." *Journal of Traumatic Stress* 17 (2004) 11–21.

Linnane, Brian F. "Celibacy and Sexual Malpractice: Dimensions of Power and Powerlessness in Patriarchal Society." In *Theology and the New Histories,* edited by Gary Macy, 227–244. Maryknoll, NY: Orbis, 1999.

———. "The Sexual Abuse Scandal in the Catholic Church: Implications for Sexual Ethics." In *A Just & True Love: Feminism at the Frontiers of Theological Ethics: Essays in Honor of Margaret A. Farley*, edited by Maura A. Ryan and Brian F. Linnane, S.J., 273–302. Notre Dame, IN: University of Notre Dame Press, 2007.

Linz, Daniel G., et al. "Effects of Long-Term Exposure to Violent and Sexually Degrading Depictions of Women." *Journal of Personality and Social Psychology* 55 (1988) 758–768.

Liotte, Giovanni. "Attachment and Dissociation." In *Dissociation and the Dissociative Disorders: DSM-V and Beyond*, edited by Paul F. Dell and John A. O'Neil, 53–65. New York, NY: Routledge, 2009.

Lipka, Hilary B. *Sexual Transgression in the Hebrew Bible.* Sheffield: Sheffield Phoenix Press, 2006.

Loader, William. *The Septuagint, Sexuality, and the New Testament: Case Studies in the Impact of the LXX in Philo and the New Testament.* Grand Rapids, MI: Eerdmans, 2004.

Logan, T. K., et al. *Women and Victimization: Contributing Factors, Interventions, and Implications.* Washington, DC: American Psychological Association, 2006.

———, et al. "Victimization Manifestations and Vulnerability Factors." In *Women and Victimization: Contributing Factors, Interventions, and Implications*, 17–49. Washington, DC: American Psychological Association, 2006.

———, et al. "Justice System Options and Responses." In *Women and Victimization: Contributing Factors, Interventions, and Implications*, 161–194. Washington, DC: American Psychological Association, 2006.

Lontes, L. A. *Child Abuse & Culture: Working with Diverse Families.* New York, NY: Guilford Press, 2005.

Loseke, Donileen, et al. (eds.). *Current Controversies on Family Violence,* 2d ed. Thousand Oaks, CA: Sage, 2005.

Lou, Mike. *Victims No Longer: Men Recovering from Incest and Other Sexual Child Abuse.* New York, NY: Harper & Row, 1990.

Luxenberg, Toni, et al. "Complex Trauma and Disorders of Extreme Stress (DESNOS) Diagnosis, Part One: Assessment." *Directions in Psychiatry* 21 (2001) 373–394.

Lyons-Ruth, Karlen and Deborah Block. "The Disturbed Caregiving System: Relations among Childhood Trauma, Maternal Caregiving, and Infant Affect and Attachment." *Infant Mental Health Journal* 17 (1996) 257–275.

———, et al. "From Infant Attachment Disorganization to Adult Dissociation: Relational Adaptations or Traumatic Experiences?" *Psychiatric Clinics of North America* 29 (2006) 63–86.

McAfee Brown, Robert. *Elie Wiesel: Messenger to All Humanity*. Notre Dame, IN: University of Notre Dame Press, 1983.

Mcann, Lisa, Laurie Anne Pearlman. "Vicarious Traumatization: A Framework for Understanding the Psychological Effects of Working with Victims." *Journal of Traumatic Stress* 3 (1990) 131–149.

Macchietto, John. "Aspects of Male Victimization and Female Aggression: Implications for Counseling Men." *Journal of Mental Health and Counseling* 14 (1992) 375–392.

MacIntosh, H. B., Susan M. Johnson. "Emotion Focused Therapy for Couples and Childhood Sexual Abuse Survivors." *Journal of Marital and Family Therapy* 34 (2008) 298–315.

MacMurray, John. *Self as Agent*. New York, NY: Humanity Press, 1991.

———. *Persons in Relation*. New York, NY: Humanity Press, 1999.

Maddock, James W. "Healthy Family Sexuality: Positive Principles for Educators and Clinicians." *Family Relations* 38 (1989) 130–136.

Maguth Nezu, Christine. "Social Problem-Solving Correlates of Sexual Deviancy and Aggression among Adult Child Molesters." *Journal of Sexual Aggression* 11 (2005) 27–36.

Mahoney, Patricia, et al. "Violence against Women by Intimate Relationship Partners." In *Sourcebook on Violence against Women*, edited by Claire M. Renzetti, et al, 143–178. Thousand Oaks, CA: Sage Publishers, 2001.

Maltas, Carolyn P. "Trauma Contagion in Partners of Survivors of Childhood Sexual Abuse." *American Journal of Orthopsychiatry* 65 (1995) 529–539.

Maltz, Wendy. "Sexual Healing from Sexual Abuse." *Siecus Report* 29 (2000) 17–23.

———. *The Sexual Healing Journey: A Guide for Survivors of Sexual Abuse*. New York, NY: HarperCollins, 2001.

———. "Treating the Sexual Intimacy Concerns of Sexual Abuse Survivors." *Sexual and Relationship Therapy* 17 (2002) 321–327.

———, et al.,. *Incest and Sexuality: A Guide to Understanding and Healing*. Lexington, MS: Lexington Books, 1987.

Manlowe, Jennifer L. *Faith Born of Seduction: Sexual Trauma, Body Image, and Religion*. New York, NY: New York University Press, 1995.

———. "Seduced by Faith: Sexual Traumas and Their Embodied Effects." In *Violence Against Women and Children: A Christian Theological Sourcebook*, edited by Carol J. Adams and Marie M. Fortune, 328–338. New York, NY: Continuum, 1998.

Mann, Ruth E., and Jo Shingler. "Schema-driven Cognition in Sexual Offenders: Theory, Assessment and Treatment." In *Sexual Offender Treatment*, edited by William L. Marshall, et al., 173–185. New York, NY: Wiley, 2006.

———, et al. "Voyeurism: Assessment and Treatment." *Sexual Deviance: Theory, Assessment, and Treatment*, 2nd ed., edited by D. Richard Laws and William T. O'Donohue, 320–355. New York, NY: The Guilford Press, 2008.

Manning, Doug. *Don't Take My Grief Away*. New York, NY: Harper & Row, 1979.

Margolin, Gayla and Elana B. Gordis. "The Effects of Family and Community Violence on Children." *Annual Review of Psychology* 51 (2000) 445–479.

Marques, Janice K., et al. "Preventing Relapse in Sex Offenders: What We learned From SOTEP's Experimental Treatment Program." In *Remaking Relapse Prevention with Sex Offenders: A Sourcebook*, edited by D. Richard Laws, Stephen M. Hudson, and Tony Ward, 321–339. Thousand Oaks, CA: Sage, 2000.

———, et al. "Effects of a Relapse Prevention Program on Sexual Recidivism: Final Results from California's Sex Offender Treatment and Evaluation Project (SOTEP)," *Sexual Abuse: A Journal of Research and Treatment* 17 (2005) 79–107.

Marshall, I. Howard. *New Testament Theology: Many Witnesses, One Gospel*. Downers Grove, IL: InterVarsity, 2004.

———. "Mutual Love and Submission in Marriage." In *Discovering Biblical Equality: Complementarity without Hierarchy*, edited by Ronald W. Pierce and Rebecca Merrill Groothuis, 186–204. Downers Grove, IL: InterVarsity, 2004.

Marshall, Peter. *The Prevalence of Convictions for Sexual Offending. Research Findings No. 55 Research and Statistics Directorate*. London: Home Office, 1997.

Marshall, William L., "The Use of Sexually Explicit Stimuli by Rapists, Child Molesters, and Nonoffenders." *The Journal of Sex Research* 25 (1988) 267–288.

———, and Howard E. Barbaree. "An Integrated Theory of Sexual Offending." In *Handbook of Sexual Assault: Issues, Theories, and Treatment of the Offender*, edited by William L. Marshall, et al., 363–385. New York, NY: Plenum Press, 1990.

———. "Current Status of North American Assessment and Treatment Programs for Sexual Offenders." *Journal of Interpersonal Violence* 14 (1999) 221–239.

———. "Diagnosing and Treating Sexual Offenders." In *The Handbook of Forensic Psychology*, 2d ed., edited by Allen K. Hess and Irving B. Weiner, 640–670. New York, NY: Wiley, 1999.

———, and D. R. Laws. "A Brief History of Behavioral and Cognitive Behavioral Approaches to Sexual Offender Treatment: Part 2. The Modern Era." *Sexual Abuse: Journal of Research and Treatment* 15 (2003) 93–120.

———, and G. A. Serran. "Current Issues in the Assessment and Treatment of Sexual Offenders." *Clinical Psychology and Psychotherapy* 7 (2000) 85–96.

Marshall, W. L. "Diagnostic Issues, Multiple Paraphilias, and Co-Morbid Disorders in Sexual Offenders: Their Incidence and Treatment." *Aggression and Violent Behavior* 12 (2007) 16–35.

Mart, Eric G. "Common Errors in the Assessment of Allegations of Child Sexual Abuse." *Journal of Psychiatry & Law* 38 (2010) 325–343.

Martin, Dale B. "Paul Without Passion: On Paul's Rejection of Desire in Sex and Marriage." In *Constructing Early Christian Families: Family as Social Reality and Metaphor*, edited by Halvor Moxnes, 201–215. New York, NY: Routledge, 1997.

Martin, Elaine K., et al. "A Review of Marital Rape." *Aggression and Violent Behavior* 12 (2007) 329–347.

———, et al. "A Review of Marital Rape." *Aggression and Violent Behavior* 12 (2007) 329–347.

Martsolf, Donna and Claire Draucker. "The Legacy of Childhood Sexual Abuse and Family Adversity." *Journal of Nursing Scholarship* 40 (2008) 333–340.

Marty, Martin. *Cry of Absence*. San Francisco, CA: Harper, 1983.

Mason, Mike. *The Mystery of Marriage: Meditations on the Miracle*. Colorado Springs, CO: Multnomah Books, 1985.

Masters, William, et al. *Human Sexuality*. Boston, MA: Little Brown, 1982.

Masterson, J. *The Narcissistic and Borderline Disorders*. New York, NY: Brunner/Mazel, 1981.

Matek, Ord. "Obscene Phone Callers." *Journal of Social Work and Human Sexuality* 7 (1988) 113–130.

Mather, C. L. *How Long Does it Hurt? A Guide to Recovering from Incest & Sexual Abuse for Teenagers, Their Friends, and Their Families-Revised Edition*. San Francisco, CA: Jossey-Bass, 2004.

Mathews, Kenneth A. *Genesis 1–11:26*, vol. 1. New American Commentary. Nashville, TN: Broadman and Holman, 1996.

Matsakis, Aphrodite. *The Rape Recovery Handbook: Step-by-Step Help for Survivors of Sexual Assault*. NP: New Harbinger Publications, 2003.

Matthews, Jane Kinder, et al. "Female Sexual Offenders: A Typology." In *Family Sexual Abuse: Frontline Research and Evaluation*, edited by Michael Quinn Patton, 199–219. Newbury Park, CA: Sage, 1991.

Matthews, V. H., and D. C. Benjamin. *The Social World of Ancient Israel 1250–587 B.C.E.* Peabody, MA: Hendrickson, 1993.

Matthews, Victor H. *Judges & Ruth*. New Cambridge Bible Commentary. Cambridge: Cambridge University Press, 2004.

Mazor, Aviva. "Relational Couple Therapy with Post-Traumatic Survivors: Links Between Post-Traumatic Self and Contemporary Intimate Relationships." *Contemporary Family Therapy* 26 (2004) 3–21.

McAlister, E. W. C. "Christian Counseling and Human Need." *Journal of Psychology and Christianity* 2 (1984) 50–60.

Bibliography

McBride, Jr., S. Dean. "Divine Protocol: Genesis 1:1–2:3 as Prologue to the Pentateuch." In *God Who Creates: Essays in Honor of W. Sibley Towner*, edited by W. P. Brown and S. D. McBride, Jr., 3–41. Grand Rapids, MI: Eerdmans, 2000.

McCall, Catherine. *When the Piano Stops: A Memoir of Healing from Sexual Abuse*. Berkeley, CA: Seal Press, 2009.

McCarty, L. "Mother-Child Incest: Characteristics of the Offender." *Child Welfare* 65 (1986) 447–458.

McConville, J. Gordon. "The Judgment of God in the Old Testament." *Ex auditu* 20 (2004) 25–42.

McCourt, Frank. *Angela's Ashes*. New York, NY: Scribner, 1999.

McCullough, Michael. E., Steven. J. Sandage, and Everett L. Worthington. *To Forgive is Human: How to Put Your Past in the Past*. Downers Grove, IL: InterVarsity Press, 1997.

———. et al. Everett L. Worthington, and K. C. Rachal. "Interpersonal Forgiving in Close Relationships." *Journal or Personality and Social Psychology* 2 (1997) 321–336.

McDarg, John. "Desire, Domination, and the Life and Death of the Soul." In *On Losing the Soul: Essays in the Social Psychology of Religion*, edited by Richard K. Fenn and Donald Capps. Albany, NY: State University of New York Press, 1995.

McElroy, Wendy. "Spousal Rape Case Sparks Old Debate." Fox News Story, February 16, 2005.

McFadyen, Alistair I. *The Call to Personhood: A Christian Theory of the Individual in Social Relationships*. Cambridge: Cambridge University Press, 1990.

———. *Bound to Sin: Abuse, Holocaust and the Christian Doctrine of Sin*. Cambridge: Cambridge University Press, 2000.

McFague, Sallie. "God as Mother." In *Weaving the Visions: New Patterns in Feminist Spirituality*, edited by Judith Plaskow and Carol P. Christ, 139–150. New York, NY: Harper and Row, 1989.

McFarlane, Alexander C. (ed). "Trauma and Its Challenge to Society." In *Traumatic Stress: The Effects of Overwhelming Experience on Mind, Body, and Society*, edited by Bessel A. van der Kolk et al., 24–46. New York, NY: The Guilford Press, 2006.

McFarlane, J., and A. Malecha. *Sexual Assault among Intimates: Frequency, Consequences and Treatments*. Washington, DC: Department of Justice, 2005.

McGee, R. et al. "Multiple Maltreatment, Attribution of Blame and Adjustment among Adolescents." *Development and Psychopathology* 13 (2001) 827–846.

McGrath-Merkle, Clare. "Generativity and the U.S. Roman Catholic Bishops' Responses to Priests' Sexual Abuse of Minors." *Journal of Religion and Health* 49 (2010) 73–87.

McGregor, Kim, et al. "Health Professionals' Responses to Disclosure of Child Sexual Abuse History: Female Child Sexual Abuse Survivors' Experiences." *Journal of Child Sexual Abuse* 19 (2010) 239–254.

McGrew Bennett, Anne. "Overcoming the Biblical and Traditional Subordination of Women." In *Feminist Theological Ethics: A Reader*, edited by Lois K. Daly, 135–145. Louisville, KY: Westminster John Knox Press, 1994.

McMinn, Mark. *Sin and Grace in Christian Counseling*. Downers Grove, IL: InterVarsity, 2008.

McKnight, Scot. *1 Peter*. NIV Application Commentary. Grand Rapids, MI: Zondervan, 1996.

McRay, B. W., et al. "What Evangelical Pastors Want to Know About Psychology." *Journal of Psychology & Theology* 29 (2001) 99–105.

Mead, Beverly F. "Coping with Obscene Phone Calls." *Medical Aspects of Human Sexuality* 9 (1975) 127–128.

Mead, James K. *Biblical Theology: Issues, Methods, and Themes*. Louisville, KY: Westminster John Knox, 2007.

Means, J. Jeffery. *Trauma and Evil: Healing the Wounded Soul*. Minneapolis, MN: Fortress Press, 2000.

Medrano, M. A., et al. "Childhood Trauma and Adult Prostitution in a Multiethnic Heterosexual Drug-using Population." *American Journal of Drug and Alcohol Abuse* 29 (1003) 463–486.

Meiselman, Karin C. *Incest: A Psychological Study of Causes and Effects with Treatment Recommendations*. San Francisco, CA: Jossey-Bass, 1978.

———. *Resolving the Trauma of Incest: Reintegration Therapy with Survivors*. San Francisco, CA: Jossey-Bass, 1990.

Melchert, T. "Clarifying the Effects of Parental Substance Abuse, Child Sexual Abuse and Parental Care Giving on Adult Adjustment." *Professional Psychology Research and Practice* 31 (2000) 64–69.

Melroy, J. Reid. "Pathologies of Attachment, Violence, and Criminality." In *Handbook of Psychology, Volume 11 Forensic Psychology*, edited by Alan M. Goldstein and Irving B. Weiner, 509–526. New York, NY: Wiley, 2003.

Mendel, Matthew Parynik. *The Male Survivor: The Impact of Sexual Abuse.* Thousand Oaks, CA: Sage, 1995.

Mendelson, Eric. "How Relevant an Issue is 'Anti-Male Sexism'?" *Standing Committee for Men Newsletter* 9 (1990) 3–5. Alexandria, VA: Amer. Coll. Personnel Assoc.

Mennen, Ferol E., and Diane Meadow. "The Relationship of Abuse Characteristics to Symptoms in Sexually Abused Girls." *Journal of Interpersonal Violence* 10 (1995) 259–274.

Menninger, Karl. *Whatever Became of Sin?* New York, NY: Hawthorn Books, 1972.

Merrill, L. L., et al. "Child Sexual Abuse and Number of Sexual Partners in Young Women: The Role of Abuse Severity, Coping Style and Sexual Functioning." *Journal of Consulting and Clinical Psychology* 71 (2003) 987–996.

Messler Davies, Jody and Mary Gail Frawley. *Treating the Adult Survivor of Childhood Sexual Abuse: A Psychoanalytic Perspective.* New York, NY: Basic Books, 1994.

Meston, C. M., et al. "The Relation between Early Abuse and Adult Sexuality." *Journal of Sex Research* 36 (1999) 385–395.

———. et al. "Women's History of Sexual Abuse, Their Sexuality, And Sexual Self-Schemas." *Journal of Consulting and Clinical Psychology* 74 (2006) 229–236.

Meyer, C. B., and S. E. Taylor. "Adjustment to Rape." *Journal of Personality and Social Psychology* 50 (1986) 1226–1234.

Meyer, Rick. *Through the Fire: Spiritual Restoration for Adult Victims of Childhood Sexual Abuse.* Minneapolis, MN: Augsburg, 2005.

Michael, Chester. *An Introduction to Spiritual Direction.* New York/Mahwah, NJ: Paulist, 2004.

Middleton, J. Richard. *The Liberating Image: The Imago Dei in Genesis 1.* Grand Rapids, MI: Baker, 2005.

Middleton-Moz, J., and L. Dwinell. *After the Tears.* Deerfield Beach, FL: Health Communications, 1986.

Milavec, Aaron. *The Didache: Faith, Hope, and Life of the Earliest Christian Communities, 50–70 C.E.* New York, NY: Newman, 2003.

Mildred, Jane. "Can We Trust What They Say? Wounded Healers and Other Myths about Child Sexual Abuse Experts." *Journal of Public Child Welfare* 4 (2010) 61–76.

Milgrom, Jacob. *Leviticus 17–22: A New Translation with Introduction and Commentary.* Anchor Bible 3A. New York, NY: Doubleday, 2000.

Miller, Alice. *Thou Shalt Not Be Aware: Society's Betrayal of the Child.* Translated by H. and H. Hannum. 1981. Reprinted, Du Sollst Nicht Merken. New York, NY: New American Library/Meridian, 1986.

———. *Breaking Down the Wall of Silence: The Liberating Experience of Facing Painful Truth.* New York, NY: Meridian, 1997.

Milner, Joel S., et al. "Paraphilia not Otherwise Specified: Psychopathology and Theory." *Sexual Deviance: Theory, Assessment, and Treatment.* 2nd ed, edited by D. Richard Laws and William T. O'Donohue, 384–418. New York, NY: The Guilford Press, 2008.

Minuchin, Salvador. *Families and Family Therapy.* Cambridge, MA: Harvard University Press, 1974.

Mitchell, Mark W. "Child Sexual Abuse: A School Leadership Issue." *Clearing House* 83 (2010) 101–104.

Moberly, Elizabeth R. *Homosexuality: A New Christian Ethic.* Cambridge, England: James Clarke & Co., 1983.

Moberly, R. W. L. *The Theology of the Book of Genesis.* Cambridge: Cambridge University Press, 2009.

Moisan, P. A., et al. "Ethnic Differences in Circumstances of Abuse and Symptoms of Depression and Anger among Sexually Abused Black and Latino Boys." *Child Abuse & Neglect* 21 (1997) 473–488.

Moltmann, Jürgen. *The Crucified God*, tran. R. A. Wilson and J. Bowden. New York, NY: Harper and Row, 1968.

———. *God in Creation: An Ecological Doctrine of Creation.* London: SCM Press, 1985.

Moltmann-Wendel, Elisabeth. *I Am My Body: A Theology of Embodiment.* trans. John Bowden. New York, NY: Continuum, 1995.

Monahan, John. "Violence Risk Assessment." In *Handbook of Psychology, Volume 11 Forensic Psychology*, edited by Alan M. Goldstein and Irving B. Weiner, 527–540. New York, NY: Wiley, 2003.

Money, John W., and Margaret Lamacz. *Vandalized Lovemaps: Paraphilic Outcome of Seven Cases in Pediatric Sexology.* Amherst, NY: Prometheus Books, 1989.

———, et al. "Paraphilia not Otherwise Specified: Psychopathology and Theory." In *Sexual Deviance: Theory, Assessment, and Treatment*. 2nd Edition. Edited by D. Richard Laws and William T. O'Donohue, 384–418. New York, NY: The Guilford Press, 2008.

Monroe, Philip G., George Schwab. "God as Healer: A Closer Look at Biblical Images of Healing with Questions for Counselors." *Journal of Psychology & Christianity* 28 (2009) 121–129.

Monson, C. M, et al. "Alcohol and Sex Offending: What Do Child Sex Offenders Think about Drinking?" *Journal of Addictions & Offender Counseling* 19 (1998) 15–27.

Moon, Gary, and David G. Benner, eds. *Spiritual Direction and the Care of Souls: A Guide to Christian Approaches and Practice*. Downers Grove, IL: InterVarsity Press, 2004.

Moore, Robert, and Douglas Gillette. *King, Warrior, Magician, Lover: Rediscovering the Archetypes of the Mature Masculine*. San Francisco, CA: Harper, 1990.

Morin, J. W., and J. S. Levenson. *The Road to Freedom*. Oklahoma City, OK: Authors, 2002.

Morin, J. W., and J. S. Levenson. "Exhibitionism: Assessment and Treatment." In *Sexual Deviance: Theory, Assessment, and Treatment,* 2nd ed., edited by D. Richard Laws and William T. O'Donohue, 76–101. New York, NY: The Guilford Press, 2008.

Mosgofian, Peter, and George Ohlschlager. *Sexual Misconduct in Counseling and Ministry*. Dallas, TX: Word, 1995.

Mounce, Robert H. *The Book of Revelation*. Grand Rapids, MI: Eerdmans, 1977.

Mulder, R. T., et al. "Relationship between Dissociation, Childhood Sexual Abuse, Childhood Physical Abuse, and Mental Illness in a General Population Sample." *American Journal of Psychiatry* 155 (1998) 806–811.

Mulholland, M. Robert. *Revelation: Holy Living in an Unholy World*. Grand Rapids, MI: Francis Asbury, 1990.

———. *Invitation to a Journey: A Road Map for Spiritual Formation*. Downers Grove, IL: InterVarsity, 1993.

Mullen, Jr., E. Theodore. "Divine Assembly." In *Anchor Bible Dictionary*, edited by D. N. Freedman, 2:214–217. New York, NY: Doubleday, 1992.

Munge, Bethany A., et al. "The Influence of Length of Marriage and Fidelity Status on Perception of Marital Rape." *Journal of Interpersonal Violence* 22 (2007) 1332–1339.

Mura, David. *A Male Grief: Notes on Pornography and Addiction*. Milkweed Editions, P.O. Box 3226, Minneapolis, MN, 55403, 1987.

Murphey, Cecil. *When a Man You Love Was Abused: A Woman's Guide to Helping Him Overcome Childhood Sexual Molestation*. Grand Rapids, MI: Kregel, 2010.

Murphy, J. *Getting Even: Forgiveness and its Limits*. Oxford, MS: Oxford University Press, 2003.

Murphy, Nancey. *Bodies and Souls, or Spirited Bodies?* New York, NY: Cambridge, 2006.

———. "The Resurrection Body and Personal Identity: Possibilities and Limits of Eschatological Knowledge." In *Resurrection: Theological and Scientific Assessments*, edited by Ted Peters, Robert J. Russell, and Michael Welker, 202–218. Grand Rapids, MI: Eerdmans, 2002.

Murphy, William D., and I. Jacqueline Page. "Exhibitionism: Psychopathology and Theory." In *Sexual Deviance: Theory, Assessment, and Treatment*, 2nd ed., edited by D. Richard Laws and William T. O'Donohue, 61–75. New York, NY: The Guilford Press, 2008.

Murray-Swank, Nicole A. "Solace for the Soul: An Evaluation of a Psycho-Spiritual Intervention for Female Survivors of Sexual Abuse." PhD diss., Bowling Green: Bowling Green University, 2003.

———, and Kenneth I. Parament. "Solace for the Soul: Evaluating a Spiritually-Integrated Counseling Intervention for Sexual Abuse." *Counseling et Spiritualité* 27 (2008) 157–174.

Murtagh, Michael P. "The Appropriate Attribution Technique (AAT): A New Treatment Technique for Adult Survivors of Sexual Abuse." *North American Journal of Psychology* 12 (2010) 313–34.

Najavits, Lisa M. "Assessment of Trauma, PTSD, and Substance Use Disorder: A Practical Guide." In *Assessing Psychological Trauma and PTSD*, edited by John P. Wilson and Terence M. Keane, 466–491. New York, NY: The Guilford Press, 2004.

Najman, J. M., et al. "Sexual Abuse in Childhood and Sexual Dysfunction in Adulthood: An Australian Population-based Study." *Archives of Sexual Behavior* 34 (2005) 517–526.

Nason-Clark, Nancy. *The Battered Wife: How Christians Confront Family Violence*. Louisville, KY: Westminster John Knox, 1997.

———, and Catherine Clark Kroeger. *Refuge from Abuse: Healing and Hope for Abused Christian Women.* Downers Grove, IL: Inter-Varsity Press, 2004.

———. "When Terror Strikes at Home: The Interface Between Religion and Domestic Violence." *Journal for the Scientific Study of Religion* 43 (2004) 303–310.

———, N. Murphy, B. Fisher-Townsend, and L. Ruff . "An Overview of the Characteristics of the Clients at a Faith-Based Batterers' Intervention Program." *Journal of Religion and Abuse* 5 (2004) 51–72.

———. "Christianity and Domestic Violence." In *Encyclopedia of Domestic Violence*, edited by Nicole Jackson, 161–166. New York, NY: Routledge, 2007.

———, Cathy Holtmann, Barbara Fisher-Townsend, Steve McMullin, and Lanette Ruff, "The RAVE Project: Developing Web-Based Religious Resources for Social Action on Domestic Abuse." *Critical Social Work* 11:1 (2009), available online at www.uwindsor.ca/units.socialwork/critical.nsf/

Nasjleti, Maria. "Suffering in Silence: The Male Incest Victim." *Child Welfare* 59 (1980) 269–275.

Nathanson, Donald L. "Shaming Systems in Couples, Families, and Institutions." In *The Many Faces of Shame*, edited by D. L. Nathanson, 246–270. New York, NY: The Guilford Press, 1987.

National Review Board for the Protection of Children and Young People. *A Report on the Crisis in the Catholic Church in the United States.* Washington, DC: United States Conference of Catholic Bishops, 2004.

Nelson, Christine. "Job: The Confessions of a Suffering Person." In *Spinning a Sacred Yarn: Women Speak from the Pulpit.* New York, NY: Pilgrim Press, 1982.

Nelson, James B. *Embodiment: An Approach to Sexuality and Christian Theology.* Minneapolis, MN: Augsburg, 1978.

———. *Body Theology.* Louisville, KY: Westminster/John Knox, 1992.

Nemiah, John C. "Dissociation, Conversion, and Somatization." In *Review of Psychiatry* 10, edited by Allan Tasman and Stephen M. Goldfinger, 248–260. Washington, DC: American Psychiatric Press, 1991.

Neuhaus, Richard John. "When Shepherds Go Astray." *First Things* 29 (1993) 55–58.

Neumann, D. A, et al. "The Long-Term Sequelae of Childhood Sexual Abuse in Women: A Meta-Analytic Review." *Child Maltreatment* 1 (1996) 6–16.

Newell, J. Philip. *Echo of the Soul: The Sacredness of the Human Body.* Harrisburg, PA: Morehouse, 2000.

Newsom, Carol A. "Angels." In *Anchor Bible Dictionary*, vol. 1, edited by D. N. Freedman, 1:248–253. New York, NY: Doubleday, 1992.

Neyrey, Jerome H. "Nudity." In *Handbook of Biblical Social Values*, edited by John J. Pilch and Bruce J. Malina, 136–142. Peabody, MA: Hendrickson, 2009.

Ngien, Dennis. "The God Who Suffers." *Christianity Today* (1997) 38–42.

Nicole Brannon, Yolanda. et al., "Attitudes about Community Notification: A Comparison of Sexual Offenders and the Non-offending Public." *Sexual Abuse* 19 (2007) 369–379.

Nicolosi, Joseph. *Reparative Therapy for the Homosexual Male.* Northvale, NJ: Jason Aronson, 1991.

Niehaus, Ashley, et al. "Sexual Self-Schemas of Female Child Sexual Abuse Survivors: Relationships with Risky Sexual Behavior and Sexual Assault in Adolescence." *Archives of Sexual Behavior* 39 (2010) 1359–1374.

Nijenhuis, Ellert R. S. "Somatoform Dissociation: Major Symptoms of Dissociative Disorders." *Journal of Trauma & Dissociation* 1 (2000) 7–32.

Niskanen, Paul. "The Poetics of Adam: The Creation of *Adam* in the Image of *Elohim*." *Journal of Biblical Literature* 128 (2009) 417–436.

Nissinen, Martti and Risto Uro. (Ed.). *Sacred Marriages: The Divine-Human Sexual Metaphor from Sumer to Early Christianity.* Winona Lake, IN: Eisenbrauns, 2008.

Nolan Fewell, Danna and David M. Gunn. *Gender, Power, and Promise: The Subject of the Bible's First Story.* Nashville, TN: Abingdon, 1993.

Noll, Jennie G. "A Prospective Investigation of the Impact of Childhood Sexual Abuse on the Development of Sexuality." *Journal of Consulting and Clinical Psychology* 71 (2003) 575–586.

———, et al. "The Cumulative Burden Borne by Offspring Whose Mothers Were Sexually Abused as Children: Descriptive Results From a Multigenerational Study." *Journal of Interpersonal Violence* 24 (2009) 424–449.

Noort, E. "The Creation of Man and Woman in Biblical and ancient Near Eastern Traditions." In *The Creation of Man and Woman: Interpretations of the Biblical Narrative: Jewish and Christian Traditions*, edited by G. P. Luttikhuizen, 6–10. Themes in Biblical Narratives, Jewish and Christian Traditions 1. Leiden: Brill, 2000.

Norberg, Tilda, and Robert Webber. *Stretch Out Your Hand: Exploring Healing Prayer*. New York, NY: United Church Press, 1990.

Nowrojee, Binaiter. *Shattered Lives: Sexual Violence During the Rwanda Genocide and its Aftermath*. New York, NY: Human Rights Watch, 1996.

Norris, Kathleen. *The Cloister Walk*. New York, NY: Riverhead Books, 1996.

North, Joanna. "Wrongdoing and Forgiveness." *Philosophy* 61 (1987) 499–508.

Nusbaum, M. R., and C. D. Hamilton. "Recognizing Sexual Problems Masquerading as Other Medical Conditions." *Medical Aspects of Human Sexuality* 1 (2002) 24–30.

Oates, R., et al. "Prior Sexual Abuse in Mothers of Sexually Abused Children." *Child Abuse and Neglect* 22 (1998) 1113–1118.

Ochberg, Frank M., ed. *Post-traumatic Therapy and Victims of Violence*. New York, NY: Bruner/Mazel Publishers, 1988.

———. "Gift from Within – PTSD Resources for Survivors and Caregivers." *Psychotherapy* 28 (1991) 5–15.

O'Connor, Kathleen M. "Lamenting Back to Life." *Interpretation* 62 (2008) 34–47.

Ogawa, John R., et al. "Development and the Fragmented Self: Longitudinal Study of Dissociative Symptomatology in a Nonclinical Sample." *Development and Psychopathology* 9 (1997) 855–879.

Olson, Dennis T. "Genesis." In *The New Interpreter's Bible: One Volume Commentary*, edited by Beverly Roberts Gaventa and David Petersen, 1–32. Nashville, TN: Abingdon, 2010.

Orlinsky, Harry. "The Hebrew Root ŠKB." *Journal of Biblical Literature* 63 (1944) 19–22.

Oswald, Roy. *Transforming Rituals: Daily Practices for Changing Lives*. Herndon, VA: Alban Institute, 1999.

Oswolt, John N. *The Bible Among the Myths: Unique Revelation or Just Ancient Literature*. Grand Rapids, MI: Zondervan, 2009.

Outka, Gene. "Equality and the Fate of Theism in Modern Culture." *Journal of Religion* 67 (1987) 275–288.

Oz, Sheri. "When the Wife Was Sexually Abused as a Child: Marital Relations Before and During Her Therapy for Abuse." *Sexual & Relationship Therapy* 16 (2001) 287–298.

Page, Stewart. "The Turnaround on Pornography Research: Some Implications for Psychology and Women." *Canadian Psychology/Psychologie Canadienne* 31 (1990) 359–367.

Pagelow, Mildred D. "Marital Rape." In *Handbook of Family Violence*, edited by Vincent B. Va Hasselt et al., chap 9. New York, NY: Plenum Press, 1988.

———. "Adult Victims of Domestic Violence." *Journal of Interpersonal Violence* 7 (1992) 87–120.

Pakhomou, Serge M. " Methodological Aspects of Telephone Scatalogia: A Case Study." *International Journal of Law and Psychiatry* 29 (2006) 178–185.

Panuzio, Jillian, et al. "Physical, Psychological, and Sexual Intimate Partner Aggression among Newlywed Couples: Longitudinal Prediction of Marital Satisfaction." *Journal of Family Violence* 25 (2010) 689–699.

Pargament, Kenneth, et al. "Patterns of Positive and Negative Religious Coping with Major Life Stressors." *Journal for the Scientific Study of Religion* 37 (1998) 710–724.

———. *Spiritually Integrated Psychotherapy*. New York, NY: The Guilford Press, 2007.

Parkinson, Patrick, et al. "Breaking the Long Silence: Reports of Child Sexual Abuse in the Anglican Church of Australia." *Ecclesiology* 6 (2010) 183–200.

Patterson, Mary. "Coming too Close, Going too Far: Theoretical and Cross-Cultural Approaches to Incest and its Prohibitions." *The Australian Journal of Anthropology* 16 (2005) 95–115.

Patton, Corrine L. "'Should Our Sister Be Treated Like a Whore?': A Response to Feminist Critiques of Ezekiel 23." In *The Book of Ezekiel: Theological and Anthropological Perspectives*, edited by Margaret S. Odell and John T. Strong, 221–227. Society of Biblical Literature Symposium 9. Atlanta, GA: Society of Biblical Literature, 2000.

Paul II, John. *Man and Woman He Created Them: A Theology of the Body*. trans. Michael Waldstein. Boston, MA: Pauline Books & Media, 2006.

Paul Kim Hyun Chul and M. Fulgence Nyengele. "Murder S/He Wrote? A Culture and Psychological Reading of 2 Samuel 11–12." In *Pregnant Passion: Gender, Sex, and Violence in the Bible*. Semeia Studies 44 (Atlanta, GA: Society of Biblical Literature, 2003) 95–116.

Paul, Pamela. *Pornified: How Pornography is Transforming Our Lives, Our Relationships, and Our Families*. New York, NY: Times Books, 2005.

Pearce, J. and T. Pezzot-Pearce. *Psychotherapy of Abused & Neglected Children.* 2nd Edition. New York, NY: The Guilford Press, 2007.

Peck, Scott M. *People of the Lie: The Hope for Healing Human Evil.* New York, NY: Simon & Schuster, 1983.

Pellauer, Mary, et al. "Resources for Ritual and Recuperation." In *Sexual Assault and Abuse: A Handbook for Clergy and Religious Professionals*, edited by Mary Pellauer, et al, 223–247. San Francisco, CA: Harper & Row, 1989.

———. et al. *Sexual Assault and Abuse: A Handbook for Clergy and Religious Professionals.* San Francisco, CA: HarperSanFrancisco, 1991.

Pennachia, M. *Healing the Whole: Diary of an Incest Survivor.* London: Cassell, 1994.

Penner, Carol. "After Sexual Violence: What Happens Next in the Community of Grace?" *Vision* 9 (2008) 58–66.

Perdahli Fis, Nese, et al. "Psychiatric Evaluation of Sexual Abuse Cases: A Clinical Representative Sample from Turkey." *Children & Youth Services Review* 32 (2010) 1285–1290.

Perkins, Pheme. "The Letter to the Ephesians: Introduction, Commentary, and Reflections." In *Second Corinthians, Galatians, Ephesians, Philippians, Colossians, 1 & 2 Thessalonians, 1 & 2 Timothy, Titus, Philemon*, 349–466. NIB 11. Nashville, TN: Abingdon, 1997.

Persons, Elizabeth, et al. "The Impact of Shame on Health-Related Quality of Life Among HIV-Positive Adults with a History of Childhood Sexual Abuse." *AIDS Patient Care & STDs* 24 (2010) 571–580.

Peter, Tracy. "Exploring Taboos: Comparing Male-and Female-Perpetrated Child Sexual Abuse." *Journal of Interpersonal Violence* 24 (2009) 1111–1128.

Peterman, Janet. *Speaking to Silence: New Rites for Christian Worship and Healing.* Louisville, KY: Westminster John Knox, 2007.

Peters, D., and L. Range. "Childhood Sexual Abuse and Current Suicidality in College Women and Men." *Child Abuse and Neglect* 19 (1995) 335–341.

Peterson, Eugene H. *A Long Obedience in the Same Direction: Discipleship in an Instant Society.* Downers Grove, IL: InterVarsity, 2000.

Phasha, Tlakale Nareadi. "Educational Resilience among African Survivors of Child Sexual Abuse in South Africa." *Journal of Black Studies* 40 (2010) 1234–1253.

Phelan, James E., Jr. "Women and the Aims of Jesus." *Priscilla Papers* 18 (2004) 7–11.

Phillips, Anthony. "Nebalah—A Term for Serious Disorderly and Unruly Conduct." *Vetus Testamentum* 25 (1975) 237–242.

Pingleton, J. P. "The Role and Function of Forgiveness in the Psychotherapeutic Process," *Journal of Psychology and Theology* 17 (1989) 27–35.

Pinhas-Hamiel, Orit. "Obesity in Girls and Penetrative Sexual Abuse in Childhood." *Acta Paediatrica* 98 (2009) 144–147.

Piper, John. *The Pleasures of God: Meditations on God's Delight in Being God.* Portland, OR: Multnomah, 1991.

Plantinga, Jr., Cornelius. *Not the Way It's Supposed to Be: A Breviary of Sin.* Grand Rapids, MI: Eerdmans, 1995.

Plato. *Phaedo.* In *The Collected Dialogues of Plato*, edited by Edith Hamilton and Huntington Cairns, 48-49. trans. Hugh Tredennick. Princeton, NJ: Princeton University Press, 1961.

Poling, James Newton. *The Abuse of Power: A Theological Problem.* Nashville, TN: Abingdon, 1991.

———, ed. *Victim to Survivor: Women Recovering from Sexual Abuse.* Cleveland, OH: United Church Press, 1999.

Pollack, William. *Real Boys: Rescuing Our Sons from the Myths of Boyhood.* New York, NY: Henry Holt and Company, 1998.

Polusny, Melissa A., and Victoria M. Follette. "Long-Term Correlates of Child Sexual Abuse: Theory and Review of the Empirical Literature." *Applied and Preventative Psychology* 4 (1995) 143–166.

Porter, Eugene. *Treating the Young Male Victim of Sexual Assault.* Syracuse, NY: Safer Society Press, 1986.

Porter, Muriel. "Sexual Abuse: Sin, Guilt and Shame in the Context of Pastoral Care in the Parish." *St Mark's Review* 205 (2008) 15–29.

Poston, Carol, and Karen Lison. *Reclaiming Our Lives: Hope for Adult Survivors of Incest.* Boston, MA: Little, Brown and Company, 1989.

Potter-Efron, Ronald, and Patricia Potter-Efron. *Letting Go of Shame.* Center City, MN: Hazelden, 1989.

Pressler, Carolyn. *The View of Women Found in the Deuteronomic Family Laws.* Berlin: Walter de Gruyter, 1993.

Procter-Smith, Marjorie. "The Whole Loaf: Holy Communion and Survival." In *Violence Against Women and Children, A Christian Theological Sourcebook,* edited by Carol J. Adams and Marie M. Fortune, 464–478. New York, NY: The Continuum Publishing Company, 1995.

———. "Review Article: Liturgical Responses to Sexual and Domestic Violence." *Journal of Religion and Abuse* 8 (2006) 39–44.

Purdy, A. *He Will Never Remember: Caring for Victims of Child Abuse.* Atlanta, GA: Susan Hunter Publishing, Inc., 1989.

Putnam, Frank W. *Diagnosis and Treatment of Multiple Personality Disorder.* New York, NY: Guildford Press, 1989.

———, et al. "Patterns of Dissociation in Clinical and Nonclinical Samples." *Journal of Nervous and Mental Disease* 184 (1989) 673–679.

———. *Dissociation in Children and Adolescents: A Developmental Perspective.* New York, NY: Guilford Press, 1997.

Quinsey, Vernon L., et al. *Violent Offenders: Appraising and Managing Risk.* 2nd ed. Washington DC: American Psychological Association, 2006.

Radford Ruether, Rosemary. *Woman-Church: Theology and Practice of Feminist Liturgical Communities.* San Francisco, CA: Harper and Row, 1985.

———. *Women-Church: Theology and Practice of Feminist Liturgical Communities.* San Fancisco, CA: Harper, 1986.

———. "Christian Anthropology and Gender: A Tribute to Jürgen Moltmann." In *The Future of Theology: Essays in Honor of Jürgen Moltmann,* edited by Miroslav Volf et al, 241–252. Grand Rapids: Eerdmans, 1996.

———. "The Image of God's Goodness: How Language Reflects Our Understanding of God." *Sojourners* 25 (1996) 30–31.

Rambo, Shelly. *Spirit and Trauma: A Theology of Remaining.* Louisville, KY: Westminster John Knox, 2010.

Ramsey, Nancy J. "Preaching to Survivors of Child Sexual Abuse." In *Telling the Truth: Preaching about Sexual and Domestic Violence,* edited by John S. McClure and Nancy J. Ramsay, 58–70. Cleveland, OH: United Church Press, 1998.

Ramsey-Klawsnik, Holly. "Elder Sexual Abuse within the Family." *Journal of Elder Abuse & Neglect* 15 (2003) 43–58.

Ramshaw, Elaine. *Ritual and Pastoral Care.* Philadelphia, PA: Fortress, 1987.

Ratner, Ellen. *The Other Side of the Family: A Book for Recovery from Abuse, Incest, and Neglect.* Deerfield Beach, FL: Health Communications, 1990.

Rauch, Mikele. "Dissecting the Lamb of God: The Other Devastation of Clergy Sexual Abuse." *Cross Currents* 54 (2004) 47–54.

Read, J., et al. "Assessing Suicidality in Adults: Integrating Childhood Trauma as a Major Risk Factor." *Professional Psychology: Research and Practice* 32 (2001) 367–372.

Read, Wendy. *A Conspiracy of Love: Living Through and Beyond Childhood Sexual Abuse.* Saskatchewan, Canada: Northstone Publishing: 2006.

———. et al, and Hillary Cashman. "Service of Acknowledgment of Organized Abuse and Cleansing of a Church Sanctuary." *Journal of Religion and Abuse* 8 (2006) 7–12.

Rediger, G. Lloyd. *Ministry and Sexuality.* Minneapolis, MN: Fortress Press, 1990.

Reeves, Nancy C. "The Effects of Post-Traumatic Stress Disorder On Spirituality." *American Journal of Pastoral Counseling* 4 (2001) 3–17.

Rego, Aloysius. *Suffering and Salvation: The Salvific Meaning of Suffering in the Later Theology of Edward Schillebeeckx.* Louvain Theological and Pastoral Monographs 33. Louvain: Peeters, 2006.

Remley, Theodore, and Barbara Herlihy. *Ethical, Legal, and Professional Issues.* Boston, MA: Merril, 2010.

Rendtorff, Rolf. *Canon and Theology: Overtures to an Old Testament Theology,* trans. and ed. Margaret Kohl. Overtures to Biblical Theology. Minneapolis, MN: Fortress, 1993.

Renvoize, Jean. *Incest: A Family Pattern.* London: Routledge & Kegan Paul, 1982.

———. *Innocence Destroyed: A Study of Child Sexual Abuse.* London: Routledge, 1993.

Rich-Edwards, Janet W., et al. "Abuse in Childhood and Adolescence as a Predictor of Type 2 Diabetes in Adult Women." *American Journal of Preventive Medicine* 39 (2010) 529–536.

Ridout, George. "The Rape of Tamar: A Rhetorical Analysis of 2 Sam 13:1–22." In *Rhetorical Criticism: Essays in Honor of James Muilenberg*, edited by Jared J. Jackson and Martin Kessler, 81–83. Pittsburgh Theological Monograph Series 1. Pittsburgh, PA: Pickwick, 1974.

Rodriguez, Ned, Hendrika Vande Kemp, and David W. Foy. "Posttraumatic Stress Disorder in Survivors of Childhood Sexual and Physical Abuse: A Critical Review of the Empirical Literature." *Journal of Child Sexual Abuse* 7 (1998) 17–45.

Rigali, Norbert J. "Moral Theology and Church Responses to Sexual Abuse." *Horizons* 34 (2007) 183–204.

Rinck, Margaret J. *Christian Men Who Hate Women*. Grand Rapids: Zondervan, 1990.

Ripley, Jennifer S., and Everett L. Worthington. "Comparison of Hope-focused Communication and Empathy-based Forgiveness Group Interventions to Promote Marital Enrichment." *Journal of Counseling and Development* 80 (2002) 452–463.

Roberto, Karen A., et al. "Sexual Abuse of Vulnerable Young and Old Men." *Journal of Interpersonal Violence* 22 (2007) 1009–1023.

Roberts, Robert C. *Taking the Word to Heart*. Grand Rapids, MI: Eerdmans, 1993.

———. "Forgivingness." *American Philosophical Quarterly* 32 (1995) 289–306.

Robertson, John, and Louise Fitzgerald. "The (Mis) Treatment of Men: Effects of Client Gender Role and Lifestyle on Diagnosis and Attribution of Pathology." *Journal of Counseling Psychology* 37 (1990) 3–9.

Robinson, Simon J. "Agape and Moral Meaning in Pastoral Counseling." *The Journal of Pastoral Care* 54 (2000) 147–159.

Rodriguez-Srednicki, Ofelia, and James A. Twaite. *Understanding, Assessing, and Treating Adult Victims of Childhood Abuse*. New York, NY: Jason Aronson, 2006.

Rogers, Daléne Fuller. *Pastoral Care for Post-Traumatic Stress Disorder: Healing the Shattered Soul*. New York, NY: The Haworth Pastoral Press, 2002.

Rogers, Sara. "Journeys Out of the Victim Role: Male Violence and the Hebrew Scriptures." *Feminist Theology* 11 (2003) 190–196.

Romans, S. E., J. L. Martin, E. Morris, G. P. Herbison, "Psychological Defense Styles in Women Who Report Childhood Sexual Abuse: A Controlled Community Study." *American Journal of Psychiatry* 156 (1999) 1080–1085.

Roodman, A. A., and G. A. Clum. "Victimization Rates and Method Variance: A Meta-Analysis." *Journal of Traumatic Stress* 21 (2001) 183–204.

Root, Maria. "Reconstructing the Impact of Trauma on Personality." In *Personality and Psychopathology: Feminist Reappraisals*, edited by Laura S. Brown and Mary Ballou, 229–266. New York, NY: The Guilford Press, 1992.

Roozendaal, B., et al. "Stress, Memory and the Amygdala." *Nature Reviews Neuroscience* 10 (2009) 423–433.

Rosner, Brian S. "Biblical Theology." In *New Dictionary of Biblical Theology*, edited by T. D. Alexander and B. S. Rosner, 3–11. Downers Grove, IL: InterVarsity Press, 2000.

Ross, Jr., Bobby. "Modern Day Lepers." *Christianity Today* 53 (December 2009) 16–17.

Ross, G., and P. O'Carroll. "Cognitive Behavioural Psychotherapy Intervention in Childhood Sexual Abuse: Indentifying New Directions from the Literature." *Child Abuse Review* 13 (2004) 51–64.

Rossetti, Stephen. "The Impact of Child Sexual Abuse on Attitudes toward God and the Catholic Church." *Child Abuse and Neglect* 19 (1995) 1469–1481.

———. *Tragic Grace: The Catholic Church and Child Sexual Abuse*. Collegeville, MN: Liturgical Press, 1996.

Rudolfsson, Lisa, and Inga Tidefors. "'Shepherd My Sheep': Clerical Readiness to Meet Psychological and Existential Needs from Victims of Sexual Abuse." *Pastoral Psychology* 58 (2009) 79–92.

Rudman, Dominic. "Reliving the Rape of Tamar: Absalom's Revenge in 2 Samuel 13." *Old Testament Essays* 11 (1998) 326–339.

Runyon, M. K., and M. C. Kenny. "Relationship of Attributional Style, Depression, and Posttrauma Distress among Children Who Suffered Physical or Sexual Abuse." *Child Maltreatment* 7 (2002) 254–64.

Rupp, Joyce. *Praying Our Goodbyes*. New York, NY: Ivy, 1988.

Ruscio, Ayelet. "Predicting the Child-rearing Practices of Mothers Sexually Abused in Childhood." *Child Abuse and Neglect* 25 (2001) 369–387.

Rush, Florence. *The Best Kept Secret: Sexual Abuse of Children*. Englewood Cliffs, NJ: Prentice-Hall, 1980.

Russell, Diana E. H. *Rape in Marriage.* Indiana: Indiana University Press, 1990.

———. "The Incidence and Prevalence of Intrafamilial and Extrafamilial Sexual Abuse of Female Children." *Child Abuse and Neglect: The International Journal* 7 (1983) 113–46.

———. *Rape, Incest and Sexual Exploitation.* Los Angeles, CA: Sage, 1984.

———. *The Secret Trauma: Incest in the Lives of Girls and Women.* New York, NY: Basic Books, 1986.

———, et al. "Pornography: Is It Harmful to Women?" In *Women, Men, & gender: Ongoing Debates*, edited by Mary Roth Walsh, 155–179. New Haven, CT: Yale University Press, 1997.

———. and Rebecca M. Bolen. *The Epidemic of Rape and Child Sexual Abuse in the United States.* Thousand Oaks, CA: Sage, 2000.

Rutter, Peter. *Sex in the Forbidden Zone: When Men in Power—Therapists, Doctors, Clergy, Teachers, and Others—Betray Women's Trust.* Los Angeles, CA: Jeremy P. Tarcher, 1989.

Ryan, Kathryn M. "Further Evidence for a Cognitive Component of Rape." *Aggression and Violent Behavior* 9 (2004) 579–604.

Ryan, Thomas. *Reclaiming the Body in Christian Spirituality.* New York, NY: Paulist, 2004.

Ryken, L., et al, eds. "Sex." In *Dictionary of Biblical Imagery*, 776–779. Downers Grove, IL: InterVarsity, 1998.

Sachs, Carolyn and Linda J. Gomberg. "Intimate Partner Sexual Abuse." In *Intimate Partner Violence: A Health-based Perspective*, edited by Connie Mitchell, Deirdre Anglin, 265–274. New York, NY: Oxford University Press, 2009.

Salter, Anna C. *Transforming Trauma: A Guide to Understanding and Treating Adult Survivors of Child Sexual Abuse.* London: Sage Publications, 1995.

———. *Predators: Pedophiles, Rapists and Other Sex Offenders.* New York, NY: Basic Books, 2004.

Sands, Kathleen M. "Clergy Sexual Abuse: Where Are The Women?" *Journal of Feminist Studies in Religion* 19 (2003) 79–83.

Sanford, Linda T. *The Silent Children: A Parent's Guide to the Prevention of Child Sexual Abuse.* New York, NY: McGraw-Hill Paper Backs, 1980.

———. *Strong at the Broken Places: Overcoming the Trauma of Childhood Abuse.* New York, NY: Random House, 1990.

Sarna, Nahum M. *Genesis.* The JPS Torah Commentary. Philadelphia, PA: The Jewish Publication Society, 1989.

Savran, George W. *Telling and Retelling: Quotation in Biblical Narrative.* Bloomington, IN: Indiana University Press, 1988.

Sawyer, Deborah F. "Sex, Sexuality." In *The New Interpreter's Dictionary of the Bible S-Z*, edited by Katharine Doob Sakenfeld, 199–205. Nashville, TN: Abingdon, 2009.

Saxe, G. N., et al. "Somatization in Patients with Dissociative Disorders." *American Journal of Psychiatry* 151 (1994) 1329–1334.

Saywitz, K., et al. "Treatment for Sexually Abused Children and Adolescents." *American Psychologist* 55 (2000) 1040–1049.

Schacht, Rebecca L. "Sexual Abuse History, Alcohol Intoxication, and Women's Sexual Risk Behavior." *Archives of Sexual Behavior* 39 (2010) 898–906.

Schaefer, Charles, and Kevin O'Connor. *Handbook of Play Therapy.* New York, NY: John Wiley & Sons, 1983.

Schaffran, Janet, and Pat Kozak. *More Than Words: Prayer and Ritual for Inclusive Communities.* Oak Park: Meyer Stone Books, 1988.

Sheinberg, Marsha, and Peter Fraenkel. *The Relational Trauma of Incest.* New York, NY: The Guilford Press, 2001.

Schene, P. "Child Abuse and Neglect Policy, History, Models, and Future Directions." In *The APSAC Handbook of Child Maltreatment*, edited by John Briere, et al, 385–397. Thousand Oaks, CA: Sage, 1996.

Schenk, Roy U. "Beyond Shame: Transforming Our Lives." In *Men Healing Shame: An Anthology*, edited by Roy U. Schenk and John Everingham, 291–301. New York, NY: Springer, 1995.

Schetky, Diane H., and Arthur H. Green. *Child Sexual Abuse: A Handbook For Health Care and Legal Professions.* Florence, KY: Routledge Publishers, 1988.

Schetky, Diane H. "A Review of the Literature on the Long-Term Effects of Childhood Sexual Abuse." In *Incest-Related Syndromes of Adult Psychopathology*, edited by R. Kluft, 35–54. Washington, DC: American Psychiatric Press, 1990.

Schloredt, K. A., and J. R. Heiman. "Perceptions of Sexuality as Related to Sexual Functioning and Sexual Risk in Women with Different Types of Child Abuse Histories." *Journal of Traumatic Stress* 16 (2003) 275–284.

Schmidt, Ruth. "After the Fact: To Speak of Rape." *Christian Century* 110 (1993) 14–17.

Schmutzer, Andrew J. "'All Those Going Out of the Gate of His City': Have the Translations Got It Yet?" *Bulletin for Biblical Research* 17 (2007) 37–52.

———. "A Theology of Sexual Abuse: A Reflection on Creation and Devastation." *Journal of the Evangelical Theological Society* 51 (2008) 785–812.

———. *Be Fruitful and Multiply: A Crux of Thematic Repetition in Genesis 1–11*. Eugene, OR: Wipf and Stock, 2009.

———. "Spiritual Formation and Sexual Abuse: Embodiment, Community and Healing." *Journal of Spiritual Formation and Soul Care* 2 (2009) 67–86.

Scholz, Susanne. "Was it Rape in Genesis 34? Biblical Scholarship as a Reflection of Cultural Assumptions." In *Escaping Eden: New Feminist Perspectives on the Bible*, edited by Harold C. Washington et al, 183–198. Sheffield: Sheffield Academic Press, 1998.

———. "Through Whose Eyes? A 'Right' Reading of Genesis 34." In *Genesis: A Feminist Companion to the Bible*, edited by Athalya Brenner, 150–171. Feminist Companion to the Bible 2/1. Sheffield: Sheffield Academic Press, 1998.

———. *Rape Plots: A Feminist Cultural Study of Genesis 34*. New York, NY: Peter Lang, 2000.

———. *Sacred Witness: Rape in the Hebrew Bible*. Minneapolis, MN: Fortress Press, 2010.

Schroeder, Joy A. "The Woman and the Dragon: Feminist Reflections on Sexual Violence, Evil, and Bodily Resurrection" *dialog* 33 (1994) 135–141.

———. *Dinah's Lament: The Biblical Legacy of Sexual Violence in Christian Interpretation*. Minneapolis, MN: Augsburg Fortress Press, 2007.

Schwartz, M. "Negative Impact of Sexual Abuse on Adult Male Gender: Issues and Strategies of Intervention." *Child and Adolescents Social Work Journal* 11 (1994) 179–194.

Scott, Kay. *Sexual Assault: Will I Ever Feel Okay Again?* Bloomington, MN: Bethany House, 1993.

Scott, Marshall S. "Honor thy Father and Mother: Scriptural Resources for Victims of Incest and Parental Abuse." *Journal of Pastoral Care* 42 (1988) 139–48.

Sedlak, A. J., et al., *Fourth National Incidence Study of Child Abuse and Neglect* (NIS–4): Report to Congress. Washington, DC: US Department of Health and Human Services, Administration for Children and Families, 2010.

Seitz, Christopher R. "Sexuality and Scripture's Plain Sense: The Christian Community and the Law of God," 319–339. In *Word Without End: The Old Testament as Abiding Theological Witness*. Grand Rapids, MI: Eerdmans, 1998.

Serrano, Alberto C. and D. W. Gunsburger. "An Historical Perspective of Incest." *Journal of Family Therapy* 5 (1983) 70–80.

Seto, Michael C. "Pedophilia: Psychopathology and Theory." In *Sexual Deviance: Theory, Assessment, and Treatment*, 2nd ed., edited by D. Richard Laws and William T. O'Donohue, 164–182. New York, NY: The Guilford Press, 2008.

Sexaholics Anonymous. *Sexaholics Anonymous*. Semi Valley, CA: SA Literature, 1989.

Sgroi, A., and B. S. Bunk. "A Clinical Approach to Adult Survivors of Child Sexual Abuse." In *Vulnerable Populations: Evaluation and Treatment of Sexually Abused Children and Adult Survivors*, vol. 1, edited by S. Sgroi, 137–186. Lexington, MA: Lexington Books, 1988.

Shapiro, Francine and Margot S. Forrest. *EMDR: The Breakthrough "Eye Movement" Therapy for Overcoming Anxiety, Stress, and Trauma*. New York, NY: Basic Books, 1997.

———, ed. *EMDR as an Integrative Psychotherapy Approach: Experts of Diverse Orientations Explore the Paradigm Prism*. Washington, DC: American Psychological Association, 2004.

Shemesh, Yael. "Biblical Stories of Rape Narratives: Common Traits and Unique Features" [in Hebrew]. In *Studies in Bible and Exegesis*. Vol. 6, edited R. Kasher and M. Zipor, 315-344. Ramat Gan, Israel: Bar-Ilan Press, 2002.

Shengold, L. *Soul Murder: The Effects of Childhood Abuse and Deprivation*. New York, NY: Ballantine Books, 1989.

Bibliography

Sherwin, Byron L. "The Human Body and the Image of God." In *A Traditional Quest*, edited by D. Cohn-Sherbok, 75–85. Sheffield: JSOT Press, 1991.

Shrier, Diane and Robert L. Johnson. "Sexual Victimization of Boys: An Ongoing Study of an Adolescent Medicine Clinic Population." *Journal of the National Medical Association* 80 (1988) 1189–1193.

Silk, K. R., S. Lee, E. M. Hill, and N. E. Lohr. "Borderline Personality Disorder and Severity of Sexual Abuse." *American Journal of Psychiatry* 152 (1995) 1059–64.

Silverman, Sue William. *Because I Remember Terror, Father, I Remember You*. New York, NY: Three Rivers Press, 1998.

Silverman, Jay G. et al. "Dating Violence against Adolescent Girls and Associated Substance Abuse, Unhealthy Weight Control, Sexual Risk Behavior, Pregnancy, and Suicidality." *Journal of the American Medical Association* 286 (2001) 572–579.

Smedes, L. B. *Forgive and Forget: Healing the Hurts We Don't Deserve*. San Francisco, CA: Harper & Row, 1998.

Simkins, Ronald A. *Creator and Creation: Nature in the Worldview of Ancient Israel*. Peabody, MA: Hendrickson, 1994.

Smith, Carol. "Stories of Incest in the Hebrew Bible: Scholars Challenging Text or Text Challenging Scholars?" *Henoch* 14 (1992) 227–242.

Smith, Daniel W., et al. "Mother Reports of Maternal Support Following Child Sexual Abuse: Preliminary Psychometric Data on the Maternal Self-Report Support Questionnaire (MSSQ)." *Child Abuse & Neglect* 34 (2010) 784–792.

Smith, Gerrilyn. *Sexual Offending Against Children*. Abingdon, New York, NY: Taylor & Francis, 1994.

Smith, Helen A. "Sexual Abuse, Sexual Orientation, and Obesity in Women." *Journal of Women's Health* 19 (2010) 1525–1532.

Smith, Jay E. "Another Look at 4Q416 2ii.21: A Critical Parallel to First Thessalonians 4:4." *Catholic Biblical Quarterly* 63 (2001) 499–504.

Smith, Michelle E. "Faith Healing." In *The Baker Encyclopedia of Psychology and Counseling*, edited by J. W. Watts and A. R. Ross, 85. Grand Rapids, MI: Baker, 2002.

Sobrino, Jon. *The Principle of Mercy: Taking the Crucified People from the Cross*. Maryknoll, NY: Orbis Books, 1994.

Sommerfeld, Leila Rae. *Beyond Our Control: Reconstructing Your Life after Sexual Assault*. Grand Rapids: Kregel, 2009.

Spencer, Dale. "Sex Offender as Homo Sacer." *Punishment & Society* 11 (2009) 219–240.

Spiegel, D. "Trauma, Dissociation and Hypnosis." In *Incest-Related Syndromes of Adult Psychopathology*, edited by R. Kluft, 247–261. Washington, DC: American Psychiatric Press, 1990.

Spielman, Larry W. "David's Abuse of Power." *Word and World* 19 (1999) 251–259.

Stanley, J. L., et al. "Gay and Bisexual Men's Age-discrepant Childhood Sexual Experiences." *Journal of Sex Research* 41 (2004) 381–389.

Steel, Chad. "Child Pornography in Peer-to-Peer Networks." *Child Abuse & Neglect* 33 (2009) 560–568.

Steele, Brandt F., and Helen Alexander. "Long-term Effects of Sexual Abuse in Childhood." In *Sexually Abused Children and Their Families*, edited by Patricia Beezley Mrazek and C. Henry Kempe. New York, NY: Pergamon Press, 1981.

Stein, M. B., et al. "Hippocampal Volume in Women Victimized by Child Sexual Abuse." *Psychological Medicine* 27 (1997) 951–959.

Steinberg, Marlene. "Advances in the Clinical Assessment of Dissociation: The SCID-D-R." *Bulletin of the Menninger Clinic* 64 (2000) 146–163.

Stepakoff, S. "Effects of Sexual Victimization on Suicidal Ideation and Behavior in U.S. College Women." *Suicide and Life-Threatening Behavior* 28 (1998) 107–126.

Sternberg, Meir. *The Poetics of Biblical Narrative: Ideological Literature and the Drama of Reading*. Bloomington, IN: Indiana University Press, 1987.

———. "Biblical Poetics and Sexual Politics: From Reading to Counter-reading." *Journal of Biblical Literature* 111 (1992) 463–488.

Stepp, Laura Session. *How Young Women Pursue Sex, Delay Love, and Lose at Both*. New York, NY: Riverhead Books, 2007.

Stoddard, Joel, et al. "Sexual and Physical Abuse: A Comparison between Lesbians and Their Heterosexual Sisters." *Journal of Homosexuality* 56 (2009) 407–420.

Stone, M. H. "Incest in the Borderline Patient." In *Incest-Related Syndromes of Adult Psychopathology*, edited by R. Kluft, 183–204. Washington, DC: American Psychiatric Press, 1990.

Stone, Robin D. "Reconciliation . . . and Moving On." *Journal of Feminist Family Therapy* 16 (2005) 71–89.

Straus, Murray A., et al. *Behind Closed Doors: Violence in the American Family*. Garden City, NY: Doubleday/Anchor, 1980.

———. "Physical Assaults by Wives: A Major Social Problem." In *Current Controversies on Family Violence*, edited by Richard J. Gelles and Donileen Robert Loseke, 67–87. Newbury Park, CA: Sage, 1993.

Streets, F. J. "Preaching and Trauma." *Living Pulpit* 14 (2005) 22–24.

St-Yves, M., and B. Pellerin. "Sexual Victimization and Sexual Delinquency: Vampire or Pinocchio Syndrome?" *Correctional Service Canada Forum* 14 (2002) 51–2.

Summers, Bonnie. "A Service of Celebration and Thanksgiving for Healing." *Journal of Religion and Abuse* 8 (2006) 13–25.

Talbert, Charles H. "Freedom and Law in Galatians." *Ex auditu* 11 (1995) 17–28.

———. *Reading Corinthians: A Literary and Theological Commentary*, rev. ed., *Reading the New Testament*. Macon: Smyth & Helwys, 2002.

———. *Romans*. Smyth & Helwys Bible Commentary. Macon, Smyth & Helwys, 2002.

Tarvis, Carol. *Anger: The Misunderstood Emotion*. New York, NY: Simon and Schuster, 1982.

Tebbutt, J., et al. "Five Years after Child Sexual Abuse: Persisting Dysfunction and Problems of Prediction." *Journal of the American Academy of Child & Adolescent Psychiatry* 36 (1997) 330–339.

Tedeschi, Richard G., Lawrence Calhoun. *Trauma & Transformation: Growing in the Aftermath of Suffering*. Thousand Oaks, CA: Sage Publications, 1995.

Terr, Lenore. *Too Scared To Cry: How Trauma Affects Children and Ultimately Us All*. New York, NY: Basic Books, 1990.

———. *Unchained Memories*. New York, NY: HarperCollins, 1994.

The Child Dissociative Checklist: Frank W. Putman, Karin Helmers, and Penelope K. Trickett. "Development, Reliability, and Validity of a Child Dissociation Scale." *Child Abuse & Neglect* 17 (1993) 731–741.

Thielman, Frank. *Theology of the New Testament: A Canonical and Synthetic Approach*. Grand Rapids, MI: Zondervan, 2005.

Thiselton, Anthony C. *The Living Paul: An Introduction to the Apostle's Life and Thought*. Downers Grove, IL: IVP Academic, 2009.

Thistlethwaite, Susan. "Every Two Minutes: Battered Women and Feminist Interpretation." In *Feminist Interpretation of the Bible*, edited by Letty Russell, 96–107. Philadelphia, PA: Westminster Press, 1985.

Thomas, Linda. "Womanist Theology, Epistemology, and a New Anthropological Paradigm." *Cross Currents* 48 (1998) 1–9.

Thomas, T. *Men Surviving Incest*. Walnut Creek, CA: Launch Press, 1989.

———. *Surviving with Serenity: Daily Meditations for Incest Survivors*. Deerfield Beach, FL: Health Communications, 1990.

Thornton, Jennifer A., et al. "Intrafamilial Adolescent Sex Offenders: Family Functioning and Treatment." *Journal of Family Studies* 14 (2008) 362–375.

Tishelman, Amy C., and Robert Geffner. "Forensic, Cultural, and Systems Issues in Child Sexual Abuse Cases—Part 1: An Introduction." *Journal of Child Sexual Abuse* 19 (2010) 485–490.

———, et al., and Robert Geffner. "Forensic, Cultural, and Systems Issues in Child Sexual Abuse Cases—Part 2: Research and Practitioner Issues." *Journal of Child Sexual Abuse* 19 (2010) 609–617.

———, et al., and Robert Geffner. "The Clinical-Forensic Dichotomy in Sexual Abuse Evaluations: Moving Toward an Integrative Model." *Journal of Child Sexual Abuse* 19 (2010) 590–608.

Tjaden, P., and N. Thoennes. *Extent, Nature, and Consequences of Rape Victimization: Findings from the National Violence against Women Survey*. Washington, DC: National Institute of Justice, 2006.

Todd, Shelley. "An Exploration of the Concept of God Espoused by Female Adult Survivors of Sexual Abuse." PhD diss., New Orleans Baptist Theological Seminary, 1991.

Todd Holeman, Virginia, and Rita W. Myers "Effects of Forgiveness of Perpetrators on Marital Adjustment for Survivors of Sexual Abuse." *The Family Journal* 6 (1998) 182–188.

Bibliography

Tomeo, Marie E., et al. "Comparative Data of Childhood and Adolescence Molestation in Heterosexual and Homosexual Persons." *Archives of Sexual Behavior* 30 (2001) 535–541.

Toronto Crisis Center. "Rape." In *No Safe Place: Violence against Women and Children*. Edited by Connie Guberman and Margie Wolfe, 62. Toronto, Canada: Women's Press, 1985.

Torre, Lilliam. "Predators of the Concept of God in a Sample of Adult Survivors of Father-Daughter Incest." PhD diss., University of Miami, 1993.

Tracy, Steven R. "Sexual Abuse and Forgiveness." *Journal of Psychology and Theology* 27 (1999) 219–229.

———. *Mending the Soul: Understanding and Healing Abuse*. Grand Rapids, MI: Zondervan, 2005.

———. "Patriarchy and Domestic Violence: Challenging Common Misconceptions." *Journal of the Evangelical Theological Society* 50 (2007) 573–594.

Tracy, Celestia, G., et al. *Mending the Soul Workbook: Understanding and Healing Abuse*. NP: Global Hope Resources, 2009.

Traina, Christina L. H. "Captivating Illusions: Sexual Abuse and the Ordering of Love." *Journal of the Society of Christian Ethics* 28 (2008) 183–208.

Trible, Phyllis. "Feminist Hermeneutics and Biblical Studies." *Christian Century*. Feb. 3–10 (1982) 116–118.

———. *God and the Rhetoric of Sexuality*. Overtures to Biblical Theology. Philadelphia: Fortress, 1984.

———. *Texts of Terror: Literary-Feminist Readings of Biblical Narratives*. Overtures to Biblical Theology. Philadelphia, PA: Fortress, 1984.

Tribune Staff. "State's Oldest Inmate, Former La Crosse Resident, Dies." *La Crosse Tribune*. January 27 (2008).

Truesdell, Donna L., et al. "Incidence of Wife Abuse in Incestuous Families." *Social Work* 31 (1986) 138–140.

Tuggle, B., and C. Tuggle. *A Healing Marriage: Biblical Help for Overcoming Childhood Sexual Abuse*. Colorado Springs, CO: NavPress, 2004.

Turell, Susan, and Mary Armsworth. "Differentiating Incest Survivors Who Self-Mutilate." *Child Abuse and Neglect* 24 (2000) 237–249.

———. et al. "Where Was God? Utilizing Spirituality with Christian Survivors of Sexual Abuse." *Women and Therapy* 24 (2001) 133–147.

Tutu, Archbishop Desmond. *No Future without Forgiveness*. New York, NY: Doubleday, 1999.

Twenge, Jean M., and W. Keith Campbell. *The Narcissism Epidemic: Living in an Age of Entitlement*. New York, NY: Free Press, 2009.

Ulanov, Ann Belford. *Picturing God*. Einsiedeln: Daimon Verlag, 2002.

Valle, L. A., and J. F. Silovsky. "Attributions and Adjustment Following Child Sexual and Physical Abuse." *Child Maltreatment* 7 (2002) 9–25.

Vander Mey, Brenda J., and Ronald L. Neff. "Adult-Child Incest: A Sample of Substantiated Cases." *Family Relations* 33 (1984) 549–557.

Van der Hart, Onno and Martin Dorahy. "History of the Concept of Dissociation." In *Dissociation and the Dissociative Disorders: DSM-V and Beyond*, edited by Paul F. Dell and John A. O'Neil, 3–11. New York, NY: Routledge, 2009.

van der Kolk, Bessel. *Psychological Trauma*. Washington, DC: American Psychiatric Publishing, 1987.

———. "The Compulsion to Repeat Trauma: Re-enactment, Revictimization, and Masochism." *Psychiatric Clinics of North America* 12 (1989) 389–411.

———, et al. *Traumatic Stress: The Effects of Overwhelming Experience on Mind, Body, and Society*. New York, NY: Guilford Press, 1996.

———. "Clinical Implications of Neuroscience Research in PTSD." *Annals of the New York Academy of Science* 1071 (2006) 277–293.

———. et al. *Traumatic Stress: The Effects of Overwhelming Experience on Mind, Body, and Society*. New York, NY: Guilford, 2007.

van der Louw, Theo A. W. *Transformations in the Septuagint: Towards an Interaction of Septuagint Studies and Translations Studies*. Contributions to Biblical Exegesis and Theology 47. Leuven: Peeters, 2007.

van Wolde, Ellen J. "Rhetorical, Linguistic and Literary Features in Genesis 1." In *Literary Structure and Rhetorical Strategies in the Hebrew Bible*, edited by L. J. de Regt, J. de Waard, and J. P. Fokkelman, 134–151. Winona Lake, IN: Eisenbrauns, 1996.

———. "The Dinah Story: Rape or Worse?" *Old Testament Essays* 15 (2002) 225–239.

van Wormer, Katherine. "Restorative Justice as Social Justice for Victims of Gendered Violence: A Standpoint Feminist Perspective." *Social Work* 54 (2009) 107–116.

Van Stone, D., and E. Lutzer. *No Place to Cry: The Hurt & Healing of Sexual Abuse.* Chicago: Moody Publishers, 1992.

Visotzky, Burton L. *The Genesis of Ethics.* New York, NY: Crown, 1996.

Volf, Miroslav. *Exclusion and Embrace: A Theological Exploration of Identity, Otherness, and Reconciliation.* Nashville, TN: Abingdon, 1996.

———. *The End of Memory: Remembering Rightly in a Violent World.* Grand Rapids, MI: Eerdmans, 2006.

Vogel, Linda. "Creating Rituals That Speak To Us and For Us in the Winter-time of Life." Paper presented at the North American Academy of Religion, Indianapolis. January 2003. http://mystagogy.info/mystagogy2/files/Creating_Rituals_for_Older_Women.pdf.

Wagner, James. *Healing Services.* Nashville, TN: Abingdon, 2007.

Waites, Elizabeth. *Trauma and Survival: Post-traumatic and Dissociative Disorders in Women.* New York, NY: Norton, 1993.

Wakabi, Wairagala. "Sexual Violence Increasing in Democratic Republic of Congo." *The Lancet* 371 (2008) 15–16.

Walker, A. M. "The Church in Trauma at Worship." *Review & Expositor* 105 (2008) 323–329.

Walker Bynum, Caroline. *The Resurrection of the Body in Western Christianity, 200–1336.* New York, NY: Columbia University Press, 1995.

Wallace, Daniel B. *Greek Grammar Beyond the Basics: An Exegetical Syntax of the New Testament.* Grand Rapids, MI: Zondervan, 1996.

Walls, Jeannette. *The Glass Castle.* New York, NY: Scribner, 2006.

Walsh, Jerome T. *Style and Structure in Biblical Hebrew Narrative.* Collegeville, MN: Liturgical Press, 2001.

Walsh, Wendy A., et al. "Prosecuting Child Sexual Abuse." *Crime & Delinquency* 56 (2010) 436–54.

Walsh, William M., and James A. McGraw. *Essentials of Family Therapy.* 2nd ed. Denver, CO: Love Publishing, 2002.

Walters, M., et al. *The Invisible Web: Gender Patterns in Family Relationships.* New York, NY: The Guilford Press, 1988.

Waltke, Bruce K. *Genesis: A Commentary.* Grand Rapids, MI: Zondervan, 2001.

———. *Old Testament Theology: An Exegetical, Canonical, and Thematic Approach.* Grand Rapids, MI: Zondervan, 2007.

Walton, Elaine. "Therapeutic Forgiveness: Developing a Model for Empowering Victims of Sexual Abuse." *Clinical Social Work Journal* 33 (2005) 193–207.

Walton, John H. *Ancient Near Eastern Thought and the Old Testament.* Grand Rapids, MI: Baker, 2006.

Ward, Tony. "Sexual Offenders' Cognitive Distortions as Implicit Theories." *Aggression and Violent Behavior* 5 (2000) 491–507.

———, and S. M. Hudson. "Finkelhor's Precondition Model of Child Sexual Abuse: A Critique." *Crime & Law* 7 (2001) 291–307.

———, and Claire Stewart. "The Treatment of Sex Offenders: Risk Management and Good Lives." *Professional Psychology* 9 (2003) 645–73.

———, et al. *Theories of Sexual Offending.* New York, NY: Wiley, 2006.

———, and Anthony R. Beech. "An Integrated Theory of Sexual Offending." In *Sexual Deviance: Theory, Assessment, and Treatment,* 2nd ed., edited by D. Richard Laws and William T. O'Donohue, 21–38. New York, NY: The Guilford Press, 2008.

Warren, K., and K. Knox. "Offense Cycles, Thresholds and Bifurcations: Applying Dynamic Systems Theory to the Behaviors of Adolescent Sex Offenders." *Journal of Social Service Research* 27 (2000) 1–27.

Warshaw, Robin. *I Never Called It Rape: The Ms. Report on Recognizing, Fighting, and Surviving Date and Acquaintance Rape.* San Francisco, CA: Harper and Row, 1988.

Watkins, W. G., and A. Bentovim. "The Sexual Abuse of Male Children and Adolescents: A Review of Current Research." *Journal of Child Psychology and Psychiatry* 33 (1992) 197–248.

Watson, David. "Investigating the Construct Validity of the Dissociative Taxon: Stability Analyses of Normal and Pathological Dissociation." *Journal of Abnormal Psychology* 112 (2003) 298–305.

Watts, Charlotte and Cathy Zimmerman. "Violence against Women: Global Scope and Magnitude." *The Lancet* 359 (2002) 1232–1237.

Weaver, Andrew J., Harold G. Koenig, and Frank M. Ochberg. "Posttraumatic Stress, Mental Health Professionals, and the Clergy: A Need for Collaboration, Training, and Research." *Journal of Traumatic Stress* 9 (1996) 847–856.

———. "Psychological Trauma: What Clergy Need to Know." *Pastoral Psychology* 41 (1993) 385–408.

Weborg, John C. Lecture Notes. Chicago, IL: North Park Theological Seminary, 2001.

Webster, Brian L. and David R. Beach. "The Place of Lament in the Christian Life." *Bibliotheca Sacra* 164 (2007) 387–402.

Weems, Ann. *Psalms of Lament*. Louisville, KY: Westminster John Knox, 1995.

Weems, Renita J. *Battered Love: Marriage, Sex, and Violence in the Hebrew Prophets*. Minneapolis, MN: Fortress Press, 1995.

Weierich, M. R. & M. K. Nock. "Posttraumatic Stress Symptoms Mediate the Relation between Childhood Sexual Abuse and Nonsuicidal Self-Injury." *Journal of Consulting and Clinical Psychology* 76 (2008) 39–44.

Weiner, Neil, and Sharon E. Robinson Kurpius. *Shattered Innocence*. Washington, DC: Taylor & Francis, 1995.

Weingarten, Kathy. *Cultural Resistance: Challenging Beliefs about Men, Women, and Therapy*. New York, NY: Harrington Park Press, 1995.

Weir, Allison. *Sacrificial Logistics: Feminist Theory and the Critique of Identity*. New York, NY: Routledge, 1996.

Weiss, Johannes. *Earliest Christianity: A History of the Period A.D. 30–150*, trans. Frederick C. Grant. 2 Vols. New York, NY: Harper & Brothers, 1937.

Welburn, Ken R., et al. "Discriminating Dissociative Identity Disorder from Schizophrenia and Feigned Dissociation on Psychological Tests and Structured Interview." *Journal of Trauma & Dissociation* 4 (2003) 109–130.

Wenham, Gordon J. *Story as Torah: Reading the Old Testament Narrative Ethically*. Grand Rapids, MI: Baker, 2000.

———. *Exploring The Old Testament: A Guide to the Pentateuch*, vol. 1. Downers Grove, IL: InterVarsity Press, 2008.

Wenninger, K. M., and J. R. Heiman. "Relating Body Image to Psychological and Sexual Functioning in Child Sexual Abuse Survivors." *Journal of Traumatic Stress* 11 (1998) 543–562.

Werner, David. *Where There is No Doctor: A Village Health Care Handbook*. Palo Alto, CA: The Hesperian Foundation, 1996.

Westerlund, Elaine. *Women's Sexuality after Childhood Incest*. New York, NY: Norton, 1992.

Westermann, Claus. "Biblical Reflection on Creator-Creation." In *Creation in the Old Testament*, edited by Bernhard W. Anderson, 90–101. Issues in Religion and Theology 6. Philadelphia, PA: Fortress, 1984.

———. *Praise and Lament in the Psalms*. Atlanta, GA: John Knox, 1981.

Westermarck, Edward. *The History of Human Marriage*. London: Macmillan, 1926.

Whiffen, Valerie E., Melissa E. Judd and Jennifer A. Aube. "Intimate Relationships Moderate the Association Between Childhood Sexual Abuse and Depression." *Journal of Interpersonal Violence* 14 (1999) 942–947.

———, et al. "Mediators of the Link between Childhood Sexual Abuse and Emotional Distress." *Trauma, Violence & Abuse* 6 (2005) 24–39.

White, James. *Sacraments as God's Self-Giving*. Nashville, TN: Abingdon, 1983.

White, Michael, and David Epston. *Narrative Means to Therapeutic Ends*. New York, NY: Norton, 1990.

WHO Multi-country Study on Women's Health and Domestic Violence against Women. Geneva: World Health Organization, 2005.

Widom, C. S., and M. A. Ames. "Criminal Consequences of Childhood Sexual Victimization." *Child Abuse & Neglect* 18 (1994) 303–318.

Wiesel, Elie. *Night*. New York, NY: Hill and Wang, 2006.

Wilcox, D. T., et al. "Resilience and Risk Factors Associated with Experiencing Childhood Sexual Abuse." *Child Abuse Review* 13 (2004) 338–352.

Wilhoit, James C. *Spiritual Formation as if the Church Mattered: Growing in Christ through Community*. Grand Rapids, MI: Baker, 2008.

Willard, Dallas. *The Great Omission: Reclaiming Jesus' Essential Teachings on Discipleship*. San Francisco, CA: HarperCollins, 2006.

Williams, James G. *Those Who Ponder Proverbs: Aphoristic Thinking and Biblical Literature*, edited by David M. Gunn. Bible and Literature Series 2. Sheffield: The Almond Press, 1981.

Wilson, Debra Rose. "Health Consequences of Childhood Sexual Abuse." *Perspectives in Psychiatric Care* 46 (2010) 56–64.

Wilson, D. R. "Health Consequences of Childhood Sexual Abuse." *Perspectives in Psychiatric Care* 46 (2010) 56–63.

Wilson, H. W., and C. S. Widom. "Does Physical Abuse, Sexual Abuse, or Neglect in Childhood Increase the Likelihood of Same-Sex Sexual Relationships and Cohabitation? A Prospective 30-year Follow-up." *Archives of Sexual Behavior* 39 (2009) 63–74.

Wilson, Robin J., et al. "Circles of Support and Accountability: Engaging Community Volunteers in the Management of High-Risk Sexual Offenders." *Howard Journal of Criminal Justice* 46 (2007) 1–15.

Wilson-Kastner, Patricia. "Theological Perspectives on Sexual Violence." In *Sexual Assault and Abuse: A Handbook for Clergy and Religious Professionals*, edited by M. Pellauer, B. Chester and J. Boyajian, 105–106. San Francisco, CA: Harper & Row, 1989.

Winter, Miriam T. *Woman Prayer, Woman Song: Resources for Ritual*. Oak Park, IL: Meyer Stone Books, 1987.

———. *Woman Word: A Feminist Lectionary and Psalter*. New York, NY: Crossroad, 1990.

Wisechild, Louise M. *The Obsidian Mirror*. Seattle, WA: Seal Press, 1998.

Wismer, Patricia L. "Evil." In *Handbook of Christian Theology*. New and Enlarged, edited by D. W. Musser and J. L. Price, 186–188. Nashville, TN: Abingdon, 2003.

Wodarski, John S., and Sandy R. Johnson. "Child Sexual Abuse: Contributing Factors, Effects, and Relevant Practice Issues." *Family Therapy* 15 (1988) 157–173.

Woititz, Janet. *Struggle for Intimacy*. Pompano Beach, FL: Health Communications, 1985.

Wolf. S.C., et al. "Community Treatment of Adults who Have Sex with Children." In *Handbook on Sexual Abuse of Children: Assessment and Treatment Issues*, edited by L. E. A. Walker. New York, NY: Springer, 1987.

Wolterstorff, Nicholas. *Lament For a Son*. Grand Rapids, MI: Eerdmans, 1987.

———. "The Remembrance of Things (Not) Past: Philosophical Reflections on Christian Liturgy." In *Christian Philosophy*, edited by Thomas Flint, 118–161. Notre Dame, IN: University of Notre Dame, 1990.

Wood, Eric, and Shelley Riggs. "Predictors of Child Molestation: Adult Attachment, Cognitive Distortions, and Empathy." *Journal of Interpersonal Violence* 23 (2008) 259–75.

Wood, Ralph C. *The Gospel According to Tolkien: Visions of the Kingdom in Middle-earth*. Louisville, KY: Westminster John Knox, 2003.

World Health Organization. "Comparative Risk Assessment: Child Sexual Abuse." Sydney, Australia: WHO Collaborating Centre for Evidence and Health Policy in Mental Health, 2001.

Worthington, Everett L., ed. *Dimensions of Forgiveness: Psychological Research and Theoretical Perspectives*. Radnor, PA: Templeton, 1998).

———. et al. "The Psychology of Unforgiveness and Forgiveness and Implications for Clinical Practice." *Journal of Social & Clinical Psychology* 18 (1999) 385–418

———. *Forgiving and Reconciling*. Downers Grove, IL: InterVarsity, 2003.

———. ed. *Handbook of Forgiveness*. New York, NY: Routledge, 2005.

———. *Forgiveness and Reconciliation: Theory and Application*. New York, NY: Routledge, 2006.

———. *A Just Forgiveness: Responsible Healing without Excusing Injustice*. Downers Grove, IL: IVP, 2009.

Wortley, Richard and Stephen Smallbone. *Child Pornography on the Internet*. Washington, DC: US Department of Justice, Office of Community Oriented Policing Services, 2006.

Wright Knust, Jennifer. *Unprotected Texts: The Bible's Surprising Contradictions about Sex and Desire*. New York, NY: HarperCollins, 2010.

Wright, M., J. Fopma-Loy, and S. Fischer. "Multidimensional Assessment of Resilience in Mothers who are Child Sexual Abuse Survivors." *Child Abuse & Neglect* 29 (2005) 1173–1193.

Wright, N. T. "The Letter to the Romans: Introduction, Commentary, and Reflections." In *Acts, Introduction to Epistolary Literature, Romans, 1 Corinthians. NIB* 10. Nashville, TN: Abingdon, 2002.

———. *Surprised by Hope: Rethinking Heaven, the Resurrection, and the Mission of the Church*. New York, NY: Harper Collins, 2008.

Wuellner, Flora. *Heart of Healing, Heart of Light: Encountering God, Who Shares and Heals Our Pain*. Nashville, TN: Upper Room, 1992.

Wyatt, G., and G. Powell (eds.). *Lasting Effects of Child Sexual Abuse*. Newbury Park, CA: Sage Publications, Inc., 1988.

———, et al. "Differential Effects of Women's Child Sexual Abuse and Subsequent Sexual Revictimization." *Journal of Consulting and Clinical Psychology* 60 (1992) 167–173.

———, et al. "The Prevalence and Circumstances of Child Sexual Abuse: Changes across a Decade." *Child Abuse and Neglect* 23 (1999) 46–50.

Wyatt, Nicholas. "The Story of Dinah and Shechem." *Ugarit-Forschungen* 22 (1990) 433–458.

Yamada, Frank M. *Configurations of Rape in the Hebrew Bible: A Literary Analysis of Three Rape Narratives*, edited by Hemchand Gossai. Studies In Biblical Literature, 109. New York, NY: Peter Lang, 2008.

Yantzi, Mark. *Sexual Offending and Restoration*. Eugene, OR: Wipf and Stock, 2009.

Yao-Hwa Sung, Elizabeth. "Culture and Hermeneutics." In *Dictionary for Theological Interpretation of the Bible*, edited by Kevin J. Vanhoozer, 150–155. Grand Rapids, MI: Baker, 2005.

Yarhouse, Mark A., et al. *Modern Psychopathologies: A Comprehensive Christian Appraisal*. Downers Grove, IL: InterVarsity Press, 2005.

———. "Same-sex Attraction, Homosexual Orientation, and Gay Identity: A Three-Tier Distinction for Counseling and Pastoral Care." *Journal of Pastoral Care & Counseling* 59 (2005) 201–212.

———. *Homosexuality and the Christian: A Guide for Pastors, Parents, and Friends*. Minneapolis, MN: BethanyHouse, 2010.

Yaron, Shlomit. "The Politics of Sex—Woman's Body as an Instrument for Achieving Man's Aims." *Old Testament Essays* 15 (2002) 269–292.

Yates, P. M., and D. A. Kingston. "The Self-regulation Model of Sexual Offending: The Relationship between Offense Pathways and Static and Dynamic Sexual Offence Risk." *Sex Abuse* 18 (2006) 256–70.

Young, Leslie. "Sexual Abuse and the Problem of Embodiment." *Child Abuse and Neglect* 16 (1992) 89–100.

Young-Eisendrath, Polly. *The Resilient Spirit: Transforming Suffering into Insight and Renewal*. Reading, MA: Persus Books, 1996.

Younger, Jr., K. Lawson. *Judges/Ruth*. NIV Application Commentary. Grand Rapids: Zondervan, 2002.

Zanarini, M. C., L. Yong, F. R. Frankenburg, J. Hennen, D. B. Reich, and M. F. Marino. "Severity of Reported Childhood Sexual Abuse and its Relationship to Severity of Borderline Psychopathology and Psychosocial Impairment among Borderline Patients." *Journal of Nervous and Mental Disease* 190 (2002) 381–387.

Zankman, S., and J. Bonomo. "Working with Parents to Reduce Juvenile Sex Offender Recidivism." *Journal of Child Sexual Abuse* 13 (2004) 139–156.

Zaphiris, Alexander G. *Methods and Skills for a Differential Assessment and Treatment in Incest, Sexual Abuse and Sexual Exploitation of Children*. Denver, CO: The American Humane Association, 1983.

Zerbe Enns, Carolyn. et al. "Working with Adult Clients Who May Have Experienced Childhood Abuse: Recommendations for Assessment and Practice." *Professional Psychology: Research and Practice* 29 (1998) 248–251.

Zimmerman, Mari West. *Take and Make Holy: Honoring the Sacred in the Healing Journey of Abuse Survivors*. Chicago, IL: Liturgy Training, 1995.

Zink, Therese, et al. "The Development of a Sexual Abuse Severity Score: Characteristics of Childhood Sexual Abuse Associated with Trauma Symptomatology, Somatization, and Alcohol Abuse." *Journal of Interpersonal Violence* 24 (2009) 537–546.

Zuravin, S., et al. "The Intergenerational Cycle of Child Maltreatment: Continuity vs. Discontinuity." *Journal of Interpersonal Violence* 2 (1996) 15–34.

Contributors

Morven R. Baker
Director
Ashland Women's Counseling Center (Ashland, OH)

Clark Barshinger
Private Practice, Clinical Psychology
Cherry Hill Center (Lake Zurich, IL)

Cheryl Clayworth Belch
(Kitchener, ON, Canada)

Richard M. Davidson
Professor of Old Testament Interpretation
Andrews University Theological Seminary (Berrien Springs, MI)

J. Edward Ellis
Associate Professor of New Testament
Olivet Nazarene University (Bourbonnais, IL)

Heather Davediuk Gingrich
Associate Professor of Counseling
Denver Seminary (Littleton, CO)

James B. Gould
Instructor of Philosophy
McHenry County College (Crystal Lake, IL)

Emily G. Hervey
Doctoral Candidate in Clinical Psychology
Regent University (Norfolk, VA)

Janelle Kwee
Assistant Professor of Counseling Psychology
Trinity Western University (Langley, BC, Canada)

Diane Mandt Langberg
Psychologist
(Jenkintown, PA)

Contributors

Philip G. Monroe
Professor of Counseling and Psychology
Biblical Seminary (Hatfield, PA)

Stephen McMullin
New Brunswick Program Director and Lecturer in Evangelism and Mission
Acadia Divinity College (Wolfville, Nova Scotia, Canada)

Kelvin F. Mutter
Psychotherapist, Family Counseling & Support Services (Guelph, ON, Canada)
Adjunct Professor in Ministry Studies, McMaster Divinity College
(Hamilton, ON, Canada)

Nancy Nason–Clark
Professor (and Chair) of Sociology and Director of the RAVE Project
University of New Brunswick (Fredericton, New Brunswick, Canada)

Patrice F. Penney
Lecturer in Psychology and Counseling
Africa International University (Kenya, Africa)

Andrew J. Schmutzer
Professor of Biblical Studies
Moody Bible Institute (Chicago, IL)

Joy A. Schroeder
Bergener Professor of Theology and Religion
Capital University and Trinity Lutheran Seminary (Columbus, OH)

Jim Sells
Professor of Counselor Education and Supervision
Regent University (Virginia Beach, VA)

JoAnn A. Shade
Corps Officer
The Salvation Army (Ashland, OH)

Justin Smith
Assistant Professor of Counseling
Phoenix Seminary (Phoenix, AZ)

Gary H. Strauss
Professor, Rosemead School of Psychology
Biola University (La Mirada, CA)

ELISABETH C. SUAREZ

Associate Professor of Counseling
Regent University (Virginia Beach, VA)

STEVEN R. TRACY

Professor of Theology and Ethics; Founder,
Mending the Soul Ministries
Phoenix Seminary (Phoenix, AZ)

JOYCE WAGNER

Director, Counseling Center
Roberts Wesleyan College (Rochester, NY)

TERRI S. WATSON

Associate Professor of Psychology
Wheaton College (Wheaton, IL)

MARK A. YARHOUSE

Professor of Psychology and Endowed Chair
Regent University (Virginia Beach, VA)